MW00791147

AUSTRALIA

The Three Sisters, a rock formation in the Blue Mountains

AUSTRALIA

CONTENTS

Intricately painted didgeridoos

DISCOVER 6

EXPERIENCE 72

NEED TO KNOW 488

DISCOVER

Melbourne's city centre skyline

WELCOME TO
AUSTRALIA

Dining out with a view of the Sydney Opera House or discovering a hidden bar in a Melbourne laneway. Learning to surf on Bondi Beach or snorkelling on the Great Barrier Reef. Sleeping under the stars or bathing in a waterfall. Whatever your dream trip to Australia entails, this DK travel guide is the perfect companion.

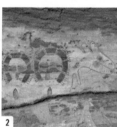

1 Surfing the waves off on Bondi Beach.

2 Detail of an Aboriginal rock-art painting.

3 A narrow, café-lined laneway in Melbourne.

4 Sunrise over Sydney Harbour Bridge.

Shaped by a beguiling mix of ancient traditions – the country's Indigenous culture is the oldest on the planet, after all – and modern, multicultural influences, Australia is famous for its easy-going, "she'll be right, mate" lifestyle and its love of the great outdoors. And what an outdoors it is. From the sun, sand and surf of the country's 10,000 beaches to the vast, arid landscape of the outback interior, Australia is an epic land of huge skies, immense rock formations and "Big Things" – roadside sculptures of everything from oversized ants to avocados.

The cities, too, are not to be missed. Sydney dazzles with its harbour attractions and historic neighbourhoods. The spirit of Sydney's rival – painfully cool Melbourne – is embodied in its graffiti-splattered laneways, trendsetting coffee shops and jubilant sports grounds. Then, there's oft-overlooked Brisbane with its burgeoning foodie scene, pretty Adelaide with its world-renowned wine and laid-back Perth with its surf culture.

With so much on offer and so much distance to cover, Australia can feel overwhelming. We've broken the country down into easily navigable chapters, with detailed itineraries, expert local knowledge and comprehensive maps to help you plan your perfect trip. Whether you're visiting just one place or roaming across this Great Southern Land, this DK travel guide will ensure that you see the very best that this vast country has to offer. Enjoy the book, and enjoy Australia.

REASONS TO LOVE
AUSTRALIA

Immense swathes of coral teeming with marine life. A landscape as varied as it is beautiful. Ancient rock-art sites and world-class vineyards. Here are just some of the reasons why we love Australia.

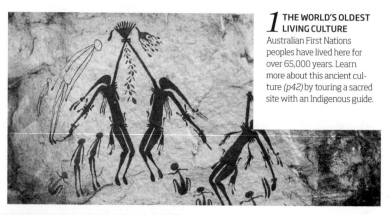

1 THE WORLD'S OLDEST LIVING CULTURE

Australian First Nations peoples have lived here for over 65,000 years. Learn more about this ancient culture *(p42)* by touring a sacred site with an Indigenous guide.

UNDERWATER WONDERLANDS 2

The world's largest – and most famous – coral reef, the Great Barrier Reef *(p384)* is truly breathtaking, but don't ignore Australia's less exposed reefs like Ningaloo *(p485)*.

3 UNIQUE WILDLIFE

Some of Australia's animals *(p58)* can't be found anywhere else. See koalas on Kangaroo Island, peek at platypuses in the Mackay Highlands, and catch kangaroos just about anywhere.

4 SYDNEY HARBOUR

Cruise it, walk around it, picnic beside it, swim in it or dine out overlooking it – however you experience Sydney's sparkling harbour, you're bound to fall in love with it.

THE OUTBACK 5

Australia's arid interior is a land of wide, open spaces and big skies, fiery sunsets and starry nights. Here, distances are great, people are few and adventure is guaranteed.

WORLD-CLASS WINES 6

At the last count, over 2,400 wineries were scattered across Australia's 65 wine regions (p50). Head to South Australia's Barossa Valley (p324) to sample some of the very best.

THE GREAT OCEAN ROAD 7

One of the world's favourite coastal drives, the Great Ocean Road *(p248)* rewards drivers with rock stacks, boundless beaches and fabulous restaurants along the way.

WORLD-CLASS MUSEUMS 8

Melbourne and Sydney's cultural colossi, like the Art Gallery of New South Wales *(p124)*, are much lauded, but there are countless other great museums elsewhere.

9 WILD SWIMMING

Swimming is not consigned to pools and beaches. Take the plunge and join the locals beneath the many thunderous waterfalls in the Kimberley and the Top End.

10 BREATHTAKING BEACHES

From buzzy Bondi to the serene stretches of white sand found in the Whitsundays, Australia's beaches *(p46)* are as diverse as they are plentiful.

WILDERNESS AT YOUR DOORSTEP 11

You're never too far away from one of the country's 600 national parks *(p40)*. The Blue Mountains, Wilsons Prom, Litchfield and Lamington are all found on city fringes.

SKIING AND SNOW SPORTS 12

It's not all about the sun, sand and surf: hit the slopes in the Snowy Mountains or strap on some snowshoes and take to the groomed trails in Falls Creek.

EXPLORE
AUSTRALIA

This guide divides Australia into
19 colour-coded sightseeing areas,
as shown on this map. Find out
more about each area on the
following pages.

Timor
Sea

Darwin

Arnhem
Land

Katherine

**DARWIN AND
THE TOP END**
p412

*Indian
Ocean*

Broome

Halls Creek

*Tanami
Desert*

**NORTHERN
TERRITORY**

Port Hedland

*Great Sandy
Desert*

Exmouth

*Gibson
Desert*

THE RED CENTRE
p430

Alice
Springs

**NORTH OF PERTH
AND THE KIMBERLEY**
p472

Carnarvon

WESTERN   AUSTRALIA

*Great Victoria
Desert*

**YORKE AND EYRE
PENINSULAS AND THE
SOUTH AUSTRALIAN
OUTBACK**
p328

Mount
Magnet

Geraldton

Nullarbor Plain

Kalgoorlie

Eucla

**SOUTH
AUSTRALIA**

Perth

Norseman

**PERTH AND
THE SOUTHWEST**
p452

*Great
Australian
Bight*

Bunbury

Esperance

Port Lincoln

Albany

*Southern
Ocean*

| 0 kilometres | 500 |
| 0 miles | 500 |

N

SOUTHEAST ASIA AND OCEANIA

INDONESIA

SOLOMON
ISLANDS

VANUATU   FIJI

Pacific Ocean

NEW
CALEDONIA

AUSTRALIA

NEW
ZEALAND

*Coral
Sea*

*Indian
Ocean*

*Gulf of
Carpentaria*

*Pacific
Ocean*

FAR NORTH
QUEENSLAND
p380

Cooktown

Cairns

Normanton

Townsville

Mount Isa

Winton

Mackay

*Simpson
Desert*

QUEENSLAND

WESTERN AND
OUTBACK QUEENSLAND
p396

Rockhampton

Gladstone

Birdsville

Charleville

SOUTHEAST
QUEENSLAND AND
THE WHITSUNDAYS
p364

Maryborough

Caloundra

BRISBANE
p348

Bourke

Lismore

THE BLUE MOUNTAINS
AND WESTERN
NEW SOUTH WALES
p156

Coffs Harbour

Port
Augusta

Broken
Hill

Dubbo

HUNTER VALLEY AND
THE NORTH COAST
p170

Whyalla

NEW
SOUTH WALES

Newcastle

Mildura

SYDNEY
p74

Adelaide

Goulburn

ADELAIDE
AND THE
SOUTHEAST
p308

Shepparton

Canberra

Albury

THE SOUTH COAST
AND SNOWY MOUNTAINS
p180

VICTORIA

CANBERRA AND THE AUSTRALIAN
CAPITAL TERRITORY
p194

Mount
Gambier

Geelong

EASTERN VICTORIA
AND THE HIGH COUNTRY
p264

THE GREAT
OCEAN ROAD AND
WESTERN VICTORIA
p244

MELBOURNE
p216

TASMANIA
p278

Hobart

GETTING TO KNOW
AUSTRALIA

Stretching about 4,000 km (2,500 miles) from east to west, and 3,860 km (2,400 miles) from north to south – without counting its islands – Australia is about the same size as Europe. To help you get familiar with this continent-sized country, we've split it into nine regions.

PAGE 74

SYDNEY

New South Wales's wonderfully multicultural capital is both cosmopolitan and historic, a financial powerhouse and champion of outdoor recreation. Locals spend much of their free time enjoying the beaches, parks and bushland that surround the city, as well as the huge harbour that bisects its centre. On the coastline are innovative museums, cutting-edge art galleries and the iconic Opera House. Add The Rocks' olde-worlde pubs, Paddington's glitzy boutiques and Darlinghurst's buzzy LGBTQ+ scene, and it's easy to see why few visitors leave Australia without seeing Sydney.

Best for
Performing arts

Home to
The Rocks and Circular Quay, City Centre and Darling Harbour, Royal Botanic Garden and the Domain, Kings Cross, Darlinghurst and Paddington, sights just beyond the city

Experience
A ferry ride across sparkling Sydney Harbour

NEW SOUTH WALES

PAGE 150

Beyond Sydney, New South Wales unfurls in sparkling beaches and awe-inspiring national parks. As a result, it's a fantastic destination for a huge variety of outdoor adventures, including snorkelling, whale-watching, kayaking and stand-up paddleboarding. Surfers flock to beach towns like Byron Bay and Narooma, while the Great Dividing Range beckons bushwalkers. The state also offers one of Australia's most surprising activities – skiing. Experience a distinctly Aussie winter in the Snowy Mountains, complete with snow-laden eucalyptuses and flat whites by the slopes.

Best for
Outdoor activities

Home to
The Blue Mountains and Western New South Wales, Hunter Valley and the North Coast, the South Coast and Snowy Mountains

Experience
Hopping between beautiful beaches, and trying a different watersport at each one

CANBERRA AND THE AUSTRALIAN CAPITAL TERRITORY

PAGE 194

Despite being the nation's capital, Canberra is a rural city, ringed by gum trees and home to fewer than 500,000 people. Don't be surprised if you spot a kangaroo hopping past Parliament House. These contradictions are the essence of the city's attraction. Beyond the "Bush Capital", the Australian Capital Territory (or ACT as it's known) is made up of forests, farmland and nature reserves, offering canoeing, camping and fishing.

Best for
The relaxed life

Home to
Parliamentary Triangle, National Museum of Australia

Experience
Cycling along the shady, green paths that encircle Lake Burley Griffin

→

PAGE 210

VICTORIA

Victoria is a tale of two halves. First there's Melbourne, the state's cultured capital. Its hidden bars, earnest spoken-word poets and oat-milk latte art may have earned the city a hipster reputation, but Melbourne's politically skewering street art, pulsating nightclubs and stellar restaurants keep things grounded. Then, there's the wild landscape of the surrounding state, with its windswept limestone stacks, blustery surf beaches and scrubby outback. For the journey of a lifetime, drive the Great Ocean Road, spot penguins at Phillip Island and admire Aboriginal rock art in the Grampians.

Best for
Urban life

Home to
Melbourne, The Great Ocean Road and Western Victoria, Eastern Victoria and High Country

Experience
Driving the iconic Great Ocean Road

TASMANIA

PAGE 278

An island located 240 km (150 miles) to the south of the mainland, Tasmania is Australia's least populous state. But don't let its diminutive size fool you: "Tassie" punches above its weight. Hobart, the state capital, is known for its cold weather and equally cool vibe. Here, you can frequent supper clubs housed in heritage buildings, browse bustling weekend craft markets and visit avant-garde art galleries. Beyond the city limits, an adventurer's paradise awaits. Hikers take on large tracts of wilderness and overland mountain treks, while others climb aboard heritage trains and gleaming sailing boats.

Best for
Hiking

Home to
Hobart, Port Arthur

Experience
Cruising along the Gordon River, taking in the mountain views along the way

SOUTH AUSTRALIA

PAGE 302

This is the unspoiled corner of Australia that few visitors discover. Beaches feel like treasured secrets, particularly around the Eyre Peninsula and the lustrous Limestone Coast, and national parks, such as the Murray River and Kangaroo Island's Flinders Chase, seem untrammelled. But this state is far from staid. Historically known as the "City of Churches", Adelaide, the capital, is now dubbed "Radelaide" for its art, dining and – of course – wine scenes. Despite being the driest state, South Australia is blessed with 18 wine regions, producing some of the country's best bottles.

Best for
Wineries

Home to
Adelaide and the Southeast, Yorke and Eyre Peninsulas and the South Australian Outback

Experience
The Blue Lake turning from grey to sapphire between November and March

$\rightarrow$

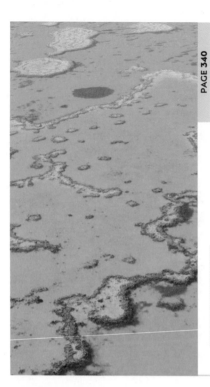

PAGE 340

QUEENSLAND

Queensland's world-famous underwater paradise, the Great Barrier Reef, needs little introduction. But this amazing reef is just one of Queensland's watery wonderlands. Go diving in the crystal-clear waters off Port Douglas, try surfing the waves off the Gold or Sunshine coasts, or take a boat trip to the paradisal Whitsundays. Out of the water, there's cosmopolitan Brisbane, vast Daintree – the world's oldest rainforest – and surprising sights, including outback pubs and oversized roadside oddities like "the Big Cassowary" and "Big Mango".

Best for
Water-based adventures

Home to
Brisbane, Southeast Queensland and Whitsundays, Far North Queensland, Western and Outback Queensland

Experience
Diving among sea anemones and giant clams on the Great Barrier Reef

NORTHERN TERRITORY

PAGE 406

This is the real outback. Tropical to the north and arid further south, the Northern Territory may be Australia's least populated region, but what it lacks in people it more than makes up for in beauty. At its heart is Uluṟu, a sacred monolith rising from the amber desert. The best way to appreciate the landscape? Get out into it. Hike the waterfalls, drive through the gigantic national parks and cruise the habitat of snapping saltwater crocodiles. Along the way, you'll get the chance to experience Aboriginal culture, seeking out ancient rock art in Kakadu and attending a dot-painting workshop in Uluṟu.

Best for
Aboriginal culture

Home to
Darwin and the Top End, The Red Centre

Experience
Watching the sunset turn Uluṟu a dusty pink

WESTERN AUSTRALIA

Australia's largest state, Western Australia has it all: bright-red deserts and forests teeming with wildlife, sun-soaked vineyards and livable cities. Take Perth – the state capital – with its outdoor lifestyle, easygoing nature and booming gourmet scene. Crystalline water and silky-soft sand draw visitors to Cable Beach, Hamelin Bay and other beautiful stretches. But it'd be a waste to spend all day lounging on the sand when there are whale sharks to watch and dolphins to spot. And don't forget the quokka – catch sight of these famously cute marsupials at Rottnest Island.

Best for
Wildlife encounters

Home to
Perth and the Southwest, North of Perth and the Kimberley

Experience
The epic grandeur of the multicoloured, curved granite cliff, Wave Rock

1 The Sydney Opera House.

2 Sydney's skyline from the Royal Botanic Garden.

3 Interactive exhibit at the Museum of Sydney.

4 Surfers at Manly Beach.

3 DAYS
in Sydney

Day 1

Morning Spend an hour or so wandering the winding streets of The Rocks (p82). Australia's oldest suburb – once notorious for its criminals, sex workers and reluctant sailors – is full of honey-coloured sandstone buildings, characterful pubs and beautifully restored terrace houses. Follow the foreshore path around the curve of Circular Quay to the Royal Botanic Garden (p122) for iconic views of the Harbour Bridge and Opera House. Then, head back to the quay and join a harbour cruise (many include lunch) or, if you're on a budget, jump on one of the ferries instead.

Afternoon Take a deep dive into Sydney's past at the Museum of Sydney (p109), then suit up and join a BridgeClimb (p53) to climb up the arches of Sydney Harbour Bridge (p88). If you don't have a head for heights, walk across the bridge below.

Evening Watch the sun set behind the Harbour Bridge with a cocktail in hand at the Opera Bar (p86) at the Sydney Opera House, and then dine out with a harbour view at Quay restaurant (p91).

Day 2

Morning Pack your swimsuit and wear your walking shoes for the 3.5-km- (2-mile-) long clifftop path from Bronte to Bondi Beach (p146). When you get there, tuck into breakfast or brunch at Bondi Trattoria (www.bonditrattoria.com.au), before going for a swim, either in the surf or at Bondi Icebergs ocean pool (p147).

Afternoon Head back into the city centre via Paddington's Oxford Street (p137) – nicknamed "the Golden Mile", it's a thriving shopping zone and former LGBTQ+ hub. Then, walk along Crown Street in Surry Hills, which is lined with quirky boutiques and vintage stores. Along the way, pop into any café or wine bar that catches your eye.

Evening Book a pre-theatre dinner at Bennelong (p86) and then enjoy a show at the world's most photographed dance hall. Don't be misled by the name – the Sydney Opera House (p86) stages everything from rock to comedy, ballet to rap.

Day 3

Morning Ride one of the world's best harbour cruises: the ferry from Circular Quay to Manly (p144). Amble down the Corso to the beach – Manly is a great place to learn to surf – or follow Marine Parade to Shelly Beach. Flanked by parklands, this stretch of sand is a local favourite.

Afternoon Back at the ferry wharf, upscale restaurant Hugos (p145) serves a very good plate of fish and chips, so settle in for a leisurely lunch before catching the ferry back to the city. Spend the rest of the afternoon browsing the stalls at The Rocks Markets (p93).

Evening Enjoy a casual meal at one of The Rocks' historic old pubs: The Fortune of War (www.fortuneofwar.com.au) is the city's oldest, The Hero of Waterloo (p92) is reputedly the most haunted and the Glenmore (p92) has a great rooftop bar.

1

2 WEEKS
on Australia's East Coast

Day 1

A two-and-a-half-hour drive north of Sydney is New South Wales's coolest city, Newcastle *(p175)*. Here, pop-up galleries, quirky boutiques and edgy places to eat compete with beautiful beaches for your attention. After a spot of gallery-hopping in town, walk the convict-built breakwater to Nobbys Head Lighthouse for great views, and then cycle the Bathers Way to the Art Deco ocean baths for a swim. In the afternoon, take the ferry across the river to Stockton Beach to see shipwrecks. Back in the city, head to the former industrial district of Honeysuckle for dinner with a view of the tugboats coming and going.

Day 2

Take the scenic coastal road to Port Macquarie *(p174)* for riverside walks, deserted beaches and sweeping coastal views. Time your arrival to catch the free 3pm talk at the state's only koala hospital *(www.koalahospital.org.au)*. Then, set off on the 9-km (5.5-mile) coastal walk between Tacking Point and Town Green,

pausing along the way for a swim. Once you reach Town Green, have a drink at The Beach House *(www.thebeachhouse. net.au)* and dinner at The Stunned Mullet *(www.thestunnedmullet.com.au)*.

Day 3

No Australian road trip is complete without seeing at least one "big thing". The supersized roadside attraction that started the national obsession is the Big Banana at Coffs Harbour *(p177)*. After stepping inside this 13-m (43-ft) sculpture, grab a chocolate-coated frozen banana from the Big Banana café. Next, drive on to Yamba *(p177)*, pausing at the town of Angourie to watch daredevils leap off the cliffs and surfers tackle the breaks. After checking into your accommodation, catch the ferry across the Clarence River to Iluka and its World Heritage-listed rainforest. Tucking into a bucket of Yamba prawns, while watching the sun set over one of the town's five beaches, is the perfect way to end the day.

1 Enjoying Flynns Beach,
Port Macquarie.

2 Walking to Nobbys Head
Lighthouse, Newcastle.

3 Tamborine Mountain.

4 Dinosaur sculpture,
Queensland Cultural Centre.

Day 4

Much of today is spent on the road.
Make your first stop Byron Bay (p177) and
stretch your legs with a walk to Cape Byron
Lighthouse, Australia's most easterly point.
Returning to town, recapture some of the
eco vibe that made Byron famous with
a sustainable lunch at The Farm (www.
thefarm.com.au). Take a detour to see the
glittering high-rise strip that is Surfers
Paradise (p370), before swapping the
neon lights for tree ferns and bedding
down near Tamborine Mountain (p372).

Day 5

One day in Brisbane (p348) is never going
to be enough, so spend your time wisely.
Rise early so you can cruise the Brisbane
River, stroll the South Bank Precinct (p354)
and go museum-hopping in the Queensland
Cultural Centre (p352) before lunch. Don't
miss a close encounter with a koala at
Lone Pine Koala Sanctuary (p361) in the
afternoon. Round off the action-packed
day with dinner in the Howard Smith
Wharves beneath the Story Bridge (p354).

Day 6

Today's first stop is Australia Zoo (p373),
the wildlife park run by the family of the
late Steve Irwin, "The Crocodile Hunter".
Continue on towards Nambour, stopping
to ride a heritage-listed pineapple train
through the sugar cane at the Big Pineapple
(www.bigpineapple.com.au). From here, it's
a 40-minute drive to Noosa (p373). Count
koalas in Noosa National Park before
boarding the little Noosa River Ferry for a
hop-on-hop-off 90-minute cruise. Noosa
is renowned for its ritzy restaurants, but
join the locals for a cheap-as-chips dinner
on the deck at the Noosa Heads Surf Life
Saving Club (www.noosasurfclub.com.au).

Day 7

If visiting between mid-July and early
November, embark on a whale-watching
cruise from Hervey Bay (p374). Out of
whale season, a day trip to K'gari (Fraser
Island; p368) – the world's largest sand
island – offers the consolation of glorious
beaches, crystalline lakes, verdant
rainforest and sightings of wild dingoes.

Day 8

On your way to Rockhampton (p377), drop into the Bundaberg Rum Distillery (p375) for a behind-the-scenes look at how this beloved rum is made – a Bundy and coke is a classic Aussie drink. "Rocky" is one of northern Australia's oldest cities and an afternoon stroll beside the Fitzroy River will lead you past a string of elegant old buildings and iconic Queensland-style pubs. Rockhampton is also the country's beef capital, so it would be rude not to try a steak here. The restaurant at the Great Western Hotel (www.greatwesternhotel.com. au) serves up some of the best cuts of beef.

Day 9

Broken River in Eungella National Park (p378), nestled in the highlands west of Mackay, is one of the only places on the planet to see platypuses in the wild. Your best chance of spotting them is in the early morning or late evening, so spend the night at Broken River Mountain Resort (www.brokenrivermr.com.au) to increase your odds. When you're not playing hide and seek with these elusive creatures, walk along the park's rainforest tracks or hike to waterfalls and swimming holes in Finch Hatton Gorge.

Day 10

Get up early and set off on the two-hour drive to Airlie Beach (p379), gateway to the Whitsunday Islands (p379). You'll want to arrive in good time to board a sailing trip to Whitehaven Beach. Day cruises depart early in the morning, but there are also half-day sails that leave around noon if you like your sleep. With some of the whitest sands in Australia, Whitehaven Beach lives up to the hype. Lunch and dinner are often included in the cruise.

Day 11

It takes around seven or eight hours to drive to Cairns from Airlie Beach, so break up the journey halfway with an overnight stop in Townsville (p392). Start by walking the Strand – a 2-km (1-mile) stretch of beach-front lined with cafés, parks and swimming enclosures. After a coffee stop, dive

1 Bundaberg Rum Distillery.

2 Paronella Park.

3 Boats moored at Airlie Beach.

4 Diving the Great Barrier Reef.

5 Aerial walkway, Daintree Rainforest Discovery Centre.

through ethereal underwater sculptures at the Museum of Underwater Art and uncover the fascinating story of the wrecked HMS *Pandora* at the Queensland Museum Tropics. End the day with dinner at foodie Flinders and Palmer streets.

Day 12

Continuing your journey to Cairns, pause at Mission Beach (p392) to see if you can spot a cassowary and to marvel at Paronella Park (p392), the ruins of a Spanish castle built by a cane cutter in the 1930s. Having finally reached Cairns (p388), cool off in the free swimming lagoon and stretch your driving legs with a stroll along the Cairns Esplanade Boardwalk (p388). Save your visit to the aquarium (p389) until after dark to see what the Great Barrier Reef looks like at night – the two-and-a-half-hour experience includes a two-course dinner.

Day 13

Top of the list for most visitors to Cairns is a trip out to the Great Barrier Reef (p384), and there is a huge range of diving and snorkelling tours available. Most all-day snorkelling trips cruise out to coral cays and islands around 90 minutes to two hours from shore, and cater to all swimming abilities. If you've always wanted to try scuba diving there are lots of places in Cairns that run introductory courses for first-timers.

Day 14

Today, trace the Great Barrier Reef Drive between Cairns and Cape Tribulation. This coastal road may be named after the reef, but this drive is really all about the Daintree National Park (p391). Watch outside your window as the rainforest spills down the mountain to meet the sea in a never-ending string of white beaches. Along the way, stop for coffee and some celebrity spotting in chic Port Douglas (p390) and join an Aboriginal tour to learn the history of the boulder-strewn Mossman Gorge. At the end of the road, check into Cape Trib Beach House (p391) to spend an unforgettable night in a 135-million-year-old coastal rainforest.

1 Melbourne at dusk.

2 The Twelve Apostles along Victoria's Great Ocean Road.

3 A Melbourne tram.

4 Pastries in the window of a cake shop on Acland Street.

5 DAYS

in Melbourne and on the Great Ocean Road

Day 1

Morning Grab a coffee from Hardware Société (*www.hardwaresociete.com*) and lose yourself in Melbourne's street-art adorned laneways. Continue your arty morning at the National Gallery of Victoria (*p222*). Then, amble along the Southbank promenade, where you'll find plenty of places to eat.

Afternoon Take the tram to St Kilda, and walk the pier and beach. Feeling hungry? Head to Acland Street, which is lined with cake shops, and try a vanilla slice at Monarch Cakes (*www.monarchcakes.com.au*).

Evening Reserve a table at Vue de Monde (*www.vuedemonde.com.au*), which has sparkling city views.

Day 2

Morning Begin your day with an amble down the leafy eastern end of Collins Street, checking out its high-end boutiques and elegant heritage buildings. Look out for No 120 Collins Street (*p228*), which was once the city's tallest building.

Afternoon Take a leisurely cruise down the Yarra River (*p242*), then jump on a tram and explore Fitzroy (*p233*) and Collingwood, two old working-class suburbs that are now crammed with chic boutiques and super-cool bars.

Evening Take your pick from the dozens of pubs, bars and restaurants on Collingwood's Smith Street.

Day 3

Morning Hit the Great Ocean Road (*p248*)– a scenic seaside drive. Stop at Torquay to learn all about surfing culture at the Australian National Surfing Museum and see it in action at Bells Beach.

Lunch overlooking Anglesea Beach at Captain Moonlite (*www.captainmoonlite.com.au*).

Afternoon Continue on to Lorne, with stops at Aireys Inlet Lighthouse, Erskine Falls and countless lookouts along the way.

Evening Enjoy a tapas feast, with plenty of seafood, at Lady Bay Restaurant (*p249*).

Day 4

Morning There are more sea views in store as you coil your way along the coast, but there's some beautiful rainforest to explore, too. Pause at the Great Otway National Park and take to the canopy on the Otway Fly (*www.otwayfly.com.au*).

Afternoon Climb to the top of Australia's oldest surviving lighthouse at Cape Otway. Then, drive on to snap a picture of the Twelve Apostles rock stacks.

Evening Overnight in Port Campbell.

Day 5

Morning Visit London Bridge that famously lost one of its arches in 1990, stranding two startled sightseers. Next, take a detour inland. Stop for icecream at Timboon (*www.timboonfineicecream.com.au*) as you drive along the Great Ocean Road.

Afternoon Southern right whales visit Logans Beach each winter, so you might spot one here. Afterwards, visit Flagstaff Hill to learn about the shipwrecked treasures that have been washed up on this stretch of coast. Arrive at Port Fairy in time for sunset.

Evening Enjoy local produce and sustainably produced wines at the historic Merrijig Inn (*www.merrijiginn.com*).

$\rightarrow$

① Vines in the Barossa Valley.

② A vintage car in Birdwood's National Motor Museum.

③ Rosé wines at a winery on St Hallett Road, Tanunda.

④ The jetty in Glenelg.

3 DAYS

in Adelaide and the Barossa Valley

Day 1

Morning Skip your hotel breakfast and join the throng of hungry locals buying, selling and tasting the best of South Australia at the Adelaide Central Market *(p312)*. Established in 1869, it's the largest undercover produce market in the southern hemisphere. There are several cafés and coffee bars scattered among the stalls, but the breakfast spaghetti carbonara at Lucia's is hard to beat *(www.lucias.com.au)*. Walk off the carbs on North Terrace, where you'll find most of the city's museums and galleries, including the South Australian Museum *(p315)*. Inside, you'll find the world's largest collection of Aboriginal Australian artifacts.

Afternoon After lunch, ride the historic tram to beachside Glenelg *(p314)*, where the city was founded back in 1836. If it's not swimming weather, stroll the jetty, browse the shops and admire the grand Victorian-era mansions on South Esplanade. Otherwise, take a dip in the sea.

Evening Book a table at Jolleys Boathouse *(www.jolleysboathouse.com)* and enjoy the view of the River Torrens glimmering in the lingering twilight.

Day 2

Morning Drive up into the Adelaide Hills, around 30 minutes southeast of the city. Settled in 1839 by Lutherans fleeing persecution, Hahndorf *(p323)* is Australia's oldest surviving German settlement. The town's main street has around 90 historic buildings, many housing craft shops, galleries, cellar doors and restaurants. For pork knuckles, sauerkraut and a vast array of wursts, call in to the Hahndorf Inn *(www.hahndorfinn.com)*.

Afternoon Take a guided tour of The Cedars – the family home and studio of Hans Heysen, one of Australia's most well-known landscape painters *(p323)*. Circle back to Adelaide via Mount Lofty for panoramic views. Then, if time, visit the National Motor Museum in Birdwood *(p322)*.

Evening With its fine city views, Penfolds' historic Magill Estate vineyard *(www.magillestaterestaurant.com)* is the perfect spot for dinner. If you're feeling flush, splurge out on a bottle of Penfolds Grange, Australia's most famous wine.

Day 3

Morning Get ready to spend the day in Australia's most acclaimed winemaking region, the Barossa Valley *(p324)*, which is around an hour's drive from Adelaide. Start in Tanunda with a tour of Seppeltsfield *(www.seppeltsfield.com.au)*, a wine estate that dates back more than 170 years. Next, travel across the vine-clad hills to Angaston and visit Yalumba *(www.yalumba.com)*, the oldest family-owned winery still operating in Australia. Stop for lunch at cooking icon Maggie Beer's Farm Shop in Nuriootpa *(www.maggiebeer.com.au)* en route.

Afternoon There are more than 150 wineries and 90 cellar doors in the Barossa. You'll find a convenient cluster along Krondorf and St Hallett roads. Four tastes are equal to a standard glass of wine, so stick to buying bottles to take home if you're driving.

Evening Check into The Louise *(www.thelouise.com.au)* and enjoy a five-course tasting menu at its restaurant, Appellation, which only uses ingredients from the Barossa.

1 The distinctive sweep of Wineglass Bay.

2 The ruins of Port Arthur.

3 Golden winery in the Tamar Valley.

4 Bridge over Cataract Gorge.

10 DAYS
in Tasmania

Day 1

Kick off your circumnavigation of "Tassie" in the north at Launceston *(p292)*. It's around an hour's drive southeast of Devonport *(p294)*, where you'll have arrived if you caught the overnight car ferry from the mainland. Spend the morning exploring the Cataract Gorge Reserve *(www.gorgechairlift.com.au)*, a not-so-little slice of wilderness within walking distance of Launceston's city centre. Don't skip riding the chairlift over the gorge. After taking it all in, lunch fireside in The Gorge restaurant, which is located in the middle of the reserve. Happily full, return to the city and spend the afternoon perusing the treasures on show at the Queen Victoria Museum and Art Gallery *(p292)*. In the evening, enjoy a fortifying ale on a tour of James Boag Brewery *(www.jamesboag.com.au)*, then head to Stillwater *(www.stillwater.com.au)* for fine riverside dining in an old mill.

Day 2

Today, you'll discover why Tasmanian wine is making a name for itself on the global stage. Follow the Tamar Valley Wine Route *(p292)*, trying some local sparkling wines along the way at the Jansz Tasmanian Wine Room *(www.jansz.com.au)* and Pipers Brook Vineyard *(www.kreglingerwineestates.com)*. The latter has a delightful café where the designated driver can enjoy some soft refreshments and everyone can refuel. Golfers won't be able to resist playing a game at nearby Barnbougle *(www.barnbougle.com.au)*, which has two stunning links courses (both ranked in Australia's top ten). But even non-golfers will enjoy the views from the on-site Lost Farm restaurant.

Day 3

Don't rush your way down the east coast or you'll regret missing out on some of Australia's prettiest beaches. First stop is the Bay of Fires *(p290)*, which is famous for its orange lichen-covered boulders. Driving on, you'll reach the Freycinet National Park *(p288)*, which is home to Wineglass Bay. Be prepared to work up a sweat on the hike up to the lookout, but the exertion will be worth it when you see the perfect crescent of sand below. This might be Tasmania's most photographed view. Back down on earth, spend the night in the national park at Freycinet Lodge *(www.freycinetlodge.com.au)*.

Day 4

Continue winding your way south along the coastline to the Tasman Peninsula *(p287)*. Your first stop is the Tasmanian Devil Unzoo *(www.tasmaniandevilunzoo.com.au)*, which is one of the only places in the world where you're almost guaranteed to see these endangered creatures. Try to time your visit with feeding time. Next, drive on to the atmospheric ruins of Port Arthur *(p286)*. This UNESCO World Heritage-listed site is one of the best-preserved penal sites in Australia. With more than 30 sand-coloured buildings studded around the pretty bay, it has the appearance of a village rather than a prison, but it was here that the British sent reoffending convicts from the mainland. In 1996, the site was also the scene of the worst mass murder in post-colonial Australian history. If you're not easily spooked, join the night-time ghost tour – it's guaranteed to send shivers down your spine. Otherwise, have dinner at the on-site 1830 Restaurant & Bar.

→

Day 5

It's around a 90-minute drive from the peninsula to Hobart *(p282)* – one of Australia's prettiest and most historic state capitals. It's a very easy city to explore on foot, so lace up your most comfortable shoes and head straight out to Salamanca Place *(p283)* and nearby Battery Point *(p282)*. Here, beautiful sandstone warehouses and cottages have been turned into art galleries and cafés. Grab a coffee to go before continuing on to Macquarie and Davey streets. These roads are lined with more than 60 heritage-listed buildings including the Tasmanian Museum and Art Gallery *(p285)*. Spend some time exploring the collection, looking out for its star exhibit – the now extinct thylacine (Tasmanian tiger). Come lunchtime, enjoy some local seafood on the wharf at Fish Frenzy *(www. fishfrenzy.com.au)*, before catching the ferry to the Museum of Old and New Art (MONA; *p284)*. This is one of the country's most irreverent art galleries, so expect some thought-provoking pieces. After a full-on day of sightseeing, head back to Salamanca Place for dinner.

Day 6

The Wild Way – the road between Hobart and Strahan – is 300 km (186 miles) long, but it will be a longer drive than you think because there are so many picture-perfect places to pull over. First, you'll reach Mount Field National Park *(p301)*. Allow an hour or so here to walk the trails in and around Russell Falls. Next, you'll hit Lake St Clair *(p296)*, where you should pause to walk around the shoreline of Cynthia Bay. Then, the road winds its way through the World Heritage-listed Franklin-Gordon Wild Rivers National Park *(p300)*, one of the last expanses of temperate rainforest in the world. Finally, you'll find yourself in Strahan, the gateway to Macquarie Harbour *(p297)*. View 42° Restaurant & Bar *(p296)* is a good choice for dinner.

Day 7

Strahan is the birthplace of the Australian conservation movement. In 1982, thousands of protestors descended on the town to stop the damming of the Gordon and Franklin rivers. For a close-up view of the

1 The Franklin River.
2 The heritage West Coast Wilderness Railway.
3 Marions Lookout.
4 Cottages in Hobart.
5 The bridge to Sarah Island.

wilderness that these protestors were trying to protect, board a Gordon River Cruise (www.gordonrivercruises.com.au). Most cruises include a walk through the ancient rainforest and a guided tour of the convict ruins on Sarah Island. On your return to Strahan, check into Risby Cove, (www. risbycove.com.au) which provides both waterfront rooms and dining.

Day 8

Take another day off from driving and ride the historic West Coast Wilderness Railway (www.wcwr.com.au). It's a full-day trip, taking you to Queenstown and back again. Along the way, the old steam train travels though steep gorges and rugged wilderness to places where there are no roads. After alighting from the train, swing by the Regatta Point Tavern (www.regatta pointtavern.com.au) for a sundowner.

Day 9

It's wilderness all the way as you drive to the iconic, saw-toothed peaks of Cradle Mountain (p296). If you're feeling energetic,

tackle the two-hour steep climb to Marions Lookout for fabulous views or the much easier stroll around Dove Lake, before checking in to Cradle Mountain Lodge (www.cradlemountainlodge.com.au).

Day 10

Call into the Wilderness Gallery (www. wildernessgallery.com.au) on your way out of Cradle Mountain to see some exceptional photography and artwork. There's more art on show in Sheffield, where the walls really do talk, or tell a story at any rate: almost all the build ings on the main street are adorned with colourful murals detailing the town's past. If you're driving to the ferry at Devonport, keep an eye out for the quirky topiary that fills just about every green space in Railton on the way. If Launceston is your final stop, spend some time in the picturesque village of Longford (p293). It's home to two World Heritage-listed properties, Brickendon and Woolmers Estate, which between them provide an absorbing glimpse into Tasmania's convict past.

1

2

7 DAYS
in the Red Centre

Day 1

Start your journey into the Red Centre at Alice Springs (*p438*). First, set out on an early morning walk to the old telegraph station, which sits beside the original spring that the town was named after in 1871 (*p440*). The Trail Station Café here does excellent coffee. Then, spend a couple of hours exploring the Alice Springs Desert Park, (*p441*) which is home to a plethora of desert wildlife. (Some of the kangaroos have a thing for shoes, so watch your laces!) Back in town, join the locals lunching at Page 27 (*3 Fan Arcade*), then zigzag down Todd Mall, visiting the Aboriginal art galleries on either side of the road. Round off the day with a "meen moolie" (fish curry) at Hanuman (*www.hanuman.com.au*).

Day 2

Pack walking shoes and plenty of water for the day ahead. Start with a sunrise hot-air balloon flight over the desert. Back down on earth, drive east through the East MacDonnell Ranges (*p442*) to see rock art at Emily Gap, striking cliff walls at Jessie

Gap and a deep semicircular canyon at Trephina Gorge. The one-hour trail around the gorge's rim rewards walkers with one fantastic view after another.

Day 3

The rocky ramparts and gorges of the West MacDonnell Ranges (*p442*) are one of the Red Centre's most arresting landscapes. Just 18 km (11 miles) from Alice Springs, you'll find the stunning Simpsons Gap, a deep cleft in the red rock range. Further on lies Standley Chasm, which is only 9 m (29 ft) wide, but 80 m (262 ft) high. Other beautiful sites in the Ranges include Ellery Creek Big Hole and Ormiston Gorge, which provide cooling waters for tired feet. Overnight beside Glen Helen Gorge (*www.discoveryholidayparks.com.au*).

Day 4

The magnificent scenery continues as you drive west to Kings Canyon (*p444*). On the way, stop off at Redbank Gorge. The gorge is a moderate 45-minute hike from the trailhead but that's enough to

1 Walking the rim of Kings Canyon.
2 Kangaroo resting in the sun.
3 Bruce Munro's *Field of Light*.
4 Sunset at Kata Tjuṯa.
5 Simpsons Gap in the West
MacDonnell Ranges.

deter many travellers, so chances are you'll have this swimming spot all to yourself. Pause your journey again at the lookout above Tnorala (Gosse Bluff). This crater was formed more than a million years ago when an asteroid hit the earth. After such an active day, you'll be ready to go to sleep as soon as you reach Kings Canyon. Kings Canyon Resort (p444) has a range of accommodation, but the best place to watch the sunset is from its caravan park.

Day 5

Get up early to beat the heat, and then set out to walk the rim of Kings Canyon. The first half hour is a thigh killer, but the rest of the trail is relatively easy. After completing the circuit, set off on the four-and-a-half-hour drive to Uluṟu-Kata Tjuṯa National Park (p434). Aim to check into Ayers Rock Resort (p437) in time to see the sunset turn Uluṟu a deep red. One of the natural world's best light shows is followed by Bruce Munro's stunning Field of Light installation, where 50,000 spindles illuminate the desert floor.

Day 6

Rise before dawn to see the sunrise light up Uluṟu (p434), and then walk the 10-km (6-mile) trail that loops around its base. The hike takes around three and a half hours to complete. Head back to Ayers Rock Resort to sit out the heat of the day poolside, then nab a table at the on-site Sounds of Silence restaurant for an unforgettable three-course meal beneath the stars.

Day 7

Uluṟu might get all the attention but Kata Tjuṯa (p436) is just as impressive and the sunrise viewing platform tends to attract much smaller crowds. Spend the rest of the morning hiking the steep 8-km (5-mile) Valley of the Winds trail, which winds past sheer rock faces to a magnificent lookout. Back at Ayers Rock Resort, learn the secrets behind the symbols on a dot-painting class with Aboriginal artists, before venturing out again to watch the sunset cast its golden light over Uluṟu. It doesn't matter how many times you've seen it before, it never fails to take your breath away.

7 DAYS
in the Kimberley

Day 1

Thought to be more than two billion years old, the Kimberley (p476) is one of the world's oldest landscapes. Your journey, however, starts in the remote farming town of Kununurra (p479). The Kimberley's eastern gateway, this town was built to service the Ord River Irrigation Project in the 1960s. After settling into your accomodation, listen to ancient stories on a walking tour with an Aboriginal guide among the beehive domes of the Bungle Bungles in Purnululu National Park (p478). Back in town, browse rare pink Kimberley diamonds and Aboriginal art, then visit the Hoochery rum distillery (www.hoochery. com.au). Watch the sun go down from the deck of the Pumphouse Restaurant (www.pumphousekununurra.com.au), a decommissioned pumping station on the Ord River.

Day 2

Take a cruise on the Ord River upstream to Lake Argyle. Expect to see plenty of birdlife and reptiles along the way: these waters are home to an estimated 35,000 freshwater crocodiles. Most of the full-day tours also include a visit to the Argyle Homestead Museum (www.argylehome steadmuseum.com.au) – the reconstructed home of the Duracks, who moved here from Ireland in the mid-1880s and are immortalized in the novel Kings in Grass Castles (1959) by Mary Durack. The building was moved from Argyle Downs Station to its present site when the station was flooded as a result of the Ord River Dam.

Day 3

Fire up the four-wheel drive, pack plenty of supplies and head west on the Gibb River Road (p478; often closed Oct–Apr). One of Australia's most legendary outback tracks, the road passes iconic boab trees and the rampart-shaped Cockburn Range on its way to El Questro, (p476) a former cattle station-turned-resort. Once you've settled into your room or tent, join a guided horse-riding trek from the resort to Emma Gorge, where you can swim beneath a waterfall and chill out in the palm-fringed Zebedee Thermal Springs.

① Aboriginal rock painting at Galvans Gorge.

② Cruising the Ord River.

③ View over Lake Argyle.

④ Boab trees at sunset.

⑤ Zebedee Thermal Springs.

Day 4

Bid farewell to the tarmac when you drive out of El Questro's front gate – you won't see another sealed road for the next three and a half days. What you will see is plenty of magnificent scenery as you bump your way along the 330-km (205-mile) red-dirt road to Mount Barnett. It might look like just about any other Australian roadhouse, but Mount Barnett is also home to Manning Gorge, another stunning swimming spot. After a long day on a dusty road, there's nothing better than a float and soak.

Day 5

There's more wild adventure in store as you continue on the Gibb River Road to Bell Gorge in the King Leopold Ranges Conservation Park. Here, the Isdell River forms a series of cascading waterfalls and deep plunge pools. Further along the road is Galvans Gorge, where you'll find yet another waterfall and pool, this time surrounded by boabs and cliff walls decorated in ancient rock art. Stop here for a late-afternoon dip.

Day 6

You probably won't be inclined to swim at today's destination, Windjana Gorge, once you see the resident crocodiles sunning themselves on the rocks. Explore the gorge on foot instead. This spectacular 100-m- (328-ft-) high gorge is actually an ancient coral reef, eroded by the Lennard River. If you look carefully on the 7-km (4-mile) walk that winds along the length of Windjana, you'll see countless fossils exposed in the limestone walls.

Day 7

Windjana Gorge is 145 km (90 miles) from Derby (p479), the official end point of the Gibb River Road. Once you reach the finishing line, celebrate with a scenic cruise around the Buccaneer Archipelago, a beautiful expanse of turquoise water studded with around 1,000 rocky islands. Then, take to the road once more. This time it's a mercifully paved and bump-free two-hour journey to Broome (p478). Arrive in time to watch the sun slide into the sea from Cable Beach.

Dazzling Beaches

Bounded by beaches on all sides, Australia offers countless opportunities to squeeze silken sand between your toes (p46). If we were forced to pick the best, the list would certainly include the vast Surfers Paradise (p370), white-sand Jervis Bay (p193), buzzing Bondi (p146) and remote Whitehaven Beach (p379). But seek out the sands and decide for yourself.

→

An aerial view of the sweeping curve of Bondi Beach, to the east of Sydney, at sunrise

AUSTRALIA FOR
NATURAL WONDERS

There's no doubt about it: Australia is staggeringly beautiful. Undersea reefs, sun-baked deserts and lush rainforests are reason to visit this country alone – but remember, these landscapes are fragile and deserve our protection.

↑ Admiring a school of snapper on the Great Barrier Reef

Underwater Wonderlands

There are many ways to explore Australia's waters and reefs. Encounter tropical fish on a snorkelling or diving trip to the Great Barrier Reef (p384), or take a boat from Exmouth (p484) to swim with gentle whale sharks or migrating humpback whales on Ningaloo Reef (p485). Do choose an eco-friendly tour operator.

TOP 3 SUSTAINABLE TRAVEL TIPS

Get the App
Download the Eye on the Reef app and log reef health and animal sightings to help scientists protect the Great Barrier Reef.

Choose Eco
Green Eco Guide and Eco Destination logos designate if an area, site or tour is sustainable.

Don't Touch
Standing on or touching reefs breaks the delicate coral and removes this animal's protective film.

Thundering Waterfalls

You'll usually hear the roar of a waterfall before you see the mist-shrouded rush of water. To experience the full force of a cascade's power, get up close: cruise to the remote King George Falls in the Kimberley *(p476)*, take to the air to see Jim Jim Falls in Kakadu *(p422)* or swim in Millaa Millaa Falls on the Waterfall Circuit from Cairns *(www.tropicalnorth queensland.org.au)*.

$\longrightarrow$

Thundering King George Falls in the Kimberley, Western Australia

Otherworldly Rock Formations

Like much of Australia's landscape, rock formations such as Uluṟu *(p434)* are sacred to Aboriginal peoples, so be respectful when visiting *(p42)*. Stick to the marked trails and follow advice from Aboriginal rangers when exploring Mount Augustus; walk through the lunar landscape of the Pinnacles *(p482)*, but don't try to climb these spiky formations; and join a guided trek to learn the sacred significance of the Bungle Bungles *(p478)*.

$\longleftarrow$

The limestone Pinnacles in Nambung National Park, Western Australia

Jurassic Rainforests

It's not all beaches and deserts: there are verdant rainforests to discover here, too. Walk the trails between lacy ferns and soaring trunks, take a river cruise beneath the boughs or get up high on the aerial walkways that wind through the canopies around the Dorrigo Rainforest Centre and the Daintree Discovery Centre *(p391)*.

Dorrigo National Park, New South Wales, part of the Gondwana Rainforests $\uparrow$

Sacred Spaces

Some sites have special spiritual significance to Australian First Nations. Uluṟu *(p434)* is believed to have been been formed by ancestral beings during the Dreamtime. Climbing is banned; walk round the base instead. Other sacred sites include Wilpena Pound in South Australia *(p332)*, Lake Mungo in Willandra Lakes Region *(p169)*, and Kakadu *(p422)* in the Top End.

→

Starry skies over Mungo National Park, part of the Willandra Lakes Region

AUSTRALIA FOR
FIRST NATIONS
CULTURE

This ancient land is steeped in thousands of years of Aboriginal history and tradition. Experience it in their art, both ancient and contemporary; in the ceremony and regalia of their festivals; and in their Dreamtime beliefs.

TIWI ISLANDS FOOTBALL AND ART FESTIVAL

The population of the Tiwi Islands doubles for the annual Football Grand Final and Art Sale, a day-long celebration of two of the most important features of Tiwi culture each March. Art centres sell works by local artists before Australian Football League players battle it out on the local oval.

→

Members of the Yarrabah community dancing at the Cairns Indigenous Art Fair

Awesome Art

Australia has 100,000 known rock-art sites. The oldest is a 17,300-year-old painting of a kangaroo in Drysdale River National Park, the Kimberley. For the largest concentration of rock art, head to Kakadu *(p422)*, which has 5,000 outdoor galleries, or follow the Quinkan Ancient Rock Art Trail through Queensland *(www.queensland.com)*. If you're interested in contemporary Aboriginal art, visit Darwin *(p416)* and Cairns *(p388)* during their August art fairs.

 INSIDER TIP
Buying Right

The most ethical way to buy Aboriginal art is from the artist directly. If this is not possible, visit a gallery that supports the Indigenous Art Code *(www.indigenous-artcode.org)*.

↑ Aboriginal rock art at Nourlangie, Kakadu National Park

First Nations-led Tours

Hear Dreamtime creation stories, sample bush tucker or try throwing a spear on ac First Nations-led tour. Explore the Daintree with Walkabout Cultural Adventures *(www.walkaboutadventures.com.au)*; spend time with the Yolŋu people with Liya Wanhurr Camping and Tours *(0499 912 119)*; and explore Sydney with DreamTime SouthernX *(www.dreamtimesouthernx.com.au)*.

← An Aboriginal guide explaining typical hunting weapons

Fabulous Festivals

For a snapshot of First Nations culture, attend an arts festival. Experience Aboriginal dance at the Cairns Indigenous Art Fair *(www.ciaf.com.au)* or Laura Quinkan Dance Festival *(www.lauraquinkanfestival.com.au)*, which features up to 1,000 performers from 20 communities across Cape York. Interested in art? Alice Springs Desert Park *(p441)* lights up with large-scale illuminations of First Nations works for ten nights during the free Parrtjima Festival each April *(www.parrtjimaaustralia.com.au)*. If it's music you're after, check out Sydney's Yabun *(www.yabun.org.au)*.

AUSTRALIAN FIRST NATIONS CULTURE

It's a mistake to think that First Nations culture is homogenous – each of the tribes or clans that existed at the time of European invasion had their own distinct culture, beliefs and language, shaped by their history and location. The tribes of northern coastal areas, such as the Tiwis Yolngu, had most contact with outsiders, especially from Indonesia, and their culture was quite different from the more isolated Pitjantjatjara of Central Australia's deserts or the Kooris from the south-east. However, there were features common to First Nations life and these have passed down the centuries to become present-day traditions.

TRADITIONAL ABORIGINAL LIFESTYLES

For tens of thousands of years, First Nations peoples were nomadic hunter-gatherers. They made lightweight, versatile tools, such as the boomerang, which they used for hunting, and built temporary mud dwellings as they moved from region to region with the seasons. Through living in small groups across a vast land, First Nations society came to be broken up into numerous clans separated by different languages and customs. Even people with a common language would live apart in extended family groups that came together only for religious ceremonies, to arrange marriages and to settle interclan disputes. Trade was also an important part of social life. Shell, ochre and wood were some of the goods exchanged along Songlines – trade routes that were passed down through the generations through song, story and dance.

The nomadic way of life largely ended when English settlers claimed vast tracts of land, but many traditions have survived. In First Nations communities, senior members are still held in great respect, and are responsible for maintaining laws and meting out punishments to those who break them or divulge secrets of ancient rituals. Such rituals are part of the First Nations belief system called Dreamtime.

FIRST NATIONS SONG AND DANCE

First Nations songs and dances have many different functions and meanings. They tell stories of Dreamtime creator spirits, pay respects to ancestors, pass on knowledge, celebrate the changing seasons and welcome a visitor or returning family member. Singers and dancers are accompanied by instruments, including the didgeridoo, a 1-m- (3-ft-) long wind instrument with a deep sound that is unique to Australia. First Nations musicians and dance troupes perform both traditional and new works at festivals held around the country throughout the year (p43).

↑ A European painting depicting Aboriginal Australians hunting

ONGOING ISSUES

It cannot be denied that First Nations peoples are still disadvantaged in comparison with non-Indigenous Australians, particularly in terms of employment, education, housing, health and life expectancy due to past government policies. Growing awareness of, and respect for, their culture and traditions is gradually leading to a more harmonious coexistence, but there is still much more work to be done.

The right to own land has long been an issue for the First Nations community; they believe that they are responsible for caring for the land entrusted to them at birth. The Land Rights Act of 1976 has done much to improve these rights. The Act established Aboriginal Land Councils which negotiate with the Australian government to claim land for its traditional owners. Where First Nations rights have been established, that land cannot be altered in any way.

In areas of large First Nations inhabitance, the government has also agreed that tribal law can exist alongside common law. This allows tribes to exact justice on members of their community according to their own belief system.

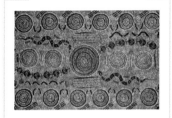

THE DREAMTIME

The Dreamtime (or Dreaming) is the English term for the laws and beliefs that form the basis of First Nations life. It all starts with the earth's creation. "Creation ancestors" are believed to have risen up from the earth's core, creating valleys, rivers and mountains. Sites where these ancestral beings are thought to have emerged from the earth are sacred and every First Nations person is believed to have descended from one of these ancestral beings, who provides them with protection: any misfortune is due to disgruntled forebears.

Did You Know?

Over 500 different Australian First Nations existed at the time of colonial invasion in 1788.

↑ Dancers performing during the Laura Quinkan Dance Festival, Cape York

Surf's Up

Every Aussie surfer's wish list should include Byron Bay *(p177),* Burleigh Heads on the Gold Coast *(p370)* and Crescent Head near Port Macquarie *(p174).* Hire boards or join a surf school at any of these locations or a popular city beach like Perth's Shoalwater Bay or Sydney's Narrabeen, Botany Bay, Bondi *(p146)* or Manly *(p144).* You'll be standing in no time. Fancy trying windsurfing or kiteboarding? Head to Lancelin or Cervantes on the west coast.

→

Surfers riding the incoming waves in the morning light

AUSTRALIA FOR
BREATHTAKING BEACHES

With over 10,000 beaches to choose from, it's inevitable that a trip to Australia will include some time spent on the sand. Here's our pick of some of the best, whether you're after a secluded spot or a family-friendly stretch.

Walking around Collaroy Beach, a family favourite near Sydney ↑

Family Friendly

Some beaches are more geared up for kids than others. Busselton's protected beach offers train rides, an underwater observatory and an inflatable water park *(p464).* A harbour beach on Sydney's north side, Clifton Gardens has a fantastic playground, huge grass reserve, and the all-important kiosk and changing rooms. Also in New South Wales is Collaroy Beach, which has rock pools and a large ocean pool providing sheltered swimming. Brisbane's Streets Beach *(p354),* on a human-made lagoon, also offers safe swimming.

BEACH SAFETY

Going to the beach is fun, but it can be dangerous too. The safest place to swim is between the red-and-yellow flags at beaches patrolled by lifeguards or surf life-savers. If you get into difficulties, raise one arm for help. Never swim alone or after drinking alcohol, and always check the water's depth before diving or jumping in to prevent spinal injuries. Check out patrolled beaches and local conditions at www.beachsafe.org.au.

Remote and Isolated

After that desert-island feeling? Take a catamaran from Airlie Beach to unspoiled Whitehaven Beach (p379) for powdery sand and turquoise water. Similarly isolated is Tasmania's Wineglass Bay (p288). Only the most determined undertake the steep 45-minute climb through Freycinet National Park to the beach, where they're rewarded with a sweep of uninterrupted white sand almost entirely to themselves.

→

Overlooking the swirling sands of Hill Inlet from Whitehaven Beach

The Hippest Stretches

Some beaches are more popular than others. Competition is tough for a patch of sand or a table overlooking the beach at permanently packed Bondi (p146). City slickers head to hip Byron Bay (p177) to soak up its alternative vibes, while the chic set descends on Noosa's Main Beach (p373) every summer, only drying off for a spot of shopping on the main strip.

←

Cape Byron Lighthouse, dominating the view from Byron Bay's beaches

Crafty Brews

Australia's brewing history dates back to Captain Cook. Nowadays, locals thirst for more than just Coopers and Foster's and Australia is home to over 500 microbreweries, including Black Brewing Co (*www.blackbrewingco.com.au*) in Margaret River and Capital Brewing Co in Canberra (*www.capital brewing.co*).

←

The bar and brewery at Black Brewing Co, Margaret River

AUSTRALIA
BY THE GLASS

Aussies love a tipple, whether it's a classy rooftop cocktail or a pint of bitter at the cricket ground. Of course, the country's experimental wine culture is world-famous but craft beer, cider and spirits round off the menu.

Grape Escapes

Wineries make a great day trip or overnight stay, and Australia has plenty of options. Swirl glasses of Pinot Noir by day then bed down in a sumptuous suite at Port Phillip Estate on the Mornington Peninsula (*www.portphillip estate.com.au*) or at Yarra Valley's lavish Chateau Yering (*www.chateauyering.com.au*). For a boutique stay in the Barossa Valley, head to plush The Louise for an unforgettable wine-filled escape (*www.thelouise.com.au*).

 INSIDER TIP
Wine Blending

Many wineries such as Penfolds (*www. penfolds.com*) and Mandoon Estate (*www. mandoonestate.com.au*), let you blend wine to suit your taste and take home a custom bottle.

Rows of vines at Chateau Yering in the Yarra Valley ↑

Outback Pubs

Australia's most remote locales, outback pubs offer an unforgettable drinking experience. These weather-beaten watering holes are surrounded by lonesome roads and endless desert – conditions that are sure to work up a thirst. The Northern Territory is home to the first outback pub, The Daly Waters Pub *(www.dalywaterspub. com)*, but Queensland has the most watering holes. Check out Betoota Hotel *(Birdsville Developmental Rd, Birdsville)* and Walkabout Creek Hotel *(27 Middleton St, Mckinlay)*, which was made famous by the film *Crocodile Dundee* (1986).

↑ Serving bottles of wine at the world-renowned Walkabout Creek Hotel

Tassie Whisky Trails

Thanks to ample barley, high-quality water and its comparatively cool climate, Tasmania has more whisky distilleries than any other state. Plot a route between tasting rooms to find your favourite single malt; most are within 90 minutes' drive of Hobart *(p282)*. Try Lark Distillery *(www.larkdistillery.com)*.

←

Explaining the whisky-making process during a tour of Lark Distillery, Hobart

Aussie Spirit

Aussie mixologists are endlessly inventive, serving up every-thing from apple brandy to green ant gin (the insects give it its citrusy notes). Hunt out unique libations on expertly cur-ated cocktail menus in Sydney, Brisbane and Melbourne, or sip on site. Bundaberg Rum's distillery runs excellent tours *(www. bundabergrum.com.au)*, as do Kangaroo Island Spirits *(www. kispirits.com.au)* and Wildbrumby *(www.wildbrumby.com)*, which creates butterscotch schnapps in the shade of Mt Kosciuszko.

→

Sunset cocktails at a rooftop bar with amazing views over Sydney

10,000

The estimated number of different Australian wines on the market at any one time.

THE WINES OF AUSTRALIA

A small consignment of vines was on board the First Fleet when it landed at Sydney Cove in January 1788, and grapes and wine have been produced in Australia virtually since European settlement. The first vineyards were created in Sydney in 1791 and over the next 40 years vines were planted in the Hunter Valley, the Barossa at Jacobs Creek, the Yarra Valley and Adelaide. In the 1960s, the introduction of international grape varieties, small oak-barrel maturation and modern winemaking technology saw the wine industry develop at pace. Since the 1990s, Australia has earned an excellent reputation for high-quality wines and there are more than 2,400 wineries operating today.

↑ A tasting at a vineyard in the Barossa wine region, South Australia

RED WINE

Australia's benchmark red is Penfolds Grange, the creation of the vintner Max Schubert in the 1950s and 60s. Due to his work, Shiraz has become Australia's premium red variety, although plenty of other red wines are also produced here, too, including Cabernet Sauvignon, Grenache and Mourvedre, which have been grown here for so long that they are classed as "old vine", can also be found in the Barossa and McLaren Vale.

 INSIDER TIP
Visiting a Winery

Wine tourism is understandably popular in Australia and information and maps are readily available at local information bureaux. Many wineries are open daily (but you should call ahead to avoid disappointment) and if they charge for tastings it will be refunded against a purchase from the "cellar door".

← Golden vines stretching into the distance in the Adelaide Hills wine region, and (inset) collecting harvested red grapes in the Barossa wine region

WHITE WINE

In the 1970s, a localized revolution in winemaking firmly established dry wines on the Australian table. These vintages were made from international grape varieties, including Chardonnay and Sauvignon Blanc, which all remain popular. Since 2000, the likes of Viognier, Pinot Gris, Riesling, Marsanne and Semillon have also been found on wine lists. Although many of these bottles are imported, a growing number are being Australian-made.

FORTIFIED WINE

Australia produces award-winning fortified and dessert wines. Australian winemakers use *botrytis cinerea*, or noble rot, to make luscious dessert wines such as De Bortoli's "Noble One", which is made with Semillon grapes from Riverina. Prefer something even sweeter? Northeast Victoria is famous for its fortified Muscats and Tokays, which are often described as liquid toffee.

SPARKLING WINE

Australia is justly famous for its sparkling wines, which range from Yalumba's Angas Brut to Seppelts Salinger. Tasmania in particular has shown considerable promise

WINE REGIONS OF AUSTRALIA

Since signing a trade agreement with the European Union, Australia has had to implement a classification system for its wine-producing regions. The whole of Australia has 28 wine zones, which can encompass a whole state (Tasmania) or part of a state (Western Victoria). Within these zones are 65 wine regions, including the centuries-old Barossa *(p324)*, Margaret River *(p464)* and Yarra Valley *(p272)*, as well as up-and-coming areas like Mudgee, Orange and Geelong.

in producing many high-quality sparkling wines, particularly Pirie from Pipers Brook. However, the real hidden gems are the sparkling red wines, which are made using the French Méthode Champenois - the wine is matured over a number of years and helped by a small drop of vintage port. The best producers of red sparkling wines are Rockford and Seppelts. These sparkling wines are available from "bottle shops" throughout the country.

Off-Road Rides

Mountain bikers are spoiled for choice when it comes to epic rides in Australia. Take on the 480-km (298-mile) Tasmanian Trail (*www.tasmaniantrail.com.au*), which winds through the Apple Isle, or the Wollemi Cycle Trail, a 442-km (275-mile) route through the Blue Mountains *(p160)*. It takes three weeks to cover the biggest of all, the Munda Biddi Trail from the south of Perth to Albany in the southwest *(www. mundabiddi.org.au)*. For a quicker thrill, ride the trails in Toohey Forest Park, near Brisbane, or the world-championship course at Smithfield in Cairns *(p388)* – this volcanic clay trail slices through dense rainforest.

AUSTRALIA FOR
THRILL SEEKERS

Australia is one big playground and there are plenty of ways to get your pulse racing and adrenaline pumping with adventures on the ground, in the air and on the water. Buckle in and enjoy a ride you won't forget.

Wet and Wild

Be prepared to get wet as you hurtle through Sydney Harbour at high speed on a jet-boat ride. Operators include Thunder Jet (*www.thunderjetboat.com. au*) and Harbour Jet *(www. harbourjet.com)*. Beyond the big city, the Blue Mountains *(p160)* are home to the world's most extensive wet sandstone canyoning system *(www. highandwild.com.au)*. The highlight of the day-long canyoning adventure? An abseil down a waterfall. Elsewhere, there are 60 rapids to tackle along the 19-km (12-mile) white-water rafting course on the Mitta Mitta River Gorge in Victoria's high country.

→

Abseiling down a waterfall in the Blue Mountains National Park

Balancing on a rock at Toohey Forest Park, near Brisbane

INSIDER TIP
Harbour Highs

Sunset climbs on the Sydney Harbour Bridge with BridgeClimb *(p88)* offer stunning views but at a premium price. To save money, book the last day-climb departure before sunset prices kick in and you'll still see the light fade and colour change over the city on your descent.

Adrenaline Highs

Scale the heights of the Sydney Harbour Bridge with BridgeClimb *(p88)* or get a bird's-eye view of the Gold Coast from the SkyPoint Climb *(www.skypoint.com.au)*. Prefer wild landscapes to cityscapes? Try bungy jumping in a rainforest at the Skypark in Cairns *(www.skyparkglobal. com)*. If you want to go even higher, skydive over Rottnest Island *(p460)*, Mission Beach *(p392)*, Byron Bay *(p177)* or Darwin *(p416)*.

Climbing the colossal Sydney Harbour Bridge with BridgeClimb

Hit the Slopes

Australian ski resorts aren't as rare as you might think: the country has 15 in all, including two located on Tasmania. If you're staying on the island, head to cheap-and-cheerful Mount Mawson *(www. mtmawson.info)* for downhill and cross-country skiing. Away from Australia's east coast, sand dunes are far more common than ski slopes. Stand up and surf or sit down and slide at Lancelin Sand Dunes *(www.lancelin.com.au)*, Port Lincoln *(p339)*, Vivonne Bay on Kangaroo Island *(p318)* or Stockton Dunes at Port Stephens *(p174)*, where you can also ride a quad bike down the sand.

Surfing down the powdery white slopes of the Lancelin Sand Dunes

Awesome Road Trips

Pack the van and a sense of adventure, and hit the highway. Follow in pioneers' footsteps on the Explorers Way, which stretches all the way from South Australia to the Northern Territory; dare to cross the barren Nullarbor Plain *(p334)*; or, for something shorter, drive the 4-km (2.5-mile) loop around The Pinnacles *(p482)*, located two hours from Perth.

Driving through The Pinnacles, Nambung National Park

AUSTRALIA FOR
EPIC JOURNEYS

If it's an adventure you're after, Australia delivers. Whether you want to experience it on foot, on the water, by rail or behind the wheel, this is a country of wild places and wide open spaces waiting to be discovered.

Rail Journeys

A big country means big train trips. The *Spirit of the Outback* takes 26 hours to rumble between Brisbane and Longreach *(www. queenslandrailtravel.com.au)*, while the Indian Pacific speeds between Sydney and Perth in just three days *(www.journeybeyond rail.com.au)*. The most epic (and luxurious) journey is *The Ghan*, which cuts across the outback between Adelaide and Darwin.

→

The Ghan, a luxury train, slicing through the outback in the Northern Territory

High-Rise Hikes

Bushwalking has long been a popular Australian pastime (p56). Lace up your hiking boots and trace Aboriginal songlines or follow in the footsteps of early European colonists on one of these trails. For alpine scenery, take on Tasmania's six-day Overland Track through the heart of the Cradle Mountain-Lake St Clair National Park (p296). Also on the island is the Three Capes Track (www.threecapestrack.com.au), a gentler, four-day coastal walk around Port Arthur (p287). On the mainland, walk north to south on Queensland's challenging five-day Scenic Rim Trail (www.parks.des. qld.gov.au). Short on time? Try the 5-km (3-mile) Echo Point to Scenic World walk, via the Giant Stairway, in the Blue Mountains (p160).

$\longrightarrow$

Hiking through the bush on the epic Overland Track, Tasmania

Coastal Cruising

There's something romantic about travelling on the water, especially with scenery like this. Soak up the paradisal landscape as you island hop around the Whitsundays with Cruise Whitsundays (www.cruise whitsundays.com) or cruise Talbot Bay in the Kimberley (p476). For city views, sail on a tall ship from Sydney's Darling Harbour (www. sydneytallships.com.au).

$\longleftarrow$

Tendering off Airlie Beach in the beautiful Whitsunday Islands

Paddle Power

Time stands still as you plough the Murray River on a historic paddle steamer (p261). Prefer to paddle under your own steam? Kayak on Pittwater, an estuary north of Sydney, with Pittwater Kayak Tours (www. pittwaterkayaktours.com.au) or go whitewater rafting on the Franklin river (www. franklinriverrafting.com).

$\longrightarrow$

Whitewater rafting the Newland Cascades on the Franklin river

HIKING AND BUSHWALKING

Aboriginal Australians were the first to traverse the country's diverse landscape on foot, looking for food and shelter. No longer necessary for survival, hiking has become a beloved Australian pastime, with locals following these ancient Aboriginal routes, as well as enjoying clifftop scrambles and forested walks. You're unlikely to hear an Australian use the word "hiking" though – "bushwalking" is used to describe walking not just in the forest and scrubland of the bush, but everywhere.

BUSHWALKING HISTORY

For thousands of years, Aboriginal people have crossed the land following songlines – sacred routes traced by creator beings during the Dreamtime. When white colonists, with no generational knowledge of the land, arrived in the 18th and 19th centuries they formed recreational walking groups to explore and demystify the seemingly impenetrable terrain. These clubs became the bedrock of modern Australia's bushwalking culture. By the 1940s, bushwalking was associated with self-sufficient, multi-day hikes into rugged areas. Nowadays the term encompasses all hiking styles, and Australia has an ever-expanding network of trails.

↑ Bushwalkers shadowing Euro Ridge on the Larapinta Trail

 TOP 5 DAY HIKES

Uluṟu Base Walk
A 10-km (6-mile) trail encircles Australia's most sacred monolith.

Mt Kosciuszko Summit
Scale Australia's highest peak on this 13-km (8-mile) circuit from Thredbo.

Wineglass Bay and Hazards Beach
Allow four or five hours for this challenging 11-km (7-mile) track.

Prince Henry Cliff Walk
One of the Blue Mountains' best hikes, this route is 7 km (4 miles) one way.

Bingi Dreaming Track
Follow ancient songlines over 13.5 km (8 miles) one way.

Walking down to Lucky Bay in the Cape Le Grand National Park ↑

COASTAL RAMBLES

Australia's jewel-like coves and dramatic cliffs beg to be explored on foot. In Western Australia, the challenging 15-km (9-mile) Coastal Trail in Cape Le Grand National Park traces dazzling beaches and rocky headlands. In Tasmania, hike the Bay of Fires to admire lichen-splashed rocks and white-sand beaches. Victoria's Great Ocean Road has numerous options for explorers of all abilities. When walking along the coast, always stick to marked trails for safety and to avoid encroaching on fragile coastal ecosystems.

LONG-DISTANCE EPICS

It's hardly surprising that this huge country is home to several long-distance hikes. Tasmania's Overland Track is a firm favourite: a six-day adventure through valleys and alpine meadows. In New South Wales, scramble across creeks and bunk down in old cattle herders' huts along the five-day Green Gully Track. Between April and September, hardy hikers can tackle the Larapinta Trail, which stretches for 223 km (140 miles) through the Northern Territory. Aussies generally have a healthy respect for nature's hidden dangers, so follow their lead by always heeding weather and fire warnings.

THE BUNDIAN WAY

Running 365 km (224 miles) between Targangal (Mt Kosciuszko) and Turemulerrer (Twofold Bay), the Bundian Way is set to become Australia's newest long-distance hike. "New" is something of a misnomer – the route follows a pathway used by the Bidawal, Jaitmathang, Ngarigo and Yuin peoples for millennia. While the route is being constructed, walk the Whale Dreaming Trail or Story Trail in Eden, which will eventually link up with the Way.

Wonderful Whale-Watching

Spring is whale-watching season in Australia. Humpback whales frolic off Hervey Bay *(p374)* from mid-July to early November, but August or September is the best time to see calves trying out new tricks. Albany's King George Sound *(p468)* welcomes resting humpbacks from June to August before southern rights arrive to breed from August to October. Southern right whales also visit South Australia between June and October, birthing their calves in the nursery waters around Head of Bight. Check SA Whale Centre's online log *(www.sawhalecentre.com.au)* to find out where these cetaceans have last been seen.

→

A humpback whale breaching within view of a whale-watching boat

AUSTRALIA FOR
WILDLIFE
ENCOUNTERS

Forget zoos and aquariums: nothing beats encounters with animals in their natural habitat. In Australia, you're sure to come face to face with both the cute and cuddly and the downright dangerous on land and in water.

Marvellous Marsupials

Kangaroos, wombats, koalas – Australia's most iconic animals are marsupials. You'll find them all on Kangaroo Island *(p318)*. For tame kangaroos, visit Pebbly Beach in Shoalhaven *(p192)*. To spot wandering wombats, head to Kangaroo Valley *(p192)* or Tasmania's Maria Island *(p290)* at dusk. Fallen for cuddly koalas? Make for the hospital at Port Macquarie *(p174)*, where injured and orphaned koalas are cared for.

 PICTURE PERFECT
Say Quokka!

Rottnest Island's quokkas are exceptionally photogenic. To get the perfect snap of these incredibly cute critters, wait until they look up towards your camera or are eating.

A female and joey red kangaroo ↑
(Macropus rufus)

Swim with Giants

To appreciate the full scale of whales and sharks, you have to get below the waterline. Swim with whale sharks from March to July and humpback whales from August to November on Ningaloo Reef (p485). Humpback whales also visit Hervey Bay (p374) between mid-July and early November. For the chance to swim with dwarf minke whales, head to Cairns (p388) or Port Douglas (p390) in June and July. Feeling brave? Go cage diving with great white sharks in Port Lincoln (p339).

← Beautiful Australian penguin standing near the water

TOP 3 WILDLIFE PARKS

Tasmanian Devil Unzoo
There are no fences at this wildlife park, just plenty of Tasmanian Devils (p299).

Lone Pine Koala Sanctuary
Admire koalas, kangaroos and other marsupials at this sanctuary (p361).

Phillip Island Nature Park
Watch from the viewing platform as little penguins waddle from the ocean to their burrow at night (p270).

Incredible Crocs

Australia is home to both saltwater and freshwater crocodiles. How do you tell them apart? "Salties" are the big ones. Watch these fearsome prehistoric creatures sunning themselves on riverbanks from the safety of a boat on the Adelaide River near Darwin (p425), the Mary River or Yellow Water Billabong in Kakadu (p422) or on the Daintree River (p391) in north Queensland.

↑ Freshwater crocodiles lounging in sun-dappled water

Modern Marvels

Australian art is constantly evolving. Discover the next big artist at the Heide Museum of Modern Art *(www.heide.com. au)* in Victoria or QAGOMA *(www.qagoma. qld.gov.au)* in Brisbane. In Sydney, check out the Museum of Contemporary Art *(p91)* and White Rabbit *(p115)*, a former Rolls-Royce showroom that now showcases contemporary Chinese art. Away from the mainland, the Museum of Old and New Art (MONA; *p284)* has been credited with transforming Tasmania into a cutting-edge cultural leader. Pieces include graphic religious depictions and a wall of vulvas.

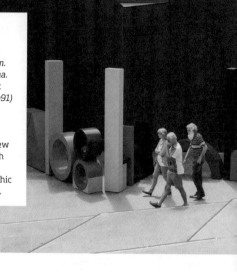

→

Outdoor sculptures at the Heide Museum of Modern Art, near Melbourne

AUSTRALIA FOR
ART LOVERS

Australian art spans a breathtaking timeline, stretching from 17,000-year-old rock etchings to millennial murals splashed across metropolises. And, although the big cities have impressive fine-art galleries, it's here – in the open air – that the country's art really comes alive.

National Galleries

State capitals hold the biggest collections of Australian art. In Canberra, the National Gallery of Australia *(p200)* houses almost 150,000 pieces, including Sidney Nolan's iconic Ned Kelly series. Nearby is the National Portrait Gallery *(p200)*, with depictions of several Aussie luminaries. In Melbourne, The National Gallery of Victoria *(p222)* explores the evolution of Australian art from Fist Nations paintings to contemporary prints.

←

Paintings in the salon of the National Gallery of Victoria

First Nations Art

Some 65,000 years of human history have gifted Australia an astounding collection of Aboriginal and Torres Strait Islander art. Get to grips with the different styles seen across the country at the National Gallery of Australia *(p200)*, which has a vast collection. Nothing beats seeing First Nations art in the great outdoors, however. Aboriginal guides lead visits in Western Australia's Burrup Peninsula *(p486)* and Queensland's remote Quinkan Country, where native fauna like dingoes and kangaroos dance across ochre rock faces. Want to have a go at making your own First Nations-style piece? Try dot-painting at Uluṟu's Maruku Arts *(www.maruku.com.au)* or Janbal Gallery near Cairns *(www.janbalgallery.com.au)*.

← Rock art in the main gallery on Injalak Hill, Arnhem Land

TOP 4 **ARTIST'S STUDIOS**

Brett Whiteley Studio
An avant-garde artist's hideaway *(www.artgallery.nsw.gov.au)*.

Margaret Olley Art Centre
A homage to the still-life artist *(www.artgallery.tweed.nsw.gov.au)*.

Hans Heysen Art Studio
Australia's oldest artist's studio *(www.hansheysen.com.au)*.

Norman Lindsay Gallery
This studio is surrounded by the misty Blue Mountains *(www.nationaltrust.org.au)*.

Public Art

Melbourne is famous for street art, and laneways like Hosier Lane and AC/DC Lane are ever-changing canvases *(p224)*. More murals can be found on Tocumwal Lane in Canberra, Anster Street in Adelaide, and in Sydney's Newtown and Enmore neighbourhoods. Artists have also transformed the outback by painting giant murals on grain silos across the country. Discover them on the 200-km (124-mile) Silo Art Trail *(www.australiansiloarttrail.com)*.

 INSIDER TIP
Gallery Nights

Major galleries, including the National Gallery of Victoria and the Art Gallery of New South Wales, host after-hours events with late viewings, drinks and live music. Book in advance.

↑ Painted silos in Grenfell, New South Wales, on the Silo Art Trail

Bush Tucker

Drawing on millennia of knowledge, Aboriginal guides lead foraging hikes, where guests nibble on medicinal plants, edible ants and native fruits while learning how to read the land. Options abound in New South Wales and around Uluṟu *(p434)*, where you can top off your experience by dining under the stars.

←

Learning traditional cooking methods in the Aurukun Wetlands

AUSTRALIA FOR
FOODIES

Australia's ever-inventive foodie scene combines Indigenous techniques with international flavours. Munch on classic Aussie dishes like meat pies, avocado on toast and bush tucker barbecue, or taste the world in the big cities and at food festivals.

Foodie Festivals

Australians celebrate their foodie scene with gusto. Taste of Summer *(www.tasteofsummer. com.au)* showcases Tasmania's produce while Taste of Kakadu *(www.parksaustralia.gov.au)* spotlights Aboriginal food culture. Narooma's Oyster Festival *(www.naroomaoysterfestival. com)* and the Truffle Kerfuffle in Manjimup *(www.trufflekerfuffle.com.au)* are popular, too.

Meet the Maker

Visiting a farmers' market is a weekend ritual for many. Standouts include Canberra's Capital Region Farmers Market (www.capitalregio farmersmarket.com.au), Sydney's Carriageworks (www.carriageworks.com.au) and Melbourne's Queen Victoria Market (www.qvm. com.au). Elsewhere, Adelaide Farmers Market (www. adelaidefarmersmarket.com. au) is cementing South Australia's status as a foodie hub and Fremantle's Freo Farmers Market (www. freofarmersmarket.com.au) promotes local food and music.

↑ A stallholder at Freo Farmers Market, held every Sunday in Fremantle

Scrumptious Seafood

Australia's coastal cities are brimming with the sea's bounty. Join fishing trips to catch native barramundi in the Northern Territory, snorkel for scallops in South Australia and watch divers seize abalone in Tasmania. Slurp juicy oysters in New South Wales, where farmers lead boat tours and shuck them on site, or learn the old ways in Queensland, where Aboriginal guides teach traditional crab-spearing.

← Barramundi, caught in Australian waters and served at a restaurant in Sydney

Food and Farm Gate Trails

Connecting different producers, food and farm gate trails are a great way to sample local flavours. Tasmania's Cradle to Coast Trail takes in olive growers, chocolatiers and dairies (www.tasting trail.com.au), while South Australia's Epicurean Way is all about local cheeses, berries and wine. Some trails are seasonal: visit mango farms in Queensland from October to April and Western Australia's truffle farms between June and September.

→ Juicy green olives, one of the delights to be sampled on the Cradle to Coast Trail

↑ A food festival celebrating local produce in Brisbane

A YEAR IN
AUSTRALIA

JANUARY

△ **Australian Open** *(mid–late Jan)*. Tennis stars battle for the year's first Grand Slam in Melbourne.

Australia Day/Invasion Day *(26 Jan)*. Many Australians celebrate the arrival of the First Fleet with concerts and fireworks, while Aboriginal communities and their allies protest with Invasion Day.

FEBRUARY

△ **Chinese New Year** *(varies, late Jan/Feb)*. Sydney's two-week lunar New Year celebrations are the largest outside of Asia, with fireworks, lanterns, dragons and lion dancers taking over the streets.

Adelaide Fringe *(mid-Feb–mid-Mar)*. The world's second-biggest arts festival takes over the South Australian capital with thousands of events.

MAY

Sydney Writers Festival *(late May)*. Australian and international authors talk about books and writing.

Ord Valley Muster *(mid–late May)*. Ten days of music, art, food and Aboriginal culture in the Kimberley.

△ **Vivid Sydney** *(late May–mid-Jun)*. Expect light installations, music and thought-provoking talks.

JUNE

Dark MOFO *(mid–late Jun)*. Hobart's cult mid-winter festival features offbeat arts and music, the huge Winter Feast and dawn Nude Solstice Swim.

△ **Alice Springs Beanie Festival** *(late Jun)*. A quirky showcase of handmade hats, including beanies crocheted by Aboriginal communities.

SEPTEMBER

△ **Carnival of Flowers** *(mid–late Sep)*. Flowers, food and music fill public parks and private gardens in Queensland's Toowoomba.

AFL Grand Final *(last Sat in Sep)*. The two top Australian Rules football teams play for the premiership trophy in Melbourne.

Riverfire *(late Sep)*. People line the banks of the Brisbane River to enjoy the fireworks.

OCTOBER

△ **Sculpture by the Sea** *(late Oct–early Nov)*. The coastal walk between Sydney's Bondi and Tamarama beaches is the location of the world's largest free public sculpture exhibition.

Grafton Jacaranda Festival *(late Oct–early Nov)*. Purple reigns when the New South Wales town of Grafton celebrates the annual jacaranda blossoms with a parade, music, exhibitions and markets.

MARCH

△ **Sydney Gay and Lesbian Mardi Gras**
(mid-Feb–early Mar). What began as a protest
march in 1978 is now a two-week-long, fun-filled
festival, ending with a huge sequin-and-glitter-
filled parade on the first Saturday in March.

Melbourne International Comedy Festival
(late Mar–Apr). One of the world's biggest
comedy festivals has Melbourne laughing
for three and a half weeks.

APRIL

△ **Byron Bay Bluesfest** *(Easter)*. A four-day music
festival with big names and a cool crowd.

Rip Curl Pro *(5 days in Apr)*. The longest-running
World Championship event on the surfing calendar is
held at rugged Bells Beach on the Great Ocean Road.

Tasting Australia *(late Apr–early May)*. Adelaide
hosts tastings, tours, masterclasses and meals.

JULY

△ **Yulefest** *(Jun–Aug)*. Christmas in Australia
is hot, so the Blue Mountains host a mid-year,
winter festival in its stead, with log fires, carols,
traditional roasts and occasional snow.

AUGUST

Garma Festival of Traditional Culture *(early Aug)*.
Guests share the cultural traditions of the Yolngu
people in Arnhem land through art, song and dance.

△ **Henley-on-Todd Regatta** *(mid-Aug)*. The
world's only boat regatta without water. Crews hold
the boat frames and run along the dry river bed.

NOVEMBER

△ **Melbourne Cup** *(first Tue in Nov)*. Punters cheer
on their horse in the "race that stops a nation" at
Melbourne's Flemington Racecourse.

Airlie Beach Festival of Music *(early Nov)*.
One of Queensland's best live-music events,
backdropped by the Whitsunday Islands.

Feast Festival *(early–late Nov)*. An LGBTQ+ arts
and cultural festival in Adelaide.

DECEMBER

Sydney to Hobart Yacht Race *(late Dec)*.
Sydneysiders line harbour vantage points to
watch yachts compete for first place.

Woodford Folk Festival *(27 Dec–1 Jan)*. The
semi-rural town of Woodford, north of Brisbane,
becomes Woodfordia village for the iconic music
and cultural festival.

△ **Sydney New Year's Eve Fireworks** *(31 Dec)*.
Hundreds of thousands of people cram the harbour
foreshore for the legendary midnight extravaganza.

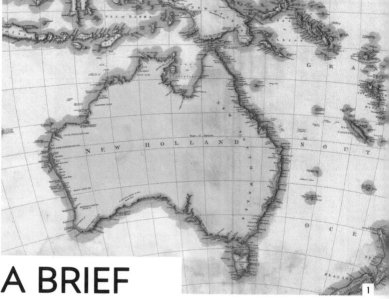

1

A BRIEF
HISTORY

Australia's unique character has been shaped by its vast and harsh landscape, a spirit of mateship forged through depressions and wars, and the many different peoples who have called this land home: from the first First Nations peoples to British convicts to today's multicultural communities.

The First Australians

The first people to settle in the land we now call Australia crossed the sea from Asia around 65,000 years ago, making them among the world's earliest mariners. Nomadic hunters-gatherers, they developed complex tools, including wooden javelins and the boomerang. Moving with the seasons, these First Nations peoples quickly spread across the continent in different clan groups, reaching Tasmania, which was then connected to the mainland, about 35,000 years ago. When the first Europeans arrived in the 17th century, Australia was home to over 750,000 First Nations peoples, living in over 500 different clan groups.

1 A map of Australia, and its neighbouring countries, drawn in 1818.

2 1819 watercolour illustration by Richard Browne, showing First Nations peoples fishing in a canoe.

3 A late 19th-century print depicting Abel Tasman's fleet.

Timeline of events

500,000,000 BCE
Australia is part of Gondwanaland with India, Africa, South America and Antarctica.

62,000 BCE
The first First Nations peoples reach Australia.

25,000 BCE
Then the largest marsupial, the *Diprotodon*, or giant wombat, becomes extinct.

20,000 BCE
Earliest evidence of the boomerang.

Foreign Forces

Europeans stumbled across Australia. The first of many accidental landings by the Dutch East India Company (VOC) was made by the ship *Duyfken* in 1606. Soon, the VOC launched decisive expeditions to learn more about this uncharted land. It was on one of these missions, in 1642, that Abel Tasman reached the island we now call Tasmania in his name. Tasman returned to map the mainland (which he proclaimed New Holland) in 1644.

British interest in New Holland, and its potential natural resources, began in the late 17th century. Privateer William Dampier became the first Briton to land on Australia when he beached the *Cygnet* near what is now Broome in 1688. Here, he encountered Aboriginal people, writing influential but ill-informed reports that they differed "little from brutes". In reality, First Nations peoples had a complex culture and, in the 18th century, clans began trading natural resources for tools with the Macassan people – Indonesian fishermen who sailed to northern Australia each December to catch trepang (sea cucumber) to sell in China.

BLOODY BATAVIA

The 1629 maiden voyage of VOC ship *Batavia* became its last when it struck a reef off Western Australia. Most of the crew swam ashore to the nearby Abrolhos Islands, but they were far from safe. When Commander Francisco Pelsaert set off for help, mutineer Jeronimus Cornelisz and his supporters killed 125 of their shipmates. It remains Australia's bloodiest shipwreck.

5,000 BCE

The dingo becomes the first domesticated animal to reach Australia.

1616

Dutch sailor Dirk Hartog accidentally reaches western Australia.

1644

Dutchman Abel Tasman proves to cartographers that Australia is an island continent.

1688

William Dampier is the first Englishman to land on Australian soil.

Cook and Convicts

In 1769, British captain James Cook set out in the *Endeavour* to find the supposed Southern Continent. When his expedition proved fruitless, he changed course for the uncharted east coast of New Holland. In 1770, Cook stepped ashore at Botany Bay, claiming the land for Britain and calling it New South Wales. Having lost many of its North American colonies after the American Revolution (1775–83), and seeking a solution to its overcrowded prisons, Britain decided to make New South Wales a penal colony. The First Fleet of 11 ships reached Sydney Cove from Portsmouth in 1788.

Creating New Colonies

Once New South Wales was established, the British set their sights on charting the surrounding land, exploiting its natural resources and establishing further settlements. Encounters with First Nations peoples along the way were often violent and many clans were massacred. The Australian states we know today were established over the course of the next 70 years and governed by the British until the 1940s. In 1788–9, Matthew Flinders and

RUM REBELLION

Australia's first, and only, military coup was staged in 1808 by the New South Wales Corps. Popularly known as The Rum Corps because of its control over the local rum trade, the Corps staged the insurrection when Governor William Bligh, of mutiny on the *Bounty* fame, tried to stop liquor being used as currency. The Corps arrested Bligh and took control of New South Wales for 23 months.

Timeline of events

1788
The First Fleet arrives in Sydney Cove to establish the convict settlement.

1793
First free settlers arrive in New South Wales.

1770
Captain James Cook claims the east coast of Australia for Britain.

1797
Merino sheep are introduced from the Cape of Good Hope.

1801–1803
Matthew Flinders circumnavigates the continent, which he names "Australia".

George Bass circumnavigated Tasmania, proving that it was an island. Due to its isolated position, the island was chosen to be a penal colony where convicts who reoffended in New South Wales would be transported. Ships arriving on the west coast founded the Swan River colony, now Perth, in 1829. Next came South Australia in 1836, which was the first colony established by free settlers rather than convicts. In contrast to other colonies, Victoria was established by negotiations between grazier John Batman and the local Aboriginal people in 1851. Queensland emerged when it separated from New South Wales in 1859.

From Boom to Bust

People had long fought over Australia's natural resources, but competition reached a fever pitch when gold was found near Bathurst, New South Wales, and at Ballarat and Bendigo in Victoria in 1851. Prospectors from around the world, particularly Europe and China, rushed to the gold fields. With new free settlers and newfound wealth, the colonies fast became progressive cities. Fortunes changed in the 1890s, however, when falling wool prices and a severe drought led to a depression.

1 Captain James Cook (1728-79). ↑

2 Settlers crossing South Australia's Nullarbor Plain.

3 Melbourne's Collins Street around 1837.

4 Gold rush miners' camp at Forest Creek, Victoria.

Did You Know?

Australia's first police force, established in 1788, was made up entirely of convicts.

1813
First currency, the holey dollar, introduced to reduce illegal rum trade.

1854
Eureka Stockade uprising by gold rush miners near Ballarat.

1838
Seven British settlers are sentenced to death for the Myall Creek massacre of 50 Aboriginal people.

1868
Transportation of convicts to Australia ends.

1876
Last Aboriginal Tasmanian, Truganini, dies.

Birth of a Nation

At the same time as more and more Asian immigrants chased the gold rush to Australia, the country's economy started to falter, causing nationalist sentiment and calls for Australian unification. In 1901, the six colonies (New South Wales, Victoria, Tasmania, Western Australia, South Australia and Queensland) formed the Commonwealth of Australia. Australia was still part of the British Empire, however, and sent forces to fight in Europe during World War I and World War II. The Australian and New Zealand Army Corps (Anzac) were the heroes at Gallipoli, Turkey, in 1915, inspiring the tradition of mateship that still defines the Australian character. This battle also encouraged an Australian independence movement, whose calls were answered in 1942 when Australia ratified the Statute of Westminister and became an autonymous dominion.

The First Nations Experience

While many Australians were enjoying their newfound independence and prosperity, the same was not true for the country's First Nations peoples. In 1951, the government launched a

1 Anzac troops in a World War I trench. ↑

2 Prime Minister Gough Whitlam (1972–5) meeting British Prime Minister Harold Wilson.

3 Sea of Hands, an annual art installation supporting Aboriginal and Torres Strait Islander land rights.

4 Fighting the 2019–20 Australian bushfires.

Timeline of events

1901
Proclamation of the Commonwealth of Australia in Centennial Park, Sydney.

1908
Canberra becomes the nation's capital.

1914–18
60,000 Australians killed in World War I.

1922
Vegemite spread is developed by an Australian chemist.

1942
Japanese Navy launch a submarine attack on Sydney Harbour during World War II.

4

policy of assimilation, placing mixed-race First Nations children in boarding schools far away from their families. These children became known as the "Stolen Generations". This policy continued until the election of Labor Prime Minister Gough Whitlam in 1972. While in office, Whitlam also launched a public inquiry into First Nations land rights, but these rights weren't enshrined into law until 1992. Australia is still working to acknowledge its traditional owners. In 2008, Prime Minister Kevin Rudd made a formal apology on behalf of the country to Australia's First Nations peoples for taking their land and trying to erase their culture.

Australia Today

Australia weathered the 2007–2008 global financial crisis thanks to a mining boom, but the country has felt the full force of climate change in the 21st century. The Great Barrier Reef has seen historic bleaching and bushfires have become an almost annual occurrence. In 2020–23, the country was also hit by floods and cyclones. Australians are used to adversity, however, and the resilience that has shaped much of the country's history is as strong as ever. The sports loving nation will host the 2032 Brisbane Olympic Games.

Did You Know?

Canberra was chosen for the capital because it was midway between bitter rivals Sydney and Melbourne.

1986

Proclamation of Australia Act breaks legal ties with Britain.

1992

High Court rules that all Australian First Nations hold valid claims to land.

2000

250,000 people join the Walk for Reconciliation on Sydney Harbour Bridge.

2010

Julia Gillard becomes first female Prime Minister of Australia.

2019–20

Bushfires burn 12.6 million hectares (32 million acres) of land across Australia.

EXPERIENCE

Surfers running on Cable Beach, Broome

SYDNEY

Sydney Harbour, with the Opera House and bridge

EXPLORE
SYDNEY

This section divides Sydney into four sightseeing areas, as shown on this map, plus an area beyond the centre. Find out more about each area on the following pages.

THE ROCKS AND CIRCULAR QUAY
p82

CITY CENTRE AND DARLING HARBOUR
p98

MILSONS POINT

Sydney Harbour Bridge

DAWES POINT

WALSH BAY

Barangaroo Reserve

Sydney Observatory

Museum of Contemporary Art

BARANGAROO

Museum of Sydney

State Libra of NS

PYRMONT

Australian National Maritime Museum

SEA LIFE Sydney Aquarium and WILD LIFE Sydney Zoo

Queen Victoria Building

Hyde Park

Sydney Town Hall

DARLING HARBOUR

Wentworth Park

Powerhouse Museum

CHINATOWN

GLEBE

ULTIMO

Paddy's Markets

FOREST LODGE

Victoria Park

CHIPPENDALE

University of Sydney

Prince Alfred Park

DARLINGTON

REDFERN

NEWTOWN

AUSTRALIA

KIRRIBILLI

SYDNEY

Sydney
Opera House

Sydney
Conservatorium
of Music

**ROYAL BOTANIC
GARDEN AND
THE DOMAIN**
p118

Art Gallery
of New
South Wales

POTTS
POINT

DARLING
POINT

St Mary's
Cathedral

WOOLLOOMOOLOO

ELIZABETH
BAY

Australian
Museum

KINGS
CROSS

RUSHCUTTERS
BAY

DOUBLE
BAY

DARLINGHURST

Sydney
Jewish Museum

EDGECLIFF

Old Gaol,
Darlinghurst

**KINGS CROSS,
DARLINGHURST AND
PADDINGTON**
p130

Trumper
Park

PADDINGTON

SURRY
HILLS

Paddington
Town Hall

WOOLLAHRA

Moore
Park

The Entertainment
Quarter

*Centennial
Park*

BONDI
JUNCTION

0 metres   500

0 yards   500

N

GETTING TO KNOW
SYDNEY

From The Rocks' historic buildings to the centre's soaring skyscrapers, the tranquillity of the Royal Botanic Garden to the buzzing atmosphere of Kings Cross, Australia's biggest city is dynamic and diverse. Becoming familiar with each area will help when planning your trip to this multifaceted metropolis.

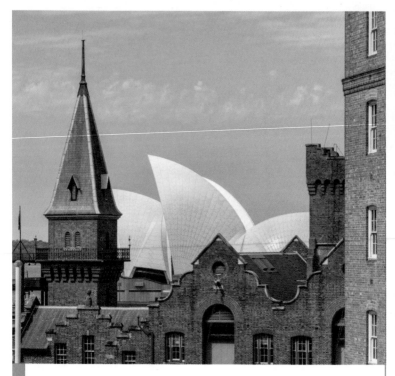

THE ROCKS AND CIRCULAR QUAY

PAGE 82

This is Sydney's waterside heart. Here, ferry horns punctuate the salty air as city workers scurry past strolling visitors hoping to catch sight of the city's dual icons – the Harbour Bridge and Opera House. To the west, in the shadow of the bridge, is The Rocks, a historic precinct made up of winding, cobbled streets and Victorian terraced houses. In the evening, the after-work crowd gathers in its quaint pubs; come the weekend, bargain-hunters flock to its markets.

Best for
Harbour life

Home to
Sydney Opera House, Sydney Harbour Bridge

Experience
Catching a show under the beautiful sails of the Opera House

CITY CENTRE AND DARLING HARBOUR

PAGE 98

Home to Sydney's best shops, massive museums and historic theatres, as well as soaring offices, the city centre is always a hive of activity. But there are some quiet moments to be found among the hustle and bustle: sipping a coffee from a hole-in-the-wall café and trundling along George Street – the city's spine – on a modern tram. Moving west, glitzy Darling Harbour is anything but quiet, especially at night, when its waterfront bars become the place to see and be seen.

Best for
Retail therapy

Home to
Australian Museum, Australian National Maritime Museum, Sydney Tower

Experience
The 360-degree views from the top of Sydney Tower

PAGE 118

ROYAL BOTANIC GARDEN AND THE DOMAIN

Sydney isn't short on recreation areas, but the Royal Botanic Garden still feels like a tranquil oasis. Its northern perimeter hugs the island-dotted harbour, making it the perfect place for a stroll. Separated from the garden by the motorway is the Domain. Overlooked by Australia's premier art gallery, this expansive and grassy patch hosts pulsating rock festivals, elegant open-air opera performances and energetic touch-football matches.

Best for
Waterfront walks

Home to
Royal Botanic Garden, Art Gallery of New South Wales

Experience
Posing for a picture-perfect Sydney selfie at Mrs Macquarie's Chair

$\rightarrow$

KINGS CROSS, DARLINGHURST AND PADDINGTON

"The Cross", "Darlo" and "Paddo" each have their own personality. To the north, Kings Cross is synonymous with strip clubs, tattoo parlours and seedy nightspots. If "The Cross" is Sydney's red light district, "Darlo" is its pink district – home to LGBTQ+ businesses and the city's annual Mardi Gras. Paddington, meanwhile, is elegance personified, with designer fashion along Oxford Street's "Golden Mile" and private art galleries in its backstreets.

Best for
The LGBTQ+ scene

Home to
Restaurants, shops and nightclubs

Experience
Sifting through handmade crafts, made by local artisans, at Paddington Markets

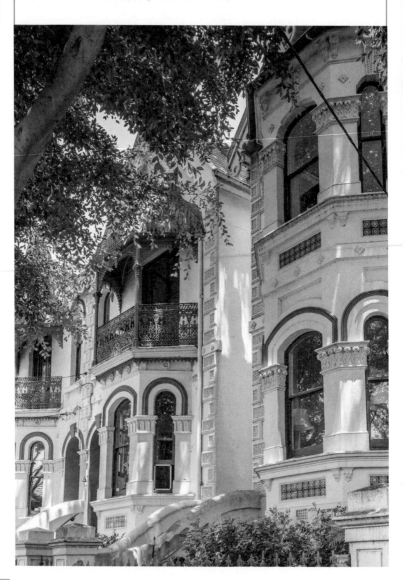

BEYOND THE CENTRE

Sydneysiders are proud of their city's setting, surrounded in all directions by deep, verdant forests, mist-shrouded mountains and glorious, sandy beaches, and spend as much time out in nature as possible. Head beyond the city limits and you'll encounter golden beaches to the east, with soft sand and roaring surf, and coastal paths buffeted by the wind, while close-knit suburbs and soaring mountains unfurl to the west. To the north, there are rugged headlands to climb, bushwalks to trek and wild amusement park attractions to ride.

Best for
Beautiful beaches and
boundless bushwalks

Home to
Manly, Bondi Beach

Experience
The clifftop coastal walk from
Bronte to Bondi

The historic Rocks and Sydney Opera House

THE ROCKS AND CIRCULAR QUAY

Once covered in bushland, the area that now forms The Rocks and Circular Quay was known as Tallawoladah by the Gadigal people, who used the area for fishing, cooking and camping. This part of Sydney is often referred to as the "birthplace of modern Australia", and it was here, in January 1788, that the First Fleet landed its human freight of convicts, soldiers and officials, declaring it the British colony of New South Wales. These European settlers carried smallpox, which spread to the Gadigal people and nearly wiped the population out. The settlers built shops and houses on the area of land they dubbed "The Rocks", which grew into a thriving trade hub for merchants and sailors. However, as wealthier residents moved out to the suburbs, The Rocks gained a reputation for squalor and crime, and in 1900 it suffered an outbreak of bubonic plague. This spurred major redevelopments in the area, which continued throughout the 20th century. Now scrubbed and polished, The Rocks forms part of the colourful promenade from the Sydney Harbour Bridge to the spectacular Sydney Opera House.

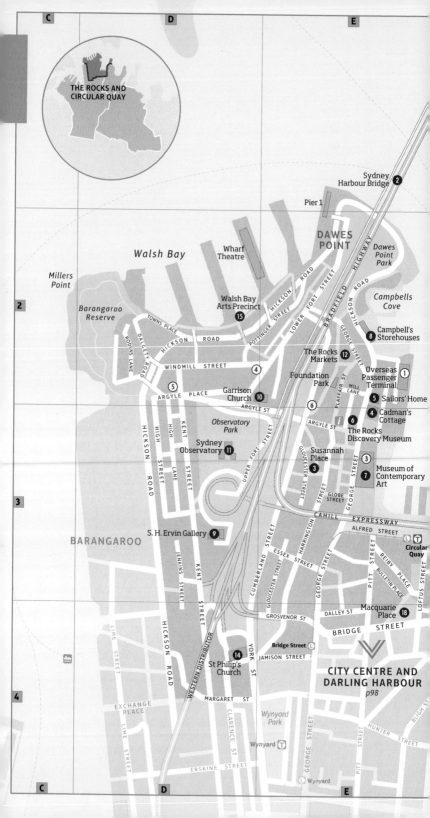

THE ROCKS AND CIRCULAR QUAY

Sydney Harbour Bridge **2**

Pier 1

DAWES POINT

Walsh Bay

Wharf Theatre

Dawes Point Park

Millers Point

Barangaroo Reserve

Walsh Bay Arts Precinct **15**

Campbells Cove

Campbell's Storehouses **8**

The Rocks Markets **12**

Overseas Passenger Terminal **1**

TOWNS PLACE

HICKSON ROAD

WINDMILL STREET

Foundation Park

Sailors' Home **5**

Cadman's Cottage **4**

Garrison Church **10**

ARGYLE PLACE

ARGYLE ST

ARGYLE ST

The Rocks Discovery Museum **6**

Observatory Park

Sydney Observatory **11**

Susannah Place **3**

Museum of Contemporary Art **7** **3**

GLOBE STREET

CAHILL EXPRESSWAY

S. H. Ervin Gallery **9**

ALFRED STREET

Circular Quay

BARANGAROO

ESSEX STREET

HARRINGTON STREET

REIBY PLACE

BULLETIN PLACE

GROSVENOR ST

DALLEY ST

Macquarie Place **18**

BRIDGE STREET

Bridge Street

JAMISON STREET

St Philip's Church **14**

CITY CENTRE AND DARLING HARBOUR
p98

MARGARET ST

Wynyard Park

Wynyard

ERSKINE STREET

LIME STREET

EXCHANGE PLACE

JENKINS STREET

KENT STREET

HICKSON ROAD

WESTERN DISTRIBUTOR

YORK ST

CLARENCE ST

GEORGE STREET

PITT STREET

HUNTER STREET

BLIGH ST

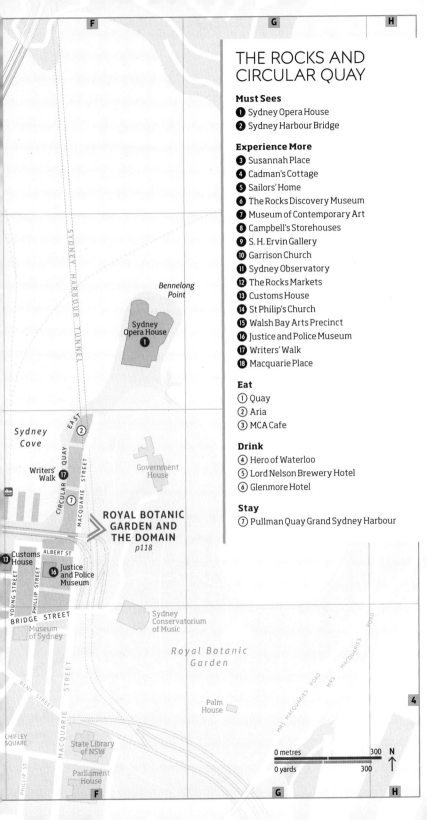

THE ROCKS AND CIRCULAR QUAY

Must Sees
1 Sydney Opera House
2 Sydney Harbour Bridge

Experience More
3 Susannah Place
4 Cadman's Cottage
5 Sailors' Home
6 The Rocks Discovery Museum
7 Museum of Contemporary Art
8 Campbell's Storehouses
9 S. H. Ervin Gallery
10 Garrison Church
11 Sydney Observatory
12 The Rocks Markets
13 Customs House
14 St Philip's Church
15 Walsh Bay Arts Precinct
16 Justice and Police Museum
17 Writers' Walk
18 Macquarie Place

Eat
1 Quay
2 Aria
3 MCA Cafe

Drink
4 Hero of Waterloo
5 Lord Nelson Brewery Hotel
6 Glenmore Hotel

Stay
7 Pullman Quay Grand Sydney Harbour

Bennelong Point

Sydney Opera House
1

Sydney Cove

Writers' Walk 17
2

CIRCULAR QUAY

MACQUARIE STREET

EAST

Government House

ROYAL BOTANIC GARDEN AND THE DOMAIN
p118

ALBERT ST

13 Customs House

16 Justice and Police Museum

YOUNG STREET

PHILLIP STREET

BRIDGE STREET

Museum of Sydney

Sydney Conservatorium of Music

BENT STREET

MACQUARIE STREET

Royal Botanic Garden

Palm House

CHIFLEY SQUARE

PHILLIP ST

MACQUARIE

State Library of NSW

Parliament House

MRS MACQUARIES ROAD

MACQUARIES ROAD

0 metres   300
0 yards   300

N

SYDNEY OPERA HOUSE

F2 Bennelong Point Circular Quay Circular Quay routes from Elizabeth St Circular Quay For tours and performances Good Fri, 25 Dec sydneyoperahouse.com

No visit to Sydney is complete without a visit to the masterpiece that is Sydney Opera House. This architectural icon has become a symbol of the city and is instantly recognizable all over the world.

There are few buildings with as distinctive a design as the Sydney Opera House. Popularly known as the "Opera House", it is, in fact, a complex of theatres and halls linked beneath its famous shells. Its birth was long and complicated: many of the construction problems had not been faced before, resulting in an architectural adventure that lasted 14 years, finally opening in 1973. Today it is Australia's most popular tourist attraction, as well as one of the world's busiest performing arts centres, hosting nearly 2,000 performances every year. The forecourt is a spectacular outdoor stage, often hosting festivals and concerts.

EAT

Bennelong
This innovative fine-dining restaurant is found right inside the Opera House.

Wed–Sun
bennelong.com.au

$$$

Midden by Mark Olive
Indigenous Australian-inspired cuisine in an open-air space with amazing harbour views.

sydneyopera house.com

$$$

DRINK

Opera Bar
Enjoy a cocktail, live music and great views.

operabar.com.au

$$$

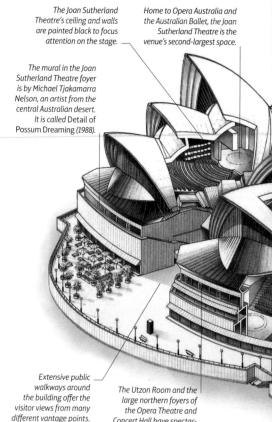

The Joan Sutherland Theatre's ceiling and walls are painted black to focus attention on the stage.

Home to Opera Australia and the Australian Ballet, the Joan Sutherland Theatre is the venue's second-largest space.

The mural in the Joan Sutherland Theatre foyer is by Michael Tjakamarra Nelson, an artist from the central Australian desert. It is called Detail of Possum Dreaming (1988).

Extensive public walkways around the building offer the visitor views from many different vantage points.

The Utzon Room and the large northern foyers of the Opera Theatre and Concert Hall have spectacular views over the harbour and can be hired for events.

Sydney Opera House lit up at night, and *(inset)* its grand Concert Hall

With seating for 2,690, the Concert Hall is the largest hall. It serves as a majestic setting for performances including music concerts, talks and comedy events.

The Monumental Steps and forecourt are used for outdoor performances.

The Playhouse, seating almost 400, is ideal for intimate productions, but is also able to present plays with larger casts.

Although fictitious, the theory that Jørn Utzon's arched roof design came to him while peeling an orange is plausible. The roof's highest point is 67 m (221 ft) above sea level.

↑ Illustration of the impressive Sydney Opera House

INSIDER TIP
Badu Gili

A spectacular, six-minute projection, *Badu Gili*, transforms the Opera House's eastern sails into a canvas for an art and light show after sunset, several times a night. This free display explores ancient Aboriginal culture.

Did You Know?

The Sydney Harbour Bridge is nicknamed "The Coathanger" because of its arch-based design.

SYDNEY HARBOUR BRIDGE

📍 E1 🏠 3 Cumberland St 🚆 Circular Quay, Milsons Point 🚢 Circular Quay
🚌 All routes to Circular Quay, 311 ⛴ Circular Quay 🕐 BridgeClimb: hours
vary, check website; Pylon Lookout: 10am–4pm Tue–Fri, 10am–6pm Sat–Mon

The magnificence of Sydney Harbour Bridge is best expressed in numbers: 1,400 workers were involved in its construction; over 150,000 vehicles cross the bridge each day; and approximately 30,000 litres (6,593 gal) of paint are required for each coat, enough to cover an area equivalent to 60 football pitches.

Prior to the construction of the Sydney Harbour Bridge in 1932, the only links between the city centre on the south side of the harbour and the residential north side were by ferry or a circuitous 20-km (12-mile) road route that involved five bridge crossings. The single-span arch bridge took eight years to build, and loans for the total cost of approximately 6.25 million old Australian pounds were only paid off in 1988. Today, the structure is a spectacular sight in its own right, but particularly memorable views are granted by taking the BridgeClimb – a three-and-a-half-hour tour up ladders, catwalks and finally the upper arch of the bridge (*www.bridgeclimb.com*).

 INSIDER TIP
Bargain Vistas

Pylon Lookout (*www. pylonlookout.com.au*) is a budget-friendly alternative to BridgeClimb. But walking along the bridge's pedestrian path is free.

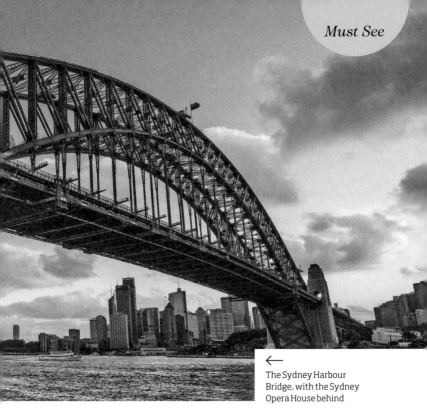

← The Sydney Harbour Bridge, with the Sydney Opera House behind

THE BRIDGE DESIGN

Planted in solid sandstone, the foundations of the bridge are 12 m (39 ft) deep. The arch was built in two halves, with steel cable restraints initially supporting each side as they grew towards the middle. Once both sides were complete, the support cables were slackened over a 12-day period to enable the two halves to join. The finished arch spans 503 m (1,650 ft) and supports the deck, which stands 59 m (194 ft) above sea level and was built from the centre outwards. Hinges at either end of the arch bear the bridge's full weight and spread the load to the foundations, with the assistance of 36-m- (188-ft)-long anchoring tunnels dug into rock. The hinges allow the structure to move as the steel expands and contracts in response to wind and extreme temperatures.

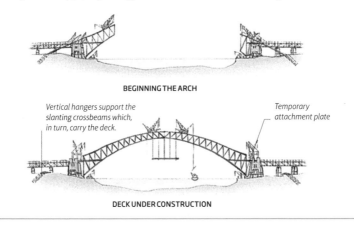

BEGINNING THE ARCH

Vertical hangers support the slanting crossbeams which, in turn, carry the deck.

Temporary attachment plate

DECK UNDER CONSTRUCTION

EXPERIENCE MORE

3

Susannah Place

📍 E3 🏠 58-64 Gloucester St, The Rocks 🚆 Circular Quay, Wynyard 🚊 Circular Quay 🚌 Circular Quay routes from Elizabeth St ⏰ 10am-5pm Thu-Sat (via guided tours only) 🚫 Good Fri, 25 Dec 🌐 mhnsw.au

This terrace of four brick and sandstone houses dating back to 1844 has a rare history of continuous domestic occupancy from the 1840s through to 1990. Built for Irish immigrants Edward and Mary Riley and their niece Susannah, these houses have remarkably survived the demolitions and redevelopments in the area.

Susannah Place is now a museum examining the living conditions of its former inhabitants. Rather than re-creating a single period, the museum retains the renovations carried out by tenants over the years – layers of different paints and wall-papers can be seen as well as various styles of storage in the basement kitchens and backyard outhouses.

↑ The charming 19th-century Cadman's Cottage, the oldest surviving dwelling in Sydney

4

Cadman's Cottage

📍 E3 🏠 110 George St, The Rocks 🚆🚊 Circular Quay 🚌 Circular Quay routes from Elizabeth St 🚫 To the public

Built in 1816 as barracks for the crews of the governor's boats, this sandstone cottage is Sydney's oldest surviving dwelling. Visitors can walk around the small, historic site, but cannot enter the building.

The cottage is named after John Cadman, a convict who was transported from England in 1798 for horse-stealing. By 1813, he was coxswain of a timber boat and later, coxswain of government craft. He was granted a pardon and in 1827 he was made boat superintendent and moved to this four-room cottage.

Cadman's Cottage was built on the foreshore of Sydney Harbour. Now, as a result of successive land reclamations, it is set well back from the water's edge.

5

Sailors' Home

📍 E2 🏠 106 George St, The Rocks 🚆🚊 Circular Quay 🚌 Circular Quay routes from Elizabeth St

These lodgings were built in 1864 for visiting sailors. The first and second floors were dormitories but these were later divided into 56 cubicles or "cabins", which were arranged around open galleries and lit by four large skylights. At the time it was built, the Sailors' Home was a welcome

→ The distinctive façade of the Museum of Contemporary Art

ARGYLE CUT

One of the most impressive engineering feats in the early days of Sydney was the Argyle Cut - a tunnel that cut through a sandstone ridge and connected The Rocks to Millers Point. Its construction first began in 1843 with convict labour chiselling the rugged rock face and was eventually completed using explosives in 1859. The cut is now a heritage-listed roadway.

alternative to the many seedy inns and brothels in the area, saving sailors from the perils of "crimping". "Crimps" would tempt newly arrived men into bars providing much sought-after entertainment. While drunk, the sailors would be sold on to departing ships, waking miles out at sea and returning home in debt.

---

dialogue with the Metropolitan Aboriginal Land Council, so that the culture and history of Aboriginal people in the area, including the impact of European settlement, is comprehensively represented.

Museum of Contemporary Art

♀E3 **♠**140 George St, The Rocks 🚆🚇Circular Quay 🚌Circular Quay routes from Elizabeth St 🕐10am-5pm Wed-Mon 🚫25 Dec 🌐mca.com.au

When Sydney art collector John Power died in 1943, he left his entire collection and a financial bequest to the University of Sydney. In 1991 the collection, which by then included works by Hockney, Warhol, Lichtenstein and Christo, was transferred to this 1950s Art Deco-style building. In addition to showing its permanent collection, the museum hosts exhibitions by local and international artists. The on-site shop sells distinctive gifts by Australian designers.

The Rocks Discovery Museum

♀E3 **♠**Kendall Lane, The Rocks 🚆🚇Circular Quay 🚌Circular Quay routes from Elizabeth St 🕐10am-5pm daily 🚫Good Fri, 25 Dec 🌐rocksdiscoverymuseum.com

This fascinating museum, in a restored 1850s sandstone house, is home to a collection of archaeological artifacts and images that detail the story of The Rocks from the pre-European days to the present. There are four permanent exhibitions, which are highly interactive and fun, making use of touch screens and audio and visual technology.
   The exhibitions at the Rocks Discovery Museum have been developed in

---

EAT

Quay
Overlooking Sydney Harbour, Quay serves exquisitely prepared dishes made with rare, local ingredients.

♀E2 **♠**Upper Level, Overseas Passenger Terminal, The Rocks 🌐quay.com.au

$$$

Aria
Feast on modern Australian food in this stunning, art-filled space.

♀F3 **♠**1 Macquarie St 🌐ariasydney.com.au

$$$

MCA Cafe
Enjoy café fare and harbour views from the terrace of the Museum of Contemporary Art.

♀E3 **♠**140 George St, The Rocks 🌐mca.com.au

$$$

Cityscape of The Rocks, with Campbell's Storehouses in the foreground ↑

DRINK

Hero of Waterloo

This sandstone pub is virtually unchanged since 1843, with live music, a rumoured smugglers' tunnel and a resident ghost.

📍 D2 🏠 81 Lower Fort, St Millers Point 🌐 heroof waterloo.com.au

---

Lord Nelson Brewery Hotel

This is Australia's oldest continually licensed pub and brewery. Try one of the six all-natural ales brewed in-house.

📍 D2 🏠 19 Kent St, The Rocks 🌐 lordnelson brewery.com

Glenmore Hotel

Head up three flights of stairs to the pub's buzzy rooftop bar and soak in the superb harbour views over a cold beer.

📍 E2/3 🏠 96 Cumberland St, The Rocks 🌐 theglenmore. com.au

8
Campbell's Storehouses

📍 E2 🏠 7-27 Circular Quay West, The Rocks 🚆 Circular Quay 🚌 Circular Quay routes from Elizabeth St

Robert Campbell, a prominent Scottish merchant in the early days of Sydney, purchased land on Sydney Cove in 1799. In 1802, he began constructing a private wharf and store-houses in which to house the tea, sugar, spirits and cloth he imported from India. The first five sandstone bays were built between 1839 and 1844, and then seven more were built between 1854 and 1861. The entire row of storehouses, including a brick upper storey, was finally completed in 1890. Eleven of the original stores are still standing, and the pulleys that were used to raise cargo from the wharf can be seen near the top of the preserved buildings.

Today, the bond stores contain fine restaurants serving different cuisines, including contemporary Australian, Chinese and Italian. The virtually unim-peded views across Circular Quay towards the Sydney Opera House (p86) and Sydney Harbour Bridge

Did You Know?

One Sydharb - a unit to measure volume - is equivalent to 500 GL, the volume of water in Sydney Harbour.

(p88) make these outdoor eating establishments very popular with locals and tourists alike.

9
S. H. Ervin Gallery

📍 D3 🏠 Observatory Hill, Watson Rd, The Rocks 🚆 Circular Quay 🚌 311 🕐 11am–5pm Tue–Sun 🚫 Public hols 🌐 shervin gallery.com.au

Housed in the historic headquarters of the National Trust of Australia, the S H Ervin Gallery explores the richness and diversity of Australian art, especially contributions made by Australian women artists. The gallery hosts changing exhibitions throughout the year as well as special events, public programmes and popular annual shows such as the Portia Geach Memorial Award and Salon des Refusés:

The Alternative Archibald and Wynne Prize, which showcases some of the works that were not selected for the prestigious Australian art prizes.

Garrison Church

D/E2 Cnr Argyle & Lower Fort sts, Millers Point Circular Quay, then walk Bridge St 311 For Sun services only churchhillanglican.com

Officially named the Holy Trinity Church, this was the colony's first military church.

English architect Henry Ginn designed the church and, in 1840, the foundation stone was laid. In 1855, it was enlarged to accommodate up to 600 people. Regimental plaques hanging along interior walls recall the church's military associations and a small cabinet displays Australian military and historical items.

Other features to look out for are the brilliantly coloured east window and the carved red cedar pulpit.

$\rightarrow$
Stalls lining George Street at The Rocks Markets

Sydney Observatory

D3 Observatory Hill, Watson Rd, The Rocks Circular Quay 311 10am-5pm daily 25 Dec powerhouse. com.au

In 1982, this domed building, which had been a centre for astronomical observation and research for almost 125 years, became the city's astronomy museum. It has interactive displays and games, along with night-sky viewings; it is essential to book for these.

The observatory building began life in the 1850s as a time-ball tower. At 1pm daily, the ball on top of the tower dropped to signal the correct time. Simultaneously, a cannon was fired at Fort Denison. This custom continues today.

During the 1880s, Sydney Observatory became world-famous when the first astronomical photographs of the southern sky were taken here. From 1890 to 1962 the observatory mapped some 750,000 stars as part of an international project that resulted in an atlas of the entire night sky.

The Rocks Markets

E2 George & Playfair sts Circular Quay Circular Quay routes 10am-5pm Sat & Sun therocks.com

More than 150 artisans set up shop under the white canvas sails that line Australia's oldest streets, transforming cobblestone backstreets into a bustling weekend market. Wares include unique pieces from local artists and designers, handcrafted jewellery, leather goods and distinctive homeware. The sounds of buskers and street entertainers create a lively atmosphere and the air is filled with the sweet, floral scents of handmade soaps and the aroma of grilled meats and freshly brewed coffee.

Customs House

📍 E/F3 🏠 31 Alfred St, Circular Quay 🚇 Circular Quay 🚌 Circular Quay routes from Elizabeth St 🕐 8am-midnight Mon-Fri, 9am-midnight Sat, 9am-5pm Sun 🚫 Good Fri, 25 Dec 🌐 sydneycustomshouse.com.au

Colonial architect James Barnet designed this 1885 sandstone Classical Revival building on the site of a previous Customs House. It recalls the days

The transparent floor at the entrance of the Customs House, and *(inset)* its façade ↑

when trading ships berthed at Circular Quay. The building stands near the mouth of Tank Stream, the European colony's freshwater supply. Among its many features are tall veranda columns of polished granite, a sculpted coat of arms and a clock face, added in 1897, which features tridents and dolphins.

A full refurbishment was completed in 2005. Facilities include a City Library with a reading room and exhibition space, and an open lounge area with a bar and an international newspaper and magazine salon. On the roof, Café Sydney offers great views.

church was a local landmark when it was first built.

The original 1793 church burned down and was replaced in 1810. Construction of the current building, designed by Edmund Blacket, began in 1848. Work was disrupted in 1851, when the stonemasons left for the gold fields, but by 1856 the church was finally completed.

A peal of bells was donated in 1888 to mark Sydney's centenary, and they still announce the services each Sunday.

STAY

Pullman Quay Grand Sydney Harbour

A short stroll from the Opera House, and with harbour views, the Pullman is the go-to hotel for sightseers.

📍 F3 🏠 61 Macquarie St 🌐 pullmanquaygrand sydneyharbour.com

$ $ $

---

14 St Philip's Church

📍 D4 🏠 3 York St (enter from Jamison St) 🚉 Wynyard 🚌 Bridge St, Wynyard 🚌 311 🕐 For Sun services only 🌐 churchhillanglican.com

Dwarfed by modern edifices today, the square tower of this Victorian Gothic

---

15

Walsh Bay Arts Precinct

📍 D2 🏠 Hickson Rd 🚌 324, 325, 311 🌐 walshbay.com.au

In the early 20th century, Walsh Bay was a busy shipping port. Its nine

200-m- (650-ft-) long wharves were built in the 1920s to serve the ships that needed to moor here. With changing shipping technology in the 1970s, the port was no longer needed and the wharves became home to a hotel, apartments, offices, restaurants and theatres. With eight performing arts companies based in the area, including Sydney Dance Company, Bangarra Dance Theatre, Sydney Theatre Company and the Australian Chamber Orchestra, it soon became known as the Walsh Bay Arts Precinct. Before taking in a show, stroll along the incorporated walkways around the wharves and then head to one of the many restaurants for a pre-show drink or dinner. The Theatre Bar at the End of the Wharf on Pier 4/5 has sweeping harbour views.

Justice and Police Museum

16

Q F3 **A** Cnr Albert & Phillip sts **T** Circular Quay, Martin Pl **C** Circular Quay **B** Circular Quay routes from Elizabeth St **Q** 10am–5pm Sat & Sun (Jan & NSW school hols: daily) **C** Good Fri, 25 Dec **W** mhnsw.au

The exhibits at this museum powerfully evoke the realities of Australian policing and justice. The buildings housing the Justice and Police Museum originally comprised the Water Police Court, designed by Edmund Blacket in 1856, the Water Police Station, designed by Alexander Dawson in 1858, and the Police Court, designed by James Barnet in 1885. Here the underworld of quayside crime, from the petty to the violent, was dealt swift and, at times, harsh justice.

Exhibits in the museum recreate this turbulent period. Formalities of the legal proceedings in the late-Victorian period can be easily imagined in the fully restored courtroom. Menacing implements, from knuckledusters to bludgeons, are displayed as the macabre relics of notorious crimes. Other interesting aspects of policing, criminality and the legal system are highlighted in special changing exhibitions.

17

Writers' Walk

Q F3 **A** Circular Quay **T C** Circular Quay **B** Circular Quay routes from Elizabeth St

This series of plaques is set in the pavement at regular intervals between East and West Circular Quay. It gives the visitor the chance to ponder the observations of famous Australian writers, both past and present, on their home country, as well as the musings of some noted literary visitors.

Each plaque is dedicated to a particular writer, consisting of a personal quotation and a brief biographical note. Australian writers in the series include the novelists Miles Franklin and Peter Carey, poets Oodgeroo Noonuccal and Judith Wright, humorists Barry Humphries and Clive James, and the influential

HIDDEN GEM
Foundation Park

After reaching the western end of Writers' Walk, extend your stroll by continuing on to Foundation Park. Here, you wander through the ruins of eight 1870s terrace houses that once stood at Gloucester Walk. Look out for hidden doors, sculptures and even a bathtub.

feminist writer Germaine Greer. Among the international writers included are Mark Twain, Charles Darwin and Joseph Conrad.

18

Macquarie Place

Q E4 **C** Circular Quay, Bridge St **B** Circular Quay routes from Elizabeth St

Governor Macquarie created this park in 1810 on what was once the vegetable garden of the first Government House. The sandstone obelisk, designed by Francis Greenway (p129), was erected in 1818 to mark the starting point for all roads in the colony. The gas lamps recall the fact that this was also the site of the city's first street lamp in 1826.

Also in the park are the remains of the bow anchor and cannon from HMS Sirius, flagship of the First Fleet, and a statue of Thomas Mort, a 19th-century industrialist.

← The recovered anchor at Macquarie Place

A SHORT WALK
THE ROCKS

Distance 1 km (0.5 miles) **Time** 15 minutes **Nearest train and light rail** Circular Quay

Named for the rugged cliffs that were once its dominant feature, this area has played a vital role in Sydney's development. In 1788, the First Fleeters under Governor Phillip's command erected makeshift buildings here, with the convicts' hard labour used to establish more permanent structures in the form of rough-hewn streets. The construction of Argyle Cut, a road carved through solid rock using just hammer and chisel, began in 1843. By 1900, The Rocks was overrun with disease; the street now known as Suez Canal was once Sewer's Canal. This walk takes you past some of the area's most significant sights.

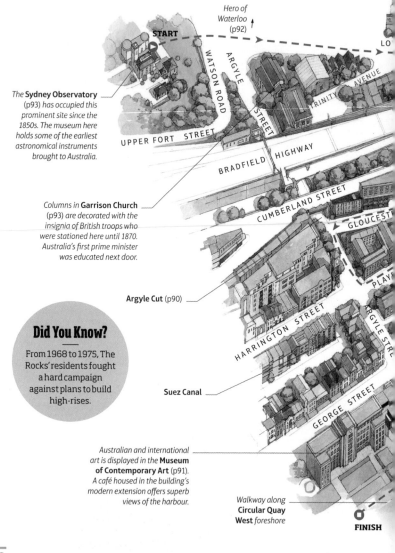

The **Sydney Observatory** (p93) *has occupied this prominent site since the 1850s. The museum here holds some of the earliest astronomical instruments brought to Australia.*

Columns in **Garrison Church** (p93) *are decorated with the insignia of British troops who were stationed here until 1870. Australia's first prime minister was educated next door.*

Argyle Cut (p90)

Did You Know?

From 1968 to 1975, The Rocks' residents fought a hard campaign against plans to build high-rises.

Suez Canal

Australian and international art is displayed in the **Museum of Contemporary Art** (p91). *A café housed in the building's modern extension offers superb views of the harbour.*

Walkway along **Circular Quay West** *foreshore*

FINISH

Locator Map
For more detail see p84

↑ Shoppers browsing the stalls at The Rocks Markets

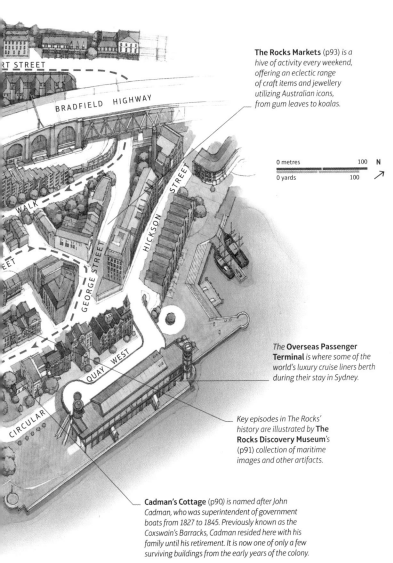

The Rocks Markets (p93) *is a hive of activity every weekend, offering an eclectic range of craft items and jewellery utilizing Australian icons, from gum leaves to koalas.*

0 metres   100   **N**

0 yards   100

The **Overseas Passenger Terminal** *is where some of the world's luxury cruise liners berth during their stay in Sydney.*

Key episodes in The Rocks' history are illustrated by **The Rocks Discovery Museum**'s *(p91) collection of maritime images and other artifacts.*

Cadman's Cottage (p90) *is named after John Cadman, who was superintendent of government boats from 1827 to 1845. Previously known as the Coxswain's Barracks, Cadman resided here with his family until his retirement. It is now one of only a few surviving buildings from the early years of the colony.*

Darling Harbour, overlooked by towering skyscrapers

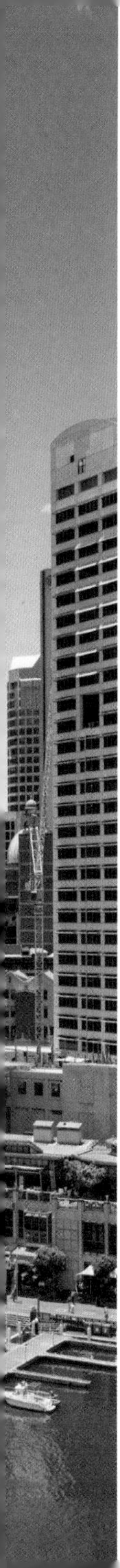

CITY CENTRE AND DARLING HARBOUR

The centre of Sydney was originally inhabited by the Gadigal people. They once had a number of trading routes running through this area, between farmed grasslands and fishing areas, and these tracks are thought to have formed the basis of several thoroughfares established by European colonizers. Among the earliest of these roadways was George Street, which was originally lined with mud and wattle huts, but came to be dominated by shops and banks following the gold rush. The country's industrial age began in Darling Harbour in 1815 with the opening of a steam mill, but later the area became run-down. In the 1980s, it was the site of low-rise, tourism-focused redevelopment, followed by another wave of redevelopment from 2016, including new entertainment facilities, high-rises and hotels, and pedestrian walkways, all revitalizing the city's heart.

CITY CENTRE AND DARLING HARBOUR

Must Sees

1. Australian Museum
2. Australian National Maritime Museum
3. Sydney Tower

Experience More

4. Queen Victoria Building
5. Strand Arcade
6. Martin Place
7. Lands Department Building
8. Museum of Sydney
9. State Theatre
10. St Mary's Cathedral
11. Great Synagogue
12. Sydney Town Hall
13. St Andrew's Cathedral
14. Hyde Park
15. Darling Harbour
16. The Goods Line
17. SEA LIFE Sydney Aquarium and WILD LIFE Sydney Zoo
18. Sydney Fish Market
19. Barangaroo
20. King Street Wharf
21. Chinatown
22. Chinese Garden of Friendship
23. Chippendale
24. Paddy's Markets

Eat

1. The Eight
2. Emperor's Garden Cakes & Bakery
3. The Malaya
4. Ester
5. LuMi

Stay

6. QT Sydney
7. Sofitel Sydney Darling Harbour

Shop

8. The Nut Shop
9. Strand Hatters
10. Andrew McDonald Shoemaker

Huge whale skeleton
hanging in the Wild
Planet exhibition ↑

Did You Know?

The museum's first
taxidermist was John
Roach, an ex-convict
who later set up a
taxidermy shop.

🛈 ⊗ 🍴 ▢ 🛍

AUSTRALIAN MUSEUM

📍F6 🏠1 William St 🚇Museum, Town Hall 🚌311, 323, 324, 325, 389
🕐10am–5pm daily 🚫25 Dec 🌐australian.museum

A treasure trove for the curious, this hub of scientific discovery and storytelling explores the richness of life in Australia and the Pacific through its natural history collections and cultural experiences.

Founded in 1827, this compelling collection was both Australia's first museum of natural history and its first public museum; today it is the nation's leading natural science museum. The main building, an impressive sandstone structure with a marble staircase, faces Hyde Park. The museum reopened in 2020 following an extensive redevelopment, which saw exhibition and public spaces expanded and improved.

The exhibitions provide a journey across Australia and the near Pacific, covering biology, and natural and cultural history.

> **The exhibitions provide a journey across Australia and the near Pacific, covering biology, and natural and cultural history.**

Key Exhibitions

Garrigarrang: Sea Country

▷ Discover the rich cultures and spiritual traditions of the Salt Water People who have lived along Australia's coastline for thousands of years. Explore creation stories and whale ceremonies from the New South Wales coast and see cultural costumes and masks from the Torres Strait.

Surviving Australia

Discover what it takes for wildlife to survive in Australia by exploring how animals have adapted to live in the nation's waterways, deserts, mountains and even backyards. Spiders, snakes and kangaroos are all covered, plus extinct species such as the Tasmanian tiger and megafauna like the giant diprotodon.

Dinosaurs

◁ Step into a prehistoric world as you walk among towering, life-size models of real dinosaur skeletons. There are displays of fossil teeth, skulls, claws and eggs, as well as the world's first anatomically correct model of a T-rex. Interactive exhibits let you smell the Mesozoic world, make dinosaur calls and experience life through the eyes of a dinosaur.

First Nations Gallery Garrigarrang and Wild Planet are on the ground floor, while the Long Gallery showcases 200 Treasures over two levels – priceless treasures on the ground floor and the stories of 100 influential Australians on level one. Birds can be found on level two, along with Surviving Australia and Dinosaurs. The museum's changing programme of events includes expert talks, workshops, screenings and exhibition tours.

200 Treasures

▷ A hundred priceless treasures from the museum's collections are showcased in the magnificent Long Gallery, alongside stories of 100 influential people who helped shape Australia. The rare objects range from an Egyptian mummy to Eric the opalised pliosaur, who lived more than 66 million years ago, while the extraordinary people covered include explorers, entrepreneurs, aviators and artists.

MR BLOBBY - THE WORLD'S "UGLIEST" FISH

The museum's collection includes a rare blobfish, or fathead sculpin, which are found northwest of New Zealand at a depth of between 1,000 m (3,280 ft) and 1,300 m (4,265 ft). The scientists and crew of the RV *Tangaroa* collected this specimen in 2003 and named it "Mr Blobby" for its large head and flabby body.

② 🛠 Ⓜ 🖥 🛍

AUSTRALIAN NATIONAL MARITIME MUSEUM

📍C5 🏠2 Murray St, Darling Harbour 🚆Town Hall Ⓛ Convention, Pyrmont Bay 🚌389 ⛴Pyrmont Bay Wharf 🕐10am–4pm daily (Jan: to 6pm) 🚫25 Dec 🌐sea.museum

Bounded as it is by the sea, Australia has a history inextricably linked to maritime traditions. The Australian National Maritime Museum explores this seafaring heritage.

The museum displays material in a broad range of permanent and temporary thematic exhibits, many with interactive elements. Along with artifacts relating to the enduring Aboriginal maritime cultures, the exhibits here survey the history of European exploratory voyages in the Pacific, the arrival of convict ships, successive waves of migration, water sports and recreation, and naval life. Historic vessels on show at the wharf include a flimsy Vietnamese refugee boat; sailing, fishing and pearling boats; a Navy patrol boat; and a World War II commando raider.

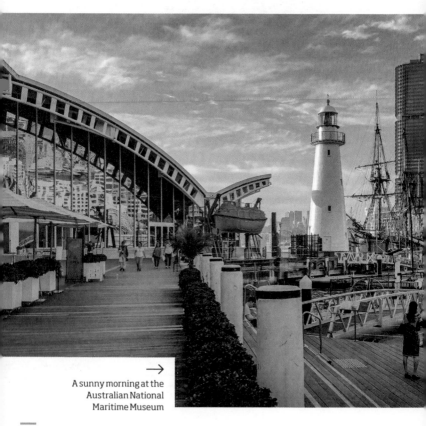

→
A sunny morning at the Australian National Maritime Museum

↑ Models of ships on display at the Australian National Maritime Museum

ACTIVITIES FOR CHILDREN

Young visitors to the museum can enjoy games, activities and excursions scheduled throughout the school and holiday calendars. Kids on Deck offers a workshop space to make art inspired by the exhibits, while self-guided activity trails take youngsters on a tour of museum exhibitions. Children can also take a peek beneath waves, talk to fish and play with seawater at the interactive Sea Science Pontoon.

Museum Highlights

HMS Onslow

▷ Experience the world of submarines in this stealthy, soundproofed submarine commissioned to watch, listen and collect information during the Cold War. A diving chamber allowed special forces to leave the boat unnoticed, while rubbish was ejected in weighted bags designed to sink so as not to reveal the sub's position.

HMS Vampire

Climb aboard the museum's largest vessel, a high-speed destroyer that served the Royal Australian Navy from 1959 to 1986. Despite having hefty firepower, including state-of-the art anti-aircraft guns and torpedo launchers, its peaceful career included escorting troops to Vietnam and HMY *Britannia* during Queen Elizabeth II's Silver Jubilee tour of Australia in 1977.

Under Southern Skies

This exhibit has more than 500 objects, including bark paintings, compasses and telescopes, which testify to incredible feats of navigation around the "Great Southern Land" of Australia. At the helm of the boats that have sailed around this vast landmass were Europeans, Makassan fishermen and traders from present-day Indonesia, Zheng He's Chinese fleet and Polynesian sailors.

Captain Cook's Endeavour

▽ One of the world's most accurate replicas of a maritime vessel, this re-creation of HMS *Endeavour* shows the true scale of Captain Cook's famous ship, which became the first European vessel to reach the east coast of Australia in 1770. It is 30 m (98 ft) long and its 28 sails are made up of almost 1 sq km (0.4 sq miles) of canvas. Step on board to experience how Cook and his crew lived on this vessel and learn more about how Cook's landing has affected the Australian experience in the past and present.

Did You Know?

If the 56 cables were untwined and laid end to end, they would reach from Sydney to New Zealand.

3 🏃 🍴 🖥 🛍

SYDNEY TOWER

📍 E5 🏠 100 Market St 🚇 St James, Martin Place, Town Hall 🚍 QVB 🚌 All city routes 🕐 10am–7pm Thu–Sun (10am–9pm during school hols) 🌐 sydneytowereye.com.au

Dominating the skyline, the iconic Sydney Tower is one of the city's tallest structures at 309 m (1,000 ft). It is certainly impressive from the ground, but the views from the top are simply breathtaking. It welcomes about one million people every year who come to admire the sights.

Sydney Tower was conceived as part of the original 1970s Centrepoint shopping centre, but was not completed until 1981. It was a complex build as the structure has to withstand earthquakes and extreme wind speeds expected only once in 500 years. Today, Sydney Tower offers visitors several different experiences. On the podium level, enjoy a multimedia journey around Australia in the 4D Experience. Views from Level 4 stretch north to Pittwater, south towards Botany Bay, west to the Blue Mountains, and along the harbour out to the open sea. Those with a head for heights can also venture outside the tower on a SKYWALK tour.

The 30-m (98-ft) spire

The water tank holds 162,000 litres (35,500 gal) and acts as a stabilizer on very windy days.

The windows comprise three layers. The outer has a gold-dust coating. The frame design prevents panes from falling outwards.

Take a virtual-reality ride across Australia in the 4D Experience that combines a 180-degree cinema, 3D technology and special effects.

Each of the 56 cables weigh seven tonnes.

The stairs are two separate, fireproofed emergency escape routes with 1,504 steps.

→

Illustration of the Sydney Tower

← Enjoying the skyline and stunning harbour views from Sydney Tower

Sydney Tower set against a jacaranda tree in bloom

GREAT VIEW
SKYWALK

Step onto the SKYWALK near the top of the tower for a bird's-eye view of the city and beyond. Sydney's highest open-air view-point, this glass walkway stands a dizzying 268 m (879 ft) above the ground.

↑ Colourful stained-glass windows inside the Queen Victoria Building

EXPERIENCE MORE

4

Queen Victoria Building

📍 E5 🏠 455 George St
🚉 Town Hall 🚆 QVB
🕐 Hours vary, check website 🌐 qvb.com.au

French fashion designer Pierre Cardin called the Queen Victoria Building "the most beautiful shopping centre in the world". This ornate Romanesque building, better known as the QVB, was once the site of the Sydney produce market. Completed to the design of City Architect George McRae in 1898, the QVB features a central copper dome and a glass roof, which lets in a flood of natural light.

The produce market closed at the end of World War I, and by the 1950s, the building was threatened with demolition. Refurbished at a cost of over A\$75 million, the QVB reopened in 1986 as a shopping gallery with over 190 shops.

Inside the QVB, suspended from the ceiling, is the Royal Clock. Designed in 1982 by Neil Glasser, it features a re-creation of Scotland's Balmoral Castle above a copy of the four dials of Big Ben. Every hour, a fanfare is played with a parade depicting various English monarchs.

QUEEN VICTORIA'S TALKING DOG

An enormous bronze statue of Queen Victoria and her favourite pet, a Skye terrier named Islay (pronounced "eye-la"), stand outside the QVB. Modelled on a sketch drawn by the queen herself, the bronze sculpture of Islay by Justin Robson was installed in 1987. Thanks to hidden speakers, the talking dog asks passers-by for donations to help deaf and blind children in New South Wales.

SHOP

The Nut Shop
A family-owned store that has been selling Vienna almonds and candied nuts since 1939.

♀E5 ☖25 Strand Arcade 🖥nutshop. com.au

Strand Hatters
Sydney's oldest hat shop has every style of handcrafted headwear.

♀E5 ☖8 Strand Arcade 🖥strand hatters.com.au

Andrew McDonald Shoemaker
Stop by the workshop of one of Australia's last remaining shoemakers who has been hand-crafting shoes, bags and belts since 1990.

♀E5 ☖121 Strand Arcade 🖥andrew mcdonald.com.au

5

Strand Arcade

♀E5 ☖412–414 George St 🚉Wynyard, St James ⏱Wynyard ⏰Hours vary, check website ⏹25 Dec, some public hols 🖥strand arcade.com.au

Victorian Sydney was a city of grand shopping arcades. The Strand, joining George and Pitt streets and designed by English architect John Spencer, was the finest of all. Opened in April 1892, it was lit both by natural light from the glass roof and by gas-powered chandeliers, each carrying 50 lamps.

After a fire in 1976, the building was restored to its original Victorian splendour. Now visitors can enjoy its stores and beautiful coffee shops.

6

Martin Place

♀E5 🚉Martin Pl ⏱Wynyard 🚌Elizabeth St routes

This plaza opened in 1891 and became a traffic-free precinct in 1971. It is busiest

> **Opened in April 1892, Strand Arcade was lit both by natural light from the glass roof and by gas-powered chandeliers, each carrying 50 lamps.**

at midday as city workers enjoy their lunch while watching free entertainment in the amphitheatre near Castlereagh Street.

Every Anzac Day (25 Apr) the focus moves to the Cenotaph at the George Street end, which was designed by Bertram MacKennal and unveiled in 1929. Past and present service personnel attend a dawn service and wreath-laying ceremony, followed by a march along Elizabeth Street.

On the southern side of the Cenotaph is the façade of the Renaissance-style General Post Office (GPO), considered to be the finest building by James Barnet, colonial architect in 1866.

A short walk away is the Dobell Memorial Sculpture. This stainless-steel sculpture of upended cubes is a tribute

↑ The majestic interior of the Strand Arcade, lined with designer shops

to Australian artist William Dobell. It was created by Bert Flugelman in 1979.

7

Lands Department Building

📍E4 🏠23 Bridge St 🚆Martin Pl, Wynyard 🚏Bridge St 🚌Elizabeth St routes 🚫To the public

Designed by James Barnet, this three-storey Classical Revival edifice dates from 1877 to 1890. Pyrmont sandstone was used for its exterior, as it was for the GPO building.

All the decisions about the subdivision of much of rural eastern Australia were made in the offices within. Statues of explorers and legislators who "promoted settlement" fill 23 of the façade's 48 niches; the remainder are still empty. After many years of use as government offices, the Lands Department Building is under restoration. Its heritage façade and interiors will be preserved and the building converted into a luxury hotel.

8

Museum of Sydney

📍F4 🏠Cnr Phillip & Bridge sts 🚆Circular Quay, Martin Pl, Wynyard 🚏Circular Quay, Bridge St, Wynyard 🚌Circular Quay routes 🕐10am–5pm daily 🚫Good Fri, 25 Dec 🌐mhnsw.au

Situated at the base of Governor Phillip Tower, the modern Museum of Sydney details the history of the city from 1788 to the present. Attractions include the archaeological remains of the colony's first Government House, as well as exhibits that explore the evolution of Sydney and honour the original inhabitants, the Gadigal people.

The Gadigal Place gallery explores the culture, history, continuity and place of Sydney's original inhabitants. The collectors' chests hold everyday items like flint and ochre. In the square outside the complex, the *Edge of the Trees* installation symbolizes the first contact between the Aboriginal people and Europeans. Inscribed are signatures of First Fleeters and the names of botanical species.

The Colony display on Level 1 focuses on Sydney during the critical decade of the 1840s: convict transportation ended, the town officially became a

city and then suffered economic depression. On Level 2, 20th-century Sydney is seen against a panorama of images.

Outside the museum, a paving pattern marks the site of the first Government House. The original foundations, below street level, can still be seen.

9

State Theatre

📍E5 🏠49 Market St 🚆Town Hall 🚏QVB 🚌Elizabeth St routes 🕐Box office: 10:30am–1:30pm Mon & Thu, 2 hours before performances 🚫Good Fri, 25 Dec 🌐statetheatre.com.au

When it opened in 1929, this cinema was hailed as the finest that local craftsmanship could achieve. The State Theatre is one of the best examples of ornate period cinemas in Australia. Its Baroque style is evident in the foyer, with its high ceiling, mosaic floor, marble columns and statues. The auditorium is lit by a 20,000-piece chandelier. The Wurlitzer pipe organ, one of only 12 worldwide that remain as originally installed, rises from below the stage before performances. This is now one of the city's special events venues.

EDGE OF THE TREES

A splendid, forest-like collection of 29 sandstone, wood and steel pillars stand to attention in the Museum of Sydney forecourt. Each pillar represents one of 29 Aboriginal clans from the area that is now Sydney. A soundscape of Koori voices recite the names of places consumed by the sprawling metropolis since colonization in 1788. The installation is called *Edge of the Trees*.

↑ The façade and towering spires of St Mary's Cathedral

St Mary's Cathedral

📍 F5 📍 St Marys Rd
🚈 St James, Martin Pl
🚌 Elizabeth St routes
🕐 6:30am-6:30pm daily; guided tours: 2pm Sun
🌐 stmaryscathedral.org.au

In 1821, Governor Macquarie laid the foundation stone for St Mary's Chapel on the first land granted to the Catholic Church in Australia.

The initial section of this Gothic Revival-style cathedral was opened in 1882 and completed in 1928, but without the twin southern spires originally proposed by the architect William Wardell. The original vision was finally achieved when the twin spires were completed in 2000. By the entrance are statues of Australia's first cardinal, Moran, and Archbishop Kelly, who laid the stone for the final stage of construction in 1913. They were sculpted by Bertram MacKennal, also responsible for the Martin Place Cenotaph (p108).

In the basement of the cathedral is the crypt, which was built to house the remains of Archbishop Kelly after his death. The magnificent Great North Window is a highlight among the cathedral's numerous stained glass windows.

Great Synagogue

📍 E6 📍 187 Elizabeth St, entrance at 166 Castlereagh St 🚈 St James, Town Hall 🚌 Town Hall 🚌 Elizabeth St routes
🕐 For services & tours only 🚪 Public and Jewish hols 🌐 greatsynagogue.org.au

Jews arrived in Australia with the First Fleet, however worship did not commence until the 1820s. The longest established Jewish Orthodox congregation in the country assembles in the Great Synagogue (consecrated in 1878). With its carved porch columns and wrought-iron gates, the synagogue is perhaps the finest work of Thomas Rowe, architect of Sydney Hospital (p128). The interior features a stunning midnight-blue ceiling adorned with gold-leaf stars.

Sydney Town Hall

📍 E6 📍 483 George St
🚈 Town Hall 🕐 8am-6pm Mon-Fri 🚪 Public hols
🌐 sydneytownhall.com.au

The steps of Sydney Town Hall have been a favourite meeting place since it opened in 1869. Standing on the site of walled burial grounds, the Town Hall itself is a fine example of High Victorian architecture. The original architect, J H Wilson, died during its construction, as did several of the architects who followed. As a result, the vestibule, an elegant salon with stained glass and a crystal chandelier, is the work of Albert Bond; the clock tower was completed by the Bradbridge brothers in 1884; and the Centennial Hall, with its imposing 19th-century Grand Organ with over 8,500 pipes, was designed by other architects and added between 1888 and 1889.

STAY

QT Sydney
Guests of this quirky boutique hotel are greeted by staff wearing theatrical costumes and wigs.

📍 E5 📍 49 Market St
🌐 qthotels.com

$$$

Sofitel Sydney Darling Harbour
Set in the harbour's tallest skyscraper, this hotel has a spectacular infinity pool.

📍 C6 📍 12 Darling Dr
🌐 sofitelsydney darlingharbour.com.au

$$$

Some people believe the Town Hall became Sydney's finest building by accident, as each architect strove to outdo similar buildings in Manchester and Liverpool. Today, it frequently acts as a venue for concerts.

St Andrew's Cathedral

E6 **Sydney Sq, cnr George & Bathurst sts** **Town Hall** **Hours vary, check website** **sydneycathedral.com**

While the foundation stone for the country's oldest cathedral was laid in 1819, the building was not consecrated until 1868. The Gothic Revival design, by Edmund Blacket, was inspired by York Minster in England. Inside are memorials to Sydney pioneers, a 1539

INSIDER TIP
Free concerts at St Andrew's

Free lunchtime concerts by the Australian Navy and New South Wales Police bands are held throughout the year. The students of St Andrew's Cathedral School also perform regularly.

Bible and beads made from olive seeds collected in the Holy Land.

The southern wall includes stones from London's St Paul's Cathedral, Westminster Abbey and the House of Lords.

Hyde Park

F5 **Elizabeth St routes**

Hyde Park was named after its London equivalent by Governor Macquarie in 1810. The fence around the park marked the outskirts of the township. Once an exercise

The Anzac Memorial at Hyde Park, and *(inset)* visitors at the Hall of Service on site

field for garrison troops, it later incorporated a racecourse and a cricket pitch. Though much smaller today than the original park, it is still a quiet haven in the middle of the bustling city centre, with many notable features.

The 30-m (98-ft) high Art Deco Anzac Memorial, opened in 1934, commemorates Australians who have died for their country. The site is made up of the Halls of Memory, Silence and Service, and a museum, hosting a military exhibition.

Sandringham Garden, filled with mauve wisteria, is a memorial to kings George V and George VI, opened by Queen Elizabeth II in 1954.

The bronze and granite Archibald Fountain commemorates the French and Australian World War I alliance. It was completed by François Sicard in 1932 and donated by J F Archibald, one of the founders of the popular Australian literary magazine, *Bulletin*.

The *Emden* Gun, on the corner of College and Liverpool streets, commemorates a World War I naval action. HMAS *Sydney* destroyed the German raider *Emden* off the Cocos Islands on 9 November 1914, and 180 crew members were taken prisoner.

Darling Harbour

⑮

📍D6 🚉Town Hall
🚉Exhibition Centre

The Eora people called the harbour Tumbalong, meaning "place where seafood is found". The first Europeans called it Cockle Bay for the masses of seashells. The then governor named it after himself in 1826.

Darling Harbour's 1988 redevelopment transformed what was once a busy industrial centre and shipping terminal for local trades into a low-rise tourism precinct, complete with the Australian National Maritime Museum *(p104)* and SEA LIFE Sydney Aquarium. In 2013, a A\$3 billion reinvention of the area combined high-rise architecture with open spaces at ground level and pedestrian-friendly walkways. The International Convention Centre (ICC) was

---

💬 INSIDER TIP
Darling Harbour Street Art Trail

Twisting lights above Little Hay Street and Steam Mill Lane, a spiral water feature on Cockle Bay promenade and a mural in Darling Square are some of the public artworks to see here.

↑ Children admiring an exhibit at the SEA LIFE Sydney Aquarium

the first landmark building to open, followed by hotels, residences and shopping facilities.

The Goods Line

⑯

📍D8 🕐Daily

Sydney's take on New York City's High Line, this partly elevated linear park runs along a disused freight line from Central Station through the city's educational, cultural and media hub to Darling Harbour. Along the way are table tennis tables, study pods, outdoor work spaces and playgrounds. You can still see some of the old tracks integrated into the plantings along the path, and some old industrial machinery has been incorporated into the park's urban sculptures. Don't miss the best view of the futuristic University of Technology Business School's Dr Chau Chak Wing building

← A bronze sculpture depicting seafarers at Darling Harbour

---

designed by Frank Gehry, affectionately known as the crumpled brown paper bag.

SEA LIFE Sydney Aquarium and WILD LIFE Sydney Zoo

⑰

📍D5 🏠1-5 Wheat Rd
🚉Town Hall 🚉Paddy's Markets 🚌389 to Maritime Museum, then a short walk
⛴Pyrmont Bay, Barangaroo
🕐Hours vary, check websites 🌐visitsealife.com; wildlifesydney.com.au

The SEA LIFE Sydney Aquarium is home to about 700 species, comprising more than 13,000 fish and other sea creatures. It strongly focuses on education, and its endangered species' breeding programme is internationally recognized. Discover sharks, rays, little penguins and dugongs in the nine themed zones, or walk through the Shark Valley tunnel, to watch giant predators cruise.

Next door at the WILD LIFE Sydney Zoo is an all-Australian line-up. More than 100 native animal species including koalas, kangaroos and Tasmanian devils are found here in re-creations of their natural habitats.

Sydney Fish Market

⑱

📍B6 🏠1 Bridge Rd, Glebe 🚉Fish Market, Wentworth Park or Glebe
⛴Fish Market 🕐Daily; hours vary, check website
🌐sydneyfishmarket.com

The modern home of Australian seafood, the Sydney Fish Market, presides over the inner harbour area of Blackwattle Bay, offering views across the bay to the Anzac Bridge.

Operating as a traditional fish market, a variety of

↑ Towering modern glass skyscrapers in Barangaroo

fishmongers and speciality food retailers sell freshly caught and prepared produce in a market hall setting.

Those who prefer not to catch or cook their own fish can dine at one of the restaurants and cafés, or buy fresh and cooked-to-order seafood to take away and enjoy on the wide promenade or in the surrounding parklands.

Barangaroo

D3 Wynyard 252, 254, 261, 288, 290, 292 Barangaroo barangaroo.com

Barangaroo became Sydney's western harbour foreshore playground when a disused container terminal was transformed into a vast waterfront precinct. To the north, Barangaroo Reserve offers exceptional views, walking and cycling paths, picnic spots and cultural tours. More than 75,000 native trees and shrubs were planted and a rocky outcrop rebuilt to replicate the area's original natural landscape.

To the south are various entertainment and performance spaces, restaurants, bars and boutique retail outlets. The waterfront Wulugul Walk connects the area to King Street Wharf and Darling Harbour. The shorter Wynyard Walk provides direct access to Barangaroo south from the city centre.

THE STORY OF BARANGAROO

Barangaroo takes its name from a powerful, independent Cammeraygal leader of the Eora Nation at the time of European colonization. She had considerable influence in the early days of the colony. While her husband Bennelong befriended colonists, Barangaroo refused their offers of food and drinks, and was appalled by their hedonistic ways. She died in 1791, shortly after giving birth.

> **To the north, Barangaroo Reserve offers exceptional views, walking and cycling paths, picnic spots and cultural tours.**

20

King Street Wharf

D5 Lime St, between King and Erskine sts Paddy's Markets 252, 254, 261, 288, 290, 292 Darling Harbour kingstreetwharf.com.au

Merchant bankers and city workers from nearby offices flock to this harbourside venue, which combines a modern glass-and-steel shrine to café society with a working wharf. The complex is full of bars and restaurants that vie for the best views of the water. The precinct provides a front row seat to the fireworks display held at 8:30pm most Saturday nights.

The area is also home to a number of low-rise residential apartments set back from the water.

EAT

The Eight
Arrive early to avoid the queues for delicious *yum cha* (dim sums served with hot tea), barbecue pork buns and mango pancakes.

Q D7 **A** Market City, 9-13 Hay St, Haymarket **w** theeightrestaurant. com.au

$$

Emperor's Garden Cakes & Bakery
Famous for its piping-hot Emperor puffs filled with vanilla custard.

Q D7 **A** Cnr Dixon & Hay sts, Haymarket

$$

The Malaya
A stalwart of the Sydney dining scene, The Malaya is renowned for its spicy Malaysian and Nonya flavours.

Q D5 **A** 39 Lime St, King St Wharf **w** the malaya.com.au

$$

Ester
Modern Australian fare, such as roasted oysters, served in a smart space.

Q D9 **A** 46-52 Meagher St, Chippendale **w** ester-restaurant.com.au

$$

LuMi
A fine-dining restaurant where modern Italian food is given a Japanese twist.

Q C4 **A** 56 Pirrama Rd, Pyrmont **w** lumidining.com

$$

㉑ Chinatown

Q E7 **A** Dixon St Plaza **T** Town Hall **D** Paddy's Markets, Chinatown **回** Routes to Central, Eddy Ave and Railway Sq

Originally set around Dixon and Hay streets, Chinatown has now expanded to fill the city's Haymarket area, stretching as far west as Harris Street, south to Broadway and east to Castlereagh Street. It is home to a mix of restaurants, noodle bars, food stalls and quirky gift shops that stay open until late. Unsurprisingly, then, Chinatown is the preferred spot for many of the city's top chefs in search of a late-night meal long after their own kitchens have closed.

The area was once little more than a run-down district at the edge of the city's produce markets, where many Chinese immigrants worked at traditional businesses. Today, Dixon Street, its main thoroughfare, has spruced-up public spaces with trees, seating, lighting and artworks, while retaining its character and heritage.

Chinatown hosts vibrant festivals and Friday-night markets, with many greengrocers, herbalists, butchers' shops, jewellers and confectioners filling the lively arcades.

Did You Know?
The Chinese New Year celebrations in Sydney's Chinatown are the biggest outside of Asia.

㉒ Chinese Garden of Friendship

Q D7 **A** Darling Harbour **T** Town Hall **D** Paddy's Markets **回回** Darling Harbour **C** 10am-5pm daily **C** Good Fri, 25 Dec **w** chinesegarden.com.au

Built in 1984, the Chinese Garden of Friendship is a tranquil refuge from the city streets. The garden's design was a gift to Sydney from its Chinese sister city of Guangdong. The Dragon Wall, in the lower section beside the lake, has glazed carvings of two dragons, one representing Guangdong and the other New South Wales. The lake is covered with colourful lotus and water lilies for much of the year. On the other side of the lake is the Twin Pavilion, which has Waratahs (New South Wales's floral symbol) and flowering

apricots carved into its woodwork in Chinese style.

The restaurant in a heritage-listed teahouse serves Chinese high tea and Sichuan cuisine.

---

23 🍴 🖥 🏛

Chippendale

📍 C/D9 🚆 Central, Redfern 🚇 Central 🚌 Eddy Ave, Railway Sq, Central, Broadway

Once a working-class neighbourhood where the air was filled with the yeasty aroma of the brewery that dominated the area, Chippendale is now a hip suburb with lanes full of small galleries and cool bars. In a major urban renewal project, the brewery site has been transformed into Central Park, a complex filled with boutique shops, cafés, restaurants, high-rise apartments with award-winning vertical gardens and thoughtfully landscaped areas for relaxing. The contemporary Chinese art collection at **White Rabbit Gallery** is not to be missed, and neither is **Spice Alley**, an outdoor hawker-style food market.

White Rabbit Gallery

🏠 30 Balfour St 🕐 10am-5pm Wed-Sun 🌐 whiterabbitcollection.org

Spice Alley

🏠 Kensington St 🕐 Hours vary, check website 🌐 spicealley.com.au

---

24 🛍

Paddy's Markets

📍 D7 🏠 Cnr Thomas & Hay sts, Haymarket 🚇 Town Hall 🚇 Paddy's Markets 🚌 Routes to Central, Eddy Ave, Railway Sq, Castlereagh St 🕐 10am-6pm Wed-Sun & public hols 🚫 25 Apr, 25 Dec 🌐 paddysmarkets.com.au

The Haymarket district, near Chinatown, is home to Paddy's Markets, Sydney's oldest and best-known market. It has been in this area, on a number of sites, since 1869. The origin of its name is uncertain, but is believed to have come from either the Chinese who previously supplied much of the produce, or the Irish who were among its main customers.

↑ Shoppers at the busy Paddy's Markets in Haymarket

Once the shopping centre for the inner-city poor, Paddy's Markets is now an integral part of the Market City Shopping Centre, which includes cut-price fashion outlet stores, an Asian food court and a cinema complex. Yet despite this transformation, the familiar clamour and chaotic bargain-hunting atmosphere of the original marketplace remain. Every week, the market is filled with up to 500 stalls selling the likes of farm-fresh produce, the latest electrical products, funky homeware and leather goods.

↑ Twin Pavilion in the serene Chinese Garden of Friendship

A SHORT WALK
CITY CENTRE

0 metres   100   N
0 yards   100

Distance 1.5 km (1 mile) **Time** 30 minutes
Nearest train Town Hall

A stroll through the bustling city centre takes in the best of the city's architectural past and present. Grand 19th-century buildings, many made from local sandstone, stand majestically beside soaring skyscrapers housing office workers and hotel guests, particularly along George Street and Martin Place. This area is also the city's commercial heart, so window-shop along the way. Glitzy designer labels dominate the retail spaces at street level in the area bounded by George, King and Castlereagh streets, while pedestrianized Pitt Street Mall and Martin Place are home to more wallet-friendly department stores and casual lunch spots.

The **Queen Victoria Building** (p107) *takes up an entire city block. This 1898 former produce market is now a shopping mall.*

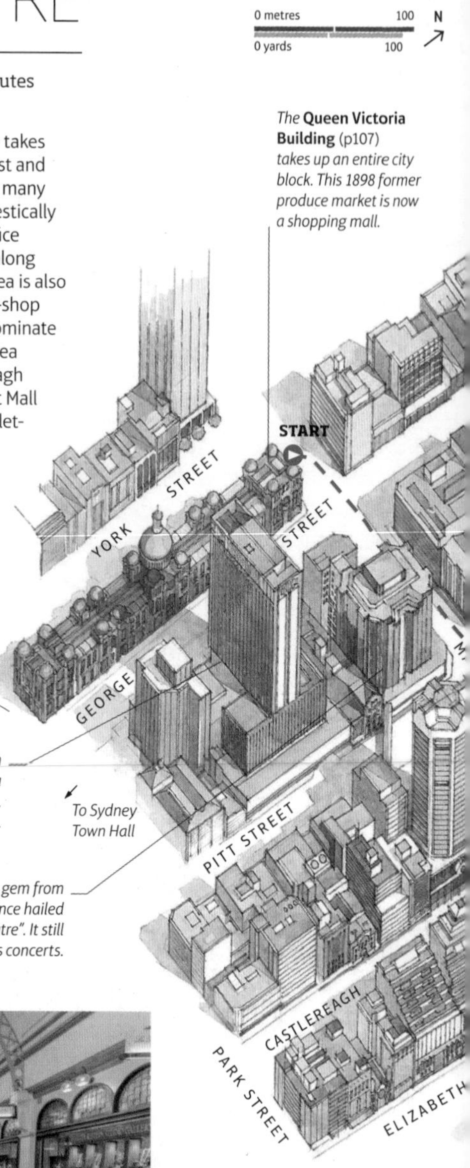

START

YORK STREET

GEORGE STREET

PITT STREET

The **Queen Victoria Statue** *was found after a worldwide search in 1983 ended in a small Irish village. It had lain forgotten since being removed from the front of the Irish Parliament in 1947.*

Marble Bar, *a grand Victorian structure with marble arches and a mahogany bar, first opened in 1893. It was beautifully restored in 2005.*

To Sydney Town Hall

The **State Theatre** (p109), *a gem from the golden age of movies, was once hailed as "the Empire's greatest theatre". It still shows films, but it also hosts concerts.*

CASTLEREAGH

PARK STREET

ELIZABETH

← The Royal Clock suspended inside the grand Queen Victoria Building (QVB)

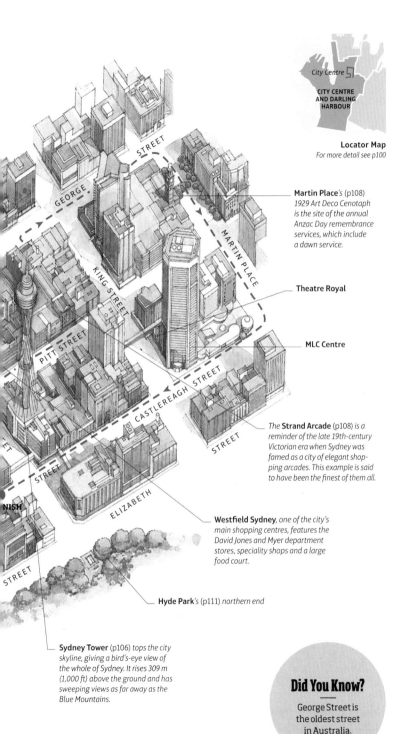

Locator Map
For more detail see p100

City Centre

CITY CENTRE AND DARLING HARBOUR

Martin Place's (p108) *1929 Art Deco Cenotaph is the site of the annual Anzac Day remembrance services, which include a dawn service.*

Theatre Royal

MLC Centre

The **Strand Arcade** (p108) *is a reminder of the late 19th-century Victorian era when Sydney was famed as a city of elegant shopping arcades. This example is said to have been the finest of them all.*

Westfield Sydney, *one of the city's main shopping centres, features the David Jones and Myer department stores, speciality shops and a large food court.*

Hyde Park's (p111) *northern end*

Sydney Tower (p106) *tops the city skyline, giving a bird's-eye view of the whole of Sydney. It rises 309 m (1,000 ft) above the ground and has sweeping views as far away as the Blue Mountains.*

Did You Know?

George Street is the oldest street in Australia.

A pond in the green and leafy Royal Botanic Garden

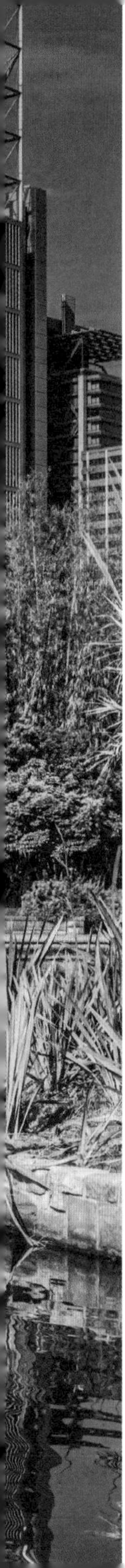

ROYAL BOTANIC GARDEN AND THE DOMAIN

This tranquil, 34-ha (84-acre) part of Sydney was set aside as parkland by the first governor of the Sydney colony in the late 18th century. Before this, the area had been used by Gadigal people for fishing, camping and important ceremonies. These people continued to meet and hunt in the area right up to the mid-19th century, when the eastern parts of the Domain were converted to housing. The expanse of public parkland that was left became increasingly popular with Europeans as a space for sport and recreation, and it continues to draw joggers, touch footballers, picnickers and sunbathers today. The Royal Botanic Garden was established on the grounds of the Domain in 1816, and has since become an area of great diversity and beauty, featuring plants from across Australia and the rest of the world.

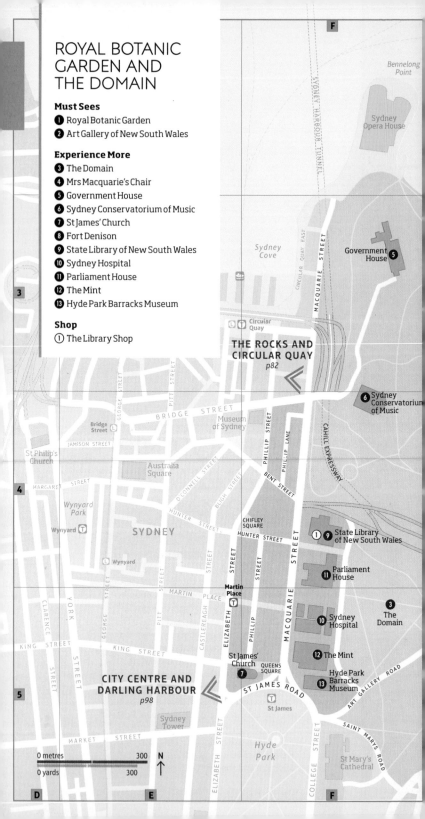

ROYAL BOTANIC GARDEN AND THE DOMAIN

Must Sees

❶ Royal Botanic Garden
❷ Art Gallery of New South Wales

Experience More

❸ The Domain
❹ Mrs Macquarie's Chair
❺ Government House
❻ Sydney Conservatorium of Music
❼ St James' Church
❽ Fort Denison
❾ State Library of New South Wales
❿ Sydney Hospital
⓫ Parliament House
⓬ The Mint
⓭ Hyde Park Barracks Museum

Shop

① The Library Shop

THE ROCKS AND CIRCULAR QUAY p82

CITY CENTRE AND DARLING HARBOUR p98

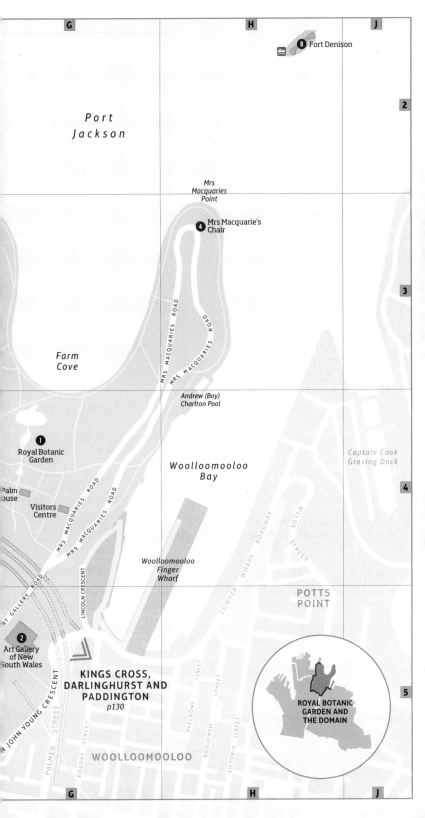

G
H
J

8 Fort Denison

Port Jackson

2

Mrs Macquaries Point

4 Mrs Macquarie's Chair

3

MRS MACQUARIES ROAD

MRS MACQUARIES ROAD

Farm Cove

Andrew (Boy) Charlton Pool

Captain Cook Graving Dock

1 Royal Botanic Garden

Woolloomooloo Bay

4

Palm House

Visitors Centre

MRS MACQUARIES ROAD

MRS MACQUARIES ROAD

WYLDE STREET

COOPER WHARF ROADWAY

Woolloomooloo Finger Wharf

ART GALLERY ROAD

LINCOLN CRESCENT

POTTS POINT

5

2 Art Gallery of New South Wales

JOHN YOUNG CRESCENT

PALMER STREET

BOURKE STREET

McELHONE STREET

VICTORIA STREET

BROUGHAM STREET

KINGS CROSS, DARLINGHURST AND PADDINGTON
p130

WOOLLOOMOOLOO

ROYAL BOTANIC GARDEN AND THE DOMAIN

G
H
J

27,000

The number of plants from around the world found in the garden.

ROYAL BOTANIC GARDEN

📍G4 🏠Mrs Macquaries Rd 🚆Martin Pl, St James, Circular Quay 🚌200, 441 ⛴Circular Quay 🕐Daily; hours vary, check website 🚫25 Dec 🌐botanicgardens.org.au

Wrapped around Farm Cove at the harbour's edge, the Royal Botanic Garden is an oasis in the heart of the city. It is Australia's oldest botanic garden, and houses an outstanding collection of plants.

Established on the site of the first European farm in the fledgling colony in 1816, the Royal Botanic Garden was at first just a series of pathways through shrubbery, before it became the oldest living scientific institution in the country. Today, the gardens cover a vast 30 ha (75 acres) of parkland and house an outstanding collection of plants native to both Australia and overseas. The diversity is amazing: there are thousands of trees, stands of bamboo, a cactus garden, a fernery and succulent garden, a rainforest walk, one of the world's finest collections of palms, a garden of herbs from around the world and another containing rare and threatened plant species. Fountains, statues and monuments are scattered throughout, as well as several restaurants and cafés.

TOP 3 GUIDED TOURS

Guided Walks
🕐10am daily
Regular 90-minute group tours with a volunteer.

Aboriginal Cultural Tour
🕐11am Thu–Sat
Discover the garden's rich Aboriginal history.

Ghostly Garden Tour
🕐Every 2nd or 3rd Fri
Hear spooky stories of the garden's past. Bring a torch.

EAT

Farm Cove Eatery
You can choose to eat in at this casual dining spot, or take away to enjoy a picnic in the garden. The menu has lots of veggie, vegan and gluten-free dishes.

🖳 botanichouse.com.au

$$$

Leaf Dept. Café
This breezy, little café in the heart of the garden serves delicious sandwiches, soups, salads and spritzes.

🖳 botanicgardens.
org.au/facility/leaf-
dept-cafe

$$$

← The green Royal Botanic Garden contrasting with the Sydney Opera House's white sails

① Pathways through the Rose Garden are shaded by trellises, which are covered in colourful blooms during the spring and summer months.

② There are several topiary works in the Royal Botanic Garden, including this one depicting a huge koala clutching a tree.

③ The Calyx, an exhibition space, features the large green wall and hosts horticultural displays. It also has a café and shop.

A selection of artworks on display at the Art Gallery of New South Wales ↑

ART GALLERY OF NEW SOUTH WALES

G5 ☐ Art Gallery Rd, The Domain ☐ 441 ☐ St James, Martin Pl ☐ Circular Quay ☐ 10am–10pm Wed, 10am–5pm Thu–Tue ☐ Good Fri, 25 Dec ☐ artgallery.nsw.gov.au

More than one million visitors a year enjoy the Art Gallery of New South Wales's changing exhibitions, annual events and incredible collection, which includes modern and contemporary works, European and Asian pieces, colonial and contemporary Australian paintings, and Aboriginal and Torres Strait Islander art.

Established in 1871, without a collection or building by 30 art-loving citizens, the gallery acquired its first artworks with government support in 1875 and found a permanent home on its present site in 1885. It doubled in size with the opening of the impressive North Building, featuring a series of light-filled pavilions and graceful terraces, and an art garden, in 2022. The North Building also includes a reclaimed underground fuel bunker that houses several art projects. The original building, now known as the South Building, combines 19th-century Grand Courts and Modernist additions, and includes Australia's first children's art library. The Yiribana Gallery is among the largest in the world to exclusively exhibit Aboriginal and Torres Strait Islander art and culture.

 INSIDER TIP
Free Tours

There are free daily guided tours on Aboriginal Art, Collection Highlights, Introductions to Exhibitions and Mystery tours. Also offered is a Welcome Wander, a talk on a theme or artist.

↑ The grand exterior of the
South Building

Gallery Guide

Two equestrian bronzes by Gilbert Bayes (1872–1953) – *The Offerings of Peace* and *The Offerings of War* – stand at the entrance of the original building, and lead to the first of 13 elegant rooms of the Grand Courts. Beyond the public art garden, the first of three art pavilions in the new building holds the Aboriginal and Torres Strait Islander art gallery. The floating gallery design flows over four lower levels that house a sculpture gallery and multiple exhibition spaces. A spiral staircase connects the pavilions to the subterranean Oil Tank Gallery.

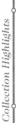

Collection Highlights

Must See

Australian Art

Occupying its own wing, this collection includes iconic paintings and sculptures from the annals of Australian art history, including the likes of Tom Roberts and Arthur Streeton. It also features 20th-century artists, such as Margaret Preston, Grace Cossington Smith, Jeffrey Smart and Brett Whiteley.

Grand Courts

▷ Built at the end of the 19th century, the Grand Courts are considered the finest Victorian-era galleries in Australia. Today, they hold more than 300 works, including 15th- to 19th-century European art, 19th- and 20th-century Australian art and contemporary works.

The Tank

A decommissioned World War II fuel bunker that once supplied the nearby Garden Island naval yard has been repurposed and transformed into a spectacular underground art space. The gallery presents large-scale contemporary works, specially commissioned installations and site-specific performances.

Asian Art

The gallery has the largest pan-Asian displays of art in the southern hemisphere, including exquisite calligraphy, traditional and modern paintings, textiles, porcelain and Buddhist art.

Contemporary Art

Explore Australia's most comprehensive representation of art from the 1960s to the present day here. The contemporary collection contains major works by more than 400 artists from Australia and across the globe, including Fiona Hall, Bill Henson, Anish Kapoor and Ai Weiwei.

Yiribana Gallery

▽ Representing Aboriginal and Torres Strait Islander artists from communities across Australia, this internationally renowned collection celebrates Australian First Nations' enduring cultural heritage and myriad contemporary expressions.

Joggers in the Domain, with the Woolloomooloo Finger Wharf in the background

 5

Government House

🗺 F3 🏛 Royal Botanic Garden (Macquarie St entrance) 🚉 Circular Quay, Martin Place 🚌 Circular Quay routes 🕙 10:30am–3pm Fri–Sun 🔒 Good Fri, 25 Dec 🌐 governor.nsw.gov.au/government-house

The official residence of the Governor of New South Wales, this is one of Australia's oldest buildings. Erected between 1837 and 1845, the turreted Gothic Revival edifice overlooks the harbour and Sydney Opera House (p86) from within the Royal Botanic Garden.

The grand interior features exquisite hand-painted stencilled ceilings and a significant number of portraits. A fine collection of 19th- and early 20th-century furnishings and decorations is housed in the ground-floor state rooms, while the upstairs rooms have been used as the private quarters of the Governor, Queen Elizabeth II and other members of the royal family and visiting heads of state.

EXPERIENCE MORE

3

The Domain

🗺 F5 🏛 Art Gallery Rd 🚌 111, 411

Once the governor's private park, the Domain is a public grass space that attracts thousands to open-air summer concerts and festival events. Since the 1890s, it has hosted Sydney's version of London's Speakers' Corner. Today, it is popular with joggers and office workers playing touch football or relaxing in their lunch hours.

Did You Know?

Under the Domain lies the Travelator – the longest moving walkway in the southern hemisphere.

4

Mrs Macquarie's Chair

🗺 H3 🏛 Mrs Macquaries Rd 🚌 111

The scenic Mrs Macquaries Road winds along much of what is now the city's Royal Botanic Garden, from Farm Cove to Woolloomooloo Bay. The road was built in 1816 at the behest of Elizabeth Macquarie, wife of Major-General Lachlan Macquarie, the then Governor of New South Wales. In the same year, a stone bench, inscribed with details of the new road and its commissioner, was carved into the rock at the point where Mrs Macquarie would often stop and admire the view.

Rounding the cove to the west leads to Mrs Macquaries Point. These lawns are a popular picnic spot with Sydneysiders, particularly at sunset.

  6

Sydney Conservatorium of Music

🗺 F3/4 🏛 Macquarie St 🚉 Martin Pl 🚌 Elizabeth St routes 🕙 8am–6pm Mon–Sat (public areas only); concerts: check website for programme 🔒 Easter Sat, 24 Dec–2 Jan, public hols 🌐 music.sydney.edu.au

When it was finished in 1821, this striking castellated colonial Gothic building was meant to be the stables and servants' quarters for the Government House, but

TOP 3 OUTDOOR EVENTS IN SUMMER

Handa Opera
For one month every year, Opera Australia *(www.opera.org.au)* stages a grand production right on the harbour. It takes place either in March or April.

Westpac OpenAir Cinema
In January or February, movies are shown on a three-storey-high screen, rising from the harbour *(www.westpacopenair.com.au)*. The Opera House *(p86)* and Harbour Bridge *(p88)* serve as a backdrop.

Carols in the Domain
The Domain hosts a family-friendly night of Christmas carols, sung by some of Australia's favourite performers, every December *(www.carolsinthedomain.com.au)*.

construction of the latter was delayed for almost 25 years. That stables should be built in so grand a style, and at such great cost, brought forth cries of outrage and led to bitter arguments between the architect, Francis Greenway *(p129)*, and Governor Macquarie – finally resulting in a decree that all future building plans be submitted to London.

Between 1908 and 1915, "Greenway's folly" underwent a dramatic transformation. A concert hall, roofed in grey slate, was built on the central courtyard and the building in its entirety was converted for the use of the Sydney Conservatorium of Music.

Popularly known as "The Con", the conservatorium continues to be a respected training ground for future musicians. The on-site café holds lunchtime concerts during the school term, and the upper level offers great harbour views.

7

St James' Church

E/F5 · **179 King St**
St James, Martin Pl
Elizabeth St routes
10am–4pm Mon–Fri, 9am–1pm Sat, 7:30am–4pm Sun; concerts: check website for programme
sjks.org.au

This fine Georgian building, built by convict labour between 1819 and 1824, was originally designed as a courthouse. The architect, Francis Greenway, had to build a church instead when plans to construct a cathedral on George Street were abandoned.

Consecrated in 1824, it is the oldest church in Sydney. In 1834, the English architect John Verge modified the design so that the pulpit faced the high-rent pews, while convicts and the military sat directly behind the preacher where the service was inaudible.

The church contains a Children's Chapel, which was created in 1929. It also exhibits a rare collection of marble tablets that honour prominent members of early 19th-century society, luckless explorers and shipwreck victims, many of whom died violently.

8

Fort Denison

H2 · **Sydney Harbour**
Circular Quay
Hours vary, check website **nationalparks.nsw.gov.au**

This impressive 18th-century fort on a small, forested island in Sydney Harbour is known as Mattewanya to its Aboriginal residents. Initially named Rock Island by early European settlers, this prominent, rocky outcrop in the harbour was also dubbed "Pinchgut", most likely because of the meagre rations given to convicts who were confined to the prison there as punishment.

In 1796, convicted murderer Francis Morgan was hanged on the island in chains. His body was left to rot on the gallows for three years as a warning to the other convicts.

Between 1855 and 1857, the Martello tower (the only one in Australia), gun battery and barracks that now occupy the island were built as part of Sydney's defences. The site was renamed after the governor of the time. The gun, fired at 1pm each day, helped mariners to set their ships' chronometers accurately.

Ferry services between Circular Quay to Manly provide a close-up view of the island en route.

↑ The heritage-listed Fort Denison in the centre of Sydney Harbour

State Library of New South Wales

📍 F4 🏛 Macquarie St
🚇 Martin Pl 🚌 Elizabeth St routes ⏰ Hours vary, check website 📅 Most public hols
🌐 sl.nsw.gov.au

The State Library is housed in two separate buildings connected by a passageway and a glass bridge. The older building, the Mitchell Library wing (1910), is a majestic sandstone edifice facing the Royal Botanic Garden *(p122)*. Huge stone columns

SHOP

The Library Shop
Specializing in Australian books, gifts and accessories, this bookshop also sells on-demand prints of photos, paintings and maps from the State Library's collections.

📍 F4 🏛 State Library of NSW, Macquarie St
🌐 shop.sl.nsw.gov.au

supporting a vaulted ceiling frame the impressive vestibule, where the floor has a mosaic replica of an old map illustrating the two voyages made to Australia by Dutch navigator Abel Tasman in the 1640s. The original Tasman Map is held in the Mitchell Library as part of its collection of historically important Australian paintings, books, documents and pictorial records.

Just beyond the main vestibule lies the Mitchell wing's vast reading room, with its huge skylight and oak panelling. There is also an attractive contemporary structure that faces Macquarie Street. It houses the State Reference Library. Beyond the Mitchell wing is the Dixson Gallery, housing cultural and historical exhibitions which change regularly.

Outside the library, facing Macquarie Street, is a statue of the explorer Matthew Flinders *(p68)*, who ventured into central Australia. On the windowsill behind him is a statue of his travelling companion, his cat, Trim.

→

Il Porcellino, the bronze boar in front of Sydney Hospital

Sydney Hospital

📍 F5 🏛 Macquarie St
📞 (02) 9382 7111 🚇 Martin Pl 🚌 Elizabeth St routes ⏰ Guided tours: hours vary, book ahead via the website
🌐 mgnsw.org.au/organisations/lucy-osburn-nightingale-museum

This imposing collection of Victorian sandstone buildings stands on the site of what was once the central section of the original convict-built Sydney Hospital. It was known locally as the Rum Hospital because the builders were paid by being allowed to import rum for resale. Both the north and south wings of the Rum Hospital survive as Parliament House and The Mint. The central wing was demolished in 1879 and the new hospital,

The huge Mitchell Library Reading Room at the State Library of New South Wales

which is still operational, was completed in 1894.

The hospital's Classical Revival building features a Baroque staircase and elegant stained-glass windows in its central hall. In the inner court-yard, there is a brightly coloured Art Deco fountain (1907).

At the front of the hospital sits a bronze boar called *Il Porcellino*. It is a replica of a 17th-century fountain in Florence's Mercato Nuovo. Donated in 1968 by an Italian woman whose relatives had worked at the hospital, the statue is a symbol of the friendship between Italy and Australia. Like his Florentine counterpart, *Il Porcellino* is supposed to bring good luck to all those who rub his snout.

Parliament House

F4 **Macquarie St**
Martin Pl **Elizabeth St routes** **9am-5pm Mon-Fri** **Public hols**
parliament.nsw.gov.au

The central section of this building, which houses the State Parliament, is part of the original Sydney Hospital. It has been a seat of govern-ment since 1829 when the newly appointed Legislative Council first held meetings here. The building was extended twice during the 19th century, and again during the 1970s and 1980s. The current building contains the chambers for both houses of state parliament, as well as parliamentary offices.

Parliamentary memorabilia is on view in the Jubilee Room, as are displays showing the house's development and the legislative history of the state of New South Wales.

FRANCIS GREENWAY, CONVICT ARCHITECT

Australian $10 notes once bore the portrait of the early colonial architect Francis Greenway. This was the only currency in the world to pay tribute to a convicted forger. Greenway was transported from England to Sydney in 1814 to serve a 14-year sentence for his crime. Under the patronage of Governor Lachlan Macquarie, who appointed him Civil Architect in 1816, Greenway designed more than 40 buildings, of which 11 survive today.

The Mint

F5 **10 Macquarie St**
St James, Martin Pl
Elizabeth St routes
9am-4pm Mon-Fri
Good Fri, 25 Dec
mhnsw.au

The gold rushes of the mid-19th century transformed colonial Australia. The Sydney Mint opened in 1854, in the south wing of the Rum Hospital, in order to turn gold into bullion and currency, but was closed in 1927. The Georgian building went into decline after it was converted into government offices. Today, the head office of the Museums of History NSW is located here, and visi-tors are allowed access only to the front part of the building.

Hyde Park Barracks Museum

F5 **Queens Square 10, Macquarie St**
St James, Martin Pl
Elizabeth St routes
10am-6pm daily **Good Fri, 25 Dec** **mhnsw.au**

Described by Governor Macquarie as "spacious" and "well-aired", the beautifully proportioned barracks are the work of Francis Greenway and are considered his master-piece. They were completed in 1819 by convict labour and designed to house 600 con-victs. Instead, the building initially housed young Irish orphans and single female immigrants, before it later became courts and legal offices. Refurbished in 1990, the barracks reopened as a museum on the history of the site and its occupants. The displays include a room recon-structed as convict quarters of the 1820s, as well as pictures, models and artifacts. Many of the objects recovered during archaeological digs at the site, and now on display, survived because they had been dragged away by rats to their nests. Today, the rodents are acknowledged as valuable agents of preservation.

Self-guided immersive tours, and an activity trail for children, tell the stories of lives impacted by the barracks' his-tory. Hyde Park Barracks is one of 11 Australian convict locations listed as UNESCO World Heritage Sites for their outstanding universal value.

↑ Imposing Hyde Park Barracks at the southern end of Macquarie Street

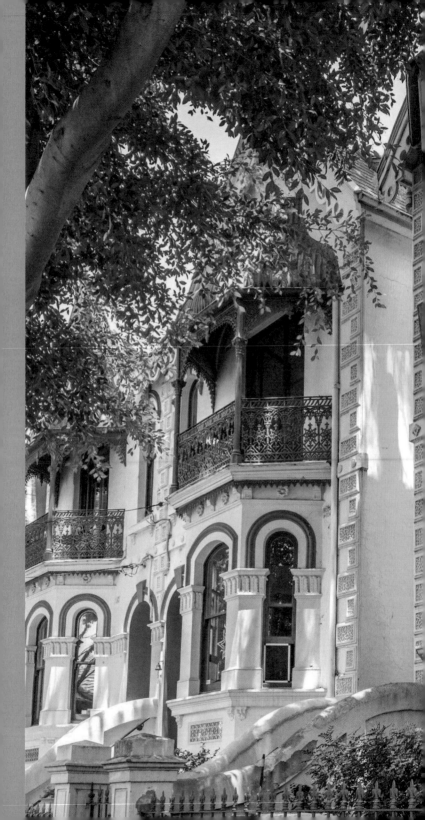

KINGS CROSS, DARLINGHURST AND PADDINGTON

As elsewhere in the city, this part of Sydney was originally inhabited by the Gadigal, a coastal people who carved out a steady existence based around fishing and hunter-gathering. Houses were built on the land here following the arrival of European colonizers in the late 18th century, though the Gadigal continued to camp, fish and hold cermonies in the area around Woolloomooloo until the 1840s. At this point much of the land was developed into residential suburbs; originally high-end, these neighbourhoods became more working class by the turn of the 20th century, after economic decline saw many of the large properties turned into boarding houses. Gentrification began in the 1960s, with artists, students and young professionals drawn to the area's cheap rents, and from the 1970s Darlinghurst became a hub for Sydney's LGBTQ+ community. Although Kings Cross has struggled to shake its reputation as a notorious red-light district, an exciting scene of restaurants, wine bars and galleries makes these neighbourhoods popular with locals and visitors alike.

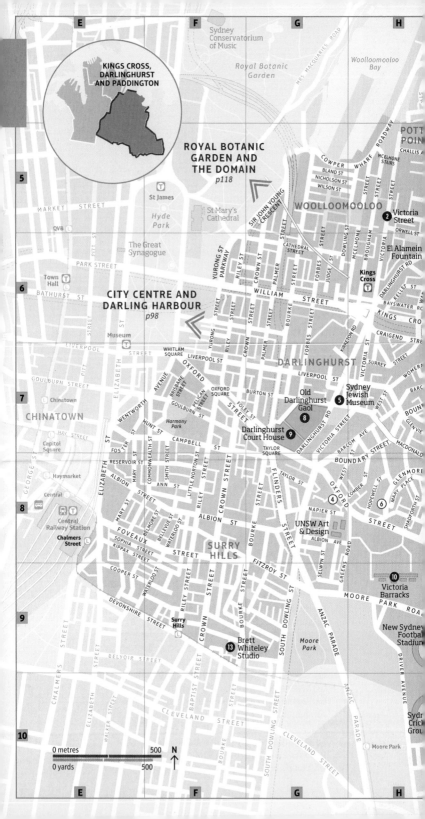

KINGS CROSS,
DARLINGHURST
AND PADDINGTON

E   F   G   H

Sydney
Conservatorium
of Music

Royal Botanic
Garden

Woolloomooloo
Bay

POTT
POIN

CHALLIS

5

ROYAL BOTANIC
GARDEN AND
THE DOMAIN
p118

COWPER WHARF ROADWAY
BLAND ST
NICHOLSON ST
WILSON ST

MCELHONE
STAIRS

WOOLLOOMOOLOO

MARKET   STREET

St James

QVB

Hyde
Park

St Mary's
Cathedral

Victoria
Street

ORWELL ST

El Alamein
Fountain

The Great
Synagogue

PARK STREET

6

Town
Hall

BATHURST   ST

CITY CENTRE AND
DARLING HARBOUR
p98

Museum

DARLINGHURST RD

KELLET   ST

BAYSWATER   RD

KINGS   CRO

CRAIGEND   STRE

Kings
Cross

SIR JOHN YOUNG CRESCENT

CATHEDRAL
STREET

YURONG ST PARKWAY

RILEY ST

CROWN ST

PALMER ST

WILLIAM   STREET

DOWLING ST

MCELHONE

BROUGHAM

FORBES   ST

JUDGE ST

LIVERPOOL   STREET

WHITLAM
SQUARE

LIVERPOOL ST

DARLINGHURST

LIVERPOOL   ST

VICTORIA   STREET

SURREY   STREET

WOMERA

7

Chinatown

CHINATOWN

HAY   STREET

Capitol
Square

Haymarket

OXFORD   STREET

BRISBANE
STREET

PELICAN
ST

AVENUE

OXFORD
SQUARE

BURTON   ST

FOLEY ST

Old
Darlinghurst
Gaol

Sydney
Jewish
Museum

BARC

BOUN

GLEN VIE

Harmony
Park

GOULBURN ST

WENTWORTH   AVENUE

HUNT ST

CAMPBELL   ST

Darlinghurst
Court House

TAYLOR
SQUARE

DARLINGHURST RD

VICTORIA STREET

OXFORD   STREET

BARCOM   AVE

BOUNDARY STREET

GLENMORE   ROAD

MACDONALD

GOULBURN   STREET

ELIZABETH   STREET

FOSTER   ST

RESERVOIR ST

COMMONWEALTH   ST

SMITH ST

ANN   ST

LITTLE NORTON ST

RILEY   STREET

CROWN   STREET

FLINDERS   STREET

TAYLOR ST

NAPIER ST

WEST   ST

COMBER   ST

HOPEWELL ST

MARY PLACE

SHADFORTH   ST

STREET

8

Central

Central
Railway Station

Chalmers
Street

GEORGE   STREET

ALBION   STREET

MARY   STREET

BELMORE ST

BELLEVUE ST

WATERLOO ST

ALBION   ST

BOURKE   STREET

UNSW Art
& Design

ALBION   AVE

SELWYN ST

GREENS   ROAD

FOVEAUX   STREET

SOPHIA   STREET

KIPPAX   STREET

SURRY
HILLS

FITZROY ST

ANZAC   PARADE

Victoria
Barracks

MOORE   PARK   ROA

New Sydney
Footbal
Stadium

9

COOPER ST

DEVONSHIRE   STREET

WATERLOO ST

RILEY   STREET

CROWN   STREET

BOURKE   STREET

SOUTH DOWLING   ST

Surry
Hills

Moore
Park

Brett
Whiteley
Studio

DRIVER   AVENUE

Syd
Crick
Grou

CHALMERS   STREET

ELIZABETH   STREET

WALKER   STREET

BELVOIR   STREET

BAPTIST   STREET

STREET

CLEVELAND   STREET

BOURKE   STREET

SOUTH DOWLING   STREET

CLEVELAND   STREET

ANZAC   PARADE

10

0 metres   500
0 yards   500

N

Moore Park

E   F   G   H

KINGS CROSS, DARLINGHURST AND PADDINGTON

Experience

1. El Alamein Fountain
2. Victoria Street
3. Beare Park
4. Elizabeth Bay House
5. Sydney Jewish Museum
6. Paddington Village
7. Paddington Markets
8. Old Darlinghurst Gaol
9. Darlinghurst Court House
10. Victoria Barracks
11. Paddington Town Hall
12. Centennial Park
13. Brett Whiteley Studio
14. The Entertainment Quarter
15. Juniper Hall

Eat

1. Saint Peter
2. Fred's
3. Tequila Mockingbird

Shop

4. Lee Matthews
5. Dinosaur Designs

El Alamein Fountain in full display at Fitzroy Gardens, Kings Cross ↑

EXPERIENCE

El Alamein Fountain

📍 H6 🏛 Fitzroy Gardens, Macleay St, Potts Point 🚌 311

Located in the heart of Kings Cross, the modernist dandelion-shaped fountain has a reputation for working so sporadically that passers-by often murmur facetiously, "He loves me, he loves me not".

Designed by Australian architect Robert Woodward, the fountain was installed in 1961 to commemorate the Australian army's role in the siege of Tobruk, Libya, and the battle of El Alamein in Egypt during World War II. Throughout the 1960s and 1970s, the El Alamein Fountain was an icon of Sydney, rivalling the Opera House (p86) and the Harbour Bridge (p88). At night, when it is brilliantly lit, the fountain looks ethereal.

> **Throughout the 1960s and 1970s, the El Alamein Fountain was an icon of Sydney, rivalling the Opera House and the Harbour Bridge.**

Victoria Street

📍 H5 🏛 Potts Point 🚌 311, 324, 325, 389

At the Potts Point end, this street of 19th-century terrace houses, interspersed with a few incongruous-looking high-rise blocks, is, by inner-city standards, almost a boulevard. The gracious street you see today was once at the centre of a bitterly fought conservation struggle, one that almost certainly cost the life of a prominent heritage campaigner.

In the early 1970s, residents, backed by the "green bans" put in place by the Builders' Labourers Federation of New South Wales, fought to prevent demolition of old buildings for high-rise towers. Juanita Nielsen, an heiress and publisher of a local newspaper, vigorously took up the conservation battle. On 4 July 1975, she disappeared without a trace. An inquest into her disappearance returned an open verdict, and the case that captivated Sydney and dominated the front pages of newspapers remains unsolved.

As a result of the actions of the union and residents, most of Victoria Street's superb old buildings still stand.

Beare Park

📍 J5 🏛 Ithaca Rd, Elizabeth Bay 🚌 311

Originally a part of the Macleay Estate, Beare Park is now encircled by a jumble of apartment blocks. A refuge from the hectic Kings Cross, it is one of few parks serving this populated area. Shaped like a natural amphitheatre, the park offers glorious views of Elizabeth Bay.

The family home of J C Williamson, a famous theatrical entrepreneur who came to Australia from America in the 1870s, formerly stood at the eastern extremity of the park.

Elizabeth Bay House

📍 J5 📍 7 Onslow Ave, Elizabeth Bay 🚌 311 ⏰ 10am–4pm Sun & Mon 🚫 25 Dec 🌐 mhnsw.au

Elizabeth Bay House contains the finest colonial interior on display in Australia. It is a potent expression of how the depression of the 1840s cut short the 1830s' prosperous optimism.

Designed in Greek Revival style by John Verge, it was built for Colonial Secretary Alexander Macleay, from 1835 to 1839. The oval saloon with its dome and cantilevered staircase is recognized as Verge's masterpiece. The exterior is less satisfactory, as the intended colonnade and portico were not finished owing to a crisis in Macleay's financial affairs.

The interior is furnished to reflect Macleay's occupancy from 1839 to 1845, and is based on inventories drawn up in 1845 for the transfer of the house and contents to his son, William Sharp. He took ownership of the house in return for paying off his father's debts, leading to a rift that was never resolved.

Macleay's original 22-ha (55-acre) land grant was subdivided for flats and villas from the 1880s to 1927.

In the 1940s, the house itself was divided into 15 flats, one of which was owned by the artist Donald Friend. In 1942, Friend saw the ferry *Kuttabul* hit by a torpedo from a Japanese midget submarine from his flat's balcony.

The house was restored and opened as a museum in 1977. It is now a property of the Historic Houses Trust of New South Wales.

Sydney Jewish Museum

📍 G7 📍 148 Darlinghurst Rd, Darlinghurst 🚌 311 ⏰ 10am–4pm Sun–Thu, 10am–3pm Fri 🚫 1 Jan, Good Fri, 25 & 26 Dec, Jewish hols 🌐 sydney jewishmuseum.com.au

Sixteen Jewish convicts were on the First Fleet *(p68)*, and many more were to be transported before the end of the convict era. As with other convicts, most would endure and some would thrive, seizing all the opportunities the colony had to offer.

Established in 1992, the Sydney Jewish Museum relates the stories of Australia's Jewish community. The permanent exhibitions on the ground floor trace the history of Judaism, the persecution

RAZOR GANG WARS

In the 1920s and early 1930s, two women, brothel owner Tilly Devine and sly-grog dealer Kate Leigh, ran vicious razor gangs that battled for control of the criminal underworld in Darlinghurst and Kings Cross. The razor gangs were named after their weapon of choice – barbers' cut-throat shaving blades.

of Jewish people (particularly at the hands of the Nazis), their migration to Australia and present-day Jewish traditions and culture in the country. The mezzanine levels 1–6 have chronological and thematic exhibitions that unravel the tragic history of the Holocaust. The harrowing events are graphically documented, from Hitler's rise to power and *Kristallnacht*, through the evacuation of the ghettos and the Final Solution, to the ultimate liberation of the infamous death camps and Nuremberg Trials. This horrific period is recalled using photographs and relics, some exhumed from mass graves, as well as audiovisual exhibits and oral testimonies.

Holocaust survivors act as guides and their presence, bearing witness to the recorded events, lends considerable power and moving authenticity to the exhibits in the museum.

↑ The lavishly furnished drawing room at the historic Elizabeth Bay House

6

Paddington Village

📍K8 🏠 Between Gipps & Shadforth sts 🚌 333, 440

Paddington began its life as a working-class suburb of Sydney. The community mainly consisted of the carpenters, quarrymen and stonemasons who supervised the convict gangs that built the Victoria Barracks (p138) in the 1840s.

Paddington grew rapidly as a commuter suburb in the late 19th century and most of the terraces were built for renting to Sydney's artisans. The artisans and their families occupied a tight huddle of spartan houses crowded into the area's narrow streets. A few of these houses still remain. Like the barracks, these dwellings and surrounding shops and hotels were built of locally quarried stone. They were decorated with iron lace, Grecian-style friezes, worked parapets and cornices, pilasters and scrolls.

With its huge plane trees shading the road and fine terrace houses on each side, Paddington Street is one of

🔍 HIDDEN GEM
Reservoir Garden

Paddington reservoir, on Oxford Street, is now a park. Inspired by the Hanging Gardens of Babylon, it has board-walks and features reminiscent of Rome's Baths of Carcella.

the oldest and loveliest of the suburb's streets. However, by the 1900s, the terraces of Paddington Village had become unfashionable and people moved out to newly emerging "garden suburbs". In the 1960s, however, their architectural appeal came to be appreciated again and the area was reborn.

Paddington's genteel streets and aesthetic sensibility make it the perfect breeding ground for many artistic endeavours. In addition to the international and Australian contemporary artists showcased by the world-leading **University of NSW Art and Design School**, small and private galleries

abound. These galleries cater to a range of interests, from music photography and limited-edition rock-and-roll prints at Blender, to paintings and sculptures at Australia's oldest Aboriginal art gallery, Cooee. Maunsell Wickes gallery hosts exhibitions by emerging and important mid-career Australian artists, while the Olsen Gallery offering is spearheaded by the works of John Olsen, one of the country's most esteemed living artists.

University of NSW Art and Design School

🏠 Cnr Oxford St & Greens Rd 🕐 10am–5pm Wed–Fri, noon–5pm Sat & Sun 🚫 Public hols 🌐 artdesign. unsw.edu.au/unsw-galleries

7

Paddington Markets

📍J9 🏠 395 Oxford St 🚌 333, 440 🕐 10am–4pm Sat 🚫 25 Dec 🌐 paddington markets.com.au

This market, which began in 1973 as Paddington Bazaar,

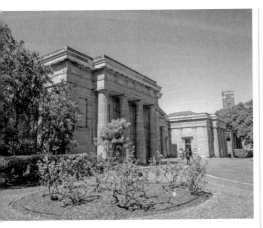

↑ Entrance to the heritage-listed Darlinghurst Court House

takes place every Saturday, come rain or shine, in the grounds of Paddington Village Uniting Church. It is probably the most vibrant in Sydney and is always buzzing with locals. Stallholders come from all over the world and young designers, hoping to launch their careers, display their wares. Other offerings are jewellery, pottery and varied arts and crafts, as well as new and second-hand clothing. Whatever you are looking for, you are more than likely to find it here.

8

Old Darlinghurst Gaol

🇶 G7 🏠 Cnr Burton & Forbes sts, Darlinghurst 🚌 333, 440 🕐 9am–5pm Mon–Fri 🚫 Public hols

Originally known as the Woolloomooloo Stockade and later as Darlinghurst Gaol, this complex is now home to the National Art School. It was constructed over a 20-year period from 1822.

Stalls selling an array of colourful items at Paddington Markets

Surrounded by walls almost 7 m (23 ft) high, the old cell blocks radiate from a central roundhouse. The building is built of stone quarried on the site by convicts, which was then chiselled by them into blocks.

No fewer than 67 people were executed here between 1841 and 1908. Perhaps the most notorious hangman was Alexander "The Strangler" Green, after whom Green Park, outside the jail, is thought to have been named. Green lived near the park until public hostility forced him to live inside the jail.

Some of Australia's most noted artists, including Frank Hodgkinson, Jon Molvig and William Dobell, trained or taught at the art school which was established here in 1921.

9

Darlinghurst Court House

🇶 G7 🏠 197 Oxford St at Taylor Square, Darlinghurst 🚌 333, 440 🕐 Feb–mid-Dec: 10am–4pm Mon–Fri 🚫 Public hols

Abutting the Old Gaol, to which it is connected by underground passages,

and facing tawdry Taylor Square, this unlikely gem of Greek Revival architecture was begun in 1835 by colonial architect Mortimer Lewis. He was only responsible for the central block of the main building, with its six-columned Doric portico with Greek embellishments. The side wings were not added until the 1880s.

Before its completion, the court building was used for church services and community functions. Today, it is still used by the state's Supreme Court, mainly for criminal cases, and these are open to the public.

SHOP

During the 1960s, Paddington became a magnet for top international designers who set up shop here, giving Oxford Street its moniker of "Golden Mile". Here are just a handful of the many stores that you'll find in this shoppers' paradise, selling everything from chic womenswear to quirky homeware at a premium price.

Berkelouw Books
🇶 G8 🏠 19 Oxford St, 🌐 berkelouw. com.au

Opus
🇶 J9 🏠 354 Oxford St 🌐 opusdesign. com.au

Lee Matthews
🇶 H8 🏠 18 Glenmore Rd 🌐 leematthews.com.au

Dinosaur Designs
🇶 J9 🏠 339 Oxford St 🌐 dinosaurdesigns. com.au

↑ The quaint timber bridge built over a pond in Centennial Park

Centennial Park

📍L10 🚆Royal Randwick 🚌Clovelly, Coogee, Maroubra, Randwick, City, Bronte, Bondi Beach & Bondi Junction routes, 333, 352, 255, 389 and 440 🌐centennialparklands. com.au

An idyllic 220-ha (544-acre) park close to the city centre, Centennial Park was formerly a common. It was dedicated "to the enjoyment of the people of New South Wales forever" in 1888. On 1 January 1901, 100,000 people gathered here to witness the Commonwealth of Australia come into being, when the first Australian federal ministry was sworn in by the first governor-general (p70).

The park has landscaped lawns, a rose garden, statues and walking paths. Once the source of the city's water supply, the swamps are now home to many species of waterbirds. Equipment hire is available, as well as barbecues and a café and restaurant. Tennis courts and an adjacent golf course with a large driving range offer sporting opportunities.

10

Victoria Barracks

📍H9 🚏Oxford St 🚌333, 440

Victoria Barracks is the largest and best-preserved group of late Georgian architecture in Australia, covering almost 12 ha (30 acres). Designed by colonial engineer Lieutenant Colonel George Barney, it was completed in 1848 using sandstone quarried by convict labour. Built to house 800 men, the barracks now operate as a centre of military administration. The 225-m (740-ft) main block has two-storey wings with cast-iron verandas flanking a central archway. The perimeter walls have foundations 10 m (40 ft) deep in places. A former gaol block now houses the **Army Museum of New South Wales**.

Army Museum of New South Wales

⏰ Feb–Nov: 10am–1pm Thu (last adm: noon), 10am–4pm first Sun of the month; ID required 🌐armymuseum-nsw.com.au

11

Paddington Town Hall

📍J8 🚏Cnr Oxford St & Oatley Rd 🚌333, 440 🔒To the public, except cinema 🌐palacecinemas.com.au

Local architect J E Kemp won a competition to design Paddington Town Hall. It was completed in 1891. No longer a centre of local government, the Classical Revival building still dominates the area and now houses the arthouse Palace Chauvel cinema.

13

Brett Whiteley Studio

📍F9 🚏2 Raper St, Surry Hills 🚆Surry Hills 🚌301, 302, 303, 372, 393 ⏰10am–4pm Thu–Sun 🌐artgallery.nsw.gov.au/ brett-whiteley-studio

The studio and home of Australian artist Brett Whiteley is tucked in a backstreet in Surry Hills. He converted the former warehouse into a studio and exhibition space in 1985 and lived there from 1987 until his death in 1992. Everything remains as Whiteley left it and haunting reminders of his legacy, such as unfinished paintings, art paraphernalia,

MARDI GRAS

Having started as a protest march, Gay Mardi Gras is now a flamboyant, sequin-infused festival of acceptance, with fairs, theatre, live music, drag shows and more. The month-long celebration culminates in a colourful parade along Oxford Street, in Paddington, and a party at Moore Park.

The scenic Entertainment Quarter, lit up with fairy lights in the evening

books and the graffiti wall he used for inspiration, are all around. The living area features memorabilia such as photos, sketchbooks, furniture and his music collection.

 14

The Entertainment Quarter

📍J10 🚇Lang Rd, Moore Park 🚉Moore Park 🚌339, 355 🌐entertainment quarter.com.au

The Entertainment Quarter is located next door to the working film studios that produced blockbusters, such as *The Matrix* and *Moulin Rouge*.

There are 16 cinema screens within the Quarters, including the Hoyts cinema complex, where you can enjoy your movie with wine and cheese, sitting on sofas. Live entertainment venues feature the latest local and international music and comedy acts. Ten-pin bowling, seasonal ice-skating and children's play areas are available. There are many restaurants, cafés and bars here as well.

The EQ Markets are held on Wednesday and Saturday where stalls feature the best of the region's produce, with many offering free tastings.

Shops are open until late every day. There is plenty of undercover parking and the quarter is a pleasant stroll from the Paddington end of Oxford Street.

 15

Juniper Hall

📍J8 🏠250 Oxford St 🚌333, 440 🔒To the public, except during Moran Art Prize exhibition 🌐juniper hall.com.au

The emancipist gin distiller Robert Cooper built this extravagant colonial Georgian building for his third wife, Sarah. He named it after the main ingredient of the gin that made his fortune.

Completed in 1824, the two-storey home is the oldest dwelling still standing in Paddington. It is also likely the largest and most extravagant house ever built in the suburb.

Juniper Hall was saved from demolition in the mid-1980s and has been restored. It is now home to the annual Moran Art Prize and holds exhibitions through the year.

EAT

Saint Peter
Sustainably sourced seafood, a no-waste philosophy and delicious flavours abound.

📍K9 🏠161 Underwood St, Paddington 🌐saint peter.com.au

$$$

Fred's
Set in a rustic country home, Fred's has a farm-to-table approach.

📍J9 🏠380 Oxford St, Paddington 🌐merivale.com/venues/freds

$$$

Tequila Mockingbird
Tapas-style sharing plates and great tequila served in a beautifully restored terrace house.

📍J8 🏠6b Heeley St, Paddington 🌐tequila-mockingbird.com.au

$$$

A SHORT WALK
PADDINGTON

Distance 1.5 km (1 mile) **Time** 20 minutes
Nearest bus 333

Paddington began to flourish in the 1840s, with the construction of the Victoria Barracks. A village emerged around the workers' cottages, and rapid development followed, with narrow Victorian terraces crowding the streets. Hard hit by the Great Depression, the area became run-down. The 1960s saw the restoration of homes and gentrification of this bohemian suburb. Today, Paddington's streets are a treasure trove of galleries, bars, shops and restaurants. A wander through the area should prove an enjoyable experience.

Five Ways *is a shopping hub that was established in the late 19th century on the busy Glenmore roadway trodden out by bullocks.*

Did You Know?

Paddington is often referred to as "Paddo" by the locals.

Duxford Street's *terrace houses in toning pale shades constitute an ideal of town planning: the Victorians preferred houses in a row to have a pleasingly uniform aspect.*

"Gingerbread" houses can be seen in **Broughton and Union streets**. *With their steeply pitched gables and fretwork bargeboards, they are typical of the rustic Gothic Picturesque architectural style.*

GLENMORE ROAD

GUR

WHITE LANE

STREET

SUF

OXFORD

STAFFORD LANE

BROUGHT

STAFFORD STREET

START

UNION STREET

UNDERWOOD STREET

WILLI

FINISH

0 metres 50
0 yards 50

N ↑

Locator Map
For more detail see p132

←

Five Ways, a picturesque
intersection with 19th- and
early 20th-century buildings

The **Korban Flaubert** *design and
sculpture studio is housed in this strikingly
modern building. It was designed to hold
Australian and international contemporary
sculpture and paintings.*

Warwick, *built in the 1860s, is a minor
castle lying at the end of a row of humble
terraces. Its turrets, battlements and
assorted decorations, in a style somewhat
fancifully described as "King Arthur", even
adorn the garages at the rear.*

Windsor Street's *terrace
houses are, in some cases,
a mere 4.5 m (15 ft) wide.*

Paddington Street (p136), *lined with
plane trees, has some of Paddington's
finest Victorian terraces which exemplify
the building boom between 1860 and
1890. Over 30 years, 3,800 houses were
built in the suburb.*

The **London Tavern** *opened in 1875, making it the
suburb's oldest pub. Like many of Paddington's pubs,
it stands at the end of a row of terraces.*

BEYOND THE CENTRE

For more than 30,000 years, the Greater Sydney area was home to 29 clans of First Australians, collectively known as the Eora Nation. Living mostly in camp-sites along rivers and the harbour foreshore, they sourced food from the sea and surrounding bushland. The arrival of European settlers in 1788 saw the construction of permanent structures in the region, and Parramatta became Australia's first inland European settle-ment. These communities continued to expand, particularly after the opening of the Sydney Harbour Bridge in 1932, which made the bush reserves and beaches of the north more easily accessible.

Must Sees

1 Manly
2 Bondi Beach

Experience More

3 Parramatta
4 Ku-ring-gai Chase National Park
5 Taronga Zoo
6 Luna Park
7 Sydney Olympic Park

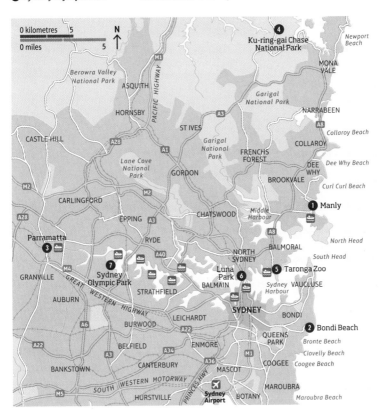

↑ Hornby Lighthouse, near Watson Bay, with views across to Manly

💬 INSIDER TIP
Learn to Surf

Where better to learn to surf than the beach in Australia where the first world surfing championship was held? See if you can master the skill of standing on a board with a lesson at the Manly Surf School *(manlysurfschool.com)*.

The beachside suburb of Manly, set on a peninsula to the northeast of Sydney ↑

❶

MANLY

🚢 Manly 🛈 Manly Wharf; www.manlyaustralia.com.au

If asked to suggest a single excursion outside the city, most Sydneysiders would nominate the 11-km (7-mile) ferry ride from Circular Quay to Manly. In a few short years, this laid-back suburb has become the hub of surf culture and a regular haunt for city dwellers.

Encompassing a narrow stretch of land lying between the harbour and the ocean, Manly is one of Sydney's most popular playgrounds. Ferries from the city arrive into Manly Wharf, which is connected to Manly's famous beach by a lively pedestrian thoroughfare known as the Corso, lined with shops, restaurants and bars. The golden sands of the beach have long drawn walkers and sunbathers, while the waves are legendary for surfing – it was here, in 1964, that the first world surfing championship was held. From the beach's southern end, the Eco-Sculpture Walk along Marine Parade takes visitors past sculptures of the area's marine life, as well as the historic Fairy Bower swimming pool, cut out of oceanside rock. The trail ends at Shelly Beach, a pretty snorkelling destination with a scenic headland lookout.

Did You Know?

Manly Cove is home to little penguins which nest near the wharf between May and February.

1 The Corso is always a hive of activity.

2 The North Head Quarantine Station at North Head, Manly, was once a quarantine facility for migrants arriving in Australia by ship.

3 Surfing is an extremely popular activity in Manly due to the excellent swell.

EAT

Hugos Manly
Watch the ferries come and go from a harbourside seat at Hugos. Here, a cool crowd indulges in cocktails and contemporary Italian fare – like squid ink linguine and pizza topped with pancetta, gorgonzola and figs – while taking in the stunning views across the water.

🏠 Manly Wharf,
1 E Esplanade 🕑 Mon
🌐 hugos.com.au

$ $ $

2

BONDI BEACH

🚌 333 🌐 hellobondi.com.au

Australia's most famous beach, this iconic, photogenic stretch of coast is the place for wriggling toes in the sand, feeling the water lapping around your ankles and soaking up the vibrant culture beyond the shoreline.

Bondi's lengthy crescent of golden sand has long drawn the sun and surf set. Initially part of a private estate following European settlement, the beach was opened to the public in 1882. It later became home to the world's first surf life-saving club, formed in 1907. The skills of the local life-savers were perhaps most famously tested on Black Sunday in 1938, when a freak wave struck the beach and 250 swimmers had to be rescued – five tragically drowned.

Today, surfers visit from far and wide in search of the perfect wave (fittingly, *bondi* is in fact an Aboriginal word for "water breaking over rocks"). People also seek out Bondi as much for its trendy seafront cafés and cosmopolitan milieu as for the world-famous beach. The pavilion, built in 1928 as changing rooms, is now a busy cultural venue.

INSIDER TIP
Sculpture by the Sea

The world's biggest free outdoor sculpture festival takes place over three weeks starting from late October. Enormous, thought-provoking artworks are installed along the clifftop walk between Bondi and Tamarama.

Did You Know?

The TV show *Bondi Rescue* follows Bondi lifeguards performing real rescues.

A game of beach volleyball in progress at the sunny Bondi Beach

EAT

Icebergs Dining Room

Enjoy an elegant fine-dining experience against a dramatic backdrop at this exceptional venue perched above the ocean baths.

🏠 1 Notts Ave
🌐 idrb.com/dining-room

$ $ $

Activities for all Seasons

Whatever the weather or time of year, Bondi has plenty to explore beyond the beach. Cultural attractions include ancient Aboriginal rock engravings at the northern cliffs and urban street art on the Graffiti Wall along the Promenade's southern end, and in summer you can catch outdoor film festivals in the pavilion. More active options include diving into the Icebergs ocean pool, where club members go winter swimming with giant ice bricks, or taking the spectacular clifftop Coastal Walk from Bondi to Coogee, past Tamarama, Bronte and Clovelly beaches.

↑ Saltwater swimming pools right at the edge of the beach at Bondi

EXPERIENCE MORE

Parramatta

🚉Parramatta 🚌Parramatta
📍346a Church St; www.
cityofparramatta.nsw.gov.
au/visiting

The fertile soil of this Sydney suburb resulted in its foundation as Australia's first rural colonial settlement, celebrating its first wheat crop in 1789. **Elizabeth Farm**, dating from 1793, is the oldest surviving residence in Australia. Once the home of John Macarthur, the farm played a major role in breeding merino sheep, which was vital to the country's economy. The house is now a museum, detailing the lives of its first inhabitants until 1850.

Old Government House, built in 1799, stands in Parramatta Park. It is the oldest intact public building in Australia. The Doric porch, added in 1816, is attributed to Francis Greenway (p129). Inside is a collection of early 19th-century furniture. St John's Cemetery on O'Connell Street is the final resting place of many First Fleet settlers (p68).

Elizabeth Farm
🖼🎫🚻 📍70 Alice St, Rosehill ⏰10am–4pm Fri & Sat (Jan: daily) 🚫1 Jan, Good Fri, 25 Dec 🌐mhnsw.au/visit-us/elizabeth-farm

Old Government House
🖼 📍Parramatta Park (entry by Macquarie St) 📞(02) 9635 8149 ⏰Thu–Sun 🚫Public hols

Ku-ring-gai Chase National Park

📍McCarrs Creek Rd, Church Point 🛈Bobbin Head Information Centre: Ku-Ring-Gai Chase Rd; (02) 9472 8949

This national park lies on the city's northernmost outskirts, 30 km (19 miles) from Sydney, and covers 15,000 ha (37,000 acres). It is bounded to the north by Broken Bay, at the mouth of the Hawkesbury River, with its eroded valleys formed during the last Ice Age. Waterways and beaches are set against the national park. Picnicking, bushwalking and windsurfing are popular.

The Hawkesbury River curls around an ancient sandstone

EAT

Bathers' Pavilion
Close to the beach, this restaurant and bistro serves superb seasonal food.

📍4 The Esplanade, Balmoral 🌐bathers pavilion.com.au

$$$

↑ Attractions at the Luna Park fair on the Sydney Harbour shore

landscape rich in Aboriginal rock art. Within the national park are hundreds of Aboriginal art sites, the most common being rock engravings thought to be 2,000 years old.

5

Taronga Zoo

🏠 Bradley's Head Rd, Mosman 🚌 100 ⛴ From Circular Quay 🕐 May-Aug & 31 Dec: 9:30am-4:30pm; Sep-Apr: 9:30am-5pm daily 🌐 taronga.org.au

Taronga opened in 1916 in its idyllic harbourside location, with sweeping views across the water. The protection and preservation of endangered creatures is at the heart of the zoo's prolific conservation programmes. Free daily presentations include the engaging Free Flight Bird Show.

→
Relaxing besides a fountain at Sydney Olympic Park

6

Luna Park

🏠 1 Olympic Dr, Milsons Point 🚇 Milsons Point 🚌 209, 230 🕐 Daily; hours vary, check website 🌐 lunaparksydney.com

This amusement park with its famous smiling face entrance has been a popular destination since 1935. Entry is free, but passes are required for the rides and entry into Coney Island. Coney Island is the world's last operating example of a true 1930s fun house, and the gentle Ferris wheel is popular for sweeping views of the harbour, especially as the sun sets.

7

Sydney Olympic Park

🏠 Sydney Olympic Park 🚇 Olympic Park 🌐 sydney olympicpark.com.au

Sydney Olympic Park was host to the 27th Olympic Games in 2000. The venues built for the Olympics, Stadium Australia and The Showground, now hold major football and cricket matches throughout the year. In summer, pack a picnic and bring a rug for the free movies, music and events on the grass at Cathy Freeman Park.

TOP 5 **BEACHES AND SWIM SPOTS IN SYDNEY**

Balmoral
🏠 Mosman
Picture-perfect beach with calm waters and a lovely esplanade walk.

Maccallum Seawater Pool
🏠 Milson Rd, Cremorne Point
Small harbour pool with stunning views of the city.

Murray Rose Pool
🏠 536 New S Head Rd, Double Bay
Great harbourside pool with a beach area.

Nielsen Park
🏠 6 Steele Point Rd, Vaucluse
Neighbourhood beach with a selection of scenic walking tracks.

Shelly Beach
🏠 Manly
Quieter than nearby Manly Beach and great for snorkelling.

Other facilities include the Aquatic Centre with a waterpark, an archery range and a Tennis Centre. There is also an arena that hosts concerts by major Australian and international acts.

NEW SOUTH WALES

Admiring the view while hiking in the Blue Mountains

Sturt Stony
Desert

Wyandra

Innamincka

Cunnamulla

Lake
Blanche

Bourke

Darling

Lake
Frome

Wilcannia

SOUTH
AUSTRALIA

Broken
Hill

**THE BLUE MOUNTAINS
AND WESTERN
NEW SOUTH WALES**
p156

Mannahill

Ivanhoe

Hillston

Port Wakefield

Renmark

Mildura

Murray

Narrandera

Adelaide

Murrayville

Deniliquin

Albury

Charlton

Shepparton

Bendigo

EXPLORE
NEW SOUTH
WALES

VICTORIA

Melbourne

Sale

Traralgon

This guide divides New South Wales into three colour-
coded sightseeing areas, as shown on this map. Find
out more about each area on the following pages.

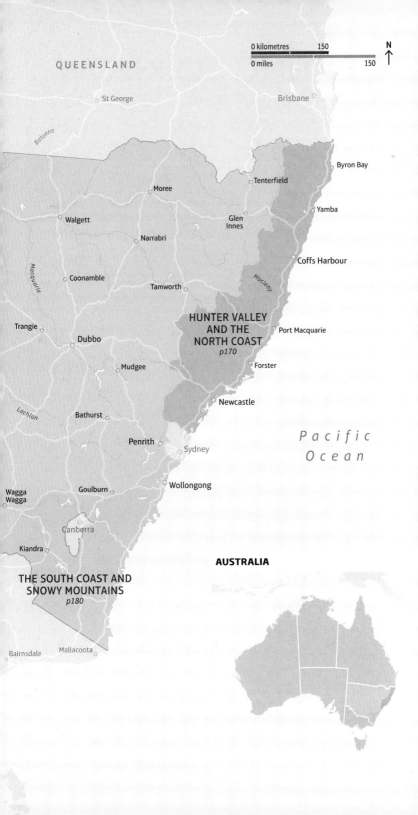

GETTING TO KNOW
NEW SOUTH WALES

Sydney is just the beginning. New South Wales offers plenty more to keep visitors entertained, from bushwalking in the fragrant Blue Mountains to surfing off the white-sand beaches near Byron Bay, wine tasting in the Hunter Valley to whale-watching off the south coast.

PAGE 156

THE BLUE MOUNTAINS AND WESTERN NEW SOUTH WALES

Bordering Sydney to the west are the beautiful Blue Mountains. Here, a eucalyptus haze hangs over vast valleys and thundering waterfalls throw up mist. Further west still, the forest gives way to a dusty, lunar landscape. Despite appearances, Western New South Wales is anything but empty. This is an ancient world of intriguing rock formations, where fossickers still dig for opals and artists chronicle local life.

Best for
Bushwalking and scenic drives

Home to
The Blue Mountains

Experience
Soaking up the view of the Three Sisters from Echo Point

PAGE 170

HUNTER VALLEY AND THE NORTH COAST

Welcome to wine – and unwind – country. The North Coast is home to some of New South Wales's coolest towns and cities, like Newcastle and Byron Bay, a hippie haven where art, yoga and all things organic rule. Sydney's hip younger sibling, Newcastle brings a buzz to the region, with locals hitting the beach by day and waterfront bars come nightfall. From here, the Hunter River flows into the Hunter Valley, where undulating vineyards are overlooked by mountains and rainforest.

Best for
Food and wine

Home to
Rural vineyards and cosmopolitan cities

Experience
Surfing the waves at laidback Byron Bay

PAGE 180

THE SOUTH COAST AND SNOWY MOUNTAINS

Only 110 km (68 miles) southwest of Sydney – and seemingly a whole world away from the capital – is the snow-capped landscape of the Snowy Mountains. This winter playground is perhaps one of the most surprising places in the country. For a more typical Australian experience, make for the coast, where beaches are separated by quaint towns, full of tearooms, antique stores and museums of local curiosities.

Best for
Skiing and snow sports

Home to
The Snowy Mountains

Experience
Hiking to the top of Australia's highest mountain – Mount Kosciuszko

The Skyway cable car gliding above the Blue Mountains

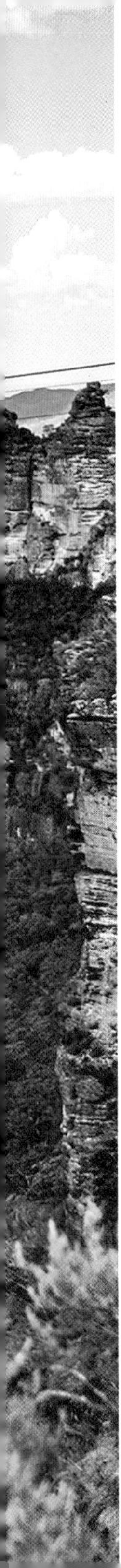

THE BLUE MOUNTAINS AND WESTERN NEW SOUTH WALES

The Gundungurra believe that the Blue Mountains were formed when Dreamtime creatures Mirigan and Garangatch fought an epic battle here. For millennia, the Gundungurra and other Aboriginal nations lived here peaceably, using ancient routes through the mountains for trade, ceremony and travel. The first European settlers were unable to find these routes and the seemingly impenetrable mountains soon became shrouded in legends as well as blue haze. It was said that fertile lands, and even China, lay beyond.

The barrier of the Blue Mountains was finally penetrated by settlers in 1813 and the rich plains beyond were soon used for sheep and cattle grazing. In the middle of the 19th century, coal, shale and gold were found here, prompting mining operations and the gold rush around Bathurst and Mudgee, and up into the New England Tablelands. The roads and railways that were built to aid miners and prospectors made this part of New South Wales accessible and it now contains more towns, a denser rural population and a more settled coastline than anywhere else in the country. Fortunately, all this development has not robbed the region of its natural beauty, from the verdant wilderness of the Blue Mountains to the lunar landscape of the Willandra Lakes Region.

Bourke

NEW
SOUTH
WALES

Tibooburra

Wilcannia

12

**BROKEN
HILL**

Ivanhoe

Dubbo

Sydney

Hay

Wagga Wagga

Canberra

0 km   250

0 miles   250

N

MOONIE HIGHWAY

St George

Westm

Talwood

Boom

Macintyre

Mungindi

Garah

More

Gwydir

GWYDIR HIGHWAY

Bellata

9 LIGHTNING
RIDGE

B55

B76

Collarenebri

Cryon

Fords
Bridge

Collerina

B71

Brewarrina

B76

Walgett

Wee Waa

Narrabri

B51

Warrego

10 BOURKE

Carinda

Pilliga

NEWELL HIGHWAY

Louth

B71

MITCHELL HIGHWAY

Quambone

Coonamble

Baradine

Mulla

B87

Coolabah

Macquarie

B55

Mt Booroondarra
441 m (1,446 ft)

Castlereagh

Mt Exmouth
1,206 m (3,956 ft)

Warrumbungle Ran

Coonabarab

Cobar

Girilambone

BARRIER HIGHWAY

Nyngan

Tooraweenah

Binnaway

Coolah

A32

Canbelego

Mullengudgery

Gilgandra

Mendooran

B55

B87

A32

Dunedoo

Nymagee

Trangie

B84

Ulan

Narromine

8 DUBBO

Gulgong

NEW   SOUTH   WALES

A32

Wellington

MUDGEE **11**

Melrose

Tullamore

Peak Hill

Mumbi

Matakana

NEWELL HWY

MITCHELL HWY

HILL END **13**

Ilfor

15

Condobolin

Parkes

Molong

Orange

SOFA

16 WILLANDRA
NATIONAL PARK

Lake Cargelligo

Forbes

Mt Canobolas
1,396 m (4,580 ft)

Bathurst

Lachlan

Hillston

Canowindra

A41

Obero

B75

B87

Girral

MID WESTERN HWY

Cowra

Shooters h
1,354 m (4,442

Booligal

B64

Trunkey

Goolgowi

West
Wyalong

Grenfell

Lake
Wyangala

Crookwe

Griffith

B87

Ardlethan

Koorawatha

Young

B81

Boorowa

Murrumbidgee

Darlington Point

A39

Grogan

Harden

Goulburn

Hay

B75

A20

Temora

B94

Cootamundra

Coolamon

A41

Coolac

Murrumbateman

A25

A23

Narrandera

STURT HIGHWAY

Coleambally

14 WAGGA
WAGGA

M31

Canberra Airport

M2

0 kilometres   80

0 miles   80

N

B72

Canberra

Binalong

Boorowa

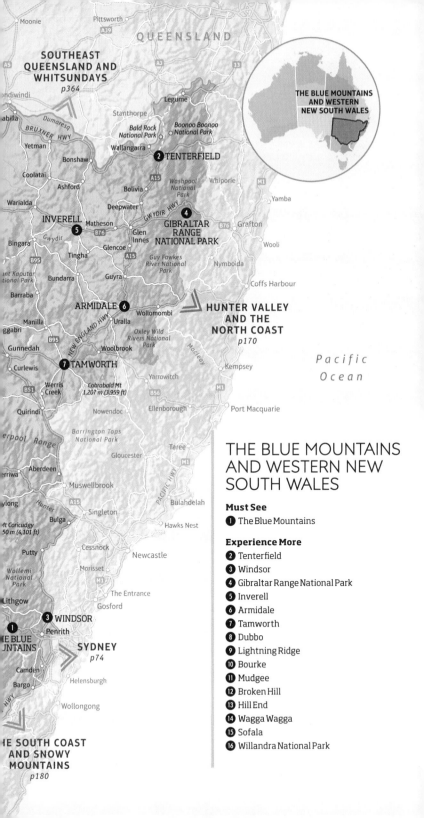

HUNTER VALLEY
AND THE
NORTH COAST
p170

Pacific
Ocean

THE BLUE MOUNTAINS
AND WESTERN NEW
SOUTH WALES

Must See

❶ The Blue Mountains

Experience More

❷ Tenterfield
❸ Windsor
❹ Gibraltar Range National Park
❺ Inverell
❻ Armidale
❼ Tamworth
❽ Dubbo
❾ Lightning Ridge
❿ Bourke
⓫ Mudgee
⓬ Broken Hill
⓭ Hill End
⓮ Wagga Wagga
⓯ Sofala
⓰ Willandra National Park

THE BLUE MOUNTAINS
AND WESTERN NEW SOUTH WALES

SYDNEY
p74

THE SOUTH COAST
AND SNOWY
MOUNTAINS
p180

Did You Know?

The region is home to about 1,500 plant species, including Wollemi pine, one of the oldest trees in the world.

THE BLUE MOUNTAINS

D6 **Great Western Hwy** **Katoomba** **Visitor centres: Hamment Pl, off Great Western Hwy, Glenbrook; Echo Point, Katoomba; 1300 653 408**

Named for the blue haze caused by the release of oil from eucalyptus trees, the Blue Mountains are an arresting sight. To best experience the landscape, get out there: climb a peak, jump in a creek or walk a trail.

The Blue Mountains have been home to Aboriginal communities for an estimated 14,000 years. The rugged terrain, with its sheer cliff faces, canyons and soaring peaks, proved a formidable barrier to white settlers, who were virtual prisoners of the Sydney Cove area. In 1813, however, three farmers set out on a well-planned mission and emerged successfully on the western side of the mountains. To aid future journeys, roads and railways were constructed in the 1870s, making the mountains an increasingly attractive resort destination. In 1959, the Blue Mountains National Park was gazetted, ensuring the preservation of the large tracts of remaining wilderness.

LEGEND OF THE THREE SISTERS

A towering sandstone formation in the heart of the park, the Three Sisters is a sacred Aboriginal site. According to an Aboriginal story, the rocks were formed when three Katoomba sisters – Gunndeoo, Wimlah and Meehni – fell in love with three brothers from the neighbouring Nepean tribe. At the time, inter-tribal marriages were forbidden so an elder turned the sisters to stone to protect them from capture, promising to turn them back when it was safe. But the elder was killed and the sisters remained rock pillars forever more.

←
The Three Sisters and surrounding peaks, as seen from Echo Point in the Blue Mountains National Park

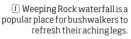

① Weeping Rock waterfall is a popular place for bushwalkers to refresh their aching legs.

② Lyrebirds are a common sight in the Blue Mountains. Male lyrebirds, like this one, have beautiful tails.

③ Rock climbing is one of the many outdoor activities popular with visitors to the Blue Mountains.

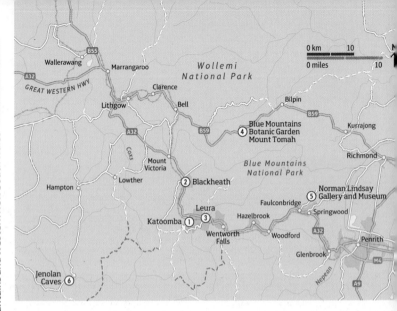

EXPLORING THE BLUE MOUNTAINS

①
Katoomba

🛈 Echo Point, Katoomba
🌐 visitbluemountains.com.au

Katoomba is the tourism centre of the Blue Mountains and a good base from which to explore the park. The town itself seems little changed from when it first attracted wealthy Sydneysiders in need of mountain air during the 1870s.

Within a few minutes' drive of the town is Echo Point, which is home to a large information centre and lookout, with views of the Three Sisters (*p160*). A short walk leads down to this striking rock formation, while further on is the Giant Staircase – steps hewn out of the rock face.

On the western side of town, the world's first glass-floor Skyway, the Scenic Skyway, traverses 205 m (670 ft) above the mountains, while the Scenic Railway offers great views as it plummets down a gorge.

---

②
Blackheath

🛈 Govetts Leap Rd; 1300 653 408

The excellent restaurants and accommodation available in Blackheath often induce visitors to stay one or two nights here. But the real draw of this area is the chance to explore the mist-enshrouded rifts and ravines of the beautiful Grose Valley.

Start at the Heritage Centre 3 km (2 miles) from Blackheath along Govetts Leap Road. Here, displays document the geological, Aboriginal and European histories of the region. Then continue to Govetts Leap, which is the starting place for a number of trails. A clifftop track leads from here to Bridal Falls, the highest waterfalls in the Blue Mountains, while an arduous 8-hour return trek takes you to Blue Gum Forest. The five-hour Grand Canyon track, meanwhile, sets off from Evans lookout and is only suited to the fittest walkers.

> **GREAT VIEW**
> ### Govetts Leap Lookout
>
> Make for this viewpoint near Blackheath for sweeping panoramas over the Grose Valley – a wilderness made up of sandstone escarpments and cliff walls, deep canyons and waterfalls.

→

The visitor centre at Mount Tomah Botanic Garden

③
Leura

🛈 Echo Point, Katoomba; 1300 653 408

This small town's tree-lined main street is home to fine art galleries, cafés, shops, restaurants and the Leuralla Toy and Railway Museum.

About 6 km (3.5 miles) away lies Everglades House, an Art Deco masterpiece. The house is best known for its Everglades gardens, which include a shaded alpine garden, a grotto pool and rhododendron stands.

④
Blue Mountains Botanic Garden Mount Tomah

📍 Bells Line of Rd ⏰ 9am-5pm daily 🚫 25 Dec 🌐 botanicgardens.org.au

Home to the Darug Aboriginal people, Mount Tomah gets its name from an Indigenous word for "fern". Since 1987, the site has acted as an annex to Sydney's Royal Botanic Garden (p122), housing species that would not survive the coastal conditions. The layout of the garden is an impressive feat

→
Admiring the limestone features at Jenolan Caves

of engineering, and the views across Grose Valley are truly breathtaking.

_____

⑤
Norman Lindsay Gallery and Museum

📍 14 Norman Lindsay Crescent, Faulconbridge ⏰ 10am-4pm Thu-Mon 🚫 25 & 26 Dec 🌐 normanlindsay.com.au

One of Australia's most recognized artists, Norman Lindsay inspired considerable controversy with his nudes and risqué novels. He bought his mountain retreat in 1913 and set about producing a large body of work, much of which reflects his rejection of the moral and sexual restraints of his era. His beautifully pre-served home is now a gallery for his paintings, cartoons, mythological garden sculp-tures and children's books. There is also a re-creation of the interior of his original studio, and a peaceful garden set amid the bushland.

⑥
Jenolan Caves

📍 Jenolan Caves Rd ⏰ 9am-4:30pm Sun-Thu (to 10:30pm Fri & Sat) 🌐 jenolancaves.org.au

More than 300 subterranean chambers make up the Jenolan Caves. The nine caves open to the public have a variety of delicate limestone formations, pools and rivers, including the ominously named Styx River.

EAT

Darleys
Local produce is transformed into artistic dishes here.

📍 Lilianfels Resort & Spa, 5-9 Katoomba 🌐 darleysrestaurant.com.au

$$$

Arrana
This sleek restaurant is tucked away in an unassuming arcade.

📍 9-12, 125 Macquarie Rd, Springwood 🌐 arrana.com.au

$$$

EXPERIENCE MORE

② Tenterfield

 G4 🚌 *i* 157 Rouse St; www.visittenterfield.com.au

The rural town of Tenterfield is often called the "Birthplace of Our Nation". It was at the town's School of Arts building on 24 October 1889 that politician Sir Henry Parkes made his "One Nation" speech. The address explained his vision of all the colonies in Australia uniting as one country and led to the creation of the Australian Federation on 1 January 1901 (p70). Due to its historic importance, the school was the first building to be acquired by the New South Wales National Trust. Other historic buildings in this small town include the Victorian mansion Stannum House, the bluestone saddlers' shop and the courthouse.

As well as its connection to Sir Henry Parkes, Tenterfield is known for Bald Rock, the second-biggest monolith in Australia after Uluru (p434) and the country's largest exposed granite rock. Located 40 km (25 miles) north of Tenterfield, Bald Rock dates back to the Lower Triassic period which was over 200 million years ago. It is 750 m (2,460 ft) long and about 200 m (650 ft) high, and offers great views of volcanic ranges to the east, Mount McKenzie to the south and Girraween National Park to the north.

③ Windsor

D6 🚌🚆 *i* Hawkesbury Valley Way, Richmond; www.discoverthehawkesbury.com.au

Windsor, named by Governor Macquarie, is one of the five "Macquarie towns". Set up on the banks of the Hawkesbury River in 1794, it provided farmers with both fertile land and the ease of river transport. In the centre of town, St Matthew's Church is a fine example of Georgian colonial architecture. Some other sights of interest include the Macquarie Arms and the **Hawkesbury Regional Museum**, which chronicles Windsor's early colonial history.

Hawkesbury Regional Museum

 ♿ 🏠 8 Baker St, Windsor 📞 (02) 4560 4655 🕐 10am–4pm Wed–Mon ⊘ Good Fri, 25 Dec

④

Gibraltar Range National Park

G4 🅿 Gwydir Hwy 🌐 nationalparks.nsw.gov.au

Situated 70 km (43 miles) east of Glen Innes, this national park is known for its giant

> As well as its connection to Sir Henry Parkes, Tenterfield is known for Bald Rock, the second-biggest monolith in Australia after Uluru and the country's largest exposed granite rock.

tors, which tower 1,200 m (4,000 ft) above sea level and are surrounded by swampland and heath. The area is beautiful in the summer when wildflowers bloom.

Gibraltar Range National Park is linked to neighbouring Washpool National Park by a 40-km (25-mile) World Heritage walk.

Away from the wilderness, Glen Innes and nearby Glencoe, Ben Lomond and Shannon Vale are in an area known as Australia's "Celtic Country" as they were settled by Welsh, Irish, Scottish and Cornish immigrants in 1852. Check out the Standing Stones in Glen Innes, which were erected in 1992 to mark the contribution of Celtic settlers to modern Australian culture.

Sapphire mining is a major industry in Celtic Country, and Glen Innes hosts a gem and mineral fair each September. Public digging ("fossicking") for sapphires, topaz, garnet and beryl is still possible near Emmaville and Torrington.

↑ The majestic Wollomombi Gorge at Oxley Wild Rivers National Park

---

5

Inverell

 G4 🚗🚌 *i* Water Towers Complex, 13-35 Campbell St; www.inverell.com.au

Inverell is known as "Sapphire City" because so many of the world's sapphires are mined in the area. Many of the buildings in the main street were built during the 1880s mining boom and are well preserved. Visit the **Inverell Pioneer Village** to see how Australians lived here in the 19th century.

Just south of Inverell lies the mighty Copeton Dam. Whitewater rafting below the dam on the wild Gwydir River is an exhilarating experience.

←

Stannum House in Tenterfield, one of the town's historic landmarks

Inverell Pioneer Village
⊕ 🏠 Tingha Rd, Inverell
⏰ 10am-4pm Tue-Fri, 9:30am-1:30pm Sat & Sun
🚪 Good Fri, 25 Dec 🌐 inverell pioneervillage.org.au

6

Armidale

 G4 🚗🚕🚌 *i* 82 Marsh St; www.armidaletourism. com.au

In the heart of the New England Tablelands, Armidale is a university city. Concerts, plays, films and lectures fill its many theatres, pubs and halls.

Some 35 buildings here are classified by the National Trust. The **New England Regional Art Museum** holds the A\$20-million Howard Hinton and Chandler Coventry collections, with works by local artists, including Tom Roberts and Norman Lindsay *(p61)*.

Armidale is surrounded by some magnificent national parks. To the east is the 90-ha (220-acre) **Oxley Wild Rivers National Park**, which has the 220-m (720-ft) high Wollomombi Gorge, one of the highest waterfalls in Australia.

New England Regional Art Museum
⊕ 🏠 106 Kentucky St
⏰ 10am-4pm Tue-Sun
🚪 1 Jan, Good Fri, 25 Dec
🌐 neram.com.au

Oxley Wild Rivers National Park
🏠 188 W North St, Walcha
⏰ Mon-Fri 🌐 nationalparks. nsw.gov.au

HOWARD HINTON COLLECTION

The mysterious art patron and benefactor Howard Hinton (1867–1948) amassed a fortune in art despite living a modest life. Slowly, he gifted it all to Armidale Teachers' College, now the New England Regional Art Museum, with which he had no known connection. It is said to be one of the best collections of Australian art.

7
Tamworth

AG5 🚗🚌 **i** The Big Golden Guitar, 2 The Ringers Rd; www.destination tamworth.com.au

A thriving rural city at the centre of fertile agricultural plains, Tamworth is best known as Australia's country music capital. Every January, thousands of fans and performers flock here for the Country Music Festival, which includes blue grass, bush ballads and the Golden Guitar Awards.

Reflecting the city's passion for country music are the Big Golden Guitar Tourist Centre, the Gallery of Stars (where Australia's country music greats are immortalized in wax), the Hall of Fame Museum (dedicated to musicians who have made a major contribution to the industry) and the Country Music Hands of Fame Cornerstone.

Tamworth is also Australia's equestrian centre. The Quarter Horse Association and Appaloosa Association are based here, and show-jumping events are regularly held in the city.

← The iconic guitar at the Big Golden Guitar Tourist Centre, Tamworth

8
Dubbo

AF5 🚗🚌 **i** Cnr Newell Hwy & Macquarie St; www. dubbo.com.au

Located at the geographical heart of the state, Dubbo is the regional capital of western New South Wales. The area, situated on the banks of the Macquarie River, was first noted for its agricultural potential in 1817 by explorer John Oxley. The city has since grown into a rural centre producing A$45 million worth of food and agricultural goods annually.

Dubbo's colonial history is evident in its period architecture. Seek out the 1876 Dubbo Museum, which has ornate ceilings and a cedar staircase, the 1890 Italianate courthouse and the Tuscan columns and terracotta tiles of the 1884 Macquarie Chambers.

At the **Old Dubbo Gaol**, visitors can hear the tragic story of Jacky Underwood, an Aboriginal Australian who was hanged for his part in the Breelong massacre of 1900, when 11 white settlers were killed. Dubbo magistrate Rolf Boldrewood drew on the characters of the gaol's inmates to write the novel *Robbery Under Arms* (1888).

The most popular sight in Dubbo is the large **Taronga Western Plains Zoo**, 5 km (3 miles) from the town. The zoo's emphasis is on breeding endangered species. Visitors can see over 1,000 animals.

Old Dubbo Gaol
♿ 🏛 Macquarie St ⏰ 9am–5pm daily 🚫 Good Fri, 25 Dec 🌐 olddubbogaol.com.au

Taronga Western Plains Zoo
♿⏱ 🏛 Obley Rd ⏰ 9am–4pm daily 🌐 taronga.org.au

→ Visitors at a winery, and *(inset)* a verdant vineyard in Mudgee

9
Lightning Ridge

AF4 🚗🚌 **i** Morilla St; (02) 6829 1670

Lightning Ridge is a small mining village and home of the treasured black opal – a rare dark opal shot with red, blue and green. Gem enthusiasts from around the world come to try their luck on the opal fields. The town treats these international visitors to a hearty welcome, with mine tours, a plethora of opal shops and hot bore spas all on offer.

10
Bourke

AF4 🚗🚌 **i** Kidman Way; www.visit bourke.com

Situated on the banks of the Darling River, part of Australia's longest river system, Bourke is a colourful town that was once the centre of the world's wool industry. It still produces 25,000 bales per year.

Bourke's heyday is evident in the colonial buildings as well as the old weir, wharf, lock and lift-up span bridge, which recall the days of the paddle-steamer trade to

 INSIDER TIP
Take a Tour

Learn about Bourke's Aboriginal history and culture on a guided tour with Bourke Aboriginal Cultural Tours *(www.bourke aboriginalculturaltours. com)*. The guides will take you to the wharf, a local art gallery and the town's First Nations radio station, 2CUZFM.

Victoria. The town's cemetery tells something of Bourke's history: Afghan camel drivers who brought the animal to Australia from the Middle East in the 19th century are buried here.

Promoted locally as the "Gateway to the 'Real' Outback", Bourke is the traditional land of the Ngemba and Barkindji peoples. During the 1940s, the town saw the arrival of many displaced Aboriginal peoples from the outback, and they settled here, resulting in a significant increase in the area's First Nations population. Nearby is the Mulgowan Aboriginal Art Site walking track, a challenging path featuring ancient rock art in unspoiled bushland.

⑪

Mudgee

Ⓐ F5 🚗 🚌 **𝒊 90 Market St; www.visitmudgeeregion. com.au**

Mudgee is a magnificent old rural town with gardens and grand buildings, many of which are protected by the National Trust. Don't miss the Regent Theatre on Church Street, the many banks, civic buildings and churches on Market Street, the railway station and the restored West End Hotel, which now houses the Colonial Inn Museum.

The town is also famous for its surrounding wineries, which are celebrated at the annual Mudgee Wine Festival, and fresh local produce, such as yabbies (crayfish), trout, lamb, peaches and asparagus.

During the 1850s and 1860s, gold was discovered to the south of Mudgee. Panning for gold in the creeks of Windeyer, which yielded alluvial gold until the 1930s, is a popular tourist activity.

Visitors can try their hand at panning for gold at the **Gulgong Gold Experience** in Gulgong, a gold rush village 33 km (20 miles) north of Mudgee.

Gulgong Gold Experience

♦ Ⓐ Tom Saunders Ave, Gulgone Ⓒ 1-3pm Wed-Fri, 10am-2pm Sat & Sun Ⓒ Public hols 🌐 gulgonggold.com.au

STAY

Zoofari Lodge
Stay at the Taronga Western Plains Zoo in Dubbo to experience an African safari in NSW.

Ⓐ F5 Ⓐ Taronga Western Plains Zoo, Dubbo 🌐 taronga.org.au/dubbo-zoo/accommodation

💲💲💲

Goonoo Goonoo Station Tamworth
Perched over Tamworth's pastoral lands, these cottages offer panoramic views.

Ⓐ G5 Ⓐ 13304 New England Hwy, Timbumburi 🌐 goonoogoonoo station.com

💲💲💲

A museum dedicated to
the 1981 Australian film,
Mad Max 2, near Broken Hill ↑

12 Broken Hill

E4 ✈🚆🚌 **𝒊** Cnr Blende &
Bromide sts; www.visit
brokenhill.com

The unofficial centre of outback
New South Wales, Broken Hill
is a mining city perched on
the edge of the deserts of
inland Australia. The town was
established in 1883, when vast
deposits of zinc, lead and silver
were discovered in a 7-km
(4-mile) long "Line of Lode" by

TOP 3 BROKEN HILL ART GALLERIES

Pro Hart
🏠 108 Wyman St
Find works by Hart, the
father of Australian
outback painting, here.

**Howard Steer
Art Studio**
🏠 721 Williams St
Humorous and vibrant
art on life in the outback.

**Broken Hill Regional
Art Gallery**
🏠 404/408 Argent St
Exhibits by established
and emerging artists.

45

The number of movies
that have been filmed
in Silverton and Broken
Hill, including
Mad Max 2.

the then-fledgling company
Broken Hill Pty Ltd. Broken Hill
has since grown into a major
town and BHP has become
Australia's biggest corporation.

Broken Hill's now declining
mining industry is still
evident; slag heaps are piled
up, there are more pubs per
head than any other city in
the state and streets are
named after metals.

It may seem surprising at
first glance, but the town's
gritty character and barren
surroundings have inspired
many artists and Broken Hill
has more than 20 art galleries
featuring works by local
desert artists.

To the northwest of Broken
Hill is Silverton, once a thriving silver mining community
and now a ghost town. It
is popular as a location for
films, such as *Mad Max 2* and
Priscilla, Queen of the Desert.

13 Hill End

D6 ✈🚆 Bathurst (75 km/
47 miles), then drive
𝒊 Hill End Heritage Centre:
1 Beyers Ave; www.visit
nsw.com

This former gold town brims
with rustic charm and
Victorian buildings. Hill End
became a boomtown in 1872
when German-born miner and
businessman Bernhardt Otto
Holtermann discovered the
world's biggest hunk of reef
gold. Today, Hill End Historic
Site preserves the town as it
was in the roaring days of the
early gold rush. The **Hill End
Heritage Centre** brings the
area's history to life, with a
preserved miner's cottage
and mining trolley.

On the outskirts of town, the
scenic Bald Hill walking loop
passes relics of old mines,
while the restored Bald Hill
mine provides a glimpse into
underground life in the craggy
mountain and gorge country.

**Hill End
Heritage Centre**
🏠 5 Beyers Ave, Hill
End 📞 (02) 6370 9050
🕐 8:30am–4pm Mon–Fri
🚫 Public hols

On the outskirts of the city, the Widadjuri track is a popular walk along the banks of the Murrumbidgee River.

The gentle town of Gundagai is located 80 km (50 miles) to the east, on the banks of the Murrumbidgee River. This was the site of one of Australia's greatest natural disasters, when floods swept away the town in 1852. Look out for Darien Pullen's sculpture of two Wiradjuri men, Yarri and Jacky Jacky, who rescued townspeople during the flood.

15

Sofala

 D6 ✈🚌 Bathurst, then drive 🛈 www.visitnsw.com

It's hard to believe that Sofala was once a thriving gold town. Today, it's one of the country's tiniest towns, with little more than 200 people living on its three streets. Gold rush-era buildings, including the Old Sofala Gaol and The Royal Hotel, dominate the charming old-world streetscape, which was immortalized in an iconic painting by Russel Drysdale. Though the last commercial mine shut in 1947, prospectors still try their luck panning for gold in the Turon River.

---

16 ✍

Willandra National Park

F5 🛈 200 Yambil St, Griffith 🕐 In wet weather 🌐 national parks.nsw.gov.au

Willandra National Park, on the edge of a riverine plain, has significant wildlife and

14

Wagga Wagga

C6 ✈🚌🚌 🛈 183 Tarcutta St; www. visitwagga.com

Named by its original inhabitants, the Widadjuri people, as "a place of many crows", Wagga Wagga has grown into a large, modern city serving the surrounding farming community. As well as wheat, barley, sheep and cattle, the fertile soil is perfect for cultivating grapes and Wagga Wagga's vineyards have won numerous accolades for their wines. Add the city's abundance of gardens, and it's no wonder that Wagga Wagga is called the "Garden City of the South".

The city's main sights are the large Botanic Gardens and the Wagga Historical Museum.

← *The Great Rescue of 1852, a sculpture in Gundagai town near Wagga Wagga*

▎**MUNGO WORLD HERITAGE AREA**

Lake Mungo, in the Willandra Lakes Region near Willandra National Park, is an area of great archaeological significance. For 40,000 years, it was a 10-m (33-ft) deep lake, around which Aboriginal people lived. The lake dried up about 14,000 years ago and its human history was forgotten until the 1960s, when winds uncovered a largely intact skeleton later called the Mungo Man.

historic values. The park covers part of the once prosperous Willandra Sheep Station and contains the homestead and shearing complexes of the former station. The homestead overlooks peaceful Willandra Creek, where grasslands and creek beds are home to kangaroos, emus and ground-nesting birds.

Around 200 km (124 miles) to the west of Willandra National Park is the Willandra Lakes Region. Designated a UNESCO World Heritage Area in 1981, this 240,000-ha (590,000-acre) area is home to exceptional examples of pre-historic civilization, including the world's oldest cremation site. The most well known of the lakes is Lake Mungo, site of the Mungo Man discovery.

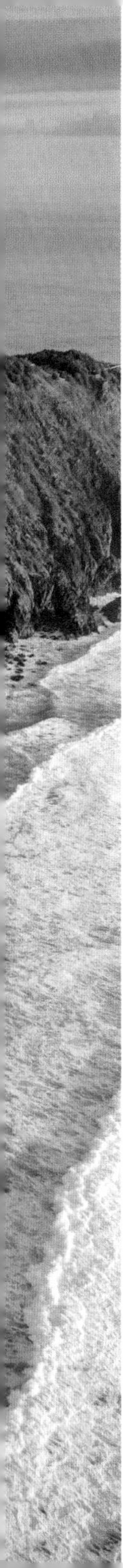

Cape Byron Lighthouse, perched on Cape Byron

HUNTER VALLEY AND THE NORTH COAST

The Woonarua, Worimi and Awabakal lived in what now comprises the Hunter Valley for 30,000 years before Europeans stumbled upon the Hunter River by accident in 1797 while searching for escaped convicts. The early settlers quickly exploited the valley's natural resources, clearing and cultivating traditional Aboriginal lands for timber and coal. This new landscape proved perfect for grape growing and, following experimental plantings by viticulturalists, the valley's first vineyards sprung up in the 1820s. Today, there are over 150 wineries in the Hunter Valley, many of them boutique, and it is one of Australia's most celebrated wine regions.

European settlement of the north coast began in 1821, with the establishment of Port Macquarie. The convicts from this penal settlement planted the area with sugar cane crops and built infrastructure, attracting free settlers. Soon the area was home to flourishing timber and sand-mining industries, and the resulting tree clearance created land for dairy farming. Another infrastructure project, the 1965 Pacific Highway, brought tourism and further development as Sydneysiders, seeking a more relaxed lifestyle, migrated to the north coast.

HUNTER VALLEY AND THE NORTH COAST

Experience

1. Port Macquarie
2. Port Stephens
3. Gosford
4. Newcastle
5. Barrington Tops World Heritage Area
6. South West Rocks
7. Lord Howe Island
8. Yamba
9. Coffs Harbour
10. Byron Bay

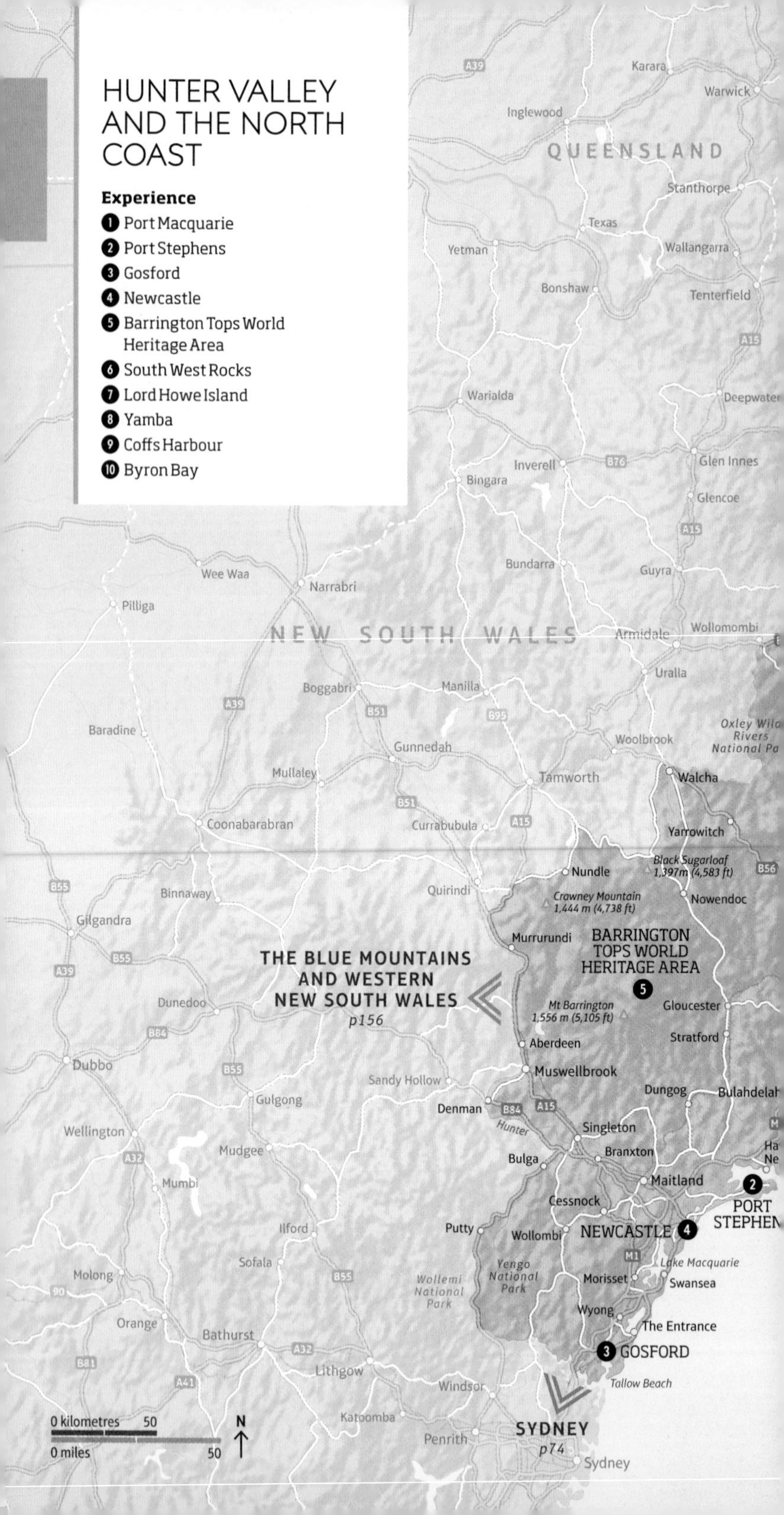

QUEENSLAND

Karara

Warwick

Inglewood

A39

Stanthorpe

Texas

Yetman

Wallangarra

Bonshaw

Tenterfield

A15

Deepwater

Warialda

Glen Innes

Inverell

B76

Bingara

Glencoe

A15

Wee Waa

Narrabri

Bundarra

Guyra

Pilliga

NEW SOUTH WALES

Armidale

Wollomombi

Boggabri

Manilla

Uralla

B51

B95

Oxley Wild
Rivers
National Pa

Baradine

Gunnedah

Woolbrook

Mullaley

Tamworth

Walcha

B51

Coonabarabran

Currabubula

A15

Yarrowitch

Nundle

Black Sugarloaf
1,397 m (4,583 ft)

B56

Quirindi

Crawney Mountain
1,444 m (4,738 ft)

Nowendoc

Binnaway

Murrurundi

BARRINGTON
TOPS WORLD
HERITAGE AREA

Gilgandra

B55

THE BLUE MOUNTAINS
AND WESTERN
NEW SOUTH WALES
p156

Mt Barrington
1,556 m (5,105 ft)

Gloucester

5

A39

B55

Dunedoo

Aberdeen

Stratford

B84

Dubbo

B55

Sandy Hollow

Muswellbrook

Dungog

Bulahdelah

Gulgong

Denman

B84   A15

Hunter

Singleton

M

Wellington

Mudgee

Bulga

Branxton

Ha
Ne

A32

Mumbi

Maitland

2

Ilford

Putty

Cessnock

PORT
STEPHEN

Molong

Sofala

Wollombi

Wollemi
National
Park

NEWCASTLE

4

90

B55

Yengo
National
Park

M1

Lake Macquarie

Orange

Bathurst

A32

Morisset

Swansea

B81

A41

Lithgow

Wyong

The Entrance

Windsor

3   GOSFORD

Katoomba

Tallow Beach

0 kilometres   50

0 miles   50

N

Penrith

SYDNEY
p74

Sydney

SOUTHEAST QUEENSLAND AND WHITSUNDAYS
p364

Woodenbong
Murwillumbah
Tweed Heads
Pottsville
Brunswick Heads
Kyogle
Nimbin
10 BYRON BAY
Bonalbo
Casino
Lismore
abulam
Ballina
Coraki
Baryulgil
Woodburn
Whiporie
Bundjalung National Park
Iluka
Jackadgery
Maclean
8 YAMBA
Ulmarra
Grafton
Yuraygir National Park
Nymboida
Wooli
Glenreagh
Corindi Beach
ingham
Woolgoolga
Dorrigo
9 COFFS HARBOUR
Ebor
Sawtell
Bellingen
Urunga
Bowraville
Nambucca Heads
omara
Macksville
Macleay
6 SOUTH WEST ROCKS
Hat Head National Park
Kempsey
Crescent Head
Point Plomer
Wauchope
1 PORT MACQUARIE
North Haven
Crowdy Bay National Park
Harrington
ee
Old Bar
abiac
Forster
all Lakes ational Park

HUNTER VALLEY AND THE NORTH COAST

Pacific Ocean

Southeast Australia
QUEENSLAND
Byron Bay
Area shown on main map
Coffs Harbour
NEW SOUTH WALES
Newcastle
7 LORD HOWE ISLAND
Sydney
Canberra
Pacific Ocean
VICTORIA
Melbourne

0 kilometres 500
0 miles 500
N

EXPERIENCE

Port Macquarie

🅐G5 ✈🚗🚌 🛈 Cnr Clarence and Hay sts; www.port macquarieinfo.com.au

Established in 1821 as a penal colony, Port Macquarie is now a popular holiday resort thanks to its 17 beaches. The 9-km- (5-mile-) long Coastal Walk from Westport Park to Tacking Point Lighthouse is a great way to take in the town's dramatic coastline. For bushwalking, make for the Kooloonbung Creek Nature Park, which offers 3 km (2 miles) of walking trails.

A five-minute drive from the town centre is Settlement Point Reserve, which has a ferry service to the more secluded North Shore beaches.

Port Stephens

🅐G5 🚗🚌 🛈 60 Victoria Parade, Nelson Bay; www. portstephens.org.au

With 26 beaches and the southern hemisphere's biggest moving sand dunes, Port Stephens abounds with sea and sand and is a haven for outdoor activities. Sandboard down the Stockton dunes, ride horses on the beaches and hike Mount Tomaree. Animal lovers should throw in a visit to Tilligerry Habitat, which is one of the best spots to see koalas in the wild.

Around 90 km (56 miles) north of Port Stephens is the Myall Lakes National Park. Home to a vast network of pristine freshwater lakes and beaches, it offers water sports such as kayaking, fishing, scuba diving and a 4WD beach safari.

Gosford

🅐E6 🚗🚌🚌 🌐 love centralcoast.com.au

Gosford is the principal town of the popular holiday region known as the Central Coast, and provides a good base for touring the surrounding area. Gosford itself sits on the calm northern shore of Brisbane Waters, an excellent spot for sailing and other recreational activities. The nearby beaches are renowned for their great surf, clear lagoons and long stretches of sand.

The town's cultural highlights include the **Gosford Regional Gallery**, which holds photography, painting, sculpture, textiles and ceramic exhibitions. Within the gallery precinct is the Edogawa Commemorative Garden, which has traditional Japanese features such as a pavilion, a Koi pond, a stone garden and a teahouse.

Take a self-guided driving tour exploring the **Central Coast Makers Trail** and meet boutique producers selling epicurean delights from nougat and chocolate to cheese, spices, craft beer, wine and coffee. You can also visit the oyster farms and discover rare pearls and shells.

Memorial Park, located in the town of The Entrance, is a short drive north of Gosford. Here, dozens of pelicans vie for fish at the feeding show that takes place at 3:30pm daily. This council-run event teaches visitors about the area's pelicans, and other bird and marine life.

There are several national parks within a short distance

of Gosford. Bouddi National Park is one of the most diverse, with sandstone cliffs, beaches and coastal heaths. Also worth a visit is the Bulgandry Aboriginal site in Brisbane Waters National Park, which has rock engravings dating back thousands of years.

Gosford Regional Gallery

 36 Webb St, East Gosford (02) 4304 7550 9:30am–4pm daily

Central Coast Makers Trail

 Various locations centralcoastmakerstrai.com.au

4
Newcastle

G5 visit newcastle.com.au

One visitor to Newcastle, Australia's second-oldest city, remarked in the 1880s: "To my mind the whole town appeared to have woke up in fright at our arrival and to have no definite ideas of a rendezvous whereat to rally". The chaos to which he referred was largely the result of the city's reliance on coal mining and vast steelworks. As profits rose, construction progressed without much

> **Today, industry is still the mainstay, but this does not detract from Newcastle's quaint beauty. The city curls loosely around a harbour.**

planning. Today, industry is still the mainstay, but this does not detract from Newcastle's quaint beauty. The city curls loosely around a harbour and its main streets rise randomly up the surrounding hills. The main thoroughfare, Hunter Street, has many architecturally diverse buildings.

One of the city's main sights is the **Newcastle Art Gallery**, which houses works by prominent 19th- and 20th-century artists, including the Newcastle-born William Dobell, Arthur Boyd and Brett Whiteley.

Queens Wharf is the main attraction of the harbour foreshore. There are great views from its promenade areas and outdoor cafés. On the southern side, Nobbys Head Lighthouse sits at the end of a long causeway; the vista back over old Newcastle makes the brief walk worthwhile. Further on lies **Fort Scratchley**, built in the 1880s. The fort did not open fire until the 1940s, when the Japanese shelled the city during World War II. Good surfing beaches

lie on either side of the harbour's entrance. Around 2 km (1 mile) from Fort Scratchley is Bogey Hole, one of Australia's oldest ocean pools and Newcastle's most photographed landmark.

The vast Lake Macquarie, 20 km (12 miles) south of Newcastle, offers nearly every kind of water sport imaginable. On the western shore, at Wangi Wangi, is Dobell House, once home to William Dobell.

Newcastle Art Gallery

 Cnr Darby & Laman sts Hours vary, check website nag.org.au

Fort Scratchley

 Nobbys Rd 10am–4pm Wed-Mon (last tour: 2:30pm) Good Fri, 25 Dec fortscratchley.com.au

---

EAT

The Flotilla
The seasonal menu highlights local produce from an open kitchen.

G5 9 Albert St, Wickham the flotilla.com.au

$$$

Bocados Spanish Kitchen
Tapas and churros are the highlights at this Spanish spot.

G5 25 King St, Newcastle bocados-spanishkitchen.com.au

$$$

← The turquoise waters of Shoal Bay Beach, located near Mount Tomaree, Port Stephens

↑ Swimmers at the Allyn River in Barrington Tops National Park, and *(inset)* an Australian azure kingfisher

❺
Barrington Tops World Heritage Area

🅰 G5 🅰 Gloucester 🛈 27 Denison St, Gloucester; www.nationalparks.nsw. gov.au

Flanking the north of the Hunter Valley is the Barringtons mountain range. One of the highest points in Australia, the "Barrington Tops", reaches 1,550 m (5,080 ft). Its 280,000 ha (690,000 acres) of forest, with 1,000-year-old trees, are protected by the Barrington Tops National Park. The rainforest was declared a World Heritage Area in 1986 and a Wilderness Area in 1996 as part of the Gondwana Rainforests of Australia (formerly the Central Eastern Rainforest Reserves). The rugged mountains, cool-climate rainforest, gorges, cliffs and waterfalls make the park a paradise for hikers, campers and bird-watchers, with bird species like the Australian azure kingfisher regularly being spotted here.

Barrington Tops is a popular weekend escape for Sydney-siders. Tourist operators organize environmentally friendly 4WD trips into the forests, with camping along the Allyn River, hiking trails at Telegherry and Jerusalem Creek and swimming in the rock pool at Lady's Well.

❻
South West Rocks

🅰 G5 🛈 1 Boatman's Cottage, Ocean Drive; www.macleayvalley coast.com.au

Located near the mouth of the Macleay River, the coastal town of South West Rocks is home to sandy beaches, national parks and exceptional diving sites, including Fish Rock Cave, which is also a breeding ground for endangered grey nurse sharks. At the idyllic Arakoon National Park, rocky headlands frame the calm waters of Trial Bay where swimmers can share the water with frolicking dolphins. Perched high above it all are the expansive ruins of the historic Trial Bay Gaol.

❼
Lord Howe Island

🅰 G5 🛈 Lord Howe Island Museum; www.lord howeisland.info

This small, yet stunning island paradise was discovered by the First Fleet's HMS *Supply (p68)* in 1788. Located 600 km (373 miles) east of Port Macquarie *(p174)*, Lord Howe is a World Heritage Site and allows only 400 visitors at a time.

Watched over by craggy volcanic peaks, the crystal-clear waters here teem with 450 species of fish and 90 species of coral, many of which don't exist anywhere else in the world. To experience the island's incredible natural attractions, climb Mount Gower, hand-feed fish on Ned's Beach, swim with the turtles, dive off Ball's Pyramid or snorkel the world's most southerly coral reef.

Lord Howe is also Australia's premier bird-watching destination, with 14 species of seabirds breeding here. Dozens of walking trails take you past nesting sites and on to breathtaking views.

→ Cape Byron Lighthouse, Byron Bay's most iconic sight

INSIDER TIP
Getting to Lord Howe Island

The fastest way to the island is a two-hour flight from Sydney. Qantas Airways operates flights daily. You can also sail to the island, but you need to apply for a public mooring before arriving.

Yamba

 G4 ℹ Grafton Regional Gallery, 158 Fitzroy St, Grafton; www.myclarence-valley.com

Set in the Clarence Valley, Yamba offers a World Heritage-listed rainforest and is the starting point for the multi-day Yuraygir Coastal Walk to Red Rock, which follows the ancient wandering trails of Australia's coastal emus. But it's the town's glorious beaches and relaxed seaside vibe that keep people coming back here. Visitors can kayak with wild dolphins in the estuary, go swimming or simply relax with a riverside picnic.

Superb surf breaks are found at Angourie, a national surfing reserve, just south of Yamba. Here, visitors swim in a former rock quarry.

 9

Coffs Harbour

G4 ℹ 35-61 Harbour Drive; www.coffscoast.com.au

The waters off the coastal city of Coffs are protected by the Solitary Islands Marine Park. Home to abundant wildlife and coral reefs, it's great for snorkelling. Bird-watchers should make for Muttonbird Island Nature Reserve, which has a large population of wedge-tailed shearwater birds.

 10

Byron Bay

G4 ℹ 80 Johnson St; www.visitbyronbay.com

Once a sleepy coastal town with a relaxed surf culture, Byron Bay has become the coast's trendiest destination thanks to an influx of celebrities that now call it home. Summer crowds come in December and January, but the laid-back vibe remains year-round. The town has trendy cafés, yoga schools, boutiques and backpacker hostels.

Surfers and sunbathers frequent Main and Wategos beaches, which are overlooked by the beautiful Cape Byron Lighthouse. This striking white tower marks Australia's most easterly point.

If you wish to escape the hubbub of town, the foodie haven of Mullumbimby is 22 km (14 miles) away. To experience the Byron Bay of old, head to Nimbin, a hippy community set on the edge of an extinct volcano 70 km (43 miles) from Byron.

 TOP 4 NORTH COAST BEACHES

Crowdy Bay
Crowdy Head, 60 km (37 miles) from Port Macquarie, is a great swimming spot.

Tallow Beach
Byron Bay's Tallow Beach is rich in birdlife.

Crescent Head
Found 21 km (13 miles) north of Port Macquarie, Crescent Head has sensational surf.

Nambucca Heads
Nambucca, near South West Rocks, has several beaches. South Beach is great for surfing, while Main Beach is best for swimming.

A DRIVING TOUR
A TOUR OF THE HUNTER VALLEY

Length 39 km (24 miles) **Stopping-off points** Pokolbin has plenty of cafés, a general store and a bush picnic area. The Mount Bright lookout gives a panoramic view over the region

The first commercial vineyards in Australia were established on the fertile flats of the Hunter River in the 1830s. Today, the region is home to more than 150 wineries and the Hunter Valley is one of the top destinations in New South Wales. This circular route takes in at all the main vineyards, some of which are worth a brief pause, while others should be lingered at for longer. Along the way, you're rewarded with some great views of the beautiful valley.

Tamburlaine is a small private producer of vegan-friendly, low- and no-added-sulphur organic wines.

*The first vintage at **Brokenwood** was picked here in 1973, and since then this winery has attracted a loyal following.*

Tyrrell's

Hunter Valley Gardens

Pokol

Brokenwood

MCDONALDS ROAD

Tamburla

*The Tyrrell family has been making wine at **Tyrrell's Vineyards** since 1858. An outdoor tasting area gives views over the vineyards.*

Ben Ean

Ben Ean vineyard and winery, formerly known as Lindemans, pours a range of wines at its cellar door, including Penfolds, Weerona and SOMM.

McWilliams Mount Pleasant Winery is home to the Mount Pleasant Elizabeth Semillon, one of Australia's best-quality white wines.

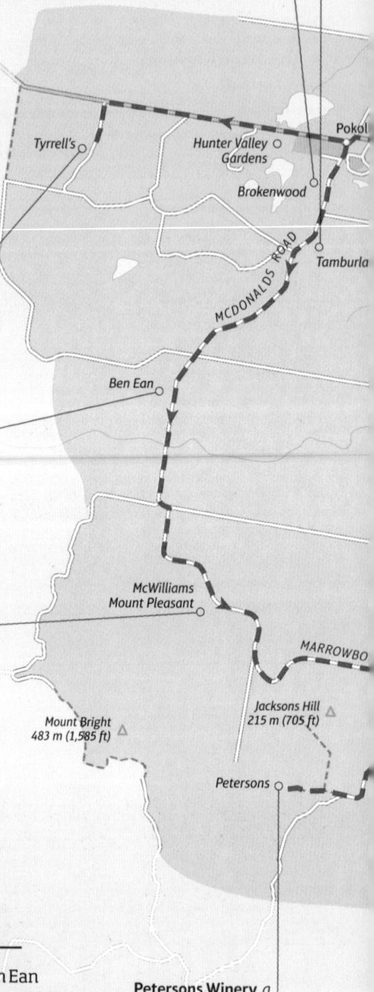

McWilliams Mount Pleasant

MARROWBO

Mount Bright 483 m (1,585 ft)

Jacksons Hill 215 m (705 ft)

Petersons

← Ben Ean vineyard and winery, bathed in sunshine, in Hunter Valley

Petersons Winery, a small family winery, is known for its experimentation with champagne-style wine production.

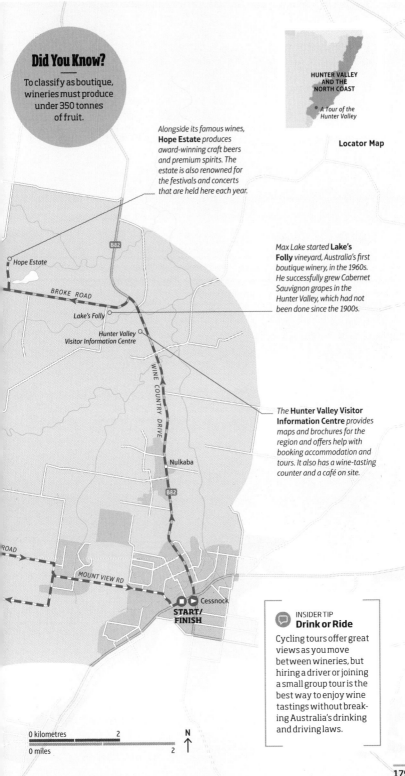

Did You Know?

To classify as boutique, wineries must produce under 350 tonnes of fruit.

*Alongside its famous wines, **Hope Estate** produces award-winning craft beers and premium spirits. The estate is also renowned for the festivals and concerts that are held here each year.*

HUNTER VALLEY AND THE NORTH COAST

A Tour of the Hunter Valley

Locator Map

*Max Lake started **Lake's Folly** vineyard, Australia's first boutique winery, in the 1960s. He successfully grew Cabernet Sauvignon grapes in the Hunter Valley, which had not been done since the 1900s.*

Hope Estate

BROKE ROAD

Lake's Folly

Hunter Valley Visitor Information Centre

WINE COUNTRY DRIVE

*The **Hunter Valley Visitor Information Centre** provides maps and brochures for the region and offers help with booking accommodation and tours. It also has a wine-tasting counter and a café on site.*

Nulkaba

ROAD

MOUNT VIEW RD

Cessnock

START/ FINISH

💬 INSIDER TIP
Drink or Ride

Cycling tours offer great views as you move between wineries, but hiring a driver or joining a small group tour is the best way to enjoy wine tastings without breaking Australia's drinking and driving laws.

| 0 kilometres | | 2 |
| 0 miles | | 2 |

N ↑

Skiing in Thredbo, a popular resort in the Snowy Mountains

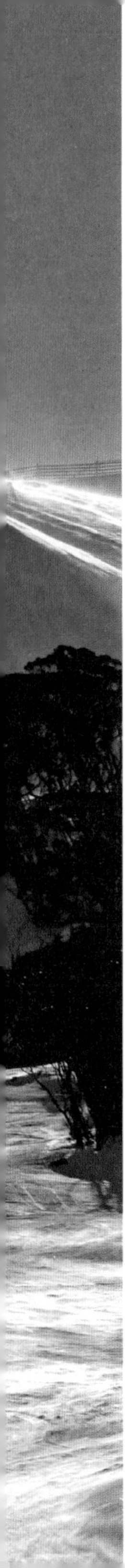

THE SOUTH COAST AND SNOWY MOUNTAINS

Aboriginal tribes, gold diggers and mountain cattlemen have all left their mark here. The temperate climate, rich soils and waterways sustained Aboriginal people for millennia. Tribal groups followed a trade route from the high country to the coast, gathering at Twofold Bay in spring for the whale migration and at ceremonial locations on Mount Kosciuszko in summer. When European settlers crossed the Blue Mountains in 1813, they pushed out the land's traditional owners, turning the southern plains into dairy and potato farms, cutting down trees for timber and boat building, and whaling and fishing the waters. High-country stockmen used the Snowy Mountains for summer grazing, sheltering in the mountain huts that still cling to the slopes. Soon, gold was found on the high plains, attracting hundreds of prospectors from around the world. Thousands more European immigrants moved here in the 1950s for the Snowy Mountains Scheme, a post-war engineering feat, cementing the region as the birthplace of multicultural Australia.

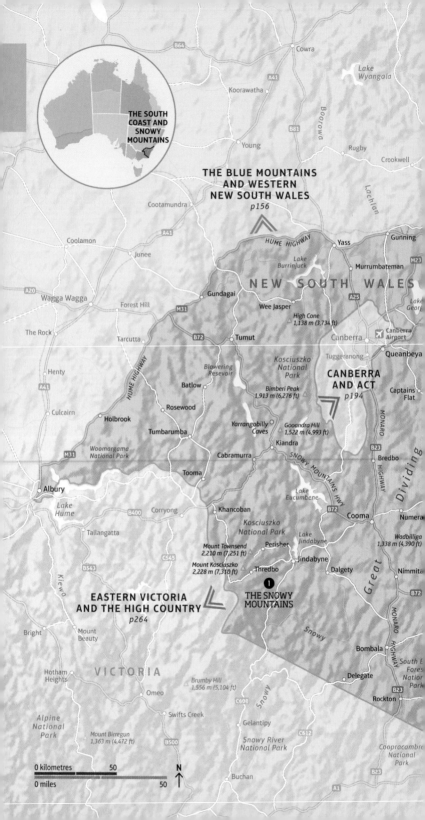

Penrith
Manly
SYDNEY
p74
Parramatta
Sydney
Liverpool
Sydney Airport
Blue Mountains
National Park
Mount Trickett
1,362 m (4,468 ft)
Lake
Burragorang
Campbelltown
M31
5 ROYAL NATIONAL PARK
Nyanga Mountain
923 m (3,028 ft)
Helensburgh
Picton
M1
Corrimal
Taralga
Berrima
Bowral
2 WOLLONGONG
Moss Vale
Port Kembla
ny Range Hill
2 m (2,500 ft)
M31
A48
3
THE SOUTHERN
HIGHLANDS
6 KIAMA
Bundanoon
7 GOULBURN
KANGAROO
VALLEY
14
15 BERRY
Seven Mile Beach
Bomaderry
12 NOWRA
Lake Bathurst
MORTON
NATIONAL PARK
4
A1
Tomerong
Hyams Beach
Murrays Beach
JERVIS BAY
17
Nerriga
Lake Conjola
Pacific
Ocean
B52
Pigeon House Mountain
719 m (2,359 ft)
16 ULLADULLA
ange
Braidwood
Nelligen
Pebbly Beach
13 BATEMANS BAY
A1
Guerilla Bay
Moruya
Deua
National
Park
Tuross Head
8 NAROOMA
8 MONTAGUE ISLAND
NTRAL TILBA **10**
adbilliga
lational
Park
Bermagui
mboka
Bega
9 TATHRA
A1
Merimbula
11 EDEN
11 BEOWA
NATIONAL PARK
PRINCES
Narrabarba

THE SOUTH COAST
AND SNOWY
MOUNTAINS

Must See
1 The Snowy Mountains

Experience More
2 Wollongong
3 The Southern Highlands
4 Morton National Park
5 Royal National Park
6 Kiama
7 Goulburn
8 Narooma and Montague Island
9 Tathra
10 Central Tilba
11 Eden and Beowa National Park
12 Nowra
13 Batemans Bay
14 Kangaroo Valley
15 Berry
16 Ulladulla
17 Jervis Bay

THE SNOWY MOUNTAINS

⚐ D7 ℹ Kosciuszko Rd, Jindabyne; www.snowymountains.com.au

Lovingly christened "The Snowies", the Snowy Mountains are a playground for the entire family, offering both seclusion and alpine adventures. Ski the snowcapped mountains, hike or mountain bike vast trails, explore underground caves or kayak rushing rivers.

Preserved within the Kosciuszko National Park, the Snowy Mountains stretch 500 km (310 miles) from Canberra to Victoria. Formed more than 250 million years ago, the range includes Australia's highest mountain, Mount Kosciuszko (or "Kossie"), and the country's only glacial lakes. In spring and summer, hikers trek past wildflower-carpeted meadows; in winter, snow gums bend beneath the cold winds, and skiers and snowboarders hit the slopes. The Snowies are home to two of Australia's largest ski resorts, Thredbo and Perisher, as well as some smaller options. The national park's perimeter is peppered with small villages. These settlements are either relics from Australia's shortest, highest and coldest gold rush of 1859 or the Snowy Mountains Scheme, a hydroelectric power plant (*p186*).

 GREAT VIEW
Black Perry Lookout

Located just off the Snowy Mountains Highway near Talbingo, this lookout offers views of Jounama Creek Valley, Bogong Peaks Wilderness and Black Perry Mountain.

Did You Know?

The Snowy Mountains receive more snow than the Swiss Alps each year.

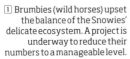

1 Brumbies (wild horses) upset the balance of the Snowies' delicate ecosystem. A project is underway to reduce their numbers to a manageable level.

2 The spectacular Blue Lake, in Kosciuszko National Park, is one of only four cirque lakes found in mainland Australia.

3 Perisher's 47 ski lifts ferry skiers and snowboarders up and down the resort's slopes.

↑ Sunset over snow-covered Mount Kosciuszko, the highest mountain in Australia

---

TOP 4 SKI RESORTS

Thredbo
This resort offers Australia's longest ski runs and a buoyant après-ski scene *(www. thredbo.com.au)*.

Perisher
Four areas – Perisher Valley, Blue Cow, Guthega and Smiggin Holes – make up this huge resort *(www. perisher.com.au)*.

Selwyn
Selwyn has the country's premier toboggan park *(www. selwynsnow.au)*.

Charlotte Pass
The park's highest resort is family friendly and offers good cross-country skiing *(www.charlottepass. com.au)*.

↑ The leafy town of Cooma,
in the heart of the
Snowy Mountains

EXPLORING THE SNOWY MOUNTAINS

 ①

Cooma

🛫🚌 ℹ119 Sharp St;
www.visitcooma.com.au

Colourful Cooma has a
rich history as a cattle,
engineering and ski town.
During construction of the
Snowy Mountains Scheme,
Cooma was also the week-
end base for the thousands
of immigrants working up
in the mountains. Stories
surviving from this era include
tales of shootouts in the main
street, interracial romances
and bush mountain feats.
Modern life in Cooma is
now much more sedate
and this sleepy rural town
acts primarily as the gateway
to the Snowy Mountains and
the southern ski slopes.

 ②

Jindabyne

ℹ49 Kosciuszko Rd;
www.destination
jindabyne.com.au

Located on expansive
Lake Jindabyne, the modern
resort town of Jindabyne
is home to the Kosciuszko
National Park information
centre, a myriad of ski shops
and lodges, and a lively
nightlife scene. During the
winter, it becomes a ski resort
town. Come summer, its
picturesque lake is awash
with recreational boats,
water-skiers and trout
and salmon fishers.

 ③

Kiandra

ℹ5 Adelong Rd, Tumut;
www.nationalparks.
nsw.gov.au

Following the discovery of
gold in the Selwyn region
in 1859, about 8,000 miners
moved to this area and
established the Kiandra
township. They built a bank,
a courthouse, a school and
hotels, but as the gold rush
lasted little more than a
year, the buildings were
soon abandoned and none
remain today. Signs along
a short heritage walking
loop detail where the original structures once stood.
Although the gold rush was
short lived, Kiandra had a
lasting influence on Australian
life. It was here, during the
gold rush, that Norwegian
miners introduced Australians
to what is now a surprising
national pastime, skiing.

SNOWY MOUNTAINS SCHEME

One of the world's most complex engineering feats, the
Snowy Mountains Scheme dammed four rivers to supply
power and water to much of inland eastern Australia.
Work began in 1949 and many of the project's 100,000
employees were migrants from post-war Europe. Around
100 temporary camps and seven townships were swiftly
built to house these workers. At the time of completion in
1974, the hydroelectric scheme consisted of seven power
stations, 16 major dams, 80 km (50 miles) of aqueducts and
145 km (90 miles) of interconnected tunnels.

2,228

The height of Mount Kosciuszko in metres (7,310 ft).

④ Kosciuszko National Park and Mount Kosciuszko

🛈 49 Kosciuszko Rd; www.snowymountains. com.au

A 6,900-sq-km (2,700-sq-mile) national park, Kosciuszko offers outdoor activities all year-round. Four ski resorts (p185) keep fans of snow sports entertained with everything from tobogganing to night skiing. Once the snow melts, fly fishing, hiking, riding and biking resume, and campgrounds fill with outdoor enthusiasts. Bushwalkers are spoiled for choice, with two tracks leading to the summit of Mount Kosciuszko. Note that many trails and roads are closed in winter (June–September).

⑤ Yarrangobilly Caves

🛈 50 Yarrangobilly Caves Rd; www.nationalparks. nsw.gov.au

Formed from limestone laid down 440 million years ago, these six caves hold wondrous formations, including stalagmites, stalactites and cave corals. Five of the caves can only be visited by guided tours, but South Glory – the largest cave in the system – can be accessed without a guide, although it's recommended to join a river walk or a guided walk to its thermal pools to best appreciate its lofty chambers. Buy tickets at the visitor centre.

⑥ Blue Lake

📍 46 km (28 miles) W of Jindabyne

This 28-m- (92-ft-) deep glacial lake is the largest cirque lake in Australia, and one of only four located on the mainland. The Blue Lake is also remarkable because its low salt content makes its water the freshest in the mainland. To reach the lake, set out on the 10-km (6-mile) circular trail from Charlotte Pass. Along the way, the track passes through snow gums and alpine meadows.

Tinkersfield
A secluded, luxury retreat found in a pristine valley minutes away from Jinbdabyne.

🏠 1 Post Office Lane, Crackenback
🌐 tinkersfield.com.au

$$$

Lake Crackenback Resort & Spa
This large lakefront property near the national park has a range of accommodation.

🏠 1650 Alpine Way, Crackenback
🌐 lakecrackenback. com.au

$$$

EXPERIENCE MORE

 2

Wollongong

🅰 **D6** 🚌🚆 **ℹ 93 Crown St;
www.visitwollongong.
com.au**

The third-largest city in the
state, Wollongong is set on
a coastline of beautiful surf
beaches, and is fast building a
reputation as a leisure centre.
North Beach is the best
known of its 17 beaches and
curves around to Flagstaff
Point. With its lighthouse,
boat harbour and seafood
restaurants, this peninsula
is popular with visitors.

Other attractions include
Australia's largest regional
art gallery and the Nan Tien
Temple, the biggest Buddhist
temple in the southern hemisphere, built for the local
Chinese community.

 3

The Southern
Highlands

🅰 **F5** 🚆🚌 **Bowral, Moss
Vale, Mittagong, Bundanoon
ℹ 62-70 Main St, Mittagong;
www.visitsouthern
highlands.com.au**

Quaint villages, country
guesthouses, homesteads
and beautiful gardens are
scattered across the lush
landscape of the Southern
Highlands. The region has
been a summer retreat for
Sydneysiders for almost 100
years. Villages such as Bowral,
Moss Vale, Berrima and
Bundanoon are also ideal
places for pottering around
antiques shops, dining on
hearty soups, sitting by open
fires and taking bushwalks and
country drives. The region's
gardens are renowned for their
blaze of colours in the spring
and autumn. The Corbett
Gardens at Bowral are a showpiece during its Tulip Festival
in September.

Bowral is also home to
the **Bradman Museum &
International Cricket Hall
of Fame**, where a collection of
photos and memorabilia commemorates the town's famous
son, cricketer Sir Donald
Bradman. He had a Test batting
average of 99.94 – an incredible
sporting achievement.

Did You Know?

As a child, Sir Donald
Bradman could hit a golf
ball with only a stump-
wide strip of wood.

Visiting the village of Berrima
is like stepping back in time.
The settlement, now home to
an abundance of antiques and
craft shops, is one of the most
unspoiled examples of a small
Australian town of the 1830s.

Popular walks in the area
include Mount Gibraltar,
Carrington Falls, the majestic
Kangaroo Valley and
the Wombeyan Karst
Conservation Reserve west
of the town of Mittagong.
The highlights of this reserve
are its five caves, which form
an imposing underground
limestone cathedral.

Bradman Museum &
International Cricket
Hall of Fame

♿♨ 🚗 St Jude St, Bowral
🕙 9am–4pm daily 🚫 Good
Fri, 25 Dec 🌐 bradman.com.au

 4

Morton National Park

🅰 **D6** 🚆 **Bundanoon**
🚌 **Fitzroy Falls** ℹ **Fitzroy
Falls; www.nationalparks.
nsw.gov.au**

Morton National Park
stretches along the rugged
hinterland from north of
the Shoalhaven Valley to
the Ulladulla area. Fitzroy
Falls are at the northern end

← Boats sitting in Wollongong's harbour, with lighthouses standing guard

of the park. At Bundanoon, magnificent sandstone country can be explored.

To the south, views of the coastline and Budawang wilderness can be found at Little Forest Plateau and the top of Pigeon House Mountain.

5

Royal National Park

⚐D6 🚆Loftus, then tram to Audley (Sun & public hols only) ⛴Bundeena from Cronulla 🛈Sir Bertram Stevens Dr, Audley; www. nationalparks.nsw.gov.au

When it was designated in 1879, the "Royal" was Australia's first national park and the second-oldest protected area in the world after Yellowstone in the entire USA. It covers 16,500 ha (37,000 acres) of spectacular landscape.

To the picturesque east, the waves from the Pacific Ocean have undercut the sandstone and produced coastal cliffs, interspersed by creeks, cascading waterfalls, lagoons and pristine beaches. Heath vegetation on the plateau merges with woodlands on the upper slopes and rainforest in the gorges. Sea eagles and terns nest in caves at the Curracurrang Rocks. This stunning park is ideal for many activities like bushwalking, swimming and bird-watching.

6

Kiama

⚐D6 🚆🚌🚗 🛈Blowhole Point Rd; www.kiama. com.au

This laidback seaside town, with a harbour, surf beaches and pretty ocean pools, is most famous for its blowhole. Plumes of seawater erupt more than 20 m (65 ft) into the air from an opening in the rock face when the swell is high. Located below the lighthouse, the easternmost viewing platform is the best spot to see the formation's full height.

Not far from the blowhole is the **Pilot's Cottage Museum**. Located in a quaint restored cottage, it explores the region's maritime history, including Aboriginal fishing techniques and the Minnamurra River Tragedy of 1893, when seven people drowned.

Pilot's Cottage Museum

🚗 ⚐Blowhole Point Rd ⏰11am–3pm Sat & Sun 🌐ekiama.com/museum/index.htm

---

7

Goulburn

⚐D6 🚆🚌 🛈201 Sloane St; www.goulburnaustralia. com.au

Goulburn is at the heart of the Southern Tablelands, with its rich pastoral heritage. Proclaimed in 1863, the town's 19th-century buildings, such as the courthouse,

→ *Big Merino*, the large sheep statue in Goulburn

TOP 5 SOUTH COAST BEACHES

Seven Mile Beach
This beach extends in a gentle arc from Gerroa to Shoalhaven Heads.

Murrays Beach
An uncrowded jewel with fine sand in Booderee National Park.

Hyams Beach
Here, tread the world's whitest sand or swim in the turquoise waters.

Lake Conjola
Fish, swim, kayak, water ski or wakeboard on this coastal waterway.

Pebbly Beach
Tame kangaroos visit this beautiful beach in Murramarang National Park at dusk and dawn.

post office and railway station, are testament to the prosperity of the district.

Today, the town is known as the "fine wool capital of the world", as marked by the *Big Merino*, a giant concrete sheep statue.

The nearby town of Yass is also known for its fine wool. Here, visit the historic Cooma Cottage, now owned by the National Trust. It was the home of explorer Hamilton Hume, between 1839 and 1873.

↑ Eastern fiddler ray and a scuba diver in the waters off Montague Island

Museum, which tells the history of the region and its historic wharf. Built in 1862 and restored by the National Trust, this is the only deep water timber wharf on Australia's east coast. It is a magnet for snorkellers and divers wanting to explore the waters below.

Beaches and waterways are plentiful around these parts and include the protected Kianinny Bay, which is excellent for swimming, snorkelling and spotting stingrays. Good surf beaches are found at Tathra, Merimbula and within the Mimosa Rocks and Bournda national parks. The pristine waters of Nelson Lake in Mimosa Rocks National Park are known for their oysters. Try them for yourself at family-run Tathra Oysters between December and June.

Away from the water, Tathra is also a premier mountain-biking destination, with almost 50 km (31 miles) of tracks all within 5 km (3 miles) of the town centre.

Tathra Wharf Museum
 ⬛2 Wharf Rd ⏰10am–3pm Sat & Sun 🌐tathrawharfmuseum.org

8

Narooma and Montague Island

⬛D6/7 ℹ️80 Princess Hwy, Narooma; www.eurobodalla.com.au, www.montagueisland.com.au

The sleepy town of Narooma is located at the mouth of the stunning Wagonga Inlet, whose perfectly turquoise waters are flanked by leafy woodlands and sandy bays. Narooma itself has several gorgeous beaches, including secluded Handkerchief Beach and Narooma Surf Beach, which is dominated by two imposing, ancient geological formations – Glasshouse Rock at the southern end and Australia Rock to the north. The latter is famous for the hole in its centre which is shaped like Australia.

Away from the sand, there are plenty of ways to enjoy the inlet. Cycle along its periphery on the Narooma to Dalmeny cycling route or stroll along the pretty Mill Bay Boardwalk on the inlet's northern side.

Beautiful Montague Island (Barranguba) lies just 9 km (5 miles) offshore. This nature reserve spans 81 ha (200 acres) and is home to fur seals, penguins and more. The waters surrounding the island teem with sea life, making them perfect for snorkelling. Visitors can stay overnight at the lighthouse keeper's residence or take day trips from Narooma. These boat tours are conducted by park rangers and can be combined with snorkelling excursions.

9

Tathra

⬛D7 ℹ️29 Market St, Merimbula; www.visittathra.com.au

A tiny fishing village on the Sapphire Coast, Tathra's main attraction is the **Tathra Wharf**

10

Central Tilba

⬛D7 ℹ️2 Bate St; www.visittilba.com.au

This delightful historic farming village is backed by the 800-m (2,600-ft) Mount

> **HIDDEN GEM**
> **Bermagui Blue Pool**
>
> Located 20 km (12 miles) to the south of Central Tilba, this natural rock pool is hidden at the base of a craggy cliff face in the town of Bermagui. Seek it out at low tide on a clear day, when the calm waters reflect the sapphire sky above.

Dromedary (also known as Mount Gulaga). A former gold-mining town, it is renowned for its 19th-century weatherboard cottages that today house various art and craft shops and galleries, as well as some of the region's finest gourmet produce stores. The Tilba cheese factory is just one of these treasures and produces bottled milk, yoghurt, cream and cheese. The milkshakes here are popular with visitors. Other edible treats can be found at the Tilba Market, which is held every Saturday morning in the town's Big Hall.

Alternative attractions include Water Tower Lookout, which offers panoramic views of the region and nearby Montague Island.

 11

Eden and Beowa National Park

🅐D7 🚌🚃🚕 ✈Weecoon St, Snug Cove; www.visit eden.com.au

Set on Twofold Bay, the southern hemisphere's third-deepest natural harbour, this coastal town was once a whaling station. Learn more about its whaling history at the **Eden Killer Whale Museum**. Exhibits here include a full-scale model of a whaling boat.

Today, whales are only hunted by whale watchers and Eden is the south coast's prime destination for spotting these huge creatures (between May and November). But whales aren't the only sea creatures that you'll see here; snorkellers and scuba divers swim with a huge variety of marine life, including blue groupers and sea dragons.

The town has a thriving fishing industry. At stunning Snug Cove you can buy blue mussels directly from fishing boats or try fresh seafood at one of the wharf's restaurants.

Located 15 km (9 miles) away from Eden, Beowa National Park is an adventurer's playground, with bushwalks in temperate rainforests and fine beaches. The challenging 6-km (4-mile) return hike to Mount Imlay rewards intrepid walkers with panoramic views of the coast.

Eden Killer Whale Museum

 🏛184 Imlay St ⏰9:15am-3:45pm Mon-Sat, 11:15am-3:45pm Sun 🌐edenkiller whalemuseum.com

STAY

Green Cape Lightstation

Perched on a peninsula some 45 km (30 miles) south of Eden, this keeper's cottage offers excellent sea views. If you're lucky, you might even catch sight of whales from the terrace.

🅐D7 📍Green Cape, Ben Boyd National Park 🌐nationalparks.nsw. gov.au

$$$

Montague Island Assistant Lighthouse Keeper's Cottage

This three-bedroom cottage is set in a nature reserve, with many opportunities for wildlife watching. It's very cosy, with fireplaces in most rooms.

🅐D7 📍Montague Island 🌐nationalparks.nsw. gov.au

$$$

← Waves crashing against the cliffs at Beowa National Park

Nowra

 D6 🚌🚗 ℹ 42 Bridge Rd, Nowra; www.shoal haven.com

A regional city at the centre of the Shoalhaven Coast, Nowra is a good base for exploring the surrounding wine country, with cellar door tastings at the historic Coolangatta Estate, Two Figs and Mountain Ridge Wines.

Nowra is also perfectly positioned to take advantage of the nearby resorts of Culburra to the south and Shoalhaven Heads to the east. The latter is located where the Shoalhaven River meets the sea, making it a popular boating and fishing spot, especially around Seven Mile Beach National Park. After spending some time on this beach, walk the Sand Track south of the Beach Road picnic area to explore the ancient forested dunes that run parallel to the sand.

Batemans Bay

D6 🌐 eurobodalla. com.au

This town marks the start of the Eurobodalla coastline, which is loved by Canberrans for its chain of quiet beaches. Boating, fishing, kayaking and paddleboarding are popular activities on the Clyde River, which enters the sea here. The Batemans Bay Snorkelling Trail comprises three terrific snorkelling spots: Maloneys Beach to the north of the township, Sunshine Cove Beach and the ancient Guerilla Bay, both to the south. At Burrewarra Point, near Guerilla Bay, an easy 1.5-km (1-mile) trail passes through mature banksia forest and offers coastal and hinterland views.

For a dose of local history, visit the Batemans Bay Heritage Museum, which is set in a 1905 courthouse in the centre of town, or stroll through the Nelligen Heritage Area, located 9 km (5.5 miles) northwest of town.

Kangaroo Valley

D6 🚌 ℹ Fitzroy Falls Visitor Centre: 1301 Nowra Rd; www.visitkangaroo valley.com.au

Towering sandstone cliffs enclose the deep valley carved by the Kangaroo River. As the name suggests, the area is great for spotting

 GREAT VIEW
Cambewarra Lookout

Visit the summit of the Cambewarra Range for views across Jervis Bay to Pigeon House Mountain in the south and Coolangatta Mountain in the north. You may be joined by lyrebirds and kookaburras.

kangaroos and wombats, particularly around the Bendeela Recreation Area.

Popular pursuits for visitors include canoeing or kayaking from the majestic Hampden Bridge to the Bendeela Recreation Area; driving to Tallowa Dam, home to large goanna and the country's biggest fish lift; and visiting Fitzroy Falls Visitor Centre for information on local history and culture, as well as easy nearby bushwalks to waterfalls.

Situated between Kangaroo Valley and the coast is the Cambewarra Range and the charming village of Cambewarra. With its relaxed pace of life, teahouses and pubs, this village makes for a great side trip from the valley.

Berry

 F5 🚌🚗 ℹ 42 Bridge Rd, Nowra; www.berry.org.au

This charming country town is a popular weekend escape for Sydneysiders. Berry's lively main street is an epicurean haven, filled with cafés, restaurants and shops selling

> **Berry's lively main street is an epicurean haven, filled with cafés, restaurants and shops selling gourmet offerings.**

↑ Watching a small group of kangaroos at Pebbly Beach near Batemans Bay

↑ Surfers at one of the many popular beaches in the Booderee National Park in Jervis Bay

gourmet offerings. As well as food, the strip is home to stylish stores, brimming with antiques, books, art, crafts and homewares. On the first Sunday of the month, more than 200 stalls selling local produce, handmade arts and crafts, leather goods, books and collectibles set up at the showground for the Berry Markets.

Berry is also a great base for exploring the surrounding Shoalhaven area and its numerous wineries, beaches, hiking trails and nature walks.

Ulladulla

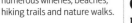🏛 D6 🛈 Shoalhaven Visitor Centre: 81B Princes Hwy; www. shoalhaven.com

A small fishing village known for its picturesque harbour, Ulladulla is flanked by the dovecote-shaped peak of Pigeon House Mountain in the Morton-Budawang National Park. It is surrounded by beaches and reef dive sites, national parks and a heath-land reserve. A bushwalk along one of the town's numerous trails offers breathtaking coastal views. Learn about the area's heritage and the Yuin people, the traditional

owners of the land, on a guided hike of the Coomee Nulunga Cultural Trail, which begins near the Warden Head Lighthouse and leads to Rennies Beach.

A short distance away from Ulladulla are a string of charming villages including Mollymook, where the Bogey Hole – a large rock tidal pool – is a favourite spot for swimming and snorkelling.

Jervis Bay

🏛 D6 🚌 🛈 11 Dent St, Huskisson; www.jervis baytourism.com.au

Apart from being a naval base, this beautiful natural harbour is a much-loved holiday destination, offering all manner of water-based activities, including dolphin- and whale-watching. Jervis Bay's main areas of development are the tiny settlements of Huskisson and Vincentia on its western coast. On the Beectroft Peninsula, to the north of the bay, Point Perpendicular grants spectacular views.

The southern sweep of the bay is dominated by the Booderee National Park, with its quiet beaches and botanic gardens (an entrance pass from the visitor centre is

compulsory). The Wreck Bay area of the park was returned to the First Nations peoples of Australia in 1995. Rangers from the community lead tours.

EAT

Rick Stein at Bannisters

Fresh seafood with an Asian touch is the order of the day at this spot in Mollymook, run by the famous British chef.

🏛 D6 🏠 191 Mitchell Parade, Mollymook Beach �🌐 bannisters. com.au/mollymook

South on Albany

Tucked down a side street in Berry, this restaurant offers three-course set menus of local dishes. Order the freshly shucked oysters to start.

🏛 F5 🏠 3/65 Queen St, Berry �🌐 southonalbany. com.au

$$$

CANBERRA AND THE AUSTRALIAN CAPITAL TERRITORY

The name Canberra is based on an Aboriginal word meaning "meeting place" and the land was seasonally inhabited by different tribes for millennia. European settlement of the area, which was then part of New South Wales, dates from 1823, when a sheep station was built on the edge of the Molonglo River. Its fortunes changed in 1908 when this tiny, rural settlement – conveniently located between Sydney and Melbourne – was chosen to be the site of the nation's capital. American architect Walter Burley Griffin won an international competition to design the city. He envisaged a spacious, low-level, modern metropolis, with its major buildings centred on the focal point of Lake Burley Griffin. While lacking the traffic and skyscrapers of Australia's other main cities, Canberra is the national capital and the centre of political and administrative power in Australia. A place of contrasts, Canberra is rural and laidback, and a young, vibrant city where almost one in three residents are university students. The Australian Capital Territory's forests, farmland and nature reserves surround the city.

Anzac Parade, as seen from the lookout on Mount Ainslie

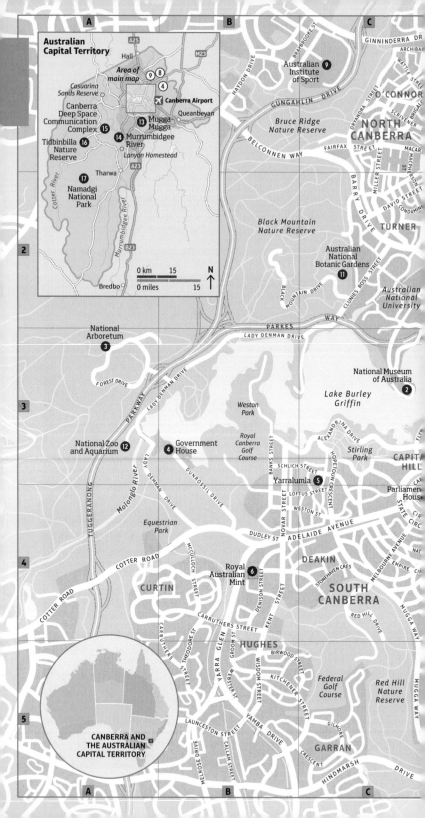

CANBERRA AND THE AUSTRALIAN CAPITAL TERRITORY

Must Sees

1 Parliamentary Triangle
2 National Museum of Australia

Experience More

3 National Arboretum
4 Government House
5 Yarralumla
6 Royal Australian Mint
7 Australian War Memorial
9 Australian Institute of Sport
10 Civic Square
11 Australian National Botanic Gardens
12 National Zoo and Aquarium
13 Mugga-Mugga
14 Murrumbidgee River
15 Canberra Deep Space Communication Complex
16 Tidbinbilla Nature Reserve
17 Namadgi National Park

Eat & Drink

3 Molly

Drink

4 Mount Majura Vineyard
5 Silo Bakery & Café
6 Capital Brewing Co

Shop

7 Old Bus Depot Markets
8 Capital Region Farmers Market
9 Handmade Market

❶

PARLIAMENTARY TRIANGLE

◎ D3 ⌂ Between Commonwealth, Kings and Constitution aves
🛈 Regatta Point, Barrine Dr, Parkes; www.visitcanberra.com.au

Canberra's major monuments, national buildings and key attractions are all situated around Lake Burley Griffin within the Parliamentary Triangle. For the quintessential Canberra day, venture inside the various buildings to discover a treasure trove of architecture, art and history, and then enjoy a leisurely stroll or cycle around the lake.

①

High Court of Australia

⌂ Parkes Place, Parkes
🚌 2, 6, 58 ◷ 9:45am–4:30pm Mon–Fri, noon–4pm Sun ⟲ Public hols
🌐 hcourt.gov.au

British and Australian legal traditions are embodied in this lakeside structure, opened in 1980 by Queen Elizabeth II. The High Court is centred on a glass public hall, designed to instil respect for the justice system. Two murals by artist Jan Sensbergs look at the Australian constitution, the role of the Federation and the significance of the High Court. There are three courtrooms, and chambers for the Chief Justice and six High Court judges. Sittings are open to the public.

On one side of the ramp at the entrance is a sculpture of a waterfall made out of granite. It is intended to convey how the decisions of this legal institution trickle down to all Australian citizens.

②

National Library of Australia

⌂ Parkes Place, Parkes
🚌 2, 6, 7, 58 ◷ 8am–8pm Mon–Thu (to 5pm Fri), 9am–5pm Sat, Sun & public hols
⟲ Good Fri, 25 Dec
🌐 nla.gov.au

This imposing five-storey library, an icon of 1960s architecture, is the repository of Australia's literary and documentary heritage. Containing more than seven

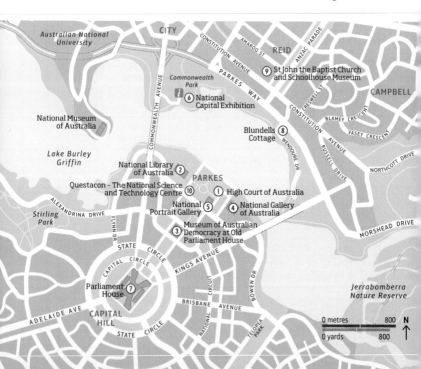

↑ The lakeside setting of Parliamentary Triangle, central Canberra

💬 **INSIDER TIP**
Behind the Scenes

The National Library doesn't just hold books, it also has a huge array of "treasures", like wanted posters and a bush-ranger's revolver. See them and more on a free behind-the-scenes tour.

million books, as well as copies of most of the news-papers and magazines ever published in Australia, thousands of tapes, manu-scripts, prints, maps and old photographs, it is the nation's largest library and leading research centre. The library also displays historic items, such as Captain Cook's original journal from his *Endeavour* voyages, in a rotating exhibit.

The building, designed by Sydney architect Walter Bunning (1912–1977) and completed in 1968, also includes some notable works of art. Foremost are the modern stained-glass win-dows by Australian architect and artist Leonard French (1928–2017), which are made of Belgian chunk glass and depict the planets. There are also the Australian life tapestries by French artist Mathieu Mategot.

③

Museum of Australian Democracy at Old Parliament House

📍 King George Terrace, Parkes 🚌 2, 6, 57, 58
🕐 9am–5pm daily 🚫 25 Dec
🌐 moadoph.gov.au

Built in 1927 as the first parliamentary building in the new national capital, Old Parliament House was the centre of Australian politics for more than 60 years. During this time, the building witnes-sed many historic moments: Australia's declaration of war in 1939; the bombing of the northern shores by Japan in 1942; the disappearance and presumed death of Prime Minister Harold Holt in 1967 and the dismissal of the Whitlam government by Sir John Kerr in 1975. It was replaced by the new Parliament House in 1988 *(p201)*.

Today the building houses the Museum of Australian Democracy. Visitors can explore the Kings Hall, the old House of Representatives and Senate chambers, and see the peephole in the wall of the prime minister's office, discov-ered during renovations.

ABORIGINAL TENT EMBASSY

This protest site has occupied the lawns of Old Parliament House since 1972. What started as a temporary demon-stration over First Nations land has become a permanent symbol for Aboriginal political rights. Despite countless attempts to shut it down, a slew of flags and powerful signs still occupy the site today. Visitors are invited to lay gum leaves on the embassy's burning ceremonial fire as a symbol of protection during their travels.

④

National Gallery of Australia

🏠 Parkes Place 🚌 2, 6, 59
🕐 10am–5pm daily
🚫 25 Dec 🌐 nga.gov.au

The diverse and multicultural spirit of the country is reflected in the 160,000 works of art on display in the National Gallery of Australia (NGA). The NGA opened in 1982, and the core of its collection consists of Australian art, from European settlement to present day, by some of its most famous artists, such as Tom Roberts, Arthur Boyd, Sidney Nolan and Margaret Preston. The oldest art in Australia is that of its Indigenous inhabitants (p61), and the Aboriginal and Torres Strait Islander art collection offers fine examples of both ancient and contemporary works. The gallery's Asian and international collections are also growing. For modern sculptures, check out the gardens.

> **The National Portrait Gallery pays homage to prominent individuals who have inspired and shaped the fabric of Australian society.**

⑤

National Portrait Gallery

🏠 King Edward Terrace, Parkes 🚌 2, 6, 59
🕐 10am–5pm daily 🚫 25 Dec
🌐 portrait.gov.au

The National Portrait Gallery pays homage to prominent individuals who have inspired and shaped the fabric of Australian society. Its mixed-media collection, which is displayed across nine gallery spaces, includes over 500 portraits of famous entertainers, scientists, artists, politicians, athletes and royalty. While the portraiture is the main event, the award-winning, 21st-century building is itself a work of art. This architectural showpiece features striking cantilever concrete blades, strips of stone and timber from each Australian state and territory, and a design that symbolizes the relationship between the visitor, space, material, light and art.

📷 PICTURE PERFECT
Commonwealth Park

Snap away in Commonwealth Park during September and October when it is home to the city's annual spring flower festival, Floriade.

---

⑥

National Capital Exhibition

🏠 Commonwealth Park
🚌 2, 4, 5, 6, 7, 10, 57, 58, 180, 181, 830 🕐 9am–5pm Mon–Fri, 10am–4pm Sat & Sun
🚫 25 Dec, public hols (except Australia Day)
🌐 nca.gov.au/attractions/national-capital-exhibition

The National Capital Exhibition features models, videos and old photographs that show the history and growth of Canberra as the federal capital of Australia. The main draw of the exhibition, however, is the view from the rotunda. Through the windows there is a clear view of Lake Burley Griffin, the Parliamentary Triangle and the Captain Cook Memorial Jet and Globe and the National Carillon. The jet

←

The striking Brutalist exterior of the National Gallery of Australia

miss the Lego scale model of the building, which was constructed from 152,690 blocks and took 740 hours to build.

 ⑧

Blundells Cottage

⌂ Wendouree Dr, Parkes
🚌 3, 56, 59, 182, 830, 842
🕙 10am-2pm Sat & Sun
🚫 25 Dec 🌐 natcap.gov.au/blundells

This small sandstone farmhouse was built in 1858 by the Campbell family, owners of a large farming property at Duntroon Station, for their head ploughman. It was later occupied by bullock driver George Blundell, his wife, Flora, and their eight children.

This excellent example of a colonial cottage conveys the remoteness of early farming life. The cottage once looked out over sheep paddocks, but these were flooded by Lake Burley Griffin.

 ⑨

St John the Baptist Church and Schoolhouse Museum

⌂ Constitution Ave, Reid 🚌 3, 56, 59, 182, 830, 842 🕙 10am-noon Wed, 2-4pm Sat & Sun
🚫 Good Fri, 25 Dec
🌐 stjohnscanberra.org/st-johns-schoolhouse

Built in 1844 from local bluestone and sandstone, the Anglican church of St John the Baptist and its adjoining schoolhouse are Canberra's oldest buildings. They were built to serve the pioneer farming families of the region. Memorials on the walls of the church

SHOP

The Parliament Shop

Not your ordinary gift shop - find bespoke glassware, cufflinks, sweet treats and one of the best collections of political books in the country.

⌂ Parliament Dr, Parliament House
🌐 aph.gov.au

commemorate early settlers, including statesmen, scientists and scholars.

Within the schoolhouse is a museum containing various 19th-century memorabilia and artifacts.

⑩

Questacon - The National Science and Technology Centre

⌂ Cnr King Edward Terrace & Parkes Pl, Parkes 🚌 2, 6, 58, 59 🕙 9am-5pm daily 🚫 25 Dec 🌐 questacon.edu.au

Questacon's mission is to prove that science is both fascinating and an everyday part of life. Within the centre's six galleries, there are over 200 hands-on exhibits, allowing visitors to freeze their shadow to a wall, play a harp with no strings, experience an earthquake or feel bolts of lightning. There are giant slides and a roller coaster simulator, too.

←

The Astronomer by Tim Wetherell at Questacon

fountain and bronze, copper and enamel globe on the edge of the lake were part of the 1970 bicentennial commemoration of the claiming of the east coast of Australia by British Navy officer Captain James Cook in 1770. The elegant fountain lifts a column of water 147 m (480 ft) out of the lake from 11am until 2pm.

The National Carillon is also visible from the rotunda. It has 55 bronze bells and there are regular recitals.

⑦ 🚲 🚭 🛍

Parliament House

⌂ Capital Hill 🚌 57, 58
🕙 9am-5pm daily (to 6pm on days parliament is sitting)
🚫 25 Dec 🌐 aph.gov.au

Parliament House is the meeting place of Australia's parliament and the centre of Australia's democracy. Opened in 1988, the building is located on Capital Hill and is the third home of the Australian Federal Parliament, having replaced the Old Parliament House *(p199)* in 1901. Parliament House stretches across a 32-ha (80-acre) site and is the focal point of Canberra.

The building contains many artifacts but don't

② Ⓜ ▣ 🛍

NATIONAL MUSEUM OF AUSTRALIA

📍C3 🏠Lawson Crescent, Acton Peninsula, Canberra 🚌53 🕐9am–5pm daily
🚫25 Dec 🌐nma.gov.au

Housed in a striking building, made up of a medley of materials, the National Museum of Australia's collection aims to unite the different peoples that call this country home. Exhibits cover 50,000 years of history, including First Nations heritage, immigration and contemporary issues.

Established by an Act of Parliament in 1980, the National Museum of Australia moved to its permanent home on the Acton Peninsula in early 2001. It shares its location with the Australian Institute of Aboriginal and Torres Strait Islander Studies. The museum brings Australian history to life through compelling objects, ideas and events, with a focus on Aboriginal cultures, European settlement and the environment.

↑ Holden Prototype No 1, one of three test cars built by hand in 1946

Exploring the Museum

Permanent exhibitions explore the people, events and issues that have shaped Australia. The museum's aim is to be a focus for sharing stories and promoting debate, and interactive displays involve visitors by inviting their contributions. Galleries include the Great Southern Land, which explores connections to the landscape and biodiversity of this ancient continent through 1,200 objects, documents and experiences. The two-level First Australians gallery traces the experiences and spirituality of Aboriginal and Torres Strait Islander peoples.

Did You Know?

The museum's unique design was inspired by the idea of a jigsaw puzzle.

↑ The interesting exterior of the National Museum of Australia lit up at night

EAT

Museum Café
Enjoy contemporary dishes that feature seasonal, locally sourced and sustainable produce at this impressive café perched on the edge of Lake Burley Griffin. It's the perfect place to take a break and refuel, whether you order a light lunch, substantial meal or coffee and cake. The waterfront views are simply stunning, whether you dine indoors behind glass windows or relax on one of the two wonderful outdoor decks.

ⓦ nma.gov.au

EXPERIENCE MORE

National Arboretum

📍 A3 🏠 Forest Dr, Molonglo Valley 🕐 Apr-Sep: 7am-5:30pm daily; Oct-Mar: 6am-8:30pm daily; Village Centre and National Bonsai and Penjing Collection of Australia: 9am-4pm daily ⓦ nationalarboretum.act.gov.au

The National Arboretum has one of the world's largest collections of rare, endangered and significant trees, with more than 44,000 species across 96.5 sq km (37 sq miles) of undulating landscape. Located 6 km (4 miles) from the centre of Canberra, this ecological site is the only monocultural arboretum of its size in the world and is home to nearly 100 forests, a bonsai collection, themed gardens and outdoor sculptures.

The arboretum's Village Centre has won numerous awards for its striking and sustainable architecture, which was designed to complement the building's setting. Inside, the Village Centre houses an information hub, restaurant, café and gift shop. Next door is the similarly acclaimed children's POD Playground

↓ The Village Centre set in the grounds of the National Arboretum

 GREAT VIEW
Mount Ainslie

Tired of the panorama from Dairy Farmers Hill? An alternative view of Canberra can be seen from the top of Mount Ainslie. Here, you'll be able to admire Walter Burley Griffin's carefully planned city design.

with giant acorn treehouses, nest swings, banksia pods and musical instruments. Its design was inspired by seeds and new life.

Guided short strolls, forest walks and bus tours depart from the Village Centre and showcase the arboretum's commitment to conservation, education, research and recreation. Outdoor enthusiasts can also enjoy more than 20 km (12 miles) of trails perfect for hiking, jogging and mountain biking. A popular route climbs up to the lookout on the peak of Dairy Farmers Hill. From here, you can enjoy 360-degree views over the capital, including Lake Burley Griffin, the Brindabella ranges and a breathtaking front look at Black Mountain Tower.

To get a feel of the arboretum ahead of your visit, download the augmented reality app and take a virtual stroll through the grounds.

Government House,
seen from across
Lake Burley Griffin ↑

SHOP

Old Bus Depot Markets
Since 1994, this Canberra market has been selling art, clothing, jewellery and food every Sunday.

📍D4 🏠21 Wentworth Ave, Kingston
🕐9:30am–2:30pm
🌐obdm.com.au

Capital Region Farmers Market
Sample the region's freshest produce at Canberra's original and biggest farmers market.

📍B1 🏠Exhibition Park, Watson 🕐7am–11:30pm Sat 🌐capitalregion farmersmarket.com.au

---

Handmade Market
Find hundreds of stalls with homeware, crafts, fashion and food here.

📍A1 🏠Exhibition Park, Watson 🕐Last weekends in Apr, Jun & Sep and the second weekend of Dec 🌐handmade canberra.com.au

---

4

Government House

📍B3 🏠Dunrossil Dr, Yarralumla 📞(02) 6283 3533 🕐Two days a year, call ahead to check
🌐gg.gov.au/about-governor-general/governor-generals-official-residences

Government House has been the official residence of the Governor General, the representative of the monarch in Australia, since 1927. The house was once part of a large sheep station called Yarralumla, which was settled in 1828, and is now where heads of state and the Royal Family stay when visiting Australia. The house is closed to the public, except on special open days; however, a lookout point on Lady Denman Drive offers good views of the residence and the large gardens.

5

Yarralumla

📍C3 🏠Yarralumla 🚌31, 901 ℹ️Canberra Visitors' Centre; (02) 6205 0044

The suburb of Yarralumla, on the edge of Capital Hill, is home to more than 80 of Australia's foreign embassies and diplomatic residences. A drive through the tree-lined streets gives a fascinating view of the architecture and cultures of each country represented, as embodied in their embassies and grand ambassadorial residences. Distinctive buildings include the vast Chinese Embassy at No 15 Coronation Drive, with its red columns, dragon statues and pagoda-shaped roofs. At No 3–5 Moonah Place, the Indian High Commission has

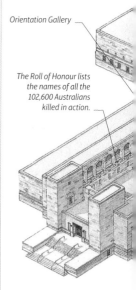

Orientation Gallery

The Roll of Honour lists the names of all the 102,600 Australians killed in action.

🔍 HIDDEN GEM
Weston Park

Situated on Lake Burley Griffin's western peninsula in Yarralumla, this park has a beach, electric BBQs, an adventure playground, cycle paths, a mini railway and miniature golf. It also offers great views of Black Mountain.

pools, a shallow moat and a white temple building in the Mughal architectural style, with a gold spire on top. The High Commission of Papua New Guinea on Forster Crescent is built as a Spirit House, with carved totem poles outside; the Mexican Embassy on Perth Avenue boasts a massive replica of the Aztec Sun Stone.

Just across Adelaide Avenue is The Lodge, the official residence of the Australian prime minister and his family.

6

Royal Australian Mint

📍 B4 🏠 Denison St, Deakin 🚌 58, 932 🕐 8:30am-5pm Mon-Fri, 10am-4pm Sat-Sun & public hols; tours: hours vary, check website 📅 Good Fri, 25 Dec 🌐 ramint.gov.au

The Royal Australian Mint is the sole producer of Australia's circulating coin currency. It has produced over 11 billion circulating coins and today has the capacity to mint over two million coins per day, or over 600 million per year. The Mint is dedicated to commemorating Australia's culture and history through its numismatic programme. When touring the Mint you'll discover the history of Australian currency and see how coins are made. You can even view the coins coming directly off the presses.

7

Australian War Memorial

📍 D2 🏠 Treloar Crescent, Campbell 🚌 54 🕐 10am-4pm daily 📅 25 Dec 🌐 awm.gov.au

The Australian War Memorial was built to commemorate all Australians who have died while serving their country. The Roll of Honour and the symbolic Tomb of the Unknown Australian Soldier serve as a reminder of the horror and sadness of war. Parts of the memorial are closed on some days each week for redevelopment until 2028.

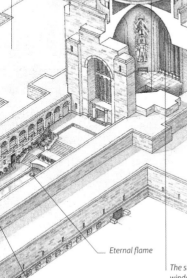

Adorning the Hall of Memory is one of the world's largest mosaics, built in part by war widows.

The Tomb of the Unknown Australian Soldier has the remains of a soldier who died during World War I.

First World War Gallery

Aircraft Hall

Second World War Gallery

Eternal flame

The Pool of Reflection is a peaceful place where families can mourn their loved ones.

The stained-glass windows depict the personal, social and fighting skills of all Australians during wartime.

↑ Illustration of the Australian War Memorial, a landmark of national importance

8

Canberra Museum and Gallery

📍 B2 🏛 Cnr London Circuit and Civic Sq, Canberra 🚌 City centre routes ⏰ 10am–4pm Mon–Fri, noon–4pm Sat & Sun 🚫 25 & 26 Dec 🌐 cmag.com.au

Located in the heart of the city centre, this vast museum focuses on the ancient history and contemporary culture of Canberra, which was chosen to be the nation's capital in 1909.

The museum's permanent Canberra/Kamberri Place and People exhibition tell the stories of the First Nations people who have always lived here, and those who have come to call the region home. Belonging and identity in communities and places (past and present) are explored

through significant and everyday objects, artworks and moving images.

The gallery is also home to The Nolan Collection, a group of significant paintings gifted to the nation by artist Sidney Nolan in 1974. Pieces displayed from the collection's 141 works change frequently and are hung alongside works by local contemporary artists.

9

Australian Institute of Sport

📍 C1 🏛 Leverrier Crescent, Bruce 🚌 R1, R9 ⏰ Visitor centre: 9am–5pm Mon–Fri; tours: 10am–2:30pm daily 🚫 25 & 26 Dec 🌐 ais.gov.au

Some of Australia's best Olympic and Paralympic athletes live and train, using the state-of-the-art equipment, at the Australian Institute of Sport (AIS). This is the national centre of the country's sports efforts. It was built in 1981 to improve the nation's sporting achievements after Australia failed

to win a single gold medal at the 1976 Montreal Olympic Games. The visitor centre has a small display of memorabilia. Behind-the-scenes tours of the facilities include Sportex, where visitors can take on high performance simulators for football, rowing, cycling, alpine skiing and wheelchair racing.

10

Civic Square

📍 D2 🏛 Civic Centre 🚌 City centre routes

The commercial heart of Canberra is undoubtedly the Civic Centre, on the north side of Lake Burley Griffin close to the northwest corner of the Parliamentary Triangle (p198). It is the centre of many administrative, legal and local government functions in Canberra, as well as having the highest concentration of offices and private sector businesses. It is also the city's main shopping area. Here, you'll find the Canberra Centre shopping mall, housing world-

1,000,000

The number of visitors who flock to the Australian Institute of Sport every year.

↑ The intriguing Kamberri Place at the Canberra Museum and Gallery

renowned Australian brands such as Aesop, Lorna Jane and Haigh's Chocolates.

As envisaged by American architect Walter Burley Griffin in his original 1911 city plan, the central civic square is a common meeting place and relaxing area. It is dominated by the graceful bronze statue of Ethos, by Australian sculptor Tom Bass, located at the entrance of the ACT Legislative Assembly. In the adjacent Petrie Plaza is a traditional carousel, a much-loved landmark among the citizens of Canberra.

Australian National Botanic Gardens

📍 C2 🏠 Clunies Ross St, Acton 🕐 8:30am-5pm daily 🚫 25 Dec 🌐 anbg.gov.au

On the slopes of Black Mountain, the Australian National Botanic Gardens hold the finest scientific collection of native plants in the country. Approximately 90,000 plants of more than 5,000 species are featured in its displays.

The Rainforest Gully, one of the gardens' most popular attractions, features plants from the rainforests of eastern Australia. One fifth of the nation's eucalyptus species are found on the Eucalypt Lawn. The Aboriginal Trail is a self-guided walk that details how First Nations communities have utilized plants over thousands of years.

National Zoo and Aquarium

📍 A3 🏠 Lady Denman Dr, Scrivener Dam 🕐 9:30am-5pm daily 🚫 25 Dec 🌐 nationalzoo.com.au

This is Australia's only combined zoo and aquarium. A wonderful collection of the nation's fish, from native freshwater river fish to brilliantly coloured cold sea, tropical and coral species, are on display in the aquarium, including some eight different species of shark. There are about 20 tanks on show, with the smaller ones containing either freshwater fish or marine animals.

↑ Rainforest gully area at the Australian National Botanic Gardens

The 9-ha (22-acre) landscaped grounds of the adjacent zoo have excellent enclosures that house numerous native animal species, such as koalas, wombats, dingoes, little penguins, Tasmanian devils, emus and kangaroos. As well as the native residents of the zoo there are many favourites from all over the world, including several big cats, primates, giraffes and African antelopes.

EAT & DRINK

Bar Rochford

A wine bar serving fine food in one of the city's oldest buildings. Set menus are offered for groups of four or more.

📍 D2 🏠 Level 1, 65 London Circuit, Canberra 🌐 barrochford.com

$$$

Raku Dining

A sleek restaurant with a great ambience, Raku is known for its Japanese fare that looks like art on a plate.

📍 D4 🏠 148 Bunda St, Civic 🌐 rakudining.com.au

$$$

Molly

This hidden, cosy speakeasy takes guests back in time, with 1920s decor and live jazz music. Choose from the whisky and cocktail list and enjoy European-style grazing plates.

📍 D2 🏠 Odgers Lane, Canberra 🌐 molly.bar

$$$

DRINK

Mount Majura Vineyard

This winery is known for its flagship Tempranillo and the region's best Riesling and Shiraz.

📍 B1 🏠 88 Lime Kiln Rd, Majura 🕐 10am–5pm daily 🌐 mountmajura.com.au

Silo Bakery & Café

Called "part Brooklyn, part wartime Parisian bakery" by *The New York Times*, this café has cool industrial decor.

📍 D4 🏠 36 Giles St, Kingston 🕐 7am–3pm Tue–Sat 🌐 silobakery.com.au

Capital Brewing Co

An award-winning brewery with an impressive range of pale ales, stouts and pilsners.

📍 E4 🏠 Bldg 3, 1 Dairy Rd, Fyshwick 🕐 From 11:30am daily 🌐 capitalbrewing.co

---

13

Mugga-Mugga

📍 A1 🏠 129 Narrabundah Lane, Symonston 📞 (02) 6237 6500 🕐 10am–1pm Sat & Sun 🌐 Late Dec–mid-Jan 🌐 historicplaces.com.au/mugga-mugga-cottage

Mugga-Mugga reflects the history of a rural working-class family who worked on Duntroon Estate. The site's main feature is a small stone cottage built for the estate's head shepherd in the 1830s. It has been adapted over time, but is still furnished with household items that belonged to the Curley family who moved to Mugga-Mugga in 1913. A galvanized iron garage near the cottage houses an exhibition on the issue of Federation.

14

Murrumbidgee River

📍 A1 🏠 ACT Parks and Conservation Service; 13 2281

A tributary of the Murray River, this river is the second-longest in Australia. It meets the Cotter River at Casuarina Sands, a beautiful place to fish and canoe. Other notable sights include Cotter Dam, which is good for picnics, swimming and camping, and **Lanyon Homestead**, a restored 1850s home. On the same property is the Sidney Nolan Gallery, which holds the Ned Kelly series of paintings.

Lanyon Homestead

   🏠 Tharwa Dr, Tharwa 🕐 10am–4pm Wed–Sun 🌐 Good Fri, 24 & 25 Dec 🌐 historicplaces.com.au/lanyon-homestead

---

15

Canberra Deep Space Communication Complex

📍 A1 🏠 Via Paddys River Rd (Tourist Dr 5) 🕐 9am–5pm daily 🌐 25 Dec 🌐 cdscc.nasa.gov

This deep-space network station is managed by the Commonwealth Scientific

↓ A satellite dish at the Canberra Deep Space Communication Complex

and Industrial Research Organization (CSIRO) and the American NASA organization. It is one of only three such deep-space tracking centres in the world linked to the NASA control centre in California. The complex has six satellite dishes, the largest of which measures 70 m (230 ft) in diameter and weighs a hefty 3,000 tonnes.

Visitors to the Space Centre can see a piece of moon rock 3.8 billion years old, examine an astronaut's spacesuit, learn about the role of the complex during the Apollo moon landings and see pictures sent back from Mars, Saturn and Jupiter. Guided tours can be taken by prior arrangement.

16

Tidbinbilla Nature Reserve

📍 A1 🚗 Via Paddys River Rd (Tourist Drive 5) 🕐 Apr-Sep: 7:30am-6pm daily; Oct-Mar: 7:30am-8pm daily 🚫 25 Dec 🌐 tidbinbilla.act. gov.au

The tranquil Tidbinbilla Nature Reserve preserves 5,450 ha (13,450 acres) of forests, grasslands, streams and mountains. It is a paradise

Tidbinbilla Nature Reserve, and (inset) kangaroos at the Namadgi National Park ↑

for wildlife lovers. Kangaroos and their joeys bask in the sun, emus strut on the grassy flats, platypuses swim in the creeks, koalas thrive on the eucalyptus branches and bower birds and superb lyrebirds can be seen in the tall forests.

Visitors can hike up to Gibraltar Rock or explore one of the 24 walking trails through wetlands and forests. The Birrigai Time Trail is a 3-km (2-mile) walk through various periods of history. The visitors' centre features Aboriginal artifacts and pioneer relics.

17

Namadgi National Park

📍 A2 ℹ️ Namadgi Visitors' Centre, Naas Rd, 2 km (1 mile) S of Tharwa; www.parks.act.gov.au

Namadgi National Park covers almost half of the Australian Capital Territory. Located only 35 km (22 miles) south

of Canberra, Namadgi is remote and solitary. It is a beautiful, harsh landscape of snow, mountains, river valleys, scenic bushwalks and Aboriginal rock art. Many days could be spent exploring the park, but even a day's walking will reward you with breathtaking views of the country. It's advisable to hire a Personal Locator Beacon from the Visitor Centre if you plan to go hiking by yourself in remote areas of the park.

🔍 HIDDEN GEM
Yankee Hat

The Aboriginal rock art at Yankee Hat is the only currently known prehistoric art site in the ACT. Located within the Namadgi National Park, the site has well-preserved paintings of animals and human-like figures.

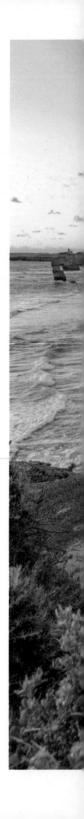

VICTORIA

The Twelve Apostles, the limestone stacks on the Great Ocean Road

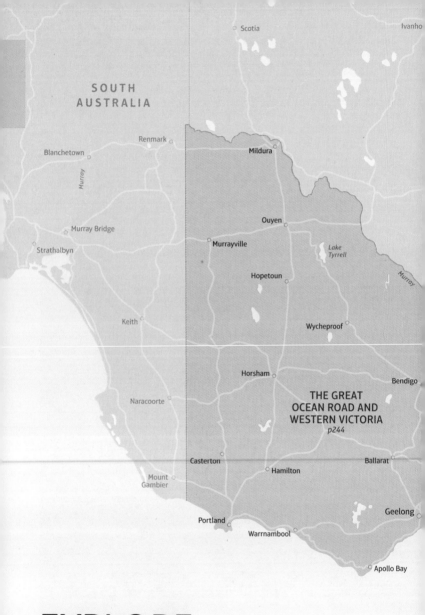

SOUTH
AUSTRALIA

Scotia

Ivanho

Renmark

Mildura

Blanchetown

Murray

Ouyen

Murray Bridge

Murrayville

Lake
Tyrrell

Strathalbyn

Hopetoun

Murray

Keith

Wycheproof

Horsham

Bendigo

Naracoorte

THE GREAT
OCEAN ROAD AND
WESTERN VICTORIA
p244

Casterton

Ballarat

Mount
Gambier

Hamilton

Geelong

Portland

Warrnambool

Apollo Bay

EXPLORE
VICTORIA

King
Island

This guide divides Victoria into three
colour-coded sightseeing areas, as
shown on this map. Find out more
about each area on the following pages.

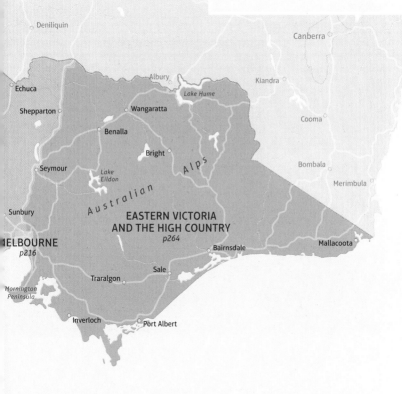

AUSTRALIA

Hillston

Hay

NEW
SOUTH WALES

Deniliquin

Canberra

Echuca

Albury

Lake Hume

Kiandra

Shepparton

Wangaratta

Benalla

Cooma

Bright

Seymour

Lake
Eildon

Australian

Alps

Bombala

Merimbula

Sunbury

EASTERN VICTORIA
AND THE HIGH COUNTRY
p264

MELBOURNE
p216

Bairnsdale

Mallacoota

Sale

Mornington
Peninsula

Traralgon

Inverloch

Port Albert

Bass
Strait

Flinders
Island

Stanley

0 kilometres   100

N

TASMANIA

0 miles   100

GETTING TO KNOW
VICTORIA

Victoria is a smorgasbord of city and country attractions, home to both Melbourne, with its world-class coffee and kaleidoscopic street art, and the rugged natural beauty of the Grampians. In between, there are vineyards and beaches to explore and – of course – the Great Ocean Road to drive.

MELBOURNE

PAGE 216

Sydney's biggest rival, Melbourne is one of the world's coolest and most cultured cities. The city's calendar is packed with major productions in grand theatres, nightly comedy in tiny venues and serious sporting events. Over 100,000 fervent fans pack the Melbourne Cricket Ground – or "the G" – for the year's biggest games, and visitors flock to the city for its Formula One Grand Prix and tennis Grand Slam. But there are also some quieter moments to be had in this city, like sipping a flat white in a street-art-splashed laneway and taking in a provocative performance-art exhibition.

Best for
Culture and coffee

Home to
Federation Square, National Gallery of Victoria

Experience
Cheering on your AFL team with the roaring crowd at "the G"

PAGE 244

THE GREAT OCEAN ROAD AND WESTERN VICTORIA

The Great Ocean Road winds along the windblown coast from Torquay to Allansford. On one side are crashing waves and limestone stacks, and on the other are rainforests with giant tree ferns. Beyond the coast, Western Victoria unfurls in a series of pretty villages and family-run wineries. The past and the present walk hand-in-hand here – stately paddle steamers meander down the serene Murray river and gold-rush towns host modern art galleries.

Best for
The ultimate road trip

Home to
The Great Ocean Road, Ballarat, Bendigo

Experience
Cruising along the Murray River on a historic paddle steamer

PAGE 264

EASTERN VICTORIA AND THE HIGH COUNTRY

Outdoor enthusiasts find paradise in this corner of Victoria. Cyclists wheel up and down the soaring peaks of The High Country, pausing at rustic cattlemens' huts and breweries along the way. In winter, skiers come here for the snow, while in summer it's the turn of bushwalkers and horse riders. If that all sounds far too energetic, head to Eastern Victoria for vast coastal beaches, including one where tiny penguins march out of the sea each night.

Best for
Outdoor attractions

Home to
Beaches and ski slopes

Experience
Watching wild penguins waddle onto Phillip Island

A café in Melbourne surrounded by street art

MELBOURNE

The traditional custodians of Melbourne are the Boon Wurrung and Woi Wurrung (Wurundjeri) peoples of the Kulin Nation. For thousands of years they lived a nomadic lifestyle in this area, hunting and gathering food, and visiting sacred sites. However, the arrival of European settlers in the 1830s brought an abrupt end to this existence, with the settlers erecting boundary fences and drastically altering the landscape to construct their new township. Named Melbourne after the British prime minister of the day, the city underwent rapid growth in the 1850s, with a huge influx of immigrants seeking their fortunes on the rich gold fields of Victoria. The enormous wealth generated by the gold rush led to the construction of grand public buildings, a development that continued throughout the land boom of the 1880s, earning the city the nickname "Marvellous Melbourne". By the end of the 19th century, the city was the industrial and financial capital of Australia. It was also the home of the national parliament until 1927, before it was moved to purpose-built Canberra *(p194)*. Melbourne was the proud host of the summer Olympics in 1956, which had a significant impact on the city's social, cultural and architectural development. The post-war period also witnessed a new wave of immigrants from Eastern Europe and the Mediterranean, who infused the city with a multicultural dynamic that continues to flourish today.

MELBOURNE

Must Sees

① Federation Square
② National Gallery of Victoria

Experience More

③ Queen Victoria Market
④ Supreme Court
⑤ Rialto Towers
⑥ St Francis's Church
⑦ Melbourne Mint
⑧ St James's Old Cathedral
⑨ Melbourne Town Hall
⑩ Block Arcade
⑪ Docklands
⑫ Royal Arcade
⑬ St Paul's Cathedral
⑭ State Library of Victoria
⑮ Immigration Museum
⑯ Regent Theatre
⑰ Scots' Church
⑱ No 120 Collins Street
⑲ Old Magistrates' Court
⑳ Old Melbourne Gaol
㉑ Museum of Chinese Australian History
㉒ Lygon Street
㉓ Chinatown
㉔ Royal Exhibition Building
㉕ Melbourne Museum
㉖ Brunswick Street and Fitzroy
㉗ Old Treasury Building
㉘ Melbourne Cricket Ground
㉙ Australian Centre for Contemporary Art
㉚ Melbourne and Olympic Parks
㉛ Australian Sports Museum
㉜ Flinders Street Station
㉝ Royal Botanic Gardens and Kings Domain
㉞ SEA LIFE Melbourne Aquarium
㉟ Eureka Tower
㊱ Polly Woodside
㊲ Rippon Lea Estate
㊳ St Kilda
㊴ Albert Park
㊵ Chapel Street
㊶ Como Historic House and Garden

Eat

① DOC Espresso
② Brunetti Oro
③ ShanDong MaMa
④ Flower Drum

Eat & Drink

⑤ MoVida
⑥ Supernormal
⑦ Pellegrini's Espresso Bar

Stay

⑧ The Como Melbourne

Shop

⑨ Rose Street Artists' Market
⑩ Northside Records
⑪ Mud Australia

Royal Park

PARKVILLE

FLEMINGTON ROAD
GATEHOUSE STR
PARK DR
COURTNEY STREET
ERROL STREET
CHETWYND STREET
QUEENSBERRY STRE
VICTORIA STRE
STANLEY ST
KING STREET
ROSSLYN STREET
DUDLEY STREET

⑧ St James's Old Cathedral

LATROBE STREET
SPENCER

Victoria Harbour

⑪ Docklands

Marvel Stadium

Spencer Street

WURUNDJERI WAY

4

Yarra River

Bolte Bridge

CITY LINK

NORTH WHARF ROAD

BOURKE STREET WEST

Docklands Park

COLLINS STREET

LORIMER STREET

LORIMER STREET

INGLES STREET

Webb Bridge

Charles Grimes Bridge

Polly Woodside ㊱

WESTGATE FREEWAY (M1)

Melbou Exhibit Centre

5

BOUNDARY STREET

INGLES STREET

NORMANBY ROAD

MONTAGUE STREET

GLADSTONE ST

CIT

MELBOURNE

0 metres   750
0 yards   750

N ↑

A   B   C

❶

FEDERATION SQUARE

📍E4 🏠Cnr Flinders & Swanston sts 🚊Swanston St and Flinders St routes 🌐fedsquare.com.au

Melbourne's Federation Square, opened in 2002, one of urban Australia's most dynamic public spaces, and a major arts, events, and food and drink hub. Bustling with activity, there's always plenty going on.

Paved with almost half a million cobblestones from Western Australia, Federation Square has as its centrepiece the stunning, glass-walled Atrium, an indoor venue for exhibitions, festivals, markets and art installations. Dotted around the rest of the area are bars, restaurants, shops and more cultural institutions, notably the Australian Centre for the Moving Image (ACMI). The centre houses Australia's national museum of cinema, TV, video games and multimedia art, as well as the Koorie Heritage Trust, which showcases the culture of southeastern Aboriginal peoples.

The large open area at the heart of Federation Square has become a favoured Melbourne meeting place, and the open-air screen often broadcasts live some of the city's big events (such as the Australian Open) and performances.

TOP 3 FESTIVALS AND EVENTS

Fed Summer
Feb
Free workshops, outdoor cinema and more.

Melbourne Food & Wine festival
Mar
Various food-oriented events around the city.

Melbourne International Comedy Festival
Late Feb-Mar
Stand-up comedy shows.

Paved with almost half a million cobblestones from Western Australia, Federation Square has as its centrepiece the stunning, glass-walled Atrium.

→

The geometrically patterned, glass-and-steel Atrium

←

Screens featuring film, games and digital culture exhibits at the Australian Centre for the Moving Image

EAT

MoVida Next Door

This branch of the excellent Spanish tapas restaurant MoVida is a more casual version of its older sibling *(p225)*, with lower prices to match. Delicious tapas dishes aside, it's a great place to linger over pre- and post-dinner drinks.

📍 164 Flinders St
🌐 movida.com.au

$$$

Chocolate Buddha

Famous for its sushi, ramen and *donburi* dishes, this stylish Japanese restaurant offers quick and friendly service. A good place for a pre-theatre meal.

📍 Cnr Flinders & Swanston sts
🌐 chocolatebuddha. com.au

$$$

←

The distinctive angular architecture of Federation Square lit up at night

NATIONAL GALLERY OF VICTORIA

📍 E4 🏠 180 St Kilda Rd and Federation Sq 🕐 10am–5pm daily 🚫 Good Fri, 25 Apr, 25 Dec 🌐 ngv.vic.gov.au

The National Gallery of Victoria (NGV) is a Melbourne icon and one of Australia's top art exhibition spaces. Touch the Waterwall on the way to the international site, then soak up the vast collection of paintings and decorative arts.

The first public art gallery in Australia, the NGV opened in 1861 and housed the original State Museum. The NGV moved to its current building on St Kilda Road in 1968, and contains the largest and widest-ranging international art collection in the whole country. Its most significant bequest was from Melbourne entrepreneur Alfred Felton in 1904. The collections of European Old Master paintings and sculptures, and of Asian and Pacific artworks and objects are outstanding, with works by Turner, Rembrandt, Tiepolo and Picasso among the many highlights. Some of the biggest temporary exhibitions to visit Australia often feature here.

The Ian Potter Centre: NGV Australia in Federation Square (p220) is an offshoot of the National Gallery of Victoria's International site on St Kilda Road. Well worth a visit, it is the first major gallery in the world to be dedicated exclusively to the display of Australian art. You could spend many hours familiarizing yourself with the extraordinary collection of Aboriginal art here. The Ian Potter Centre: NGV Australia's other star attractions include the famed Heidelberg School collection (showcasing painters such as Tom Roberts and Frederick McCubbin) as well as works by other renowned Australian artists, including Sidney Nolan, Arthur Boyd, Russell Drysdale and Brett Whiteley.

↑ Fountains along the Waterwall at the entrance to the NGV

> 💬 INSIDER TIP
> **NGV Friday Nights**
>
> The NGV is anything but a static gallery space. Check the website for NGV Friday Nights, which give late-night access to exhibitions at the gallery. The back gardens host live music, DJ sets, bars and food.

→ A gallery of paintings at the NGV, also featuring sculptures by English artist Jonathan Owen

EXPERIENCE Melbourne

Did You Know?

Picasso's *The Weeping Woman*, stolen from the NGV in 1986, was later found in a train station locker.

↑ The world's largest stained-glass ceiling, by artist Leonard French, in the Great Hall

↑ Visitors exploring Melbourne's lively Queen Victoria Market in the evening

EXPERIENCE MORE

3

Queen Victoria Market

📍 D3 🏛 Elizabeth, Franklin, Peel & Victoria sts 🚇 Flagstaff & Melbourne Central (Elizabeth St exit) 🚊 Elizabeth St routes 🕐 Hours vary, check website 🚫 Public hols 🌐 qvm.com.au

The city's main fresh produce and general goods market has a strange history: it occupies the site of the original Melbourne General Cemetery. In 1877, the idea of converting part of the cemetery into a marketplace seemed practical, as it only involved relocating three graves. However, the choice later created controversy as the market became more popular and needed more land. In 1917, Parliament granted the removal of 900 remains – the rest still lie there, mainly under the car park.

Today, the market has more than 600 stalls selling fish, meat, fruit, vegetables, organic food and clothing.

PICTURE PERFECT
Street Art

Street art is all around in Melbourne's laneways. Hit up Hosier Lane opposite Federation Square, Centre Place between Collins Street and Flinders Lane, and AC/DC Lane (named after Australian rock royalty) for the best graffiti.

4

Supreme Court

📍 D3/4 🏛 210 William St 🚇 Flagstaff 🚊 City Circle & Bourke St routes 🕐 9:30am–4pm Mon–Thu, 9:30am–5pm Fri 🌐 supremecourt.vic.gov.au

When the Port Phillip district was still part of the New South Wales colony, criminal and important civil cases were heard in Sydney. To ease the inconvenience, Melbourne's first resident judge arrived in 1841 to help set up a Supreme Court. Following the Separation Act of 1851, which established the Colony of Victoria, the city set up its own Supreme Court. It moved to the present building, with a design inspired by Dublin's Four Courts, in 1884.

This imposing Classical-style building has multiple street façades. Internally, a labyrinthine plan is centred on a beautiful domed library (now classified by the National Trust). The statue of Justice, defying tradition, is not blindfolded: rumour has it that a judge persuaded the authorities that Justice should be "wide-eyed if not innocently credulous".

The public can visit the court and observe proceedings (barring special circumstances). The courts sit 10am–4:15pm.

5

Rialto Towers

📍 D4 🏛 525 Collins St 🚇 Southern Cross Station 🚊 Collins St routes 🕐 7am–7pm daily 🌐 rialto.com.au

Rialto measures 253 m (830 ft) from ground up. It has 58 floors

> **St James's Old Cathedral was relocated to its present site between 1913 and 1914. The stones were numbered to ensure that the original design was replicated.**

above street level and 8 below. The structure was built in 1986 by developer Bruno Grollo, who was responsible for the Eureka Tower (*p237*). The former observation deck on the 55th floor now houses the Vue de Monde restaurant, including the Lui Bar. It is one of the most spectacular places to dine, with panoramic views over the city. The bar is open to non-diners.

St James's Old Cathedral was relocated to its present site between 1913 and 1914. The stones were numbered to ensure that the original design was replicated.

---

❻
St Francis's Church

📍 D3 🏠 326 Lonsdale St
🚇 Melbourne Central
🚊 Elizabeth St routes
🕐 Hours vary, check website
🌐 stfrancismelbourne.com

Attracting thousands of visitors each week, St Francis's Church is a hub for Roman Catholic life in Melbourne. Built between 1841 and 1845, it is one of Victoria's oldest church. Renowned for its beauty, it began as a simple Neo-Gothic building and has undergone several major alterations.

During one restoration effort, treasures from the 1860s, such as a painting of angels, stars and a coat of arms, were discovered and beautifully restored. The church has one of Australia's most celebrated resident choirs.

---

❼
Melbourne Mint

📍 D3 🏠 280 William St
🚇 Flagstaff 🚊 24, 30
🚌 Lonsdale & Queen sts routes 🔒 To the public
🌐 melbournemint.com.au

This former Mint, built between 1871 and 1872, contains two courts which were used to cope with the overflow from the Supreme Court.

When it opened in 1872 it processed finds from the Victoria gold fields and was a branch of the Royal Mint of London. The Melbourne site ceased production in 1967 and was relocated to Canberra. Although the building is closed to the public, visitors can still take in its imposing structure from the outside.

---

❽
St James's Old Cathedral

📍 C3 🏠 Cnr King & Batman sts 🚇 Flagstaff 🚊 30, 75
🚌 220 🕐 9am–3pm Mon-Fri; service: 10am Sun
🔒 Public hols 🌐 sjoc.org.au

St James's was the first Anglican cathedral in the city, used until St Paul's opened

←
The beautifully adorned ceiling and windows of St Francis's Church

in 1891 (*p227*). It was relocated to its present site between 1913 and 1914. The stones were numbered to ensure that the original design was replicated.

St James's was designed in a Colonial Georgian style. The foundations are made of bluestone and the main walls were constructed with local sandstone. The cathedral was opened for worship on 2 October 1842, but was not consecrated until 1853. Charles Perry, the city's first bishop, was enthroned here in 1848. The cathedral is still used for regular services. There's also a small museum that contains photographs, historic documents and cathedral mementos.

EAT & DRINK

MoVida
An iconic Spanish tapas bar, tucked away down a graffiti-laden alley.

📍 E4 🏠 1 Hosier Lane
🌐 movida.com.au

💲💲💲

Supernormal
A cutting-edge spot famous for pan-Asian and Szechuan cooking.

📍 E4 🏠 180 Flinders Lane 🌐 supernormal.net.au

💲💲💲

Pellegrini's Espresso Bar
One of the city's most famous espresso bars, Pellegrini's has been in business since 1954.

📍 E3 🏠 66 Bourke St
📞 (03) 9662 1885

💲💲💲

9

Melbourne Town Hall

E4 Swanston St
Flinders St Swanston &
Collins sts routes 9am-
6pm Mon-Fri, 9am-5pm
Sat & Sun (ground level
foyer only) Public hols
melbourne.vic.gov.au

The Town Hall was designed by
Reed & Barnes and completed
in 1870. The portico was added
in 1887. An adjacent administration block and the council's
second chamber were added
in 1908. This chamber combines a Renaissance-style
interior with Australian motifs,
such as a ceiling plasterwork
of gum nuts.

A fire in 1925 destroyed
much of the interior, including
the main hall which had to be
rebuilt. At the entrance, there
are four motifs on the city's
coat of arms: a whale, a ship,
a bull and a sheep, signifying
the colonial industries. In 1942,
the College of Arms ordered an
inversion of the motifs according to heraldic convention.

The main hall often hosts
public events and features a
three-storey-high pipe organ.

10

Block Arcade

D4 282 Collins St
Flinders St Swanston
& Collins sts routes 9am-
5pm daily Good Fri,
25 Dec theblock.com.au

Built between 1891 and 1893,
with period details including
a mosaic floor and a central
dome, Melbourne's most

> **The Melbourne
> Docklands are
> also home to the
> 120-m- (394-ft-) tall
> Melbourne Star
> Ferris wheel, the
> crowning glory of
> the city's skyline.**

opulent shopping arcade was
named after the promenade
taken by fashionable society
in the 1890s. Known as "doing
the block", the walk involved
strolling down Collins Street
between Elizabeth and
Swanston streets.

The arcade was restored
in 1988. It still includes the
Hopetoun Tea Rooms, which
have been in place since the
structure was opened. Guided
arcade tours are available.

11

Docklands

C4 Southern Cross
Station City Circle 11,
35, 48, 70, 75 Yarra
River Shuttle

The redevelopment of
Melbourne Docklands
makes it worth visiting for
the modern architecture
alone. The total redevelopment area is 200 ha (490
acres), with 3 km (2 miles) of
Yarra River frontage. It is also
home to the 120-m- (394-ft-)
tall Melbourne Star Ferris
wheel. Though its panoramic
rides closed down indefinitely
in 2021, it's still the crowning
glory of the city's skyline.

The area has a beautiful
harbour and marina, public
spaces (including Docklands
Park, Harbour Esplanade and
Grand Plaza), historic wharves,
shops and restaurants. There
is also urban art by renowned
Australian artists such as Bruce
Armstrong. Several events,
including the Summer Boat
Show, take place here, and
the weekly Docklands Sunday
Community Market is held
on Newquay Promenade.

Did You Know?

More than one-third
of Melbourne's
residents were
born overseas.

12

Royal Arcade

D4 Elizabeth, Bourke &
Little Collins sts Flinders
St Bourke, Elizabeth &
Collins sts routes Hours
vary, check website
royalarcade.com.au

Melbourne's oldest surviving
arcade features boutiques
selling everything from antique
jewellery to fine chocolates. It is
part of a network of lanes and
arcades which sprang up to
divide the big blocks of the city
grid into smaller segments.

↑ Boats at the Docklands harbour, with the
Melbourne Star in the background

The splendid reading room at the State Library of Victoria ↑

The original arcade, built in 1869 and designed by Charles Webb, runs between Little Collins Street and Bourke Street Mall. An annexe, with an entrance on Elizabeth Street, was added in 1902. A statue of Father Time, originally on the Bourke Street façade, is now located inside the arcade.

The arcade famously houses the statues of Gog and Magog, mythical representations of the conflict between the ancient Britons and the Trojans. They are modelled on identical figures in the Guildhall in London. Between them is Gaunt's Clock, crafted by Thomas Gaunt.

St Paul's Cathedral

📍E4 🏛Cnr Swanston & Flinders sts 🚃Flinders St 🚋Swanston, Flinders & Collins sts routes 🕐10am–6pm Mon–Fri, 10am–5pm Sat; services: 8am, 10am & 4pm Sun 🌐cathedral.org.au

St Paul's Cathedral, one of Melbourne's most famous architectural landmarks, was completed in 1891. Construction, however, was plagued by difficulties, with dissension between the architect, William Butterfield, and the Cathedral

Erection Board. Building began in 1880, but Butterfield tendered his resignation in 1884. The final stages of construction were supervised by architect Joseph Reed, who also designed many of the fittings.

There are many outstanding internal features, including the reredos (altar screen) made in Italy from marble and alabaster inset with glass mosaics. The organ, made by T C Lewis & Co of London, is the best surviving work of this great organ-builder. The cathedral also has a peal of 13 bells – a rarity outside the British Isles.

The cathedral underwent a five-year restoration, which included upgrading the spectacular stained-glass windows.

State Library of Victoria

📍D3 🏛328 Swanston St 🚃Melbourne Central 🚋Swanston & La Trobe sts routes 🕐10am–6pm daily 🗓1 Jan, Good Fri, 25 & 26 Dec 🌐slv.vic.gov.au

Counted among the city's most distinguished institutions, the State Library was founded in 1854. It is Australia's oldest public library, holding more

than two million books – among the most renowned are folios from Captain James Cook and the body armour worn by 19th-century bushranger Ned Kelly (p229).

At the library's centre is the octagonal reading room with a soaring, domed ceiling. It was laid out in 1913 and can hold 32,000 books across its six storeys. Renovations that were completed in 2019 have transformed the elegant Neo-Classical Ian Potter Queen's Hall into a public reading room.

Immigration Museum

📍D4 🏛400 Flinders St 🚃Southern Cross Station 🚋Collins St routes 🕐10am–5pm daily 🗓Good Fri, 25 Dec 🌐museumsvictoria.com.au/immigrationmuseum

The Immigration Museum explores the stories of people from all over the world who have migrated to Victoria. Located in the Old Customs House, it uses moving images, personal and community memories and memorabilia to re-create the journey and arrival of immigrants. It also explores the impact of immigration on Aboriginal peoples.

16

Regent Theatre

📍 E4 🏠 191 Collins St
🚇 Flinders St 🚊 Swanston
& Collins sts routes
🌐 marrinergroup.com.au/
regent-theatre

When the Regent Theatre's auditorium was destroyed by fire in April 1945, the Lord Mayor of Melbourne promised the public that it would be rebuilt, despite the scarcity of building materials due to World War II – such was the popularity and local importance of the theatre.

Known as "Melbourne's Palace of Dreams", it was first opened in 1929. Its lavish interiors emulated both the glamour of Hollywood and the impressive design of New York's Capitol Theater.

The building had two main venues. An auditorium upstairs, for live stage and musical entertainment, was known as the Regent Theatre. Downstairs, the Plaza Theatre was originally a ballroom but, following the success of the "talkies", it was converted into a cinema.

The advent of television led to dwindling cinema audiences, and the Regent Theatre closed for almost 30 years. The complex was later restored in 1996 and is now listed by the National Trust. Today, it mostly hosts musical theatre. Ticket-holders can admire the beautiful interiors before seeing the latest show.

17

Scots' Church

📍 E4 🏠 99 Russell St (cnr
Collins St) 🚇 Flinders St &
Parliament 🚊 Swanston &
Collins sts routes ⏰ 9am–
5pm Mon-Fri; services:
11am & 5pm Sun 🌐 scots
church.com

Scots' Church, completed in 1874, was intended at the time to be "the most beautiful building in Australia". It was designed by Joseph Reed in a "decorated Gothic" style, with bluestone used in the foundations and local Barrabool stone in the superstructure.

There is also an old assembly hall here, which was completed in 1913.

💬 INSIDER TIP
Free Ride

The City Circle Tram offers free travel in Melbourne's CBD area, located between Queen Victoria Market and the Docklands. Visit www.ptv.vic.gov.au for a map.

↑ Regent Theatre, one of Melbourne's grand historic buildings

18

No 120 Collins Street

📍 E3/4 🏠 120 Collins St
🚇 Flinders St & Parliament
🚊 Collins St routes

Built in 1991, this landmark office block, located in the city's central business district, was designed by Daryl Jackson and Hassell Architects. Until 2005, its communications tower was the highest building in the entire country, at 265 m (869 ft). Original 1908 Federation-style professional chambers, built on the grounds of the 1867 St Michael's Uniting Church, are incorporated into the building.

19

Old Magistrates' Court

📍 D3 🏠 Cnr La Trobe &
Russell sts 📞 (03) 9656
9889 🚇 Melbourne Central
🚊 La Trobe & Swanston sts
routes ⏰ During school hols

The Melbourne Magistrates' Court (also known as City Court) occupied this building until 1995. The area was formerly known as the police precinct because the court lies opposite the former police headquarters, a striking Art Deco skyscraper that was completed in the early 1940s, and next door to the Old Melbourne Gaol.

Built in 1911, the court's façades are made of native Moorabool sandstone. The intricate, Romanesque design features gables, turrets and arches. The building originally contained three courtrooms. Court One is open to the public during school holidays as part of the Old Melbourne Gaol Crime and Justice Experience.

Old Melbourne Gaol

📍 D3 🏛 Russell St 🚇 Melbourne Central 🚊 La Trobe & Swanston sts routes 🕐 10am–5pm Wed-Sun 🚫 Good Fri, 25 Dec 🌐 oldmelbournegaol. com.au

Visiting the Old Melbourne Gaol, Victoria's first extensive gaol complex, is a chilling experience, especially on a night tour. Between 1845 and 1929, it was the site of 133 executions. While much of the original complex has been demolished, the imposing Second Cell Block still stands and is today home to a fascinating museum.

Conditions in the gaol, based on London's Pentonville Model Prison, were grim, leading to many tragic and grisly accounts of prisoners' lives and deaths. When first incarcerated, prisoners were held in solitary confinement and were not permitted to mix with other prisoners until a later date, set according to their specific sentence.

Exhibits showing these conditions include prisoners' chains and a frame used for flogging. But perhaps the most compelling exhibits are the many accounts of prisoners who were condemned to die at the gaol, accompanied by their death masks. The death mask of outlaw Edward "Ned" Kelly is without a doubt the most famous of those on display – his execution, which took place when he was just 25 years old, is one of the gaol's most notorious. Visitors can also see the original gallows where executions occurred.

NED KELLY

Ned Kelly, the famous Australian bushranger, was executed at the Old Melbourne Gaol on 11 November 1880. A crowd of 5,000 waited outside the gaol when he was executed, most to lend their support to a man perceived to be rightfully rebelling against the English-based law and police authorities. The controversy over whether Kelly was hero or villain continues to this day.

Included with a ticket to the Old Melbourne Gaol is admittance to the former city Watch House, which served as a central "lock up" for police from 1908 to 1994. With a Charge Sergeant as a guide, visitors are "arrested" and processed through the lock up, experiencing first hand an environment that has not changed since the police and inmates left it. The Watch House has a long and fascinating history, with characters such as the 1920s gangster Squizzy Taylor, last man hanged Ronald Ryan and infamous criminal Chopper Read all having been locked up here. The experience is enhanced by informative multimedia displays that illustrate the stories of former inmates.

←

The haunting cell blocks at the Old Melbourne Gaol complex

EAT

DOC Espresso
Casual yet classy, this contemporary Italian joint specializes in homemade pasta and cakes, plus great coffee and cocktails.

📍E2 📍326 Lygon St, Carlton 🅦docgroup.net

$$$

Brunetti Oro
Sample mouthwatering tartlets and pizzas, washed down with negronis and proper espresso at this Melbourne institution.

📍E2 📍250 Flinders Lane 🅦brunettioro.com.au

$$$

ShanDong MaMa
Tucked away in an unassuming shopping arcade, ShanDong MaMa feeds the city's obsession with dumplings.

📍E3 📍Mid City Arcade, 200 Bourke St 📞(03) 9650 3818

$$$

Flower Drum
Considered to be Australia's best Cantonese restaurant, Flower Drum serves beautifully prepared dishes in a large dining room decorated with Chinese art. The restaurant is popular with celebrities, and retains an accommodating and relaxed vibe.

📍E3 📍17 Market Lane 🅦flowerdrum.melbourne

$$$

21

Museum of Chinese Australian History

📍E3 📍22 Cohen Pl (off Little Bourke St) 🚇Parliament 🚊Swanston & Bourke sts routes 🕐10am–4pm daily 🗓1 Jan, Good Fri, 25 Dec 🅦chinesemuseum.com.au

Situated in the heart of Chinatown, this museum opened in 1985 to preserve the heritage of Australians of Chinese descent. The subjects of its displays range from the influx of Chinese gold-seekers in the 1850s to exhibitions of contemporary Chinese art, thus offering a comprehensive history of the Chinese community in Victoria.

The second floor holds touring exhibitions from China and displays of Chinese art. On the third floor is a permanent exhibition covering aspects of Chinese-Australian history, including elaborate costumes and temple regalia. In the basement, another permanent exhibition traces the experiences of Chinese gold miners – visitors step into a booth which creaks and moves like a transport ship, then view dioramas of life in a gold field and a tent theatre used by Chinese performers to entertain miners.

The museum also houses the beautiful Melbourne Chinese dragon, the head of which is the largest of its kind anywhere in the world. A guided heritage walk through Chinatown is also available.

22

Lygon Street

📍D3 📍Lygon St, Carlton 🚊1, 8 🚌200, 207, 955, 966

This Italian-influenced street is one of the best-known café, restaurant and delicatessen areas in central Melbourne. The strong Italian tradition of the street began at the time of

mass post-World War II immigration. With a general exodus to the suburbs in the 1940s, house prices in Carlton dropped and new immigrants were able to buy the area's 19th-century houses and shops. The immigrant community was central in protecting these Victorian and Edwardian houses, which were built with gold-rush wealth, from government plans to fill the area with low-income Housing Commission homes.

↑ Restaurants and cafés offering outside seating on Lygon Street

↑ The Facing Heaven Archway on Chinatown's main street

Did You Know?

Unique to Australians of Italian descent, the Italo-Australian dialect combines modern Italian with English.

A distinctive architectural trait of the street's two-storey shops is their verandas, built to protect both customers and merchandise from the sun. With its European feel, Lygon Street is well suited to host the Carlton Italian Festa, a celebration of Italian Australian culture.

The street is only one block from the main University of Melbourne campus, making it a popular spot for students.

Chinatown

📍 E3 🏠 Little Bourke St
🚉 Parliament 🚃 Swanston & Bourke sts routes

When Chinese immigrants began arriving in Melbourne to seek gold during the 1850s, many of the city's European residents were unfriendly towards them. Competition over labour opportunities, coupled with the racial slurs and negative stereotypes published by newspapers, created an intensely hostile environment for Chinese migrants.

The very first Chinese immigrants landed in Australia as early as 1818, but it was during the late 1840s that larger contingents arrived. These newcomers took on the cheap labour previously assigned to the convict settlements, which had been decreasing. This wave of immigration was harmonious until the 1850s, when a vast influx of Chinese visitors – who came not for labour, but to seek their fortune in the Victorian gold fields – arrived. The large numbers of immigrants and a decline in gold finds made the Chinese population in Australia targets of vicious and organized riots.

This attitude was sanctioned by government policy. The Chinese were charged a poll tax in most states of £10 each – a huge sum, particularly as many were of low income.

Even harsher was a restriction on the number of passengers that boat-owners could carry. This acted as a disincentive for them to bring Chinese immigrants to Australia. What resulted were "Chinese marathons", as new arrivals dodged the tax by landing in "free" South Australia and walking to the gold fields, covering distances of up to 800 km (500 miles).

The Chinese population established a city base during the 1850s, utilizing the cheap rental district of Melbourne's city centre. Traders could live and work in the same premises and act as a support network for other Chinese immigrants. The community largely avoided prejudice by starting up traditional Asian businesses, which included market gardening, laundering, green grocers and furniture-making (but work had to be stamped "Made by Chinese labour").

Today, Chinatown is known for its restaurants and Chinese produce shops, with the community's calendar culminating in its New Year celebrations in January or February.

← The majestic, World Heritage-listed exterior of the Royal Exhibition Building, and *(inset)* the ornate interior of its dome

24

Royal Exhibition Building

📍 E2/3 🏠 9 Nicholson St, Carlton 🚇 Parliament 🚋 Nicholson & Victoria sts routes 🕐 Daily (via guided tours only) 🌐 museums victoria.com.au/reb

The city's only World Heritage-listed site is adjacent to Melbourne Museum and offers an interesting 19th-century counterpoint to its neighbour's modern architecture. Designed by Cornish architect Joseph Reed, the Royal Exhibition Building was built for the 1880 International Exhibition and is one of the few remaining structures from the 19th-century world fairs.

Among the city's grandest structures, the building is surrounded by the ornamental Carlton Gardens. Book tickets ahead for hour-long guided tours of the complex.

25

Melbourne Museum

📍 E2 🏠 Carlton Gardens 🚋 86, 96 🕐 10am–5pm daily 🚫 Good Fri, 25 Dec 🌐 museumvictoria.com. au/melbournemuseum

Housed in an ultra-modern facility in verdant Carlton Gardens, the Melbourne Museum has exhibits over six levels. Diverse displays offer insights into science, technology, the environment, the human mind and body, Australian society and Aboriginal peoples.

One of the highlights is Bunjilaka, the Aboriginal Centre which combines exhibition galleries with a performance space. *Wurreka*, the 50-m- (150-ft-) long zinc wall etching at the entrance is by Aboriginal artist Judy Watson. On the Milarri Garden trail, you can learn about the traditional uses of endemic plants and also explore a cave decorated with Aboriginal paintings.

The Forest Gallery is a living, breathing exhibit, featuring 8,000 plants from 120 different species. It is also home to around 20 different vertebrate species, including snakes, birds, fish and hundreds of insects. This gallery explores the complex ecosystem of Australia's temperate forests, using plants and animals as well as art and multimedia installations.

There is also a dedicated gallery for children, featuring a dinosaur dig to excavate fossils, a discovery garden and museum objects, as well as Aboriginal storytelling and sculptures.

One of the most popular exhibits is in the Australia Gallery. It displays the life of Phar Lap, the champion Australian racehorse of the early 1930s. Exhibits include race memorabilia of the period and the taxidermy form of Phar Lap himself, which is preserved in an Art Deco-inspired showcase. Other curiosities on show in the museum include dinosaur skeletons, a taxidermy hall with more than 500 stuffed species and a 3D volcano.

INSIDER TIP
Early Risers

Café tables can be hard to come by in Fitzroy and Brunswick, especially on weekends. Grab a classic Melbourne brunch during the week, or arrive before 10am on Saturday or Sunday to avoid queues.

Brunswick Street and Fitzroy

F2 Brunswick St 11

Bordering the university suburb of Carlton, Fitzroy was the natural choice for a post-1960s population of students, who took advantage of the area's cheap post-war Housing Commission properties. Despite becoming gentrified since this era, Fitzroy's main strip, Brunswick Street, still maintains a young, alternative air and a cosmopolitan street life.

Today, Brunswick Street features a vibrant array of cafés, restaurants and trendy shops; especially popular are the numerous vintage stores where locals hunt for second-hand treasures. A little to the south is Gertrude Street, which has an eclectic mix of record stores, bars and modern galleries.

Nearby Johnston Street is home to a few tapas and Mexican bars and a Spanish grocery. In late February, the area hosts The Fiesta, an outdoor festival celebrating Hispanic-Latin American culture. Also nearby lies Smith Street, which has outgrown its formerly seedy reputation to become a hotspot for some of the trendier restaurants and bars in the city. All the streets in this area are most lively on Friday and Saturday nights and easily accessible on a tram.

Old Treasury Building

E3 Old Treasury Building, Spring St (top of Collins St) 11, 109 10am–4pm Sun-Fri Good Fri, 25 & 26 Dec oldtreasurybuilding.org.au

Melbourne's beautiful, 19th-century Old Treasury Building was designed in 1857 by John James Clark, a 19-year-old architectural prodigy. It provided secure storage for all the gold that flooded into the city from the wealthy Victorian gold fields. The building also served as office accommodation for the Governor of Victoria (a role it still fulfils today).

As well as an opportunity to see the building itself, a visit to the old treasury includes a look into the gold vaults that lie just beneath the building. The vaults contain a dynamic multimedia exhibition, *Built on Gold*, which tells the story of how Melbourne rapidly developed into a city of enormous wealth in a remarkably short period of ten years. In this time it progressed from a small 19th-century outpost to a vibrant city with several impressive buildings, grand boulevards, a dynamic theatre culture and a passion for sport and political activism.

SHOP

Rose Street Artists' Market
This Saturday market brings together Melbourne's original handicraft vendors and jewellery makers.

F3 60 Rose St rosestmarket.com.au

Northside Records
Search for old-school musical treasures at this local favourite. Funk and soul records are the speciality here, but hip-hop and R&B vinyls also feature.

F3 236 Gertrude St northsiderecords.com.au

Mud Australia
This small, intimate shop sells colourful handmade porcelain homeware, lighting fixtures and decorative items.

F3 181 Gertrude St mudaustralia.com

↑ Colourful shops and restaurants lining Brunswick Street

28

Melbourne Cricket Ground

📍 F4 🏠 Yarra Park, Jolimont 🚉 Jolimont 🚊 48, 70, 75 (special trams run on sports event days) 🌐 mcg.org.au

Melbourne Cricket Ground (MCG), or "the G", is Australia's premier sports stadium and a cultural icon. The land was granted in 1853 to the Melbourne Cricket Club (MCC), itself conceived in 1838.

The MCG predominantly hosts cricket and Australian Rules Football; it acts as the site for test matches and one-day international match and for the Australian Football League (AFL) Grand Final, which is held on the last Saturday of September (p64). Non-sporting events, such as music concerts, are also held here.

There have been numerous stands and pavilions over the years, each superseded at different times by reconstructions of the ground. An 1876 stand, destroyed in a fire eight years after being built, was reversible, with spectators able to watch cricket on the ground and football in the park in winter. Following massive redevelopment of the ground ahead of the 2006 Commonwealth Games, the MCG can now seat crowds of more than 100,000.

Guided tours are offered from 10am

to 3pm daily and usually take visitors behind the scenes to the players' changing rooms, and the Melbourne Cricket Club (MCC) Museum. It traces the history of the MCG with an impressive collection of information and artifacts. The Mythical Ashes is a fascinating display of Ashes mementos.

29

Australian Centre for Contemporary Art

📍 E5 🏠 111 Sturt St, Southbank 🚉 Flinders St 🚊 St Kilda Rd routes 🕐 10am–5pm Tue–Fri, 11am–5pm Sat & Sun 🚫 1 Jan, Good Fri, 25 & 26 Dec 🌐 acca.melbourne

Spread over four different galleries, and filled with cutting-edge Australian art, the Australian Centre for Contemporary Art (ACCA) is one of the country's most dynamic creative spaces. Even the building itself – an uneven rust-red shell designed by Wood Marsh Architects in 2002 – is considered a striking piece of art.

In addition to an impressive calendar of rotating exhibitions, the ACCA has multiple spaces for performance arts and a fantastic permanent collection. Its most famous work is Ron Robertson-Swann's *Vault*, popularly known as "The Yellow Peril". This large, abstract and eye-catching sculpture has been here since 2005, having previously occupied various inner-city public spaces – dividing opinion wherever it went – since its creation in 1980.

← A statue of W H Ponsford, an Australian cricketer, outside the Melbourne Cricket Ground

30

Melbourne & Olympic Parks

📍 F4 🏠 Batman Ave 🚉 Flinders St & Richmond 🚊 70 🕐 For events, check website; for tours of Rod Laver Arena, call 1300 836 647 🌐 mopt.com.au

Melbourne Park (formerly the National Tennis Centre) is the city's sports and large-scale concerts venue. Events include the Australian Open (p64), one of the four Grand Slam competitions of tennis, played under Rod Laver Arena's retractable roof. There are also 22 outdoor and seven indoor tennis courts for public use.

Next to Melbourne Park is the John Cain Arena, home to Melbourne Vixens netball team. It also has a stadium for cycling, dance performances, family shows, concerts and other entertainment. Opposite the park is the Holden Centre, which was originally built for the 1956 Olympics but has been redeveloped. Near the Olympic Park is the training

← Melbourne Park, with the Rod Laver Arena in the foreground

566

The number of medals that Australia has won in the Olympic Games since 1896.

ground for Collingwood Football Club. The AAMI Park is also a venue for soccer and rugby events. Its exterior is covered with thousands of LEDs that light up at night.

Australian Sports Museum

Q F4 **M** Melbourne Cricket Ground, Yarra Park, Jolimont **R** Richmond **E** 48, 70, 75 **O** Hours vary, check website **C** Good Fri, 25 Dec **W** australian sportsmuseum.org.au

Following its redevelopment for the 2006 Commonwealth Games, the Melbourne Cricket Ground has become the home of the Australian Sports Museum. This award-winning museum honours all things sporting, with a focus on national favourites – Aussie Rules Football, cricket and horse racing – as well as large global events such as the Olympic Games.

Located across two levels of the refurbished 1956 Olympic Stand is Australia's largest collection of sports-related memorabilia. Using state-of-the-art technology, the museum also features a number of famous sports personalities sharing first-hand accounts of their sporting story. The Olympic Museum offers a range of displays noting the history of all summer Olympic meets. The Australian Cricket Hall of Fame, which opened with ten Australian players as initial members in 1996, includes Sir Donald Bradman. Each player is presented through a comprehensive historical display.

After you've wandered through the museum, you can take a tour of the arena, the Ponsford Stand, the football and cricket changing rooms, heritage artworks, the corporate suites and the terrace, which offers spectacular views of Melbourne's skyline.

FOOTY FEVER

Melbourne is the spiritual home of Australian Rules Football (or "footy" as locals call it). The first game was played here in 1858, and it's now a local institution - the Australian Football League (AFL) Grand Final at the MCG draws nearly 100,000 spectators each September. The most successful teams include the Essendon Bombers, Carlton Blues, Collingwood Magpies, Richmond Tigers and Hawthorn Hawks.

↑ The exterior of Flinders Street Station, and *(inset)* travellers waiting under the iconic clocks

in French Renaissance style, it features bright-yellow brickwork and an impressive copper dome.

32 🍴 🛍 🛍

Flinders Street Station

📍 E4 📍 Cnr Flinders & Swanston sts 🚆 13 16 38 🚋 Swanston & Flinders sts routes

Flinders Street Station is the central metropolitan train terminus of Melbourne and one of the city's favourite meeting places. Generations of Melburnians have met each other on the corner steps of the station "under the clocks".

The Flinders Street site has been part of the public transport network since the city's early days. In 1854, the first steam train in Australia left Flinders Street Station, then a small wooden building. The present station building, completed in 1910, is one of the grandest in the city. Built

33 🚴 🍴 🛍 🛍

Royal Botanic Gardens and Kings Domain

📍 E5–F5 📍 St Kilda Rd 🚋 3, 5, 6, 8, 16, 64, 67, 72 🕐 Hours vary, check website 🌐 rbg.vic.gov.au

These adjoining gardens, established in 1852, form the green heart of Melbourne on what was originally a

swamp on the edge of the city. The Botanic Gardens house one of the finest collections of botanic species in the world and are highly regarded for their landscape design. William Guilfoyle, curator of the gardens between 1873 and 1909, used his knowledge of English garden design to create this horticultural paradise.

The gardens are home to a huge variety of plants, from endemic desert plants in the Arid Garden to the huge Algerian Oak in the centre of the Oak Lawn. Attractions include Guilfoyle's Volcano, a 19th-century water reservoir that affords great views of the city, the Ornamental Lake, the Italianate Government House and the Ian Potter Foundation Children's Garden. There's also the

---

RISING

First held in 2021, RISING *(www.rising.melbourne)* is an exciting addition to Melbourne's festival calendar. Held in May or June each year, the event aims to make art public, diverse and accessible for the widest possible audience. Expect a roster of free and ticketed events, including street art displays and installations as well as live music and other performances.

Shrine of Remembrance that honours Australian soldiers who gave their lives in war.

Kings Domain was once an inner-city wilderness but is now a gracious parkland. Its civic function grew over the years, with the establishment of its monuments, statues, cultural venues and the hilltop residence of the Governor of Victoria.

The highlight of Kings Domain is the Pioneer Women's Memorial Garden, which is located between the Royal Botanic Gardens and the Yarra River. Inaugurated in 1934 on Melbourne's 100th anniversary, the garden honours the contribution of the city's women in its early history. It's a tranquil oasis, with a symmetrical layout, disrupted by a bronze statue by Charles Web Gilbert, a fountain and a sundial. On weekends, it's a popular spot for weddings.

34

SEA LIFE Melbourne Aquarium

📍 D4 🏛 Cnr Flinders & King sts 🚇 Southern Cross, Flinders St 🚊 70 🕐 Hours vary, check website 🌐 visitsealife.com

Featuring species from the Australian, southern and tropical oceans, SEA LIFE Melbourne Aquarium allows visitors to see some of the colourful inhabitants of the deep. Among the exhibits is the enormous Oceanarium, approached through a viewing cylinder and housing sharks and rays as well as vibrant fish. Another underwater wonderland worth seeing is the Coral Atoll exhibit. It is home to a variety of colourful fish, including Dory, the famous southern blue tang. There is also an immersive digital installation, the Interactive Wonder Wall, that allows kids to colour their own jellyfish on an interactive screen and then watch it float. The highlight of any visit to SEA LIFE Melbourne Aquarium is watching the resident king and gentoo penguins – it's the only place in Victoria where you can see these birds. Entrance tickets to the aquarium must be booked in advance.

35

Eureka Tower

📍 D4 🏛 7 Riverside Quay 🕐 Hours vary, check website 🌐 melbourneskydeck.com.au

This 297-m (974-ft) tower was named after the Eureka Stockade, a rebellion that took place during the Victoria gold rush (p69). Its gold crown and gold-plated windows refer back to this era. Visitors travel to the Skydeck on the 88th floor, which has numerous viewfinders and a moving viewpoint called "The Edge" – a glass cube that slowly slides out 3 m (10 ft) from the side of the building.

 PICTURE PERFECT
Edge of the World

Not afraid of heights? Take a photo of yourself in "The Edge". The highest public vantage point in the southern hemisphere, Eureka Tower's glass cube will make it seem like the city is literally at your feet.

36

Polly Woodside

📍 C5 🏛 21 S Wharf Promenade, South Wharf 🚇 Southern Cross 🚊 12, 96, 109 🚏 Grimes St Bridge 🕐 Hours vary, check website 🌐 nationaltrust.org.au

This is an 1885 barque built in Belfast. When it was retired in the 1960s, it was the only deep-water commercial ship still afloat in Australia. Even in 1885, the ship was rare, as only one in four were built with sails at that time. Most of the last 40 years of its working life were spent as a coal hulk. Donated to the National Trust in 1968, the ship has since been restored. Interactive displays explore life at sea and working on Melbourne's docks. Tour days are infrequent; book in advance via the website.

The elegant *Polly Woodside* ship, docked at the South Wharf
↓

37 ⊘ ⊗ ⊡ 🗋

Rippon Lea Estate

📍 F2 **🏠 192 Hotham St, Elsternwick** **🚉 Rippon Lea** **🚋 67** **🚌 216, 219** **🕐 May-Aug: 10am-4pm daily; Sep-Apr: 10am-5pm daily** **🚫 Good Fri, 25 Dec** **🌐 ripponleaestate.com.au**

Rippon Lea Mansion, designed by Joseph Reed and built in 1868, is now part of the National Trust's portfolio. The house is a much-loved fixture of the city's heritage. The first family of Rippon Lea were the Sargoods, who held many balls during the 1880s and 1890s. The next owner, Premier Sir Thomas Bent, sold off parts of the estate in the early 1900s. The Nathans bought Rippon Lea in 1910 and restored its reputation as a family home. Benjamin Nathan's daughter Louisa Jones added a ballroom and swimming pool, which were the venue for parties in the 1930s and 1940s.

The sprawling gardens around the mansion include a lake populated with black ducks and tortoises, a fernery with hundreds of species of ferns and palms, an orchard and other features of historical and architectural interest.

→ Scenic St Kilda Pier, which looks out onto Port Phillip Bay

38

St Kilda

📍 F2 **🚋 12, 16, 96** **🚌 246, 600, 623, 606** **⛴ St Kilda Pier**

Situated 6 km (4 miles) south of the city centre, pretty St Kilda is a seaside suburb with a charisma of its own. St Kilda Pier and Luna Park sign are still a magnet for visitors, as are the neighbourhood streets, which feature many Art Deco apartment blocks.

St Kilda's main streets are Fitzroy and Acland. The latter, home to cafés and cake shops, is packed with visitors on Sundays. Fitzroy Street is filled with upmarket restaurants and shops. Rejuvenated in the 1980s, the beachside esplanade attracts crowds to its busy arts and crafts market each Sunday.

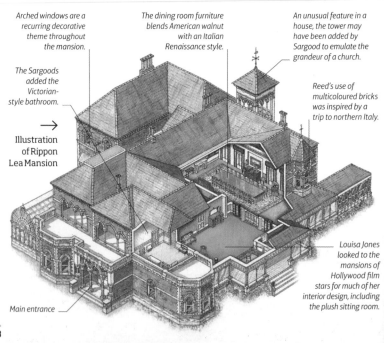

Arched windows are a recurring decorative theme throughout the mansion.

The dining room furniture blends American walnut with an Italian Renaissance style.

An unusual feature in a house, the tower may have been added by Sargood to emulate the grandeur of a church.

The Sargoods added the Victorian-style bathroom.

Reed's use of multicoloured bricks was inspired by a trip to northern Italy.

→ Illustration of Rippon Lea Mansion

Louisa Jones looked to the mansions of Hollywood film stars for much of her interior design, including the plush sitting room.

Main entrance

 TOP 5 **MELBOURNE BEACHES**

St Kilda
Palm- and café-lined beach, with a historic pier and plenty of kite-surfing opportunities.

Brighton
Famous for its colourful bathing boxes, Brighton is very family-friendly.

Williamstown
Scenic "Willy" has great views of the city skyline.

Elwood
Lined with cafés, this busy bay has excellent swimming spots.

Black Rock
This crescent-shaped beach is one of the city's prettiest bay beaches.

39
Albert Park

F1 Canterbury Rd, Albert Rd & Lakeside Dr 1, 12, 96 parks.vic.gov.au

Encompassing the remains of a former natural swampland, Albert Park Lake is the centre-piece of a 225-ha (555-acre) parkland, which includes sporting fields, a public golf course and other recreational facilities. However, it is now predominantly known as the site of the annual Australian Formula One Grand Prix.

The park is also home to the Melbourne Sports and Aquatic Centre, where locals come for sailing sessions. Wetlands have been added to the area to safeguard the resident birdlife.

STAY

The Como Melbourne
Mingle with celebrities at The Como, which is all about elegance, fine facilities and discreet, professional service.

F1 630 Chapel St, South Yarra como melbourne.com.au

$$$

40
Chapel Street

F1 South Yarra, Prahran and Windsor South Yarra, Prahan 6, 8, 78 chapel street.com.au

Chapel Street, the centre of Melbourne's nightlife and shopping scene, is lined with boutiques selling local and international designs. Upmarket restaurants and cafés abound and the nearby Prahran Market sells some of the city's best fresh produce. The market also contains many Greek and Italian delis.

Crossing Chapel Street is Toorak Road, whose "village" is patronized by Melbourne's wealthiest community. To the west is Greville Street with its cafés, bars and chic second-hand shops.

41
Como Historic House and Garden

F1 Cnr Williams Rd & Lechlade Ave, South Yarra South Yarra 8 Hours vary, check website Good Fri, 25 Dec nationaltrust.org.au

Begun in 1847 by Edward Eyre Williams, Como House was occupied by the Armytage family for almost a century (1865–1959). One of Como's highlights is its vast collection of original furnishings. These include pieces collected by the Armytage matriarch, Caroline, while on a Grand Tour of Europe during the 1870s, and include marble and bronze statues. The tour was undertaken as an educational experience for her nine children after the death of her husband, Charles Henry.

Set in the picturesque remnants of its once extensive gardens, the house overlooks Como Park and the Yarra River. The original facets of the magnificent grounds, designed by William Sangster (who also had an input at Rippon Lea), remain: the fountain terrace, croquet lawn and hard-standing area at the front of the house.

Como was managed by the Armytage women from 1876 until it was purchased by the National Trust in 1959. The house has undergone major restoration work over the years since then. Guided tours run on select dates; check the website for more details.

A SHORT WALK
PARLIAMENT AREA

Distance 1.6 km (1 mile) **Time** 25 minutes
Nearest tram Parliament

The Parliament precinct on Eastern Hill is an area of great historic interest and a lovely place for a stroll. Early founders of the city noted the favourable aspect of the hill and set it aside for Melbourne's official and ecclesiastical buildings. The streets still retain the elegance of the Victorian era; the buildings, constructed with revenue from the gold rush, are among the most impressive in the city. The Fitzroy Gardens, on the lower slopes of the hill, date back to the 1850s and provide a peaceful retreat complete with woodlands, glades, seasonal plantings and magnificent elm tree avenues.

The Renaissance Revival-style **Old Treasury Building** (p233) now holds permanent and temporary exhibitions.

↑ The impressive Victorian-era façade of Hotel Windsor

Did You Know?

Cooks' Cottage was deconstructed brick by brick and packed into 253 cases and 40 barrels.

The **Hotel Windsor**, with its long and ornate façade, was built in 1883 and is the grandest surviving hotel of its era in Australia.

The beautiful bluestone **Stanford Fountain** is the centrepiece of the Gordon Reserve. It was sculpted by the prisoner William Stanford.

ST.

SPRING STREET

MACARTHUR STREET

TREASURY PLACE

LANSDOWNE STREET

WELLINGTON PARADE

Cooks' Cottage, originally built in 1755, was the English home of the parents of Captain James Cook. It was shipped to Australia in 1934 and now houses displays about Cook and 18th-century life.

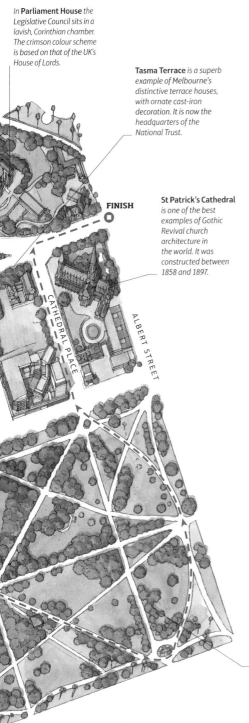

In **Parliament House** the Legislative Council sits in a lavish, Corinthian chamber. The crimson colour scheme is based on that of the UK's House of Lords.

Tasma Terrace is a superb example of Melbourne's distinctive terrace houses, with ornate cast-iron decoration. It is now the headquarters of the National Trust.

FINISH

St Patrick's Cathedral is one of the best examples of Gothic Revival church architecture in the world. It was constructed between 1858 and 1897.

CATHEDRAL PLACE

ALBERT STREET

MELBOURNE

Parliament Area

Locator Map
For more detail see p219

↑ Wandering along a tree-shaded path in the elegant Fitzroy Gardens

| 0 metres | 100 | N |
| 0 yards | 100 | ↗ |

James Sinclair was head gardener when the superb formal **Fitzroy Gardens** were first laid out, featuring follies, winding paths, a fern gulley and avenues of elms.

A SHORT WALK
THE YARRA RIVER

Distance 2.9 km (1.8 miles) **Time** 35 minutes
Nearest tram Flinders Street

The Yarra River winds for 240 km (150 miles) from its source in Baw Baw National Park to the coast, emptying in Port Phillip Bay. The river has always been vital to the city, not just as its major natural feature, but also in early settlement days as its gateway to the rest of the world. Today, the Yarra is a symbol of the boundary between north and south Melbourne and many citizens live their whole lives on one side or the other. Since the 1980s, the rejuvenation of the central section of the river has given the Southbank an important focus. The river is also used for sport: rowers in training are a daily sight and cycle trails run along much of the river. This walking route takes you past many of the Southbank's main attractions.

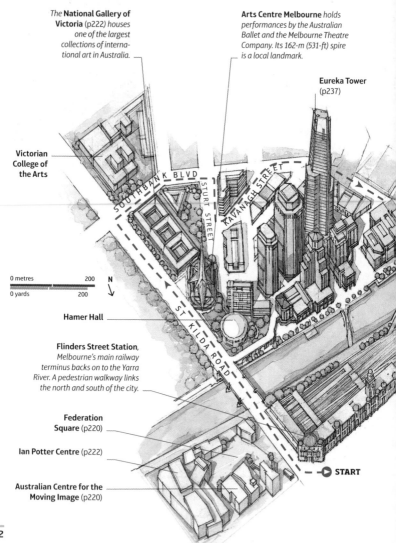

The **National Gallery of Victoria** *(p222) houses one of the largest collections of international art in Australia.*

Arts Centre Melbourne *holds performances by the Australian Ballet and the Melbourne Theatre Company. Its 162-m (531-ft) spire is a local landmark.*

Eureka Tower (p237)

Victorian College of the Arts

SOUTHBANK BLVD

STURT STREET

KAVANAGH STREET

ST KILDA ROAD

0 metres 200
0 yards 200

N

Hamer Hall

Flinders Street Station, *Melbourne's main railway terminus backs on to the Yarra River. A pedestrian walkway links the north and south of the city.*

Federation Square (p220)

Ian Potter Centre (p222)

Australian Centre for the Moving Image (p220)

➤ START

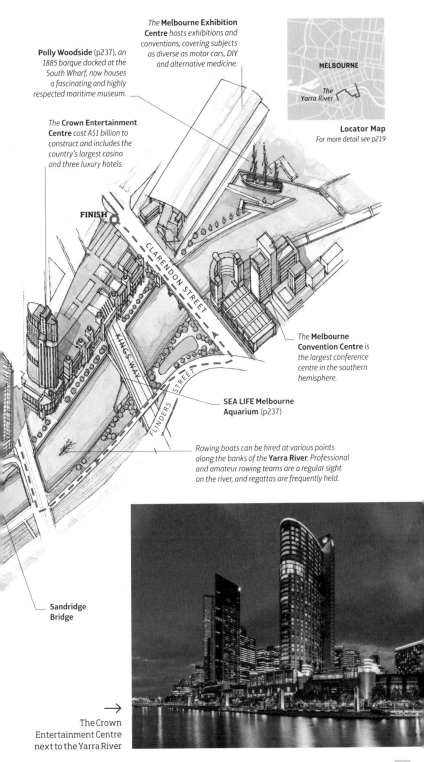

The **Melbourne Exhibition Centre** hosts exhibitions and conventions, covering subjects as diverse as motor cars, DIY and alternative medicine.

Polly Woodside (p237), an 1885 barque docked at the South Wharf, now houses a fascinating and highly respected maritime museum.

The **Crown Entertainment Centre** cost A$1 billion to construct and includes the country's largest casino and three luxury hotels.

MELBOURNE

The Yarra River

Locator Map
For more detail see p219

FINISH

CLARENDON STREET

KINGS WAY

FLINDERS STREET

The **Melbourne Convention Centre** is the largest conference centre in the southern hemisphere.

SEA LIFE Melbourne Aquarium (p237)

Rowing boats can be hired at various points along the banks of the **Yarra River**. Professional and amateur rowing teams are a regular sight on the river, and regattas are frequently held.

Sandridge Bridge

→ The Crown Entertainment Centre next to the Yarra River

THE GREAT OCEAN ROAD AND WESTERN VICTORIA

Western Victoria spans the bare beauty of the semi-arid Mallee in the north to the steep slopes of the Grampians and rugged coastline in the south. For millennia, the First Australians of the northwest gathered for trading and summertime ceremonies near what is now Terang. And in the southwest, the Gunditjmara people established a successful aquaculture, farming fish and eels through a complex network of channels and traps.

It was these bounties of the sea that attracted Victoria's first European settlers, who established ports and towns in the early 1830s to support whaling and fishing along the southwestern coast. This appropriation of land and resources resulted in violent clashes with the Gunditjmara, who were ultimately displaced from their hunting grounds.

Fortune-seeking prospectors descended on the region in the mid-19th century, after gold was discovered in Ballarat in 1851. They were followed soon afterwards by thousands of settlers who set up home in the wheat and sheep belt of the Mallee between 1880 and 1930. Railway lines were constructed and towns built every 16 km (10 miles) in what remains an agricultural heartland. Infrastructure along the coast also expanded with the construction of the Great Ocean Road, which was built to provide employment to returned World War I servicemen. Today it is one of Australia's most celebrated attractions, with a reputation as one of the world's most scenic drives.

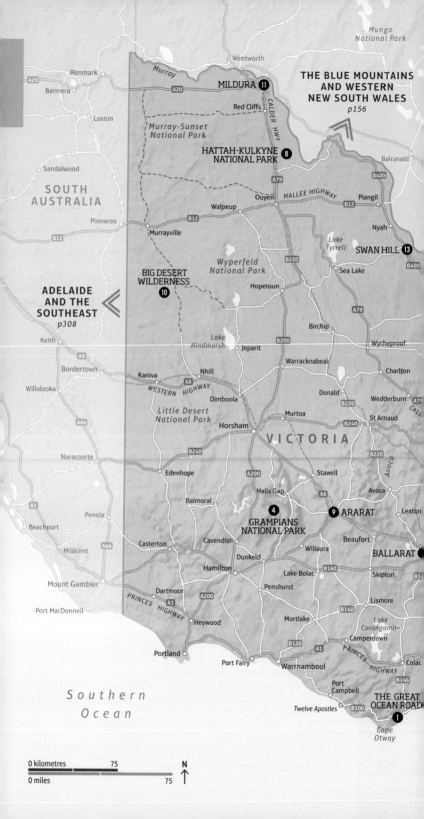

THE GREAT
OCEAN ROAD AND
WESTERN VICTORIA

Must Sees
1 The Great Ocean Road
2 Ballarat
3 Bendigo

Experience More
4 Grampians National Park
5 Werribee Park
6 Bellarine Peninsula
7 Geelong
8 Hattah-Kulkyne National Park
9 Ararat
10 Big Desert Wilderness
11 Mildura
12 Castlemaine
13 Swan Hill
14 Maldon
15 Echuca

THE GREAT OCEAN
ROAD AND
WESTERN VICTORIA

Did You Know?

It took 3,000 World War I soldiers almost 13 years to build the Great Ocean Road by hand.

Cycling along a winding stretch of the magnificent Great Ocean Road shoreline ↑

❶

THE GREAT
OCEAN ROAD

🅰 B7 🏠 Torquay to Allansford 🌐 visitgreatoceanroad.org.au

The Great Ocean Road bucks and weaves along a glorious coastline, following Victoria's southwest shore. Breezy seaside towns, world-class surf beaches, an emerging culinary scene and breathtaking natural wonders can all be found along this stretch of tarmac.

Built as a post-war employment project and as a memorial to those who died in World War I, the Great Ocean Road stands among Australia's elite coastal drives. Spectacular natural landmarks abound, including the much-photographed Twelve Apostles and London Bridge, while lively beach towns, such as Anglesea and Lorne, provide the perfect places to pause. The road also offers plenty of opportunity for wildlife-spotting: look out for koalas along the Kennett River and whales off the coast of Warrnambool.

↑ The Twelve Apostles limestone stacks off the Port Campbell shore

EAT

Aireys Pub
Enjoy locally sourced produce and malty ales at this brewpub.

🏠 45 Great Ocean Rd, Aireys Inlet 🌐 aireys pub.com.au

Lady Bay Restaurant
Dig into seasonal Victorian produce, including pub classics and great seafood.

🏠 2 Pertobe Rd, Warrnambool 🌐 ladybayresort-restaurantand-bar.com.au

↑ Visitors at Australia's oldest-running lighthouse, Cape Otway Lighthouse

↑ Memorial Arch, commemorating the soldiers who built the Great Ocean Road

A DRIVING TOUR
THE GREAT OCEAN ROAD COASTLINE

Length 280 km (174 miles) **Stopping-off points** There are numerous places en route to hop out of the car and soak in the ocean views, go for a swim or grab a bite at a café

The Great Ocean Road is one of the world's great scenic drives. Close to Melbourne, pretty towns are linked by curving roads with striking views at every turn. Inland, the road cuts through the Otways, a forested landscape, ecologically rich and visually splendid. Between Port Campbell and Port Fairy is a landscape of rugged cliffs and swirling seas. The giant eroded monoliths, the Twelve Apostles, in Port Campbell National Park, are an awesome spectacle. To the far west, old whaling ports provide an insight into one of Australia's early industries; at Warrnambool, southern right whales can still be spotted between May and October.

💬 INSIDER TIP
Take it all in

The drive is doable in a day, but rather than rushing to see the major sights, stay overnight en route and allow yourself plenty of time to also visit the many coastal towns and national parks.

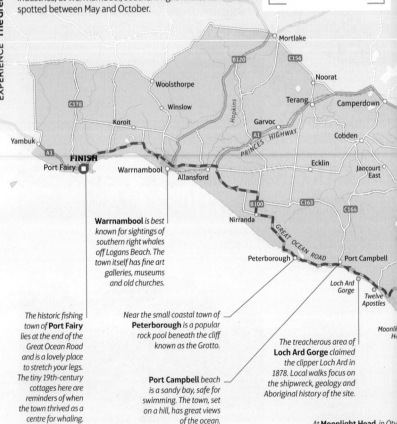

Warrnambool is best known for sightings of southern right whales off Logans Beach. The town itself has fine art galleries, museums and old churches.

The historic fishing town of **Port Fairy** lies at the end of the Great Ocean Road and is a lovely place to stretch your legs. The tiny 19th-century cottages here are reminders of when the town thrived as a centre for whaling.

Near the small coastal town of **Peterborough** is a popular rock pool beneath the cliff known as the Grotto.

Port Campbell beach is a sandy bay, safe for swimming. The town, set on a hill, has great views of the ocean.

The treacherous area of **Loch Ard Gorge** claimed the clipper Loch Ard in 1878. Local walks focus on the shipwreck, geology and Aboriginal history of the site.

At **Moonlight Head**, in Otw[...] National Park, massive cliffs g[...] way to rock platforms. Embed[...] anchors are reminders of the sh[...] lost along this perilous coastl[...]

0 kilometres 20

0 miles 20

N ↑

THE GREAT OCEAN
ROAD AND
WESTERN VICTORIA

*The Great Ocean Road
Coastline*

Locator Map

↑ Split Point Lighthouse overlooking
the coast at Aireys Inlet

Begin your tour at **Bells
Beach**. *Here, a natural
underwater rock platform
contributes to the excellent
surfing conditions. Bells hosts
an international surfing
competition at Easter.*

Aireys Inlet, *a tiny town, is famous
for its red-and-white Split Point
Lighthouse, a filming location for
several movies and TV series. Not
far from here is Memorial Arch,
the road's iconic wooden gateway.*

*The Great Ocean Road leads to
the* **Point Addis** *headland car
park, which has spectacular
views of waves beating the
rocks. There are also steps
leading down the cliff to get
closer to the rolling surf.*

Winchelsea

Moriac

M1

PRINCES HIGHWAY

A1

B100

START

Torquay

Colac

Birregurra

Bells Beach

Anglesea

Point Addis

Deans Marsh

Aireys Inlet

C151

Memorial Arch

Gellibrand

Forrest

C119

Otway Ranges

C155

GREAT OCEAN ROAD

Lorne

C159

Aire

Wye River

Lorne *is a charming
seaside village that
has excellent cafés
and restaurants. The
nearby forests provide
a paradise for walkers.*

Lavers Hill

B100

Wongarra

Skenes Creek

Apollo Bay

Johanna
Beach

Cape
Otway

Fishing is the main activity at
Apollo Bay, *and fishing trips
can be taken from the town's
wharf. The town itself has a
relaxed village atmosphere
and good restaurants.*

Johanna Beach, *another
of Victoria's renowned surf
beaches, is backed by
rolling green hills. The area
is quite remote, but popular
with campers in summer.*

Did You Know?

At least 638
shipwrecks lie off-
shore from the Great
Ocean Road.

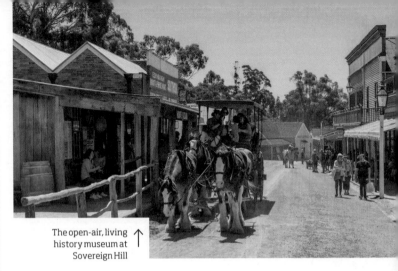

The open-air, living history museum at Sovereign Hill ↑

The Great Ocean Road and Western Victoria

EXPERIENCE

BALLARAT

🅰 B7 ➡ 12 km (7 miles) from city centre 🚉 Lydiard St
🚌 Ballarat Railway Station ℹ Ballarat Town Hall, 225 Sturt St; www.visitballarat.com.au

In 1851, the cry of "Gold!" shattered the tranquillity of this pastoral district. Within months, thousands of fortune-seekers poured into the area, transforming Ballarat from a peaceful sheep station into a bustling city. Although the gold rush petered out in the late 1870s, the two decades of wealth can still be seen in the city's lavish buildings, broad streets and ornate statuary.

① Lydiard Street

The wealth of the gold fields is reflected in Lydiard Street's well-proportioned streetscape, which is lined with buildings of exemplary quality and design.

At the northern end lies the railway station. Built in 1862, it features an arched train entrance and Tuscan pilasters. Nearby, a neat row of four banks was designed by prominent architect Leonard Terry whose concern for a balanced streetscape is clearly expressed in their elegant façades. Then there's Her Majesty's Theatre, a handsome venue in continuous operation since 1875, which is opposite the historic Craig's Royal Hotel.

② Art Gallery of Ballarat

🏛 40 Lydiard St North ⏰ 10am–5pm daily 📅 25 & 26 Dec 🌐 artgalleryof ballarat.com.au

This stunning art gallery has gained a reputation as the largest and arguably best

Did You Know?

The city has the greatest concentration of public statuary in any Australian city.

provincial art institution in Australia. More than 11,000 works chart the course of Australian art from colonial to contemporary times. Look out for works by gold field artists, such as Eugene von Guerard, whose work *Old Ballarat as it was in the summer of 1853–54* is an extraordinary evocation of the town's early tent cities. The gallery hosts cutting-edge temporary exhibitions as well.

③ Eureka Centre

🏛 102 Stawell St ⏰ 10am–5pm daily 🌐 eurekacentre ballarat.com.au

Occupying the site of the 1854 Battle of the Eureka Stockade, this museum tells the story of the miners' rebellion against unfair working conditions. The rebellion was a formative moment in Australian democracy, and is widely seen as the starting point for workers' rights in the country. Since the battle, the blue-and-white Eureka flag – part of the Art Gallery of Ballarat's collection and currently on loan to the town hall – symbolizes egalitarianism but has been hijacked by the country's far-right movements. Many Australians are uncomfortable with its usage.

diggers' huts, tents, old meeting places and the Chinese Village. (Many of the miners were Chinese immigrants, who chose to stay once the gold rush ended.)

This site also includes the nearby Gold Museum, which focuses on the uses of gold throughout history.

To visit Sovereign Hill, book tickets in advance online.

---

⑤ Ⓜ Ballarat Botanical Gardens

🏛 Wendouree Parade ⏰ Hours vary, check website 🚫 25 Dec 🌐 ballaratbotanical gardens.com.au

These gardens speak of Ballarat's pursuit of Victorian gentility. The rough-and-ready atmosphere of the gold fields could be easily overlooked here among the statues, lush green lawns and a wide variety of plants. The focus of the gardens has always been aesthetic rather than botanical, although four different displays are exhibited each

Must See

STAY

Craig's Royal Hotel
This 1860s hotel has hosted many famous guests, including British royalty. To fully appreciate its grandeur, book a table for High Tea.

🏛 10 Lydiard St
🌐 craigsroyal.com.au

$$$

year in the Robert Clark Conservatory. The most famous of these is the lovely begonia display, part of the Begonia Festival held here each March.

As well as plants, the gardens are home to some impressive statuary. In the Statuary Pavilion, Classical figures in provocative poses circle the splendid centrepiece, *Flight from Pompeii*. There is also the Avenue of Prime Ministers, a double row of staggered busts of every Australian prime minister to date.

---

④ ✏ Ⓜ Sovereign Hill

🏛 Bradshaw St ⏰ 10am-5pm Tue-Sun 🚫 25 Dec 🌐 sovereignhill.com.au

Sovereign Hill is the gold fields' living museum and offers visitors the chance to explore this period of Australia's history. Blacksmiths, hoteliers, bakers and grocers in period dress ply their trades on the main streets, amid the re-created

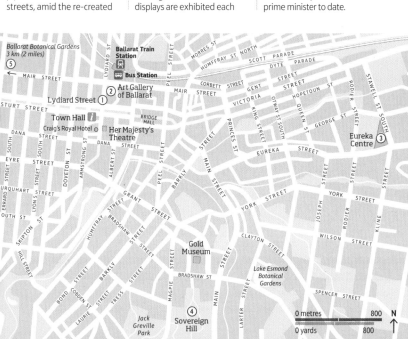

BENDIGO

🅰C6 ✈🚆🚌 ℹ 51-67 Pall Mall; www.bendigotourism.com

Bendigo celebrated the gold rush like no other city, and with good reason – the finds here were legendary. In 1851, the first year of gold mining, 23 kg (50 lbs) of gold were extracted from only one bucketful of dirt. When the surface gold began to disappear, the discovery of a gold-rich quartz reef in the 1870s reignited the boom. As the wealth of the city's residents grew, so did the scale and extravagance of Bendigo's buildings. Learn more about the city's architecture, and changing fortunes, on the self-guided heritage walk from the information centre or the vintage "talking tram".

①
Joss House

🏠 Finn St, Emu Point
🕐 10:30am–3pm Sat & Sun
🌐 bendigojosshouse.com

A pillar of Bendigo's Chinese community since it was built in 1871, this bright-red temple is both a historical landmark and a functioning temple. It's the only survivor of seven such temples that were built to serve the large number of Chinese miners who settled here during the gold-rush era.

BENDIGO'S HERITAGE TRAMS

Melbourne's trams may be better known, but Bendigo's are just as charming. As you trundle around town in an atmospheric streetcar, hopping on and off as you please, this "talking tram" tells you about the city's history, pointing out interesting sights along the way (www.bendigotram ways.com). Blues fan? Ride the tram while tapping your feet to local blues and roots artists; check for upcoming live music events on the website (www.bendigo tramways.com/tours/ blues-tram).

②
Golden Dragon Museum

🏠 1-11 Bridge St 🕐 9:30am–5pm Tue–Sun 🌐 golden dragonmuseum.org

In the middle of the 19th century, one-fifth of Bendigo's population identified as Chinese and the community continues to play an important role in city life. Opened in 1991, the Golden Dragon Museum charts the history of Bendigo's Chinese community, from the first settlers to their millennial descendants, as well as exploring the lives of those who settled elsewhere in Victoria's gold fields and beyond. The extraordinary collection is made up of thousands of objects, textiles, photographs, records and oral histories, including an impressive collection of processional dragons. Look out for the world's longest dragon, which measures an incredible 125 m (410 ft) long. After taking in the collection, head out to the Yi Yuan Gardens, which were modelled on those at Beijing's Imperial Palace.

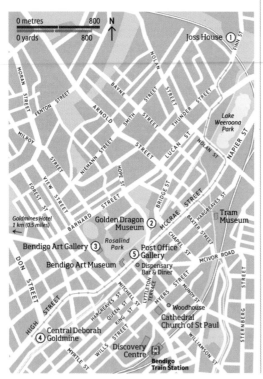

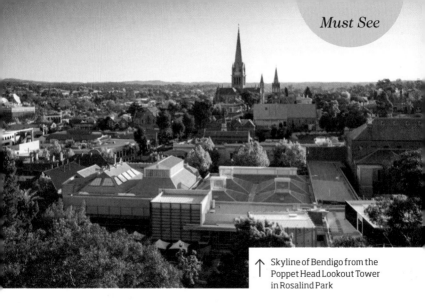

↑ Skyline of Bendigo from the Poppet Head Lookout Tower in Rosalind Park

Did You Know?

More than 700,000 kg (700 tonnes) of gold was dug up around Bendigo during the gold rush.

 ③

Bendigo Art Gallery

🏠 42 View St 🕐 10am–5pm daily 🚫 25 Dec 🌐 bendigoregion.com.au/bendigo-art-gallery

Founded in 1887, Bendigo Art Gallery is one of Australia's oldest and most respected regional art galleries. Its stellar collection has an emphasis on 19th-century European and Australian art, as well as contemporary local pieces. The paintings, sculptures, ceramics, decorative arts and photography on display include works by Australian artists Brett Whiteley, Russell Drysdale and Arthur Boyd.

The gallery is also known for its impressive calendar of temporary exhibitions. Check the website to see what's on.

④

Central Deborah Goldmine

🏠 76 Violet St 🕐 9:30am–4:30pm daily 🌐 central-deborah.com

To understand what life was really like for Bendigo's miners, there's nothing better than going deep underground yourself. A fully operational mine during the gold rush, the Central Deborah Goldmine is now an interactive museum, where visitors can pan for gold, admire a replica of the Hand of Faith (a 27-kg/60-lb gold nugget discovered nearby) and descend 228 m (748 ft) beneath the surface into an old mine.

⑤

Post Office Gallery

🏠 51-67 Pall Mall 🕐 9am–5pm daily 🌐 bendigoregion.com.au/bendigo-art-gallery/post-office-gallery

This grand building is a satellite space of Bendigo Art Gallery and hosts an exciting exhibition programme of local history, arts and crafts.

EAT

Gold Mines Hotel

This restaurant serves local meat dishes using traditional wood-fired cooking techniques.

🏠 49-57 Marong Rd 🌐 goldmineshotel.com

$$⑤

Woodhouse

Steaks are smoked with red gum here and it makes all the difference.

🏠 101 Williamson St 🌐 thewoodhouse.com.au

$$$

DRINK

Dispensary Bar & Diner

Choose from over 100 craft beers, 80 single malts, 70 types of gin and as many cocktails at this popular bar.

🏠 9 Chancery Lane 🌐 dispensarybendigo.com

The Pinnacle, rising above a vast expanse of Western Victoria, Grampians National Park ↑

EXPERIENCE MORE

4

Grampians National Park

 B7 🚇 Stawell 🚌 Halls Gap 🛈 Brambuk National Park and Cultural Centre, 277 Grampians Rd, Halls Gap; www.parks.vic.gov.au

The mountains, cliffs and sheer rock faces of the Grampians rise like a series of waves above the flat western plains. Within this national park, the third largest in Victoria, is a remarkable diversity of wildlife and natural features.

There are craggy slopes, cascading waterfalls and sandstone mountaintops, all formed 400 million years ago by an upthrust of the earth's crust. It has been known as *Gariwerd* for thousands of years to local Aboriginal peoples, for whom it is a sacred place, and 80 per cent of Victoria's Aboriginal rock art is here. The Brambuk National Park and Cultural Centre in Halls Gap displays the region's Aboriginal cultures through multimedia exhibits and artifacts and is partly run by local Aboriginal communities who conduct tours to the sites.

The Grampians offer many different experiences for visitors. Day trips take in the spectacular MacKenzie Falls and the Balconies rock formation. Longer stays offer bush camping, wildflower studies, exploration of the Victoria Valley over the mountains from Halls Gap and overnight hiking trips in the south of the park. Experienced rock climbers come from around the world to tackle the

Did You Know?

MacKenzie Falls, in the Grampians National Park, is the largest waterfall in Victoria.

challenging rock forms in the park and also at the nearby Mount Arapiles.

Excellent maps of the area and guides to the best walks are all available at the park's visitors' centre.

5

Werribee Park

 C7 🚗 K Rd, Werribee 🚇 Werribee 🕐 Daily 🌐 parks.vic.gov.au

From 1860 until 1890, the wool boom made millionaires of Australia's sheep farmers, with the Chirnside family of Werribee Park and later of Victoria's Western District among the richest and most powerful. Their former mansion is a striking Italianate house, built between 1874 and 1877. It has now been restored to reflect the lifestyle of wealthy pastoral families. A wing added in the 1930s has been converted into a luxury hotel.

6

Bellarine Peninsula

🅰C7 🚌Geelong 🅸1251-1269 Bellarine Hwy, Wallington; www.visit geelongbellarine.com.au

At the western entrance to Port Phillip Bay, the Bellarine Peninsula is one of the city's summer resorts. The golden-sand beaches of Barwon Heads, Point Lonsdale and Ocean Grove mark the start of the Great Ocean Road (p248) and its famous surf beaches.

The village of Point Lonsdale lies at the entrance to the Heads – it was once considered Australia's most dangerous harbour entrance, and is still Victoria's most hazardous beach due to its rough seas and whirlpools. Across the swirling water (known as the Rip) is Point Nepean. It is on the Mornington Peninsula in Eastern Victoria (p271), only 3 km (2 miles) from Point Lonsdale.

The town of Queenscliff faces Port Phillip Bay so its beaches are calm. During the 1880s, Queenscliff was a fashionable resort for Melburnians – its elegant hotels, such as the Vue Grand, are reminders of that opulent era. St Leonards and Portarlington are also popular holiday villages.

The peninsula has around 20 wineries, most offering cellar door sales and tastings.

7

Geelong

🅰C7 🚆🚌 🅸26-32 Moorabool St; www.visit geelongbellarine.com.au

The second-largest city in the state, Geelong has a rural and industrial past. Located on Corio Bay, the city offers many

DRINK

Basils Farm
Set on the Bellarine Peninsula, this winery is known for its Prosecco, Chardonnay and Pinot Noir. Sample the wines with a meal at Basils Café or head to the cellar door for tastings.

🅰C7 🅰43-53 Nye Rd, Swan Bay Ⓦbasilsfarm. com.au

recreational activities thanks to its waterfront precinct and surf beaches.

The wooden 1930s bathing complex at Eastern Beach, with its lawns, sandy beach and shady trees, was restored to its former Art Deco glory in 1994. Steampacket Place and Pier were part of an extensive redevelopment project that saw the gradual renovation of the old warehouses into a thriving waterfront quarter filled with excellent seafood restaurants, cafés, shops and hotels. Opposite Steampacket Place are the historic wool stores, with the largest housing the award-winning **National Wool Museum**. It traces Australia's wool heritage from the shearing shed to the fashion catwalks.

A short drive from Geelong is the Brisbane Ranges National Park, near Anakie, with lovely walks and native wildflowers. Nearby is Steiglitz, a ghost town from the 1850s gold rush. Few buildings remain of this once thriving town, among them is the elegant 1870s courthouse, which is closed to the public.

National Wool Museum
⊚⊜ 🅰26-32 Moorabool St 🕙10am-3pm daily 🅲Good Fri, 25 & 26 Dec Ⓦgeelong australia.com.au/nwm

---

Next to the mansion and its formal gardens, which are a popular picnic area, is the Victoria State Rose Garden. Laid out in a symbolic Tudor Rose-shaped design, it contains more than 5,000 rose bushes of different varieties and colours that bloom from October to May. Also attached to Werribee Park is **Werribee Park National Equestrian Centre**. The largest equestrian centre in Victoria, it houses two large indoor areas, multiple outdoor arenas, polo fields, 180 stables and 250 campsites. It also hosts some of Australia's premier show-jumping and polo events. For bird-watchers, the nearby Western Treatment Plant and the Point Cook Coastal Park offer magnificent views of rare bird species.

Werribee Park National Equestrian Centre
⊛⊛ 🕙Hours vary, check website Ⓦwpnec.com.au

> **The golden-sand beaches of Barwon Heads, Point Lonsdale and Ocean Grove on the Bellarine Peninsula mark the start of the Great Ocean Road.**

8

Hattah-Kulkyne National Park

B6 Mildura
Mildura; www.parks.vic.gov.au

Unlike its drier Mallee region counterparts, Hattah-Kulkyne National Park has many lakes that are linked to the mighty Murray River through a complex billabong (natural water hole) overflow system.

Its perimeters are typical dry Mallee country of low scrub, mallee trees and native pine woodland, but the large lakes, including Hattah, Lockie and Mournpoul, are alive with

---

HATTAH LAKES

The national park's 20 freshwater lakes are part of a wetlands eco-system. The lakes fill seasonally by creeks connected to the Murray River. Since 2010, after years of drought, the Australian government had to pump 11 billion litres (2.4 billion gal) of water into the lakes, through a long process known as environmental watering. More recently, regular rainfall has allowed fish and waterbirds to thrive.

---

bird and animal life. Ringed by massive red gums, the surrounding habitat is home to an abundance of emus, goanna lizards and kangaroos. The freshwater lakes teem with fish, while ibis, pelicans, black swans and other waterbirds flock on the surface and surrounding shores.

The lakes are ideal for canoeing, and the twisting wetlands and billabongs along the Murray River and in the Murray-Kulkyne section of the park make for fine fishing, picnics, camping and bird-watching spots.

9

Ararat

B7 82 Vincent St; www.ararat.vic.gov.au

Just over 200 km (124 miles) northwest of Melbourne, the city of Ararat is situated close to both Grampians National Park (p256) and Victoria's gold fields, and it's to the latter that the town owes its existence. Ararat is located on the lands of the Djab Wurrung Aboriginal peoples but in 1857, soon after Chinese miners discovered gold nearby, it became Australia's only Chinese-built town. The story of this heritage is told at the **Gum San Chinese**

> The freshwater lakes at Hattah-Kulkyne National Park teem with fish, while ibis, black swans and other waterbirds flock on the surface.

Heritage Centre, which has exhibitions on the experience of Chinese miners and immigrants in the 19th century, as well as information on the community's ongoing presence in the area.

Gum San Chinese Heritage Centre
31-33 Lambert St
10am-3pm Thu-Sun & public hols 25 Dec
ararat.vic.gov.au

10

Big Desert Wilderness

B6 Hopetoun 75 Lascelles St, Hopetoun; www.parks.vic.gov.au

Victoria is so often seen as the state of mountains, green hills, river valleys and beaches that many visitors don't realize that a large part of the west of the state consists of mallee scrubland and arid desert. These are areas of beauty and solitude, with

sand hills, dwarf she-oaks, lizards, snakes and dry creek systems. Big Desert Wilderness Park and Murray-Sunset National Park are true deserts, with hot days and freezing nights. The latter is also home to the endangered black-eared miner, as well as Victoria's largest flower, the Murray lily.

To the south, Wyperfeld and Little Desert national parks are not true deserts, as they contain lake systems that support diverse flora and fauna, including a variety of reptiles.

The 19th-century Queen Anne-style house Rio Vista in Mildura, and *(inset)* its restored interiors ↑

River, situated in the middle of a red sandy desert. That year, two Canadian brothers, William and George Chaffey, came to town directly from their successful irrigation project in California and began the first large-scale irrigation scheme in Australia. Since their efforts, the red soil, fed by the Murray and Darling rivers, has become

a expansive plain of farms stretching for nearly 100 km (60 miles).

Today, Mildura is a modern city with a thriving tourist trade. The former home of William Chaffey, the **Rio Vista**, is worth a visit. Built in 1890, it has been restored with its original furnishings and is now an Arts Centre.

Grapes, olives, avocados and citrus fruit are grown successfully in the region and the area is rapidly expanding its vineyards and wineries. The stark desert of Mungo National Park is only 100 km (60 miles) to the northeast of town.

 Mildura

🅰B6 ➡🚌🚏 🚉180-190 Deakin Ave; www.midura.vic.gov.au

In 1887, Mildura was little more than a village on the banks of the Murray

 ←

Scrubland surrounding one of the freshwater lakes in Hattah-Kulkyne National Park

 INSIDER TIP
Hit the Beach

Mildura may be more than 400 km (249 miles) from the coast, but you can still spend a day at the beach. Just a few minutes' drive from the city centre, Apex River Beach Holiday Park *(www.apexriverbeach. com.au)* has a long sandy beach on a bend of the Murray River.

Rio Vista

♿ 🏠199 Cureton Ave
🕙10am–5pm daily 🚫Good Fri, 25 Dec 🌐milduraarts centre.com.au

↑ Pioneer Settlement Museum, a re-creation of a 19th-century river town in Swan Hill

Castlemaine

🅰B7 🚃🚌 ℹ️ Market Bldg, 44 Mostyn St; www.bendigo region.com.au

The elegance of this small city reflects the fact that gold finds here were brief but extremely prosperous. The finest attraction is the Palladian-style Market Hall, built in 1862. It has a portico and a large arched entrance leading into its restrained interior. The building is now the Visitors' Information Centre.

Buda Historic Home and Garden was occupied from 1863 to 1981 by two generations of Hungarian silversmith Ernest Leviny and his family. The house displays an extensive collection of arts and crafts works. The property is known for its 19th-century garden.

Castlemaine is also home to many writers and artists from Melbourne and has lively cafés, restaurants and museums.

The **Victorian Goldfields Railway** is a steam heritage train linking Castlemaine with

Did You Know?

Australia's longest river, the Murray runs for 2,508 km (1,558 miles), via NSW, Victoria and South Australia.

its neighbour Maldon. Running alongside the railway line is a scenic cycle trail.

Buda Historic Home and Garden

🖐️ 🅰42 Hunter St 🕐 Hours vary, check website 🕑 Good Fri, 25 Dec 🔘 budacastle maine.org

Victorian Goldfields Railway

🖐️🔘🔘 🔘 vgr.com.au

Swan Hill

🅰B6 🚃🚌 ℹ️ Cnr McCrae & Curlewis sts; www.swan hill.vic.gov.au

Black swans are noisy birds, as the explorer Major Thomas Mitchell discovered in 1836 when his sleep was disturbed by their early morning calls on the banks of the Murray River. That's how the vibrant river town of Swan Hill got its name, and the black swans are still a prominent feature.

One of the most popular attractions of Swan Hill is the **Pioneer Settlement Museum**, a 3-ha (7-acre) living and working re-creation of a river town in the Murray-Mallee area during the period from

1830 to 1930. The settlement buzzes with the sound of printing presses, the blacksmith's hammer and general daily life. "Residents" dress in period clothes and produce old-fashioned goods to sell to tourists. Some of the log buildings are made of Murray pine, a hardwood tree impenetrable to termites. The sound-and-light show at night (bookings essential) is particularly evocative, providing a 45-minute journey through the town with sound effects, such as pounding hooves and a thundering steam locomotive.

Pioneer Settlement Museum

🖐️🔘 🅰125 Monash Dr 🕐9:30am–4:30pm daily 🕑25 & 26 Dec 🔘 pioneer settlement.com.au

Maldon

🅰C7 🚃🚌 ℹ️ 93 High St; www.maldon.org.au

The perfectly preserved town of Maldon offers an

→

The restored paddle steamer PS *Britannia* docked on the Murray River, Echuca

outstanding experience of an early gold-mining settlement. This tiny town is set within one of the loveliest landscapes of the region. The hills, forests and superb trees are an attractive setting for the narrow streets and 19th-century buildings. Maldon was declared Australia's "First Notable Town" by the National Trust in 1966. Cafés, galleries and museums cater to the stream of tourists.

Other attractions include Carman's Tunnel, an old gold mine, and a round-trip ride aboard the Victorian Goldfields Railway to Muckleford and Castlemaine. Visit at Easter to see the glorious golden leaves of the plane, oak and elm trees. There is also an Easter Fair, including an Easter parade and a street carnival.

> **The perfectly preserved town of Maldon offers an outstanding experience of an early gold-mining settlement.**

THE MURRAY RIVER PADDLE STEAMERS

Between the 1860s and 1880s, Australia's economy "rode on the sheep's back" – from Victoria to central Queensland, wool was king. But the only way to transport it from remote sheep stations to coastal ports was by river, so paddle steamers regularly plied the Murray, Murrumbidgee and Darling river systems. Towing barges loaded with wool, they reached the Port of Echuca after sailing for days from inland Australia. However, by the 1890s railway lines had crept into the interior and the era of the paddle steamer was gone. Now the Port of Echuca is once again home to paddle steamers, such as the restored PS *Adelaide* and PS *Success* (www.portofechuca.org.au).

Echuca

🅰C6 🚉🚌 ℹ2 Heygarth St; www.echucamoama.com

Ex-convict and entrepreneur Henry Hopwood travelled to the Murray River region in 1853, at the end of his prison sentence. He seized upon the need for a river punt at the Echuca crossing by setting up a ferry service, as well as the Bridge Hotel. However, Echuca really came into its own in 1864 when the railway from Melbourne reached the port. Suddenly the town, with its paddle steamers on the river, became the largest inland port in Australia. Today, the port area features horse-drawn carriages, working steam engines and old-fashioned timber mills. Tours of the area are available, along with regular river trips on a paddle steamer. Visit the Star Hotel and discover the secret tunnel that let patrons leave after hours. There is also a paddle steamer display opposite the hotel.

Around 30 km (19 miles) upstream from Echuca is Barmah Forest, the largest red gum forest in the world. A drive in the forest, with its 500-year-old river red gums and important Aboriginal sites, is highly recommended, as is the wetlands ecocruise that operates out of Barmah (www. botanicatours.com).

A DRIVING TOUR
DAYLESFORD AND THE MACEDON RANGES

Length 215 km (133 miles) **Stopping-off points** There are numerous places to stay and eat along the route, particularly at Woodend and Daylesford

Daylesford and the Macedon Ranges lie to the northwest of Melbourne. The landscape is dotted with vineyards, small townships, craft markets and bed-and-breakfasts. This tour follows the Calder Highway, once taken by gold prospectors to the alluvial fields of Castlemaine and Bendigo, before heading west into the spa country around Daylesford. The region's wealthy past is reflected in the 19th-century bluestone buildings, including wool stores and stately homes.

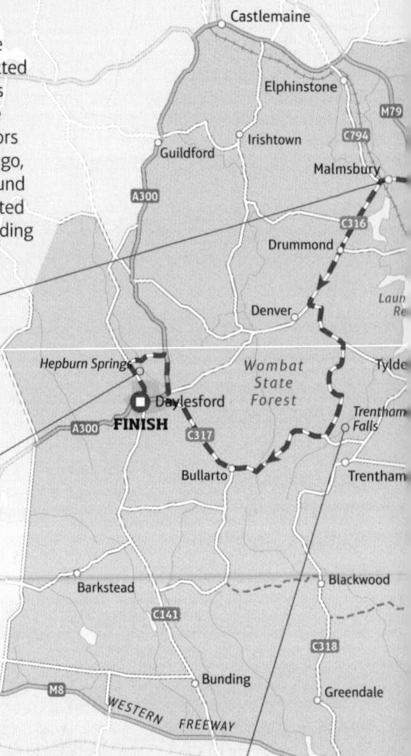

During the gold rush, the peaceful hamlet of **Malmsbury** was a busy stop for prospectors on their way to the gold fields.

The **Hepburn Mineral Springs Reserve** is a large area of native bushland. It is an idyllic place for walkers and those who want to "take the waters" from the old-fashioned pumps.

Castlemaine

Elphinstone

M79

Irishtown   C794

Guildford

Malmsbury

A300

C316

Drummond

Denver   Laun Re

Hepburn Springs

Wombat State Forest   Tylde

Daylesford   Trentham Falls

A300   **FINISH**   C317

Bullarto   Trentham

Barkstead   Blackwood

C141

C318

Bunding   Greendale

M8   WESTERN FREEWAY

Trentham Falls, Central Victoria's largest single-drop falls at 33 m (108 ft) high, are a few minutes' walk from Falls Road.

← The impressive Trentham Falls thundering over a basalt cliff

Did You Know?

This area has the richest concentration of natural mineral springs in Australia.

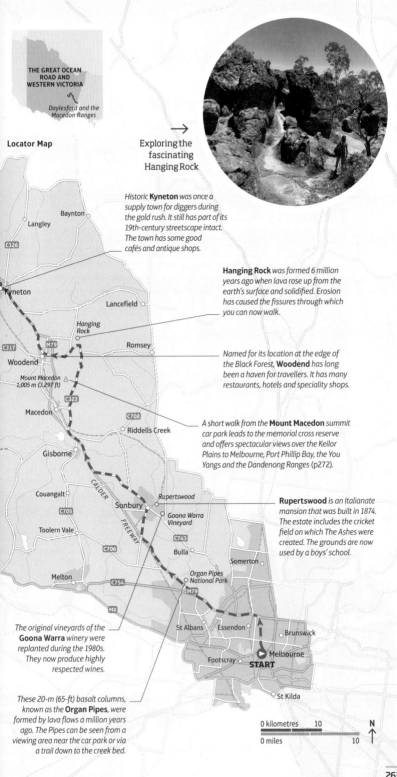

Locator Map

→

Exploring the fascinating Hanging Rock

Historic **Kyneton** was once a supply town for diggers during the gold rush. It still has part of its 19th-century streetscape intact. The town has some good cafés and antique shops.

Hanging Rock was formed 6 million years ago when lava rose up from the earth's surface and solidified. Erosion has caused the fissures through you can now walk.

Named for its location at the edge of the Black Forest, **Woodend** has long been a haven for travellers. It has many restaurants, hotels and speciality shops.

A short walk from the **Mount Macedon** summit car park leads to the memorial cross reserve and offers spectacular views over the Keilor Plains to Melbourne, Port Phillip Bay, the You Yangs and the Dandenong Ranges (p272).

Rupertswood is an Italianate mansion that was built in 1874. The estate includes the cricket field on which The Ashes were created. The grounds are now used by a boys' school.

The original vineyards of the **Goona Warra** winery were replanted during the 1980s. They now produce highly respected wines.

These 20-m (65-ft) basalt columns, known as the **Organ Pipes**, were formed by lava flows a million years ago. The Pipes can be seen from a viewing area near the car park or via a trail down to the creek bed.

Langley · Baynton · Kyneton · Lancefield · Hanging Rock · Romsey · Woodend · Mount Macedon 1,005 m (3,297 ft) · Macedon · Riddells Creek · Gisborne · Couangalt · Toolern Vale · Sunbury · Rupertswood · Goona Warra Vineyard · Bulla · Somerton · Melton · Organ Pipes National Park · St Albans · Essendon · Brunswick · Footscray · Melbourne START · St Kilda

C326 · C317 · M79 · C322 · C708 · CALDER FREEWAY · C705 · C743 · C706 · C754 · M8 · M79

0 kilometres 10
0 miles 10

N ↑

EASTERN VICTORIA AND THE HIGH COUNTRY

Eastern Victoria centres around the Victorian Alps, the southwestern portion of the Australian Alps. Aboriginal peoples from different tribes would meet on the peaks to trade, settle disputes and hold ceremonies; and on the high plains in summer to feast on the Bogong moth. Early European settlers were also seasonal visitors, retreating from the area's grazing lands and gold mines once the winter drew harsh. The region was relatively disconnected until a series of railways and roads, including the Great Alpine Road, were built in the early 20th century when the demand for timber grew frenzied due to the post-war population boom.

It was around this time that Victorians started enjoying snow sports, with the government building Mount Buffalo chalet and ski field in 1910. Driven predominantly by ski clubs, winter sports grew slowly at first, but took off in the 1960s, when Austrian immigrants like Hans Grimus and Peter Zirknitzer opened rental businesses and lodges in the area. Today, Australians and visitors flock here in the winter to downhill ski among the snow gums at village resorts such as Mount Buller and Falls Creek.

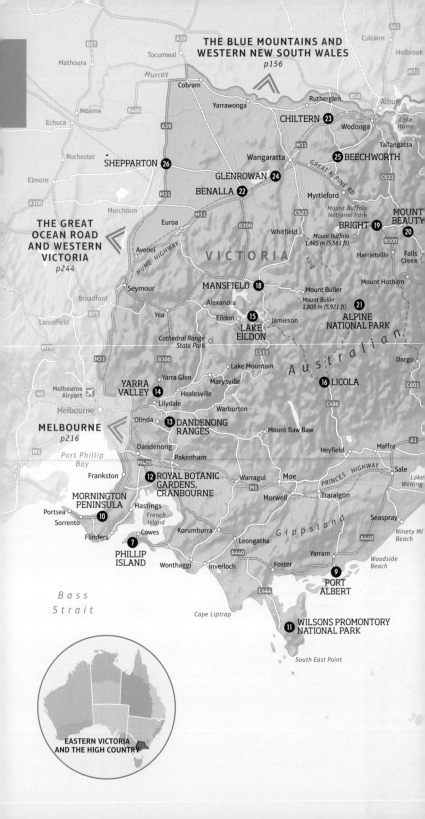

THE BLUE MOUNTAINS AND
WESTERN NEW SOUTH WALES
p156

Culcairn

Holbrook

Mathoura

Tocumwal

B57

A39

A41

B31

Moama

Murray

Cobram

Rutherglen

B58

Albury

Echuca

B400

Yarrawonga

Wodonga

Lake
Hume

Rochester

CHILTERN 23

Taltangatta

Elmore

A39

SHEPPARTON 26

Wangaratta

M31

BEECHWORTH 25

Murchison

Glenrowan 24

GREAT ALPINE RD

B531

A300

BENALLA 22

Myrtleford

C521

Mount Buffalo
National Park

MOUNT
BEAUTY 20

Euroa

B300

Whitfield

BRIGHT 19

THE GREAT
OCEAN ROAD
AND WESTERN
VICTORIA
p244

HUME HIGHWAY

Avenel

Mount Buffalo
1,695 m (5,561 ft)

Harrietville

B500

Seymour

V I C T O R I A

King

Falls
Creek

Broadford

MANSFIELD 18

Mount Buller

Mount Hotham

Lancefield

B75

Alexandra

Mount Buller
1,805 m (5,921 ft)

ALPINE
NATIONAL
PARK 21

Yea

Eildon

LAKE
EILDON 15

Jamieson

Australian

M79

Cathedral Range
State Park

C511

Dargo

M31

B300

Lake Mountain

A8

Melbourne
Airport

YARRA
VALLEY 14

Yarra Glen

Marysville

LICOLA 16

C601

Lilydale

Healesville

C486

Melbourne

Olinda

DANDENONG
RANGES 13

Warburton

MELBOURNE
p216

M1

Dandenong

Mount Baw Baw

Heyfield

Maffra

A1

Port Phillip
Bay

M420

Pakenham

PRINCES HIGHWAY

Sale

ROYAL BOTANIC
GARDENS,
CRANBOURNE 12

Warragul

Moe

Lake
Welling

Frankston

M1

Traralgon

Morwell

MORNINGTON
PENINSULA 10

Hastings

Seaspray

Portsea

French
Island

Korumburra

Ninety Mi
Beach

Sorrento

Cowes

Leongatha

A440

Flinders

Gippsland

Woodside
Beach

PHILLIP
ISLAND 7

Wonthaggi

Inverloch

Foster

Yarram

PORT
ALBERT 9

B a s s
Strait

C444

Cape Liptrap

WILSONS PROMONTORY
NATIONAL PARK 11

South East Point

EASTERN VICTORIA
AND THE HIGH COUNTRY

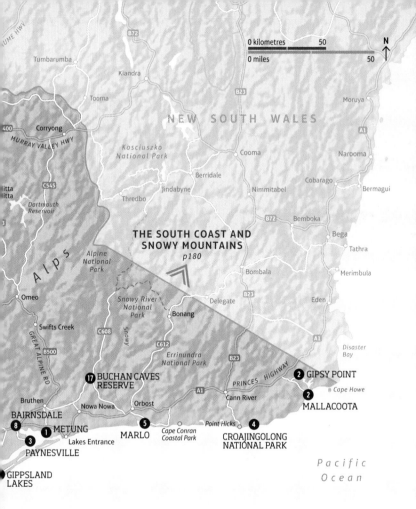

EASTERN VICTORIA
AND THE HIGH COUNTRY

Experience

1 Metung
2 Gipsy Point and Mallacoota
3 Paynesville
4 Croajingolong National Park
5 Marlo
6 Gippsland Lakes
7 Phillip Island
8 Bairnsdale
9 Port Albert
10 Mornington Peninsula
11 Wilsons Promontory National Park
12 Royal Botanic Gardens, Cranbourne
13 Dandenong Ranges
14 Yarra Valley
15 Lake Eildon
16 Licola
17 Buchan Caves Reserve
18 Mansfield
19 Bright
20 Mount Beauty
21 Alpine National Park
22 Benalla
23 Chiltern
24 Glenrowan
25 Beechworth
26 Shepparton

EXPERIENCE

1

Metung

 C7 www.visiteastgippsland.com.au

Metung is one of the loveliest towns anywhere along the Gippsland coastline. It is spread across a hilly peninsula and encompassed by water on three sides. The town has a few cafés, a pub, a village green and a coastal boardwalk, all surrounded by eucalyptus trees that draw plenty of birds.

It is a quieter, more charming alternative to the nearby Lakes Entrance township. Boating excursions are a popular way to explore the lakes and estuaries around. Metung is popular among locals and it's enjoyed as a slightly upscale coastal retreat for visitors from Melbourne.

Did You Know?

In the language of the Gunaikurnai people, Metung translates as "mainland" or "ti-tree river bend".

2

Gipsy Point and Mallacoota

 D7 70 Maurice Ave; www.visitmallacoota.com.au

These two settlements on the Gippsland coastline are easily accessible off Princes Highway despite being isolated towns.

With its calm waterways and densely forested tracts, Gipsy Point is great for bird-watching, bushwalking and picnicking in the summer. Mallacoota, by contrast, is a quintessential coastal town, with cafés and supermarkets. There are also opportunities for boating here.

Both suffered terribly during the bushfires in 2019 and 2020, but the area had begun to recover within months.

3

Paynesville

 C7 Bairnsdale 240 Main St, Bairnsdale; www.visitpaynesville.com.au

This appealing coastal town acts as a gateway for Ninety Mile Beach, Raymond Island

PICTURE PERFECT
Koala-rama

Catch the ferry from Paynesville to Raymond Island, home to one of the largest koala colonies in the country. Keep a respectful distance and zoom in to capture a joey on a mother's back.

and the wider Gippsland Lakes region. It was founded in 1879 and was originally known by the local Aboriginal name, Toonalook (meaning "the place of many fish").

The 3-km (2-mile) Sunset Cove Walk is perfect for a stroll. Look out for pelicans and dolphins. Swimming, fishing, boating and other water-based activities are popular here.

4

Croajingolong National Park

 D7 parks.vic.gov.au

Classified as a World Biosphere Reserve, the Croajingolong National Park is a magnificent stretch of

 Boats moored at a creek in Metung on a beautiful summer morning

rugged and coastal wilderness. Its isolated beaches and dense forests are ideal for hiking, bird-watching, canoeing and surfing. Although Croajingolong National Park was extensively damaged during the bushfires between 2019 and 2020, regrowth began within months and many of the region's native animals have now returned. The impact on tours and accommodation, however, is still continuing.

Within the park lies Point Hicks, where Captain Cook and his crew, on board the *Endeavour*, caught their first sight of Australia in 1770. A monument and a lighthouse stand on the site.

Marlo

🄰D7 🚍 🆆visiteast gippsland.com.au/marlo

Situated at the mouth of the great Snowy River, which meanders through far eastern Gippsland, quiet little Marlo is a popular holiday destination, particularly with avid anglers. It is a pretty place that has managed to avoid the feel of a tourist town. This may be due in part to its location down a quiet road south of the main Princes Highway.

Marlo serves as a supply town for those visiting Cape Conran Coastal Park – one of Victoria's most beautiful stretches of coastline. As a consequence, there are some excellent beaches close to Marlo, but the town itself faces onto the more tranquil waters of an estuary.

Gippsland Lakes

🄰C7 🚉Bairnsdale
🛈240 Main St, Bairnsdale; www.visiteastgippsland. com.au

The lagoons, backwaters, islands and lakes of this region make up Australia's biggest inland waterway. The Gippsland Lakes region is spread across more than 350 sq km (135 sq miles). Included here are two protected areas – Lakes National Park and Gippsland Lakes Coastal Park – which encompass large lakes, including Lake Wellington, Lake Victoria and Lake King.

Fed by a total of three rivers (Mitchell, Tambo and Nicholson), the lakes meet the sea at the appropriately named township of Lakes Entrance. These shimmering lakes have islands with abundant wildlife and sheltered inlets ideal for

kayaking and canoeing. Lakeside settlements are home to large sailing and fishing fleets, and the many activities on offer here include boating, fishing, swimming and hiking.

TOP 5 GIPPSLAND BEACHES

Squeaky Beach
Framed by granite boulders, mountain views and fern gullies, the beach has grains of quartz in the sand.

Golden Beach
This sandy beach, formerly known as Letts Beach, benefits from access to both the ocean and the Gippsland Lakes.

Woodside Beach
Woodside is popular with families, walkers and surfers.

Ninety Mile Beach
One of Australia's longest unbroken stretches of sand.

Norman Bay Beach
Patrolled in summer, this sheltered beach is ideal for swimming.

7

Phillip Island

🗺️C7 🚌Cowes ⛴️Cowes
ℹ️895 Phillip Island Tourist Rd, Newhaven; www.visitphillipisland.com.au

Phillip Island's penguin parade is an extraordinary natural spectacle. Every evening at sunset, hundreds of penguins at Summerland Beach waddle from the ocean to their burrows in the spinifex tussocks (spiky clumps of grass).

At Seal Rocks, off the rugged cliffs at the western end of the island, is Australia's largest fur seal colony. Approximately 25,000 seals can be seen playing, resting or feeding their pups. Visitors can watch from the clifftop or on an organized boat trip. There is also a large koala colony on Phillip Island.

Cape Woolamai, with its red cliffs and wild waters, has walking

trails, bird-watching and surfing opportunities. Cowes is ideal for dining, relaxing or swimming.

The island is popular during motor racing events so reserve accommodation in advance.

INSIDER TIP
Check for Penguins

When driving on Phillip Island's southwest coast, check under your vehicle before setting out to make sure that no little penguins have taken shelter from the sun or other vehicles.

8

Bairnsdale

🗺️C7 🚃🚌 ℹ️240 Main St; www.visiteastgippsland.com.au

The town of Bairnsdale was established in 1844 and is considered the commercial capital of East Gippsland. It's also an emerging culinary destination. The Gunaikurnai people are the traditional custodians of this land set on a bend of the Mitchell River.

Sights here include the **Krowathunkooloong Keeping Place**, where you can get insights into Aboriginal hunting, fishing and mythology, and **St Mary's Church**, which has Italianate-style painted walls and ceilings, plus beautiful carved statuary set in its exterior walls.

Krowathunkooloong Keeping Place
♿ 🏠37–53 Dalmahoy St ⏰Hours vary, check website 🌐gegac.org.au

St Mary's Church
♿ 🏠23 Pyke St ⏰9am–4pm Mon–Fri 🌐stmarysbairnsdale.net

9

Port Albert

🗺️C7 🌐portalbert.vic.au

Located 236 km (146 miles) southeast of Melbourne, this is the oldest port in Gippsland. It was founded in 1841 and used as a waystation by gold miners heading for the Walhalla and

Beautiful frescoes at St Mary's Church in Bairnsdale, and *(inset)* its splendid façade
↓

↑ A rock formation at Portsea on the Mornington Peninsula

Omeo gold fields in the 1850s. Quaint wooden buildings with shady verandas line the streets, and many carry plaques detailing their original purpose.

The **Maritime Museum** here tells the story of Port Albert's original Aboriginal inhabitants as well as the area's naval history.

Maritime Museum

⊛ ◪ 78 Tarraville Rd
◷ Summer: 10am–4pm Thu–Mon; winter (except for school hols): 10am–4pm Sat & Sun ⌨ portalbertmaritime museum.com.au

 ⑩

Mornington Peninsula

◪ C7 ◪ Frankston ◪ Stony Point, Sorrento ◪ 359B Point Nepean Rd, Dromana; www.visitmornington peninsula.org

Only an hour's drive from Melbourne is the Mornington Peninsula. From Frankston down to Portsea near its tip, the area is an ideal get away. The sheltered beaches facing the bay are perfect for windsurfing, sailing or paddling, while the rugged coast fronting the Bass Strait has rocky reefs, rock pools and surf beaches.

The Red Hill wineries are winning awards and gaining a reputation for their fine Chardonnays and Pinot Noirs. Sip a glass of wine in historic Sorrento or take a ferry across the narrow Rip to the beautiful 19th-century town of Queenscliff (p257).

Running the length of the peninsula, the Mornington Peninsula National Park has lovely walking tracks. The beach at the tip of The Heads and Cheviot Beach, where Prime Minister Harold Holt disappeared while swimming in 1967, are both beautiful spots.

The village of Flinders is a peaceful, chic seaside resort, while Portsea is the summer playground of Melbourne's rich and famous. Options a little more off the beaten track

include the remote French Island, a short ferry trip from Crib Point or Cowes. It has no mains electricity or water, and residents either live without these facilities or use solar and wind technology. The island also teems with wild life, including rare potoroo.

 ⑪

Wilsons Promontory National Park

◪ C7 ◪ 1 Ring Rd, Tidal River ⌨ parks.vic.gov.au

The Prom, as locals call this national park, is the southernmost tip of mainland Australia. It is the remnant of a land bridge that connected Tasmania to the rest of the country until around 12,000 years ago. The landscape takes in remote, white-sand beaches, dense forests and dramatic rock formations. Nearly 90 km (55 miles) of hiking trails lace the peninsula, and this is one of the best places in Victoria to see wildlife, including emus, kangaroos, wallabies, wombats, echidnas, koalas and more than 200 different bird species.

⑫

Royal Botanic Gardens, Cranbourne

◪ C7 ◪ Off South Gippsland Hwy, 1000 Ballarto Rd ◪◪ Cranbourne ◷ 9am–5pm daily ◷ 25 Dec ⌨ rbg.vic.gov.au

The Royal Botanic Gardens (p236) in Melbourne are the city's pride, but they have not concentrated exclusively on native flora. The Cranbourne Botanic Gardens fill that niche. Amid the lakes, hills and dunes of this bushland park, banksias, wattles, grevilleas, casuarinas, eucalyptus and pink heath bloom, while wrens, honeyeaters, galahs, rosellas, cockatoos and parrots nestle among the gardens' trees.

HAROLD HOLT

Australian prime minister Harold Holt disappeared at Portsea's Cheviot Beach in 1967. His body was never found, leading to various speculations. Some believe he was assassinated by the CIA, some that he faked his death to be with a lover. Another rumour is that he was a spy who defected to China. Bizarrely, his death is commemorated by the Harold Holt Memorial Swimming Centre in Melbourne.

13 Dandenong Ranges

⚠C7 🚆Ferntree Gully &
Belgrave 🚌From nearby
towns 🛈Ferntree Gully;
www.parks.vic.gov.au

Since the mid-19th century,
the Dandenong Ranges have
been a popular retreat for
Melbourne residents. The cool
of the ash forests, fern gullies
and bubbling creeks provides
a welcome relief from the
midsummer heat.

The gardens of the
Dandenongs, many of which
were once privately owned,
are great for walks and picnics.
Particularly popular is the Alfred
Nicholas Memorial Garden at
Sherbrooke with its wide variety of trees around a boating
lake. Flowers abound at the
National Rhododendron
Gardens at Olinda and Tesselaar
Flower Farm at Silvan, home to
the annual tulip festival *(Sep-
mid-Oct)*. A steam train, *Puffing
Billy*, runs several times daily
from Belgrave through 24 km
(15 miles) of gullies and
forests to Emerald Lake
and on to Gembrook.

The superb lyrebird makes
its home in Sherbrooke Forest
and the 7-km (4-mile) Eastern
Sherbrooke Lyrebird Circuit
Walk offers a chance to view
these shy birds. Another walk
is the 15-km (9-mile) path from
Sassafras to Emerald.

Healesville Sanctuary, with
its 30 ha (75 acres) of natural
bushland, is the best place to
see Australian animals in relatively relaxed captivity. Look
out for rare species such as
platypuses and tree-kangaroos.
Book tickets in advance.

Healesville Sanctuary

🎫 🚌Glen Eadie Ave,
Healesville ⏰9am–5pm
daily 🌐zoo.org.au

> The cool of the ash
> forests, fern gullies
> and bubbling creeks
> in the Dandenong
> Ranges provides a
> welcome relief from
> the midsummer heat.

cool-climate wineries *(p50)*.
They are known for their
Méthode Champenoise sparkling wines, Chardonnays and
Pinot Noirs. Most are open daily
for wine tastings. Several also
have restaurants, serving food
to accompany their fine wines.

Just past the bush town of
Yarra Glen is the historic Gulf
Station. Owned by the National
Trust, it provides a traditional
glimpse of farming life at the
end of the 19th century.

🏔 **GREAT VIEW**
Black Spur

The Black Spur road
passes through 30 km
(19 miles) of rainforest
from Healesville to
Marysville. Giant trees,
lush ferns and sweep-
ing panoramas make
this one of Victoria's
most scenic drives.

14 Yarra Valley

⚠C7 🚆Lilydale 🚌Heales-
ville service 🛈Healesville;
www.visityarravalley.
com.au

The beautiful Yarra Valley,
located at the foot of the
Dandenong Ranges, is home
to some of Australia's best

15 Lake Eildon

⚠C7 🚌Eildon 🛈Main
St, Eildon; www.lake
eildon.com

Lake Eildon, the catchment
for five major rivers, is a vast
irrigation reserve that turns
into a recreational haven in
summer. Surrounded by the

The steam train *Puffing Billy* chugging through the Dandenong Ranges

Great Dividing Range and Fraser and Eildon national parks, the lake is a good location for fishing, hiking, water-skiing, horse-riding and house-boat holidays. Kangaroos, koalas and rosellas abound near the lake, and trout and Murray cod are common here and in the Upper Goulburn River. Canoeing on the river is popular. Accommodation in the area ranges from rustic cabins and campsites in Fraser National Park to five-star lodges and guesthouses.

Licola

C7 **Heyfield**
**Licola Wilderness Village, Jamieson Rd;
www.licola.org.au**

Licola is a tiny village set on the edge of Victoria's mountain wilderness. North of Heyfield and Glenmaggie, follow the Macalister River Valley north to Licola. The 147-km (90-mile) journey from here to Jamieson, along unsealed roads, takes in the magnificent scenery. Only 20 km (12 miles) from Licola is Mount Tamboritha and the start of the popular Lake Tarli Karng bushwalk in the Alpine National Park, also a good base for those keen to explore the surrounding country. The village store has information.

Licola is owned by the Lions Club of Victoria (the only privately owned town in the state). The club has developed the Lions Wilderness Village, which provides campsites and activities for young people.

Awe-inspiring, colourful limestone formations at the Buchan Caves

Buchan Caves Reserve

D7 **Buchan** **By appt only** **25 Dec** **parks.vic.gov.au**

Some of the most spectacular limestone formations in Australia can be found at Buchan Caves Reserve. Two of the finest are Fairy Cave and Royal Cave, which are both lit and have walkways; guided tours are conducted throughout the day, alternating between the two caves. Dating back 300–400 million years, the caves and the stalactites and stalagmites were made by ancient rivers coursing and seeping through the limestone rock. Royal Cave also has colourful calcite-rimmed pools. Entry to the reserve, where there are picnic facilities and a spring-fed pool suitable for swimming, is free. There are also campsites and walking trails, while the nearby township of Buchan offers other accommodation. The reserve is a wildlife refuge to native animals such as kangaroos, possums, bellbirds and lyrebirds.

EAT

Dudley's of Olinda
Tucked away in Mount Dandenong, this fabulous restaurant offers delicious wood-fired pizzas, as well as a variety of pastas and other Mediterranean dishes.

C7 **540 Mt Dandenong Tourist Rd, Olinda** **dudleys olinda.com.au**

Oakridge
Arguably the highlight of the winery restaurants in the Yarra Valley, Oakridge creates remarkable dishes with organic and sustainable ingredients.

C7 **864 Maroondah Hwy, Coldstream** **oakridgewines.com.au**

Mansfield

🅰C7 🚌 ℹ175 High St, Mansfield; www.mansfield mtbuller.com.au

A country town surrounded by mountains, Mansfield is the southwest entry point to Victoria's alpine country. A memorial in the main street, near the 1920s cinema, commemorates the death of three troopers shot by Ned Kelly (p229) and his gang at nearby Stringybark Creek in 1878.

The scenery of Mansfield became famous as the location for the 1982 film *The Man from Snowy River*, based on the poet "Banjo" Paterson's legendary ballad of the same name. Today, visitors can ride a horse or bike on one of the many trails, or visit the Mansfield Zoo, which offers sleepovers between May and September, allowing visitors to witness nocturnal animals after dark.

The downhill slopes of the Mount Buller ski resort are less than one hour's drive from Mansfield. Mount Stirling offers year-round activities, such as mountain bike riding.

ACCESSING THE SLOPES

When travelling to the ski resorts, be aware that roads are sealed to all resorts except Dinner Plain, Mount Baw Baw and Mount Stirling. By law, vehicles must carry chains. Coaches run from Melbourne to every resort except Mount Baw Baw. Aircraft and helicopters from Melbourne and Sydney fly to Mount Hotham and Mount Buller. There is also a helicopter shuttle that flies between Mount Hotham and Falls Creek.

🅱

Bright

🅰C7 🚌 ℹ119 Gavan St, Bright; www.visitbright. com.au

Bright is a picturesque town near the head of the Ovens River Valley, with the towering rocky cliffs of Mount Buffalo to the west and the peak of the state's second-highest mountain, Mount Feathertop, to its south. The trees along Bright's main street flame into spectacular colours of red, gold and copper for its Autumn Festival in April and May. In winter, the town turns into a gateway to the snow fields, with the resorts of Mount Hotham and Falls Creek in the Victorian Alps close by. In summer, fly-fishing for trout and swimming in the Ovens River are popular activities.

The spectacular **Mount Buffalo National Park** is popular all year round; visitors can camp amid the snow gums by Lake Catani and walk its mountain pastures and peaks, fish for trout, hang-glide off the granite tors over the Ovens Valley, or rock-climb the sheer cliffs. There is also a range of walking trails with wonderful views of Buckland Valley.

Did You Know?

Mount Buffalo was named for its supposed resemblance to a reclining buffalo.

Sheer cliffs and imposing granite tors in Mount Buffalo National Park, near Bright

→

A cross-country skier on a snow gum-lined trail in Falls Creek, Alpine National Park

Other activities on offer include canoeing, caving, horse-riding, paragliding and, in winter, cross-country skiing.

Mount Buffalo National Park

 ⊘ 🅰 Mount Buffalo Rd
🅦 parks.vic.gov.au

20

Mount Beauty

🅰 C7 😑 🛈 31 Bogong High Plains Rd, Mt Beauty; www.visitmountbeauty.com.au

This town is a good base for exploring the Kiewa Valley, with its tumbling river and dairy farms. Also nearby is the wilderness of the Bogong High Plains and the Alpine National Park, with their walks, wildflowers and snow gums. In summer, Rocky Valley Dam on the Bogong High Plains is popular for boating, kayaking and swimming. There are beautiful bushwalks, and at the top of the High Plains, there are opportunities for fishing, mountain biking, horse-riding and hang-gliding.

21

Alpine National Park

🅰 C7 😑 🅦 parks.vic.gov.au/places-to-see/parks/alpine-national-park

Australia is not famous for winter sports, but it offers excellent skiing and snow-boarding opportunities in scenic resorts. Most of these fall within Alpine National Park, Victoria's largest national park, and are open from June to late September. Given that the season is so short, conditions can vary.

Mount Buller, Falls Creek and Mount Hotham are the main resort villages, and the whole region is very fashionable. There are chic lounge bars, top-end lodges and fine dining prepared by some of Melbourne's best chefs.

Within the national park, Mount Bogong, Victoria's highest mountain, rises an impressive 1,986 m (6,516 ft). Some of the mountain's trails can be challenging but offer stunning views of the Bogong High Plains. The 655-km (393-mile) Australian Alps Walking Track runs from Walhalla to the Brindabella Ranges outside Canberra. The walk passes through magnificent tall forests and stunted snow gum.

┌──────────────────────────┐

TOP 5 SKIING DESTINATIONS

Mount Buller
The most accessible, busiest and trendiest of the major resorts.

Falls Creek
Australia's only real ski-in ski-out resort village. It also offers the country's longest green run and plenty of options for freestylers.

Mount Hotham
Suited for intermediate to more advanced skiers.

Lake Mountain
This resort is ideal for cross-country skiing.

Mount Baw Baw
An excellent option for beginners, families and skiers on a budget.

└──────────────────────────┘

㉒ Benalla

C7 3 Church St; www.enjoybenalla.com.au

The rural town of Benalla is where Ned Kelly (p229) grew up and first appeared in court at the age of 15. Today, it is most famous for the **Benalla Art Gallery**, which houses a fine collection of Australian art from the 19th century to the present day.

The town also has Australia's longest-running gliding club, thanks to the air thermals rising from both the hot plains and nearby mountains.

Benalla Art Gallery

 97 Bridge St Mar–Aug: 10am–4:30pm Wed–Mon; Sep–Feb: 10am–5pm Wed–Mon benallaart gallery.com.au

> **HIDDEN GEM**
> **Street Art**
>
> The streets of Benalla have been transformed by local and international artists. The murals take centre stage during the annual Benalla Street Art Wall to Wall Festival (www.benallastreetart. com) in March or April.

↑ Striking street art mural on a building in Benalla

㉓ Chiltern

C6 30 Main St; www.explorechiltern. com.au

This quiet village was once a booming gold-mining town with 14 suburbs. Located 1 km (half a mile) off the Hume Highway, halfway between the towns of Wodonga and Wangaratta, Chiltern features colonial architecture and receives only a trickle of visitors, unlike other Victorian boomtowns such as Ballarat.

The town has three National Trust properties: the Federal Standard newspaper office, Dow's Pharmacy and Lake View House. The last is the former home of Henry Handel Richardson, the pen name of Australian author Ethel Richardson, who wrote *The Getting of Wisdom*. The house has been restored with period furniture, and gives an insight into the life of the wealthy at the turn of the 20th century.

The Grapevine Hotel (formerly the Star Hotel and Theatre), built in 1866, has the largest grapevine in the southern hemisphere. It was planted in 1867.

㉔ Glenrowan

C6 Wangaratta 41 Gladstone St; www. visitwangaratta.com.au

Glenrowan was the site of the last stand by Australia's most notorious bushranger, Ned Kelly (p229), and his gang. In a shoot-out with police in 1880, on Siege Street near the town's railway station, Kelly was finally captured after more than two years on the run. During this time he had earned a status as a Robin Hood-type character among Victoria's bush poor, particularly its Irish Catholic farming families. Kelly knew the country

around Glenrowan, especially the Warby Ranges, in great detail and often used Mount Glenrowan, west of town, as a lookout. He was later hanged at Old Melbourne Gaol (p229).

Today, Glenrowan thrives on its association with Kelly as a tourist attraction. A 6-m- (20-ft-) high statue of the bushranger in his iconic iron armour greets visitors at the entrance. There are also various displays, such as a replica of his homestead and re-enactments of the full story of Kelly.

㉕ Beechworth

C6 103 Ford St; www.explorebeechworth. com.au

Beautifully situated in the foothills of the Victorian Alps, Beechworth was the centre of the great Ovens gold fields during the 1850s and 1860s. At the height of its boom, the town had a population of 42,000 and 61 hotels.

Today, visiting Beechworth is like stepping back in time. One of the state's best-preserved

↑ Main square of the historic town of Beechworth, and *(inset)* Ned Kelly Vault at the town's courthouse

gold rush towns, it contains more than 32 19th-century buildings now classified by the National Trust. Its tree-lined streets feature granite banks and a courthouse, hotels with wide verandas and dignified brick buildings on either side. The majority of these are still in daily use, modern life continuing within edifices of a bygone era. Many of the old buildings are now restaurants and bed-and-breakfasts. Visitors can stand in the dock of the courthouse where Ned Kelly *(p229)* was finally committed for his trial in Melbourne and marvel at the old channel blasted through the granite to create a flow of water in which miners panned for gold.

The evocative Chinese cemetery serves as a poignant reminder of the hundreds of Chinese who worked and died on the gold fields.

㉖

Shepparton

🅰C6 ✈🏛🚌 ℹ530 Wyndham St; www. visitshepparton.com.au

Located in the heart of the fertile Goulburn River Valley, Shepparton is called the "food bowl of Australia". The plains around the town support Victoria's most productive pear, peach, apricot, plum, cherry and kiwi fruit farms. A summer visit to the town's biggest fruit cannery, SPC, when fruit is being harvested, reveals a hive of activity. The fruit also makes excellent cider. Try some at Cheeky Grog Co, 12 km (7 miles) north of the city; make an appointment ahead of your visit.

The area's sunny climate is ideal for grapes. The wineries of Mitchelton and Tahbilk, 50 km (30 miles) south of the city, are open for tours and tastings.

TOP 5 NORTH-EASTERN WINERIES

Campbells Wines
This family-run winery in Rutherglen has made Cabernet Sauvignon since the 1870s.

Chambers Rosewood Vineyards
This Rutherglen winery is renowned for its reds.

Morris Wines
Based in Rutherglen, Morris has been making Shiraz, Chardonnay and fortified wines for more than 160 years.

Brown Brothers
One of Australia's most respected vineyards, Milawa's Brown Brothers is an innovative winemaker, producing spicy red blends alongside buttery Chardonnay.

Buller Wines
This Rutherglen-based winery is best known for its muscat and ports.

TASMANIA

Tasmania wasn't always an island: it separated from the mainland around 12,000 years ago. Tasmania's Aboriginal population predates this event, however, with some rock art dating from at least 35,000 years ago. Dutch navigator Abel Tasman, after whom the state is now named, was the first European to reach the island, but it was the British who built the earliest real settlement – Hobart – in 1804. From here, Europeans spread throughout the state, with convicts building and working the new farms and villages. As the Europeans advanced, the Tasmanian Aboriginal population depleted due to violent attacks by the colonists and infectious diseases. The last Aboriginal Tasmanian was said to have died in 1876. Around 20,000 Tasmanians claim Aboriginality today, however, and the population is as fiercely proud of their landscape as their forebears. One-fifth of the state is protected as a World Heritage Area and the island saw the rise of the world's first green political party, the "Tasmanian Greens".

Orange, lichen-covered rocks in the Bay of Fires

TASMANIA

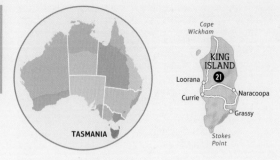

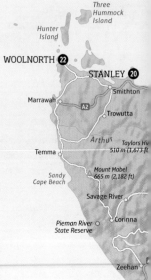

Cape Wickham
KING ISLAND 21
Loorana
Naracoopa
Currie
Grassy
Stokes Point
Three Hummock Island
Hunter Island
WOOLNORTH 22
STANLEY 20
Smithton
Marrawah
A2
Trowutta
Arthur
Taylors Hi
510 m (1,673 ft
Temma
Mount Mabel
665 m (2,182 ft)
Sandy Cape Beach
Savage River
Pieman River State Reserve
Corinna
Zeehan
Strahan
MACQUARIE HARBOUR 24
Southern Ocean

TASMANIA

Must Sees

1. Hobart
2. Port Arthur

Experience More

3. Tasman Peninsula
4. Freycinet National Park
5. Richmond
6. New Norfolk
7. Oatlands
8. Bothwell
9. Bicheno
10. Ben Lomond National Park
11. Bay of Fires
12. Maria Island
13. Ross
14. Launceston
15. Longford
16. Flinders Island
17. Devonport
18. Hadspen
19. Burnie
20. Stanley
21. King Island
22. Woolnorth
23. Cradle Mountain-Lake St Clair National Park
24. Macquarie Harbour
25. Bruny Island
26. Franklin-Gordon Wild Rivers National Park
27. Mount Field National Park

↑ Melbourne

Bass Strait

Palana

FLINDERS ISLAND 16

Emita

Strzelecki National Park

Lady Barron

Cape Barren Island

Clarke Island

Wynyard

JRNIE 19

Penguin

A10

Gunns Plains

Varatah

Cradle Valley

DEVONPORT 17 **Devonport Airport**

Beaconsfield

George Town

B82

Bridport

Derby

Scottsdale

A3

Gladstone

Mount William National Park

11 **BAY OF FIRES**

St Helens

Sheffield

Deloraine

Liena

HADSPEN 18 14 **LAUNCESTON**

Perth

Launceston Airport

Scamander

Mathinna

St Marys

A3

CRADLE MOUNTAIN– LAKE ST CLAIR NATIONAL PARK 23

Mount Ossa △ 1,617 m (5,300 ft)

LONGFORD 15

A5

Central Plateau Conservation Area

BEN LOMOND NATIONAL PARK 10

A4

Fingal

Avoca

Douglas Apsley National Park

9 **BICHENO**

Walls of Jerusalem National Park

Liawenee

Conara

Campbell Town

uenstown

Miena

A10

Lake St Clair

Derwent Bridge

ROSS 13

Swansea

Coles Bay

Lake Echo

Interlaken

A5

4 **FREYCINET NATIONAL PARK**

FRANKLIN– ORDON WILD RIVERS NATIONAL PARK 26

7 **OATLANDS**

BOTHWELL 8

A10

Hamilton

Lake Gordon

MOUNT FIELD NATIONAL PARK 27

Kempton

A1

Triabunna

Orford

A3

12 **MARIA ISLAND**

Maria Island National Park

Strathgordon

B61

Maydena

6

5 **RICHMOND**

NEW NORFOLK

Pontville

Sorell

Forestier Peninsula

Hobart International Airport

HOBART 1

A9

Lake Pedder

Huonville

Kingston

3 **TASMAN PENINSULA**

2 **PORT ARTHUR**

Huon

Cygnet

Kettering

South West National Park

25 **BRUNY ISLAND**

Dover

Adventure Bay

Southport

Recherche

0 kilometres   50

0 miles   50

N ↑

HOBART

🅐F6 ✈20 km (12 miles) NE of the city 🚌Tasmanian Redline, Transit Centre, 230 Liverpool St, www.tasredline.com.au 🛈20 Davey St; www.discovertasmania.com.au

Spread over seven hills between the banks of the Derwent River and the summit of Kunanyi/Mount Wellington, Australia's second-oldest city has an incredible waterfront location, similar to that of its "big sister", Sydney. Hobart began life on the waterfront and the maritime atmosphere is still an important aspect of the city. From Old Wharf, where the first Europeans settled, round to the fishing village of Battery Point, the area known as Sullivans Cove is still the hub of this cosmopolitan city. It is the centre of attention in late December every year as the finish line of the famous Sydney to Hobart Yacht Race.

> **Did You Know?**
>
> Hobart is home to the oldest brewery in Australia, the Cascade Brewery, founded in 1832.

settlement and wharves. The site was originally home to a gun battery, positioned there to ward off potential enemy invasions. The old guardhouse, built in 1818, now lies within a leafy park, just a few minutes' walk from busy Hampden Road with its antiques shops, art galleries, tearooms and restaurants.

Battery Point retains a strong sense of history, with its narrow gas-lit streets lined with tiny fishers' and workers' houses, cottage gardens and colonial mansions and pubs. Book online for the Hobart Historic Walk (*www.hobart historictours.com.au*), which takes place daily at 2pm and departs from the Travel & Information Centre on Davey and Elizabeth streets.

Narryna Heritage Museum

🏠103 Hampden Rd, Battery Point 🕙10am–4pm Tue–Sat 🚫1 Jan, Good Fri, 25 Apr, 25 & 26 Dec 🌐narryna.com.au

Set inside an 1834 Georgian house in Battery Point, the Narryna Heritage Museum is the oldest folk museum in Australia. Beautiful grounds make a fine backdrop for an impressive collection of early Tasmanian pioneering relics.

Battery Point

This maritime village grew up on the hilly promontory adjacent to the early

↑ Hobart and beyond, as seen from Kunanyi/ Mount Wellington

③

Salamanca Place

Once the haunt of sailors and workmen, and the site of early colonial industries, from jam-making to metal foundry and flour milling, this graceful row of sandstone warehouses at Salamanca Place is now the heart of Hobart's lively atmosphere and creative spirit.

Kunanyi/Mount Wellington towers above the buildings lining the waterfront, which have been converted into art galleries, antique stores and antiquarian book shops. The **Salamanca Arts Centre** houses artists' studios, theatres and galleries. The area also has some of the city's best pubs, cafés and restaurants.

The Salamanca Market is held every Saturday from 8:30am to 3pm. Take home fresh produce or gourmet treats, look for antique treasures or while away time listening to the tunes of busking musicians.

Salamanca Arts Centre

⌂ 77 Salamanca Place, Battery Point ◷ Daily; hours vary, check website 𝕎 sac.org.au

> This graceful row of sandstone ware-houses at Salamanca Place is now the heart of Hobart's lively atmosphere and creative spirit.

④

Castray Esplanade

Castray Esplanade was originally planned in the 19th century as a riverside walking track, and it still provides visitors with the most pleasurable short stroll within the city. En route are the old colonial Commissariat Stores. These have been beautifully renovated for inner-city living, architects' offices and art galleries, focusing on Tasmanian arts and crafts.

Must See

⑤

Parliament House

⌂ Salamanca Pl ◷ 8am-5pm Mon-Fri ◷ Public hols 𝕎 parliament.tas.gov.au

One of the oldest civic buildings in Hobart, the Parliament House was originally designed by colonial architect John Lee Archer as a customs house on reclaimed marshy land. It was constructed by convicts between 1835 and 1841. Since then, it has been the meeting place of the Government of Tasmania.

It is partly open to the public through tours on non-sitting days at 9:30am and 2:30pm. The tours focus on the history of the house and the role of the parliament.

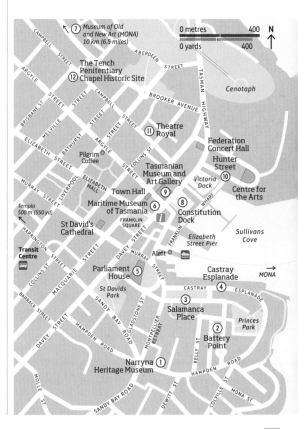

⑥
Maritime Museum of Tasmania

📍 Cnr Davey & Argyle sts
🕐 9am-5pm daily
🚫 25 Dec 🌐 maritime tas.org

Steeped in seafaring history, the Maritime Museum of Tasmania is housed in the Carnegie Building, which used to be the former Hobart Public Library. This major attraction, which records Tasmania's maritime history, is an impressive source of information for the community. It contains a fascinating collection of old relics, manuscripts and voyage documents, as well as an important and extensive collection of photographs.

 GREAT VIEW
Atop Kunanyi/ Mount Wellington

Hike or take the Kunyani/ Mount Wellington Explorer tour bus to the top of Mount Wellington for views that seemingly go on forever, taking in the city of Hobart and a faraway horizon across southern Tasmania.

↑ Brett Whiteley's *The Naked Studio* (1981) in the Museum of Old and New Art (MONA)

⑦
Museum of Old and New Art (MONA)

📍 655 Main Rd, Berriedale
🕐 10am-5pm Thu-Mon
🌐 mona.net.au

This museum is carved out of a sandstone cliff. It houses an extensive collection that ranges from ancient Egyptian mummies to some of the world's most unusual contemporary art. It is also home to an on-site winery that specializes in producing small batch premium wines.

⑧
Constitution Dock

📍 Davey St

The main anchorage for fishing boats and yachts also serves as the finish line of the annual Sydney to Hobart Yacht Race. This famous race attracts an international field of competitors.

Constitution Dock borders the city and the old slum district of Wapping, which has now been redeveloped. Many of the old warehouses have been restored to include

restaurants and cafés. One houses the eccentric restaurant, the Drunken Admiral.

Tasmanian Museum and Art Gallery

◫ 40 Macquarie St ◷ 26 Dec-Mar: 10am-4pm daily; Apr-24 Dec: 10am-4pm Tue-Sun ◷ Good Fri, 25 Apr, 25 Dec ◱ tmag.tas.gov.au

This 1863 building, designed by colonial architect Henry Hunter, is home to a collection of prints and paintings of Tasmania, Aboriginal artifacts and botanical displays that aim to value the history and culture of the Tasmanian Aboriginal peoples.

Hunter Street

Once joined to Hobart Town by a sandbar and known as Hunter Island, this historic harbourside locale is an art and culture precinct. It is lined with colonial warehouses and was once the site of the Jones & Co IXL jam factory. At the heart of this redevelopment is the award-winning Henry Jones Art Hotel.

---

⑪

Theatre Royal

◫ 29 Campbell St ◱ theatreroyal.com.au

Built in 1837, this is the oldest theatre in Australia. Almost gutted by fire in the 1960s, the ornate decor has since been restored and can be admired during a guided tour.

---

⑫

The Tench Penitentiary Chapel Historic Site

◫ Cnr Brisbane & Campbell sts ◷ Tours: 10:30am-2:30pm Wed-Sun ◷ 1 Jan, Good Fri, 24-26 Dec ◱ nationaltrust.org.au / places/penitentiary

The Tench Penitentiary Chapel Historic Site, designed by architect John Lee Archer, is built in the shape of a crucifix. Once a barracks for convicts sent to Australia from the UK, this building was later the Hobart Gaol for more than 100 years.

A guided tour takes in the former chapel, cells and gallows, and tells of incredible stories about the solitary cells and underground tunnels. Book ahead to visit.

Must See

EAT

Pilgrim Coffee
Visit this cool café for creative wraps, light mains, burgers and artisanal coffee.

◫ 54 Liverpool St
☎ (03) 6234 1999

$ $ $

Aløft
One of Tasmania's finest kitchens, Aløft offers set menus, featuring fresh fish and seafood, and vegetarian options. Book well in advance.

◫ Brooke St Pier
◱ aloftrestaurant.com

$ $ $

Templo
This Hobart treasure seats just 25. The four-course lunch menu is excellent value.

◫ 98 Patrick St
◱ templo.com.au

$ $ $

↑ Hobart and Kunanyi/ Mount Wellington seen from Constitution Dock

❷ 🗡 ⛰ 🍴 🍽 🏛

PORT ARTHUR

🅰 F6 🏠 Hwy A9 🕐 9am–5pm daily 🌐 portarthur.org.au

The extraordinary, still-intact ruins of Port Arthur evoke its poignant history. With its dramatic natural setting down on Tasmania's beautiful southeastern coast, it is hard to imagine the grim things that took place here, not least the tragic events of the 1996 massacre.

Port Arthur was set up in 1830 as a timber station and a prison settlement for repeat offenders. Transportation from the mainland ceased in 1853, but the prison was operational until 1877, by which time some 12,000 men had passed through what was regarded as the harshest such institution in the British Empire. Punishments included sensory deprivation and extreme isolation. In 1895 and 1897, when the authorities were trying to distance themselves from its grim past, many buildings were destroyed by fire, including the Old Prison House. A conservation project was undertaken to restore the ruins between 1979 and 1986.

↑ Buildings and ruins of the prison at Port Arthur

One of the first houses at Port Arthur is the Commandant's House, a restored cottage furnished in early 19th-century style.

The Semaphore was a series of flat, mounted planks that could be arranged in different ways to send messages.

The sandstone hospital building was completed in 1842. The basement housed the kitchen and a morgue, known as the "dead room".

The Paupers' Mess was the dining area for poor ex-convicts.

The Guard Tower was built in 1835 to prevent escapes from the settlement and pilfering from the Commissariat Store, which the tower overlooked.

The penitentiary was thought to be the largest in Australia at the time of its construction in 1844. It housed almost 500 prisoners.

Completed in 1836, the church was never consecrated because it was used by all denominations. The building was gutted by fire in 1884, but the ruins have been preserved.

Government Cottage was built in 1853 and was used by visiting dignitaries and officials.

MASON COVE

CHAMP STREET

TARLETON STREET

JETTY ROAD

CH

Must See

1996 MASSACRE AND GUN CONTROL

On 28 April 1996, Port Arthur became the scene of an unimaginable tragedy, when a lone gunman came to the island, killed 35 people and injured 23 more. It is regarded as the worst mass murder in post-colonial Australian history, and has since resulted in the State and Federal governments passing strong gun control laws that are counted among the strictest in the world. A moving memorial to the victims of this violence now stands on the site.

By 1872, Port Arthur's asylum housed more than 100 convicts with mental illness. When the settlement closed, it became the town hall, but now serves as a museum and café.

The Separate Prison was thought to provide "humane" punishment. Convicts lived separately in 50 cells, referred to by a number.

Trentham Cottage was owned by the family who lived here after the site closed. The refurbished interior has early 20th-century furnishings.

↑ Illustrated layout showing the prison buildings at Port Arthur

↑ A scenic hiking trail overlooking the Southern Ocean in Cape Hauy, Tasman National Park

EXPERIENCE MORE

Tasman Peninsula

🅰F6 🅸 Arthur Hwy, Port Arthur; www.discover tasmania.com.au

Southeast of Hobart, the Tasman Peninsula is one of Australia's most remarkable stretches of coastline. Port Arthur may be the most popular sights, but the nearby **Tasman National Park** is one of the state's best. The park is traversed by the Three Capes Track, a jaw-dropping trek that snakes along the clifftops for much of its 46 km (29 miles). Look out for dramatic rock formations all along this coast, especially close to Eaglehawk Neck, a narrow isthmus or land bridge that connects the peninsula to the rest of Tasmania. The rock formations include the Tasman Blowhole, the perfectly formed Tasman Arch, Devil's Kitchen, a deep, partially enclosed canyon where the waters of the Southern Ocean foam and roil, and the bizarre, tooth-like jagged cliffs at Cape Raoul and Cape Hauy. There is also the Totem Pole, a slender finger of rock at Cape Hauy beloved by climbers. Another unusual geological phenomenon is the Tessellated Pavement, a naturally formed collection of square rock pools over-looking the Southern Ocean.

On the northern promontory of Tasman Peninsula is the World Heritage-listed **Coal Mines Historic Site**. It has evocative convict-era sandstone buildings that were abandoned in 1848. Located close to Eaglehawk Neck is Doo Town, a quiet village where every house has "doo" in the name.

Tasman National Park
🕐 Daily 🌐 parks.tas.gov.au/explore-our-parks/tasman-national-park

Coal Mines Historic Site
🏠 Coal Mines Rd, Saltwater River 🕐 Dawn-dusk daily 🌐 coalmines.org.au

Did You Know?

At 300 m (980 ft), Cape Pillar - on the Three Capes Track - has the southern hemisphere's tallest sea cliffs.

Richmond Bridge spanning Coal River in Richmond ↑

STAY

Daisy Bank Cottages
Stay in a beautifully converted sandstone Richmond cottage, built in the 1930s.

🅰F6 🏠78 Middle Tree Rd, Richmond 🌐daisybank cottages.com.au

⑤⑤⑤

The Woodbridge
This heritage-listed hotel in New Norfolk feels like a home away from home.

🅰F6 🏠6 Bridge St, New Norfolk 🌐woodbridge nn.com.au

⑤⑤⑤

Ratho Farm
Rooms are set in restored convict cottages at this Bothwell hotel.

🅰F6 🏠2122 Highland Lakes Rd, Bothwell 🌐rathofarm.com

⑤⑤⑤

---

④

Freycinet National Park

🅰F6 🚌From Bicheno 🛈138 Freycinet Dr; www. parks.tas.gov.au

The Freycinet Peninsula on Tasmania's east coast is a long, narrow neck of land jutting south, dominated by the granite peaks of the Hazards Mountain Range. Named after an early French maritime explorer, the peninsula consists of ocean beaches to the east and secluded coves and inlets to the west. The fishing village of Coles Bay lies in the largest cove, backed by the Hazards.

Freycinet National Park on the tip of the peninsula is criss-crossed with walking tracks along beaches, over mountains, around headlands and across lagoons. The most popular walk takes hikers up and over the mountains to Wineglass Bay. The blue waters of the bay are cupped against a crescent of golden sand, which inspired the name.

The drive up the east coast is a highlight of Tasmania. There are superb ocean views and marshlands inhabited by black swans. Small towns such as Orford and Swansea are good for overnight stays.

---

⑤

Richmond

🅰F6 🚌 🛈Old Hobart Town, Bridge St; www. richmondvillage.com.au

In the heart of the countryside, 26 km (16 miles) from Hobart, lies the quaint village of Richmond. This was the first area granted to free settlers from England for farming, and at its centre they established a township reminiscent of their homeland. Richmond now includes some of Australia's oldest colonial architecture. Most of the buildings were constructed by convicts, including the sandstone bridge built in 1823, the gaol of 1825 and the Roman Catholic Church of 1834.

Today, Richmond is a lively centre for rural artists and artisans. On the main street, between the old general store and post office, they occupy many of the historic homes.

---

⑥

New Norfolk

🅰F6 🚌 🛈Circle St; www. newnorfolk.org

From Hobart, the Derwent River heads north, then veers west through the

7

Oatlands

F6 | 13 Smith St, Longford; www.southern midlands.tas.gov.au

Oatlands was one of a string of military stations established in 1813 during the construction of the old Midlands Highway by convict chain gangs. Colonial Governor Lachlan Macquarie ordered the building of the road in 1811, to connect the southern settlement of Hobart (p282) with the northern settlement of Launceston (p292). He chose locations for the townships en route, naming them after places in the British Isles. The road ran through the area of Tasmania corresponding in name and geography to that of the British Midlands region, but since the 1990s it has been dubbed the Heritage Highway.

Oatlands soon became one of the colonial coaching stops for early travellers. Today, it has the richest endowment of Georgian buildings in the country, mostly made of local sandstone, including the 1829 courthouse and St Peter's Church (1838) which is classified by the National Trust. Its most distinctive building is the Callington Flour Mill. No longer operational, it is now home to a whisky distillery.

Did You Know?

Ratho Farm in Bothwell is home to the oldest golf course in the southern hemisphere.

8

Bothwell

 F6 | 4 Market Place; www.ausgolfmuseum.com

Nestled in the Clyde River Valley, Bothwell's wide streets are set along the Bothwell River, formerly known as the "Fat Doe" river after a town in Scotland. The area's names were assigned by early Scottish settlers, who arrived from Hobart Town in 1817 with their families and 18-litre (5-gal) kegs of rum loaded on bullock wagons.

The town's heritage is now preserved with some 50 National Trust buildings dating from the 1820s, including the Castle Hotel, the Masonic Hall (now an art gallery), Bothwell Grange Guest House and the Old Schoolhouse, now home to the Australasian Golf Museum and the town's visitors' centre. The stone heads above the door of the Presbyterian St Luke's Church depict a Celtic god and goddess.

The town lies at the centre of the historic sheep-farming district of Bothwell. There are several cheese-makers and a renowned whisky distillery in the area, too. It is also the gateway to the ruggedly beautiful Central Plateau Conservation Area – a tableland that rises abruptly from the flat countryside to an average height of 600 m (nearly 2,000 ft).

Derwent River Valley. The hop farms and oast houses along the willow-lined river are testimony to the area's history of brewing.

At the centre of the valley, 38 km (24 miles) from Hobart, is the town of New Norfolk. Many of the first settlers in the region abandoned the colonial settlement of Norfolk Island to come here, hence the name. One of Tasmania's classified historic towns, it contains many interesting buildings, such as the Bush Inn of 1815, which claims to be one of Australia's oldest licensed pubs.

←

The beautiful Georgian Callington Flour Mill in Oatlands

❾ Bicheno

⚑ F6 ⊕ tasmania.com/points-of-interest/bicheno

Together with Coles Bay, Bicheno is the holiday centre of Tasmania's east coast. In summer, the bay is very popular due to its sheltered location, which means temperatures are always a few degrees warmer than elsewhere in the state.

The area is also home to Tasmania's smallest national park, the 16,000-ha (40,000-acre) Douglas Apsley National Park. It contains the state's largest dry sclerophyll forest, patches of rainforest, river gorges, waterfalls and spectacular views along the coast. This varied landscape can be taken in along a three-day north-to-south walking track through the park. The north of the park is only accessible by 4WD. Walking, hiking and bush camping opportunities are also available to visitors.

Other attractions in the area include the Apsley Gorge Vineyard, planted with Pinot Noir and Chardonnay, and a penguin breeding colony that stretches for 3 km (2 miles).

❿ Ben Lomond National Park

⚑ F6 ▦ When ski slopes are open ▯ 167 Westbury Rd, Prospect, Launceston; www.parks.tas.gov.au

In the hinterlands between the Midlands and the east coast, 50 km (30 miles) southeast of Launceston, Ben Lomond is the highest mountain in northern Tasmania and home to one of the state's two main ski slopes. The 16,000-ha (40,000-acre) national park surrounding the mountain covers an alpine plateau of barren and dramatic scenery, with views stretching over the northeast of the state. The vegetation includes alpine daisies and carnivorous sundew plants. The park is also home to wallabies, wombats and possums. From Conara Junction on the Heritage Highway, take the Esk Main Road east before turning off towards Ben Lomond National Park.

The mountain's foothills have been devastated by decades of mining and forestry, and many of the townships, such as Rossarden and Avoca, have since suffered an economic decline. The road through the South Esk Valley along the Esk River loops back to the valley's main centre of Fingal. From here, you can continue through the small township of St Marys before joining the Tasman Highway and heading up the east coast.

💬 INSIDER TIP
Bay of Fires

Hike the Bay of Fires and beyond with an Aboriginal guide on the four day immersive Wukalina Walk and experience natural beauty, culture and bush tucker.

⓫ Bay of Fires

⚑ F6 ⊕ discovertasmania.com.au/regions/east-coast/bay-of-fires

One of the prettiest stretches along Tasmania's east coast, the Bay of Fires has gorgeous white-sand beaches backed by big boulders covered in orange lichen – hence the name. The rocks really do look as if they're on fire, close to sunset.

The area is ideal for camping and watersports. There are walking trails as well. Nearby St Helens has Tasmania's largest fishing fleet, while **Mount William National Park** is remote and spectacular – head for Eddystone Point Lighthouse to see wombats, wallabies and Forester (eastern grey) kangaroos, especially around Stumpys Bay.

Mount William National Park
⊕ parks.tas.gov.au

⓬ Maria Island

⚑ F6 ▦ ▯ Triabunna Wharf; www.encounter-maria.com.au

Located off Tasmania's east coast, Maria Island is

↑ Accommodation gracing the lush ski slope at Ben Lomond mountain

Hiking past the magnificent sandstone Painted Cliffs at Maria Island

 13

Ross

🗺️ F6 🚌 🛈 Tasmanian Wool Centre: Church St; www.taswoolcentre.com.au

Set on the banks of the Macquarie River, Ross, like Oatlands (p289), was once a military station and coaching stop along the Midlands Highway. It lies at the heart of the richest sheep farming district in Tasmania, internationally recognized for its fine merino wool. Some of the large rural homesteads in the area have remained within the same families since the 1820s when the village was settled.

Its most famous sight is Ross Bridge, built by convict labour and opened in 1836. It features 186 unique carvings by convict sculptor Daniel Herbert, who was given a Queen's Pardon for his intricate work. The town centres on its historic cross-roads, the Four Corners of Ross: "Temptation, Damnation, Salvation and Recreation". These are represented respectively on each corner by the Man-O-Ross Hotel, the jail, the church and the town hall.

a wonderful place to see wildlife, engage in outdoor activities and learn about local history. First settled by whalers and sealers, the island became home to a penal colony called Darlington in 1825. It was later abandoned in favour of Port Arthur. The convict ruins here remain on the UNESCO World Heritage List. In the late 19th century, the island was leased by flamboyant Italian entre-preneur Diego Bernacchi who planted grapes, cultivated silkworms and established a cement factory here. By the 1930s, the island was home to only a handful of farmers. However, its fortunes revived after it was declared a national park in 1972. The island is now a veritable playground for visitors.

After arriving at Darlington by ferry, walk along one of the numerous trails or set off by bike to see seabirds, endemic mammals or even whales. Often visited at low tide are the impressive

Painted Cliffs. These are towering, beautifully coloured sandstone cliffs on the western side of the island that have been eroded into superb wave-like patterns by centuries of wind and waves. Fossil Cliffs plunge down into the ocean and offer stunning views all around, and the white-sand beaches lead to beautiful, turquoise waters.

MARIA ISLAND'S NATIVE SPECIES

Maria Island is Tasmania's modern-day Noah's Ark. Since the 1960s, several species facing extinction on the Tasmanian mainland have been reintroduced to the island. In 2012, Tasmanian devils were returned to Maria Island and the population has grown to nearly 100. The island's other animals have been learning to live with the world's largest carniv-orous marsupial ever since.

SHOP

Old Umbrella Shop
Seemingly unchanged since the 1920s, this National Trust-registered shop is partially a museum. The Schott family has been making and repairing umbrellas here since 1860.

F6 60 George St, Launceston national trust.org.au/places/old-umbrella-shop

A café on a street corner in Longford, housed in a historic building

14

Launceston

F6 68-72 Cameron St; 1800 651 827

In colonial days, the coach ride between Tasmania's capital, Hobart, and the township of Launceston took a full day, but today the 200-km (125-mile) route is flat and direct. Nestling in the Tamar River Valley, Launceston was settled in 1804 and is Australia's third-oldest city. It has a charming ambience, with old buildings, parks, gardens, riverside walks, craft galleries and hilly streets lined with weatherboard houses.

The two-pronged **Queen Victoria Museum and Art Gallery** is excellent. Its Queen Victoria Art Gallery has the country's largest provincial display of colonial art, along with an impressive modern collection. The paintings by English-born Australian artist John Glover as well as Aboriginal artifacts and colonial relics are the star attractions. The main museum building is in the restored railway yards and has fascinating natural history displays and a planetarium. There is also a café and a shop on the premises.

A short stroll over the North Esk River takes you to the City Park. Laid out in the early 19th century, it has ample lawns, Victorian-era monuments, playgrounds and an enclosure of Japanese macaques (a gift from Launceston's sister city in Japan, Ikeda).

At the edge of the park is **Design Tasmania**. Set in a converted church, this gallery-shop show-cases Tasmanian crafts and home furnishings.

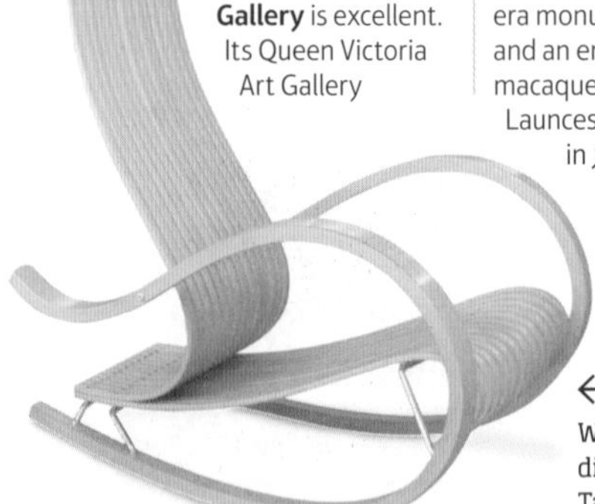

Wooden chair displayed at Design Tasmania, Launceston

Back on the other side of the river is the **National Automobile Museum of Tasmania**. This is one of Australia's best motor vehicle museums. If you love classic cars and motorbikes, you could easily spend hours here.

North of Launceston, the Tamar Valley is one of Tasmania's premier wine-producing regions. It is well known for its Chardonnay, Sauvignon Blanc, Riesling, Pinot Gris and Pinot Noir varieties *(www.tamarvalleywine route.com.au)*.

Cataract Gorge Reserve is alive with birds, wallabies, pademelons, potoroos and bandicoots, only a 15-minute walk from the city centre. A chairlift, believed to have the longest central span in the world, provides a striking aerial overview.

In nearby Underwood is the award-winning **Treetops Adventure**, which combines the tranquillity of the forest with adventurous

The Tamar Valley is one of Tasmania's premier wine-producing regions. It is well known for its Chardonnay, Sauvignon Blanc, Riesling, Pinot Gris and Pinot Noir varieties.

canopy tours. These take place in all weathers, and there is also a night-time ride. Visitors can enjoy a unique view of the beautiful forest environment from above.

Queen Victoria Museum and Art Gallery

😊 🏛️ 🏠 Museum: 2 Wellington St, Royal Park, Launceston; Gallery: 2 Invermay Rd, Inveresk ⏰ 10am-4pm daily ⏰ Good Fri, 25 Dec 🌐 qvmag.tas.gov.au

Design Tasmania

🏠 Cnr Brisbane & Tamar sts ⏰ 10am-3pm Wed-Sat, 10am-2pm Sun ⏰ Public hols 🌐 designtasmania.com.au

National Automobile Museum of Tasmania

🚗 🏠 84 Lindsay St, Invermay ⏰ 9am-5pm daily 🌐 namt.com.au

Treetops Adventure

🚠 🚼 🏠 66 Hollybank Rd, off the Launceston-Lilydale Rd, Underwood ⏰ 9am-5pm daily 🌐 treetops adventure.com.au

---

Longford

🗺️ F6 ℹ️ JJ's Bakery, 52 Wellington St; www.tasmania.com/points-of-interest/longford

In the 1830s, the Norfolk Plains was a farmland district owned mainly by wealthy settlers who had been enticed to the area by land grants. The small town of Longford is located about 20 km (12 miles) south of Launceston. It is still the centre of a rich agricultural district with its many historic inns and churches, and the

town has the greatest concentration of colonial mansions in the state.

Among these are two UNESCO World Heritage-listed sites. **Woolmers** is a former pastoral property with wonderfully preserved period furnishings. The farm at **Brickendon** was built by convicts and is surrounded by expansive gardens. Woolmers and Brickendon are connected by the themed Convict Trail Walk, which runs for nearly 3 km (2 miles). Woolmers is also home to the National Rose Garden, which is the venue for the Festival of Roses every November. Both properties are open for public tours.

Another attraction here is Christ Church. It was built in 1839 using Hadspen freestone. The stained-glass window was designed by architect William Archer and the church's clock and bell were gifts from King George IV. A short distance to the west of town is the Woodstock Lagoon Wildlife Sanctuary, known for its large waterfowl population.

Woolmers

🚠 🚼 🏠 658 Woolmers Lane ⏰ 10am-3:30pm Wed-Sun ⏰ Public hols 🌐 woolmers.com.au

Brickendon

🚠 🚼 🏠 236 Wellington St ⏰ Jun-Sep: 10am-4pm daily; Oct-May: 9:30am-5pm daily 🌐 brickendon.com.au

---

 GREAT VIEW
Brady's Lookout

Once the secret hideout of bushranger Mathew Brady, this spot affords one of the best panoramas in the state. Set 20 km (12 miles) from Launceston, the platforms grant views of the Tamar Valley and Ben Lomand, 120 km (75 miles) to the south.

Dramatic coastline in the
Strzelecki National Park,
Flinders Island ↑

 16

Flinders Island

🅰F6 ✈From Launceston,
Melbourne 🚢From Bridport
ℹ4 Davey St; (03) 6359
5002

On the northeastern tip of
Tasmania, in the waters of the
Bass Strait, Flinders Island is
the largest within the Furneaux
Island Group. These 50 or so
dots in the ocean are what
remains of a land bridge that
once spanned the strait to
the continental mainland.

The most famous – and
tragic – event in Flinders Island's
history was when Reverend
George Augustus Robinson
transported 133 Aboriginal
Tasmanians here in the 1830s to
"save" the Aboriginal population

 INSIDER TIP
Look for Topaz

On the northern coast of
Flinders Island, walk the
beaches at Tanners Bay
and Killiecrankie Bay at
low tide and look for
Killiecrankie Diamonds,
an ice-blue or rose-gold
topaz that's distinctive
to the area.

in Tasmania from extinction by
"civilizing" and converting them
to Christianity. In 1847, greatly
diminished by disease and
despair, the 47 survivors were
sent to Oyster Cove, a sacred
Aboriginal site, and the plan
was deemed a failure. Within
a few decades, all full-blooded
Aboriginal Tasmanians had died.

Much of Flinders is preserved
as a natural reserve, including
Strzelecki National Park, which
is a particularly popular area
with hikers. Off the island's
south coast is Cape Barren
Island, home to the Patriarch
Sanctuary, a protected
geese reserve.

The island can be reached
by air from Launceston and
Melbourne. There is also a
ferry trip aboard the *Matthew
Flinders*, which sets sail from
the coastal town of Bridport.

 17

Devonport

🅰F6 ✈🚂🚌🚢 ℹ145 Rooke St;
www.visitdevonport.com.au

Spirit of Tasmania, an overnight
car and passenger ferry, sails
from the Port of Melbourne to
Devonport several times each
week. Named after Devon

in England, the third-largest
city of the state is strategically
sited as a river and sea port –
it lies at the junction of the
Mersey River and the Bass
Strait, on the north coast.
The dramatic rocky head-
land of Mersey Bluff is 1 km
(half a mile) from the city
centre. It is linked by a coastal
reserve and parklands. Take
a short, self-guided walk from
near the Bluff's lighthouse
to see rock paintings and
carvings. Along the way, the
route circles around the
former Tiagarra Aboriginal
Cultural Centre and Museum,
which is only open by appointment for groups of ten visitors
or more.

 18

Hadspen

🅰F6 🚌 ℹ68-72 Cameron
St, Launceston; 1800
651 827

Heading west along the Bass
Highway, a string of historic
towns pepper the countryside
from Longford through to
Deloraine, surrounded by
the Great Western Tiers
Mountains. The tiny town of
Hadspen is a picturesque

Did You Know?

Heritage, a speciality cheese factory in Burnie, is one of the largest in the southern hemisphere.

strip of Georgian cottages and buildings which include an old 1845 coaching house.

The town is also home to one of Tasmania's most famous historic homes. Built in 1819 on the bank of the South Esk River, the **Entally House**, with its gracious veranda, has its own chapel, stables, horse-drawn carriages and 19th-century furnishings.

Entally House

◎◉ ☐782 Meander Valley Rd, via Hadspen ☐Sep-Apr: 11am-4pm Fri & Sat ☐1 Jan 25-28 Dec, public hols ☒entallyestate.com.au

---

⑲ Burnie

☐F6 ☐☐ ⑰77-79 Wilmot St; www.burnie.tas.gov.au

Further along the northern coast from Devonport is Tasmania's fourth-largest city, Burnie, which was founded in 1829. Along its main streets are many attractive 19th-century buildings decorated with wrought ironwork. Previously, Burnie's prosperity centred on a thriving wood-pulping industry. The area's history throughout the 19th and 20th centuries is showcased at the Burnie Regional Museum. Here, displays depict the pastoral lives of early European

settlers and include a replica shoemaker's shop and blacksmith's forge. The museum and a small art gallery are housed in the **Burnie Arts and Function Centre**, which also hosts local theatre productions, live performances and arts events throughout the year.

Today, Burnie is known for its food. To enjoy some of the region's produce, visit Delish Fine Foods (www.delish burnie.com), which sells award-winning products such as delicious creamy Camemberts and sharp blue cheeses with signature flavour. Burnie also has a number of lush gardens, including Fern Glade, where platypuses are often seen feeding at dusk and dawn. Situated on Emu Bay, it has a number of natural attractions include forest reserves, fossil cliffs, water-falls and canyons and panoramic ocean views from nearby Round Hill.

Burnie Arts and Function Centre

☐77-79 Wilmot St ☐9am-5pm Mon-Fri and for performances ☒burniearts.net

Stanley

☐F6 ☐ ⑰12 Nelson St, Smithdon; www.stanley-andtarkine.com.au

The rocky promontory of Circular Head, known locally as "the Nut", rises 152 m (500 ft) above sea level and looms over the fishing village of Stanley. A chairlift up the rock face offers striking views.

Stanley's main street runs towards the wharf, lined with fishers' cottages and blue-stone buildings dating from the 1840s. There are inns and restaurants serving fresh, local seafood here.

Nearby, **Highfield Historic Site** was the original head-quarters of the Van Diemen's Land Company, a London-based agricultural holding set up in 1825. The home and grounds of its colonial overseer are open for tours.

Highfield Historic Site

◎◉ ☐Green Hills Rd, via Stanley ☐9:30am-4:30pm daily ☐25 Dec ☒parks.tas.gov.au

→

The descending chairlift from Circular Head offering views of Stanley

EAT

King Island Bakehouse

King Island's best bakery does great Aussie pies, including ones filled with local crayfish or wallaby.

 E6 5 Main St, Currie, King Island (03) 6462 1337

$ $ $

Wild Harvest

Wild Harvest has a farm-to-table, seasonal menu, with a focus on local seafood, as well as some unusual additions such as muttonbird or wallaby.

 E6 4 Bluegum Dr, Grassy, King Island wildharvest kingisland.com.au

$ $ $

King Island Dairy – Cheese Store

King Island cheeses are famous throughout Australia. Most of its cheddars, blues, bries and camemberts have won awards. Order a cheese platter to try them all.

 E6 869 North Rd, Loorana, King Island kingislanddairy. com.au

$ $ $

View 42° Restaurant & Bar

One of the best seafood spots in Tasmania, View 42° serves up generous all-you-can-eat buffets.

 E6 1 Jolly St, Strahan strahan village.com.au

$ $ $

21
King Island

E6 5 George St, Currie; (03) 6462 1778

Lying off the northwestern coast of Tasmania in the Bass Strait, King Island is a popular location for wild-life lovers. Muttonbirds and elephant seals are among the animals to be seen here.

Divers frequent the island, too, fascinated by the shipwrecks that lie nearby. The island is also noted for its cheese, beef and seafood.

22
Woolnorth

E6 Via Smithton www.woolnorthtours. com.au

This huge dairy farming property is located on the outskirts of Smithton. At present, Woolnorth is the only remaining land-holding of the Van Diemen's Land Company. Half-day tours of the property feature its historic precinct and wind farm. They also include a trip to secluded Cape Grim, remarkable for for having the cleanest air in the world. It is advisable to book your tour in advance.

23
Cradle Mountain-Lake St Clair National Park

F6 Cradle Mountain, Lake St Clair Cradle Mountain, (03) 6492 1110; Lake St Clair, www.parks.tas.gov.au

The distinctive jagged peaks of Cradle Mountain act as a symbol of the state's natural environment. The second-highest mountain in Tasmania, Cradle Mountain reaches 1,560 m (5,100 ft) and is located at the northern end of the 161,000-ha (400,000-acre) national park, which bears its name and stretches 80 km (50 miles) south to the shores of Lake St Clair.

The park was founded in 1922 by Austrian nature enthusiast Gustav Weindorfer. His memory lives on in his forest home Waldheim Chalet, now a heritage lodge in Weindorfer's Forest. Nearby, at Ronny Creek, is the registration point for the celebrated Overland Track, which

Did You Know?

Lake St Clair is the deepest freshwater lake in Australia.

↑ A walkway running alongside Dove Lake beneath Cradle Mountain in the national park

traverses the park through rainforest, alpine moors, buttongrass plains and waterfall valleys. Walking the track takes an average of six days, with overnight stops in tents or huts. At the halfway mark is Mount Ossa, the state's highest peak at 1,617 m (5,300 ft). In May, the park is ablaze with the autumn colours of Tasmania's deciduous beech *Nothofagus gunnii*, commonly known as "Fagus".

 24

Macquarie Harbour

E6 **Strahan** **The Esplanade, Strahan; (03) 6472 6800 or 1800 352 200**

Off the wild, western coast of Tasmania there is nothing but vast stretches of ocean until the southern tip of Argentina, on the other side of the globe. The region bears the full brunt of the "Roaring Forties" – the name given to the tremendous winds that whip southwesterly off the Southern Ocean.

In this hostile environment, Tasmania's First Nations peoples survived for thousands of years before European convicts were sent here in the 1820s and took over the land. Their harsh and isolated settlement was a penal

The restored 1896 West Coast Wilderness Railway, linking Strahan and Queenstown, and *(inset)* its interior ↑

station on Sarah Island, situated in the middle of Macquarie Harbour.

The name of the harbour's mouth, "Hell's Gates", reflects conditions endured by both seamen and convicts – shipwrecks, drownings, suicides and murders all occurred here. Abandoned in 1833 for the "model prison" of Port Arthur *(p286)*, Sarah Island and its penal settlement ruins can be viewed on a guided boat tour from the fishing port of Strahan.

The small town of Strahan grew around an early timber industry supported by convict labour. It became well known in the early 1980s when protesters from across Australia came to Strahan to fight government plans to flood the wild Franklin River for a hydroelectric scheme. A fascinating exhibition at the town's visitor centre charts the drama of Australia's most famous environmental protest.

Strahan today is one of the state's loveliest towns, with its old timber buildings, a scenic port and a natural backdrop of fretted mountains and dense bushland. One of its main attractions is the West Coast Wilderness Railway *(www.wcwr.com.au)*, which travels 35 km (22 miles) across rivers and mountains to the mining settlement at Queenstown.

THE BLOCKADES

In 1982, Tasmania's government began building a dam to flood the World Heritage-listed Gordon and Franklin rivers. The resulting protest, the Franklin River Blockade, attracted 6,000 protestors and kickstarted the green movement in Australia. The blockade ended in 1983 when the Labor Party won the national elections and ended the construction of the dam.

TASMANIA'S WILDLIFE AND WILDERNESS

Tasmania's landscape varies dramatically within its small area. Some parts of the island have swathes of lush, green pastures; to the west, the state is wild and untamed, while inland lie glacial mountains and wild rivers. This diverse landscape is the habitat of flora and fauna unique to the island, such as the eastern quoll, red-bellied pademelon and, of course, the Tasmanian devil. To ensure the longevity of these animals, the landscape must be preserved.

Did You Know?

The thylacine was the world's largest carnivorous marsupial until its extinction in 1936.

MOUNTAIN WILDERNESS

Inland southwest Tasmania is dominated by its glacial mountain landscape, including the beautiful Cradle Mountain. To the east of Cradle Mountain is the isolated Walls of Jerusalem National Park, with five rocky mountains. To the south is Mount Field National Park, an alpine area of glacial tarns and eucalyptus forests.

COASTAL WILDERNESS

The climate of Tasmania's eastern coastline is often balmy. The western coast, however, bears the full brunt of the Roaring Forties winds, whipped up across the vast expanses of ocean between the island state and the nearest land in South America. As a result, the landscape is lined with rocky beaches and raging waters, the scene of many shipwrecks during Tasmania's history.

RIVER WILDERNESS

The southwest of Tasmania is well known for its wild rivers, particularly among avid whitewater rafters. The greatest wild river is the 120-km (75-mile) Franklin River, protected within Franklin-Gordon Wild Rivers National Park. This is the only undammed wild river left in Australia, and despite its sometimes calm moments it often rages fiercely through gorges, rainforests and heathland.

PRESERVING TASMANIA'S WILDERNESS

An inhospitable climate, rugged landforms and the impenetrable scrub are among the factors that have preserved Tasmania's wilderness. Although there is a long history of human habitation (Aboriginal sites date back 35,000 years), the population has always been small. The first real human threat occurred in the late 1960s when the Tasmanian government's hydro-electricity programme drowned Lake Pedder. The latest threat to the landscape is tourism. While many places of beauty are able to with-stand visitors, others are not and people are discouraged from visiting these areas.

Cradle Mountain, the natural symbol of the state of Tasmania ↑

TASMANIA'S FLORA AND FAUNA

① Bennett's Wallaby
Sometimes called the red-necked wallaby because of the red-tinted fur on its back, the Bennett's wallaby *(Macropus rufogriseus)* is native to Tasmania's mountain regions. A shy animal, it is most likely to be spotted at either dawn or dusk.

② Banksia
Distinctive for its seed pods, this shrub comes in many varieties in Tasmania. The *Banksia serrata*, or saw banksia, has serrated leaves and large yellow flower spikes, while *Banksia marginata*, known as the silver banksia, has narrrow leaves and smaller yellow flower spikes.

③ Tasmanian Devil
The world's largest carnivorous marsupial, the Tasmanian devil *(Sarcophilus harrisii)* is an iconic symbol of the island. In recent years, the devil facial tumour disease has drastically reduced the population and, in 2008, the Tasmanian devil was declared endangered. Work is underway to save it.

④ Eastern Quoll
A small, carnivorous marsupial, the eastern quoll *(Dasyurus viverrinus)* once thrived all over Australia. The species has been considered extinct on the mainland since the 1960s, but the absence of introduced predators, like foxes, might have ensured its survival on Tasmania.

⑤ Huon Pine
A towering conifer, Huon pine *(Lagarostrobus franklinii)* is found in the south-west and in the south along the Franklin Gordon rivers. It is prized for its ability to withstand rot, making it a popular boat building material. Some examples are more than 2,000 years old.

⑥ Brown Trout
Introduced to the island in the 19th century from Europe, brown trout *(Salmo trutta)* is now abundant in the wild rivers and lakes of Tasmania. It is a popular catch with fly-fishers; the largest recorded brown trout, caught in the Huon River in 1887, was 13.27 kg (29 lb).

⑦ Deciduous Beech
Deciduous beech *(Nothofagus gunnii)* is the only such native beech in Australia. The spectacular golden colours of its leaves fill the island's mountain areas during the autumn. The best seasonal displays are found in Mount Field National Park and at the northern end of Cradle Mountain Lake St Clair National Park.

25
Bruny Island

⚑F7 🌐brunyisland.org.au

On Hobart's back doorstep, yet a world away in landscape and atmosphere, is the Huon Valley and D'Entrecasteaux Channel. The Huon Trail winds its way from Hobart, through the Huon Valley and D'Entrecasteaux Channel to Bruny Island. In total, the trip south from Hobart, through the town of Huonville, the Hartz Mountains and Southport, the southern-most town in the country, is only 100 km (60 miles), but take your time and soak up the views of the orchards, craft outlets and vineyards along the way.

Near the end of the trail is the attractive marina of Kettering, the departure point for a regular ferry service to Bruny Island, which is a pop-ular holiday destination in Tasmania. "Island" is

INSIDER TIP
Bruny Island Cruises

Explore Bruny Island on a wilderness boat trip run by Bruny Island Cruises (www.bruny cruises.com.au). Boats depart from Adventure Bay at regular intervals each day.

something of a misnomer. It is actually two islands joined by a narrow neck. Once home to a thriving colonial whaling industry, Bruny Island is now a haven for bird-watchers, boaters, swimmers and camel riders along its sheltered bays, beaches and lagoons. Visitors should note that there are no taxis or public transport on the island. The only way to travel is by car. The south island townships of Adventure Bay and Alonnah are very

close and can be reached by only a half-hour drive from the ferry terminal in the north.

Bruny Island has a tragic history. The islands were home to Truganini, of the Wuenonne people of Bruny Island, said to have been one of Tasmania's last full-blooded Aboriginal peoples. She died here in 1876. It was also from the aptly named Missionary Bay on the island that Reverend Robinson (p294) began his ill-fated campaign to round up the Indigenous inhabitants of Tasmania for incarceration.

26
Franklin-Gordon Wild Rivers National Park

⚑F6 🚌Strahan ℹThe Esplanade, Strahan; www. parks.tas.gov.au

One of Australia's great wild river systems flows through southwest Tasmania. This spectacular region consists of high ranges and deep gorges. The Franklin-Gordon Wild Rivers National Park extends southeast from Macquarie Harbour (p297) and is one of four national parks in the western part of Tasmania that make up the Tasmanian Wilderness World Heritage Area (p298). The park takes its name from the Franklin and Gordon rivers, both of which were saved by conservationists in 1983 after the Franklin River Blockade (p297).

Within the national park's 442,000 ha (1,090,000 acres) are vast tracts of cool tem-perate rainforest, as well as waterfalls and dolerite- and quartzite-capped mountains. The flora within the park is as varied as the landscape, with impenetrable horizontal scrub, lichen-coated trees, pandani

←

Bruny Island Neck, an isthmus connecting the two Bruny islands

↑ The multitiered Russell Falls in Mount Field National Park

plants and the endemic conifers, King William, celery top and Huon pines. The easiest way into this largely trackless wilderness is via a boat cruise from the town of Strahan. Visitors can disembark and take a short walk to see a 2,000-year-old Huon pine. The park also contains the rugged peak of Frenchmans Cap, accessible to experienced bushwalkers, and the Franklin River's renowned rapids.

The Wild Way, linking Hobart with the west coast, runs through the park. Sections of the river and forest can be reached from the main road along short tracks. Longer walks into the heart of the park require a higher level of survival skills and equipment.

Mount Field National Park

AF6 **i**Lake Dobson Rd, at the entrance to the park; www.parks.tas.gov.au

Little more than 70 km (45 miles) from Hobart along the Maydena Road is Mount Field National Park. Its proximity and beauty make it a popular location with nature-loving tourists. Just a day trip from Hobart, it offers easy access to a diversity of Tasmanian vegetation and wildlife along well-maintained walking tracks.

The most popular walk in the park is also the shortest: the ten-minute trail to Russell Falls starts out from just within the park's entrance through a temperate rainforest environment. Other walks set off from Lake Dobson car park, which is 15 km (9 miles) from the park's entrance up a steep gravel path.

Another popular trail is the 10-km- (6-mile-) long walk to Tarn Shelf, which is a bushwalker's paradise, especially in autumn, when the glacial lakes, mountains and valleys are spectacularly highlighted by the red and orange hues of the deciduous beech trees. Longer trails lead up to the higher peaks of Mount Field West and Mount Mawson, which is southern Tasmania's premier ski slope.

EAT

Bruny Island Cheese and Beer Co
Sample artisan cheeses and home-brewed beers.

AF7 **⌂**1807 Bruny Island Main Rd **W**bruny islandcheese.com.au

---

Get Shucked
An oyster farm and bar with great views.

AF7 **⌂**1735 Bruny Island Main Rd **W**get shucked.com.au

DRINK

Bruny Island House of Whisky
Taste some of the state's best single malts here.

AF7 **⌂**360 Lennon Rd **W**tasmanianhouse ofwhisky.com.au

SOUTH
AUSTRALIA

A road winding through the Flinders Ranges

EXPLORE SOUTH AUSTRALIA

This guide divides South Australia into two colour-coded sightseeing areas, as shown on this map. Find out more about each area on the following pages.

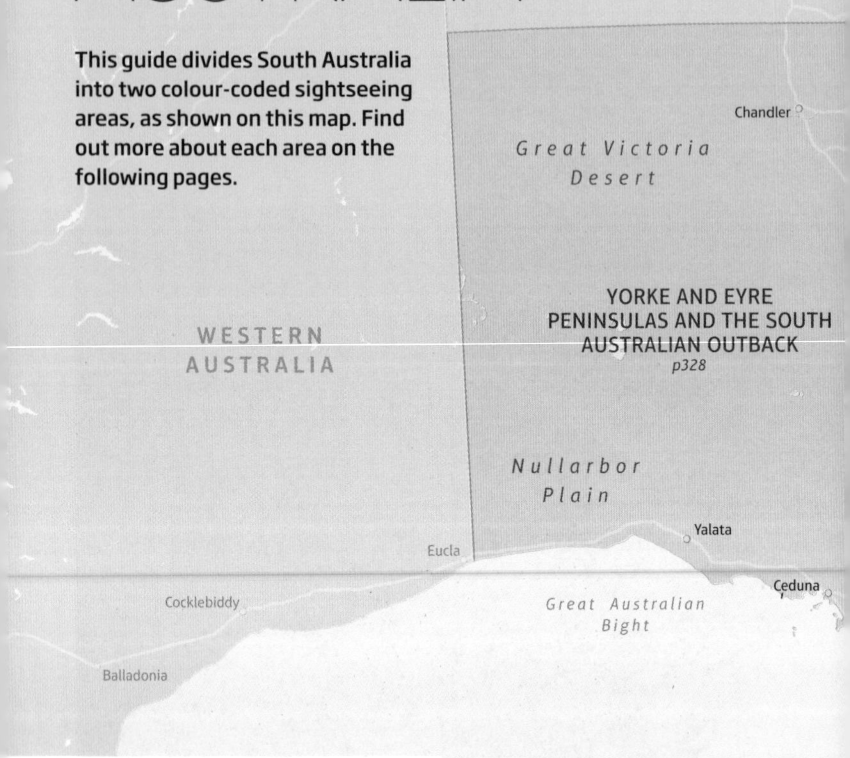

Alice Springs

NORTHERN TERRITORY

Yulara

Erldunda

Chandler

Great Victoria Desert

WESTERN AUSTRALIA

YORKE AND EYRE PENINSULAS AND THE SOUTH AUSTRALIAN OUTBACK
p328

Nullarbor Plain

Eucla

Yalata

Ceduna

Cocklebiddy

Great Australian Bight

Balladonia

AUSTRALIA

Southern Ocean

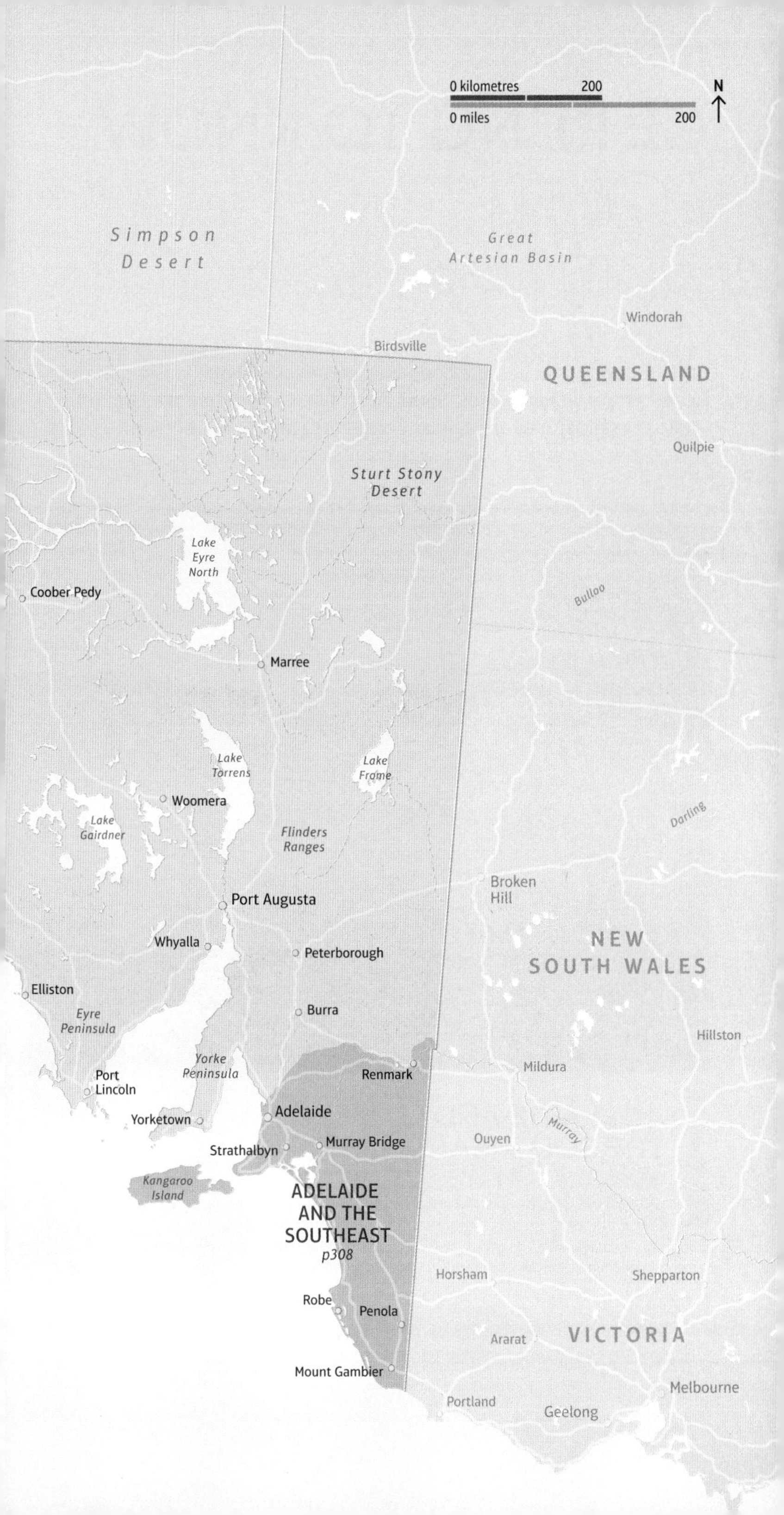

0 kilometres 200

0 miles 200

N

Simpson Desert

Great Artesian Basin

Birdsville

Windorah

QUEENSLAND

Quilpie

Sturt Stony Desert

Coober Pedy

Lake Eyre North

Marree

Bulloo

Lake Torrens

Lake Frome

Woomera

Lake Gairdner

Flinders Ranges

Darling

Broken Hill

NEW SOUTH WALES

Port Augusta

Whyalla

Peterborough

Hillston

Elliston

Eyre Peninsula

Burra

Mildura

Yorke Peninsula

Port Lincoln

Renmark

Ouyen

Murray

Yorketown

Adelaide

Murray Bridge

Strathalbyn

Kangaroo Island

ADELAIDE AND THE SOUTHEAST
p308

Horsham

Shepparton

Robe

Penola

Ararat

VICTORIA

Mount Gambier

Portland

Geelong

Melbourne

GETTING TO KNOW
SOUTH
AUSTRALIA

With its sandy beaches and deep-blue crater lakes, wildlife watching and wine-tasting opportunities, South Australia is an outdoor playground. While the landscapes are epic, the cities are small in scale (even Adelaide feels like a big country town), which adds to their charm.

PAGE 308

ADELAIDE AND THE SOUTHEAST

The once sleepy city of Adelaide is now a cultural hub, with international performing arts festivals, a world-class wine scene, gourmet local produce and a bustling central market. Leaving the city, historic towns give way to the mighty Murray River and a dramatic coastline, with spectacular limestone cliffs and caves, and abundant wildlife, including fur seals, penguins and seabirds. Wildlife encounters await off the coast too, with sea lion and koala colonies on Kangaroo Island.

Best for
Wine and wildlife

Home to
Adelaide, Kangaroo Island

Experience
Wine tasting in the beautiful Barossa Valley

PAGE 328

YORKE AND EYRE PENINSULAS AND THE SOUTH AUSTRALIAN OUTBACK

Red earth, deep craters and dusty roads characterize the South Australian Outback. This vast desert wilderness is punctuated by opal-mining towns, where people live in underground dugouts to escape the searing heat above. Looking for something more comfortable? Try the beautiful beaches of the Yorke and Eyre Peninsulas.

Best for
Rugged scenery

Home to
Flinders Ranges

Experience
Spending a night in an underground hotel in Coober Pedy

The sun setting over a vineyard in the Barossa Valley

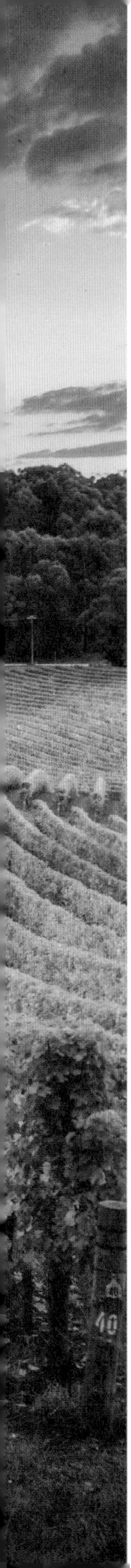

ADELAIDE AND THE SOUTHEAST

Home to the Aboriginal Kaurna people for more than 50,000 years, this region was settled by Europeans in 1836 when Governor John Hindmarsh proclaimed the area a British colony. The settlement was based on a theory of free colonization funded solely by land sales, and no convicts were transported here. Many of the first settlers were nonconformists from Great Britain seeking a more open society. Other early migrants included Lutherans escaping persecution in Germany. They settled in Hahndorf and the Barossa, where they established a wine industry.

Colonel William Light, the Surveyor General, carefully planned the elegant city of Adelaide in 1836, installing a grid pattern, and pretty squares and gardens, all surrounded by parkland. Wealth from agriculture and mining paid for many of Adelaide's fine Victorian buildings. In the mid-20th century, the city established a significant manufacturing industry, in particular of motor vehicles and household appliances. Today, Adelaide still has a booming technology industry.

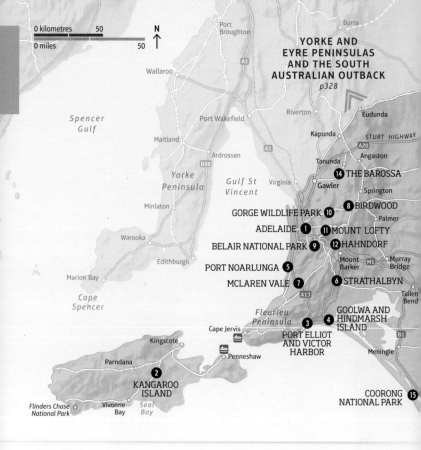

YORKE AND EYRE PENINSULAS AND THE SOUTH AUSTRALIAN OUTBACK *p328*

14 THE BAROSSA

8 BIRDWOOD

10 GORGE WILDLIFE PARK

1 ADELAIDE

11 MOUNT LOFTY

BELAIR NATIONAL PARK **9**

12 HAHNDORF

PORT NOARLUNGA **5**

MCLAREN VALE **7**

6 STRATHALBYN

3 PORT ELLIOT AND VICTOR HARBOR

4 GOOLWA AND HINDMARSH ISLAND

2 KANGAROO ISLAND

COORONG NATIONAL PARK **15**

Southern Ocean

ADELAIDE AND THE SOUTHEAST

Must Sees

1 Adelaide
2 Kangaroo Island

Experience More

3 Port Elliot and Victor Harbor
4 Goolwa and Hindmarsh Island
5 Port Noarlunga
6 Strathalbyn
7 McLaren Vale
8 Birdwood
9 Belair National Park
10 Gorge Wildlife Park
11 Mount Lofty
12 Hahndorf
13 Murray River
14 The Barossa
15 Coorong National Park
16 Robe
17 Mount Gambier
18 Beachport
19 Penola
20 Naracoorte Caves National Park

↑ The serene Torrens River flowing through the heart of Adelaide

1

ADELAIDE

🔼A6 ✈West Beach, 10 km (6 miles) W of the city 🚆North Terrace (suburban); Richmond Rd, Keswick (interstate) 🚌Central Bus Station, Franklin St ℹ25 Pirie St; www.experienceadelaide.com.au

With its gracious stone buildings and garden squares, not to mention its unhurried way of life, Adelaide is a joy to explore. While Adelaide values its past, it is very much a modern city that prides itself on being an important bastion of traditional arts and culture. Expect acclaimed festivals and streetside cafés galore.

Central Market

📍Gouger St ⏰Tue–Sat; hours vary, check website 🚫Public hols 🌐adelaidecentralmarket.com.au

Just west of Victoria Square, Adelaide Central Market has provided a profusion of tastes and aromas in the city for more than 150 years. The changing ethnic pattern of Adelaide society is reflected in the diversity of produce available today. Asian shops now sit beside older European-style delicatessens, and part of the area has become Adelaide's own little Chinatown. Around the market are restaurants and cafés.

Adelaide Town Hall

📍128 King William St ⏰9am–5pm Mon–Fri 🚫Public hols 🌐adelaidetownhall.com.au

Built in 1866, the Adelaide Town Hall fast became the most significant structure on King William Street. The building, designed in Italianate style by the Mayor of the city, Edmund Wright, was the city's premier venue for concerts and civic receptions, and it is still used as such today. Notable features include the regal clock tower at the centrepiece of its façade, as well as the grand staircase and decorative ceiling inside.

Victoria Square

📍King William & Franklin sts

Set in the centre of the city, Victoria Square is home to some of Adelaide's most important edifices, many of them government buildings built during the colonial era.

On the north side of the square is the impressive General Post Office with its clock tower. Opened in 1872, it was hailed by English novelist Anthony Trollope as the "grandest edifice in the town".

To the east is St Francis Xavier Catholic Cathedral. The cathedral's construction started in 1851, but plans for its expansion were hampered due to lack of funds. It was finally completed in 1996, when the spire was added.

South of the square stands the Three Rivers Fountain designed by sculptor John

Did You Know?

Adelaide is the only capital city in Australia that was never settled by convicts.

④
Edmund Wright House

⌂ 59 King William St
Ⓦ experienceadelaide.
com.au

Originally built for the Bank of South Australia in 1878, this finely proportioned structure was set to be demolished in 1971. However, a general outcry led to its public purchase and restoration, and the building was renamed after its main architect, Edmund Wright. The skill and workmanship is displayed in the building's design. In 2019, the house was purchased by a Sydney investor after remaining empty for four years. Its future status has not yet been determined.

Further north along King William Street stands one of Adelaide's finest statues, the South African War Memorial, which is dedicated to those who lost their lives in the Boer War.

Dowie in 1968. Each statue represents one of the three rivers from which Adelaide draws its water: the Torrens, the Onkaparinga and the Murray. Further south of here is the historic Magistrates Court and the grand Supreme Court.

EAT

Chianti
This family-run restaurant has been serving fresh pasta, chargrilled steaks and homemade gelato since 1985.

⌂ 160 Hutt St
Ⓦ chianti.au

Ⓢ Ⓢ Ⓢ

Bakery on O'Connell
Outstanding 24-hour bakery serving savoury pies, gourmet donuts and lamingtons, along with vegan options.

⌂ 128-130 O'Connell St
Ⓦ bakeryonoconnell.
com.au

Ⓢ Ⓢ Ⓢ

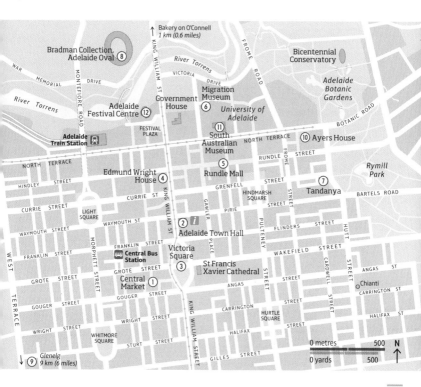

⑤ Rundle Mall

📍Rundle Mall ⏰Daily ❌Good Friday, 25 Dec & public hols 🌐rundle mall.com

Adelaide's main shopping area is centred on Rundle Mall, with its mixture of small shops, boutiques and department stores. Several arcades run off the mall, including Adelaide Arcade. Built in the 1880s, it has Italianate-style elevations at both ends and a central dome. The interior was modernized in the 1960s, but has since been fully restored to its former glory.

⑥ Migration Museum

📍82 Kintore Ave ⏰10am–5pm daily ❌25 Dec 🌐migration.history. sa.gov.au

The thought-provoking Migration Museum is located behind the State Library in what was once Adelaide's Destitute Asylum. It reflects the cultural diversity of South Australian society by telling the stories of people from many different parts of the world who came here to start a new life.

Permanent exhibitions examine different waves of migration: pre- and post-World War II, the "White Australia" policy and the changing fabric of South Australian society. The Memorial Wall acknowledges that many people were forced to leave their homelands.

⑦ Tandanya

📍253 Grenfell St ⏰10am–5pm Mon-Sat ❌Public hols 🌐tandanya.com.au

Tandanya, the Kaurna Aboriginal people's name for the Adelaide area (it means "place of the red kangaroo"), is an excellent cultural institute celebrating the Aboriginal and Torres Strait Islander art and cultures. Established in 1989, it is the first Aboriginal-owned and run arts centre in Australia. The institute features First Nations art galleries, educational workshops and areas for performing. The gift shop sells a wide range of artifacts, arts and crafts.

⑧ Bradman Collection, Adelaide Oval

📍War Memorial Dr ⏰8:30am–5pm Mon-Fri (hours vary on event days) 🌐adelaide oval.com.au

The world-class Bradman Collection at Adelaide Oval – one of the world's best cricket grounds – pays homage to the legendary sportsman Sir Donald Bradman, who batted many memorable innings here. Exhibits

← *The Immigrants* sculpture at the Migration Museum

 GREAT VIEW
Rooftop Views
Climb the roof of the Adelaide Oval's Western Stand for the city's best views (roofclimb.com. au). While standing 50 m (164 ft) above the beautiful sports ground, you'll be able to see out across the city to the rolling Adelaide Hills.

include memorabilia from 50 years of his career and his later life. At the entrance is a sculpture of him executing his signature stroke: the cover drive.

⑨ Glenelg

🚋 ℹ️1 Moseley Sq; www.glenelg.com.au

A 20-minute tram ride from the city centre takes you to this historic seaside neighbourhood, the oldest colony on mainland South Australia. The town hall is a great first port of call to understand Glenelg's Aboriginal heritage, as is the Bay Discovery Centre. To see Glenelg's beautiful Victorian mansions and summer gardens, walk along the South Esplanade. Catching a cruise to watch the sunset is another popular activity, where there is a good chance of spotting dolphins around the hulls.

⑩ Ayers House

📍288 North Terrace 🚌99c 🌐ayershousemuseum. org.au

Ayers House is one of the best examples of Victorian architecture in Australia. It was the home of Sir Henry Ayers, a former Premier of South Australia and an influential businessman, from 1855 until

14 Pieces outside the South Australian Museum, and *(inset)* some of its acclaimed Aboriginal artifacts ↑

his death in 1897. The original house was quite simple but was expanded over the years with the growing status and wealth of its owner. The final form of this elegant mansion is due largely to the noted colonial architect Sir George Strickland Kingston. After 50 years of operating as a museum, Ayers House was closed to visitors in 2021. Following a flurry of petitions and legal challenges, the Ayers House Bill was introduced in 2023 to secure the future of this heritage building. With an upcoming $5.7 million restoration, the timeline for reopening is unclear.

 South Australian Museum

⌂ North Terrace ⏰ 10am-5pm daily ✖ Good Fri, 25 Dec 🌐 samuseum.sa. gov.au

With an entrance framed by huge whale skeletons, this museum has five floors of interesting collections, including an Egyptian room and natural history exhibits.

In cooperation with the Australian Government's Return of Cultural Heritage Program, the museum is working with Aboriginal communities to return sacred objects from their collections to their original tribes.

 Adelaide Festival Centre

⌂ King William St ⏰ 9am-5pm Mon-Fri ✖ Public hols 🌐 adelaidefestivalcentre. com.au

Although it has been around since 1973, this centre was re-launched in 2020 at a stunning new location that is a triumph of contemporary architecture. Known as Australia's first capital city arts venue, it is a cultural centre, performing arts venue and centrepiece for Adelaide's full calendar of cultural events and festivals.

TOP 4 ADELAIDE FESTIVALS

Adelaide Fringe
Mid Feb- mid-March
Annual arts and comedy festival.

Adelaide Festival
Mar
Hosts music, theatre and visual arts.

WOMADelaide
Mar
Celebrates all cultures via music, dance and art.

OzAsia Festival
Oct & Nov
Cultural event that showcases artists from all over Asia.

A SHORT WALK
ADELAIDE

Distance 2 km (1.5 miles) **Time** 30 minutes
Nearest bus 98A and 98C

Adelaide's cultural centre, which lies between the grand, tree-lined North Terrace and the River Torrens, is a lovely area to explore on foot. This route starts near the Adelaide Botanic Garden and then heads along North Terrace. Here, you'll find a succession of imposing 19th-century public buildings, including the state library, museum and art gallery, and two university campuses. The walk ends at Adelaide Festival Centre. Situated on the bank of the river, this multipurpose complex enjoys a picturesque setting and is a perfect place to enjoy an evening stroll.

INSIDER TIP
Ride for Free

The free City Connector bus service runs on two loops – an inner-city loop and an extended route around North Adelaide – providing a useful link to major city attractions. The tram is also free to ride within city limits.

START

*The **Migration Museum** (p314) tells the stories of the thousands of people from more than 100 nations who left everything behind to start a new life in South Australia.*

*Visitors can hire paddleboats to travel along the gentle **River Torrens** to see views of Adelaide from the water.*

VICTO

KINTORE AVENUE

KING WILLIAM ROAD

Adelaide Festival Centre (p315) is a multipurpose arts complex and includes an outdoor amphitheatre. In March, it hosts the renowned annual Adelaide Festival.

*Ten marble Corinthian columns grace the façade of **Parliament House**, which was completed in 1939, more than 50 years after construction first began.*

FINISH

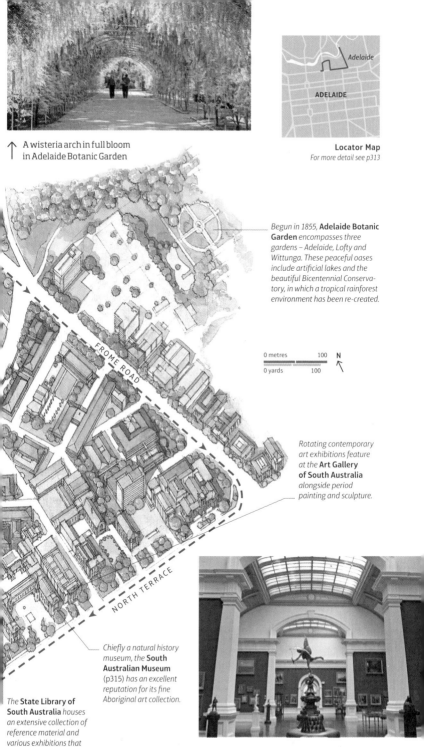

↑ A wisteria arch in full bloom in Adelaide Botanic Garden

Locator Map
For more detail see p313

ADELAIDE

Adelaide

Begun in 1855, **Adelaide Botanic Garden** encompasses three gardens – Adelaide, Lofty and Wittunga. These peaceful oases include artificial lakes and the beautiful Bicentennial Conservatory, in which a tropical rainforest environment has been re-created.

FROME ROAD

0 metres 100 N
0 yards 100

Rotating contemporary art exhibitions feature at the **Art Gallery of South Australia** alongside period painting and sculpture.

NORTH TERRACE

Chiefly a natural history museum, the **South Australian Museum** (p315) has an excellent reputation for its fine Aboriginal art collection.

The **State Library of South Australia** houses an extensive collection of reference material and various exhibitions that explore the region's history and culture.

↑ Sculptures and paintings on display at the Art Gallery of South Australia

KANGAROO ISLAND

🅰 A6 ⛴ SeaLink ferry connection from Cape Jervis
ℹ Kangaroo Island Visitor Information Centre, 43 Howard Dr, Penneshaw; www.kangarooisland visitorcentre.com.au

A compact and beautiful natural setting with a wild coastline and plenty of native vegetation, Kangaroo Island is an exceptional destination for seeing native Australian wildlife.

Australia's third-largest island, Kangaroo Island has 4,405 sq km (1,701 sq miles) of high cliffs, wild beaches and sandy plains. Located 16 km (10 miles) off the Fleurieu Peninsula, the island was the site of South Australia's short-lived first official free settlement, established at Reeves Point in 1836. Today, this isolated and sparsely populated island is a haven for a variety of animals and birds, many protected in its 19 conservation and national parks, and five wilderness protection areas. The interior is dry, but supports tracts of mallee scrub, and eucalyptus. The north coast has sheltered beaches ideal for swimming, while the south coast, battered by the Southern Ocean, has more than 85 shipwrecks.

STAY

Sea Dragon Lodge
Located close to Kangaroo Island's easternmost tip, Sea Dragon Lodge offers the ultimate in luxury, from deluxe rooms to the fine restaurant. There are sweeping ocean views to boot.

🏠 2575 Willoughby Rd 🌐 seadragonlodge. com.au

$ $ $

Highlights

Seal Bay

▶ The south coast windswept beach of Seal Bay is home to a large colony of Australian sea lions.

Remarkable Rocks

▽ At Kirkpatrick Point to the southwest stands a group of large rocks. Aptly named Remarkable Rocks, they have been eroded into unusual formations by the winds and sea.

Ligurian Bees

▶ Kangaroo Island Bee Sanctuary has the last population of pure-breed Ligurian bees, the descendants of a population brought here in the 1880s.

Meeting a Kangaroo

In Flinders Chase National Park, kangaroos will sometimes approach visitors (but you should never feed them).

↑ Peering through Admirals Arch, a natural rock formation sculpted over thousands of years

GETTING AROUND THE ISLAND

There is no public transport on the island and so visitors must travel either on a tour or by car (available for hire at Kingscote Airport), bike or foot. Though the roads to the main sights are good, many roads are unsealed and extra care should be taken. Due to limited visibility and animal activity, avoid driving at night.

The beautiful pristine waters at the island's Emu Bay, near Kingscote

EXPERIENCE MORE

Port Elliot and Victor Harbor

📍A6 🚉 ℹ️10 Coral St, Victor Harbor; www.encountervictorharbor.com.au

Port Elliot, together with nearby Victor Harbor, has long been a favourite place to escape Adelaide's summer heat. Port Elliot, established in 1854 as a port for the Murray River trade, is the prettier of the two towns, with a small museum and a handful of cafés and restaurants. The town also has a safe swimming beach and a fine clifftop walk that offers superb views of the Encounter Bay coastline. Surfing is also popular out beyond Horseshoe Bay.

Victor Harbor gained notoriety as a whaling station during the early 19th century. Today, the southern right whales frolic offshore from June to September. One popular excursion from this town is taking the horse-drawn tram out to see the penguins on rocky Granite Island.

Goolwa and Hindmarsh Island

📍A6 ℹ️4 Goolwa Terrace, Goolwa; www.visit alexandrina.com

Goolwa is an attractive, historic town – its main street is lined with beautiful Georgian architecture. The town has served as a port since the 1850s and is also a gateway to Coorong National Park (p325) and two small, but significant wine regions: Currency Creek and Langhorne Creek. The quiet destination of Hindmarsh Island can also be reached by bridge from Goolwa. The construction of the bridge was controversial and went against the wishes of the local Ngarrindjeri people who campaigned against it in

Did You Know?

Lonely Island, on Hindmarsh Island, is an island within an island (Hindmarsh) within an island (Australia).

1994. On the island there are several good vantage points from which visitors can see the mouth of the Murray River.

Port Noarlunga

📍A6 ℹ️Port Noarlunga Jetty; (08) 8384 0666

Port Noarlunga features a fabulous beach and a protected reef with marine ecosystems that can be explored by snorkellers and scuba divers on a fully marked 800-m (2,600-ft) underwater trail. Nearby, the historic hamlet of Old Noarlunga takes you back to

TOP 5 BEACHES IN THE REGION

Port Noarlunga Beach
A beautiful arc of sand with gentle waves.

Beachport Surf Beach
Excellent for swimming, surfing and boogie boarding (p326).

Waitpinga Beach
A surfing beach an hour south of Adelaide.

Coorong National Park Beaches
This wildly beautiful park has ocean and lagoon beaches (p325).

Emu Bay Beach
Kangaroo Island's best swimming beach is a gently curving shoreline where fine sand meets turquoise water.

the 1840s with atmospheric stone cottages and the village's landmark stone church. Old Noarlunga's village green is a lovely place for a picnic.

Southport Beach, the area's second beach, is a stunning spot where the ocean and the Onkaparinga River meet. The staircase that leads down to the beach is a great place to soak up the view and take some memorable photos.

6
Strathalbyn

🅰A6 🚉 ℹ️Railway Station, 20 South Terrace; www.visitalexandrina.com

This designated heritage town, situated on the banks of the Angas River, was originally settled by Scottish immigrants in 1839. Links with its Scottish ancestry can still be seen today in much of the town's architecture, reminiscent of small highland towns in Scotland.

Strathalbyn is dominated by St Andrew's Church with its sturdy tower. A number of original buildings have been preserved. The police station, built in 1858, and the 1867 courthouse together house the National Trust Museum. The prominent two-storey London House, built as a general store in 1867, has, like a number of buildings in or near the High Street, found a new use as an antiques store.

About 16 km (10 miles) southeast of the town, on the banks of the Bremer River, is Langhorne Creek, renowned as one of the earliest wine-growing regions in Australia; wine has been produced here since the 1850s.

↑ The spectacular avant-garde d'Arenberg Cube, set among Mourvèdre vines in McLaren Vale

7
McLaren Vale

🅰A6 🚗🚌 ℹ️796 Main Rd; www.mclarenvaleand fleurieucoast.com.au

McLaren Vale, less than an hour's drive from Adelaide, is an important wine-producing region in South Australia. It has more than 160 wineries that produce award-winning Shiraz wines and Grenache and Cabernet Sauvignon. Around half of the vineyards are open for tastings and offer platters of local produce to accompany the wines. The vale is also home to many fine restaurants. It is ideal for walking and cycling, with plenty of designated paths.

DRINK

d'Arenberg Cube
On the top floor of this building is a tasting room, which offers fine wines and gorgeous views of McLaren Vale.

🅰A6 🏠58 Osborn Rd, McLaren Vale
🕙10:30am–4:30pm daily
🌐darenberg.com.au

↑ Southport Beach, situated next to the Onkaparinga River estuary, Port Noarlunga

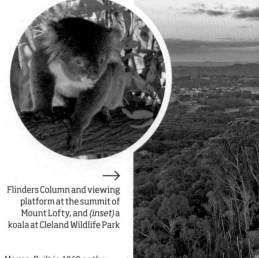

8
Birdwood

A6 ℹ️68 Mount Barker Rd, Hahndorf; www.visit adelaidehills.com.au

Nestled in the Adelaide Hills is the town of Birdwood. In the 1850s, wheat was milled in this town and the old wheat mill now houses Birdwood's most famous asset: the country's largest collection of vintage, veteran and classic motor cars, trucks and motorbikes. The **National Motor Museum** has more than 400 on display and is considered to be one of the best collections of its kind in the southern hemisphere.

National Motor Museum
⊕ 🏠Shannon St ⏰10am-5pm daily 🚫25 Dec 🌐motor.history.sa.gov.au

9
Belair National Park

🅰️A6 🚆From Adelaide ⏰Summer: 8am-9pm daily; winter: 8am-7pm daily 🚫25 Dec 🌐parks.sa.gov.au

Established in 1891, Belair is the oldest national park in South Australia. Tennis courts and pavilions are available for hire and there are picnic facilities throughout the park. Meander through the eucalyptus forests and valleys, and see kangaroos, emus, echidnas and other wildlife. In spring, plants like golden wattles and orchids bloom

Within the park lies the **Old Government**

Flinders Column and viewing platform at the summit of Mount Lofty, and (inset) a koala at Cleland Wildlife Park

House. Built in 1860 as the governor's summer residence, it offers a glimpse into the life of the Victorian gentry.

The park is closed in summer on days of high fire danger.

Old Government House
⊕ ⏰1-4pm 1st and 3rd Sun of month & public hols 🚫Good Fri, Jul, 25 Dec 🌐old governmenthouse.org.au

10
Gorge Wildlife Park

🅰️A6 🏠30 Redden Drive, Cudlee Creek 🚌Adelaide ⏰9am-5pm daily 🚫25 Dec 🌐gorgewildlifepark.com.au

Situated on 5.5 ha (14 acres) of land, Gorge Wildlife Park

A vehicle on display at the National Motor Museum

is home to an abundance of native Australian species, including kangaroos, dingoes, wombats, wallabies and fruit bats. There are also birds – from large ostriches to small fairy wrens – and a colony of free-flying rainbow lorikeets. A number of native reptile species can be found in the reptile house, including bearded dragons and turtles. The most popular residents, however, are the koalas, which can be seen in the trees. The park also offers a kiosk, a souvenir shop, picnic areas and free gas BBQs.

11
Mount Lofty

🅰️E5 🚌Mount Lofty Summit Rd 🌐parks.sa.gov.au

The hills of the Mount Lofty Ranges form the backdrop to Adelaide. The highest point, Mount Lofty, reaches 710 m (2,329 ft) and offers a fine view of the city from the modern lookout at the summit, where there is also an interpretive centre. The hills are dotted

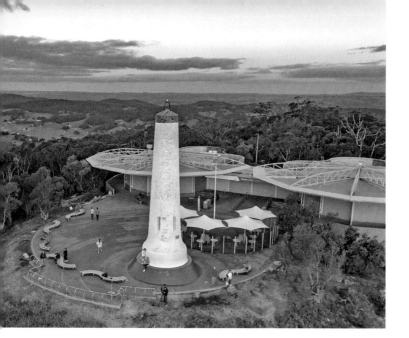

with grand summer houses to which Adelaide citizens retreat during the summer heat.

Just below the summit is the **Cleland Wildlife Park** where visitors can stroll among the kangaroos and emus, take photographs of koalas or walk through the aviary to observe native birds at close quarters.

About 6 km (3.7 mile) south of here by car, Mount Lofty Botanic Gardens feature temperate-climate plants such as rhododendrons and magnolias.

Cleland Wildlife Park

 365 Mount Lofty Summit Rd, Crafers ⏰9:30am–5pm daily 🗓25 Dec 🖥clelandwildlife park.sa.gov.au

Did You Know?

The most common location for snow in South Australia is the summit of Mount Lofty.

12

Hahndorf

🅰A6 🚌From Adelaide ℹ68 Mount Barker St; www.hahndorfsa.org.au

Hahndorf is Australia's oldest surviving German settlement. The first settlers arrived in 1839 aboard the *Zebra* under the command of Captain Dirk Hahn. They settled in the Adelaide Hills and established Hahndorf (Hahn's Village).

The town's tree-lined main street has many examples of classic German architecture, such as houses with *fachwerk* timber framing filled in with wattle and daub, or brick.

Just outside Hahndorf is **The Cedars**, the former home of South Australia's best-known landscape artist, Sir Hans Heysen. His home and his studio are open to the public. To the south of the town is Nixon's Mill, a stone mill built in 1842.

The Cedars

 Heysen Rd ⏰10am–4:30pm Tue–Sun & public hols 🗓Good Fri, 25 & 26 Dec 🖥hansheysen.com.au

---

EAT

Inglewood Inn
Upscale pub tucked away in the middle of the Adelaide Hills.

📍1931 North East Rd, Inglewood 🖥inglewoodinn.com.au

$$$

German Arms Hotel
Tuck into German classics at this spot.

🅰A6 📍69 Main St, Hahndorf 🖥german armshotel.com.au

$$$

Bangkok Noi
Enjoy Thai cuisine at this Hahndorf joint.

🅰A6 📍13–15 Mount Barker Rd, Hahndorf 🖥bangkoknoi hahndorf.com.au

$$$

13

Murray River

🅐 B6 🚌 From Adelaide.
🅘 84 Murray Ave, Renmark;
www.discoverrenmark.
com.au

Australia's largest river is a vital source of water in the driest state in the country. As well as supplying water for Adelaide, it supports a vigorous local agricultural industry that produces more than 40 per cent of all Australian wine. The river is also popular for houseboating, water-skiing and fishing.

The town of Renmark, close to the Victoria border, lies at the heart of the Murray River irrigation area and is home to the Riverlands' first winery.

Just south of Renmark, Berri is the site of the largest combined distillery and winery in the southern hemisphere. The Murray River meanders through Berri and on to Loxton before winding up towards the citrus centre of Waikerie. Surrounded by over 5,000 ha (12,000 acres) of orchards, Waikerie is a favourite gliding centre.

Another 40 km (25 miles) downstream, the river reaches Morgan, its northernmost point in South Australia, before it turns south towards the ocean. The **Morgan Museum**, located in the old landseer warehouse, tells the story of what was once the second-busiest port in the state. Local crafts are for sale in the original railway ticket office.

Beautiful vineyards set against rolling hills in the Barossa Valley ↑

Morgan Museum

♿ 🏠 Railway Terrace, Morgan ⏰ 10am–4pm Mon–Fri 🌐 visitmorgan.com.au

---

14

The Barossa

🅐 A6 🅘 66–68 Murray St, Tanunda; www.barossa.com

The Barossa, which contains both the Barossa and Eden valleys, is one of Australia's most famous and widely acclaimed wine regions. First settled in 1842 by German Lutheran immigrants, villages were established at Bethany, Langmeil (now Tanunda), Lyndoch and Light Pass. Signs of German traditions can be seen in the 19th-century buildings, churches and in the food, music and festivals.

Among the many wineries in the region is Seppeltsfield. Located between Tanunda and Greenock, it was established in 1851. A historic complex of stone buildings, it is reached via an avenue of palm trees and offers a variety of experiences,

↑ The winding Murray River passing through South Australia

INSIDER TIP
Barossa Vintage Festival

Harvest is a time for celebration in the Barossa Valley. Close to Easter, the Barossa Vintage Festival *(www.barossavintagefestival.com.au)* has week-long festivities with music, dancing and more.

Did You Know?

South Australia produces more than half of Australia's total wine volume.

including segway tours, wine tastings and cellar tours. Renowned chef Maggie Beer's Farm Shop and Eatery is another popular site. Also stop by the Barossa Farmers Market, held on Saturday mornings, to sample exceptional produce.

 15

Coorong National Park

🅰A6 ℹ️49 Princes Hwy, Meningie; www.coorong. sa.gov.au

This park is a series of lagoons separated from the ocean by a sandhill peninsula, which extends for 130 km (80 miles) southeast from where the Murray River enters the sea. It's an extraordinarily rich ecosystem, and its combination of freshwater and saltwater, and the varied habitats of sand dunes, lagoons and low-lying coastal scrub, help to support the wildlife. The park, with more than 240 bird species, is a bird-watcher's paradise, although it is also ideal for beach fishing, walking and canoeing. The Coorong was the setting for the well-known Australian children's book *Storm Boy* (1964), a story of a boy and his friendship with a pelican, and two films of the same name.

 16

Robe

🅰A7 ℹ️Lot 131, Mundy Terrace; www.robe.sa.gov.au

Robe is a pretty fishing port that has many charming buildings, a swimming beach and a rugged shoreline. In 1865, more than 16,500 Chinese people landed here and walked to Victoria's gold fields to avoid immigration tax that had to be paid upon landing in the state. These days, the port is known for its historic buildings, wineries and craft breweries. Robe is also a popular summer resort town for people from Adelaide and Melbourne and can get busy during the summer and school holidays, but it's wonderfully relaxed the rest of the year.

DRINK

The Barossa is loved by sommeliers and oeno-philes alike. Here are our picks of the wineries.

Seppeltsfield
🅰A6 🏠730 Seppelts-field Rd, Seppeltsfield
🌐seppeltsfield.com.au

Langmeil
🅰A6 🏠Cnr Langmeil & Para rds, Tanunda
🌐langmeilwinery. com.au

Yalumba
🅰A6 🏠40 Eden Valley Rd, Angaston
🌐yalumba.com

🔟7️⃣ Mount Gambier

🅰B7 🚗🚌 ℹLady Nelson Visitor Centre, 35 Jubilee Hwy; www.mountgambier point.com.au

The city of Mount Gambier is located on the slopes of an extinct volcano. Established in 1854, it is now surrounded by farming country and large pine plantations. The volcano has four crater lakes which are attractive recreation spots, with walking trails, picnic facilities and a wildlife park. The Blue Lake, up to 75 m (245 ft) deep, is a major draw between November and March when its water mysteriously turns an intense blue. From April to October, it remains a slate grey.

There are also a number of caves to explore within the city. Engelbrecht Cave is popular with cave divers.

PICTURE PERFECT
Umpherston Sinkhole

Mount Gambier's Sunken Garden might seem straight out of a fantasy tale. Take a picture of its circular shape from the viewing decks and walk amid vines and palms, keeping an eye out for possums after dusk.

1️⃣8️⃣ Beachport

🅰A7 🚌 ℹMillicent Rd; www.wattlerange.sa.gov.au

Historic Beachport was first settled as a whaling station in the 1830s. In 1941, two sailors were killed by a German land-mine here, making them the first casualties of World War II on Australian soil. Today, the town is a quiet, unspoiled haven dotted with stone buildings, such as the Old Wool and Grain Store housing the local museum, beneath the Norfolk pine trees. The jetty here runs out into the sea for a remarkable 772 m (2,500 ft). There's plenty to do here, especially water activities – go swimming (or floating) at the Pool of Siloam, a salt lake that is 700 per cent more salinated than the sea.

COONAWARRA'S TERRA ROSSA

Coonawarra's wine region sits atop a limestone ridge overlaid by rich red soil, 15 km (9 miles) by 2 km (1 mile), known as Terra Rossa: this light clay allows optimum water and air-flow to nourish grapes, thereby producing stellar wines like the famous Coonawarra Cabernet Sauvignon. Surrounding swamps makes this area all the more remarkable.

1️⃣9️⃣ Penola

🅰B7 🚌 ℹ27 Arthur St; www.wattlerange.sa.gov.au

One of the oldest towns in the Southeast, Penola is the commercial centre of the Coonawarra wine region, where the first winery was built in 1893. There are now more than

Inside a cave in the Naracoorte Caves National Park ↑

25 wineries, most of which are open for sales and tastings.

Penola itself is a quiet town that takes great pride in its history. A heritage walk takes visitors past most of its early buildings, including the restored Sharam Cottages, which were built in 1850 as the first dwellings in Penola. This town is well known for being the home of St Mary MacKillop, Australia's first saint. To learn about her life, visit the centre established in her name.

Situated 40 km (25 miles) north of Penola, Bool Lagoon Game Reserve (designated a wetland of international significance by Ramsar), is an important refuge for an assortment of native wildlife, including more than 150 species of birds. The park provides an opportunity to observe many of these local and migratory birds.

←

The scenic town of Beachport along the Limestone Coast, and *(inset)* a man fishing on one of its sandy beaches

20

Naracoorte Caves National Park

🗺️ B7 🚌 From Adelaide
🕐 9am–5pm daily (last tour: 3:30pm) 🗓️ 25 Dec 🌐 nara coortecaves.sa.gov.au

Located 12 km (7.5 miles) south of Naracoorte is the Naracoorte Caves National Park. Within this 600-ha (1,500-acre) park, there are 28 known caves, out of which only four are open to the public. The most notable is the Victoria Fossil Cave, which is on the World Heritage List as a result of the fossil deposits discovered here in 1969. The site offers self-guided, guided and adventure-caving tours year-round.

The spectacular Alexandra Cave is full of delicate needle-like stalactites and massive twisting columns. The tour of this cave offers a good introduction to the geological processes that form caves.

Thousands of bent-wing bats come to breed in the Bat Cave from November to February. They can be seen leaving the cave en masse at dusk to feed. Entry to Bat Cave is prohibited, but visitors can view the roosting bats via infrared cameras in the park.

The lunar landscape of Coober Pedy

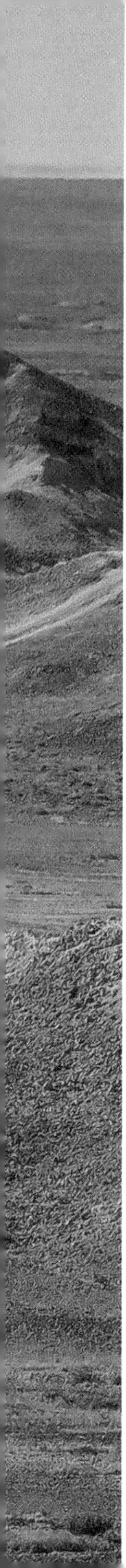

YORKE AND EYRE PENINSULAS AND THE SOUTH AUSTRALIAN OUTBACK

The Nauo of the Eyre Peninsula and the Narungga of the Yorke Peninsula were no strangers to European encroachment. Both Aboriginal peoples had been raided by whalers and sealers before the British colonized the area in 1836. Within a decade, their population had been devastated by violent encounters with settlers and the introduction of new diseases. At the same time, the colony of South Australia was suffering financial problems partly due to economic mismanagement. These were largely remedied by the discovery of copper at Kapunda, north of Adelaide, in 1842, and at Burra, near Clare, in 1845. As these resources were depleted, fresh discoveries were made in the north of the Yorke Peninsula, in the area known as Little Cornwall, at the town of Wallaroo and Kadina in 1859 and at Moonta in 1861. By the 1870s, South Australia was the British Empire's leading copper producer, and copper, silver and uranium mining still boosts the state's economy today.

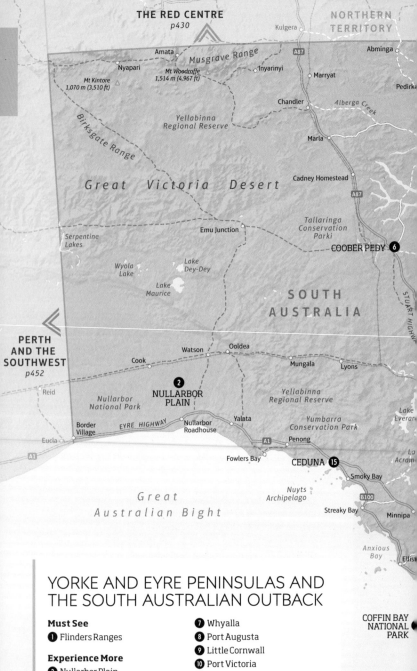

THE RED CENTRE
p430

Kulgera

NORTHERN TERRITORY

Amata

Abminga

Musgrave Range

Nyapari

A87

Pedirka

Mt Kintore
1,070 m (3,510 ft)

Mt Woodroffe
1,514 m (4,967 ft)

Inyarinyi

Marryat

Birksgate Range

Chandler

Alberga Creek

Yellabinna
Regional Reserve

Marla

Great Victoria Desert

Cadney Homestead

A87

Serpentine
Lakes

Emu Junction

Tallaringa
Conservation
Parki

COOBER PEDY **6**

Wyola
Lake

Lake
Dey-Dey

SOUTH
AUSTRALIA

Lake
Maurice

STUART HIGHWAY

PERTH
AND THE
SOUTHWEST
p452

Watson

Ooldea

Cook

Mungala

Lyons

Reid

Nullarbor
National Park

2
NULLARBOR
PLAIN

Yellabinna
Regional Reserve

Lake
Everar

Border
Village

EYRE HIGHWAY

Nullarbor
Roadhouse

Yalata

Yumbarra
Conservation Park

Eucla

A1

Penong

La
Acram

A1

Fowlers Bay

CEDUNA **15**

Smoky Bay

Great
Australian Bight

*Nuyts
Archipelago*

B100

Streaky Bay

Minnipa

Anxious
Bay

Ellis

YORKE AND EYRE PENINSULAS AND
THE SOUTH AUSTRALIAN OUTBACK

Must See

1 Flinders Ranges

Experience More

2 Nullarbor Plain
3 Witjira National Park
4 Munga-Thirri-Simpson
Desert Conservation Park
5 Kati Thanda-Lake Eyre
National Park
6 Coober Pedy

7 Whyalla
8 Port Augusta
9 Little Cornwall
10 Port Victoria
11 Yorketown
12 Clare Valley
13 Coffin Bay National Park
14 Port Lincoln
15 Ceduna

COFFIN BAY
NATIONAL
PARK

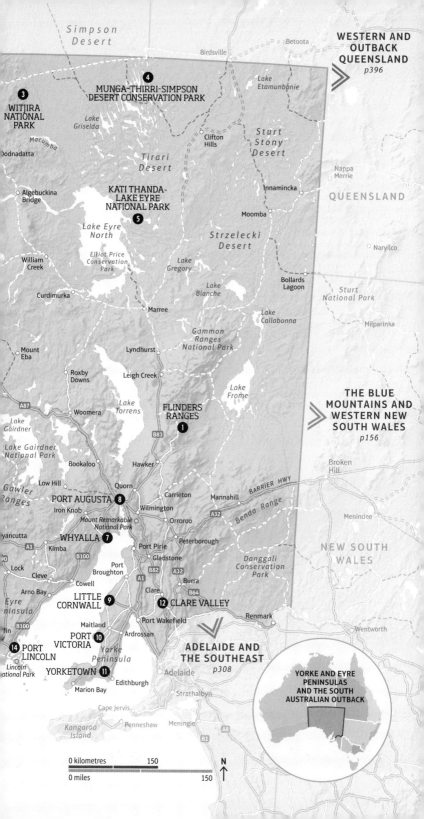

Simpson
Desert

Betoota

**WESTERN AND
OUTBACK
QUEENSLAND**
p396

Birdsville

④

**MUNGA-THIRRI-SIMPSON
DESERT CONSERVATION PARK**

Lake
Etamunbanie

③

**WITJIRA
NATIONAL
PARK**

Lake
Griselda

Clifton
Hills

*Sturt
Stony
Desert*

Oodnadatta

Macumba

*Tirari
Desert*

Nappa
Merrie

QUEENSLAND

Innamincka

Algebuckina
Bridge

**KATI THANDA-
LAKE EYRE
NATIONAL PARK**

⑤

Lake Eyre
North

Moomba

Naryilco

William
Creek

*Elliot Price
Conservation
Park*

*Strzelecki
Desert*

Lake
Gregory

Curdimurka

Lake
Blanche

Bollards
Lagoon

*Sturt
National Park*

Marree

Milparinka

Mount
Eba

*Gammon
Ranges
National Park*

Lyndhurst

Lake
Callabonna

Roxby
Downs

Leigh Creek

A87

Woomera

*Lake
Torrens*

**FLINDERS
RANGES**

①

Lake
Frome

*Lake
Gairdner*

**THE BLUE
MOUNTAINS AND
WESTERN NEW
SOUTH WALES**
p156

*Lake Gairdner
National Park*

Bookaloo

B83

Hawker

Broken
Hill

*Gawler
Ranges*

Low Hill

Quorn

Carrieton

Mannahill

BARRIER HWY

PORT AUGUSTA **⑧**

Wilmington

Benda Range

Menindee

Iron Knob

Orroroo

A32

⑦ **A1** **WHYALLA**

*Mount Remarkable
National Park*

Peterborough

NEW SOUTH
WALES

yancutta

Kimba

Port Pirie

*Danggali
Conservation
Park*

B100

Gladstone

Lock

*Port
Broughton*

A32

Cleve

Cowell

A1

Clare

Burra

B64

*Eyre
ninsula*

Arno Bay

**LITTLE
CORNWALL** **⑨**

B82

⑫ **CLARE VALLEY**

Renmark

B100

Maitland

Port Wakefield

Wentworth

fin

**⑭ PORT
LINCOLN**

**PORT
VICTORIA** **⑩**

Ardrossan

*Yorke
Peninsula*

**ADELAIDE AND
THE SOUTHEAST**
p308

*Lincoln
ational Park*

YORKETOWN **⑪**

Adelaide

**YORKE AND EYRE
PENINSULAS
AND THE SOUTH
AUSTRALIAN OUTBACK**

Edithburgh

Marion Bay

Strathalbyn

Cape Jervis

Penneshaw

Meningie

*Kangaroo
Island*

A8

B1

0 kilometres   150

0 miles   150

N
↑

FLINDERS RANGES

This mountainous terrain extends for 400 km (250 miles) from Crystal Brook, north of the Clare Valley, into South Australia's outback. A favourite with bushwalkers, they offer a range of stunning scenery and wildlife, much of it protected.

In the southern part of the Flinders Ranges is Mount Remarkable National Park, known for its abundant wildflowers and excellent walking trails. About 50 km (30 miles) north is the town of Quorn, start of the restored Pichi Richi Railway where visitors can board a heritage steam train and ride through rocky plains and rolling hills. North of Quorn lie the dramatic Warren, Yarrah Vale and Buckaring gorges, each threaded with walking and cycling trails through native pines and high cliffs capped with gum trees. Much of the central Flinders Ranges are contained within the Flinders Ranges National Park. The park's best-known feature is Wilpena Pound (Ikara), an elevated natural basin covering some 90 sq km (35 sq miles) with sheer outer walls 500 m (1,600 ft) high. To the north is Gammon Ranges National Park, just outside of which is Arkaroola, a tourist village with a wildlife sanctuary and a state-of-the-art observatory.

Oodnadatta Track

Running for 620 km (385 miles) between Marla and Marree, the Oodnadatta Track is one of Australia's best-loved outback roads. It skirts Kati Thanda-Lake Eyre, Australia's largest lake (often an expanse of salt pans) and crosses the old Great Northern Railway (along which the iconic *Ghan* railway travelled from 1929 to 1980). To drive it, you'll need a 4WD vehicle.

GREAT VIEW
The Breakaways at Sunset

For outback views, go to Kanku-Breakaways Conservation Park, 30 km (20 miles) north of Coober Pedy. At sunset, the earth turns an array of reds and yellows. There are frequent tours here from Coober Pedy.

Did You Know?

The Flinders Ranges are among the oldest landscapes in the world.

1 Yellow-footed rock wallabies are a common sight in Flinders Ranges National Park.

2 The Pichi Richi Railway is a heritage steam train that runs in the Flinders Ranges.

3 The majestic Flinders Ranges towers over the surrounding landscape.

The Flinders Ranges National Park's best-known feature is Wilpena Pound (Ikara), an elevated natural basin.

↑ Undulating road in the rugged Bunyeroo Valley in the Flinders Ranges

STAY

Prairie Hotel
A luxurious haven deep in the outback, the Prairie Hotel offers 12 tasteful rooms along with tours, locally sourced food and a brewery.

🅰E4 📍Cnr High St & West Terrace, Parachilna
🅦 prairiehotel.com.au

$$$

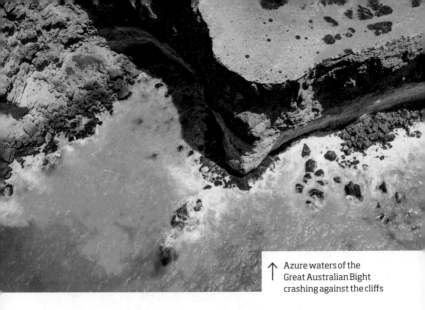

↑ Azure waters of the Great Australian Bight crashing against the cliffs

EXPERIENCE MORE

 2

Nullarbor Plain

🅐 C4 🚊 Port Augusta
🚌 Ceduna 🛈 58 Poynton St,
Ceduna; www.ceduna
tourism.com.au

The huge expanse of the
Nullarbor Plain stretches
from Nundroo, about 160 km
(100 miles) west of Ceduna, to
the distant Western Australia
border 330 km (200 miles)
away, and beyond into Western Australia. This dry, dusty
plain can be crossed by rail on
the Trans-Australian Railway or
by road on the Eyre Highway.
The train travels further
inland than the road, its route
giving little relief from the flat
landscape. The highway lies

Did You Know?

A 340-km (210-mile)
stretch of desert on the
Nullarbor has its own
time zone based on the
quarter hour.

nearer the coast, passing a
few sights of interest, such as
Nullarbor Links, the world's
longest 18-hole golf course,
with one hole in each town or
roadhouse along the highway.
Visitors should plan ahead if
they intend to drive as there
are few petrol stations.

Just south of the small town
of Nundroo lies Fowlers Bay.
Good for fishing, it is popular
with anglers seeking solitude.
West of here, the road passes
through the Yalata Aboriginal
Lands. Bordering Yalata to
the west is the vast Nullarbor
National Park. This runs from
the Nullarbor Roadhouse
hamlet, 130 km (80 miles)
west of Nundroo, to the
border with Western Australia
200 km (125 miles) away. The
Eyre Highway passes through
the park, close to the coastal
cliffs, with spectacular views
over the Great Australian Bight.

The world's longest cave
system runs beneath the
plain, and the border area has
many underground caves and
caverns. These should only
be explored by experienced
cavers, however, as many are
flooded and dangerous.

3

Witjira National Park

🅐 D4 🌐 eparks.sa.gov.
au/parks

About 200 km (125 miles) north
of Coober Pedy lies the town of
Oodnadatta, where drivers can
check the road and weather
conditions before heading
north to Witjira National Park.

Witjira has dunes, saltpans,
boulder plains and coolibah
woodlands, but it is famous for
its hot artesian springs.
Dalhousie Springs supply
essential water for Aboriginal
Australians, pastoralists and
wildlife, including water snails,
unique to the area.

4

Munga-Thirri-Simpson Desert Conservation Park

🅐 E4 🕐 1 Dec–15 Mar
🌐 parks.sa.gov.au

Located within Australia's
driest region, the Munga-
Thirri-Simpson Desert
Conservation Park adjoins

both Queensland and the Northern Territory. It is the largest national park in Australia. The region is an almost endless series of sand dunes, lakes, spinifex grassland and gidgee woodland.

The landscape is home to some 180 bird, 92 reptile and 44 native mammal species, some of which have developed nocturnal habits as a response to the aridity of the region.

OUTBACK DRIVING

Driving into the outback is a serious undertaking. Almost every year, unprepared travellers either die from exposure to the heat after getting lost or stuck on remote trails, or end up the recipients of costly rescue missions. Anyone embarking on a 4WD trip should inform themselves of the risks and prepare accordingly: carry plenty of water and adequate supplies of fuel and food, and let someone know when and where you're going and expect to return. It's advisable to travel in a convoy, and to carry a satellite phone or HF radio. If you get stuck or break down, always stay with your vehicle.

Kati Thanda-Lake Eyre National Park

◆E4 🕙 1 Dec–15 Mar
🌐 environment.sa.gov.au

Kati Thanda-Lake Eyre National Park encompasses all of Lake Eyre North and extends eastwards into the Tirari Desert. Lake Eyre/Kati Thanda is Australia's largest salt lake, 15 m (49 ft) below sea level at its lowest point, with a salt crust said to weigh 400 million tonnes. Vegetation is low, comprising mostly blue bush, samphire and saltbush. On the rare occasions when the lake floods, it alters dramatically: flowers bloom and birds such as pelicans and gulls appear, turning the lake into a breeding ground. In summer, the temperature can soar to more than 50° C (122° F).

The harsh, desert environment of the lake makes the terrain difficult to navigate. Do not walk or drive on the lake; the seemingly hard surface can often hide soft mud underneath, making it easy to get stuck, but hard to get out of. In the event of a breakdown, stay with your vehicle. An alternative way to see the park is to take a two-hour scenic flight from the small town of William Creek, located along the Oodnadatta Track *(p332)*.

Coober Pedy

◆D4 🚗 🚌 ℹ️ Lot 773, Hutchison St; www.cooberpedy.com

One of Australia's most famous outback towns, Coober Pedy is an unusual settlement in the heart of an extremely hostile landscape. Frequent duststorms and a never-ending desert landscape with abandoned mines contribute to the town's desolate appearance, yet the small population is wonderfully multicultural, hailing from over 45 nations.

Opal was discovered here in 1915, and today Coober Pedy produces a large percentage of the world's supply. Mining claims here are limited to one per person. For this reason opal mining is the preserve of individuals, not large companies, and this adds to the town's "frontier" quality.

Coober Pedy's name comes from the Aboriginal *kupa piti*, meaning "white man in a hole", and it is apt indeed. The hotels, houses and churches are built underground. This way, the residents escape the extreme temperatures.

A most remarkable subterranean structure is the richly decorated **Serbian Orthodox Church**, dug into the rock in 1993.

Serbian Orthodox Church
🏠 Potch Gully Rd 📞 (08) 8672 3048 ◯ Daily

→
An underground church inside an old opal mine in Coober Pedy

➐ Whyalla

🅰E5 🚆🚌 ℹ Lincoln Hwy;
www.whyalla.com

At the gateway to the Eyre Peninsula, Whyalla is the state's largest provincial city. Once a shipping port for iron ore, the city was transformed in 1939 when a blast furnace, a harbour and a shipyard were established. The first ship built in the yard, the HMAS *Whyalla*, is on display at the **Whyalla Maritime Museum** and can be accessed through guided tours only. Bookings are essential.

Although an industrial centre, the city has public artworks, fine beaches and good fishing spots. Whyalla's foreshore is home to a busy marina, gardens and cafés.

Whyalla Maritime Museum

⊗⊗ 🅰 Lincoln Hwy
🕐 10am–4pm daily
🚫 Good Fri, 25 Dec
🅦 whyalla.sa.gov.au

> **INSIDER TIP**
> **Look Out For Cuttlefish**
>
> From mid-May to July, giant cuttlefish ply the waters of the Upper Spencer Gulf Marine Park off Whyalla. They change colour in an instant – a spectacular sight to see on a swim.

↑ HMAS *Whyalla* (1941) docked 2 km (1 mile) from the sea at the Whyalla Maritime Museum

➑ Port Augusta

🅰E5 🚆🚌🚗 ℹ 41 Flinders Terrace; (08) 8641 9193

Situated at the head of Spencer Gulf, Port Augusta is at the crossroads of Australia; here lies the intersection of the Sydney–Perth and Adelaide–Alice Springs railway lines, as well as the major Sydney–Perth and Adelaide–Darwin highways. Once an important port, the city's power stations produce 40 per cent of the state's electricity. The coal-fired Northern Power Station, which dominates the city's skyline, was shut down in 2016.

Port Augusta is also the beginning of South Australia's outback region. The **Wadlata Outback Centre** imaginatively tells the story of the Far North from 15 million years ago, through Aboriginal and European history and up to the present day.

Arid Lands Botanic Garden, a 200-ha (500-acre) site, is an important research and education facility, as well as a recreational area. It also affords panoramic views of the Flinders Ranges (*p332*) to the east.

Wadlata Outback Centre

 🅰 41 Flinders Terrace
🕐 9am–4pm Mon–Fri, 10am–3pm Sat & Sun 🚫 25 Dec
🅦 wadlata.sa.gov.au

Arid Lands Botanic Garden

☺ 🅰 144 Stuart Hwy
🕐 7:30am–sunset daily
🚫 1 Jan, Good Fri & 25–26 Dec 🅦 aalbg.sa.gov.au

➒ Little Cornwall

🅰E5 🚌 Kadina ℹ Old Railway Stn, Blanche Terrace, Moonta; (08) 8825 1891

The towns of Moonta, Kadina and Wallaroo were established after copper discoveries on Yorke Peninsula in 1859 and 1861. Collectively the towns are known as "The Copper Coast", and Moonta as "Australia's Little Cornwall". Miners from Cornwall, England, came here in the 19th century seeking their fortunes. The biennial festival "Kernewek Lowender" (meaning "Cornish Happiness") celebrates this Cornish heritage.

Wallaroo, the site of the first copper ore smelting works, was also a shipping port for ore. The **Wallaroo Heritage and Nautical Museum** traces the history of the town.

Moonta, once home to Australia's richest copper mine, contains many sites in the **Moonta Mines State Heritage Area**. Also of interest is the Moonta Mines Railway, a restored light-gauge locomotive.

The Cape Spencer Lighthouse in Innes National Park, Yorke Peninsula, and *(inset)* the remains of *Ethel*

Kadina, where copper was originally found, is the Yorke Peninsula's largest town. The **Farm Shed Museum and Tourism Centre** has interesting displays on mining and folk history of the area.

Wallaroo Heritage and Nautical Museum

⊗ 🅐 Jetty Rd 🕒 10am–4pm daily 🚫 25 Dec 🔗 national trust.org.au

Moonta Mines State Heritage Area

⊗ 🅐 Blanche Terrace 📞 (08) 8825 1891 🕒 9am–5pm daily 🚫 Good Fri & 25 Dec

Farm Shed Museum and Tourism Centre

⊗ 🅐 50 Mines Rd, Kadina 📞 (08) 8821 2333 🕒 9am–5pm Mon–Fri, 10am–4pm Sat & Sun 🚫 Good Fri & 25 Dec 🔗 moontaheritage.com.au

---

 Port Victoria

🅐 A6 ℹ️ The Foreshore; www.visityorkepeninsula. com.au

Lying on the west coast of the Yorke Peninsula, Port Victoria is today a holiday destination, popular with anglers, swimmers and divers. In the early 20th century, however, it was a busy sea port with large clippers and windjammers loading grain bound for the northern hemisphere. The last time a square rigger used the port was in 1949. The story of these ships and their epic voyages is told in the Maritime Museum, located adjacent to the jetty.

About 10 km (6 miles) off the coast lies Wardang Island, around which are eight known shipwrecks dating from 1871. Divers can follow the Wardang Island Maritime Heritage Trail to view the wrecks. Boats to the island can be chartered, but permission to land must be obtained from the Community Council in Point Pearce, the nearby Aboriginal settlement that administers the island.

 Yorketown

🅐 A6 🚌 ℹ️ 33 Stansbury Rd; www.visityorke peninsula.com.au

Yorketown is the commercial centre of the earliest settled area on the southern Yorke Peninsula. It lies at the heart of a region scattered with nearly 200 salt lakes, many of which turn pink at various times of the year, depending on the changing salinity of the water. From the late 1890s until the 1930s, salt harvesting was a major industry in this region.

Approximately 70 km (40 miles) southwest of the town is the spectacular Innes National Park. The park's geography changes from salt lakes and low mallee scrub inland to sandy beaches and rugged cliffs along the coast. Kangaroos and emus are commonly seen, but other native inhabitants, such as the large mallee fowl, are more difficult to spot.

There is good surfing, reef diving and fishing in the park, especially at Browns Beach, Pondalowie Bay, Chinamans Beach and Shell Beach. Other beaches are considered unsafe for swimming. Also in the park are the remains of the shipwrecked barque *Ethel*, which ran aground in 1904 and now lies below the limestone cliffs of Ethel Beach.

Clare Valley

⚐ A6 🚌 Clare 🛈 8 Spring Gully Rd, Clare; www.clarevalley.com.au

Picturesque Clare Valley is a premium wine-producing region. At its head lies the town of Clare. There are many historic buildings here, such as the Old Police Station and Courthouse Museum, housed in an 1850s station building, and Wolta Wolta, an early pastoralist's home built in 1846, where visitors can stay.

Sevenhill Cellars, 7 km (4 miles) south of Clare, is the valley's oldest vineyard. It was established by Austrian Jesuits in 1851 to produce altar wine for the colonies. East of Sevenhill is **Martindale Hall**, an elegant 1879 mansion.

Lying 12 km (7 miles) north of Clare is **Bungaree Station**. This merino sheep-farming complex was established in 1841 and is maintained as a working 19th-century model. The exhibits here reveal the life and work at the station.

Northeast of Clare is Burra town, a State Heritage Area that was home to the largest mine in Australia. The 19th-century Burra Mine Site is now an exciting industrial archaeological site. Attractions include Morphett's Engine House Museum (open every morning), Bon Accord Mining Museum and Paxton Square Cottages. Many old buildings have been restored, as have a number of the shops and houses. To access the site, visitors need to purchase a permit from the **Burra & Goyder Visitor Centre**.

Sevenhill Cellars

⚐ 111C College Rd, Sevenhill 5453 🕒 10am–5pm daily 🚫 1 Jan, Good Fri, 25 & 26 Dec 🌐 sevenhill.com.au

Martindale Hall

⚐ 1 Manoora Rd, Mintaro 5415 🕒 10am–4pm Wed–Mon 🚫 1 Jan, Good Fri, 25 & 26 Dec 🌐 martindalehall.com.au

Bungaree Station

⚐ 431 Bungaree Rd, Clare 🕒 Via guided tours only, check website 🌐 bungareestation.com.au

Burra & Goyder Visitor Centre

⚐ 2 Market St, Burra 🕒 Hours vary, check website 🚫 25 Dec 🌐 visitburra.com

---

⑬

Coffin Bay National Park

⚐ D5 🚌 Port Lincoln 🌐 parks.sa.gov.au

Coffin Bay National Park lies to the west of the southern tip of the Eyre Peninsula. This coastal wilderness has exposed cliffs, sheltered sandy beaches, rich birdlife and great fishing. Wildflowers bloom in the park early spring to early summer.

There are several scenic drives through the park (some roads are accessible to 4WD vehicles only). Conventional vehicles can take the sealed Coffin and Avoid Bay roads to Yangie and Avoid bays. Access to Gunyah Beach is by dirt road.

EAT

1802 Oyster Bar

This bar serves Coffin Bay oysters, said to be the best in the country.

⚐ D5 ⚐ 61 Esplanade, Coffin Bay 🌐 1802 oysterbar.com.au

⑂⑂⑂

Ceduna Oyster Barn

Enjoy fresh oysters or try the sushi, fish and chips, or salad bowls.

⚐ D4 ⚐ Lot 20 Eyre Hwy, Ceduna 📞 0497 085 549

⑂⑂⑂

↑ Neatly planted vines in the Clare Valley region of South Australia

↑ Turquoise waters at a beach in Coffin Bay National Park

To the east of Point Avoid, Almonta Beach is one of Australia's best surfing beaches.

Coffin Bay town is a popular centre for windsurfing, sailing, swimming and fishing. It is also famous for its oysters. The Oyster Walk is a pleasant walking trail along the foreshore through native bushland.

---

⑭
Port Lincoln

🅰D5 🚗🚌 ℹ️60 Tasman Terrace; www.portlincoln. com.au

Port Lincoln sits on the shore of Boston Bay, one of the world's largest natural harbours. A fishing centre, it is home to Australia's largest tuna fleet.

Though the annual Tunarama Festival and its famous "tuna toss" no longer take place, marine life is still the primary reason to visit Port Lincoln.

Take a boat trip to Dangerous Reef or the Neptune Islands to view great white sharks from the relative safety of the boat or submerged cage. In the middle of the bay lies Boston Island, a working sheep station.

There are several buildings of note here. South of Port Lincoln, **Mikkira Station** is one of the country's oldest sheep stations. It is ideal for picnics or camping, with a restored pioneer cottage and a koala colony. The **Koppio Smithy**

Museum, located in the Koppio Hills 40 km (25 miles) north of Port Lincoln, is an agricultural museum with a furnished 1890 log cottage and a 1905 smithy.

Just 20 km (12 miles) south is Lincoln National Park with its rocky hills, sheltered coves, sandy beaches and high cliffs. Emus and parrots are common here and ospreys and sea eagles frequent the coast. West of the park, Whalers Way offers dramatic coastal scenery. This land is private and entry is via a permit from the visitors' centre.

Mikkira Station

⊗ 🏠Mikkira Lane, off Fishery Bay Rd 🚫When over 30°C (86°F) 🌐mikkirakoalas.com

Koppio Smithy Museum

⊗ 🏠RSD 1951 Koppio Rd, Koppio 🕐10am-5pm Tue-Sun 🚫Good Fri, 25 Dec 🌐nationaltrust.org.au

---

⑮
Ceduna

🅰D4 🚗🚌 ℹ️58 Poynton St; www.cedunatourism. com.au

At the top of the west side of the Eyre Peninsula, Ceduna is the most westerly significant town in South Australia before the start of the Nullarbor Plain. This town's name comes from the Aboriginal word *cheedoona*, meaning "a place to rest".

Within the town is the **Ceduna School House Museum**, with its collections of restored farm equipment from early pioneer days. It also has a display on the British atomic weapons tests held at nearby Maralinga in the 1950s, and some Aboriginal artifacts.

An 1850s whaling station on St Peter Island, off the coast of Ceduna, is now a base for whale-watchers. Southern right whales can be seen close to the shore from June to October.

The oyster-farming industry has established itself west and east of Ceduna at Denial and Smoky bays. Between Ceduna and Penong, a hamlet 75 km (45 miles) to the west, there are detours to surfing beaches including the Cactus Beach.

Ceduna School House Museum

⊗ 🏠2 Park Terrace 🕐10am-noon Mon, Tue, Fri & Sat, 2-4pm Wed, 10am-4pm Thu 🚫25 Dec 🌐nationaltrust.org.au

---

WILDLIFE OF THE EYRE PENINSULA

An enormous variety of wildlife inhabits the Eyre Peninsula. Kangaroos, hairy-nosed wombats *(right)*, emus, wedge-tailed and sea eagles, ospreys, albatrosses and petrels can be seen here. The most spectacular sight are the southern right whales which breed at the head of the Great Australian Bight.

QUEENSLAND

The sprawling Great Barrier Reef

EXPLORE
QUEENSLAND

This guide divides Queensland into four colour-coded
sightseeing areas, as shown on this map. Find out more
about each area on the following pages.

Torres Strait
Islands

Bamaga

Weipa

Cape York
Peninsula

Gulf of
Carpentaria

Borroloola

Daly Waters

Dunbar

Burketown

Normanton

*Tanami
Desert*

Renner
Springs

Tennant Creek

Mount Isa

Cloncurry

NORTHERN
TERRITORY

Winton

Boulia

Alice
Springs

*Simpson
Desert*

*Great
Artesian
Basin*

Erldunda

Birdsville

SOUTH
AUSTRALIA

Lake
Eyre
North

Moomba

Coober
Pedy

| 0 kilometres | 250 |
| 0 miles | 250 |

N
↑

AUSTRALIA

Coral
Sea

Pacific
Ocean

Cooktown

FAR NORTH
QUEENSLAND
p380

Port Douglas

Cairns

Mount Garnet

Innisfail

Mission Beach

*Hinchinbrook
Island*

Greenvale

Townsville

Charters Towers

Bowen

*Whitsunday
Islands*

Hughenden

Mackay

Clermont

St Lawrence

Longreach

Rockhampton

WESTERN AND
OUTBACK QUEENSLAND
p396

Gladstone

Bundaberg

SOUTHEAST
QUEENSLAND AND
THE WHITSUNDAYS
p364

Fraser Island

Maryborough

Charleville

Mitchell

Chinchilla

Noosa

Caloundra

Cunnamulla

St George

Toowoomba

BRISBANE
p348

Gold Coast

Byron Bay

Bourke

NEW SOUTH
WALES

Inverell

GETTING TO KNOW
QUEENSLAND

Life in Queensland revolves around the state's 7,000-km- (4,350-mile-) long coastline. This northeastern corner of Australia is rich in marine life and Aussie surf culture. But there's a lot more to experience on land, too, in Queensland's mountains, rainforests and small towns.

BRISBANE

PAGE 348

Queensland's capital was once seen as a bit of a cultural backwater, but no more: Brisbane is enjoying a riverside renaissance. Snaking its way through the city, the Brisbane River is the heart of "Brissie's" cultural and social life – from the thriving performing arts precinct and beach-style lagoon at South Bank to Riverside Markets in the Botanic Gardens. Join the locals in restaurants under the Story Bridge, at rooftop bars overlooking the river and strolling along the Riverwalk, a suspended path that stretches from the Central Business District to trendy New Farm.

Best for
Riverside dining

Home to
Queensland Cultural Centre

Experience
Strolling along the winding Riverwalk path, which floats on the Brisbane River

SOUTHEAST QUEENSLAND AND THE WHITSUNDAYS

Adventure awaits in this diverse region. Experience a white-knuckle ride at the quartet of theme parks on the glitzy Gold Coast, explore rusted shipwrecks on K'gari (Fraser Island) or take a boat trip to the unspoiled Whitsundays and snorkel on the edge of the Great Barrier Reef. Inland, Southeast Queensland is no less enchanting, with waterfalls to find and birds to spot in the tranquil hinterland.

Best for
Family-friendly adventures

Home to
K'gari (Fraser Island)

Experience
Feeling the impossibly soft sand of Whitehaven Beach between your toes

$\rightarrow$

FAR NORTH QUEENSLAND

This is the only place on earth where two UNESCO World Heritage-listed areas sit side-by-side – the Daintree Rainforest and the Great Barrier Reef. On land are soaring canopies, crocodile-haunted rivers and walking tracks, while below the sea lie coral cities, clownfish-friendly anemones and diving sites. After days spent exploring the rainforest and reef, indulge in Queensland's famously laid-back lifestyle, staying in friendly hostels in relaxed towns or luxurious hotels on unspoiled islands.

Best for
Coral reefs and rainforest

Home to
Great Barrier Reef, Cairns

Experience
Snorkelling on the iconic Great Barrier Reef.

WESTERN AND OUTBACK QUEENSLAND

This is Australia's wild west, made up of pioneering outback towns with small populations and big hearts. Cowboys are a common sight, with sun-toughened stockmen and women still working the land on horseback. But this is also where the Qantas airline was founded, where bush poets found inspiration to write national anthems and where fossilized dinosaur footprints tell a story millions of years in the making.

Best for
Classic country towns

Home to
Carnarvon National Park

Experience
Walking in the footsteps of dinosaurs at Lark Quarry

Kayaking past Brisbane's Central Business District

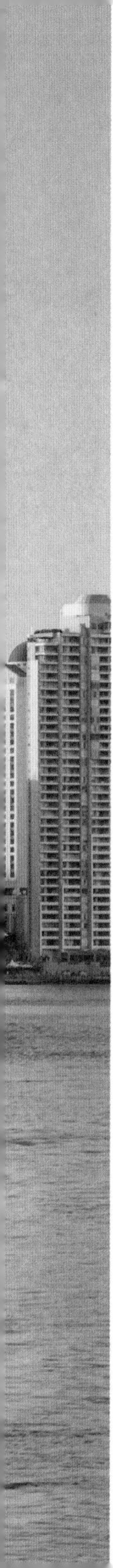

BRISBANE

For thousands of years, the Brisbane River and its surrounding grasslands and forests provided rich resources for the Jagera and Turrbal Aboriginal clans who lived here. Timber was used to create tools and shelter, and creeks and swamps offered a ready supply of food and reeds to make jewellery, baskets and nets. This way of life continued until 1824, when a convict jail was built here to provide secure facilities for some of the more intractable convicts in the Sydney penal settlement. (The inland location and the fact that the river had a bend in it made escape more difficult.) Free settlers began arriving in 1837, although they were not permitted to move closer than 80 km (50 miles) to the famously harsh penal settlement. This set a pattern of decentralization which is still evident today: Brisbane consists of several distinct communities as well as the central area. The city's growth was rapid and, in 1859, when Queensland became a self-governing colony, Brisbane was duly named as the state capital.

As Queensland's natural resources, including coal, silver, lead and zinc, were developed, so its major city flourished. Brisbane's status as a truly modern city, however, is relatively recent, beginning with a mining boom in the 1960s. Hosting the Commonwealth Games in 1982 and the 1988 World Expo were also milestones, bringing thousands of visitors to the city. Today, Brisbane is a cosmopolitan place, with some superb restaurants and streetside cafés, a lively arts scene centred around its vibrant cultural precinct and an impressive year-round schedule of festivals. In 2032, Brisbane will host the Olympics Games.

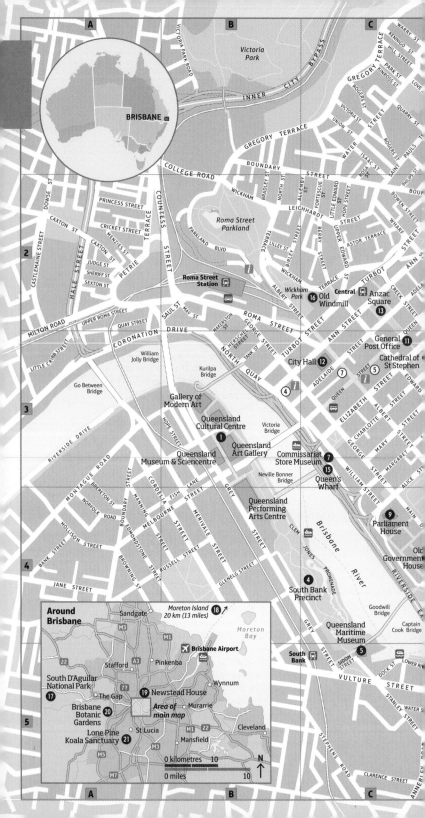

Map Labels

Inset map (top left):
BRISBANE

Main map streets and landmarks:

A
B
C

WARRY ST
KENNIGO ST
HILL STREET
PARK ST
KINROSS ST
LOVE...

Victoria Park

VICTORIA PARK ROAD

GREGORY TERRACE

ROGERS ST
VICTORIA ST

INNER CITY BYPASS

UNION ST
WATER ST
SAINT PAULS TE
ROGERS ST
PHILIP ST
BOU...

DOWSE ST

COLLEGE ROAD

GREGORY TERRACE

BOUNDARY STREET

WICKHAM STREET

PRINCESS STREET

COUNTESS TERRACE

CAXTON ST

CRICKET STREET

MENZIES ST

PETRIE TERRACE

JUDGE ST

SHERIFF ST

SEXTON ST

CASTLEMAINE STREET

HALE STREET

CAXTON ST

BRADLEY ST
NORTH ST
ALLENBY ST
FORTESCUE ST
LITTLE EDWARD ST
HOPE STREET
UPPER EDWARD STREET
BOWEN STREET
WHARF

LEICHHARDT

BERRY STREET

LILLEY ST
BIRLEY ST
ASTOR TERRACE
ANN STREET

Roma Street Parkland

PARKLAND BLVD

WICKHAM TERRACE

ALBERT STREET

Wickham Park

ROMA STREET

TURBOT CREEK ADELA...

Roma Street Station

16 Old Windmill

Central

13 Anzac Square

MILTON ROAD

UPPER ROMA STREET

QUAY STREET

SAUL ST
MAY ST

WAKERSTON ST

GEORGE STREET

ROMA STREET

TURBOT STREET

ANN STREET

QUEEN

CORONATION DRIVE

HERSCHEL STREET

TANK ST

NORTH QUAY

11 General Post Office

William Jolly Bridge

Kurilpa Bridge

City Hall 12

Cathedral of St Stephen

LITTLE CRIBB STREET

Go Between Bridge

RIVERSIDE DRIVE

HOPE STREET

7

4

ADELAIDE STREET

5

QUEEN STREET

ELIZABETH STREET

EDWARD STREET

ALBERT STREET

CHARLOTTE STREET

MARY STREET

GEORGE STREET

Gallery of Modern Art

Queensland Cultural Centre 1

Victoria Bridge

Queensland Art Gallery

MONTAGUE ROAD

Queensland Museum & Sciencentre

Commissariat Store Museum 7

15 Queen's Wharf

CORDELIA STREET

FISH LANE

MELBOURNE STREET

MERIVALE STREET

GREY STREET

Neville Bonner Bridge

WILLIAM STREET

ALICE STREET

MARGARET STREET

BRERETON ST

MANNING STREET

BOUNDARY STREET

EDMONDSTONE STREET

RUSSELL STREET

BROWNING STREET

Queensland Performing Arts Centre

CLEM JONES PROMENADE

Brisbane River

9 Parliament House

NORFOLK ROAD

MOLLISON STREET

BANK STREET

JANE STREET

GLENELG STREET

Old Government House

RIVERSIDE EX

South Bank Precinct 4

Goodwill Bridge

Captain Cook Bridge

Queensland Maritime Museum

South Bank

5

GREY STREET

SIDON STREET

DOCK ST

LOWER RI

VULTURE STREET

STANLEY STREET

WATER STREET

STEPHENS ROAD

CLARENCE STREET

ANNERLEY...

Around Brisbane (inset, bottom left)

Around Brisbane

Sandgate

Moreton Island 20 km (13 miles) 18

Moreton Bay

M3

M1

Stafford

Pinkenba

Brisbane Airport

A3

South D'Aguilar National Park

17

The Gap

22

77

19 Newstead House

Wynnum

Murarrie

Area of main map

Brisbane Botanic Gardens 20

St Lucia

M1

22

Cleveland

Lone Pine Koala Sanctuary 21

Mansfield

M5

M3

M7

0 kilometres   10

0 miles   10

N

BRISBANE

Must See
1. Queensland Cultural Centre

Experience More
2. St John's Anglican Cathedral
3. Story Bridge
4. South Bank Precinct
5. Queensland Maritime Museum
6. Fortitude Valley and Chinatown
7. Commissariat Store Museum
8. Brisbane City Botanic Gardens
9. Parliament House
10. Cathedral of St Stephen
11. General Post Office
12. City Hall
13. Anzac Square
14. Old Government House
15. Queen's Wharf
16. Old Windmill
17. South D'Aguilar National Park
18. Moreton Island
19. Newstead House
20. Brisbane Botanic Gardens
21. Lone Pine Koala Sanctuary

Eat & Drink
① 1889 Enoteca

Stay
② The Calile
③ W Brisbane

Shop
④ Queen Street Mall
⑤ James Street
⑥ Brisbane Arcade

❶ 🏃🏻 🎏 🍴 ☕ 🛍

QUEENSLAND
CULTURAL CENTRE

📍B3 🏛Grey St, South Brisbane 🕐Hours vary, check website
🌐arts.qld.gov.au/about-us/our-spaces/cultural-precinct

With a spectacular setting on the South Bank, the Queensland
Cultural Centre is the undisputed hub of Brisbane's arts scene.
Surrounded by pretty plazas and lush green gardens, the complex
incorporates the Queensland Art Gallery (QAG), the Gallery of
Modern Art (GOMA), the Queensland Museum, the State Library
of Queensland and the Queensland Performing Arts Centre (QPAC).

This vibrant arts and entertainment centre is
known as the cultural centrepiece of the state,
attracting more than 7 million visitors a year.
It is home to an impressive collection of international and domestic art, published literary
works, exhibits across life sciences, natural
history and technology, and world-class
theatre, concert and cinema facilities.

←
Browsing the artworks on display
at the Queensland Art Gallery

QUEENSLAND ART GALLERY GUIDE

The collection is housed over three levels. Fine collections of Asian and International art from the 12th century are on Level 2. Aboriginal Australian art is on Level 4. Level 3 contains the Australian art collection. The work in this gallery is complemented by the contemporary art housed in GOMA. QAGOMA's Children's Art Centre presents engaging exhibitions and events for all ages. Also of interest is the Watermall's indoor water feature.

Visitors will be equally impressed by the architectural grandeur of the centre's five cultural institutions, with the heritage-listed QPAC, QAG and Queensland Museum all examples of late-20th-century International Style architecture. Its more modern counterparts, the GOMA, built in 2006, and the renovated State Library of Queensland, have both won prestigious awards for their striking construction and design.

On the centre's doorstep are a myriad of restaurants, cafés, bars and bookshops, with open landscaped plazas, luscious subtropical gardens, sculptures and fountains peppered around the grounds.

Highlights of the Centre

Queensland Museum & SparkLab

▷ This natural history museum is filled with models, both prehistoric and current, including a large-scale model of Queensland's unique dinosaur, the Muttaburrasaurus, in the Lost Creatures gallery on level 2. The SparkLab offers interactive science exhibitions.

Gallery of Modern Art (GOMA)

Australia's largest gallery of modern and contemporary art focuses on 20th- and 21st-century works from Australia, Asia and the Pacific. The cinemas here feature films by influential and popular directors and artists.

Queensland Art Gallery

First established in 1895, QAG has a fine collection of Australian art, including works by Sidney Nolan and Margaret Preston, together with Aboriginal Australian art. The international collection includes 15th-century European art and Asian art from the 12th century. QAG and GOMA together create QAGOMA, Australia's second-largest public art museum, offering distinct yet complementary experiences.

State Library of Queensland

◁ The State Library houses collections from around the world. Its extensive resources cover all interests and most of its services are free. There are innovative exhibitions, an Asia Pacific Design Library and The Edge, a digital culture space.

Queensland Performing Arts Centre (QPAC)

The QPAC is one of Australia's leading centres for live performances. There are five performance spaces including the grand 2,000-seat Lyric Theatre, a striking 1,500-seat venue with a rippled glass façade, a concert hall and smaller theatres staging opera, ballet, music and theatrical productions.

↑ Queensland Performing Arts Centre on the waterfront in South Bank, Brisbane

353

EXPERIENCE MORE

EXPERIENCE Brisbane

2

St John's Anglican Cathedral

D2 **373 Ann St** **Brisbane Central** **Free Loop** **Riverside Centre** **9:30am–4:30pm services: hours vary, check website** **stjohnscathedral.com.au**

Designed along French Gothic lines in 1888, with the foundation stone laid in 1901, St John's Anglican Cathedral is regarded as one of the most splendid churches in the southern hemisphere. The interior is of Helidon sandstone and many examples of local needlework, wood, glass and stone craft are on display, including over 400 cushions that depict Queensland's flora and fauna.

In 1859, Queensland was made a separate colony at the adjacent Deanery – which was also the temporary residence of Queensland's first governor.

3

Story Bridge

D2 **Level 1, 170 Main St, Kangaroo Point**

Brisbane's iconic Story Bridge was constructed during the Great Depression. With a bridge already across the Brisbane River, this was more a means of creating jobs and boosting the city's morale.

The **Story Bridge Adventure Climb** is a spectacular way to see the city. Climbs take place during the day and at night. The guided tour explains the history of the bridge and the city's transition from a 19th-century penal settlement to a 21st-century metropolis. The summit affords superb views.

Story Bridge Adventure Climb

 For tours daily **storybridgeadventure climb.com.au**

4

South Bank Precinct

C4 **Brisbane River foreshore** **South Bank** **Cultural Centre bus station, South Bank Busway routes, George St nr Adelaide St routes** **South Bank 3** **visit. brisbane.qld.au/places-to-go/inner-city/south-bank**

Brisbane River's South Bank was the site of Expo '88 and is now a 17-ha (42-acre) centre of culture, entertainment and recreation. Known as the parklands, it includes the Queensland Performing Arts Centre, the State Library, the Queensland Museum & Science Centre, the Conservatorium, Queensland Art Gallery and Gallery of Modern Art *(p352)*, Opera Queensland, two colleges and an exhibition centre. The area abounds with restaurants, cafés and weekend market stalls. There is even an artificial lagoon, Streets Beach, with a sandy beach.

South Bank is also home to the Wheel of Brisbane and Goodwill Bridge, a 450-m (1,500-ft) pedestrian bridge-linking the area with the city centre and Botanic Gardens. There's also a third pedestrian walkway that runs over the river, the Neville Bonner Bridge.

STREETS BEACH

Streets Beach, in the South Bank Precinct, is Australia's only artificial, inland beach. It holds enough water to fill almost three Olympic-size swimming pools and is surrounded by palm trees and white sands from the Rous Channel in northern Brisbane's Moreton Bay.

↑ Brightly painted *paifang* entrance gate to Brisbane's Chinatown

 5

Queensland Maritime Museum

📍 C5 🏛 End of Goodwill Bridge, South Bank 🚉 South Bank 🚌 South Bank Busway & Cultural Centre routes to Mater Hill or South Bank 🚏 Maritime Museum, South Bank 🕐 10am-4pm Wed-Fri, 9:30am-4:30pm Sat & Sun 🚫 Good Fri, 25 Apr (am), 24-26 Dec 🌐 maritime museum.com.au

This museum lists among its exhibits shipbuilders' models, reconstructed cabins from early steamers and relics from shipwrecks in the area. In the dry dock, as part of the National Estate, sits HMAS *Diamantina*, a frigate that served during World War II.

The museum is also home to *Ella's Pink Lady*, the yacht Queenslander Jessica Watson used to become the youngest person to sail solo and unassisted around the world. Also on display is the pearling lugger *Penguin* and the bow of a Japanese pleasure boat, a *yakatabume*, donated to the city by Japan after Expo '88.

6

Fortitude Valley and Chinatown

📍 D1 🏛 Ann and Wickham sts, Fortitude Valley 🚉 Brunswick St 🚌 Buses to cnr Wickham & Brunswick sts, Brisbane Explorer

The ship *Fortitude* sailed from England and up the Brisbane River in 1859 with 250 settlers on board, and the name stuck to the valley where they disembarked. For a time, the area was the trading centre of the city and some impressive buildings were erected during the 1880s and 1890s.

After a long period of deterioration, the city council began to revive the district in the 1980s. It is now the alternative centre of Brisbane, with great restaurants and shops. McWhirter's Emporium, an Art Deco landmark, was once a department store. Shops now occupy the lower levels with apartments above. Shoppers also hit the outdoor market in Brunswick Street on weekends.

Also within the valley is Brisbane's Chinatown, a bustling area of Asian restaurants, supermarkets, cinemas and martial arts centres. Look out for the lions at the entrance, which were turned around when a feng shui expert considered their original position to be bad for business.

EAT & DRINK

1889 Enoteca
Expect quality Italian wines and Roman cuisine with a twist at this romantic spot.

📍 D5 🏛 12 Logan Rd, Woolloongabba 🚫 Mon 🌐 1889enoteca.com.au

⑤⑤⑤

Agnes
Sample dishes prepared in a wood-fired oven. There's also a wine bar and rooftop terrace.

📍 D1 🏛 22 Agnes St, Fortitude Valley 🚫 Sun 🌐 anyday.com.au

⑤⑤⑤

↑ The Story Bridge, spanning the Brisbane River, lit up at night

7

Commissariat Store Museum

📍 C3 🏠 115 William St
🚇 South Brisbane, Central
🚌 Free Loop 🚢 North Quay
🕐 10am–4pm Tue–Fri
🚫 Good Fri, Easter Sun,
25 & 26 Dec 🌐 commissariat
store.org.au

The Commissariat Store, constructed by convict labour in 1829, is the only surviving building from Brisbane's penal colony days open to the public. Having been restored in 2000, it now houses the Royal Historical Society of Queensland, which preserves the state's history.

8

City Botanic Gardens

📍 D4 🏠 Alice St 🚇 Brisbane
Central 🚌 Free Loop
🚢 Edward St 🕐 Daily
🌐 brisbane.qld.gov.au

Set on the Brisbane River, the city's first Botanic Gardens are the second-oldest botanic gardens in Australia. Their peaceful location is a welcome haven from the city's high-rise buildings.

In its earliest incarnation, the area was used as a vegetable garden by convicts. It was laid out in its present form in 1855 by the colonial botanist Walter Hill, who was also the first director of the gardens. An avenue of bunya pines

dates back to the 1850s, while an avenue of weeping figs was planted in the 1870s.

Hundreds of waterbirds, such as herons and plovers, come to the lakes that dot the gardens. Brisbane River's renowned mangroves are now a protected species and can be admired from a specially built boardwalk. Free guided walks take place at 11am and 1pm from Monday to Saturday.

9

Parliament House

📍 C4 🏠 Cnr George & Alice sts 🚇 Brisbane Central 🚌 40, Free Loop 🚢 Gardens Point 🕐 9am–4:15pm Mon–Fri (on sitting days) 🚫 Public hols 🌐 parliament.qld.gov.au

Queensland's Parliament House was designed in French Renaissance style by architect Charles Tiffin. Begun in 1865, it was completed in 1868. Tiffin added features more suited to

 ←

A sculpture at the Brisbane City Botanic Gardens

> **INSIDER TIP**
> **Free River Cruise**
>
> The free CityHopper ferry service along the Brisbane River is one of the most scenic ways to see the inner city. You can hop on or hop off at any of its seven stops. The service runs every 30 minutes from 5:30am to midnight daily.

Queensland's tropical climate, such as shady colonnades, shutters and an arched roof, which is made from Mount Isa copper (p404). Other notable features are the cedar staircases and the intricate gold leaf detailing on the Council Chamber ceilings. Parliament House is also noted for being the first legislative building in the British Empire to be lit by electricity.

The building is still used for its original purpose and the public is permitted to watch when parliament is sitting. Unlike other state parliaments, consisting of an Upper and Lower House, Queensland has only one parliamentary body. A government-issued ID is required to enter the

premises. Free guided tours take place on weekdays; check the website for times.

Cathedral of St Stephen

C3 249 Elizabeth St Brisbane Central Free Loop Eagle St Pier 8am–6pm Mon–Fri, 7am–6pm Sat & Sun cathedralofststephen.org.au

Early settlers provided the funds for this lovely English Gothic-style Catholic cathedral, designed by noted colonial architect Benjamin Backhouse and completed in 1874. The main façade features restored twin spires on each side of the stained-glass windows.

Next door is St Stephen's Chapel, the original cathedral.

> **Parliament House is noted for being the first legislative building in the British Empire to be lit by electricity.**

The English Gothic-style nave at the Cathedral of St Stephen

It was designed by A W Pugin, an English architect who also worked on London's Houses of Parliament. Guided tours of the cathedral start at 10:30am on weekdays, following mass. Check the website for details.

General Post Office

C3 261 Queen St Brisbane Central Free Loop Eagle St Pier, Riverside 8:30am–5pm Mon–Fri, 9am–12:30pm Sat heritage.brisbane.qld.gov.au

Built between 1871 and 1879, this attractive Neo-Classical building was erected to house the city's first official postal service. It replaced the barracks for female convicts that were previously on the site. The building continues to operate as central Brisbane's main post office.

The Post Office Square, opposite the General Post Office, is a pleasant place to relax, while looking out over the landscaped greenery and fountains of Anzac Square, just opposite (p358).

SHOP

Queen Street Mall
This bustling mall is Brisbane's go-to shopping spot. It is full of arcades, department stores, designer boutiques, local labels and dining options.

C3 Queen St, Brisbane

James Street
Dubbed Brisbane's "Rodeo Drive", this high-end shopping district has local and international luxury retailers and award-winning restaurants.

E1 James St, Fortitude Valley jamesst.com.au

Brisbane Arcade
Built in the 1920s, this heritage-listed shopping arcade is home to some of the city's best fashion boutiques as well as antiques and gift shops.

C3 160 Queen St Mall, Brisbane brisbanearcade.com.au

↑ Pretty Post Office Square in front of the General Post Office building

STAY

The Calile

An urban hotel with a tropical resort feel, The Calile is located in Fortitude Valley's James Street. It has retro-looking, pastel-coloured rooms, an elegant pool and superior city views.

📍 E1 🏠 8 James St, Fortitude Valley 🌐 thecalilehotel.com

$$$

W Brisbane

Located in North Quay, this luxurious riverside hotel is an oasis from the city hubbub. It has high-quality furnishings, cutting-edge design and a decadent pool with stunning views.

📍 B3 🏠 81 North Quay, Brisbane 🌐 marriott.com

$$$

---

⑫ City Hall

📍 C3 🏠 King George Sq, Adelaide and Ann sts 🚆 Brisbane Central, Roma St 🚌 Free Loop 🚢 North Quay ⏰ 8am–5pm daily (from 9am Sat & Sun) 🌐 brisbane.qld.gov.au

Completed in 1930, the Neo-Classical City Hall is home to Brisbane City Council. Brisbane's early settlement is depicted by a beautiful sculpted tympanum above the main entrance. In the King George Square foyer, examples of traditional crafts-manship are evident in the floor mosaics, ornate ceilings and woodwork carved from Queensland timbers. City Hall's 92-m (300-ft) Italian Renaissance-style tower gives a panoramic view of the city.

Contemporary and Aboriginal art is housed in the **Museum of Brisbane** on level 3. Free tickets for the clocktower are available at the museum, with small group departures every 15 minutes. Also within City Hall is the Shingle Inn, an iconic, restored 1936 walnut-panelled café/bakery.

The attractive King George Square, facing City Hall, has several interesting statues, including *Form del Mito* by Arnaldo Pomodoro. The work's geometric forms and polished surfaces reflect the changing face of the city from morning to night. The bronze *Petrie Tableau*, by Tasmanian sculptor Stephen Walker, was designed for Australia's bicentenary.

Museum of Brisbane

 ⏰ 10am–5pm Tue–Sun 🚫 Public hols 🌐 museumofbrisbane.com.au

60,000

Queenslanders fought in World War I.

---

⑬ Anzac Square

📍 C2 🏠 Ann & Adelaide sts 🚆 Brisbane Central 🚌 Free Loop 🚢 Waterfront Place, Eagle St Pier

Commemorating those who have given their life for the country, Brisbane's war memorial is centred on Anzac

Square, a park planted with rare boab (baobab) trees, among other flora. The Eternal Flame burns in a Greek Revival cenotaph at the Ann Street entrance. Beneath the cenotaph is the Shrine of Memories, containing various tributes and wall plaques.

Old Government House

14

C4 **Queensland University of Technology, Gardens Point, 2 George St** **Brisbane Central** **Free Loop** **Gardens Point** **10am-4pm Tue-Fri, 10am-2pm Sun** **Public hols** **ogh.qut.edu.au**

The state's first Government House was completed in 1862. The graceful sandstone building served not only as the state governor's residence, but also as the administrative and social centre of the state until 1910. It was then occupied by the fledgling University of Queensland. Reopened in 2009, it now has an art gallery dedicated to the works of William Robinson, one of Australia's greatest living landscape artists.

 Admiring the Old Windmill weather observatory in Brisbane

Queen's Wharf

15

C3 **Queens Wharf Rd, Brisbane City** **queenswharfbrisbane.com.au**

A vibrant waterfront lifestyle hub offering an array of cultural, retail, dining and entertainment offerings,

Queen's Wharf is the result of urban renewal that saw beautiful but neglected heritage buildings restored and repurposed. New meets old with soaring new buildings transforming Brisbane's skyline through landmark architecture.

Old Windmill

16

C2 **Wickham Terrace** **Brisbane Central** **Free Loop, 30** **To the public**

Built in 1828, the Old Windmill is one of two buildings still standing from convict days, the old Commissariat Store (p356) being the other survivor. Originally the colony's first industrial building, it later served as a time signal, with a gun fired and a ball dropped each day at exactly 1pm.

The mill is now a weather observatory. The windmill is not open to the public, but it makes a striking photograph.

← The Anzac Square park, surrounded by towering buildings, and (inset) the Eternal Flame on the square

17

South D'Aguilar National Park

📍A5 🚌385 🌐; parks.des.
qld.gov.au/parks/daguilar

South D'Aguilar National Park, within the D'Aguilar Mountain Range, stretches for more than 50 km (30 miles) north-west of Brisbane. Covering more than 28,500 ha (70,250 acres) of natural bushland and eucalyptus forests, it offers driving routes with breath-taking views over the countryside. The most scenic route is along Mount Nebo Road. Another drive extends from Samford up to the charming mountain village of Mount Glorious and down the other side. It is worth stopping from time to time to hear the distinctive calls of bellbirds and whipbirds.

Situated 6 km (4 miles) past Mount Glorious is the Wivenhoe Outlook, with spectacular views down to Lake Wivenhoe, an artificial lake created to prevent the Brisbane River from flooding the city. Just north of Mount Glorious is the entrance to Maiala Recreation Area, where there are picnic areas, some wheelchair accessible, and several walking trails. The rainforest here abounds with animal life. Other excellent walks are at Manorina and Jolly's Lookout, which has a lovely picnic area. Also in the park is the Westridge Outlook, a boardwalk with great views.

At the **South East Queensland Wildlife Centre at Walkabout Creek** there is a re-created freshwater environment. Water dragons, pythons, catfish and rainbow fish flourish within these natural surroundings. Visitors also have the chance to see the extraordinary lungfish, a unique species equipped with both gills and lungs. There is a café on site, which looks out over the beautiful bush landscape around the centre.

About 4 km (2 miles) from the centre is Bellbird Grove, which includes a collection of Aboriginal bark huts. There are picnic areas here and at Ironbark Gully and Lomandra.

South East Queensland Wildlife Centre at Walkabout Creek

♿🅿️ 📍60 Mt Nebo Rd, The Gap ⏰9am–4pm daily 🚫25 Apr (am) & 25 Dec 🌐parks.des.qld.gov.au

18

Moreton Island

📍B4 ⛴🚌 🌐tangalooma.
com/moreton-island

The third-largest sand island in the world, Moreton Island is a 90-minute, 40-km (25-mile) ferry ride from Brisbane. This subtropical national park has white sandy beaches, colourful marine life and countless

---

TOP 3 WEEKEND MARKETS

The Market Folk
🌐themarketfolk.com.au
Organize fashion, art and skincare markets in various locations.

West End Markets
🌐goodwillprojects.com.au/
markets/west-end
Community market under a canopy of fig trees in Davies Park.

Collective Markets
🌐collectivemarkets.com.au
South Bank's eclectic market runs weekly from Friday through Sunday afternoon.

↑ Boats floating in the blue waters of Moreton Bay, Moreton Island

outdoor activities, including wild dolphin feeding, shipwreck diving, sandboarding, camping and snorkelling. This scenic nature reserve is also home to the towering Mount Tempest, the highest vegetated sand dune in the world, standing at 285 m (935 ft). There is a steep, 2-km (1-mile) lookout track to the dune peak, but it is not for the faint-hearted. Here, you'll be rewarded with views of Moreton Bay and the Coral Sea, and, on a clear day, the volcanic peaks of the Glass House Mountains.

---

⑲
Newstead House

 A5 🏠 **Newstead Park, Breakfast Creek Rd, Newstead** 🚉 **Bowen Hills** 🚌 **300, 306, 322** 🚢 **Newstead Point** 🕐 **Temporarily, check website** 🌐 **newstead house.com.au**

Built in 1846 for Patrick Leslie, one of the first European settlers in the Darling Downs region, this is the oldest surviving colonial home in the city. The charming building was sold in 1847 to magistrate Captain John Wickham. The

centre of the new colony's social life, Newstead House was the scene of lavish parties. A huge fig tree, under which carriages once waited, still graces the drive. While the house is closed for heritage conservation works, visitors can explore the grounds of Newstead Park, a hidden oasis with fabulous views of the Brisbane River.

---

⑳
Brisbane Botanic Gardens and Mount Coot-tha

 A5 🏠 **Mt Coot-tha Rd, Toowong** 🚌 **471** 🕐 **Apr-Aug: 8am–5pm daily; Sep-Mar: 8am–6pm daily** 🌐 **brisbane.qld.gov.au**

Brisbane Botanic Gardens, in the foothills of Mount Coot-tha Forest Park, 8 km (5 miles) from the city centre, were founded in 1976 and feature more than 20,000 specimens, from 5,000 species of herbs, shrubs and trees, laid out in themed beds. Highlights include eucalyptus groves, a Japanese Garden, a Lagoon and Bamboo Grove, and the National Freedom Wall (celebrating 50 years of peace). Many arid and tropical plants, usually seen in greenhouses, thrive in the outdoor setting here. There is also a Bonsai House and rainforest sections. Free guided walks are held at 11am and 1pm Mon–Sat (check the website for details).

Mount Coot-tha Forest Park offers spectacular views and picnic areas. The Aboriginal name means "place of wild honey", a reference to the tiny bees found in the area. On a clear day, the summit provides a panorama of the skyscrapers of central Brisbane, the winding river, Moreton and Stradbroke islands, the

→
Koalas hanging onto branches at Lone Pine Koala Sanctuary

Did You Know?
In a day, koalas can eat 1 kg (2 lb) of eucalyptus leaves and sleep for up to 18 hours.

Glasshouse Mountains and the Lamington Plateau backing onto the Gold Coast (p370). The park also offers walking trails and free guided tours.

㉑
Lone Pine Koala Sanctuary

🏠 **A5** 🏠 **Jesmond Rd, Fig Tree Pocket** 🚌 **430, 445** 🚢 **North Quay** 🕐 **9am–5pm daily** 🕐 **25 April (am)** 🌐 **lonepinekoalasanctu ary.com**

The oldest koala sanctuary in Australia, Lone Pine is also the world's largest, home to more than 130 koalas, as well as kangaroos, emus, possums, dingoes, wombats, reptiles and many Australian birds.

A pleasant and scenic way to get to Lone Pine Sanctuary is on a 45-minute river cruise with Mirimar Cruises (www. mirimarcruises.com.au). Tickets include the return trip and Lone Pine entry (with three hours at the park). Trips depart from Cultural Centre pontoon.

A SHORT WALK
CENTRAL BRISBANE

Distance 2 km (1.5 miles) **Time** 30 minutes
Nearest bus Free loop

A stroll around central Brisbane takes you past a
blend of glass-and-steel high-rises and graceful
19th-century constructions. The latter fortunately
managed to survive the frenzy of demolishing old
buildings that took place throughout the country
during the 1970s. Redevelopment of the area
brought a series of towers, which soar almost 200 m
(656 ft) skyward and loom over preserved heritage
buildings, including the former government
printing office. Early 20th-century buildings dot
Charlotte and Elizabeth streets, while the former
port and naval offices give the streetscape
along Edward Street its heritage charm.

*The **Cathedral of
St Stephen** (p357) is
one of the landmarks
of Brisbane's city centre.
Particularly notable are
its white twin spires.*

*__Elizabeth Arcade__ is the
city's hotspot for Korean
and other Asian restaurants,
tea shops and dessert cafés.*

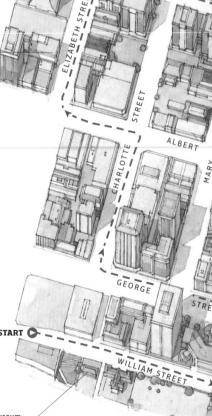

↑ Stained-glass windows
behind the organ in the
Cathedral of St Stephen

START ▶

*The **Commissariat Store Museum**
(p256), which details Queensland
history, is housed in former 19th-century
granary stores. The building's original
façade has been preserved.*

The grand façade of Brisbane's Parliament House ↑

Locator Map
For more details see p350

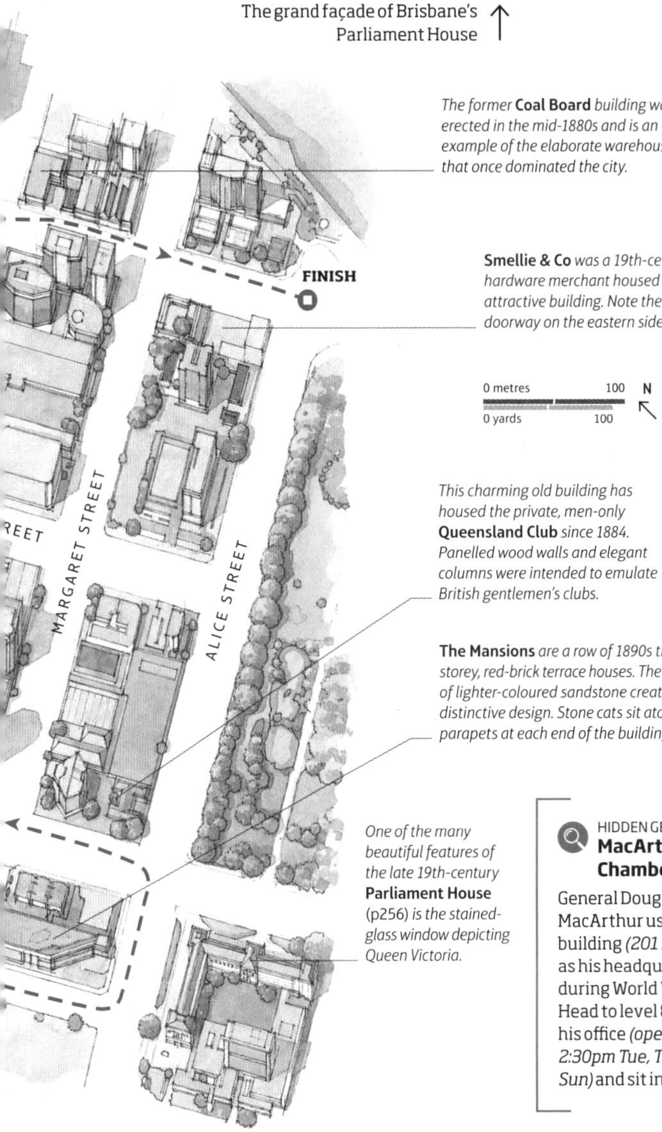

The former **Coal Board** building was erected in the mid-1880s and is an example of the elaborate warehouses that once dominated the city.

FINISH

Smellie & Co was a 19th-century hardware merchant housed in this attractive building. Note the Baroque doorway on the eastern side.

0 metres   100   N
0 yards   100

This charming old building has housed the private, men-only **Queensland Club** since 1884. Panelled wood walls and elegant columns were intended to emulate British gentlemen's clubs.

The Mansions are a row of 1890s three-storey, red-brick terrace houses. The arches of lighter-coloured sandstone create a distinctive design. Stone cats sit atop the parapets at each end of the building.

MARGARET STREET

ALICE STREET

One of the many beautiful features of the late 19th-century **Parliament House** (p256) is the stained-glass window depicting Queen Victoria.

 HIDDEN GEM
MacArthur Chambers Hotel

General Douglas MacArthur used this building *(201 Edward St)* as his headquarters during World War II. Head to level 8 to see his office *(open 10am–2:30pm Tue, Thu and Sun)* and sit in his chair.

Seventy-Five Mile Beach on K'gari (Fraser Island)

SOUTHEAST QUEENSLAND AND THE WHITSUNDAYS

The fertile lands of Southeast Queensland supported a number of different Aboriginal groups, including the Yugarapul, Yugambeh and Quandamooka, while the Whitsundays were home to the Ngaro people. European settlers first arrived in the region in the 1840s, and soon pushed out the land's traditional owners, forcing them onto missions, reserves and even penal colonies. This paved the way for pastoralists eager to exploit the potential farmland. Sugar production had begun by 1869 in the Bundaberg area, and by the 1880s it was a flourishing industry. However, this success was built on the exploitation of Kanakas – labourers from the South Sea Islands, who were paid a pittance, housed in substandard accommodation and given the most physically demanding jobs; some were even kidnapped from their homeland. It was not until Federation, when the British colonies in Australia joined together in 1901, that this practice stopped but by then some 60,000 labourers had been brought to Queensland.

In tandem with this agricultural boom, southern Queensland thrived in the latter half of the 19th century when gold was found in the region. Mining and agriculture continued to be mainstays of the economy throughout the 20th century, but the area increasingly became known for its coastal features. As early as 1917, the southern coast was being described as a "surfer's paradise", giving rise to the resort of that name in the 1930s, and visitors have continued to flock here ever since.

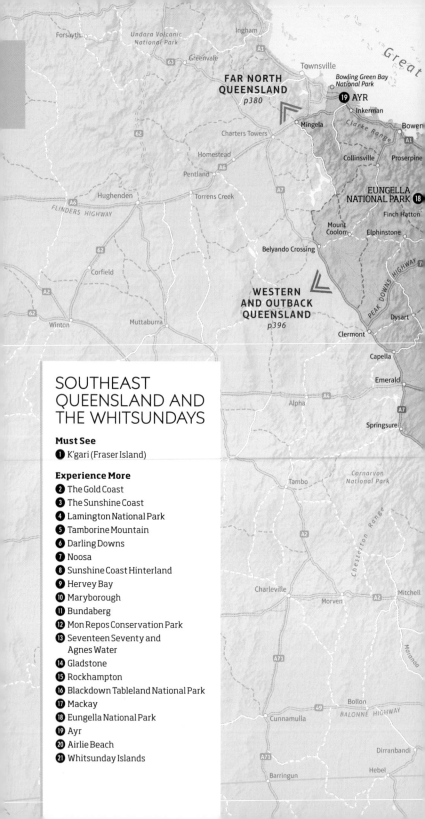

Forsayth
Ingham
Undara Volcanic
National Park
Greenvale
Townsville
Great
63
A1
**FAR NORTH
QUEENSLAND**
p380
Bowling Green Bay
National Park
19 AYR
Inkerman
Mingela
Bowen
62
Charters Towers
Clarke Range
A1
Homestead
Collinsville
Proserpine
A6
Pentland
A7
**EUNGELLA
NATIONAL PARK** 18
Hughenden
Torrens Creek
Finch Hatton
A6
FLINDERS HIGHWAY
Mount
Coolom
Elphinstone
Belyando Crossing
62
PEAK DOWNS HIGHWAY
Corfield
**WESTERN
AND OUTBACK
QUEENSLAND**
p396
Dysart
A2
Muttaburra
Winton
Clermont
Capella
Emerald
Alpha
A4
A7
Springsure
*Carnarvon
National Park*
Tambo
Chesterton Range
A2
Charleville
Morven
A2
Mitchell
Maranoa
Bollon
49
BALONNE HIGHWAY
Cunnamulla
Dirranbandi
A71
Barringun
Hebel

SOUTHEAST QUEENSLAND AND THE WHITSUNDAYS

Must See
❶ K'gari (Fraser Island)

Experience More
❷ The Gold Coast
❸ The Sunshine Coast
❹ Lamington National Park
❺ Tamborine Mountain
❻ Darling Downs
❼ Noosa
❽ Sunshine Coast Hinterland
❾ Hervey Bay
❿ Maryborough
⓫ Bundaberg
⓬ Mon Repos Conservation Park
⓭ Seventeen Seventy and
    Agnes Water
⓮ Gladstone
⓯ Rockhampton
⓰ Blackdown Tableland National Park
⓱ Mackay
⓲ Eungella National Park
⓳ Ayr
⓴ Airlie Beach
㉑ Whitsunday Islands

0 kilometres 100
0 miles 100
N ↑

SOUTHEAST QUEENSLAND AND WHITSUNDAYS

21 WHITSUNDAY ISLANDS
0 AIRLIE BEACH
Conway National Park

Barrier Reef

17 MACKAY
Sarina
Koumala
Duke Islands
Carmila
St Lawrence
Broad Sound
Reef Point

Pacific Ocean

Connors Range
Isaac
Broadsound Range
Marlborough
A1
Mount Etna National Park
Yeppoon
Great Keppel Island
Capricorn Group
Heron Island

Mackenzie
CAPRICORN HIGHWAY
Blackwater
A4
15 ROCKHAMPTON
Mount Morgan
Duaringa
Curtis Island
14 GLADSTONE
Bunker Group

16 BLACKDOWN TABLELAND NATIONAL PARK
Dawson
DAWSON HWY
60
Rannes
A3
Biloela
Miriam Vale
BRUCE HIGHWAY
13 SEVENTEEN SEVENTY AND AGNES WATER

Palm Grove National Park
Moura
Theodore
Monto
A1
MON REPOS CONSERVATION PARK
12
11 BUNDABERG
Hervey Bay
Great Sandy National Park

Isla Gorge National Park
QUEENSLAND
Burnett
9 HERVEY BAY
1 K'GARI (FRASER ISLAND)

Taroom
Mundubbera
A3
10 MARYBOROUGH
Mary

Euromba
A5
Auburn
Tin Can Bay
Great Sandy National Park

Roma
Miles
A2
Murgon
Gympie
7 NOOSA
WARREGO HIGHWAY
Chinchilla
Kingaroy
Maroochydore
3 THE SUNSHINE COAST
Condamine
Mapleton
SUNSHINE COAST HINTERLAND **8**
Surat
Dalby
Maleny
Meandarra
A5
49
Jondaryan
A2
A17
Caboolture
Moreton Island
M1
Moonie
Toowoomba
Brisbane
North Stradbroke Island
A7
MOONIE HIGHWAY
Millmerran
Ipswich
6 DARLING DOWNS
A3
A15
5 TAMBORINE MOUNTAIN
St George
Moonie
2 THE GOLD COAST
Goondiwindi
Inglewood
Warwick
4 LAMINGTON NATIONAL PARK
Queen Mary Falls National Park
Stanthorpe

NEW SOUTH WALES
Macintyre

HUNTER VALLEY AND THE NORTH COAST
p170

① 🏍 🍴 ☕ 🛍

K'GARI
(FRASER ISLAND)

🅰 G4 🚢 From Urangan, River Heads & Inskip Point
ℹ Hervey Bay; 1800 811 728

A UNESCO World Heritage Site, this spectacular natural area is known for its white-sand beaches, towering dunes, emerald-green lakes and luscious rainforests.

Set off the Queensland coast near Maryborough (p374), K'gari (Fraser Island) is the largest sand island in the world, measuring 123 km (76 miles) in length and 25 km (16 miles) across. This green-and-gold isle is also home to half of the world's perched lakes (depressions in the dunes that have become permanently filled with rainwater). As a result, it's the only place on earth where a rainforest grows on sand dunes.

Called K'gari ("paradise") by the Butchulla people, who have occupied the land for up to 50,000 years, the island has over 350 species of birds, rare frogs and wild dingoes (do not feed them and keep your distance). Marine life, such as dolphins, turtles and – in summer – humpback whales, can be found in the clear waters.

THE LEGEND OF K'GARI

The Butchulla people called the island *K'gari* after a Dreamtime legend that says K'gari, a goddess, was sent to earth with Yendingie, messenger of the god Beeral, to find land for humans. She fell in love with the area and didn't want to leave, so Yendingie transformed her into the island.

← The stunning turquoise waters surrounding Waddy Point on the island of K'gari

Must See

STAY

Kingfisher Bay Resort
Enjoy the views at this private, award-winning eco-resort tucked away in the natural landscape.

🏠 Kingfisher Bay
🌐 kingfisherbay.com

$$$

Cathedrals on Fraser
This dingo-fenced campground is nestled behind the magnificent Cathedral dunes. It offers self-catering cabins, canvas tents and a general store.

🏠 Lot 53, Fraser Island Rd 🌐 cathedrals onfraser.com.au

$$$

1 Wild dingoes are a common sight on K'gari.

2 *Maheno* is the only visible shipwreck on the island, but 22 others can be found offshore.

3 K'gari's deepest lake, Lake Wabby is a popular swimming spot. It is found in Great Sandy National Park on the eastern side of the island.

EXPERIENCE MORE

❷ The Gold Coast

 G4 ✈🚉🚌 W destination goldcoast.com

Queensland's famous Gold Coast extends 75 km (45 miles) south of Brisbane and is a flashy metropolis of holiday apartments, luxury hotels, shopping malls, nightclubs, a casino and, above all, 42 km (25 miles) of golden sandy beaches. The area's liveliest spot is without a doubt Surfers Paradise, with block after block of modern, high-rise developments and endless dining and entertainment options. This is where you'll find Q1 – the Gold Coast's tallest building, plenty of watersport options and night markets on the beachfront every Wednesday, Friday and Saturday.

About 28 km (17 miles) south on the Queensland-New South Wales border is Coolangatta. This relaxed town has some of the best surfing waters in the area and relatively uncrowded beaches. Surfing lessons are available and visitors can hire surfboards. Head 30 km (18.5 miles) north of the Gold Coast and you'll find the spectacular Sanctuary Cove, a resort on Hope Island, home to a world-class marina, delectable dining options and competition-grade golf courses. Further north of Sanctuary Cove, about 87 km (55 miles) ahead, is the unspoiled paradise of North Stradbroke Island. This stunning sand island offers peaceful but relatively basic accommodation. Catching crabs, scuba diving, surfing and bird-watching are popular activities.

↑ A family playing in the water at a beach on the Sunshine Coast

❸ The Sunshine Coast

 G4 ✈🚉🚌 W visit sunshinecoast.com

The Sunshine Coast lies 105 km (65 miles) north of Brisbane and consists of nine regions covering 2,254 sq km (870 sq miles) of spectacular coast and rich, luscious hinterland. A more restrained and elegant version of the Gold Coast, but with an equally laid-back vibe, this beautiful part of northeastern Australia has over 100 sun-drenched beaches, 211 km (131 miles) of coastline overlooking the Coral Sea, incredible natural landscapes and a near-perfect climate.

TOP 5 GOLD COAST THEME PARKS

Dreamworld
W dreamworld.com.au
Australia's largest theme park with some of the world's best rides.

Sea World
W seaworld.com.au
Marine park with many family-friendly rides.

Wet'n'Wild
W wetnwild.com.au
Australia's biggest water park, surrounded by subtropical gardens.

Movie World
W movieworld.com.au
This is an exciting cinema-themed park.

WhiteWater World
W dreamworld.com.au
This water park is right next door to Dreamworld.

Sunset over the spectacular Surfers Paradise Beach on Australia's Gold Coast ↑

In the region's northern part is Cooloola's Great Sandy National Park. This slice of coastal paradise has over 1,300 plants, 700 native animals and is home to 44 per cent of Australia's bird species. Visitors can enjoy a range of outdoor activities such as swimming, canoeing, camping, 4WD and hiking among its many attractive lakes and waterways, sclerophyll woodland and high sand dunes. Double Island Point, which sits on the tip of the park's headland, has a calm lagoon which is perfect for a dip, and an active lighthouse that offers stunning views of pristine beaches, lush bushland and sparkling ocean as far as the eye can see.

Further north, near the national park's border, is Carlo Sand Blow, known for its windswept, moon-like appearance. The area is best explored via a 4WD along Cooloola's beach drive between Noosa North Shore and Rainbow Beach. The journey passes the iconic Teewah Coloured Sands, a stretch of vibrant sand cliffs rising to a height of 182 m (600 ft). These steep dunes are a mix of yellow, brown and red hues, which are produced by natural, iron-rich minerals in the soil. Towards the southern part of the Sunshine Coast, 50 km (31.5 miles) from Brisbane, is Moreton Bay. This popular holiday destination is the access point for around 370 islands, the most popular being Moreton and Bribie. Fishing, bird-watching and boating are the main activities here. The area is well known for its mouthwatering seafood, especially the local bay lobster known as the "Moreton Bay bug".

Inland, a cool alternative to the warm coastal weather is the most westerly part of the region's hinterland, Conondale Range. Part of the Great Dividing Range, the third-longest mountain range in the world, the region flourishes with arts and crafts communities, superb bush-walking and great panoramas.

> **The Sunshine Coast has over 100 sun-drenched beaches, 211 km (131 miles) of coastline overlooking the Coral Sea and incredible natural landscapes.**

EAT

Sum Yung Guys
Popular spot serving great pan-Asian cuisine.

🅰 G4 🏠 1/205 Weyba Rd, Noosaville 🔳 sum yungguys.com.au

$$$

Orleans
Classic New Orleans cuisine with a modern French Orléans twist.

🅰 G4 🏠 24 Duporth Ave, Maroochydore, Sunshine Coast 🔳 orleansrb.com

$$$

Social Eating House & Bar
One of the best places to eat on the Gold Coast.

🅰 G4 🏠 3 Oracle Blvd, Broadbeach 🔳 social eatinghouse.com.au

$$$

④

Lamington National Park

 G4 Canungra
 parks.des.qld.gov.au/
parks/lamington

Set within the McPherson Mountain Range, Lamington National Park is one of Queensland's most popular parks. It contains 200 sq km (78 sq miles) of thick wooded country, with more than 160 km (100 miles) of walking tracks through subtropical rainforests. Some 150 species of birds, such as the Albert's lyrebird, make bird-watching a popular pastime here. The global importance of the area was recognized in 1994, when Lamington was declared a World Heritage Area.

Nearby Macrozamia National Park is home to macrozamia palms (cycads), one of the oldest forms of vegetation still growing in the world.

---

⑤

Tamborine Mountain

 G4   visittamborine
mountain.com.au

Tamborine Mountain is nestled in the scenic hinterland between the Gold Coast and Brisbane. Attractions include the 12-ha (30-acre) rainforest, waterfalls, gorges and hiking trails. Tamborine Rainforest Skywalk, situated 30 m (98.5 ft) above the forest floor, promises sweeping views, while Thunderbird Park, a rainforest playground, features high rope courses for all abilities. In town, be sure to stop at the award-winning Tamborine Mountain Distillery to taste a range of locally made spirits and liqueurs.

---

⑥

Darling Downs

 G4 Toowoomba
 visitdarlingdowns.
com.au

Stretching west of the Great Dividing Range, this fertile region encompasses some of the most productive agricultural land in Australia, as well as one of the most historic areas in Queensland.

The main centre of the Downs is Toowoomba, one of the state's biggest cities. Early settlers transformed this one-time swamp into the present "Garden City", famous for its Carnival of Flowers.

About 45 km (28 miles) northwest of Toowoomba is **The Woolshed at Jondaryan**, a memorial to the early settlers of the district. South of Toowoomba is Warwick, the oldest town in the state after Brisbane. It is known for its roses and 19th-century

SHOP

Eumundi Markets
Established in 1979, Eumundi is Australia's biggest and best arts and crafts market. You'll find furniture, ceramics, clothing, jewellery and fresh produce here.

 G4 80 Memorial Drive, Eumundi
 8am–2pm Wed, 7am–2pm Sat
 eumundimarkets. com.au

↑ A trail in the lush Lamington National Park, and *(inset)* a bowerbird at the park

 7

Noosa

🅰️G4 🚆🚌 Ⓦ visit noosa.com.au

This coastal town, 148 km (92 miles) north of Brisbane, is famous for its luxury resorts and surf beaches. Visitors will enjoy the buzz of stylish Hastings Street – voted the best main street in Australia – with its cafés, restaurants, bars, boutique shops and art galleries, all set by Noosa Heads Main Beach. This beach is connected to an extensive river system that leads inland to Noosaville, the quieter, but equally beautiful riverside suburb.

Noosa's extensive waterways and everglade system are one of only two in the world and can be explored by boat, kayak, kitesurf or on foot. No visit to the area is complete without a trip to the 4,000-ha (9,884-acre) national park on its fringe. Its most popular spot is the Laguna Lookout platform, which offers panoramic views.

 8

Sunshine Coast Hinterland

🅰️G4 Ⓦ visitsunshine coast.com/place/the-hinterland

To the west of the Sunshine Coast is the Blackall Range. The area has become a centre for artists and artisans, with several guesthouses and some fine restaurants. The most attractive centres are Montville and Maleny. The drive from Maleny to Mapleton is one of the best in the region, with views across to Moreton Island, encompassing pineapple and sugar cane fields.

Consisting of ten volcanic cones, the nearby Glasshouse Mountains were formed 20 million years ago. The craggy peaks were named by Captain Cook in 1770 as they reminded him of the glass furnaces in his native Yorkshire.

Not far from here is **Australia Zoo**, the legacy of the late "Crocodile Hunter" and conservationist Steve Irwin. Spanning 82 ha (700 acres), the zoo houses over 1,200 animals native to Australia, Southeast Asia and the African Savannah. This wildlife park is renowned for its conservation programmes and protection of 182,000 ha (450,000 acres) of vital flora and fauna habitat.

Australia Zoo
♿ 🏠1638 Steve Irwin Way
🕘9am–5pm daily 🚫25 Dec
Ⓦaustraliazoo.com.au

Did You Know?

Steve Irwin Day (15 Nov) remembers the "Crocodile Hunter's" conservation work.

---

sandstone buildings. The town also claims one of the oldest rodeos in Australia, dating from 1857.

About 60 km (40 miles) south of Warwick is Stanthorpe, which is one of the few wine regions in the state. Nearby, Queen Mary Falls National Park is a 78-ha (193-acre) rainforest park with picnic areas and a waterfall.

The Woolshed at Jondaryan

♿ 🏠264 Jondaryan-Evanslea Rd, Jondaryan
🕘9am–3pm Mon–Fri
🚫24–26 Dec Ⓦjondaryan woolshed.com

GREAT BEACH DRIVE

Don't miss the exhilarating drive and scenic ferry ride from the charming town of Noosa to the tip of K'gari (Fraser Island, *p368*), the largest sand island in the world. This striking journey takes visitors along a sand road, running next to the sparkling Pacific Ocean and passing some of Australia's most picturesque beaches, lighthouses and lush bushland. Guided tours are available to book; if you want to drive yourself, you'll need a permit and a 4WD vehicle.

9

Hervey Bay

🅰G4 ⊞⊞⊞ 🛈227
Maryborough-Hervey Bay
Rd, Torquay; www.
visitfrasercoast.com/
destination/hervey-bay

As recently as the 1970s,
Hervey Bay was just a string of
five fishing villages. However,
the safe beaches and mild
climate have quickly turned it
into a metropolis of over
40,000 people and one of the
fastest-growing holiday
destinations in Australia.

The main town in Hervey
Bay is Urangan, located on
Dayman Point. The area has
14 km (8.5 miles) of beaches
with calm waters and no jellyfish. The water is warm enough
for swimming throughout the
year. Fishing is also a popular
activity here and there are
plenty of picnic spots, markets
and a marina and pier, both
perfect for strolls. Boats to
K'gari (Fraser Island, p368)
depart from the marina.

Hervey Bay is also
considered the best place in
Australia for whale-watching;
visit between mid-
July and early
November.

Statue of
the character
Mary Poppins in
Maryborough

HERVEY BAY WHALE-WATCHING

See humpback whales up
close at Hervey Bay. Every
year, these magnificent
creatures migrate more
than 11,000 km (7,000
miles), from the Antarctic
to northern Australian
waters, to mate and calve.
On their return, between
July and November, they
rest here to allow their
calves to grow before
they begin their final
journey back to Antarctica.

10

Maryborough

🅰G4 ⊞⊞⊞ 🛈City Hall, 368
Kent St; www.visitfraser
coast.com/destination/
maryborough

Situated on the banks of the
Mary River, Maryborough is
famed as the hometown of
P L Travers, author of *Mary
Poppins* (1934), but it also has
a strong link with Australia's
colonial history. Founded in
1843, the town provided
housing for Kanakas' labour
(p365) and was the only port,
apart from Sydney, where
free settlers could enter. This
resulted in a thriving town –
the array of impressive
buildings reflects the wealth
of the town's citizens.

Many of these buildings
survive, earning Maryborough
the title of "Heritage City". A
few private residences also
date from the 19th century.
Architectural styles range
from simple workers' cottages
to old "Queenslanders". The
latter are known for their
verandas and are distinctive
to the state; they are set high
off the ground in order to
catch the cooler air currents.

11

Bundaberg

🅰G4 ⊞⊞⊞ 🖥bundaberg
region.org

Bundaberg, the sugar city
of central Queensland, is
62 km (38 miles) north of
Hervey Bay. It is the home
of Bundaberg ("Bundy") rum,
the biggest-selling spirit label
in Australia.

Bundaberg is an attractive
town with many 19th-century
buildings. History lovers will
enjoy the 1-km (half-a-mile)
heritage walk past the School
of Arts, Post Office, War
Memorial, Linden Medical
Centre, Old Australia Bank
and Holy Rosary Church
buildings, among other
architectural sights.

As well as its distilling
history, the city is proud of its
most famous son, Bert Hinkler
(1892–1933), who was the first
man to fly solo from England
to Australia in 1928. His
original "Ibis" aircraft is
displayed in the **Hinkler Hall
of Aviation** located in the
Bundaberg Botanic Gardens.
While here, you can take a
stroll around the 27-ha
(66-acre) landscape which

**Bundaberg's famous son, Bert
Hinkler (1892-1933), was the first
man to fly solo from England to
Australia in 1928.**

> **Did You Know?**
>
> P L Travers' muse for the character of Mary Poppins was her great aunt from Maryborough.

features 10,000 trees and shrubs, an Australian rainforest, Japanese and Chinese gardens, a lake and boardwalks.

About 15 km (9 miles) east, you'll find the seaside town of Bargara with two picturesque beaches. Offshore, Lady Elliott and Lady Musgrave islands are popular spots for scuba diving and snorkelling with turtles and manta rays.

Hinkler Hall of Aviation
Young St, Botanic Gardens 9am–3pm daily Good Fri, 25 Apr, 25 Dec discoverbundaberg.com.au/hinkler-hall-of-aviation

Bundaberg Botanic Gardens
6 Mount Perry Rd discoverbundaberg.com.au/bundaberg-botanic-gardens

12

Mon Repos Conservation Park

G3 parks.des.qld.gov.au/parks/mon-repos

Mon Repos Beach, 15 km (9 miles) from Bundaberg, is one of the most significant and accessible turtle rookeries on the Australian mainland. Egg-laying of loggerhead and other turtles takes place from November to March. By January, the first young turtles begin to hatch and make their way down to the ocean.

An information centre within the environmental park has videos and other information about these fascinating reptiles. Supervised public night-viewing ensures that the turtles are not unduly disturbed (book in advance; *www.bundabergregion.org*).

Just behind Mon Repos Beach is an old stone wall built by Kanakas and now preserved as a memorial to these South Sea Island inhabitants *(p365)*.

DRINK

Bundaberg Rum Distillery
Take a tour, explore the museum, blend your own rum and finish with a drink at the bar at this unmissable distillery.
G4 Hills St, Bundaberg East
bundabergrum.com.au

Bundaberg Barrel
Home to the best ginger beer in Australia, Bundaberg Barrel offers guided tastings, self-guided walks and "guess the flavour" games at the Smellography Wall. All guests can take home an assorted pack of six brews.
G4 147 Bargara Rd, Bundaberg East
bundabergbarrel.com

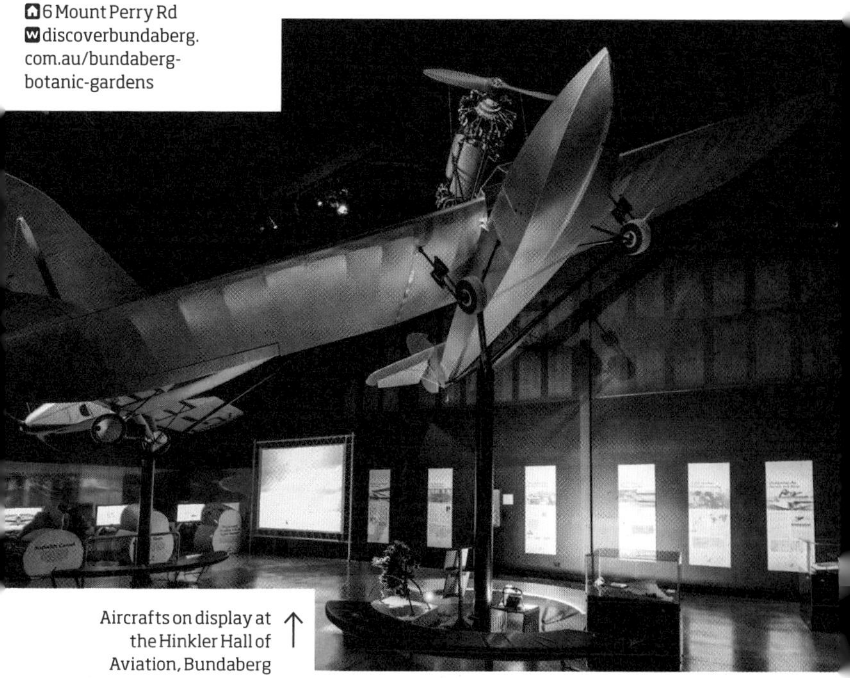

Aircrafts on display at the Hinkler Hall of Aviation, Bundaberg ↑

EAT

Lightbox Espresso & Wine Bar

Known for its modern Australian dishes, excellent coffee and good beer and wine.

🅐 G3 🏠 56 Goondoon St, Gladstone 🅦 lightbox gladstone.co

$ $ $

STAY

1770 Beach Shacks

A beachfront pole house in a tropical setting.

🅐 G3 🏠 578 Captain Cook Drive, Seventeen Seventy 🅦 1770beach shacks.com

$ $ $

Hedlow Retreat

Canoe, fish, bushwalk and star gaze on a farm just a 25-minute drive from Rockhampton.

🅐 G3 🏠 74 C H Barretts Rd, Barmoya 🅦 hedlow retreat.com.au

$ $ $

13 Seventeen Seventy and Agnes Water

🅐 G3 🚗🚌 ℹ 71 Springs Rd, Agnes Water; www. visitagnes1770.com.au

Seventeen Seventy, also written as 1770, is a pretty seaside town 129 km (80 miles) north of Bundaberg. Its name commemorates the year Captain James Cook (*p68*) and the crew of the HMS *Endeavour* arrived here. The only town in the world with a number for a name, 1770 is home to the northernmost surf beach in Queensland. The 1770 peninsula, surrounded by the Coral Sea and Bustard Bay, is one of the few places on Australia's east coast where you can watch the sun set over the ocean.

About 9 km (5.5 miles) south of 1770 lies its twin town Agnes Water, which has rich wildlife, pristine beaches, scenic walking trails, estuaries and national parks. Both coastal villages serve as departure points for cruises and tours to the Great Barrier Reef.

14 Gladstone

🅐 G3 🚗🚌 ℹ Gladstone Marina, Bryan Jordan Drive 🅦 gladstoneregion.info

Gladstone is a town dominated by industry. The world's largest alumina refinery is located here, processing bauxite mined in Weipa on the west coast of Cape York Peninsula. Five per cent of the nation's wealth and 20 per cent of Queensland's wealth is generated by Gladstone's industries. The town's port, handling more than 35 million tonnes of cargo a year, is one of the busiest in Australia.

There are many attractive sights in and around the town. The main street has an eclectic variety of buildings, including the Grand Hotel, rebuilt to its 1897 form after a fire destroyed the original in 1993. The town's Botanic Gardens consist entirely of native Australian plants. About 20 km (12 miles) south lies the popular holiday location of Boyne Island.

Gladstone is also the access point for Heron Island, considered to be one of the most desirable of all the Great

> **The 1770 peninsula, surrounded by the Coral Sea and Bustard Bay, is one of the few places on Australia's east coast where you can watch the sun set over the ocean.**

→ The tranquil shoreline of Round Hill Creek in Seventeen Seventy

Barrier Reef islands, with its wonderful coral and diving opportunities. Other islands in the southern half of the reef can also be accessed from here by boat or helicopter.

15

Rockhampton

🅰 G3 🈁🚌 ℹ️ Capricorn Info Centre, Tropic of Capricorn Spire, Gladstone Rd; www.explorerockhampton.com.au

Situated 40 km (25 miles) inland, on the banks of the Fitzroy River, Rockhampton is often known as the "beef capital" of Australia. The town is also the administrative and commercial heart of central Queensland. A spire marks the fact that, geographically, the Tropic of Capricorn runs through the town.

Rockhampton was founded in 1854 and contains many restored 19th-century buildings. Quay Street flanks the tree-lined river and has been classified by the National Trust. The **Botanic Gardens** have a fine collection of tropical plants. There is also on-site accommodation.

Set on an ancient tribal meeting ground, the **Aboriginal Dreamtime Cultural Centre** is owned and operated by local Aboriginal people.

→

Gudda Gumoo gorge at Blackdown Tableland National Park

Exhibits here give an insight into their life and culture.

The heritage township of Mount Morgan lies 38 km (25 miles) southwest of Rockhampton. An open-cut mine of first gold, then copper, operated here for 100 years until the minerals ran out in 1981.

Some 25 km (15 miles) north of Rockhampton is Mount Etna National Park, containing limestone caves. These can be accessed via tours with **Capricorn Caves**. A major feature is "cave coral" – stone-encrusted tree roots that have forced their way through the rock. The endangered ghost bat, Australia's only carnivorous bat, nests in these caves.

The stunning sandy beaches of Yeppoon and Emu Park are 40 km (25 miles) northeast of the city. Rockhampton is also the access point for Great Keppel Island.

Capricorn Caves

🈁🈁🈁🈁 🏠 Olsens Caves Rd, The Caves ⏰ 8:30am-4pm daily 🌐 capricorncaves.com.au

Botanic Gardens

🏠 Spencer St ⏰ 6am-6pm daily 🌐 rockhamptonregion.qld.gov.au

Aboriginal Dreamtime Cultural Centre

🈁🈁 🏠 Bruce Hwy ⏰ 9am-3pm Mon-Fri 🚫 Public hols 🌐 dreamtimecentre.com.au

---

16

Blackdown Tableland National Park

🅰 G3 🌐 parks.des.qld.gov.au/parks/blackdown-tableland

Between Rockhampton and Emerald, along a 20-km

(12-mile) unsealed detour off the Capricorn Highway, is Blackdown Tableland National Park. A dramatic sandstone plateau that rises to 600 m (2,000 ft) the Tableland offers spectacular views, escarpments, open forest and cascading waterfalls. Wildlife includes gliders, possums, rock wallabies and the occasional dingo.

Emerald is a coal mining centre and the hub of the central highland region, 75 km (45 miles) west of the park; the town provides a railhead for the surrounding agricultural areas. Its ornate 1900 railway station is one of the few survivors of a series of fires that occurred between 1936 and 1969, which destroyed much of the town's heritage. About 60 km (37 miles) southwest of Emerald is Cullin-la-ringo, where there are headstones marking the mass grave of 19 European settlers killed in 1861 by local Aboriginal peoples.

More in tune with its name, Emerald is also the access point for the largest sapphire fields in the world. The lifestyle of the gem diggers is fascinating, making it a popular tourist area.

❶⓻ Mackay

🅰G3 ➕🚇🚌 🅦mackay isaac.com

Situated 335 km (208 miles) north of Rockhampton is the prosperous sugar town of Mackay. The town is blessed with a balmy climate thanks to the surrounding mountains trapping the warm coastal air, even in winter. Spanning the coastline are 30 beautiful white-sand beaches, lined with casuarina trees.

The town centre has many historic buildings worth visiting, including the Customs House and Commonwealth Bank, both classified by the National Trust. There is an architecturally acclaimed art gallery, botanic gardens and a free, family-friendly swimming lagoon and water park on the banks of the Pioneer River. Just north of the town centre is the Mackay Marina, a pleasant place for a walk, and the Pine Islet Lighthouse, one of the only working kerosene lighthouses left in the world.

About 27 miles (38 km) south of Mackay is Sarina, located at the foothills of the Connors Range. Attractions here include *Buffy the Big Cane Toad* statue, pretty beaches and the local sugar mill, the **Sarina Sugar Shed**, which offers guided tours.

Sarina Sugar Shed

🕙 🅰Field of Dreams Parkland, Railway Sq 🕒9am–4pm daily 🕒Good Fri, 25 & 26 Dec 🅦sarina sugarshed.com.au

❶⓼ Eungella National Park

🅰G3 🚇Mackay 🚌Mackay 🅦parks.des.qld.gov.au/ parks/eungella

Around 80 km (50 miles) west of Mackay is the Eungella National Park, the main wilderness area on the central Queensland coast. The park encompasses some 50,000 ha (125,000 acres) of the rugged Clarke Ranges. Volcanic rock covered with rainforest and subtropical flora is cut by steep gorges, crystal clear pools and impressive waterfalls tumbling down the mountainside.

Finch Hatton Gorge, an oasis of waterfalls, swimming holes, lush flora and volcanic boulder formations, is the main destination for tourists. Endemic wildlife here includes gliders, ring-tailed possums, bandicoots and pademelons (a type of wallaby). Broken River is one of the few places in Australia where platypuses can be spotted at dusk and dawn. The Sky Window lookout affords spectacular

views of Pioneer Valley. There are also many walking tracks that weave through the rainforest. One of the most popular trails starts at the Finch Hatton picnic area. Eungella is also the starting point for the 56-km (35-mile) Mackay Highlands Great Walk.

❶⓽ Ayr

🅰F2 🚇🚌 🅸Plantation Park, Bruce Hwy; www. visitburdekin.com.au

The busy town of Ayr, at the heart of the Burdekin River Delta, is the major sugar cane-growing area in Australia.

Within the town itself is the modern Burdekin Cultural Complex, which includes a 530-seat theatre, a library and an art gallery. Among its art collection are the renowned "Living Lagoon" sculptures by the contemporary Australian sculptor Stephen Walker. The Ayr Nature Display consists of a rock wall made from 2,600 pieces of North Queensland rock, intricate pictures made from preserved insects and a display of Australian reptiles, shells, fossils and Aboriginal artifacts. In Plantation Park

↑ Pine Islet Lighthouse, overlooking boats in Mackay Harbour

Did You Know?

The Whitsundays should really be called "Whitmondays" – but Captain Cook got his days mixed up.

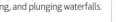
↑ People swimming in the lagoon on a sunny day at Airlie Beach, a popular resort town

is the Juru walking trail and *Gubulla Munda*, a giant snake sculpture 15 m (50 ft) long.

About 55 km (35 miles) north of Ayr is Alligator Creek, which is the access point for Bowling Green Bay National Park. Here geckos and cicadas live alongside each other in a lush landscape. Within the park are rock pools, perfect for swimming, and plunging waterfalls.

20
Airlie Beach

Ⓐ G3 **▢▢▢** **ⓦ** queens land.com

A popular holiday destination along Queensland's east coast, Airlie Beach is the gateway to the beautiful Whitsundays. Located 150 km (93 miles) north of Mackay, this relaxed coastal town features palm trees, beaches, waterfront parks, alfresco dining, hotels, shops and art galleries. Along the foreshore, visitors can stroll around the picturesque marina, go for a dip in the freshwater lagoon overlooking Pioneer Bay, or meander along the waterfront Bicentennial Walk. On Saturdays, markets selling locally made jewellery, clothes and crafts pop up along the esplanade. Visitors looking for a more tranquil spot should consider the Conway National Park, which borders Airlie Beach and is full of lush tropical rainforest, waterfalls, secluded beaches and panoramic walking trails.

21
Whitsunday Islands

Ⓐ G3 **▢** Hamilton Island; Proserpine **▢** Proserpine **▢** Airlie Beach **▢** Port of Airlie, Airlie Beach **ⓦ** australia.com/en/places/ whitsundays-and-surrounds

The Whitsunday Islands are an archipelago of 74 islands, situated within the Great Barrier Reef Marine Park, approximately 1,140 km (700 miles) north of Brisbane and 640 km (400 miles) south of Cairns. These islands and sandy atolls are among Australia's most stunning holiday destinations. Whitehaven Beach on Whitsunday Island is recognized as one of the world's best beaches, with 9 km (6 miles) of pure white silica sand and turquoise sea.

Only a few of the islands offer accommodation; these include family friendly Hamilton and Daydream, and luxurious Hayman. Some 66 islands remain uninhabited today. A wide range of accommodation is available. Pick from the luxury hotels, hostels, guesthouses and self-catering apartments.

There are many activities on offer in the area, including scuba diving, whale-watching, seaplane flights and charter sailing. Many companies at Airlie Beach, on the mainland, offer sailing packages, which feature diving or snorkelling and a night or two moored on the Great Barrier Reef.

TOP 5 **WHITSUNDAY BEACHES**

Whitehaven Beach
A slice of paradise on Whitsunday Island. It's said to be Australia's best beach.

Betty's Beach
This hidden cove is at the northern tip of Whitehaven Beach.

Chalkies Beach
This beach, on Haslewood Island, is known for its reef.

Chance Bay
Spot sea turtles from this pretty Whitsunday Island beach.

Catseye Beach
The biggest beach on Hamilton Island, Catseye is ideal for water sports.

Gazing out from Mount Alexandra Lookout in Daintree National Park

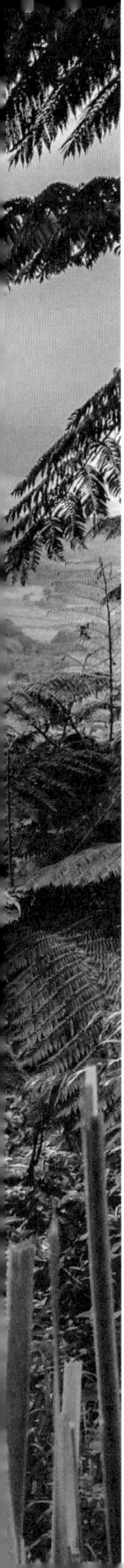

FAR NORTH QUEENSLAND

Aboriginal Australians thrived in the lush vegetation and rugged landforms of what is now known as Far North Queensland. Living on the mainland and nearby islands, they travelled by simple canoe and built complex systems of fish traps and weirs in coastal areas and inland rivers.

European explorers first visited this area in 1606, when the Dutch ship *Duyfken* landed in the vicinity of Weipa on the Cape York Peninsula. Well over a century later in 1770, Captain James Cook berthed his damaged ship, the *Endeavour*, in what is now Cooktown, while charting the coast. There was little attempt at settlement for the next 100 years, however, due to the harsh conditions on overland expeditions, which often resulted in conflict with the Aboriginal population.

This changed following a gold-mining boom in the late 19th century, which saw a series of thriving towns established. Although the gold had largely dried up by the beginning of the 20th century, the region experienced a second boom with the rise of tourism in the 1970s. The regular game-fishing trips of Hollywood star Lee Marvin brought attention to Cairns as a gateway to the Great Barrier Reef, and today this stretch of coast is a bustling holiday haven lined with resorts.

FAR NORTH
QUEENSLAND

Badu Island   *Moa Island*
18 **TORRES STRAIT**
ISLANDS
Thursday Island
Prince of Wales   *Cape York*
Island
Bamaga
Injinoo ○

Jardine
River
National
Park

Cape
Grenvil

Mapoon ○   *Bromley*
(Ampulin)
National Park
16
CAPE YORK PENINSULA
AND THE TIP

Weipa ○   *Iron Range*
National Park
[81]
Lockhart
River
Boyd Point

Aurukun ○   Archer Riv
Roadhous
Archer Bend
National Park
Cape Keer-weer   *Mungkan*   Coen ○
Kandju
National Park   [81]

Holroyd   Yarraden ○

Edward River ○
Pormpuraaw ○
Mitchell and
Alice Rivers
National Park
Kowanyama ○
Mitchell
Dunbar ○   *Palmer*

Yagoonya ○
Staaten
Gulf of   *Staaten River*
Carpentaria   *National Park*
Red
Mornington
Island   *Gilbert*   **QUEEN**

Hells Gate   Karumba ○
Roadhouse
Normanton ○   **WESTERN AND**
○ Burketown   [83]   [1]   **OUTBACK**
QUEENSLAND
Doomadgee ○   *p396*

Gregory Downs ○

○ Iffley

Burke and Wills
Roadhouse

0 kilometres   100   **N**
0 miles   100   ↑

Malpas-Trenton ○

FAR NORTH QUEENSLAND

Must Sees
1 Great Barrier Reef
2 Cairns

Experience More
3 Kuranda
4 Palm Cove
5 Port Douglas
6 Daintree National Park
7 Green Island
8 Wooroonooran National Park
9 Townsville and Magnetic Island
10 Mission Beach
11 Hinchinbrook Island
12 Babinda and the Boulders
13 Atherton Tablelands
14 Laura
15 Rinyirru (Lakefield) National Park
16 Cape York Peninsula and the Tip
17 Cooktown
18 Torres Strait Islands

Coral Sea

Port Stewart

Cape Melville

Cape Bowen

Lizard Island

RINYIRRU (LAKEFIELD) NATIONAL PARK 15

GREAT BARRIER REEF 1

Endeavour

17 COOKTOWN

LAURA 14

Black Mountain National Park

Lakeland Downs

Ayton

Cape Tribulation

DAINTREE NATIONAL PARK 6

Mungana

Chillagoe

Mossman

PORT DOUGLAS 5

PALM COVE 4

Cairns International Airport

KURANDA 3

7 GREEN ISLAND

Mareeba

2 CAIRNS

Gordonvale

Yungaburra

12 BABINDA AND THE BOULDERS

ATHERTON TABLELANDS 13

8 WOOROONOORAN NATIONAL PARK

Ravenshoe

Innisfail

Mount Garnet

Forty Mile Scrub National Park

10 MISSION BEACH

Tully

Dunk Island

Herbert

Girringun National Park

Cardwell

11 HINCHINBROOK ISLAND

Greenvale

Ingham

rsayth

Rollingstone

Townsville Airport

9 TOWNSVILLE AND MAGNETIC ISLAND

Blackbraes National Park

Lyndhurst

Clarke

AND

SOUTHEAST QUEENSLAND AND THE WHITSUNDAYS
p364

①

GREAT BARRIER REEF

A F1 **W** gbrmpa.gov.au

A natural wonder of the world, the Great Barrier Reef is the largest reef system on earth and, astoundingly, is visible from space. This impressive underwater landscape supports a diverse range of marine life, making it one of the most biodiverse places on the planet.

Stretching more than 2,300 km (1,400 miles) along Australia's northeastern coast, the Great Barrier Reef is made up of almost 3,000 separate coral reefs and around 2,000 islands. The colourful reefs here are home to over 9,000 species, including turtles, sea snakes, sharks and countless types of fish.

The reef is under threat due to climate change and pollution, which have caused significant damage. Happily, most visits to the reef should be relatively sustainable, as the Great Barrier Reef Marine Park Authority (GBRMPA) only allows tour operators with eco-tourism certifications to operate in this now-fragile environment. Many tours include diving and snorkelling, which allow visitors to immerse themselves in the reef's vibrant underwater world. It's also possible to visit some of the islands: Heron Island offers excellent snorkelling, as well as turtle-spotting from October to March, while Lady Elliot Island, with its impressive eco-resort, is the perfect place to spend a night on the reef.

STAY

Reefworld
Sleep under the stars on a moored pontoon or in a full-glass room under the Coral Sea.

W cruisewhitsundays. com/experiences

$$$

→

Scuba diving over a coral reef teeming with fish

Activities at the Reef

↑ A green turtle, one of the reef's many marine animals

Scuba Diving

The Great Barrier Reef is one of the most popular, as well as one of the more reasonably priced, places to learn to dive in the world. The best places to find dive schools are Townsville *(p392)* or Cairns *(p388)*, although many schools exist along the coast. Some boat trips also offer hand-held dives for complete beginners, while others offer night dives.

Reef Checks

▷ Play a part in reef conservation and volunteer to be part of one of many citizen-science projects led by the Great Barrier Reef Foundation and other reef charities such as Reef Check Australia. Collect data on reef fish, coral, waterways, mangroves and more in your own time and contribute to research, education and the ongoing preservation of this fragile natural ecosystem. CoralWatch provides citizen scientists with a handy coral health chart, while GBRMPA's Eye on the Reef app makes uploading your findings easy.

Snorkelling

◁ Snorkelling offers the chance to see the Great Barrier Reef's beautiful tropical fish at close range. It requires less training and equipment than diving - all you really need is a snorkel, the ability to swim and fairly good fitness. Many boat companies offer snorkelling trips or you can snorkel straight from some of the reef's islands.

Clean up the Reef

Funded by the Australian government's Reef Trust, the ReefClean project was set up to remove and prevent marine debris (human-made litter) in the Great Barrier Reef area. Join a beach clean run by organizations such as Eco Barge Clean Seas to help keep the reef litter-free.

Glass-bottomed Boat Tours

▷ Don't want to get your feet wet? Try a glass-bottomed boat tour. Glass windows allow visitors to spy the rich reef life right below, including colourful corals and vibrant shoals of fish. Many boats also offer sunbathing areas and the opportunity to go snorkelling.

GREAT BARRIER REEF

Coral reefs are among the oldest and most primitive forms of life, dating back at least 500 million years. The Great Barrier Reef started forming 18,000 years ago. Today, it is the largest reef system in the world, covering an area of approximately 350,000 sq km (135,000 sq miles) between Bundaberg and the tip of Cape York. Despite its name, the Great Barrier Reef is actually made up of thousands of islands and separate reefs of differing types. Each of these ecosystems is home to a huge variety of marine life.

LIFE ON THE GREAT BARRIER REEF

More than 2,000 species of fish and innumerable species of hard and soft coral are found in the waters of the Great Barrier Reef. The diversity of life forms, such as echinoderms (including sea urchins), crustaceans and sponges, is extra-ordinary. The reef also supports an array of invertebrates, such as the graceful sea slug, some 12 species of sea grasses and 500 types of algae. Above the water, the reef islands and coral cays support a wonderfully colourful variety of tropical birdlife.

Moray eels grow to 2 m (6 ft) in length, but are gentle enough to be hand-fed by divers.

Hard coral is formed from the outer skeleton of polyps. The most common species is staghorn coral.

Wobbegongs are members of the shark family. They sleep during the day under rocks and caves, camouflaged by their skin tones.

Soft coral has no outer skeleton and resembles the fronds of a plant, rippling in the waves.

Manta rays are huge fish, measuring up to 6 m (20 ft) across.

Butterfly fish

Thankfully, clownfish have an immunity to the stinging tentacles of sea anemones, among which they reside.

The crown of thorns starfish contributes to reef life by destroying old coral and allowing new coral to generate. It feeds mainly on staghorn coral.

Potato cod are often happy to swim alongside divers.

The seabed of the Barrier Reef is 60 m (195 ft) deep at its lowest point.

Giant clams, which are large bivalves, are protected by Australian law to save them from extinction.

Great white sharks are occasional visitors to the reef. They usually live in the open ocean and swim in schools.

Did You Know?

The Great Barrier Reef is home to a third of the world's coral.

Gobies feed on sand, ingesting the organic matter. They are found near the shoreline.

Batfish swim in large groups and colonize areas of the reef for long periods before moving on elsewhere. They mainly feed on algae and sea jellies.

Blenny

Schultz pipefish

Goatfish

↑ Soldierfish around a coral colony on the Great Barrier Reef

HOW THE REEF WAS FORMED

The growth of coral reefs is dependent on sea level - coral cannot grow above the water line or below 30 m (100 ft). As sea level rises, old coral turns to limestone, on top of which new coral can build, eventually forming barrier reefs. The Great Barrier Reef formed when the sea level rose after the end of the last Ice Age.

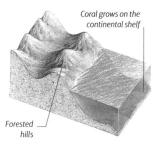

Coral grows on the continental shelf

Forested hills

Approximately 18,000 years ago, during the last Ice Age, waters were low, exposing a range of forested hills. Coral grew in the shallow waters of the continental shelf.

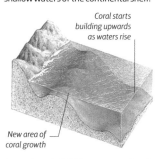

Coral starts building upwards as waters rise

New area of coral growth

Approximately 9,000 years ago, after the Ice Age, the water level rose to submerge the hills. Coral began to grow in new places.

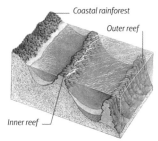

Coastal rainforest

Outer reef

Inner reef

Over succeeding millennia, coral formed on the continental shelf (the outer reef), while reefs, coral cays and lagoons formed around the former hills (the inner reef).

❷

CAIRNS

🅰F2 ✈6 km (3.5 miles) N of the city 🚉Cairns railway station, Bunda St 🚌Lake St Terminus, Lake St; Trinity Wharf, Wharf St 🚢Reef trips, Pier Point Rd ℹ1/34 The Esplanade; www.queensland.com

Perhaps best known as a jumping-off point for trips to the Great Barrier Reef, Daintree Rainforest and Atherton Tablelands, Cairns itself has plenty to offer visitors who pause here. Stately museums and buzzing bars, a human-made lagoon popular with swimmers and ancient mudflats abundant with native birdlife all await in this corner of Northern Queensland.

①

Cairns Esplanade and Lagoon

🅰Esplanade 🕐 Lagoon: 6am-9pm Thu-Tue & public hols, noon-9pm Wed 🆆cairns.qld.gov.au

Stretching for 2.5 km (1.5 miles) along the city's foreshore, the Cairns Esplanade Boardwalk offers scenic views of the Trinity Inlet. This tropical paradise is peppered with play grounds, restaurants, shops and more, including an artificial lagoon.

②

Flecker Botanic Gardens

🅰Collins Ave, Edge Hill 🕐Gardens: 7:30am-5:30pm daily; visitor centre: hours vary, check website 🆆cairns.qld.gov.au

Dating from 1886, the Flecker Botanic Gardens are home to more than 100 species of palm trees, plus many other tropical plants. The gardens include an area of Queensland rainforest, with native birdlife, as well as the Centenary Lakes, which were created in 1976 to mark the city's first 100 years.

③

Cairns Museum

🅰City Place, cnr Lake & Shield sts 🕐10am-4pm Mon-Sat 🕐1 Jan, Good Fri, 25 Apr, 25 Dec 🆆cairns museum.org.au

Housed in the 1907 School of Arts building, this museum is a fine example of the city's early architecture. Among the exhibits are the contents of an old Chinese joss house.

---

④

Reef Fleet Terminal

🅰Pier Point Rd

This jetty is more than just the departure point for cruises to the Great Barrier Reef – it's a nexus of city life. Here, locals come to browse the adjacent Pier Marketplace's boutiques, restaurants and markets. From August to December, tourists crowd Marlin Jetty to see the anglers return with their catch. Cairns is Australia's game-fishing capital.

From the terminal, catch a bus to the small village of Kuranda (p390) in the Atherton Tablelands, which has become an arts and crafts centre. Nearby is the Tjapukai Cultural Centre, home to the Aboriginal Tjapukai Dance Theatre.

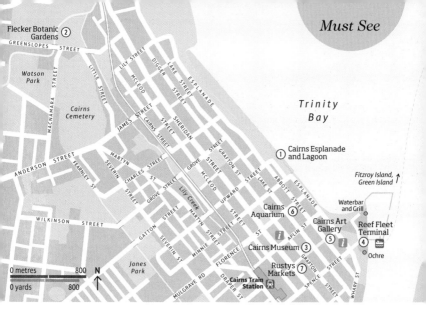

Flecker Botanic Gardens ②
GREENSLOPES STREET
Watson Park
Cairns Cemetery
Trinity Bay
Cairns Esplanade and Lagoon ①
Fitzroy Island, Green Island ↑
Waterbar and Grill
Cairns Aquarium ⑥
Cairns Art Gallery ⑤
Reef Fleet Terminal ④
Ochre
Cairns Museum ③
Rustys Markets ⑦
Jones Park
Cairns Train Station

0 metres 800 N
0 yards 800

---

⑤ Cairns Art Gallery

🏠 Cnr Abbott and Shields sts 🕐 9am–5pm Mon–Fri, 10am–5pm Sat, 10am–2pm Sun 🌐 cairnsartgallery.com.au

Opened in 1995, this art gallery is one of the largest public galleries in regional Queensland. It has works from award-winning national and international artists, including an impressive permanent collection dedicated to the Aboriginal cultural heritage of Far North Queensland.

⑥ Cairns Aquarium

🏠 5 Florence St 🕐 9:30am–3:30pm daily (last adm: 2:30pm) 🌐 cairns aquarium.com.au

This is the only aquarium in the world dedicated to protect and conserve the habitats and species of Tropical North Queensland. As well as vast tanks filled with over 16,000 fish, reptiles and marine mammals, the aquarium houses a turtle rehabilitation centre.

---

⑦ Rustys Markets

🏠 Cnr Grafton and Sheridan sts 🕐 5am–6pm Fri–Sat, 5am–3pm Sun 🌐 rustys markets.com.au

Established in 1975, this market is one of the most well known in Australia. It features more than 180 stalls stocked with local fruits, vegetables and freshly baked goods. You can also find clothing and accessories here, as well as an abundance of bric-a-brac.

EAT

Ochre

At Ochre take in sweeping views of the Trinity Inlet while enjoying Australian dishes made using bush ingredients.

🏠 6/1 Marlin Parade 🌐 ochrerestaurant. com.au

Waterbar and Grill

Offering wonderful seafood, this waterfront restaurant has often been hailed "the best steakhouse in town".

🏠 1 Pier Point Rd 🌐 waterbarandgrill. com.au

←

The tropical setting of the Cairns Esplanande and Lagoon at dusk

EXPERIENCE MORE

③

Kuranda

 F2 🚍🚌 From Cairns
🛈 Cnr Coondoo & Therwine sts; www.kuranda.org

On the eastern edge of the Atherton Tablelands is the tiny village of Kuranda, 30 km (19 miles) north of Cairns. A hippie hangout in the 1960s, it has since developed into an arts and crafts centre with stunning street art and outdoor markets. In the village centre is the **Australian Butterfly Sanctuary**, the largest butterfly flight aviary in the southern hemisphere. Other popular attractions in the area are the 7.5-km (4.5-mile) **Skyrail Rainforest Cableway** and the **Kuranda Scenic Railway**, both with great views across Barron Gorge and the heritage-listed Wet Tropics rainforest.

Australian Butterfly Sanctuary

🏠 8 Rob Veivers Dr
🌐 australianbutterflies.com

Skyrail Rainforest Cableway

🏠 6 Skyrail Dr, Smithfield
🌐 skyrail.com.au

Kuranda Scenic Railway

🏠 Coondoo St 🌐 ksr.com.au

---

④

Palm Cove

 F2 ✈ To Cairns, then bus or car 🛈 119–121 Williams Esplanade; www.tropical northqueensland.org.au

A relaxed coastal village 26 km (16 miles) north of Cairns, Palm Cove is Australia's spa capital. It is lined with boutique holiday resorts, pristine beaches, award-winning restaurants and 500-year-old Melaleuca trees. There are also plenty of water sports available here, such as sailing, jetty fishing and kayaking. Visitors should try a sunset or sunrise kayak over the coral reefs of Haycock and Double islands where stingrays, shovelnose sharks and turtles can be spotted.

⑤

Port Douglas

 F2 🚌 🌐 visitportdouglas daintree.com

Situated 75 km (47 miles) from Cairns, Port Douglas was once a tiny fishing village. Today, it is a major tourist centre, but it has managed to preserve its charming village atmosphere. The beautiful Four-Mile Beach, at the end of Macrossan Street, is a very popular walking spot. Many 19th-century buildings still line the street and modern shopping centres have been

---

 GREAT VIEW
Rex Lookout

Located between Palm Cove and Port Douglas, where the rainforest meets the sea, Rex is a striking vantage point. It has scenic views of Oak Beach, Trinity Bay and the Coral Sea. It is also a good spot for hang-gliding and paragliding.

↑ The scenic Cape Tribulation Beach, and *(inset)* the Rex Creek Bridge at the Daintree National Park

designed to blend with the town's original architecture. The port was set up during the gold rush of the 1850s, but it was superseded by Cairns as the main port of the area. The construction of the luxurious Sheraton Mirage Resort in the early 1980s heralded the beginning of a tourism boom. Port Douglas is an alternative departure point to Cairns for Great Barrier Reef tours.

Daintree National Park

🄰F2 ✈To Cairns, then train, bus or car 🚗Cnr Cape Tribulation & Tulip Oak rds, Cow Bay; www.discover thedaintree.com

This park, north of Port Douglas, covers more than 76,000 ha (188,000 acres). The Cape Tribulation section of the park is a place of great beauty, and one of the few spots where the rainforest meets the sea. The park's largest section lies inland from Cape Tribulation. Although it is a mostly inaccessible, mountainous area, it encompasses the Mossman Gorge, which offers an easy and accessible 2.2-km (1.5-mile) Dreamtime Walk through the rainforest. Led by local Aboriginal people, it covers cultural sites and includes a traditional smoking ceremony. Daintree River cruises are also on offer here, with crocodile sightings being a major draw.

Green Island

🄰F2 🚢From Cairns 🌐greenislandresort.com.au

Green Island is one of the few inhabited coral cays of the Great Barrier Reef *(p384)*.

STAY

Immerse yourself in nature and stay in the heart of the heritage-listed Daintree Rainforest.

Ferntree Rainforest Lodge

🄰F2 🏠36 Camelot Close, Cape Tribulation 🌐ferntreerainforest hotel.com

$$$

Cape Trib Beach House

🄰F2 🏠152 Rykers Rd, Cape Tribulation 🌐cape tribbeach.com.au

$$$

Silky Oaks Lodge

🄰F2 🏠Finlayvale Rd, Mossman 🌐silkyoaks lodge.com.au

$$$

Daintree Eco Lodge

🄰F2 🏠3189 Mossman-Daintree Rd, Daintree 🌐daintree-ecolodge. com.au

$$$

Despite its small size (a walk around the entire island takes approximately 15 minutes), it is home to a peaceful eco-resort.

Green Island's proximity to the mainland means its coral is not as colourful as the outer reef, but it offers snorkelling from the shore and visitors can spot sea turtles feeding on sea grass from the long jetty. Its accessibility by ferry from Cairns makes it popular with day-trippers.

The island's Marineland Melanesia complex is home to Cassius, the world's largest crocodile in captivity.

↑ A colourful cassowary bird at the Wooroonooran National Park

8

Wooroonooran National Park

F2 Innisfail Anzac Memorial Park, cnr Gladdy St & Bruce Hwy; 142 Victoria St, Cardwell; www.parks.des.qld.gov. au/parks/wooroonooran

Wooroonooran National Park contains the state's two highest mountains. Bartle Frere, reaching 1,611 m (5,285 ft), and Bellenden Ker, rising to 1,591 m (5,220 ft), are often swathed in clouds. Cassowaries (large flightless birds that are under threat of extinction) can be spotted on the mountains.

Much of this national park is wilderness, although tracks do exist. A popular area is Josephine Falls, south of the park, about 8 km (5 miles) from the Bruce Highway.

4,000
The number of cassowaries left in the world.

9

Townsville and Magnetic Island

F2 Bulletin Square; www.townsville northqueensland.com.au

The state's second-largest city, Townsville is known for its sunny beachfront. It was founded by Robert Towns, who began the practice of enslaving Kanakas from the Pacific Islands and bringing hundreds of them to Australia as cheap labour.

Another attractions is the **Queensland Museum Tropics**, which displays artifacts from the shipwreck *Pandora*. Townsville is also an access point for the Great Barrier Reef (*p384*) including the **Museum of Underwater Art** where divers and snorkellers can explore public art installations.

Situated 8 km (5 miles) offshore is Townsville's official suburb, Magnetic Island. The only reef island with a significant permanent population, it was named by Captain Cook who believed that magnetic fields were causing problems with his compass. Today, almost half of the island is a national park.

Queensland Museum Tropics

 Flinders St East
🕐 9:30am–4pm daily
🚫 Good Fri, 25 Apr, 25 & 26 Dec 🔳 museum.qld.gov. au/tropics

Museum of Underwater Art

Various dive sites, check website 🔳 moua.com.au

10

Mission Beach

F2 Tully Mission Beach 55 Porter Promenade; www. missionbeachtourism.com

Located between Cairns and Townsville, Mission Beach

🔍 HIDDEN GEM
Paronella Park

This park, between Mission Beach and Wooroonooran National Park, is home to the ruins of a Spanish-style castle. Built in 1935 by Spaniard José Paronella, the site has a spectacular 15-m (49-ft) waterfall.

comprises four beach villages linked by 14 km (9 miles) of golden sand. Its boutiques, galleries and restaurants are set against a rainforest backdrop and views across to nearby Dunk Island. Day trips from Mission Beach are popular, affording snorkelling, diving and windsurfing.

11

Hinchinbrook Island

F2 Ingham Cardwell Lucinda, Cardwell 🔳 parks.des.qld.gov.au/ parks/hinchinbrook

Covering 635 sq km (245 sq miles), and separated from the mainland town of Cardwell by a mangrove-fringed channel,

Hinchinbrook is the largest island national park in Australia. Dense, pristine rainforest makes the island popular with bushwalkers, and many scale 1,121-m (3,678-ft) Mount Bowen, Hinchinbrook's highest point. Along the trails, walkers might spot the island's native wildlife, including the magnificent blue Ulysses butterfly.

 Babinda and the Boulders

A F2 **ℹ** Cnr Munro St & Bruce Hwy, Babinda; (07) 4067 1008

Reminiscent of early 20th-century Queensland, the rural town of Babinda is lined with veranda-fronted houses and a wooden pub.

The Babinda Boulders, 7 km (4 miles) inland, are water-worn rock shapes and a popular photographic subject.

 Atherton Tablelands

A F2 **ℹ** Cnr Silo Rd & Main St, Atherton; www.athertontablelands.com.au

Rising sharply from the coastal plains of Cairns, the northern landscape levels out into the lush Atherton Tablelands.

At their highest point, the tablelands are 900 m (3,000 ft) above sea level. The cool temperature, heavy rainfall and rich volcanic soil make this one of the richest farming areas in Queensland. For many decades, tobacco was the main crop, but now farmers have diversified into peanuts, macadamia nuts, sugar cane, bananas and avocados.

The town of Yungaburra, with its many historic buildings, is listed by the National Trust. Nearby is the famed "curtain fig tree", where the aerial roots, growing down from the tree tops, form a 15-m (50-ft) screen. Southwest of Yungaburra is the eerie, green crater lake at Mount Hypipamee, which is 60 m (200 ft) in diameter.

Millaa Millaa contains the most spectacular waterfalls of the region. A 15-km (9-mile) sealed circuit drive takes in the Zillie and Ellinjaa falls. The pretty Mungalli Falls are also nearby. Atherton is the region's main town, named after its first European settlers, John and Kate Atherton, who set up a cattle station here in the 19th century where the agricultural centre of Mareeba now stands.

EAT

A Touch of Salt
This award-winning restaurant is one of the best places to eat in Townsville. It offers high-quality dishes, an extensive wine list and great waterfront views.

A F2 **🏠** 86 Ogden St, Townsville **w** atouch ofsalt.com.au

$$$

Saltwater Magnetic Island
A casual, fine-dining restaurant on Magnetic Island, this unlicensed venue serves modern Australian-Asian fusion cuisine. It specializes in seafood and poultry.

A F2 **🏠** 53 Sooning St, Nelly Bay, Magnetic Island **📞** (07) 414 352 762

$$$

↑ Babinda Creek flowing past the large granite Babinda Boulders

Performers at the
Laura Quinkan
Dance Festival

14
Laura

F2 **To Cairns, then
bus or car** **Ang-Gnarra
Aboriginal Corporation, Lot
2, Peninsula Development
Rd; www.anggnarra.
org.au**

Located at the base of the
Cape York Peninsula, this town
is a typical Australian outback
community. In the late 19th
century, Laura was the rail
terminus for the Palmer River
gold fields and some 20,000
people passed through
each year. Today, it is almost
forgotten, but the discovery
in 1959 of Aboriginal rock art
sites of great antiquity is
reviving interest in the area.
One of the most notable cave
sites is the Giant Horse Gallery,
which contains huge horse
paintings thought to record
the first sightings of European
navigators. The town is also
home to the Laura Quinkan
Dance Festival, an annual
Aboriginal celebration in June.

15
Rinyirru (Lakefield) National Park

F2 **Cooktown**
**Nature's Powerhouse,
Botanic Gardens, Walker
St, Cooktown; www.parks.
des.qld.gov.au/parks/
rinyirru-lakefield**

Covering approximately
540,000 ha (1,300,000 acres),
Rinyirru (Lakefield) National
Park is the second-largest
national park in Queensland.
It encompasses a wide variety
of landscapes, including river
forests, plains, mangroves,
sandstone hills and coastal
flats. The centre of the
park abounds with birds.

Camping is the only
accommodation option
and a permit must be
obtained at the park's
self-registration stations.
The park is largely inaccessible during the wet season
between December and
June when the rivers flood
the plains.

16
Cape York Peninsula and the Tip

F1 **To Cairns, then
4WD** **Walker St;
www.cooktownand
capeyork.com**

Cape York Peninsula, situated
at Australia's northernmost
tip, is one of the last untouched
wilderness spots in the world.
Covering 200,000 sq km
(77,220 sq miles) – roughly an
area as large as Great Britain –
the region is home to many
Aboriginal and Torres Strait
Islander communities. It also
has more national parks than
anywhere else in Queensland.
The landscape varies according
to the time of year: from
November to March, the rivers
are swollen and the landscape
is green; during the dry winter
months, the riverbeds are
waterless and the countryside
is bare and arid.

The region is dotted with
beachfront campgrounds,
fishing holes, waterfalls and
wetlands, and is a popular
bucket-list destination for
4WD enthusiasts, who come
here to tackle the iconic
350-km- (217-mile-) long
Old Telegraph Track (OTT).
History buffs can explore

> One of the most notable cave sites in Laura
> is the Giant Horse Gallery, which contains
> huge horse paintings thought to record
> the first sightings of European navigators.

the ruins at the abandoned Somerset pioneer settlement, which is scattered with masonry and rusted cannons. At low tide, Aboriginal rock art painting can be found in the cave at the nearby beach. Somerset is also home to the famous sign that marks Australia's northernmost tip.

Cooktown

🏛F2 🚉🛏🍴 ℹ️ Nature's Powerhouse, Botanic Gardens, Walker St; www.cooktownand capeyork.com

When the *Endeavour* was damaged by a coral reef in 1770, Captain Cook and his crew spent six weeks in this area while repairs to the ship were made. Cooktown's claim to fame, therefore, is that it was the site of the first white settlement in Australia.

Like most towns in the area, Cooktown originally serviced the gold fields and its present-day population is half the 4,000 inhabitants who once sustained its 50 pubs. However, many of its historic buildings survive, including the Westpac Bank, originally the Old National Bank, with its stone columns supporting an iron-lace veranda. The **Cooktown Museum**, which houses the old anchor from the *Endeavour*, started life in the 1880s as a convent. In the cemetery of the town, a memorial and numerous gravestones are testimony to the difficulties faced by the many Chinese immigrants who came to the gold fields in the 1870s.

Between Cooktown and Bloomfield, Black Mountain National Park is named after the geological formation of huge black granite boulders. The boulders were formed around 260 million years ago below the earth's surface and were gradually exposed as surrounding land surfaces eroded away.

Cooktown Museum

⊛ 🏠 Cnr Helen & Furneaux sts 🕐 9am–2pm Wed–Sat 🚫 Dec & Jan 🌐 nationaltrust qld.org.au

---

Torres Strait Islands

🏛F1 🚠 From Cairns 🚢 From Cairns ℹ️ Cairns; www.torres.qld.gov.au/tourism

The Torres Strait divides the northern coastline of Australia from Papua New Guinea and is dotted with numerous islands. Only a few of these islands are inhabited and have been governed by Queensland since 1879.

Thursday Island is the "capital" island and was once the centre of the local

274
—
The number of islands in the Torres Strait, of which 17 are inhabited.

> **TORRES STRAIT ISLANDER CULTURE**
>
> Along with Aboriginal peoples, the Torres Strait Islander peoples were the first inhabitants of Australia. Distinct from mainland First Australians, their culture is a blend of Australian, Papuan and Austronesian elements and their own art, languages and practices. The Tagai is their spiritual belief system and shapes their law and customs. It is centred around the stories of the stars and the islanders' seafaring life. The Dhari, a feathered-and-pearl headdress, is the symbol of the islanders and their customs.

pearling industry. Many Japanese pearlers who lost their lives in this occupation are buried in the island's cemetery. In 1891, Green Hill Fort was built to prevent invasion by the Russians.

Murray Island was the birthplace of Eddie Mabo, who, in 1992, won his claim to traditional land in the Australian High Court and changed First Nations-European relations for ever more.

→
The scenic view from Thursday Island, Torres Strait

WESTERN AND OUTBACK QUEENSLAND

These vast red plains and desert dunes have been home to dinosaurs and Aboriginal clans, aviators and bush poets. When Europeans arrived in the 1800s, they found a land rich in minerals – particularly gold. When mining declined at the end of the 19th century, the Aboriginal people who had acted as the prospectors' guides gained employment as stockmen and farmworkers on outback stations. Highly regarded for their horsemanship, they often rode barefoot, tagging and herding livestock over vast distances. Stories of these pastoral people inspired bush poet Banjo Paterson to write *Waltzing Matilda*, a ballad about an itinerant farm worker who stole a sheep, in 1895. Today, it is the country's unofficial anthem. The region also has links to another part of Australia's cultural heritage. Qantas, the country's national airline, was founded at Winton in 1920, moved to Longreach in 1922 and commenced its first regular passenger service between Charleville and Cloncurry that same year. But despite its globetrotting history, Western and Outback Queensland remains a distinctly Australian corner of the country.

DARWIN AND
THE TOP END
p412

THE RED
CENTRE
p430

YORKE AND EYRE
PENINSULAS
AND THE SOUTH
AUSTRALIAN
OUTBACK
p328

0 kilometres 150

0 miles 150

N

Dunbar

Staaten River
National Park

Red

Wellesley
Islands

Hell's Gate
Roadhouse

KARUMBA **7**

NORMANTON AND **6**
GULF SAVANNAH

BURKETOWN **9**

Blackbull

Croydon

Georgetow

Doomadgee

A1

A1

Forsayt

Lawn Hill
National Park

Gregory
Downs

83

Norman

Saxby

Gregor

Gregory

Leichhardt

84

Burke and Wills
Roadhouse

Iffley

BARKLY HIGHWAY

66

Camooweal

A2

Lake
Julius

83

84

Sedan
Dip

Flinders

FLINDERS HIGHW

NORTHERN
TERRITORY

MOUNT ISA **8**

Cloncurry

A6

Julia
Creek

Richmond

Corfield

McKinlay

LANDSBOROUGH

Urandangi

Duchess

A2

HIGHWAY

Dajarra

83

Selwyn

Range

WINTON **2**

Middleton

Bladensburg
National Park

Burke

Hamilton

62

Lark Quarry

BOULIA **4**

QUEENSLAND

Mulligan

Goneaway
National Park

Astrebla Downs
National Park

Stonehenge

Bedourie

Great
Artesian
Basin

Lake Macbattie

Jundah

Windorah

14

83

Betoota

BIRDSVILLE **3**

Lake Yamma
Yamma

Eromanga

Sturt Stony
Desert

Simpson
Desert

Cooper Creek

Bullo

WESTERN AND
OUTBACK
QUEENSLAND

SOUTH
AUSTRALIA

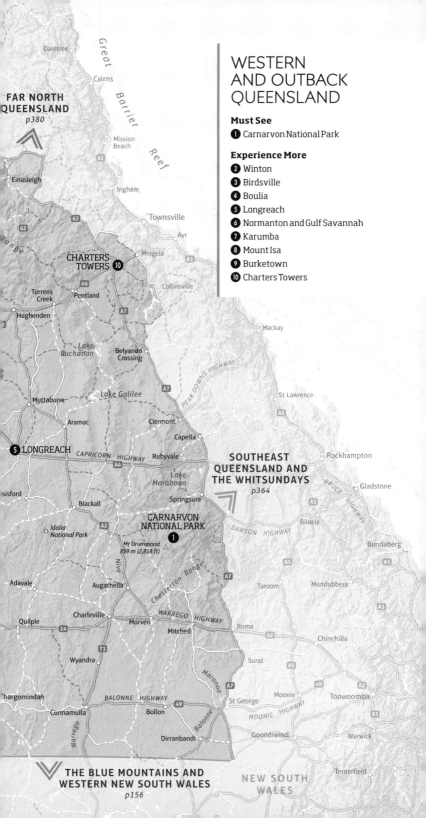

FAR NORTH
QUEENSLAND
p380

WESTERN
AND OUTBACK
QUEENSLAND

Must See
1 Carnarvon National Park

Experience More
2 Winton
3 Birdsville
4 Boulia
5 Longreach
6 Normanton and Gulf Savannah
7 Karumba
8 Mount Isa
9 Burketown
10 Charters Towers

SOUTHEAST
QUEENSLAND AND
THE WHITSUNDAYS
p364

THE BLUE MOUNTAINS AND
WESTERN NEW SOUTH WALES
p156

NEW SOUTH
WALES

❶ 🛍️

CARNARVON NATIONAL PARK

🅰️F3 ℹ️ Yeppoon Visitor Centre, Scenic Highway, Yeppoon; www.parks.
des.qld.gov.au/parks/carnarvon-gorge

Nestled among Central Queensland's rugged Sandstone Belt, Carnarvon National Park is a tranquil oasis on the edge of the outback. The area is best known for the majestic Carnarvon Gorge, a thriving ecosystem and stunning examples of Aboriginal rock art.

Covering some 2,980 sq km (1,150 sq miles), Carnarvon National Park is a 200-million-year-old landscape dotted with towering sandstone cliffs and lush green forest. Cutting through it is the stunning Carnarvon Gorge, a 32-km (20-mile) canyon carved by the waters of Carnarvon Creek. The gorge consists of beautiful white cliffs, crags and pillars of stone, which harbour plants and animals that have survived through centuries of evolution, including prehistoric cycads and Carnarvon Fan Palms.

The area is also rich in Aboriginal culture, with three rock art sites open to the public. One highlight is the Art Gallery, a 62-m- (203-ft-) long sandstone wall decorated with thousands of engravings, paintings and stencils of things like hands, animal tracks and boomerangs.

GREAT VIEW
Boolimba Bluff

The challenging 6.4-km (4-mile) Boolimba Bluff track leads to a lookout overlooking Carnarvon Gorge. From here, you'll get panoramic views over the canyon and across to the distant ranges of Boolimba Bluff.

STAY

Carnarvon Gorge Wilderness Lodge
By Carnarvon Creek, this secluded resort has 28 luxury lodges.

📍 O'Briens Rd, Carnarvon Gorge
🕒 Nov–Mar 🌐 wild ernesslodge.com.au

$ $ $

Breeze Holiday Parks Carnarvon Gorge
Pick from campsites, cottages, studios or glamping tents.

📍 O'Briens Rd, Carnarvon Gorge
🌐 breezeholidayparks.com.au/parks/carnarvon-gorge/

$ $ $

↑ The waterfall and pool at Moss Garden, located at the end of Carnarvon Gorge

→ Painting at Cathedral Cave, a major Aboriginal cultural site in the park

Did You Know?
—
Even during months with no rain, Carnarvon Creek always has flowing water.

↑ Crossing the creek in Carnarvon Gorge, surrounded by lush forest and sandstone cliffs

↑ Dinosaur Canyon at the Australian Age of Dinosaurs Museum, Winton

EXPERIENCE MORE

② Winton

🅰F3 ➕🏨🚌 ℹ️50 Elderslie St; www.experience winton.com.au

Birthplace of the song *Waltzing Matilda* and home to a great many agricultural and mining operations, the town of Winton is perhaps best known as the Hollywood of the outback. It has acted as the backdrop for countless films over the years. To see some of these movies for yourself, head to the **Royal Theatre Winton**, which was built in 1918, and screens classic movies.

One of the quirkiest attractions in Winton is the Musical Fence, a wire fence that can be played as a musical instrument. Here, visitors create their own bush orchestra. Winton is also home to the **Australian Age of Dinosaurs Museum**, which showcases the largest collection of Australian dinosaur fossils in the world.

In Lark Quarry, 110 km (68 miles) southwest of Winton, is the **Dinosaur Stampede National Monument**, the world's only known site of a dinosaur stampede.

3,300

The number of preserved dinosaur footprints at Lark Quarry.

WALTZING MATILDA

Bush ballad *Waltzing Matilda* is Australia's unofficial national anthem. It was penned in 1895 by famous Australian poet Banjo Paterson and tells the story of a swagman ("matilda" is slang for swag) who commits suicide instead of running from the law. Paterson's friend, Christina Macpherson, then added music adapted from Bonnie Wood of Craigielea, a Scottish marching song. The song's first public performance was on 6 April 1895 at the North Gregory Hotel in Winton.

Royal Theatre Winton

🅰69 Elderslie St 🌐royal theatrewinton.com.au

Australian Age of Dinosaurs Museum

🅰Lot 1, Dinosaur Dr 🌐aus tralianageofdinosaurs.com

Dinosaur Stampede National Monument

🅰Lark Quarry Access & Jundah Cork Rd, Opalton 🌐dinosaurtrackways.com.au

STAY

North Gregory Hotel
Built in 1879, this famous hotel has a restaurant, beer garden, an outdoor hydrotherapy spa and live entertainment.

🅐F3 🅐67 Elderslie St, Winton 🅦northgregory hotel.com

$$$

Birdsville Hotel
This award-winning outback hotel, built in 1884 and refurbished in 1980, has 28 modern rooms and serves traditional pub fare.

🅐E3 🅐Adelaide St, Birdsville 🅦birdsville hotel.com.au

$$$

---

❸
Birdsville

🅐E3 🔁 🛈9 Burt St; www. outbackqueensland.com. au/town/birdsville

Less than 15 km (9 miles) from the South Australian border is Birdsville. This rural town is the starting point for the iconic 517-km (321-mile) Birdsville Track and the gateway to the Simpson Desert, the world's largest parallel sand dune desert. The biggest sand dune here is the 40-m- (131-ft-) high Big Red. The desert's vibrant red dunes are best experienced at sunset.

Birdsville also attracts visitors to its quintessential outback pub, as well as the Big Red Bash – the world's most remote music festival – and the annual Birdsville Races, which are popular for betting and socializing.

❹
Boulia

🅐E3 🔁🚌 To Longreach, then by car 🛈Herbert St; www.boulia.qld.gov.au

The outback town of Boulia first stepped onto the world stage in 1918, when the Min Min lights first appeared. This mysterious phenomenon saw glowing, disc-like shapes floating in the sky above the nearby town of Min Min. The Min Min Encounter, a 45-minute theatrical experience incorporating animatronics and fibre optics, re-enacts the sightings and includes a brief history of the town.

The Boulia Heritage Complex is also worth a visit for its 19th-century stone house, Aboriginal artifacts and fossils dating from the Cretaceous Era. Look out for a plesiosaur fossil that is 80 per cent complete.

---

❺
Longreach

🅐F3 🔁🚌 🛈99A Qantas Park, Eagle St; www. experiencelongreach. com.au

Situated in the centre of Queensland, Longreach is the principal town in this part of the state. From 1922 to 1934, it was the operating base of Australian airline Qantas. At the Longreach Airport is the **Qantas Founders Museum**, where visitors can walk the wing of a Boeing 747 and tour a fully equipped jumbo jet.

Across the highway, the **Australian Stockman's Hall of Fame** is a fascinating tribute to outback men and women. Aboriginal artifacts and documented tales of the early European settlers are presented and examined in the five themed galleries.

A visit to Longreach isn't complete without a trip on the award-winning **Cobb & Co Stagecoach Experience**, an atmospheric, old-fashioned ride through the town, and along a stretch of the original Longreach-Windorah mail route, in a restored stagecoach.

Another essential Longreach journey is a cruise down the Thomson River. There are several local operators running sunset and dinner tours that offer stunning 360-degree river and floodplain views.

Qantas Founders Museum
🕘 🅐Sir Hudson Fysh Dr 🅦qfom.com.au

Australian Stockman's Hall of Fame
🕘🕘🕘 🅐Landsborough Hwy 🅦stockmans halloffame.com.au

Cobb & Co Stagecoach Experience
🅐Kinnon & Co's The Station Store, 126 Eagle St 🅦out backpioneers.com.au

→
An exhibit at the Australian Stockman's Hall of Fame

Magpie geese in the Cumberland Chimney Wetlands, Gulf Savannah

on a morning nature cruise with **Croc & Crab Tours**. On board, you'll experience live crab pot-handling, crocodile spotting and bird-watching along the Norman River and Six Mile Creek, but the real highlight is at lunchtime when freshly cooked Gulf prawns, tropical fruit and refreshments are served. This operator also offers an evening cruise around Sand Island, with breathtaking sunset views over the Gulf of Carpentaria.

Croc & Crab Tours
 🏠 40 Col Kitching Dr
🌐 crocandcrab.com.au

Normanton and Gulf Savannah

🅰E2 🚌 Normanton
ℹ Cnr Landsborough & Caroline sts, Normanton; (07) 4747 8422

The 350,000 sq km (135,000 sq miles) between the east coast and the Gulf of Carpentaria make up the Gulf Savannah, Queensland's most northwesterly region. Flat and covered in savannah grasses, abundant with wildlife, this is Australia's remotest landscape. The economic base of the area is fishing and cattle.

Situated 70 km (45 miles) inland on the Norman River, Normanton is the largest town in the region. It began life as a port, handling copper from Cloncurry and then gold from Croydon. The famous *Gulflander* train still commutes between Normanton and Croydon once a week.

En route from Normanton to the Gulf of Carpentaria, savannah grasses give way to glistening salt pans. Once the rains come in November, however, this area becomes a wetland and a breeding ground for millions of birds, crocodiles, prawns and barramundi.

EAT

Sunset Tavern
A casual, waterfront tavern serving fresh seafood. It's a great place to watch the sun set over the Gulf of Carpentaria.

🅰E2 🏠 Esplanade, Karumba 📞 (07) 4745 9183

💲💲💲

Grants Pies and Cakes
A favourite with the locals, this spot offers hot pies, sausage rolls and tasty sweet treats.

🅰E3 🏠 179 Camooweal St, Menzies, Mount Isa 📞 (07) 4743 9050

💲💲💲

Karumba

🅰E2 ✈🏠🚌 ℹ149 Yappar St; www.barracentre.com.au

Karumba lies 70 km (43 miles) north of Normanton and sits at the mouth of the Norman River, the access point for the Gulf of Carpentaria. Despite its untamed, frontier-town feel, this quiet coastal settlement is the headquarters of a multi-million-dollar prawn and fishing industry. To best get to know the town, do as the locals do and take to the water

Mount Isa

🅰E3 ✈🏠🚌 ℹ19 Marian St; www.discovermountisa.com.au

Mount Isa is the only major city in far western Queensland. Its existence is entirely based around the world's largest silver and lead mine, which still dominates the town. Ore was first discovered here in 1923 by prospector John Campbell Miles and the first mine was set up in the 1930s. In those early days, "the Isa" was a shanty town, and Tent House, now owned by the National Trust, is an example of the half-house-half-tents that housed most early European settlers. Also in town is **Outback at Isa**, which incorporates the Riversleigh Fossil Centre and Isa Experience Gallery, and runs mine tours.

One of the most popular events in the town's calendar is the Mount Isa Rodeo, which is held in August. With prize money totalling more than A$100,000, riders come from all over the world to take part.

While in the area, visit Cloncurry, 120 km (75 miles) east of Mount Isa, which was the departure point for the Queensland and Northern Territory Aerial Service's (QANTAS) first flight in 1921. Qantas is now Australia's national airline.

Outback at Isa

⊗ ⊛ 🏠 19 Marian St
🕐 Daily 🚫 Good Fri, 25 Dec
🌐 discovermountisa.com.au

THE ROYAL FLYING DOCTOR SERVICE

The Royal Flying Doctor Service was founded by John Flynn, a Presbyterian pastor who was sent as a missionary to the Australian outback in 1912. The young cleric was disturbed to see that many of his congregation died due to the lack of basic medical care and he founded the Australian Inland Mission. Today, the service deals with some 130,000 patients a year, and most outback properties have an airstrip where the Flying Doctor can land. Emergency medical help is rarely more than two hours away and advice is available over a special radio channel.

Burketown

🅰 E2 🚗 🛈 19 Musgrave St, cnr Burke St, (07) 4745 5111; City Council, 65 Musgrave St; www.burketown.com.au

Situated 30 km (18 miles) from the Gulf of Carpentaria, Burketown was once a major port servicing the hinterland. The town has a rich history; in the 1950s, it found fame as the setting for Neville Shute's famous novel about life in an outback town, *A Town Like Alice*. It is also known for the World Barramundi Fishing Championship and the spectacular propagating roll cloud known as a Morning Glory,

which appears here in the early mornings from September to November.

About 150 km (90 miles) west of Burketown is Hell's Gate, so named in the 20th century because it was the last outpost where the state's police guaranteed protection.

Charters Towers

🅰 F3 🚗🚌 🛈 74 Mosman St; www.visitcharterstowers.com.au

Following the 1871 discovery of gold in the area, it became Queensland's second-largest town, with a population of 27,000. For a glimpse of the town's gold-mining days, check out the old Charters Towers Stock Exchange Arcade, and the surrounding group of 19th-century buildings, in the city centre. This international centre of finance was the only such exchange in Australia outside a capital city.

Charters Towers fell into decline when the gold ran out in the 1920s (although gold is still mined here, as well as copper, lead and zinc). Its economy now depends on the beef industry and its status as the educational centre for Queensland's outback and Papua New Guinea.

←

Alfresco dining at popular waterfront Sunset Tavern in Karumba

NORTHERN TERRITORY

Walking through a canyon in the Uluṟu-Kata Tjuṯa National Park

EXPLORE
NORTHERN
TERRITORY

This guide divides the Northern
Territory into two colour-coded
sightseeing areas, as shown on
this map. Find out more about
each area on the following pages.

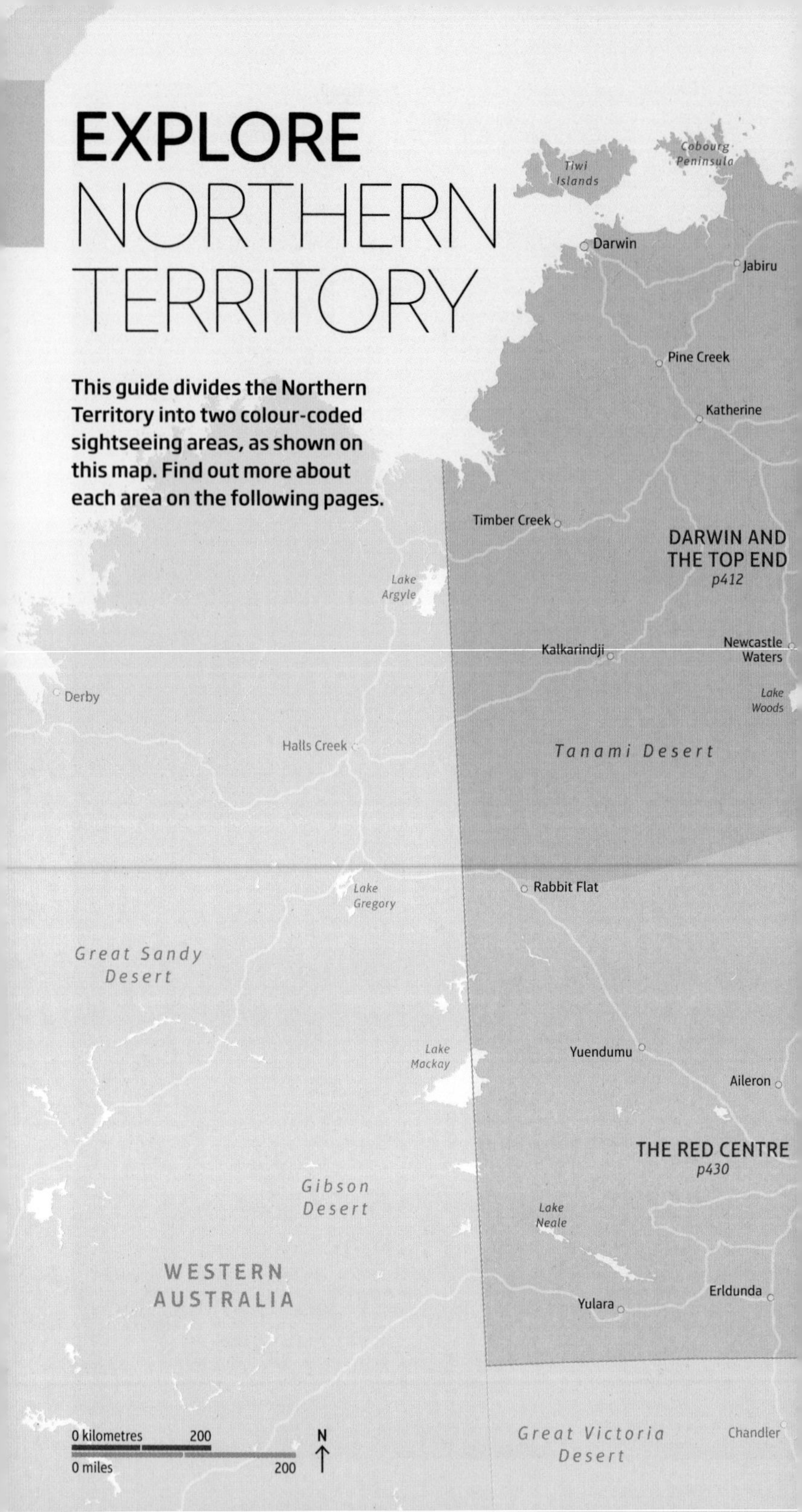

*Tiwi
Islands*

*Cobourg
Peninsula*

Darwin

Jabiru

Pine Creek

Katherine

Timber Creek

**DARWIN AND
THE TOP END**
p412

*Lake
Argyle*

Kalkarindji

Newcastle
Waters

*Lake
Woods*

Derby

Halls Creek

Tanami Desert

*Lake
Gregory*

Rabbit Flat

*Great Sandy
Desert*

*Lake
Mackay*

Yuendumu

Aileron

*Gibson
Desert*

*Lake
Neale*

THE RED CENTRE
p430

WESTERN
AUSTRALIA

Yulara

Erldunda

0 kilometres   200

0 miles   200

N

*Great Victoria
Desert*

Chandler

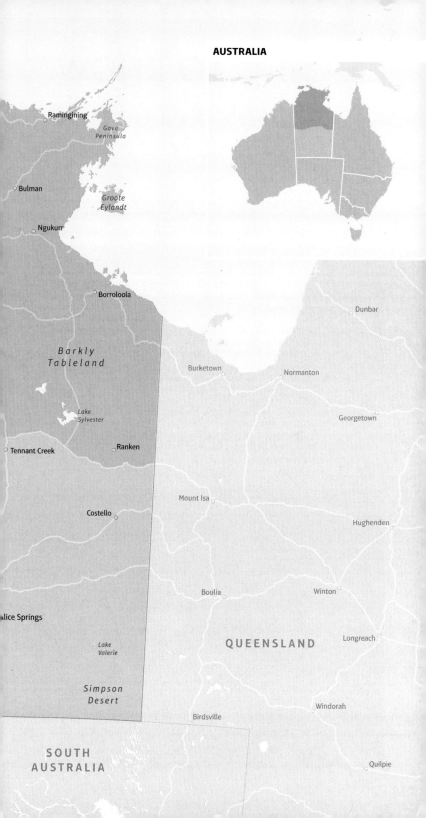

AUSTRALIA

Ramingining

Gove
Peninsula

Bulman

Groote
Eylandt

Ngukurr

Borroloola

Dunbar

Barkly
Tableland

Burketown

Normanton

Lake
Sylvester

Georgetown

Tennant Creek

Ranken

Mount Isa

Costello

Hughenden

Boulia

Winton

Alice Springs

Longreach

QUEENSLAND

Lake
Valerie

Simpson
Desert

Windorah

Birdsville

SOUTH
AUSTRALIA

Quilpie

GETTING TO KNOW
NORTHERN TERRITORY

Moving inland from the coast, the Northern Territory slowly transforms from the tropical north to the so-called Red Centre – the vast desert around Alice Springs. In between are abundant natural wonders, sacred to the local Aboriginal people, including Katherine Gorge and Kata Tjuṯa and Uluṟu.

PAGE 412

DARWIN AND THE TOP END

Unhurried Darwin is the gateway to the Top End, a land of incredible rock formations and gorgeous gorges. Aboriginal art abounds in galleries and museums, and traditional owners lead cultural tours in the Kakadu and Litchfield national parks. Located close to Indonesia, Darwin itself is infused with Southeast Asian influences, from the food served in its restaurants to the languages heard on the streets. Darwiners love the waterfront, which provides a welcome escape from the heat with its safe swimming lagoons, beachfront restaurants and sunset markets, bursting with food, stalls and entertainment.

Best for
Natural beauty

Home to
Darwin, Kakadu National Park

Experience
The beauty of ancient rock art in Kakadu National Park

THE RED CENTRE

Why is it called the Red Centre? It's obvious when you see the colour of the sand that carpets much of the heart of Australia. This area may be dominated by desert plains, weathered mountain ranges and rocky gorges, but it's far from empty. Here, you'll find some of the country's most important sites to the First Nations people, including Uluṟu, Kata Tjuṯa and Alice Springs. "Alice", as it's known to its locals, is the physical and spiritual heart of the Red Centre, with a booming Aboriginal arts, crafts and cultural scene that reflects the enterprising people who have long lived in this remote outpost.

Best for
Aboriginal history and culture

Home to
Uluṟu-Kata Tjuṯa National Park, Alice Springs

Experience
Dining in the desert while watching the sunset cast different colours on Uluṟu

Jim Jim Falls in Kakadu National Park

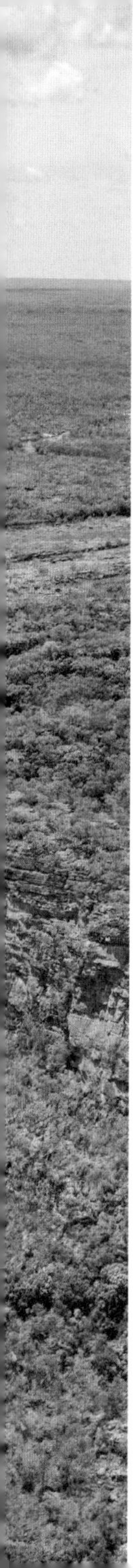

DARWIN AND THE TOP END

The Port of Darwin was first named in 1839, when British captain John Lort Stokes, commander of HMS *Beagle*, sailed into an azure harbour of sandy beaches and mangroves, and named it after his friend Charles Darwin. Although the biologist would not publish his theory of evolution, the *Origin of the Species,* for another 20 years, it proved to be a wonderfully apt name for this tropical region, teeming with unique and ancient species of birds, plants, reptiles and mammals.

The Top End is also home to one of the world's oldest races. This is where humans first set foot on the Australian landmass some 65,000 years ago, leaving a legacy of rock art that now reveals their spiritual beliefs, changing cultural practices and historic events, including the development of the boomerang, and interactions with Makassan traders and European colonizers. Although numbers have depleted over the years, over 40 different Aboriginal language groups reside in the Northern Territory today and around 30 per cent of the state's population identifies as Aboriginal.

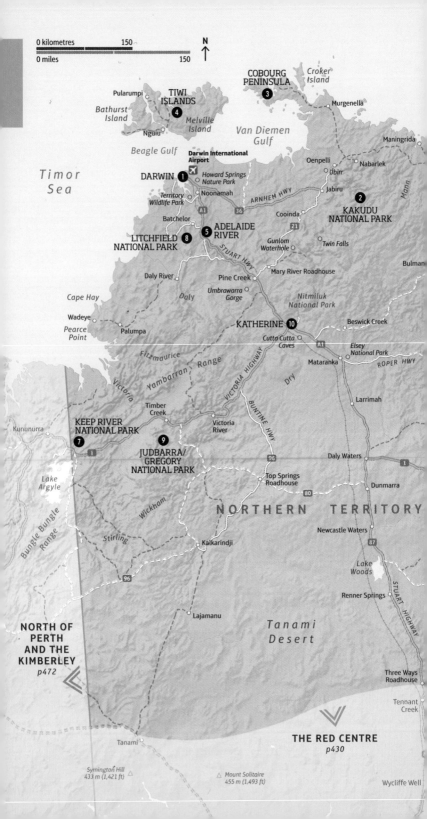

0 kilometres 150
0 miles 150
N

COBOURG PENINSULA 3
Croker Island

Murgenella
Pularumpi **TIWI ISLANDS** 4
Bathurst Island
Nguiu *Melville Island*
Van Diemen Gulf
Maningrida
Mann

Beagle Gulf
Darwin International Airport
Timor Sea
DARWIN 1
Howard Springs Nature Park
Oenpelli
Ubirr
Nabarlek
Noonamah
ARNHEM HWY
Jabiru
Territory Wildlife Park
A1
36
KAKUDU NATIONAL PARK 2
Cooinda
Batchelor
5 **ADELAIDE RIVER**
21
LITCHFIELD NATIONAL PARK 8
Gunlom Waterhole
Twin Falls
Bulman
STUART HWY
Daly River
Pine Creek
Mary River Roadhouse
Cape Hay
Daly
Umbrawarra Gorge
Nitmiluk National Park

Wadeye
Fitzmaurice
KATHERINE 10
Beswick Creek
Pearce Point
Palumpa
Cutta Cutta Caves
A1
Elsey National Park
Mataranka
ROPER HWY
Victoria
Yambarran Range
VICTORIA HIGHWAY
Dry
Larrimah
Timber Creek
KEEP RIVER NATIONAL PARK 7
Victoria River
BUNTINE HWY
Kununurra
1
9 **JUDBARRA/ GREGORY NATIONAL PARK**
96
Daly Waters
1
Lake Argyle
Top Springs Roadhouse
Dunmarra
Wickham
80
NORTHERN TERRITORY
Bungle Bungle Range
Stirling
Newcastle Waters
87
Kalkarindji
Lake Woods

NORTH OF PERTH AND THE KIMBERLEY
p472
96
Renner Springs
Lajamanu
Tanami Desert
STUART HIGHWAY
Three Ways Roadhouse
Tennant Creek

Tanami
THE RED CENTRE
p430

Symington Hill 433 m (1,421 ft)
Mount Solitaire 455 m (1,493 ft)
Wycliffe Well

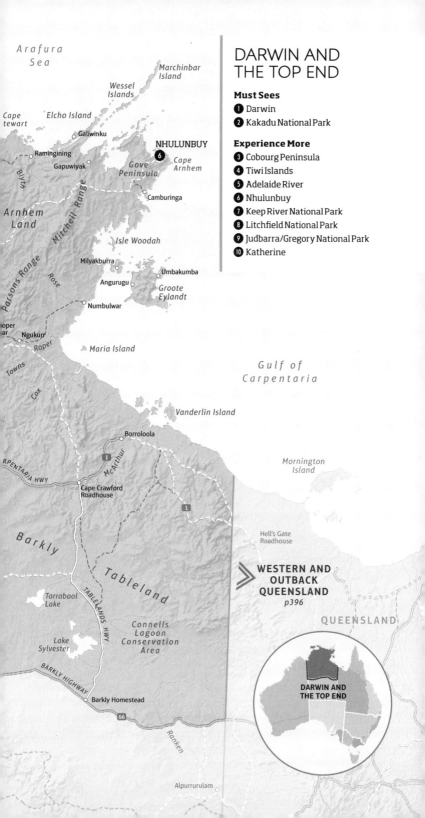

DARWIN AND THE TOP END

Must Sees
1. Darwin
2. Kakadu National Park

Experience More
3. Cobourg Peninsula
4. Tiwi Islands
5. Adelaide River
6. Nhulunbuy
7. Keep River National Park
8. Litchfield National Park
9. Judbarra/Gregory National Park
10. Katherine

Arafura Sea

Marchinbar Island

Wessel Islands

Cape tewart

Elcho Island

Galiwinku

Ramingining

Gapuwiyak

NHULUNBUY
6
Gove Peninsula
Cape Arnhem

Camburinga

Blyth

Mitchell Range

Arnhem Land

Parsons Range

Rose

Isle Woodah

Milyakburra

Umbakumba

Angurugu

Groote Eylandt

Numbulwar

oper ar

Ngukurr

Roper

Towns

Maria Island

Cox

Gulf of Carpentaria

Vanderlin Island

Borroloola

1

McArthur

RPENTARIA HWY

Cape Crawford Roadhouse

1

Mornington Island

Hell's Gate Roadhouse

WESTERN AND OUTBACK QUEENSLAND
p396

Barkly

Tableland

QUEENSLAND

TABLELANDS HWY

Tarrabool Lake

Connells Lagoon Conservation Area

Lake Sylvester

BARKLY HIGHWAY

Barkly Homestead

66

Ranken

DARWIN AND THE TOP END

Alpururulam

The modern skyline of Darwin, located at the tip of the Northern Territory

DARWIN

 C1 15 km (9 miles) NE of the city Smith St Mall, Karama, Casuarina & Palmerston shopping centres Cullen Bay Marina Cnr Smith & Bennett sts; (08) 8980 6000

Prior to European settlement in 1864, the area of Darwin was inhabited by the Larrakia people. In its short history, as an outpost of the British Empire and later a modern city, it has experienced the 1890s gold rush, life as an Allied frontline during World War II and destruction following Cyclone Tracy in 1974. Today, Darwin is a relaxed and multicultural city.

① Bicentennial Park

 The Esplanade

A collection of World War II memorials can be found in this leafy park. One marks an attack by Japanese bombers on 19 February 1942 that sank 21 of the 46 US and Australian naval vessels, killing 243 people.

② Old Admiralty House

 Cnr Knuckey St & The Esplanade

This house was once the headquarters of the Australian Navy. It was built in the 1930s by the territory's principal architect, Beni Carr Glynn Burnett, in an elevated tropical style using louvres, open eaves and three-quarter-high walls.

③ Parliament House

 Mitchell St, State Sq
 7am–6pm Mon–Fri, 9am–6pm Sat & Sun parliament.nt.gov.au

Near the edge of the sea cliffs is the new Parliament House. The architecture borrows from both Middle Eastern and Russian styles, this imposing building is home to the Territory's 25 parliamentarians. It has a granite and timber interior filled with Aboriginal art. Self-guided tours can be undertaken all year round, and free 90-minute guided tours are available every Friday at 10:30am from April to October.

④ Darwin Waterfront

 7 Kitchener Dr
 Hours vary, check website
 waterfront.nt.gov.au

Darwin Waterfront Precinct, the city's hub of lifestyle and

EAT

Alfonsino's

In the heart of Darwin, this popular restaurant offers authentic Italian cuisine. Dishes include antipasti, wood-fired pizza, handmade pasta and traditional desserts.

 20/69 Mitchell St
 alfonsinos.com

 $ $ $

hospitality, is linked to the CBD via a footbridge. Here, visitors can find restaurants, hotels, bars, a waterpark and a number of playgrounds. At the end of Stokes Hill Wharf is the Royal Flying Doctor Service.

glory, the buildings now serve the Office of the Administrator. Although closed to the public, it is worth pausing in front of the buildings to admire the architecture.

 INSIDER TIP
Deckchair Cinema

Catch an arthouse or blockbuster film at this independent outdoor cinema on Darwin's harbourside. Screenings are held seven nights a week from April to November.

⑤ Street Art

🏠 **Austin Lane** 🌐 **darwin streetartfestival.com.au**

Local, national and international artists have created vibrant murals on the city's walls, with Austin Lane alone featuring 21 murals along a 370 m (1,215 ft) stretch of laneway. West Lane has more gems. Download the Darwin Street Art Festival app for an interactive guided tour.

⑥ Old Police Station and Courthouse

🏠 **Cnr Smith St & The Esplanade**

The 1884 limestone Old Police Station and Courthouse were damaged by Cyclone Tracy. Restored to their original

⑦ Old Town Hall

🏠 **Smith St**

The limestone ruin of the Old Town Hall lies at the end of Smith Street. The original council chambers, built in 1883, became a naval workshop and store in World War II. Later the building became a bank then a museum, before being shattered by Cyclone Tracy. Curved brick paving built against the remaining wall symbolizes the fury of the cyclone's winds.

⑧ Brown's Mart

🏠 **12 Smith St** 🌐 **browns-mart.com.au**

Opposite the town hall ruins is Brown's Mart, built during the gold boom in 1885. A former mining exchange, it now houses an intimate

theatre. The iconic space hosts bands, plays, workshops and other live shows.

⑨ Government House

🏠 **The Esplanade** 🌐 **govhouse.nt.gov.au**

The 1871-built Government House, or the House of Seven Gables, is Darwin's oldest surviving edifice. It has withstood bomb raids, cyclones, earthquakes and infestations of white ants. This gracious sandstone building with stunning tropical gardens is the residence of the Administrator of the Northern Territory.

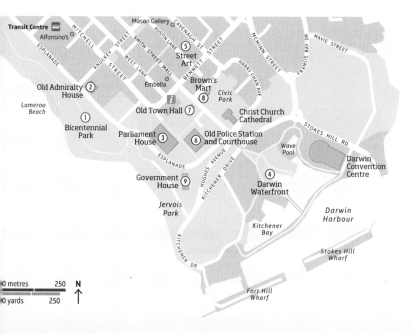

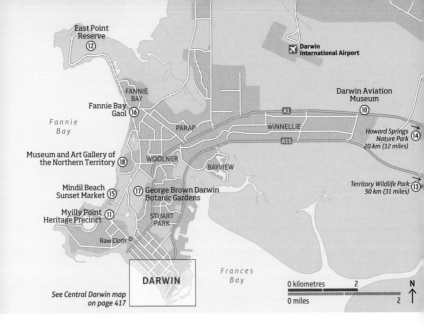

East Point
Reserve
⑫

✈ Darwin
International Airport

Darwin Aviation
Museum
⑩

FANNIE
BAY
Fannie Bay
Gaol ⑯

Fannie
Bay

PARAP

WINNELLIE

A1

A15

Howard Springs
Nature Park ⑭
20 km (12 miles)

Museum and Art Gallery of
the Northern Territory ⑱

WOOLNER

BAYVIEW

Territory Wildlife Park ⑬
50 km (31 miles)

Mindil Beach
Sunset Market ⑮

⑰ George Brown Darwin
Botanic Gardens

Myilly Point
Heritage Precinct ⑪

STUART
PARK

Raw Cloth

Frances
Bay

DARWIN

See Central Darwin map
on page 417

0 kilometres   2

0 miles   2

N

BEYOND THE CENTRE

See Central Darwin map on page 417

⑩

Darwin Aviation Museum

🅰 557 Stuart Hwy,
Winnellie 🚌 5, 8 🕐 9am–
5pm daily 🚫 Good Fri, 25 &
26 Dec 🌐 darwinaviation
museum.com.au

Found 6 km (4 miles) from
the city centre, the Aviation
Museum displays historic and
wartime aircraft. Its exhibits are
dominated by a B-52 bomber,
one of only two in the world on
display outside the US.

⑪

Myilly Point Heritage Precinct

🅰 Burnett Place & Kahlin
Ave, Larrakeyah 🕐 10am–
1pm daily 🚫 Jan & Dec
🌐 northernterritory.com

The heritage precinct is home
to four of Darwin's last remaining pre-World War II houses,
built between 1936 and 1939.
The most charming is the two-
storey Burnett House, which is
furnished with original decor.
A high tea is held here monthly.

> **DARWIN FESTIVAL**
>
> Held in August each
> year, this 18-day arts
> festival is a celebration
> of Darwin's Aboriginal
> and multicultural
> heritage. It features
> concerts, workshops
> and film screenings,
> as well as theatre,
> dance and comedy
> performances.

⑫

East Point Reserve

🅰 East Point, Darwin
🕐 5am–11pm daily
🌐 darwin.nt.gov.au/
community/community-
facilities/east-point-
reserve

Darwin's largest park, set on
the shores of the picturesque
Fannie Bay, is popular with families for year-round swimming
in Lake Alexander. Nearby, on
Alex Fong Lim Drive, is the
Defence of Darwin Experience
(www.magnt.net.au), which has
a collection of military equipment plus memorabilia from
World War II and the bombing
of Darwin Harbour.

↑ Supermarine Spitfire on display at the
Darwin Aviation Museum

SHOP

Embella
Find locally designed jewellery, plus clothing and skincare products.

🏠 Star Village Arcade, 32 Smith St Mall
🌐 embella.com.au

Mason Gallery
See works by Aboriginal artists from the Central Desert, Arnhemland and Western Desert regions.

🏠 7/21 Cavenagh St
🌐 mason gallery.com.au

Raw Cloth
Local atelier that sells unique dresses from around the globe.

🏠 132 Smith St
📞 (08) 8982 2305

---

15) Mindil Beach Sunset Market

🏠 Mindil Beach ⏰ 4-9pm Thu & Sun 🌐 mindil.com.au

Thursday and Sunday nights during the dry season are when Darwinians flock to Mindil Beach at dusk to enjoy some 60 outdoor food stalls, street theatre, live music and over 200 craft stalls.

---

16) Fannie Bay Gaol

🏠 Cnr East Point Rd & Ross Smith Ave, Fannie Bay
⏰ 10am-2pm Wed-Sun
🌐 magnt.net.au/fannie bay-gaol

This historic prison was opened in 1883 and was in use until 1979. Though part of the complex was damaged by Cyclone Tracy in 1974,

it has since been renovated and now houses an interesting museum.

---

17) George Brown Darwin Botanic Gardens

🏠 Gardens Rd, Stuart Park ⏰ 7am-7pm daily
🌐 nt.gov.au

Just north of the city centre, the 42-ha (100-acre) George Brown Darwin Botanic Gardens are home to more than 1,500 tropical species. Established in the 1870s, this beautiful park contains around 400 palm varieties and wetland mangroves. The lush rainforest path is a favourite among visitors.

---

13) Territory Wildlife Park

🏠 Cox Peninsula Rd, Berry Springs ⏰ Apr-Sep: 9am-4pm daily; Oct-Mar: 9am-3pm daily ❌ 25 Dec 🌐 territorywildlifepark.com.au

Only 60 km (37 miles) from Darwin is the Territory Wildlife Park, which features hundreds of unique local species. Nearby, Berry Springs Nature Reserve has a series of deep pools that make for great swimming.

---

14) Howard Springs Nature Park

🏠 Howard Springs Rd
⏰ Daily 🌐 nt.gov.au

A nature park, 35 km (22 miles) south of Darwin, Howard Springs has clear, spring-fed pools, filled with barramundi and turtles.

The rainforest path in the George Brown Darwin Botanic Gardens, and *(inset)* a desert rose flower ↓

⑱ 🍴 🖥 🛍

MUSEUM AND ART GALLERY OF THE NORTHERN TERRITORY

🏠 Conacher St 🚌 4, 6 🕐 9am–5pm Mon–Fri, 10am–5pm Sat & Sun
📅 1 Jan, Good Fri, 25 & 26 Dec 🌐 magnt.net.au

Located on traditional Larrakia land overlooking the Arafura Sea, this excellent museum is the state's premier artistic, scientific and cultural institution, attracting thousands of visitors each year.

The Museum and Art Gallery of the Northern Territory (MAGNT) has exhibitions on regional Aboriginal art and culture, maritime history, visual arts and natural history. Its collection of Aboriginal art is considered one of the best in the world, with some particularly fine carvings and bark paintings. Other displays include a chilling exhibition on Cyclone Tracy and descriptions of the evolution of the Top End's unique and curious wildlife. The latter features the popular stuffed crocodile named "Sweetheart".

> **The museum's collection of Aboriginal art is considered one of the best in the world.**

① The museum is housed in a simple yet stylish building surrounded by palm trees.

② Within the museum's collection are some interesting animal specimens, including these snakes.

③ MAGNT hosts the annual Telstra National Aboriginal and Torres Strait Islander Art Awards (NATSIAA).

DRINK

Darwin Ski Club
Across from the museum is the ski and sailing club, a local secret that delights visitors. This family-friendly spot has festoon lights draped between palm trees, a relaxed, beachy atmosphere, an affordable menu and unparalleled sunset views, making it the perfect choice.

⌂ 20 Conacher St, Fannie Bay 🌐 darwin skiclub.com.au

←
Large wooden sailing boats in the maritime display at MAGNT

Watching the sunset at Ubirr, a rock formation in Kakadu National Park

KAKADU NATIONAL PARK

D1 **Hwy 36** **Bowali Visitors' Centre, Kakadu Hwy, 2.5 km (1.5 miles) S of Jabiru; www.parksaustralia.gov.au/kakadu**

Kakadu National Park is one of the most extraordinary places in Australia. It's home to diverse landscapes, unique flora and fauna, and ancient rock art galleries that showcase the enduring link between the land and its Aboriginal custodians, the Bininj/Mungguy people.

Covering a vast swathe of land, Kakadu is Australia's biggest national park and a UNESCO World Heritage Area, thanks to both its cultural and natural value. The landscape here is incredibly varied and includes stony plateaux, savannah woodlands, red escarpment cliffs and glimmering wetlands, all of which are home to a wealth of plants and animals. It's especially key for birdlife: more than one-third of all bird species recorded in Australia live in Kakadu. The park is also home to 20,000-year-old Aboriginal rock art galleries that recount the history and culture of the Bininj/Mungguy people. These are best visited with a local guide.

 INSIDER TIP
Best Time to Go

If you're looking to save money, visit Kakadu in the wet season (November to April). Not only is accommodation much cheaper, but - as it's also less crowded - you'll likely get the waterfalls and walking trails all to yourself.

STAY

Mercure Crocodile Hotel

This tranquil resort makes a good base for exploring the park. It has an excellent restaurant on-site, which serves local bush tucker.

⌂ Flinders St, Jabiru
ⓦ kakadutourism.com/
accommodation/
mercure-crocodile-hotel

⑤⑤⑤

Cooinda Lodge and Camping Ground

Set beside Yellow Water Billabong, the lodge offers rooms, while the campsite has more than 200 pitches. The camping ground also has 20 glamping tents, which each have a queen-size bed, a fridge and air-conditioning, and are decorated with local art.

⌂ 1 Kakadu Hwy, Jabiru
ⓦ kakadutourism.com/
accommodation/
cooinda-lodge

⑤⑤⑤

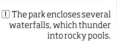

① The park encloses several waterfalls, which thunder into rocky pools.

② Many animals, including cockatoos, call the park home.

③ Boats take visitors on trips through the park's tranquil and biodiverse wetlands.

↑ Walking past the ruins of
the Victoria Settlement,
Cobourg Peninsula

EXPERIENCE MORE

Cobourg Peninsula

D1 **Venture North
Australia, Darwin; www.
northernterritory.com**

The Cobourg Peninsula is one
of the most remote parts of
Australia. It is only accessible
by vehicle during the dry season and with an access permit.
To reach the peninsula, you
have to travel through the
closed Aboriginal Arnhem
Land and the wild coastal
beaches of Garig Gunak Barlu
National Park. The number of
vehicles allowed to enter the
region each week is restricted
and there are permit fees,
too, so going on a tour is a
convenient option.

Garig Gunak Barlu National
Park dominates the peninsula.
Two attempts by the British
to settle this area in the early
1800s were abandoned due to
the inhospitable environment
and malaria epidemics. The

ruins of Victoria Settlement
can be reached by boat from
Smith Point. The Venture
North company (www.venture
north.com.au), which tours the
region, has a safari-style camp
overlooking the calm waters of
Port Essington.

Tiwi Islands

C/D1 **northern
territory.com/darwin-and-
surrounds/destinations/
tiwi-islands**

Just 80 km (50 miles) north
of Darwin lie the Tiwi Islands,
the collective name given
to the small island of Bathurst
and its larger neighbour,
Melville. The latter is the
second-largest island off the
Australian coast after Tasmania.
Both islands are veritable tropical paradises, with beautiful
waters, sandy beaches and
lush forest, and are rich in

history and Aboriginal culture.
The islands' inhabitants, the
Tiwi people, had little contact
with peoples on the mainland
until the 20th century.

Of the two Tiwi Islands,
only Bathurst can be visited
on tours from Darwin. Day trips
with Tiwi Tours or SeaLink (May
to October) offer a glimpse of
the unique blend of Aboriginal,
Indonesian and Tiwi traditions.
Tourists can visit Aboriginal art
centres, Tiwi printworks for
screen-printed fabrics and
a *pukumani* burial site.

INSIDER TIP
**Watch a Tiwi
Islands Match**

Head to the islands
in March for the Tiwi
Islands Football Grand
Final and Art Sale *(p42)*.
Watch an Aussie Rules
match and then check
out the reasonably
priced local art.

⑤ Adelaide River

🗺️D1 **🚌 To Darwin, then bus or car** **ℹ️ Tarkarri Rd, Batchelor; www.tourism topend.com.au**

Located on Stuart Highway, 114 km (71 miles) south of Darwin, this rural township is best known for being home to the **Adelaide River War Cemetery**, Australia's largest and only war cemetery. It is the resting place for 63 civilians and 434 service men and women who were killed during the World War II air raids on Darwin in 1942. Also honoured here are 287 service personnel who lost their lives in Timor and other northern regions.

In the town's centre is the **Adelaide River Railway Heritage Precinct**. Built in 1889 to service the Pine Creek gold fields, the railway was a major transportation hub when the town served as a military base for the Australian and American armed forces in World War II. Today, the railway precinct displays some of the original train infrastructure and memorabilia.

Around 14 km (9 miles) south from the town is Robin Falls, a three-tier waterfall where swimming is permitted.

Adelaide River War Cemetery

📍 105 Memorial Terrace
🌐 cwgc.org

Adelaide River Railway Heritage Precinct

📍 51 Stuart Hwy
🌐 enjoy-darwin.com/adelaide-river-railway.html

---

⑥ Nhulunbuy

🗺️E1 **🚌** **ℹ️ 19 Westal St; www.eastarnhemland.com.au**

The remote coastal town of Nhulunbuy sits on the northeastern tip of Arnhem Land on the Gove Peninsula. Nhulunbuy is located on leased Aboriginal land. While visitors are free to travel within the town, a permit is required if they wish to enter areas outside the leased land.

The town has a long mining history and the peninsula was a strategic air base during World War II. Today, Nhulunbuy is a laid-back town surrounded by pristine beaches and lush wetlands. It is a popular base for exploring the wild terrain of Arnhem Land and the glorious Bremer Island, 41 km (25.5 miles) offshore. The waters surrounding this island are home to four of the world's seven sea turtle species.

Close to Nhulunbuy is the town of Yirrkala, which is home to the **Buku-Larrnggay Mulka Centre**, a well-known museum and arts centre. The highlight here are the Yirrkala Church Panels, a precursor to the Yirrkala Bark Petitions.

A Gumatj ceremonial site about 40 km (25 miles) from Nhulunbuy is Gulkula. It hosts the annual Garma Festival in August. This four-day event is a celebration of the Yolngu culture, one of the oldest living cultures in the world, dating back almost 60,000 years. The festival is arguably Australia's most significant First Nations event, attracting thousands of business leaders, politicians, academics and journalists.

Buku-Larrnggay Mulka Centre

📍 138 Tuffin Rd, Yirrkala
🌐 yirrkala.com

THE YIRRKALA BARK PETITIONS

The Yirrkala Bark Petitions were the first traditional documents by Aboriginal Australians to be recognized by the Australian Government in the country's history. The petitions were presented to the Australian Parliament in 1963 by the Yolngu peoples of Arnhem Land to assert their rights to the traditional land on the Gove Peninsula. Although the petitions were unsuccessful, they symbolize the Aboriginal Australians' ongoing fight for land rights. Today, the bark petitions are on display at Parliament House *(p201)* in Canberra alongside the country's constitution and the Magna Carta.

↑ A grassy, windswept beach at Yirrkala, near Nhulunbuy, East Arnhem

ABORIGINAL LANDS

Aboriginal people are thought to have lived in the Northern Territory for between 40,000 and 50,000 years. The comparatively short 200 years of European settlement have damaged their ancient culture immensely, but traditional Aboriginal communities have survived more intact in the Northern Territory than in other states. Today, nearly one-third of the Northern Territory's population are First Nations people and they own almost 50 per cent of the land through native title legislation enacted by the federal government. This is important because, for Aboriginal people, the concept of land ownership is tied to a belief system that instructs them to care for their ancestral land.

THE GURINDJI STRIKE

In 1966, 200 Gurindji workers walked off a cattle station in Kalkarindji (then called Wave Hill), demanding the return of their lands. The "Wave Hill Walk-Off" lasted seven years and led to the passing of the Aboriginal Land Rights Act in 1976.

ABORIGINAL TOURISM

Most visitors who come to the Northern Territory are keen to learn more about the region's unique Aboriginal culture. There are now many Aboriginal owned and operated organizations, which take tourists into areas that would otherwise be inaccessible, and explain Aboriginal beliefs, including the sanctity of the land. Excursions available include boat trips in Kakadu National Park (p422) with a Guluyambi guide; bush camping with the Manyallaluk community near Katherine (p429); or a multi-day cultural tour in Arnhem Land with Bawaka Experience. Also well worth visiting are the information and cultural centres, such as those in Kakadu and Uluṟu-Kata Tjuṯa national parks (p422, p434), where the original owners share their creation stories and culture, adding another layer to visitors' appreciation of these special places.

Did You Know?

The Jawoyn believe that Bolung (the rainbow serpent) inhabits Nitmiluk's second gorge.

Walking along Nitmiluk, or Katherine Gorge, in the lands owned by the Jawoyn people ↑

ULURU

This large sandstone formation has many sites sacred to the Anangu people around its base. Most are closed to the public, but it is possible to walk around the entire perimeter of Uluru, and learn the associated creation stories.

ABORIGINAL ROCK ART

Located in Kakadu National Park, Ubirr is one of the finest Aboriginal rock art sites in the Northern Territory. Its paintings date from between 16,000 BCE to the present day.

BURRUNGGUI

Also known as Nourlangie Rock, Burrunggui is sacred to its traditional Aboriginal owners, who believe that this sandstone formation is the home of the Lightning Dreaming.

ABORIGINAL ART

The Papunya Tula Art Movement began in 1971 when white school teacher Geoffrey Bardon encouraged some Aboriginal men to paint a school wall. The murals sparked tremendous interest in the community and, in 1972, the artists established their own company, which they named after the settlement of Papunya and Tula, a nearby hill and Honey Ant Dreaming site.

1 Uluru is preserved in the Uluru-Kata Tjuta National Park.

2 Many of the paintings in Ubirr, such as this barramundi, are depicted in X-ray style.

3 Burrunggui is in Kakadu National Park.

4 Many Aboriginal paintings, such as this bark painting, depict Dreamtime beings.

ABORIGINAL CULTURE AND LAW

Every Aboriginal clan lives according to a set of laws linking the people with their land, their kinship and their ancestors. These laws are embedded in Aboriginal creation stories, which tell how the creator spirits and ancestors shaped and named the land, and also form a belief system which directs all aspects of Aboriginal life (p45). Aboriginal people have three levels of kinship: their moiety, totem group and skin name. These decide their links with the land, their place in the community and the creation stories they inherit.

↑ Ancient rock art at the Keep River National Park

HIDDEN GEM
 Umbrawarra Gorge

Just a two-hour drive southwest of Litchfield National Park is the Umbrawarra Gorge, surrounded by steep red cliffs, rocky pools and a beach. The best time to visit is in the dry season from May to September.

thinnest part exposed to the sun. Also popular are the sandstone block formations further south, known as the "Lost City" due to their resemblance to ruins.

STAY

Cicada Lodge
This lodge, in the Nitmiluk National Park, has 18 modern rooms, each with Aboriginal artworks and a balcony.

🅰 D1 🏠 Gorge Rd, Katherine 🅦 cicada lodge.com.au

$$$

Banubanu Beach Retreat
Just off the Nhulunbuy coast, this resort offers stunning beachfront bungalows.

🅰 E1 🏠 Bremer Island 🅦 banubanu.com

$$$

Nitmiluk Campground
Stay in a cabin, a tent or a caravan near the Nitmiluk Gorge. The park has a pool and a bistro.

🅰 D1 🏠 Gorge Rd, Katherine 🅦 nitmiluk tours.com.au

$$$

7
Keep River National Park

🅰 C2 🛈 Victoria Hwy; www.nt.gov.au

Located only 3 km (2 miles) from the Western Australian border, Keep River National Park contains the dramatic Keep River gorge and some of Australia's most ancient rock art sites. The park, once the location of an ancient Aboriginal settlement, has some superb walking trails for all levels of trekkers.

8
Litchfield National Park

🅰 C1 🅦 nt.gov.au

The spectacular Litchfield National Park is located 129 km (80 miles) south of Darwin and is very popular with Darwinians. There are waterfalls, gorges and deep, crocodile-free pools for swimming at Florence Falls, Wangi, in the wet season, and Buley Rockhole. The park also has amazing magnetic termite mounds. They are so-called because they point north in an effort by the termites to control temperature by having only the mound's

9
Judbarra/Gregory National Park

🅰 C2 🛈 Timber Creek, Bullita; www.nt.gov.au

Divided into two sections, this massive national park is 280 km (174 miles) by road southwest of Katherine. The park's eastern part contains a 50-km (31-mile) area of the Victoria River gorge, which is accessible by a boat ramp.

In the park's larger western section, many parts of the Victoria River are crocodile-infested and a "no swimming" policy covers the entire park. Take a boat trip to see the crocs up close. Also in the west of the park are the dolomite blocks and huge cliffs of the Limestone Gorge.

Katherine

D1 🚗🚌 **Cnr Katherine Terrace & Lindsay St; www. visitkatherine.com.au**

Situated on the banks of the Katherine River, 320 km (200 miles) south of Darwin, this town is a thriving regional centre and a major tourist destination. Home for thousands of years to the Jawoyn people, Katherine River has long been a rich source of food for the Aboriginal people. The river was first crossed by white explorers in 1844, and the area was not settled by Europeans until 1872, with the completion of the Overland Telegraph Line.

The quaint O'Keeffe House, built by the army as an officers' mess using bark, cypress pine and flywire during World War II,

is open to the public on Wednesday and Saturday mornings from April to October.

Only 30 km (20 miles) from town lies the famous Nitmiluk (Katherine Gorge) National Park, which is made up of 13 separate gorges carved out by torrential seasonal rains cutting through 1,650-million-year-old cliffs of red sandstone. The best way to explore the park is by guided or self-guided boat or canoe trips. There are also cruise trips run by the Jawoyn people, who own the park and run it in conjunction with the Parks and Wildlife Commission of the Northern Territory. The park has around 100 km (60 miles) of marked trails, such as the spectacular lookout walk and the five-day, 72-km (45-mile) Jatbula Trail to Edith Falls, which can also be reached by car from the Stuart Highway.

Just 27 km (17 miles) south of Katherine are the Cutta Cutta caves – limestone rock formations 15 m (50 ft) under

Bushwalkers on the Jatbula Trail, and *(inset)* canoeists in the Nitmiluk (Katherine Gorge) National Park ↓

the earth's surface. They are home to both the rare orange horseshoe bat and the brown tree snake.

Further southeast, 110 km (70 miles) from Katherine, lies the town of Mataranka. This is "Never Never" country, celebrated by pioneer Jeannie Gunn in her 1908 novel, *We of the Never Never*, about life at nearby Elsey Station at the turn of the century. About 8 km (5 miles) east of Mataranka is Elsey National Park. Here, visitors can swim in the hot waters of the Mataranka Thermal Pool. Built in 1916, **Mataranka Homestead** is now a tourist resort, which includes a motel, cabins and campsites.

Mataranka Homestead
🍴🛏️🚻 **W** mataranka homestead.com.au

THE RED CENTRE

Located at the centre of the Australian continent, this region's signature colour is red: red sand, soil, rocks and mountains are all pitched against a typically blue sky. The Red Centre contains some of the finest natural scenery in the world, much of it dating back about 800 million years. At that time, central Australia was covered by an inland sea; here sediments were laid down which form the basis of some of the region's best-known topographical features today. These include the huge monolith Uluru, the domes of Kata Tjuta, the giant boulders of Karlu Karlu/Devil's Marbles and the majestic MacDonnell Ranges.

Aboriginal people have lived in the region for more than 30,000 years, and their ancient tradition of rock painting is one of many tribal rituals still practised. The land was wrestled from its original owners by European settlers, who first arrived in the area during the 1860s, but much of the territory has now been returned to its Aboriginal owners by the Australian government, and today many Aboriginal people are actively involved in tourism.

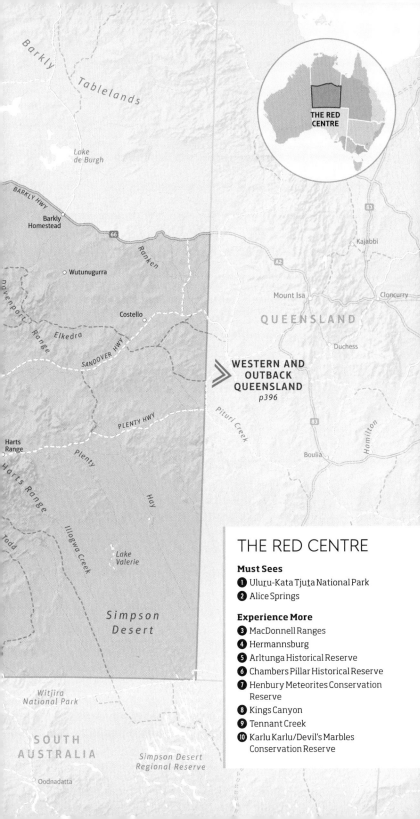

Barkly Tablelands

Lake de Burgh

BARKLY HWY

Barkly Homestead

`66`

Ranken

○ Wutunugurra

Costello

Davenport Range

Elkedra

SANDOVER HWY

PLENTY HWY

Harts Range

Harts Range

Plenty

Hay

Illogwa Creek

Todd

Lake Valerie

Simpson Desert

Witjira National Park

SOUTH AUSTRALIA

Simpson Desert Regional Reserve

Oodnadatta

THE RED CENTRE

`83`

Kajabbi

`A2`

Mount Isa

Cloncurry

QUEENSLAND

Duchess

> WESTERN AND OUTBACK QUEENSLAND p396

Pituri Creek

`83`

Hamilton

Boulia

THE RED CENTRE

Must Sees

❶ Uluṟu-Kata Tjuṯa National Park

❷ Alice Springs

Experience More

❸ MacDonnell Ranges

❹ Hermannsburg

❺ Arltunga Historical Reserve

❻ Chambers Pillar Historical Reserve

❼ Henbury Meteorites Conservation Reserve

❽ Kings Canyon

❾ Tennant Creek

❿ Karlu Karlu/Devil's Marbles Conservation Reserve

❶

ULURU-KATA TJUTA NATIONAL PARK

🅰C3 🅰Hwy 4 ➡Connellan Airport, 5 km (3 miles) N of Yulara/
Ayers Rock Resort (book a rental car in advance) 🆆parksaustralia.
gov.au/uluru

It is impossible to arrive at Uluru-Kata Tjuta National
Park and not be filled with awe. The sheer size of the
world's largest monolith, Uluru (Ayers Rock), rising from
the flat desert plain, is a moving and impressive sight.

An iconic World Heritage Site, the Uluru-Kata Tjuta National Park
covers 463 km (288 miles) and is home to Uluru and the rock
formations of Kata Tjuta, with their deep valleys and gorges. The
whole area is sacred to the Anangu people, who are the traditional
custodians of the land. In 1985, the park was handed back to the
Anangu and it is leased to the Australian government and jointly
managed. Within the park is a cultural centre, which details the
lives of the Anangu and the area's history. Outside the park
is the town of Yulara, offering accommodation and restaurants.

> **GREAT VIEW**
> **Uluru at Sunset**
>
> Nothing compares to
> the breathtaking sight
> of Uluru at sunset. As
> the sun goes down, the
> colour of the sacred rock
> changes from vibrant
> red and orange, to gold,
> dusty pink and purple. If
> this is the only thing
> you see in the north,
> you won't regret it.

Taking in the magnificent view
of Uluru, with the domes of
Kata Tjuta in the distance ↑

↑ Visitors at the Walpa Gorge enjoy the changing colours at sunset

Closing the Climb

Uluṟu has been sacred to the Aṉangu people for thousands of years, and climbing it was not allowed. From the 1930s, however, visitors were traversing Uluṟu, with annual numbers often reaching the tens of thousands. In the 1980s, the authorities and the Aṉangu began to discuss this controversial practice and its impact, including the degradation to the rock's surface, the contamination of water holes and the growing pollution. By the 1990s, the Aṉangu placed signs at Uluṟu's base request-ing visitors to refrain from ascending the rock, and with time, instances of climbing reduced. By 2017, the site's management banned the practice, which came into effect on 26 October 2019.

TOP
5 **FLORA AND FAUNA TO SPOT**

Thorny Devil
These small lizards are covered in spikes and feed only on ants – they can eat thousands a day.

Perentie
Australia's largest goanna is extremely shy and difficult to find.

Spinifex Hopping Mouse
At night, these mice can be seen jumping in open spaces.

Sturt's Desert Rose
This mauve flower is the Northern Territory's official floral emblem.

Striped Mintbush
The white flowers of this mint-scented shrub have purple stripes.

EXPLORING ULURU-KATA TJUTA NATIONAL PARK

① Uluru

This single piece of sandstone is huge. It stretches 3.6 km (2.25 miles) long and 2.4 km (1.5 miles) wide, stands 348 m (1,142 ft) above the plains and extends 5 km (3 miles) beneath the desert surface.

Uluru is an outstanding natural phenomenon, best observed by taking a guided walk at the rock's base and watching its changing colours at dusk.

There are a number of walking trails around Uluru. The three-hour, 9.5-km (6-mile) tour around the base gives the greatest sense of its size

and majesty. Sacred sights en route are closed to the public. The Mala (hare wallaby) walk takes in several caves; some feature rock art. The Mala people, the ancestors of the Anangu people, stayed in these caves when they first arrived at Uluru. The Liru (snake) walk starts at the cultural centre and winds through a mulga forest. The Kuniya (python) walk takes you to the Mutijulu water hole on the southern side of Uluru where the Anangu people tell creation stories and display art portraying them. Details of all walks can be found at Uluru-Kata Tjuta Cultural Centre.

THE ANANGU OF ULURU

Archaeological evidence suggests that Aboriginal people have lived at Uluru for at least 22,000 years and that both Uluru and Kata Tjuta have long been places of ceremonial and cultural significance to them. The traditional custodians of Uluru and Kata Tjuta are the Anangu people. They believe that both sites were formed during the creation period by ancestral spirits who also gave them the laws and rules of society that they live by today. The Anangu believe they are responsible for the protection of these lands.

② Kata Tjuta

Kata Tjuta, meaning "many heads", is a collection of massive rounded rock domes, 42 km (25 miles) to the west of Uluru. Beyond lies a vast, remote desert; permits from the Central Land Council, 4WDs and full travel survival kits are needed to travel here.

Kata Tjuta is a system of gorges and valleys that are haunting, quiet and spiritual. To the Anangu people, it is of equal significance to Uluru, and access to certain areas is restricted. The tallest rock, Mount Olga, is 546 m (1,790 ft)

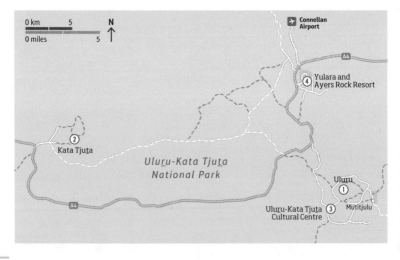

↑ Walking through the Olgas in the Kata Tjuṯa National Park

Did You Know?

The nearby, flat-topped Mount Connor is often mistaken for Uluṟu, and has been nick-named "fooluru".

high, nearly 200 m (660 ft) higher than Uluṟu. There are two main walking trails. The Valley of the Winds is a steep, rocky walk that takes about three hours; it is partially closed when the temperature exceeds 36° C (97° F). The Walpa Gorge walk leads up the pretty Olga Gorge to its dead-end cliff face and a rock pool. Walkers may spot the small brown spinifex bird, the thorny devil spiked lizard or the striped mintbush.

③

Uluṟu-Kata Tjuṯa Cultural Centre

🄰 Uluṟu Rd 🕐 7am-6pm daily (last adm: 5:30pm); information desk: 8am-5pm 🆆 parksaustralia.gov.au/uluru

Near the base of Uluṟu is an award-winning cultural centre, with multilingual displays, videos and exhibitions. It is an excellent introduction to the park and well worth visiting before exploring the rock and its surrounding area. The Nintiringkupai display focuses on the history and management of the park. The Tjukurpa display, with its art, sounds and videos, explores the beliefs and law of the Aṉangu people. Attached to the cultural centre is the Maruku Arts and Craft shop, where you can watch artists at work and see dance and music performances. The traditional art on bark and canvas tells Tjukurpa (the ancestral stories of Uluṟu).

Yulara and Ayers Rock Resort

🆆 ayersrockresort.com.au

Set 20 km (12 miles) north of Uluṟu, just outside the national park boundary, the township of Yulara serves as a good base for exploring Uluṟu and Kata Tjuṯa. It is an environmentally friendly tourist town well equipped to welcome thousands of annual visitors. The Ayers Rock Resort takes up most of Yulara and offers a wide range of accommodation options, from five-star luxury hotels to camping grounds.

The visitors' centre at Yulara has information about the park's geology, flora and fauna. It also sells souvenirs and can help arrange tours. Every day at 9am there is a free guided walk through the resort gardens, highlighting bush foods and local flora used in traditional medicine. Free daily cultural experiences with Indigenous guides include demonstrations of hunting and food gathering, weapons and tools, and a didgeridoo workshop. A stargazing Astro Tour, which combines creation stories with astronomy, is also available – the low humidity and minimal unnatural light provide excellent viewing conditions.

The shopping centre in Yulara includes a post office, bank, supermarket and childcare centre, along with plenty of great dining options.

 PICTURE PERFECT
Field of Light

Stretching for miles, this striking light installation at the base of Uluṟu, created by British artist Bruce Munro, has 50,000 solar-powered stems. Sparkling in different colours, these make for a truly memorable photo.

Alice Springs, the third-largest town in Australia's Northern Territory ↑

②

ALICE SPRINGS

 D3 ✈ 14 km (9 miles) S of town ⬜ George Crescent ℹ Cnr Todd St Mall & Parsons St; www.discovercentral australia.com

The Arrernte people have lived in this area for around 30,000 years. A European settlement was established here in the 1888 and named after the Alice Spring permanent water hole but, with no rail link until 1929 and no surface road link until the 1940s, the town grew slowly. Now considered a great base for exploring central Australia, Alice Springs has become a key tourist destination in the region.

①
Old Courthouse

⬜ Cnr Parsons & Hartley sts ⬜ On request

Built in 1928 by architect Emil Martin, the Old Court-house was in operation until 1980, when new law courts were opened. It is interesting architecturally.

②
Anzac Hill

⬜ Anzac Hill Rd

At the northern end of Alice Springs, Anzac Hill overlooks the city and offers fine views of the MacDonnell Ranges. Named after the 1934 Anzac memorial at the site, the hill

is a perfect vantage point for visitors to familiarize themselves with the city's layout, as well as for viewing the area at sunrise or sunset.

③
Stuart Town Gaol

⬜ 8 Parsons St ⬜ Feb–mid-Dec: 10:30am–2:30pm Mon-Fri 🌐 nationaltrust.org.au

The oldest building in central Alice Springs is the Stuart Town Gaol, which operated as a gaol between 1909 and 1938 – when a new prison was built on Stuart Terrace. The gaol is now open to the public, but book ahead to be granted access.

④
Megafauna Central

⬜ 21 Todd St Mall ⬜ 10am-4pm Mon & Wed–Fri, 10am-2pm Sat & Sun 🌐 magnt. net.au/alcoota

This archaeological museum in the centre of Alice Springs is free for visitors and show-cases the unique megafauna that roamed Central Australia nearly eight million years ago. The museum's collection includes an impressive fossil display and lifesize replicas of the 30 species from the Miocene epoch found at the Alcoota Scientific Reserve fossil site, 150 km (93 miles) northeast of Alice Springs. Highlights of the museum include the giant crocodile display and the world's largest bird. There is also an aug-mented reality experience that will take you on a trip back in time.

> **Megafauna Central's collection includes an impressive fossil display and lifesize replicas of the 30 species from the Miocene epoch found at the Alcoota Scientific Reserve fossil site.**

Must See

EAT

Bella Alice

An affordable, no-frills pizza place set in an outdoor food market. Fare includes wood-fired pizzas, homemade pasta and traditional Italian desserts, such as Sicilian cannoli and salted caramel tiramisu.

⌂ 57 Todd Mall
⏰ Dinner only ⓦ bella-alicesprings.com.au

$ $ $

Bean Tree Cafe

A café nestled in the lush Olive Pink Botanic Garden that is perfect for breakfast, lunch or coffee. The menu includes salads, tarts and cakes.

⌂ 27 Tuncks Rd
ⓦ opbg.com.au/bean-tree-cafe

$ $ $

---

⑤

The Residency

⌂ Cnr Parsons & Hartley sts ⏰ 10am-3pm Mon-Fri ⏰ Dec-Mar, public hols ⓦ heritagealicesprings.com.au

The Residency was built in 1927 by Emil Martin, who also built the Old Courthouse, for the regional administrator of Central Australia. It was the home of Alice Springs' senior public servant until 1973. The building was opened to the public in 1996 and houses a local history display.

⑥

School of the Air Visitor Centre

⌂ 80 Head St ⏰ Hours vary, see website ⏰ 24 Dec-mid-Jan ⓦ schooloftheair.net.au

Covering an area of 1,300,000 sq km (521,000 sq miles) across the Northern Territory, northern South Australia and eastern Western Australia, this is the world's largest classroom. The school was established in 1951 to provide education to children in remote areas via a two-way radio system. It now uses modern technology for this.

Royal Flying Doctor Service Visitor Centre

🏠 8-10 Stuart Terrace ⏰ Mid-Jan-Dec: 9:30am-5pm Mon-Sat, noon-5pm Sun & public hols 🚫 Good Fri, 25 & 26 Dec 🌐 rfdsalice-springs.com.au

This centre can only be visited with a guide; visitors are taken on a 45-minute tour of the base that includes the Radio Communications centre, where staff recount the history of the service and explain the day-to-day operations. There is also a museum containing old medical equipment, model aircrafts and an original Traeger Pedal Radio. The visitor centre has a café and a souvenir shop.

Alice Springs Telegraph Station Historical Reserve

🏠 Off Stuart Hwy ⏰ 9am-5pm daily 🚫 25 Dec 🌐 alicespringstelegraphstation.com.au

The site of the first European settlement in Alice Springs, this reserve features the original buildings and equipment of the telegraph station that was built in 1871. A small museum describes the task of setting up the station and running the overland telegraph.

Adelaide House Museum

🏠 Todd Mall 📞 (08) 8952 1856 ⏰ Mar-Nov: 10am-4pm Mon-Fri, 10am-noon Sat 🚫 Good Fri

Adelaide House Museum, Alice Springs' first hospital, opened in 1926. It was designed by John Flynn, founder of the Royal Flying Doctor Service, and is preserved as a museum dedicated to his memory.

Araluen Arts Centre

🏠 61 Larapinta Drive ⏰ 10am-4pm Tue-Sat (Nov-Feb: also 10am-2pm Sun) 🌐 araluenartscentre.nt.gov.au

This leading institution for visual and performing arts in Central Australia focuses on Aboriginal art. The centre hosts annual exhibitions, films and performances across four gallery spaces (including Albert Namatjira Gallery, named after the Australian artist) plus a theatre and a sculpture garden. The annual Desert Mob exhibition, which is held here each September,

TOP 3 ABORIGINAL ART GALLERIES

Mbantua Gallery
Home to works by artists of the Utopia region (www.mbantua.com.au).

Yubu Napa Art Gallery
Plenty of workshops, talks and events for kids (www.yubunapa.com).

Tjanpi Desert Weavers
Modern fibre art by women from the central and western deserts (www.tjanpi.com.au).

---

is said to be one of the most important Aboriginal art and cultural events in Australia.

National Pioneer Women's Hall of Fame

🏠 Old Alice Springs Gaol, 2 Stuart Terrace 📞 (08) 8952 9006 ⏰ Mid-Feb-mid-Dec: 11am-3pm Mon-Fri

The interesting displays in this museum document the

↑ Alice Springs Telegraph Station Historical Reserve, built during British colonial times

CATERPILLAR DREAMING

The Arrernte people believe in the Aboriginal legend, called Caterpillar Dreaming, which centres on the creation of the MacDonnell Ranges. It says the mountains' contours were formed after a battle between three caterpillars and their enemy, the stink bugs. Some Arrernte people believe they descend from the caterpillars.

impressive achievements of Australia's pioneering women.

Museum of Central Australia

🏠 Alice Springs Cultural Precinct, Memorial Ave 🕐 10am-4pm Mon-Fri, 10am-2pm Sat & Sun 🔒 Good Fri, two weeks in Dec 🌐 magnt.net au/museum-of-central-australia

This museum, situated in Alice Springs' Cultural Precinct, focuses on local natural history with displays of fossils, flora and fauna, meteorite pieces, as well as minerals. It also houses Arrernte art and artifacts.

Central Australian Aviation Museum

🏠 6 Memorial Ave 🕐 Apr-Nov: 11am-3pm Wed-Fri, 11am-2:30pm Sat & Sun 🌐 centralaustralian-aviationmuseum.org.au

The Central Australian Aviation Museum was founded in 1977 and occupies the site of the first airfield in Alice Springs. It pays tribute to the people who pioneered avionics in this region and is home to an extensive collection of aircraft, complete with some early flying doctor planes, a restored DC-3 and a DH-114 Heron 2D. The museum's exhibits and displays also include radio and aviation hardware, engines, films, photographs, books and several other historical memorabilia.

Olive Pink Botanic Garden

🏠 27 Tuncks Rd 🕐 8am-6pm daily 🔒 Good Fri, 25 Dec 🌐 opbg.com.au

This beautiful space is the legacy of Australian botanical illustrator, anthropologist, gardener and activist Olive Pink – who fought for the rights of the Aboriginal peoples in the 1930s. Today, the 16-ha (40-acre) gardens host more than 2,500 plants from more than 600 central Australian plant species, including 40 that have been declared threatened or rare.

Did You Know?

Beanies are so popular here that the town hosts an annual Beanie Festival in June.

The gardens are also home to an impressive sculpture trail, a thriving birdlife and many roaming black-footed rock wallabies.

The complex provides access to the 30-minute track leading to the Annie Meyer Hill lookout; this moderate walk offers breathtaking views over Alice Springs, Todd River and the MacDonnell Ranges.

Alice Springs Desert Park

🏠 Off Larapinta Drive 🕐 7:30am-6pm daily (last adm: 4:30pm) 🔒 25 Dec 🌐 alicesprings desertpark.com.au

The Alice Springs Desert Park, located on the western edge of town, provides an excellent introduction to Central Australia's striking landscapes. Three habitat types can be found here: desert river, sand country and woodlands. Visitors can also see many of the birds and animals of Central Australia at close range.

National Road Transport Hall of Fame

🏠 1 Norris Bell Ave 🕐 Mid-Jan-mid-Dec: 9am-3pm daily 🌐 roadtransport hall.com

This museum pays homage to all the great trucks, buses and other vehicles that have crossed the Australian continent. *The Ghan*, which was the first train to run from Adelaide to Alice Springs in 1929, is commemorated with a fascinating collection of vintage memorabilia. Another highlight of the museum is the 1934 AEC roadtrain, the only one of its kind in existence.

EXPERIENCE MORE

3

MacDonnell Ranges

🅰D3 🚉To Alice Springs, then car ℹ️41 Todd Mall, Alice Springs; www.discovercentralaustralia.com

The majestic MacDonnell Ranges are the remnants of an eroded, ancient mountain chain once as monumental as the Himalayas. Running like two huge spines on either side of Alice Springs, they are split into the West MacDonnells (Tjoritja) and the East MacDonnells.

A number of striking gorges can be found in the western range, including Simpsons Gap – located 23 km (14 miles) from Alice Springs. This scenic spot is home to a number of rare local plant species and is also a good place to spy black-footed rock-wallabies. West of Simpsons Gap is Standley Chasm, a narrow gorge whose sheer rock faces glow a glorious red under the midday sun. Serpentine Gorge, 45 km (28 miles) further west, is another narrow gorge created by an ancient river. A walking track leading to a lookout gives a fine view of its winding path. Another impressive gorge in the area is Ormiston Gorge. Pushed up out of Ormiston Creek, the 300-m- (985-ft-) high walls of this rock formation are an awesome sight. The gorge consists of two layers of quartzite, literally doubled over each other, thus making it twice the height of others in the region.

Hikers exploring the West MacDonnells often stop at Ellery Creek Big Hole for a cooling swim. This 18-m- (60-ft-) deep permanent water hole is within Ellery Gorge.

INSIDER TIP
The Larapinta Trail

Keen walkers will enjoy this 223-km (138.5-mile) bushwalking trail from Alice Springs through the West MacDonnells to Mount Sonder. The track has 12 sections, and you can opt for a self-guided walk, or join a guided one over seven days.

Running straight through the heart of the West MacDonnells is the iconic Mereenie Loop Road (Red Centre Way). This 690-km (428-mile) drive goes past Uluṟu and Kata Tjuṯa (p434), Alice Springs (p438) and Kings Canyon (p444).

↑ Swimming in the Ellery Creek Big Hole, found in the West MacDonnells

Did You Know?

The Finke River, or Larapinta (Arrernte), is considered to be the oldest riverbed in the world.

On the other side of Alice Springs, the East MacDonnells have some beautiful sites that can be accessed via the Ross Highway. Close to town is Emily and Jessie Gaps Nature Park, which features significant rock paintings by the Eastern Arrernte people. Further east, Corroboree Rock, a strangely shaped outcrop, has a crevice that was once used to store sacred Eastern Arrernte objects. Further north lies the most spectacular of the East MacDonnell sights, Trephina Gorge. It has colourful quartzite cliffs, red river gums and the largest ghost gum tree in Australia. The surrounding area also has an abundance of wildlife and features walking tracks and water holes, the most notable of which is the dramatic John Hayes Rockhole, with steep rock walls.

↑ The Lutheran Mission chapel in the Hermannsburg Historic Precinct

 4

Hermannsburg

D3 **To Alice Springs, then car** **47 Raberaba Circuit; www.hermanns burg.com.au**

Along Larapinta Drive, 126 km (78 miles) west of Alice Springs, is the small Aboriginal settlement of Hermannsburg, locally known as Ntaria. The area is best known as the birthplace of famous landscape watercolour artist Albert Namatjira. His memorial in the town consists of a 6-m- (20-ft-) tall monument that commemorates his legacy.

Most of the township is contained within the heritage-listed **Hermannsburg Historic Precinct**, one of the few surviving evangelical bush missions in Australia. Owned by the Western Arrernte people, the precinct features a museum devoted to the Lutheran Mission that operated here and an art gallery.

Around 20 km (12 miles) south of Hermannsburg lies the spectacular **Finke Gorge National Park**, home to Palm Valley, an unusual tropical oasis in the dry heart of the country with rare palms.

Hermannsburg Historic Precinct

⊛ ⊝ ⌂ Larapinta Dr ⊙ Daily
⌧ Good Fri, 25 Dec

Finke Gorge National Park

⌂ ⌨ Alice Springs
ⓦ nt.gov.au

ALBERT NAMATJIRA

Aboriginal painter Albert Namatjira (1902–59) is one of the most celebrated Aboriginal artists in Australian history. Born and raised in Hermannsburg, he was taught to paint at the Hermannsburg Lutheran Mission by Aboriginal artist Rex Battarbee. Namatjira was known for his distinct style, which was influenced by European techniques, seen in his signature watercolour landscapes. He quickly rose to international fame and caught the attention of Queen Elizabeth II, who awarded him the Queen's Coronation Medal in 1953. Today, his works can be found in art galleries all around the world.

5
Arltunga Historical Reserve

🅰D3 🚗🚌 Alice Springs
ℹ️ Arltunga Rd, Atitjere;
www.nt.gov.au

Located around 110 km (68 miles) east of Alice Springs is Arltunga, Central Australia's first official town. Once a thriving gold-rush town, this 5,000-ha (12,355-acre) heritage-listed site is now an outdoor museum that pays tribute to the 300 miners who came here in search of gold from as early as 1887. At the reserve, visitors can learn about Arltunga's fascinating gold-rush history and go on a range of self-guided walks around the site's attractions, such as the Government Battery and Cyanide Works, Police Station, old mine workings and abandoned residential areas.

→
The spectacular Kings Canyon, and (inset) a beautiful spinifex pigeon

6
Chambers Pillar Historical Reserve

🅰D3 🚗🚌 Alice Springs
🌐 nt.gov.au

Located 160 km (110 miles) south of Alice Springs, with the final section of the journey accessible only by 4WD vehicles, Chambers Pillar is a sacred Aboriginal site.

The pillar, a 50-m- (165-ft-) high sandstone obelisk, was also used by explorers as an important navigational landmark during early colonial exploration. The pillar is made of mixed red-and-yellow sandstone deposited more than 350 million years ago. Many of the explorers, such as John Ross who visited the area in 1870, carved their names and inscriptions into the rock.

7
Henbury Meteorites Conservation Reserve

🅰D3 🚗🚌 Alice Springs
🌐 nt.gov.au

This cluster of 12 craters, located 145 km (89 miles) southwest of Alice Springs, was formed by a meteorite that crashed to earth several thousand years ago. It is believed that local Aboriginal people witnessed the event,

as one of the Aboriginal names for the area suggests a fiery rock falling to earth. The largest crater in the group is 180 m (590 ft) across and 15 m (50 ft) deep.

8
Kings Canyon

🅰D3 🚗 Alice Springs
🚌 Alice Springs, Yulara
🌐 nt.gov.au

This spectacular sandstone gorge, set within Watarrka National Park, has walls more than 100 m (330 ft) high that have been formed by millions of years of erosion – fossilized tracks of ancient marine creatures can even be seen in them. Several scenic walking tracks take visitors around the rim of the gorge, granting stunning views of the valley below.

Watarrka National Park has many water holes and areas of lush vegetation with more than 600 plant species. The park also provides a habitat for more than 100 bird species and 60 species of reptiles.

STAY

Kings Canyon Resort
This laid-back resort has basic rooms, and glamping, camping and caravan sites.

🅰D3 📍Luritja Rd, Watarrka National Park 🌐 kingscanyonresort.com.au

$$$

Kings Creek Station
A working cattle station, 36 km (22 miles) from Kings Canyon, with air-conditioned bush tents and luxury glamping sites.

🅰D3 📍Kings Creek Caravan Rd, Petermann 🌐 kingscanyonstation.com.au

$$$

> **Karlu Karlu/Devil's Marbles Conservation Reserve features a series of huge, spherical, red-granite boulders, scattered across a shallow valley in the Davenport Ranges.**

 9

Tennant Creek

🅰 D2 🚌 🛈 Battery Hill Mining Complex, Peko Rd; www.discoverthebarkly.com

Nearly 500 km (310 miles) north of Alice Springs, Tennant Creek is the second-largest town in the Red Centre and a major stopover along Stuart Highway, between Darwin and South Australia. It was chosen as the site of a telegraph station on the Overland Telegraph Line in 1872. The town grew after gold was discovered here in 1932. The **Battery Hill Gold Mining and Heritage Centre** has two museums, an underground mine and the Tennant Creek Visitor Centre.

Other attractions include Lake Mary Ann, an ideal spot for sailing and swimming, just 5 km (3 miles) out of town. The remote **Tennant Creek**

Telegraph Station, 12 km (8 miles) north of the town, is now a historical reserve. To access its buildings, take a key from the visitor centre.

Battery Hill Gold Mining and Heritage Centre

♿ 🅿 🏠 Battery Hill, Peko Rd 📞 (08) 8962 1281 🕐 Daily 🚫 Good Fri, 7, 8 & 25 Dec

Tennant Creek Telegraph Station

🏠 Stuart Hwy 📞 (08) 8962 4499

 10

Karlu Karlu/Devil's Marbles Conservation Reserve

🅰 D2 🚌 🛈 160 Peko Rd; www.nt.gov.au

Around 104 km (65 miles) south of Tennant Creek, this reserve

has a series of huge, spherical, red-granite boulders, scattered across a shallow valley in the Davenport Ranges. The result of geological activity from 1,700 million years ago, the boulders were created when molten lava was compressed to create huge domes just below the earth's surface. Subsequent erosion of the overlying rock exposed the marbles.

The reserve offers several walks, including the Nyanjiki Lookout, which provides spectacular panoramic views, and the shorter Karlu Karlu walk. There's also a simple bush camping area at the southern end of the reserve.

 PICTURE PERFECT
Karlu Karlu

The Karlu Karlu, also known as the Devil's Marbles, are 6-m- (20-ft-) high geological wonders. The best time to capture this fascinating sight is early morning or late afternoon when they glow red in the rising or setting sun.

WESTERN AUSTRALIA

Bathurst Lighthouse overlooking The Basin, Rottnest Island

EXPLORE
WESTERN
AUSTRALIA

This guide divides Western Australia into
two colour-coded sightseeing areas, as
shown on this map. Find out more about
each area on the following pages.

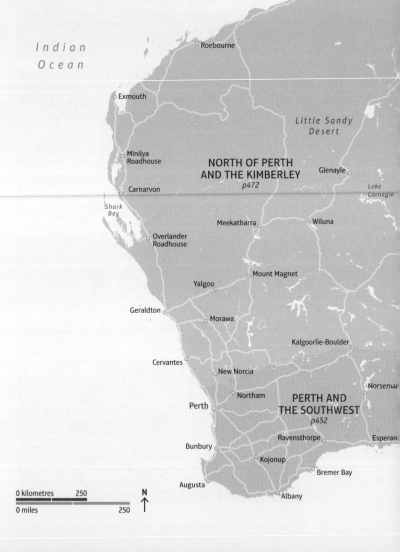

Indian
Ocean

Derby

Broome

Roebourne

Exmouth

Little Sandy
Desert

Minilya
Roadhouse

**NORTH OF PERTH
AND THE KIMBERLEY**
p472

Glenayle

Carnarvon

*Lake
Carnegie*

*Shark
Bay*

Meekatharra

Wiluna

Overlander
Roadhouse

Mount Magnet

Yalgoo

Geraldton

Morawa

Kalgoorlie-Boulder

Cervantes

New Norcia

Norsemar

Northam

**PERTH AND
THE SOUTHWEST**
p452

Perth

Ravensthorpe

Esperan

Bunbury

Kojonup

Augusta

Bremer Bay

Albany

0 kilometres   250

0 miles   250

N
↑

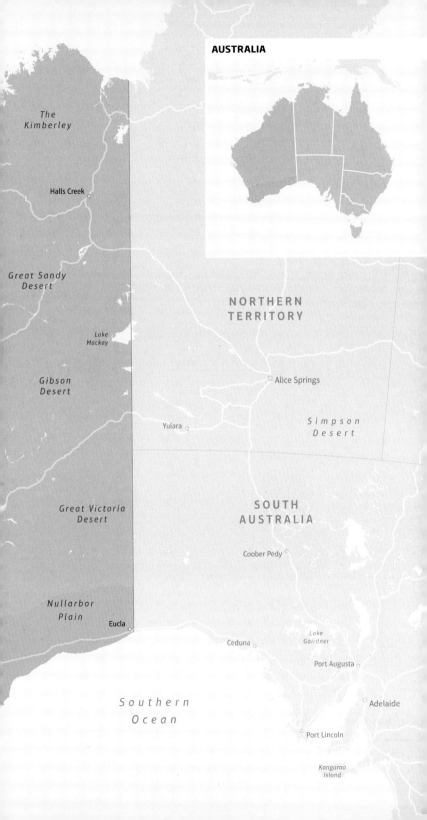

GETTING TO KNOW
WESTERN AUSTRALIA

Australia's largest state also has the country's longest coastline. This 12,895-km (8,012-mile) stretch is famed for its white-sand beaches and spectacular pink sunsets. Inland, Western Australia has a very different look: red deserts, towering forests and tiny settlements with a frontier feel.

PERTH AND THE SOUTHWEST

PAGE 452

Most of Western Australia's 2.5 million population lives in the coastal capital of Perth. Stretching out from the ocean, and with the mighty Swan River carving a path through its centre, this laid-back city is oriented around the water. In their downtime, locals drink and dine at riverfront restaurants, lounge and swim on the many beaches, and try to catch the perfect wave. Outside the city, Western Australia's rich soil fuels forests and wildflowers, vineyards and farms.

Best for
Wine and waves

Home to
Perth, Rottnest Island, Fremantle

Experience
Saying "g'day" to a friendly quokka on Rottnest Island

NORTH OF PERTH AND THE KIMBERLEY

The further you move away from Perth, the bigger Australia seems to get. In the far north is the Kimberley, a sparsely populated region punctuated by cattle stations the size of small countries. In between are mysterious cave systems and massive meteorite craters, beautiful swimming holes and thundering waterfalls. The coast, meanwhile, is all about wildlife, with protected coral atolls teeming with tropical fish, whale sharks, dugongs and dolphins.

Best for
Wildlife encounters

Home to
The Kimberley, Shark Bay World Heritage Area

Experience
Swimming with gentle whale sharks on Ningaloo Reef

Perth's red-brick Town Hall, dwarfed by a modern skyscraper

PERTH AND THE SOUTHWEST

Western Australia's pretty capital, Perth, is the most isolated city in the world, closer to Southeast Asia than it is to any other Australian city. Due to its distance from other British colonies, it was not until 1826 that the first British settlement occurred in Albany. Three years later, Captain James Stirling founded Perth, the capital of the Swan River Colony. Within 20 years, most of the Indigenous groups that had lived here peaceably for over 47,000 years had been forcibly ejected from the region, imprisoned or stricken by European diseases. Convicts arrived in 1850 and helped to build public buildings and the colony's infrastructure, until transportation to Western Australia ceased in 1868.

The beginning of the 20th century saw huge changes: a telegraph cable was laid connecting Perth with South Africa and London, and, in 1917, the railway arrived to join Kalgoorlie with the eastern states. The new infrastructure attracted waves of immigrants, first in the 1920s, when returning World War I servicemen were drafted to the area to clear and develop land under the Group Settlement Scheme, and again after World War II. Today, Perth and the Southwest still have Australia's largest percentage of foreign-born residents, connecting this isolated city to cultures from around the world.

PERTH AND THE SOUTHWEST

Must Sees
1. Perth
2. Rottnest Island
3. Fremantle

Experience More
4. Busselton
5. Margaret River
6. Leeuwin-Naturaliste
   National Park
7. Bunbury
8. Bridgetown
9. Pemberton
10. D'Entrecasteaux National Park
11. Manjimup
12. Denmark
13. Albany
14. Stirling Range National Park
15. York
16. Northam
17. Wave Rock
18. Kalgoorlie-Boulder
19. Norseman
20. Esperance
21. Nullarbor Plain

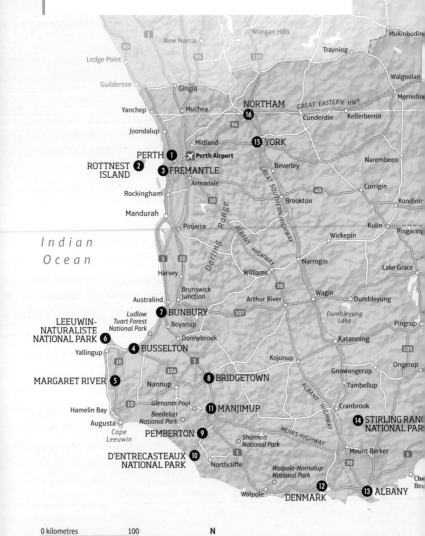

Perth skyscrapers rising above the recreational area of Elizabeth Quay

❶

PERTH

🅰A5 ✈16 km (10 miles) NE of the city 🚆11 km (7 miles) NE of the city 🚉Perth 🚢Barrack St Jetty ℹ55 William St; www.visitperth.com

The capital of Western Australia, Perth is known for its laid-back atmosphere, beautiful beaches and colourful laneways. The city centre is bordered to the south and east by the Swan River, and to the north by Northbridge, Perth's premier restaurant and nightlife district.

① Perth Cultural Centre

🏛Between William, Francis, Beaufort & Roe sts 🌐perthculturalcentre.com.au

The Perth Cultural Centre, a pedestrianized area, is home to many prestigious museums. **The Art Gallery of Western Australia** houses modern Aboriginal and Australian art and some international pieces. Head upstairs to AGWA Rooftop bar, the state's largest, for stunning views of the city. Opposite the gallery is the **Western Australian Museum Boola Bardip**, which hosts exhibitions on diverse topics. There's also the Perth Institute

of Contemporary Arts (**PICA**), a visual and performance arts venue; The Blue Room, an independent theatre; the State Library and State Theatre Centre of Western Australia.

The Art Gallery of Western Australia

🏛Roe St 🕐10am-5pm Wed-Mon 🚫Good Fri, 25 Dec 🌐artgallery.wa.gov.au

Western Australian Museum Boola Bardip

🏛Beaufort St 🕐9:30am-5pm daily; 25 Apr: 1-5pm 🚫Good Fri, 25 Dec 🌐museum.wa.gov.au

PICA

🏛51 James St 🕐10am-5pm Tue-Sun 🌐pica.org.au

②   DFES Education and Heritage Centre

🏛25 Murray St 🕐10am-3pm Tue-Thu 🚫Public hols 🌐dfes.wa.gov.au

In 1979, the old fire station became a fascinating museum charting the history of the fire service in Perth and Western Australia, as well as a fire safety centre. Exhibits here include a selection of well-preserved old fire appliances and reconstructions of fire station rooms.

③ St Mary's Cathedral

🏛25 Victoria Sq 🕐Hours vary, check website 🌐stmaryscathedralperth.com.au

After a major restoration project was carried out, St Mary's Cathedral is now an architectural delight. The building has retained its stained-glass windows and rich heritage, while also providing a modern space which seats 1,400 people. St Mary's is renowned for its superb choir.

(4)

Perth Mint

📍 310 Hay St ⏰ 9am–5pm daily ⏰ Public hols 🌐 perthmint.com.au

Perth Mint was opened in 1899, under British control, to refine gold from Western Australia's many gold fields in order to make British sovereigns and half-sovereigns.

Although it no longer produces coins for circulation, the mint produces proof coins and specialist pure precious-metal coins, making it Australia's oldest operating mint. The mint has an interesting exhibition with coins, precious metal exhibits and displays on gold mining and refining. In addition, every hour a "Gold Pour" takes place in the Melting House that has been in operation for over a century.

(5)

Elizabeth Quay

📍 The Esplanade 🌐 elizabethquay.com.au

The spectacular waterfront precinct of Elizabeth Quay, located along the Swan River, buzzes with restaurants, bars and cafés. It also features a pedestrian bridge. It's best experienced in summer, when plenty of food trucks set up shop.

EAT

Wildflower
An abundance of seasonal farm-foraged and Indigenous ingredients is a highlight of the dishes at this memorable roof-top restaurant.

📍 1 Cathedral Ave 🌐 wildflowerperth.com.au

$$ ⓢ

(6)

Yagan Square

📍 Wellington St 🌐 yagansquare.com.au

Yagan Square has infused new life into the Horseshoe Bridge area, with its bars and restaurants, plus art displays and cultural shows. There are many architectural nods to the outback and Indigenous Noongar cultures here, too.

← Sculpture of gold miners outside the entrance to Perth Mint

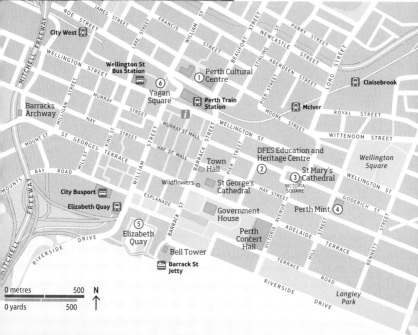

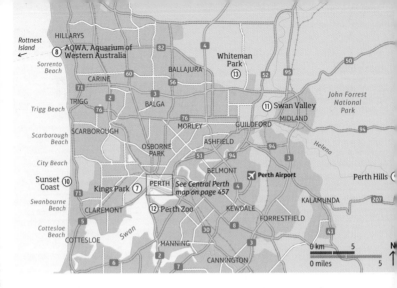

GREATER PERTH

⑦ Kings Park

🏠 Fraser Ave, Kings Park
🕐 Daily 🌐 bgpa.wa.gov.au

Established at the end of the 19th century on Mount Eliza, Kings Park is 400 ha (1,000 acres) of both wild and cultivated areas overlooking the Swan River. Most of the park is bushland, which can be seen from the DNA Tower.

A landscaped parkland area on the eastern side includes the 17-ha (42-acre) Western Australian Botanic Garden. Treetops Walkway, a 629-m- (689-yd-) long elevated path, offers another perspective of the area. The Anzac Bluff State War Memorial is dedicated to the Western

Australians who died in the two world wars. The Minmara Gun Gun and Pioneer Women's Memorial are monuments to the women who helped build the Swan River Colony and, later, the state.

⑧ AQWA, Aquarium of Western Australia

🏠 Hillarys Boat Harbour, 91 Southside Dr, Hillarys
🕐 10am–5pm daily
🚫 25 Dec 🌐 aqwa.com.au

At Hillarys Boat Harbour, to the north of Perth's Sunset Coast, is Australia's largest single aquarium complex. A transparent submerged tunnel allows visitors to view native sea creatures, including sharks and stingrays.

⑨ Perth Hills

🏠 Via Great Eastern Hwy

Only 30 minutes' drive from Central Perth, Perth Hills lies in the Darling Range and offers a wide range of bush-related activities. Conserved since 1919 as the catchment area for the Mundaring Weir, which provided water for the southern gold fields in the 19th century, the hills are well served with barbecue and picnic areas, as well as a number of campsites; the landscaped gardens at Mundaring Weir are a lovely backdrop for picnics.

On the northern edge of Perth Hills is John Forrest National Park, Western Australia's first national park. It features swathes of woodland and heath-land; several trails skirt through the park, leading

---

WILDFLOWERS OF KINGS PARK

Even if you can't make it to the famed wildflower fields of the west, Kings Park puts on a show right in the centre of town. There are more than 3,000 native plants and the flowers bloom to spectacular effect in spring. If you are here in September, attend the Kings Park Festival, where the flowers are both a backdrop and the main event.

→

Waves rolling to shore at Cottesloe Beach, Perth's most famous beach

to beautiful pools and waterfalls, including the scenic Hovea Falls. The hills are also dotted with vineyards and breweries, which have become increasingly popular.

---

 ⑩
Sunset Coast

 Via West Coast Hwy

Perth's Sunset Coast is lined with 50 km (31 miles) of white sandy beaches, many of them virtually deserted during the week. There are beaches to suit all tastes here. Cottesloe Beach, Perth's most popular coastal spot, offers safe swimming, stunning scenery and a range of swanky restaurants and takeaways, making it a big hit among tourists. To the north is Sorrento Beach, which is similarly good for families, and Swanbourne Beach, a naturist beach.

Scarborough Beach is very popular with surfers, but only experienced swimmers are advised to take to the waters here as strong currents can make it dangerous on windy days. Trigg Beach, just above Scarborough, is also a good surfing and snorkelling spot.

Visitors should note that many of the city's beaches lack large areas of shade; it is therefore advisable to come well equipped with sunscreen for a day at the beach.

> **The Swan Valley area offers an appealing mix of award-winning wineries, breweries and top-notch gourmet restaurants.**

⑪
Swan Valley

Guildford Courthouse, cnr Meadow & Swan sts, Guildford; www.swan valley.com.au

Western Australia's oldest wine-growing region is only a 25-minute drive from Perth. The historic Guildford suburb is the gateway to this area, which offers an appealing mix of award-winning wineries, breweries and top-notch gourmet restaurants.

---

⑫
Perth Zoo

20 Labouchere Rd
9am–5pm daily
perthzoo.wa.gov.au

Perth Zoo is located in South Perth, a ferry-ride away from the city centre. Dedicated to conservation, the complex has all the features of an international-standard zoo. Attractions include a Nocturnal House, a wildlife park, an African savannah exhibit, an Australian walkabout and an Asian rainforest zone. Free guided walks and talks are also held on a daily basis. The zoo also has a great breeding and conservartion programme that encourages animal adoptions.

---

⑬
Whiteman Park

Entry off Drumpellier Dr, exit Lord St, Whiteman
8:30am–6pm daily
whitemanpark.com.au

Northeast of the city centre is Whiteman Park. Visitors can tour the park on a 1920s tram or by train. A craft village displays local craftsmanship and there is a motor museum with a collection of vehicles from the last 100 years. Inside is Caversham Wildlife Park, home to 200 species of native Australian animals, from koalas to Tasmanian devils.

STAY

Discovery Rottnest Island

Set right by Pinky Beach, this eco-camp has large safari tents, some with ocean views.

🏠 Strue Rd 🌐 discovery holidayparks.com.au

$(\text{\$})(\text{\$})(\text{\$})$

EAT

Hotel Rottnest

Known for its massive beer garden near Thomson Bay, this place offers gourmet pizzas and bistro bites.

🏠 1 Bedford Ave 🌐 hotelrottnest.com.au

$(\text{\$})(\text{\$})(\text{\$})$

The Basin, a popular spot for swimming and snorkelling on Rottnest Island ↑

ROTTNEST ISLAND

🗺 A5 ⛴ From Perth, Fremantle, Hillarys Boat Harbour ℹ Thomson Bay near Main Jetty; www.rottnestisland.com

Wildly beautiful, Rottnest Island combines the dramatic Indian Ocean coastline with plenty of wildlife – look out for cute little quokkas (a type of wallaby) that can be spotted all over the island. Hire a bike, jump in a boat or lace up your hiking boots and explore this paradise.

Less than 20 km (12 miles) west of Fremantle lies the idyllic island of Rottnest. Private cars are not allowed here, so the only way to get around is by bicycle, bus or on foot.

After the arrival of the Europeans in 1831, the island was used as an Aboriginal prison between 1838 and 1904. In 1917, in recognition of its scenic beauty and rich birdlife, the island became a protected area and today it is a popular tourist destination. Rottnest's oldest settlement, Thomson Bay, dates from the 1840s. The island's other settlements, all built in the 20th century, are found at Longreach Bay, Geordie Bay and Kingstown. Rottnest's rugged coastline comprises beaches, coves

and reefs, ideal for many water-based activities, salt lakes and several visible shipwrecks. The Wadjemup Museum, housed in the old granary, is a great place to discover more about Rottnest. Exhibits cover the island's geology, its many shipwrecks, flora and fauna, and memorabilia of the early settlers and convicts.

> **Rottnest's rugged coastline comprises beaches, coves and reefs - ideal for many water-based activities - salt lakes and several visible shipwrecks.**

↑ The quokka, usually found in areas of undergrowth on Rottnest Island

↑ Dramatic rock formation at Little Parakeet Bay on the northern side of the island

THE QUOKKA

When Willem de Vlamingh, a Dutch sea captain, first visited Rottnest in 1696, he noted animals that were a bit bigger than a cat. Thinking they were a species of rat, he called the island the "rats' nest". In fact these were a type of wallaby, which the Aboriginal people called quokkas. There is a small population in Western Australia, but Rottnest is the best place to see quokkas – they are often visible at dusk. Due to their grin-like facial expressions, quokkas are known as the "world's happiest animal". But remember, they are wild and should not be touched or fed, and photos should be taken from a distance.

❸

FREMANTLE

Ⓐ A5 **🚉** Elder Pl **🚌** Elder Pl **🛈** Town Hall, Kings Sq,
8 William St; www.fremantle.wa.gov.au

The port city of Fremantle was founded in 1829, at the mouth of the Swan River. During World War II, the city became a submarine base. Today, it is an artsy area, featuring Victorian-era buildings, a thriving bar and restaurant scene, quirky breweries and a famed Cappuccino Strip.

① The Round House

Ⓐ Captains Lane **☎** (08) 9336 6897 **🕐** 10:30am–3:30pm daily

Built in 1830, this is the state's oldest public building and Fremantle's first gaol. It is now a popular tourist attraction, with views of Bathers Beach and Rottnest Island (p460). Beneath the prison is a tunnel, dug in 1837 to allow whalers to transfer cargo from the jetty to the High Street. Entry is by donation, with free tours daily to see the Cannon Firing Ceremony at 1pm.

② Western Australian Shipwrecks Museum

Ⓐ Cliff St **🕐** 9:30am–5pm daily (25 Apr: 1–5pm) **🚫** 1 Jan, Good Fri, 25 & 26 Dec **🌐** museum.wa.gov.au

Housed in the Commissariat building, an 1850s convict-built government storehouse, the Shipwrecks Museum is a centre for maritime archaeology and exploration (entry by donation). The highlight here is a reconstruction of part of the hull of the Dutch East Indiaman *Batavia* from timbers found at the site of its wreck off the Abrolhos Islands, where it had run into cliffs in 1629 (p482).

---

③ Fremantle Markets

Ⓐ Cnr South Terrace & Henderson St **🕐** Yard: 8am–6pm Fri–Sun & public hols; Hall: 9am–6pm Fri–Sun & public hols **🚫** 25 Dec **🌐** fremantlemarkets.com.au

In 1897, a competition was held to design a building to act as Fremantle's market hall. The winning design still stands today, having been renovated in 1975. There are more than 150 stalls offering everything from vegetables to opals.

Did You Know?

The Nyungar name for the area is *Walyalup* (the place of walyo), while locals call Fremantle "Freo".

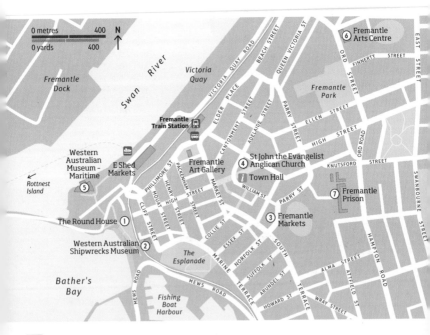

Sailing boats moored at Fremantle harbour, with the city spread out behind ↑

(4)
St John the Evangelist Anglican Church

⌂ Cnr Adelaide & Queen sts
🕐 Hours vary, check website
🌐 fremantleanglican.com

A charming church completed in 1882, St John the Evangelist replaced a smaller church on the same site. Its Pioneer Window tells the story of a settler family across seven generations, from their departure from England in the 18th century, to a new life in Western Australia. The ceiling and altars are made of local jarrah wood.

(5)
Western Australian Museum - Maritime

⌂ Victoria Quay 🕐 9:30am-5pm daily (25 Apr: 1-5pm)
📅 1 Jan, Good Fri, 25 & 26 Dec
🌐 visit.museum.wa.gov.au

This museum offers an insight into the city's wartime and maritime history through a range of immersive exhibits. Here, visitors can board the popular HMS *Ovens* to see what life is like on a submarine. The museum also houses the *Australia II*, a racing yacht with the winged keel that won the America's Cup in 1983.

(6)
Fremantle Arts Centre

⌂ Cnr Ord & Finnerty Vale sts 🕐 10am-5pm daily
📅 Public hols 🌐 fac.org.au

This beautiful Gothic Revival mansion with its shady gardens was first conceived as an asylum. The main wing was built between 1861 and 1865, and an extension was added between 1880 and 1902.

The building, which later became the wartime headquarters for US forces, was slated for demolition in 1967. However, principally through the efforts of the mayor of Fremantle, it was rescued and converted into the Fremantle Arts Centre.

The centre is now one of Western Australia's most dynamic multi-arts organisations, offering a rich programme of exhibitions, residences, art courses, music and events. It also showcases local contemporary artists, with many of the works for sale.

During the summer months (October to March), the centre's Sunday Music series takes place from 2 to 4pm. The outdoor event is free and features an extensive line-up of established local acts, touring artists and up-and-coming musicians.

(7)
Fremantle Prison

⌂ 1 The Terraces 🕐 9am-5pm daily 📅 Good Fri, 25 Dec 🌐 fremantleprison.com.au

In the 1850s, when the first convicts arrived in the Swan River Colony, the need arose for a large-scale prison. Fremantle Prison, an imposing building with limestone cell blocks, was built by those first convicts in 1855. It was used as a maximum-security prison until 1991. Today, visitors can tour the cells, chapel and gallows room and stay in budget accommodation located in the women's prison block.

PRISON BREAK

Although Fremantle was among Australia's most remote penal colonies, in 1876 six Irish prisoners mounted a daring escape, first on horseback, then by rowing out to a US ship. With soldiers in hot pursuit (but unwilling to fire on a ship flying a US flag in international waters), the escapees sailed to New York and received a hero's welcome.

→

Busselton Jetty, the longest wooden jetty in the southern hemisphere

EXPERIENCE MORE

Busselton

A5 ⬆🚌 *i* **17 Foreshore Parade; www.margaret river.com**

Set on the shores of Geographe Bay, Busselton offers plenty of beaches and an array of water-based activities, including fishing, scuba diving and whale-watching. Opposite the jetty is Shelter Brewing Co., a giant brew-house and restaurant. The foreshore is dominated by the Busselton Jetty, below which lies one of the country's biggest artificial reefs, home to 300 marine species and 13 underwater sculptures.

Some of Busselton's oldest surviving buildings are located at the Old Courthouse site. At present, local crafts are sold in the old jail cells, and other outbuildings function as a studio space for artists.

About 10 km (6 miles) north of Busselton is **Wonnerup House**. It was built by pioneer George Layman in 1859 and is currently owned by the National Trust. Three other buildings share this site, the earliest of which dates back to the 1830s. The buildings stand in pretty grounds and exhibit various Layman family memorabilia and various artifacts.

About 20 km (12 miles) north of Busselton is the beautiful Ludlow Tuart Forest National Park, the largest area of tuart trees left in the world.

Wonnerup House

 🏠935 Layman Rd ⏰10am–4pm Thu–Mon 🚫Good Fri, 25 Dec 🌐nationaltrust.org.au

---

Margaret River

A5 ⬆🚌 *i* **100 Bussell Hwy; www.margaret river.com**

The town of Margaret River, near the Indian Ocean, was settled by Europeans in the 1850s. The town is known for its wineries and culinary delights and is a jumping-off point to visit the area's timber forests, bays and beaches.

The town has many galleries, studios and food and beverage specialists. Mingle with local producers at the Margaret River Farmers Market on Saturdays. The year-round morning market features food trucks with vendors selling fresh produce, baked goods and coffee.

Mix cellar-door tastings, fine dining and contemporary art at **Leeuwin Estate Winery**. The vineyard brings together the region's essence under one roof. Margaret River has more than 95 wineries, breweries, and chocolate and cheese factories to check out.

Leeuwin Estate Winery

🏠Stevens Rd ⏰Cellar door: 10am–5pm daily 🌐leeuwin-estate.com.au

---

Leeuwin-Naturaliste National Park

A5 🏠36 km (22 miles) W of Busselton ⬆🚌 Busselton 🌐parks.dpaw.wa.gov.au

Leeuwin-Naturaliste National Park is a 19,000-ha (46,950-acre)

> INSIDER TIP
> ### Cape to Cape
>
> Drive the scenic 110 km (68 miles) between Cape Naturaliste and Cape Leeuwin. Along the way, the road passes hills corduroyed with vines, the dazzling Ngilgi Cave and the Boranup Karri Forest.

Ngilgi Cave, in the south of the park, is just one of an estimated 200 underground caves along the Leeuwin-Naturaliste Ridge that runs from Busselton to Augusta.

protected area of scenic coastline, caves, heathlands and woodlands. Its rugged limestone coast with long beaches and sheltered bays faces the Indian Ocean. It has long been popular as a holiday destination and has excellent opportunities for swimming, surfing and fishing.

Ngilgi Cave, in the south of the park, is just one of an estimated 200 underground caves along the Leeuwin-Naturaliste Ridge that runs from Busselton to Augusta. Open to the public, it is a fairyland of limestone formations, reflected in dark underground waters.

 7
Bunbury

🅰A5 🚗🚆🚌 🛈13A Prinsep St; www.visitbunbury geographe.com.au

The city of Bunbury lies about 168 km (104 miles) south of Perth. Since the 19th century it has grown into a thriving port and hub for the southwest region. It is a popular holiday destination too, with many watersport activities.

Historic buildings in the city include the Rose Hotel, built in 1865, with intricate ironwork detail. The Anglican St Boniface Cathedral contains pretty stained glass. Nearby are the Bunbury Art Galleries, housed in the former Sisters of Mercy convent built in the 1880s.

On the city's beachfront is the **Dolphin Discovery Centre**, with fascinating audiovisual exhibits. In front of the centre, wild dolphins regularly appear off the beach. The centre also organizes cruises and a swim-with-the-dolphins tour.

Run by the Bunbury Historical Society, the **King Cottage Museum** exhibits local artifacts dating from the 1880s to the 1920s and a wealth of photographs.

Dolphin Discovery Centre
♿ 🏠Koombana Dr 🕐Hours vary, check website 🗓25 Dec 🌐dolphindiscovery. com.au

Bunbury Farmers Market
🏠2 Vittoria Rd 🕐Hours vary, check website 🌐bunburyfarmers-market.com.au

EAT & DRINK

Swings & Roundabouts
Enjoy Mediterranean-inspired dishes in an outdoor setting with lovely vineyard views.

🅰A5 🏠2807 Caves Rd, Yallingup 🌐swings. com.au

💲💲💲

Beerfarm
Head here for boutique beers and American-inspired barbeque eats with a view of rolling farmland.

🅰A5 🏠177 Gale Rd, Metricup 🌐beerfarm. com.au

💲💲💲

de'sendent
This late-night spot uses high-end ingredients sourced from local suppliers and has an extensive wine list.

🅰A5 🏠3/152 Bussell Highway, Margaret River 🌐desendent.com

💲💲💲

The Tree Top Walk in the lush Valley of the Giants, Denmark

8

Bridgetown

 A5 ⊟ **i** 154 Hampton St; www.bridgetown.com.au

Nestled amid rolling hills on the banks of Blackwood River, Bridgetown began as a single one-room homestead in the 1850s. It was built by settler John Blechynden and can still be seen standing next to the second home he built, Bridgedale House. Both are National Trust properties.

The town's visitor centre is home to a municipal history museum and the unusual Brierly Jigsaw Gallery, which has hundreds of puzzles.

Sutton's Lookout, off Philips Street, offers panoramic views of the town and surrounding countryside. The Blackwood River and local jarrah and marri forests afford opportunities for walks and drives, and several water-based activities, including canoeing and marron fishing.

9

Pemberton

 A5 ⊟ **i** 29 Brockman St; www.pembertonvisitor.com.au

At the heart of karri country, Pemberton has the look and feel of an old timber town. The Pemberton Tramway, originally built to bring the trees to mills in town, now takes visitors through the forests. The **Pemberton Pioneer Museum** is a fascinating tribute to the pioneers of the area. Cool off at the 1920s, forest-lined Pemberton Pool.

Southeast of the town lies Gloucester National Park, home to some of the tallest karri fire-lookout trees in the world. Southwest of Pemberton is the Warren National Park with its cascades, swimming holes and fishing spots. Attractive Beedelup National Park is northwest of Pemberton.

Pemberton Pioneer Museum

⌂ Brockman St ⊙ Daily ⊘ Good Fri, 25 & 26 Dec ⊡ pembertonvisitor.com.au

10

D'Entrecasteaux National Park

 A5 ⊙ 40 km (25 miles) S of Pemberton ⊟ Northcliffe, then taxi ⊡ parks.dpaw.wa.gov.au

D'Entrecasteaux National Park, 40 km (25 miles) southwest of Pemberton, is a wild and rugged park with dramatic coastal cliffs, pristine beaches and excellent coastal fishing. At Point Ann, you can watch whales up close from platforms on the beach. Much of the park, including some isolated beach campsites, is only accessible by 4WD.

11

Manjimup

 A5 ⊟ **i** 151 Giblett St; www.manjimupwa.com

If you are travelling south from Perth, Manjimup acts as the gateway to the great Karri Forest, which the southwest is famous for. The town was settled in the late 1850s, and has been associated with the timber industry ever since.

Manjimup Timber and Heritage Park is home to the Timber Museum, Historical Hamlet and Bunnings Age of Steam Museum. A sculpture of a woodsman at the entrance commemorates the region's timber industry pioneers.

About 21 km (13 miles) west of Manjimup on Graphite Road lies Glenoran Pool, a pretty swimming hole on the Donnelly River. The adjacent One-Tree Bridge is the site where early settlers felled a huge karri and used it to carry a bridge across

FIRE LOOKOUTS

The forests of the southwest once had a unique system of fire-lookout trees, which were first built in the 1930s. Three karri tree towers – 61-m (200-ft) Gloucester Tree, 75-m (246-ft) Dave Evans Bicentennial Tree and 51-m (167-ft) Diamond Tree – remain but are now closed to the public. When they're open, visitors can climb the trees via spikes embedded in their trunks.

Did You Know?

Karri trees live for around 350 years, but some are known to be even older than that.

the river. Nearby are the Four Aces, four giant karri trees in a straight line, thought to be up to 300 years old.

Manjimup Timber and Heritage Park

🏠 151 Giblett St 🕐 Daily; Timber Museum: 9am–4:30pm daily 🚫 25 Dec 🌐 manjimupheritagepark. com.au

Denmark

B5 🚌 ℹ️ 73 Southcoast Hwy; www.denmark. com.au

Lying on Western Australia's southern coastline, Denmark was founded as a timber company settlement in 1895, but by the 1920s it was a fully fledged town. Today, it attracts a host of visitors, many of whom come seeking the good surf of the Southern Ocean and Ocean Beach, which is the setting for international surfing competitions. There are unique swimming spots at Greens Pool and neighbouring Elephant Rocks too. The area is also known for its large population of artists and artisans. Check out the Butter Factory Studios to see contemporary work by artists from the south coast.

Denmark's oldest building is St Leonard's Anglican Church, built by volunteers in 1899. Its Scandinavian-style pitched roof and interior detail are reminders of the Norwegian timber workers who lived in the town at that time.

A short walk from the church is Berridge Park. Hugging the Denmark river, the park often hosts open-air, riverfront concerts.

From Denmark's main street, it's a short walk through well-kept woodlands to Wilson Inlet, a shallow, seasonal estuary for the Denmark and Hay rivers offering spectacular views and great fishing spots.

A 55-km (34-mile) drive from town is the Valley of the Giants, where you can climb into the forest canopy along a 600-m (1,968-ft) ramp as part of the stunning Tree Top Walk, which ranges over colossal and rare tingle trees.

STAY

Cape Howe Cottages

Located close to Denmark, these gorgeous self-contained cottages are surrounded by native bush. Sit on your cottage's deck and unwind while listening to birdsong.

🅰️ B5 🏠 322 Tennessee Rd South, Albany 🌐 capehowe.com.au

$$$

TIN HORSE HIGHWAY

On either side of Kulin, a town between Albany and York, the roadside is decorated with more than 70 tin horses in a range of quirky themes. Crafted by local farmers, each trying to outdo the other, new tin horses are erected in the middle of the night in the weeks leading up to the region's annual October horse races.

13

Albany

A B5 🚉🚌 ℹ️ 221 York St; www.amazingalbany.com.au

Albany was first visited by Captain Vancouver in 1791, but it wasn't until 1826 that the British settled here. Until Fremantle harbour was built, Albany was the colony's main port and its harbour is still the commercial heart of the city.

Albany features many heritage buildings, such as the 1848 **St John the Evangelist Anglican Church**, the first Anglican church consecrated in Western Australia, and the pre-1836 Patrick Taylor Cottage, the oldest building in the city.

On Albany's foreshore is the **Museum of the Great Southern**, home to a replica of the brig *Amity*, which brought the first settlers here from Sydney in 1826.

Another side of Albany's history can be explored at **Albany's Historic Whaling Station** on Cheyne Beach, the world's largest whaling museum. From July to October, migrating whales can sometimes be seen offshore.

The **National Anzac Centre** was opened in 2014 to commemorate those who fought at Gallipoli during World War I.

A mega-mural of a rare sea dragon, painted by artists Yok and Sheyro, runs across four working silos along the harbour. The colourful artwork forms part of the region's PUBLIC Silo Trail.

St John the Evangelist Anglican Church

🏠 York St ⏰ Daily 🌐 anglicanchurchalbany.org.au

Museum of the Great Southern

🏠 Residency Rd ⏰ 10am-4pm daily 🌐 visit.museum.wa.gov.au/greatsouthern

Albany's Historic Whaling Station

♿♿😊 🏠 81 Whaling Station Rd, Torndirrup ⏰ 9am-5pm daily 🚫 25 Dec 🌐 discoverybay.com.au

National Anzac Centre

♿ 🏠 67 Forts Rd ⏰ 9am-4pm daily 🚫 25 Dec 🌐 nationalanzaccentre.com.au

14

Stirling Range National Park

A B5 🚌 Albany ℹ️ Albany Hwy, Albany; www.exploreparks.dbca.wa.gov.au

Overlooking the farmland to the north of Albany is the Stirling Range National Park. The mountain peaks, noted for their colour changes from purple to red to blue, rise to more than 1,000 m (3,300 ft) above sea level and stretch for more than 65 km (40 miles). The highest peak is Bluff Knoll, which reaches 1,099 m (3,605 ft). Due to its sudden rise from the surrounding plains, the park has an unpredictable climate, which encourages a wide range of unique flora and fauna species. Flowering plants are best seen from September to November. The park offers many graded and signposted walks in the mountains and there are several picturesque barbecue and picnic areas.

15

York

A A5 🚌 ℹ️ 81 Avon Terrace; www.visit.york.wa.gov.au

The town of York was founded in 1831. Now registered as a historic town, it retains many mid-19th-century buildings, the majority of which are on Avon Terrace, the main street. The cells of York's Old Gaol, in use from 1865 until 1981, provide a chilling insight into the treatment of 19th-century offenders. Other historic buildings include Settler's House (1860s) and Castle Hotel, established in 1853. Nearby stands the **York**

TOP 5 WILDFLOWER HOTSPOTS

Leeuwin-Naturaliste National Park
This park *(p464)* fills with orchids from September to November.

Kalbarri National Park
Wildflowers bloom from August to September.

Kennedy Range National Park
More than 80 wildflower species blossom after heavy rains.

Inland from Geraldton
From August to October, Route 123 features spectacular displays.

Fitzgerald River National Park
Over 1,250 unique floral species bloom from August to October.

Motor Museum, with one of the largest collections of veteran cars and vehicles in Australia. These include the 1886 Benz (the world's first car) and the very rare 1946 Holden Sedan Prototype.

Also of note is the York Residency Museum, housing an extensive collection of artifacts and photos, and York's 1892 flour mill, which has been converted into the Jah-Roc Mill Gallery, selling furniture made from jarrah wood.

York Motor Museum
🅰 116 Avon Terrace ⏰ 9am–4pm daily 🌐 york motormuseum.com

16
Northham

🅰 A5 🚌 ℹ️ 2 Grey St; www.northam.wa.gov.au

At the heart of the Avon Valley, Northam is Western Australia's largest inland town. Settled as an agricultural centre early in the colony's history, the town became a gateway to the gold fields of Kalgoorlie-Boulder *(p470)* for prospectors in the 1890s. It retains many historic buildings, including the Old Girls' School (1877) – now the town's Art Centre, St John's Church (1890) and Morby Cottage (1836).

At the centre of town, on the Avon River, Bilya Koort Boodja focuses on Noongar culture and the community's ties with the environment. Next to the centre, spanning the river, is one of the longest pedestrian suspension bridges in the country.

17
Wave Rock

🅰 B5 🏠 Wave Rock Rd, Hyden 🚌 Hyden ⏰ 9am–5pm daily 🚫 25 Dec 🌐 waverock.com.au

In Western Australia's wheat belt, 5 minutes' drive east of the small settlement of Hyden, stands one of the state's most surprising rock formations. A great granite wave-shaped rock has been created from a huge outcrop by thousands of years of erosion, its reaction with rainwater giving it red and grey stripes. Other rock formations nearby include the Breakers and Hippo's Yawn. Facing Wave Rock, Lace Place is the unusual location for the largest collection of lacework in the southern hemisphere. Guided tours of the area can be organized by prior arrangement.

About 18 km (11 miles) northeast of Hyden is located Mulka's Cave, where many rock paintings created by the Aboriginal people can be seen.

↑ The incredible Wave Rock formation, resembling an oceanic wave

Kalgoorlie-Boulder

B4 **316 Hannan St; www.kalgoorlie tourism.com**

Kalgoorlie and the nearby town of Boulder, with which it was amalgamated in 1989, constantly remind visitors of the gold rush. Gold was first discovered here by Irishman Paddy Hannan in 1893, and, within weeks, the area was besieged with prospectors. Gold fields in other areas soon dwindled, but this field has yielded rich pickings to this day, bolstered by nickel finds in the 1960s. Today, gold is mined in the world's largest open-cut mine and more than 150,000 visitors a year come to see historic Kalgoorlie.

A variety of heritage trails and tours are available, and details can be found at the tourist office. The **Museum of the Goldfields** chronicles the history of the gold rush through an impressive collection of gold nuggets and jewellery, as well as natural history displays. Visitors can ride in a glass lift for magnificent views of the gold fields, or step back in time at a 1930s miner's cottage.

The ornate buildings, erected during the boom years, are best seen on Hannan Street, in the York and Exchange hotels, classic examples of gold rush architecture, and Kalgoorlie Town Hall.

Around Kalgoorlie-Boulder are ghost towns, such as Ora Banda and Broad Arrow, deserted by prospectors in search of new mines. Some 183 km (114 miles) north of Kalgoorlie-Boulder is Lake Ballard, a stunning salt lake. Its plains are home to "Inside Australia" – the country's largest outdoor art gallery, featuring 51 black steel sculptures by British artist Antony Gormley.

Museum of the Goldfields

 17 Hannan St **10am-3pm daily (25 Apr: 1-3pm)** **1 Jan, Good Fri, 25-26 Dec** **visit.museum.wa.gov.au**

SKYLAB

On 11 July 1979, the debris of NASA's first space station, Skylab, rained down on Balladonia on the Nullarbor Plain after weeks of worldwide speculation about where it would crash-land. At the time, the local Shire Council issued a $400 fine to NASA for littering and later US President Jimmy Carter personally called the Balladonia Roadhouse to apologize for Skylab falling on them. Pieces of the space station are on display at the Esperance Museum.

Norseman

B5 **78 Prinsep St; www.dundas.wa.gov.au**

At the start of the Eyre Highway, Norseman is the gateway to the Nullarbor Plain and the eastern states beyond. Like Kalgoorlie-Boulder, the town stands on a gold field, discovered when a horse pawed the ground, uncovering gold deposits. In gratitude, miners named the town after the horse, and its statue was erected in the main street. Many visitors try fossicking, or learn more about the history of gold mining in the area at **The Norseman Historical Museum**, which is housed in the old School of Mines. Nearby, Beacon Hill offers a panoramic view of the town and surrounding countryside.

The Norseman Historical Museum

 43 McGrath St **10am-1pm Mon-Thu** **Good Fri, Easter Mon, 25 Apr, 25 Dec** **ourgems.com.au**

Esperance

B5 **Historic Museum Village, Dempster St; www.visitesperance.com**

Although this area was visited by Europeans as far back as 1627, it was not until

↑ Exhibits at the Museum of the Goldfields, Kalgoorlie-Boulder

1863 that British colonists established a settlement here. Fronting the Southern Ocean, this part of the coast is said to have some of the most beautiful beaches in Australia. Offshore is the Recherche Archipelago, with its 105 islands, one of which, Woody Island, is a wildlife sanctuary and can be visited.

In Esperance itself, the Historic Museum Village includes the town's art gallery, and Esperance Municipal Museum contains regional artifacts. Lucky Bay, in the nearby Cape Le Grand National Park, has been "scientifically proven" to have the whitest sand in Australia; kangaroos bathing in the sea here is a fairly common sight. Also not far from town is the glorious Great Ocean Drive, a 40-km (25-mile) loop that takes you past superb

beaches, including Twilight Beach and Lovers Cove, and some of Western Australia's most dramatic coastal scenery.

21
Nullarbor Plain

🅰 C4 🚉 Kalgoorlie 🚌 Norseman 🛈 78 Prinsep St, Norseman; www. dundas.wa.gov.au

The Nullarbor Plain stretches across the southeast of the state and into South Australia (p302). "Nullarbor" derives from the Latin meaning "no trees", but there are lots of trees and vegetation here.

Only one road, the Eyre Highway, leads across the plain and driving it is one of Australia's greatest road trip adventures. A few roadhouses are dotted along the historic drive. Cocklebiddy, around 438 km (270 miles) east of Norseman, has one of the world's longest cave dives and, at Eucla, 10 km (6 miles) from the state border with South Australia, a telegraph station's remains can be seen. Nearby is the Eucla National Park, which offers some fine views of coastal cliffs.

Did You Know?

A 146-km (91-mile) stretch of road on the Eyre Highway is Australia's longest straight road.

 Wooden staircase leading down to Twilight Beach near Esperance

---

EAT

FishFace
The local seafood couldn't be any fresher than it is at FishFace. Order takeaway fish and chips or enjoy a sit-down meal of oysters and a fishy dish from the à la carte menu.

🅰 B5 🏠 1 James St, Esperance 🆆 fishface esperance.com

$\$$$\$$$ⓢ

Loose Goose
At this bar and restaurant, delicate seafood dishes are accompanied by a range of craft beers.

🅰 B5 🏠 9 Andrew St, Esperance 🆆 loose gooseesperance.com.au

$\$$$\$$$ⓢ

Exploring Cathedral Gorge, Purnululu (Bungle Bungle) National Park

NORTH OF PERTH AND THE KIMBERLEY

Aboriginal peoples first set foot on the Australian land mass in the north of Western Australia some 65,000 years ago. This region was also the site of the second European landing, by Dutch navigator Dirk Hartog, in 1616. In 1688, English navigator William Dampier charted some of the coast and, on a later voyage, reached Shark Bay and the area around Broome. Despite these early European voyages, the area was not settled until the Benedictines set up a mission in New Norcia in the 1840s. By the 1860s, settlements had sprung up along the coast, most significantly at Cossack, where a pearling industry attracted immigrants from Japan, China and Indonesia. Immigration was also stimulated in 1885, when gold was struck at Halls Creek, and the northern part of the state was finally on the map. In the 1960s, mining came to prominence again with the discovery of such minerals as iron ore, nickel and oil, particularly in the Pilbara region. Today, mining still drives a large part of the region's economy, but even isolated spots, such as the Kimberley and the resorts of Coral Bay and Broome, are receiving more visitors every year.

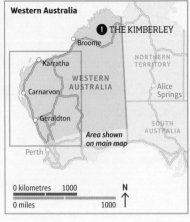

THE KIMBERLEY ❶
Broome

NORTHERN TERRITORY

Karratha
WESTERN AUSTRALIA
Carnarvon
Alice Springs

Geraldton
SOUTH AUSTRALIA

Area shown on main map

Perth

0 kilometres 1000

0 miles 1000

N

Indian Ocean

Monte Bello Islands

Barrow Island

Muiron Islands
Onslow

EXMOUTH ❽

CAPE RANGE NATIONAL PARK ❾
Learmonth

Nanutarra Roadhouse

NINGALOO REEF MARINE PARK ❿

Coral Bay

NORTH WEST COASTAL HIGHWAY

Red Bluff Lake Macleod Minilya Roadhouse

Quobba
Quobba Blowholes

KENNEDY RANGE NATIONAL PARK ⓬

Gascoyne

CARNARVON ⓫

Gascoyne Junction

Dorre Island *Shark Bay*

Dirk Hartog Island Monkey Mia *Wooramel*

Denham Wooramel Roadhouse

SHARK BAY WORLD HERITAGE AREA ❷
Overlander Roadhouse

NORTH WEST COASTAL HWY

Wannoo Billabong Roadhouse

Zuytdorp Cliffs

KALBARRI NATIONAL PARK ❼
Kalbarri

Binnu

Northampton Mullewa

HOUTMAN ABROLHOS ISLAND PARK ❺

GERALDTON ❻

Dongara

Beekeepers Nature Reserve

Eneabba

Leeman

60

Cervantes

THE PINNACLES ❸

Lancelin

NORTH OF PERTH AND THE KIMBERLEY

Must Sees
❶ The Kimberley
❷ Shark Bay World Heritage Area

Experience More
❸ The Pinnacles
❹ New Norcia
❺ Houtman Abrolhos
❻ Geraldton
❼ Kalbarri National Park
❽ Exmouth
❾ Cape Range National Park
❿ Ningaloo Reef Marine Park
⓫ Carnarvon
⓬ Kennedy Range National Park
⓭ Dampier
⓮ Roebourne
⓯ Karijini National Park
⓰ Cossack Historic Town
⓱ Murujuga National Park

❶

THE KIMBERLEY

🅐 B2 ✈ Broome International Airport ✈ East Kimberley
Regional Airport ℹ Victoria Hwy, Kununurra; www.
australiasnorthwest.com

One of the world's last wilderness frontiers, the Kimberley
is a vast, remote upland region of dry, red landscape. Deep
rivers cut through ancient mountain ranges, and parts of
the coastline experience the second-highest tidal range
in the world. Enjoy views of the wide horizons and serene
beaches as you explore the ancient gorges and rock pools.

> **Did You Know?**
>
> A 17,300-year-old
> kangaroo painting,
> found in the Kimberley,
> is Australia's oldest
> known rock art.

The Kimberley in northwestern Australia
covers 423,000 sq km (164,000 sq miles) and
has a population of less than 40,000. Geologi-
cally, it is one of the oldest regions on earth.
Its rocks formed up to 2,000 million years ago.
First Nations people have lived here for thousands of years, but this ancient land – dotted
with bottle-shaped boab (baobab) trees – has
been a tourist attraction only since the 1980s.

Seasonal climatic extremes add to the area's
sense of isolation as the harsh heat of the
dry season and the torrential rains of the wet
hamper access to the hostile terrain. April
to September is the best time to visit the
country's natural wonders such as Wolfe
Creek Meteorite Crater, Horizontal Falls and
the Bungle Bungles. To the south lie the huge,
inhospitable Great Sandy and Gibson deserts.

STAY

El Questro
Wilderness Park

Perched on the cliffs of
Chamberlain Gorge, this
working cattle station
offers different types
of accommodation in an
area replete with water-
falls and hiking trails.

🅐 El Questro Rd, Durack
🌐 elquestro.com.au

Cable Beach
Club Resort

Set alongside one of the
world's longest beaches,
this resort features
vast tropical gardens,
several restaurants
and a spa.

🅐 1 Cable Beach Rd,
Cable Beach 🌐 cable
beachclub.com

$$$

↑ The 1,500-year-old Prison Boab (baobab) tree in Derby

FIRST NATIONS POPULATIONS OF THE KIMBERLEY

The Kimberley region is home to more than 100 different First Nations communities, who speak over 40 dialects. Most live in remote communities and some are traditional custodians of vast tracts of territory. Even the towns of Derby, Halls Creek, Wyndham and Fitzroy Crossing have significant First Nations populations. Rock art and many other archaeological studies have revealed that First Nations people have been living in the Kimberley for up to 40,000 years.

↑ Captivating landscape of the Bungle Bungle, Purnululu National Park

The gorge at Bandilngan (Windjana Gorge) National Park just off Gibb River Road

EXPLORING THE KIMBERLEY

Gibb River Road

Originally built to transport livestock from the cattle stations to the ports of Derby and Wyndham, this 660-km (410-mile) road is one of the country's best off-road adventures. It offers wonderful views of the scenery as it passes through Kimberley's escarpment country and heads towards three national parks that together make up the ancient Devonian Reef System, dating back nearly 375 million years: Danggu Geikie Gorge, a stunning waterway with towering weathered cliffs; Dimalurru (Tunnel Creek), the state's oldest cave system; and Bandilngan (Windjana Gorge), with its freshwater crocodile population. Along the way, stretch your legs to reach river gorges and waterfalls. You can also take a refreshing dip in the freshwater swimming holes in this area.

Throughout the wet season (October to April), the road is often closed or has restricted access. It is advisable to plan your trip while keeping these in mind.

Halls Creek

🚌 ℹ️ 2 Hall St; www.halls creektourism.com.au

The site of Western Australia's first gold rush in 1885 is now a mining centre. It has a vertical wall of quartz – the China Wall. **Wolfe Creek Crater National Park** has the world's second-largest meteorite crater.

Wolfe Creek Crater National Park

🚗 152 km (94 miles) S of Halls Creek 🕐 May-Oct 🌐 parks.dpaw.wa.gov.au

---

③

Broome

✈️🚌 ℹ️ 1 Hamersley St; www.visitbroome.com.au

First occupied by Europeans in the 1860s, Broome became Western Australia's most profitable pearling region. Pearl divers from Asia swelled the town in the 1880s, giving it the multicultural character that remains today. The town's past can be seen in original stores, and the Chinese and Japanese cemeteries that contain graves of hundreds of pearl divers.

Just outside town is the Cable Beach, a popular sunset spot. It is the most famous of Broome's natural attractions. Other notable sights include Roebuck Bay and Gantheaume Point, home to dinosaur footprints.

---

④

Purnululu (Bungle Bungle) National Park

🚌 Halls Creek 🕐 Apr-Nov: daily 🌐 parks.dpaw.wa. gov.au

Reached by a rough 4WD track, this large national park features some of the most iconic landscapes in Western Australia. The traditional owners of the land are the Gija (or Kija) and Jaru. The park is famous for the Bungle Bungle Range. It has many rare beehive-shaped

> Derby is the gateway to a region of stunning gorges. Points of interest here include the Marsh exhibition, Mowan-jum Art & Cultural Centre and Norval Gallery.

domes of rock encased in a skin of silica and cyano-bacterium. A great way to see the landscape is from the air. Helicopter flights leave from the park's Bellburn Airstrip and from Kununurra.

⑤
Derby

🚻🚌 **ℹ** 30 Loch St; www.derbytourism.com.au

Derby is the gateway to a region of stunning gorges. Points of interest here include the Marsh exhibition, Mowanjum Art & Cultural Centre and Norval Gallery.

South of town is the 1,500-year-old Prison Boab (baobab) tree, 14 m (45 ft) in circumference. At the end of the 19th century, it was used to house prisoners overnight before their final journey to Derby Gaol.

⑥
Kununurra

ℹ 75 Coolibah Dr; www.visitkununurra.com

This young frontier town was built to house workers on the Ord River Irrigation Scheme, which created Lake Argyle – the country's second-largest human-made reservoir. Take a cruise on the Ord River and visit the Argyle Homestead, the former home of the Duracks, one of Australia's best-known pioneering families.

⑦
Wyndham

🚻🚌 **ℹ** 6 Koolama St; www.swek.wa.gov.au

The port of Wyndham was established in 1888, partly to service the Halls

Creek gold rush and partly as a centre for the local pastoral industry. It also provided supplies, which were carried by Afghan camel-trains, for cattle stations in northern Kimberley. The town's Afghan cemetery is a reminder of those traders who were essential to the survival of pioneer home-steads in the interior.

The part of the town known as Old Wyndham Port was the original town site and still contains a number of 19th-century buildings. The Port Museum displays a vivid photographic history of the port.

🗻 GREAT VIEW
On Top of the Bastion

Watch the five rivers meet and enter the Cambridge Gulf and surrounding mangroves from the Five Rivers Lookout in Wyndham. This incredible view is best at sunrise or sunset.

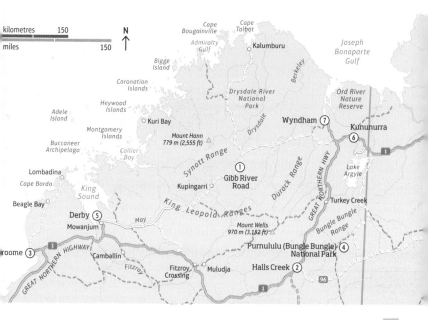

2 Ⓜ 🍴 🖥 🎒

SHARK BAY WORLD HERITAGE AREA

🔺A4 📍Off Northwest Coastal Hwy 🚌From Perth ℹ️53 Knight Terrace, Denham; Dolphin Info Centre, Monkey Mia; www.sharkbay.org

World Heritage-listed Shark Bay is located at Australia's westernmost point and covers an area of more than 22,000 sq km (8,500 sq miles). Visitors flock here for the pristine beaches, burned-red bluffs, rare stromatolites and abundant wildlife.

The waters, islands and peninsulas of Shark Bay are home to many endangered species of plants and animals, and various unusual natural processes have, over the millennia, given rise to some astounding natural features and spectacular coastal scenery. The only way to travel around the area is by car, and large areas are only accessible by 4WD.

At the small beach of Monkey Mia, wild dolphins come to shore almost every morning and there are boat trips from here that go in search of dugongs, turtles and dolphins. Nearby, at the tip of Peron Peninsula, is the Francois Peron National Park, where red desert sands meet the ocean. Lying to the south is Eagle Bluff, which has panoramic views to offshore islands, where nesting eagles are often spotted. Dirk Hartog Island National Park, in the west, is where Dutchman Dirk Hartog became the first European to set foot in Australia and leave behind an artifact (an inscribed pewter plate) in 1616. It is home to Turtle Bay, where thousands of loggerhead turtles return each year to nest.

Did You Know?

Shell Beach consists of billions of tiny cockle shells, piled up to a depth of some 10 m (33 ft).

1 Hamelin Pool in Shark Bay has a huge collection of stromatolites, which are formed by cyanobacteria, the earliest life on earth.

2 Francois Peron National Park has a variety of bird species, including the Australian pelican.

3 Numerous tropical fish swim among the coral in Shark Bay's waters.

↑ Limestone rock formations at a beach on the wind-swept Peron Peninsula

STAY

Monkey Mia Dolphin Resort
Set by the beach, this resort offers a range of options, from campsites to luxury rooms.

⌂ 1 Monkey Mia Rd, Monkey Mia ⓦ parks andresorts.rac.com.au

 $$$

Dirk Hartog Island Eco Lodge
Stay in former shearers' quarters at this retreat located right by the stunning waters of Dirk Hartog Island. There are plenty of activities to choose from.

⌂ 62 Dirk Hartog Island Dr ⓦ dirkhartog island.com

$$$

EXPERIENCE MORE

❸ The Pinnacles

🅰 A4 🛈 Cadiz St, Cevantes; www.visitpinnacles country.com.au

The eerie desert landscape of Nambung National Park comprises beach and sand dunes, with the dunes extending inland from the coast. It is best seen in spring when wildflowers bloom and the heat is not oppressive.

The park is famous for the Pinnacles, a region of curious limestone pillars, the tallest of which stand 4 m (13 ft) high. Visitors can take a 3-km (2-mile) driving trail or a shorter walking trail that leads to lookouts with stunning views of the Pinnacles and the coastline. The stones are at their most spectacular in the golden early-morning or late-after-noon light. Most of the park animals are nocturnal, but some, including kangaroos, emus and many reptiles, may be seen in the cool of dawn or dusk.

❹ New Norcia

🅰 A5 🚌 🛈 New Norcia Museum and Art Gallery, Great Northern Hwy; www. newnorcia.wa.edu.au

One of Western Australia's most important heritage sites is New Norcia, 130 km (80 miles) northeast of Perth. A mission was established here by Spanish Benedictine monks in 1846, and it is still home to a small monastic community who own and run the historic buildings. There are daily tours of the monastery and visitors can stay at a guesthouse.

The town, known for its Spanish colonial architecture, has a pretty cathedral, built in 1860, at its centre. The **New Norcia Museum and Art Gallery** has some fine art treasures and artifacts tracing the town's history.

New Norcia Museum and Art Gallery

⊘ 🅰 Great Northern Hwy ⏰ Daily 🚫 25 & 26 Dec 🌐 new norcia.wa.edu.au/museum

> West of Geraldton lie more than 100 coral islands called the Houtman Abrolhos – the southernmost coral island formation in the world.

❺ Houtman Abrolhos Islands National Park

🅰 A4 🚌 Geraldton 🚢 From Geraldton 🛈 24 Chapman Rd, Geraldton; www. visitgeraldton.com.au

About 60 km (37 miles) west of Geraldton lies the Houtman Abrolhos Islands National Park. The archipelago is made of 210 islands and is the site of the 1629 shipwreck *Batavia*, which is still visible today. While you cannot stay on the islands, visitors can take a day trip to snorkel along the coral reef at the East Wallabi Islands. The **WA Department of Fisheries** has information on visiting.

WA Department of Fisheries

🌐 fish.wa.gov.au

❻ Geraldton

🅰 A4 🚉🚌 🛈 24 Chapman Rd; www.visitgeraldton. com.au

Geraldton lies on Champion Bay, about 425 km (265 miles) north of Perth. The regional hub attracts visitors for its crayfish restaurants and whale-watching tours, as well as ample windsurfing opportunities.

← The striking limestone Pinnacles in the Nambung National Park

↑ The striking Museum of Geraldton and *(inset)* some of the exhibits in its Shipwreck Gallery

The history of European settlement in the area extends back to 1629 when two crew members of the Dutch ship *Batavia* were marooned here. In 1721, the Dutch ship *Zuytdorp* was wrecked, and it is thought that survivors settled here briefly. Champion Bay was first mapped in 1849, and a lead mine was established shortly afterwards. Geraldton grew up as a lead shipping point, and is now a port city.

There are many historic buildings in the city. The **Museum of Geraldton** houses the Shipwrecks Gallery, which contains relics of the area's early shipwrecks. The Old Railway Building has exhibits on local history, wildlife and geology. Geraldton has two cathedrals: the modern Cathedral of the Holy Cross and the Byzantine-style

St Francis Xavier Cathedral. Point Moore Lighthouse, with its distinctive red and white stripes, has been in continuous operation since 1878. The 1876 **Lighthouse Keeper's Cottage**, the town's first lighthouse, now houses Geraldton's Historical Society. Also in town is the **City of Greater Geraldton Regional Art Gallery**, exhibiting the work of local artists.

A number of viewpoints, such as Separation Point Lookout and Mount Tarcoola Lookout, give panoramic views of the city and the azure ocean.

Museum of Geraldton
🏠 2 Museum Place, Batavia Coast Marina 🕓 9:30am-3pm daily 🚫 Public hols 🌐 visit.museum.wa.gov.au

Lighthouse Keeper's Cottage
♿ 🏠 355 Chapman Rd 🕓 Hours vary, contact the Geraldton Visitor Centre

City of Greater Geraldton Regional Art Gallery
🏠 24 Chapman Rd 📞 (08) 9964 7170 🕓 9am-4pm Mon, Tue, Thu & Fri, 9:30am-1:30pm Wed, Sat & Sun

EAT

Saltdish
Geraldton's coolest café does everything well, especially the local seafood.

🗺️ A4 🏠 35 Marine Terrace, Geraldton 📞 (08) 9964 6030

$⑤$⑤$

Burnt Barrel
Visit this barbecue joint, located north of Geraldton, for smoked pulled pork or ribs and craft beer.

🗺️ A4 🏠 305 Nanson-Howatharra Rd, Nanson 🌐 burntbarrel.com

$⑤$⑤$

↑ Nature's Window framing the Murchison River, Kalbarri National Park

7

Kalbarri National Park

 A4 🚌 Kalbarri 🛈 70 Grey St, Kalbarri; www.kalbarri.org.au

The magnificent landscape of Kalbarri National Park includes stunning coastal scenery and beautiful inland gorges lining the Murchison River. The park has several coastal and river walking trails which lead to breathtaking views and fascinating rock formations. The trails vary in length, from two-hour strolls to four-day hikes. Highlights of the park include Hawks Head, a picnic area with views of the gorge; Nature's Window, where a rock formation frames a view of the river; Ross Graham Lookout, where visitors can bathe in the river pools and the Kalbarri Skywalk (Kaju Yatka), twin platforms that extend over the gorge rim. By the ocean, Pot Alley provides views of the rugged coastal cliffs, while Rainbow Valley is made up of layers of multicoloured rocks.

The access town for the park, Kalbarri, is situated on the coast and offers good facilities. The best time to visit is from July to October, when the weather is dry and the temperatures are pleasant.

8

Exmouth

 A3 ✈🚌 🛈 2 Truscott Crescent; www.ningaloocentre.com.au

Situated on the eastern side of the Exmouth Peninsula, this small town was originally built in 1967 to service the local airforce base. A military presence is still in evidence, but today the town is more important as a tourist stop, used as a base for exploring the Ningaloo Reef Marine Park and the Cape Range National Park. Giant turtles and whale sharks can frequently be seen from the nearby coastline.

Slightly outside of town, at Vlaming Head, lies the wreck of the SS *Mildura*, a cattle transporter that sank in 1907 and is still visible from the shore.

🔍 HIDDEN GEM
Burringurrah

One of the world's largest monoliths, Burringurrah rises up from Mount Augustus National Park, 508 km (315 miles) east of Exmouth. Drive around the 49-km (30-mile) road that rings its base, or hike it if you're brave.

Nearby stands the Vlamingh Lighthouse, offering panoramic views across the entirety of the peninsula.

9

Cape Range National Park

🅰 A3 🛈 Milyering Discovery Centre, Yardie Creek Rd; www.parks.dpaw.wa.gov.au

Cape Range National Park contains a low mountain range with spectacular gorges and rocky outcrops. This area was originally under water and it is possible to discern the fossils of ancient coral in the limestone. Local wildlife includes kangaroos, emus and large lizards. There are two main wilderness walks, but visitors should not attempt these in summer as temperatures can reach as high as 50° C (120° F).

Yardie Creek is on the western side of the park, only 1 km (0.5 miles) from the ocean. A short walk along gorge cliffs leads to the spectacular canyon, where you may catch sight of rock wallabies on the far canyon wall. A cruise through the gorges is also available.

Ningaloo Reef Marine Park

A3 Exmouth
Milyering Discovery Centre, Yardie Creek Rd, Cape Range National Park; www.parks.dpaw.wa. gov.au

Ningaloo Reef extends over 300 km (186 miles) along the west coast of Exmouth Peninsula and is the largest fringing barrier reef in the world. In many places, this park lies very close to the shore, and its still waters, especially Turquoise Bay and Coral Bay, are popular with snorkellers. Apart from numerous types of coral and brightly coloured fish, the marine park also protects a number of species. Several beaches here are used by sea turtles as mating and breeding areas. Further offshore, it is possible to see whale sharks from late March to July or August. You can also swim alongside these graceful creatures safely on a whale-shark experience offered by a handful of tour operators.

Visitors can camp on the park's coastline at several sites. Fishing is another popular pursuit here, but catches are very strictly controlled. So be mindful of what you catch.

WHALE SHARKS

The endangered whale shark is the world's largest fish and can grow up to 18.8 m (62 ft). It's a gentle, slow-moving creature that filter-feeds on plankton and small fish with its enormous mouth, which can be 1.5 m (5 ft) wide and contains around 300 rows of teeth. Whale sharks inhabit tropical oceans.

Did You Know?

The first images of the 1969 Moon landing were relayed by the Carnarvon Tracking Station.

Carnarvon

A4 21 Robinson St; www.carnarvon.org.au

The town of Carnarvon, at the mouth of the Gascoyne River, acts as the commercial and administrative centre for the surrounding Gascoyne region, the gateway to Western Australia's north. Tropical fruit plantations line the river here, some offering tours and selling produce along the popular Fruit Loop trail.

The town is also home to the 1887 Jubilee Hall, which houses a fine arts and crafts centre, and the interactive **Carnarvon Space & Technology Museum**. The latter occupies a former NASA OTC Satellite Earth Station that was used during the 1960s Gemini and Apollo space missions.

About 70 km (43 miles) north of Carnarvon lie the Blowholes, a spectacular

↑ The OTC satellite dish at the Carnarvon Space & Technology Museum

coastal rock formation where air and water is forced through holes in the rocks in violent spurts up to 20 m (66 ft) high.

Carnarvon Space & Technology Museum

Mahony Ave
Apr-Sep: 9am-4pm daily; Oct-Mar: 10am-2pm daily carnarvon museum.org.au

Kennedy Range National Park

A3 Gascoyne Junction Rd, Gascoyne Junction parks.dpaw.wa.gov.au/ park/kennedy-range

Inland from Carnarvon, this national park contains some of the world's oldest rock formations and remarkable examples of Badimaya and Wajarri Aboriginal rock art. The park is one of the most remote stretches of Western Australia and exploring in a 4WD is only for hardcore adventurers. The park also features shorter walks, several campsites and excellent bird-watching.

STAY

Sal Salis Ningaloo Reef

Luxury tents in a stunning setting make Sal Salis a great place to stay. Guests can watch kangaroos around the camp, swim to the reef or simply enjoy the bar.

🅰A3 🏠Yardie Creek Rd, Cape Range National Park 🌐salsalis.com.au

$⑤$⑤$⑤$

Karijini Eco Retreat

This Indigenous-owned, award-winning eco-retreat is a good base for exploring Karijini National Park. Sleep in safari tents and dine in a great restaurant.

🅰A3 🏠Weano Rd, Karijini 🌐karijini ecoretreat.com.au

$⑤$⑤$⑤$

Dampier

🅰A3 🚆🚌 ℹLot 4548 De Witt Rd, Karratha; www. karrathaiscalling.com.au

Dampier stands on King Bay on the Burrup Peninsula, facing the 40 or so islands of the Dampier Archipelago. The town, 20 km (12 miles) west of Karratha, was established and still acts as a service centre and port for mining areas inland. The town has Australia's largest desalination plant, which can be seen from the Dampier Solar Evaporated Salt Mine Lookout. Dampier is also a popular base for offshore and beach anglers. Every August, game-fishing enthu-siasts converge here for the Dampier Classic and Game Fishing Classic.

The Burrup Peninsula is one of the most renowned ancient Aboriginal art sites in Australia, created by the Yapurrara Aboriginal peoples.

The Dampier Archipelago, within 45 km (28 miles) of the town, offers a range of activities, such as game fishing and whale-watching. Sport fishing here is particularly good, with reef and game species such as tuna, trevally and queenfish on offer. Almost half of the islands in the archipelago are nature reserves and can only be accessed by boat.

Roebourne

🅰A3 🚌

About 14 km (9 miles) inland, Roebourne, established in 1866, is the oldest town in the Pilbara. It retains several late 19th-century stone buildings – the Old Gaol, which now houses the tourist office and a craft gallery, and the Holy Trinity Church. Roebourne also marks the start of the 52-km (32-mile) Emma Withnell Heritage Trail, which takes a scenic route from here to Cossack and Point Samson. Trail guides are available at the tourist office.

Some 150 km (93 miles) inland lies the 200,000-ha (500,000-acre) Millstream-Chichester National Park with its sparkling freshwater pools.

> Karijini National Park's landscape features rolling hills covered in eucalyptus trees, arid shrubland, and deep chasms and gorges walled in by red-rock cliffs.

Karijini National Park

🅰 A3 🅸 Banyjima Drive; www.parks.dpaw.wa.gov.au

Set in the Hamersley Range, in the heart of the Pilbara region, Karijini National Park covers some 600,000 ha (1,500,000 acres). It is the second-largest national park in the state after Purnululu National Park *(p478)*.

The park's landscape features rolling hills covered in eucalyptus trees, arid shrubland, and deep chasms and gorges walled in by red-rock cliffs. Around Dales Gorge, the beautiful Fortescue Falls cascades down in steep rapids. In the northwestern corner of the park, Hamersley Gorge is a classic outback water hole with moss-covered rocks and waterfalls. Other stunning attractions are the Kalamina Gorge and Weano Gorge – the latter's Handrail Pool is an otherworldly, cavern-like water hole in elemental hues of red, blue and green.

The best times to visit the park are in winter, when the days are temperate, and in spring, when wildflowers bloom.

Cossack Historic Town

🅰 A3 🚌

In 1863, the town of Tien Tsin Harbour was established and quickly became the home of a burgeoning pearling industry that attracted people from as far away as Japan and China. The settlement was renamed Cossack in 1872 after a visit by Governor Weld aboard HMS *Cossack*. However, the town's moment soon passed. The pearling industry moved on to Broome *(p478)* and by 1910 Cossack's harbour had silted up. In the late 1970s, restoration work of this ghost town began and today, under the management of the Shire of Roebourne, it has become a curiosity that continues to fascinate many visitors.

Murujuga National Park

🅰 A3 🚗 Burrup Peninsula Road 🌐 parks.dpaw.wa.gov.au/park/murujuga

North of Dampier, Murujuga National Park on the Burrup Peninsula is an ancient storehouse of petroglyphs. More than one million engravings, some dating back 47,000 years, adorn the rocks; they have deep significance for Ngarda-Ngarli, the traditional custodians of this area. The most well-known site is Deep Gorge, with petroglyphs depicting Australia's native wildlife. **Ngurrangga Tours** in Roebourne runs tours into Deep Gorge and beyond.

Ngurrangga Tours
🏠 42 Roe Street, Roebourne
🌐 ngurrangga.com.au

←

Rock climbing along a steep gorge in Karijini National Park, and *(inset)* colourful spring wildflowers blanketing the park

NEED TO KNOW

The Great Ocean Road, hugging the coast

BEFORE
YOU GO

Things change, so plan ahead to make the most of your trip. Be prepared for all eventualities by considering the following points before you travel.

AT A GLANCE

CURRENCY
Australian Dollar
(A$/AUD)

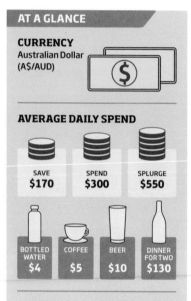

AVERAGE DAILY SPEND

SAVE	SPEND	SPLURGE
$170	**$300**	**$550**

BOTTLED WATER	COFFEE	BEER	DINNER FOR TWO
$4	**$5**	**$10**	**$130**

CLIMATE

 Summer (Nov–Mar) sees the longest days; winter (Jun–Aug) has the shortest.

 Temperatures average 28°C (82°F) in summer and 18°C (64°F) in winter.

 The heaviest rainfall occurs between November and April in the north. The interior is dry year-round.

ELECTRICITY SUPPLY
Power sockets are type I, fitting two- and three-pronged plugs. Standard voltage is 240–250v AC, 50 Hz.

Passports and Visas

For entry requirements, including visas, consult your nearest Australian **embassy** or check the **Australian Department of Home Affairs** website. Visitors need a passport valid for longer than their intended stay and a visa to enter Australia. Only New Zealand passport holders can apply for a visa on arrival. The eVisitor visa (subclass 651) and Electronic Travel Authority (subclass 601) are free and allow multiple visits within a 12-month period with a maximum stay of three months each time. The visitor visa (subclass 600), which allows a stay of up to 12 months, starts at $370. Visa eligibility can vary.
Australian Department of Home Affairs
W immi.homeaffairs.gov.au
Embassies
W dfat.gov.au

Government Advice

It is important to consult both your government and the Australian government's advice before travelling. The **UK Foreign, Commonwealth & Development Office (FCDO)**, the **US State Department** and the website of the **Australian Government** offer the latest information on security, health and local regulations.
Australian Government
W australia.gov.au
UK Foreign, Commonwealth & Development Office (FCDO)
W gov.uk/foreign-travel-advice
US State Department
W travel.state.gov

Customs Information

Find information on the laws relating to goods and currency taken in or out of Australia on the **Australian Border Force** website. Note that some foods, plant material and animal products are not allowed into Australia. Prohibited items include fresh and packaged food, eggs, meat, plants, seeds, skins and feathers.
Australian Border Force
W abf.gov.au

Insurance

We recommend taking out a comprehensive insurance policy covering theft, loss of belongings, medical care, cancellations and delays, and read the small print carefully.

Australia has reciprocal health care agreements with a number of countries. Visitors from the United Kingdom are entitled to free emergency treatment, and some subsidized health services, through Australia's **Medicare** system. Visitors from the United States are not covered.

Medicare
w servicesaustralia.gov.au

Vaccinations

For information regarding COVID-19 vaccination requirements, consult government advice. A yellow fever certificate is required if you have come from, or visited, an infected country in the six days before your arrival in Australia.

Booking Accommodation

Australia offers a wide variety of accommodation, from luxury hotels to budget hostels. Availability and rates vary enormously depending on the time of year. Book well in advance for travel at Christmas, New Year and Easter, and during festivals and school holidays.

Money

Contactless payments are widely used in Australia, and almost all establishments accept major credit, debit and prepaid currency cards. Very few outlets insist on cash, but small stores may impose a surcharge for card payments under A$10–15, so it is useful to carry some cash in small denominations. There is no need to tip anywhere but the fanciest of restaurants, where you should add 10 per cent to the total bill.

Travellers with Specific Requirements

Inclusive Tourism Australia provides information for people with specific requirements, including directories of assisted holiday providers, support services and accessible facilities, accommodation and experiences.

Most public transport services in Australia are accessible and wheelchair-accessible taxis (called "multi-purpose" taxis in Western Australia) can be booked through major taxi companies.

Theatres and concert halls offer accessible seating and options for visually and hearing impaired visitors, including captioned, audio-described and Auslan-interpreted (signed) performances. Major galleries run guided tactile and sensory tours. Check individual websites for details.

Inclusive Tourism Australia
w inclusivetourism.com.au

Language

Australia has no official language, but English is the most widely spoken. Over 250 Aboriginal languages existed before European settlement, but now only around 100 survive.

Opening Hours

Situations can change quickly and unexpectedly. Always check before visiting attractions and hospitality venues for up-to-date opening hours and booking requirements.

Monday Many restaurants close.
Thursday Large stores have extended opening hours, closing as late as 9pm.
Sundays Some sights and stores close early.
November to April Much of the Northern Territory's Top End closes for the wet season.
Public holidays Most stores and attractions are closed on Christmas Day and Good Friday.

PUBLIC HOLIDAYS	
1 Jan	New Year's Day
26 Jan	Australia Day
Mar/Apr	Easter
25 Apr	Anzac Day
2 Jun	King's Birthday (except QLD & WA)
25 Dec	Christmas Day
26 Dec	Boxing Day

GETTING AROUND

Whether you're planning a city break, outback adventure, coastal getaway or all of the above, here's all you need to know to navigate this vast country.

AT A GLANCE

PUBLIC TRANSPORT COSTS

SYDNEY

$4

One-way
Bus, light rail

MELBOURNE

$4.50

One-way
Bus, train, tram

PERTH

$3.40

One-way
Bus, train

TOP TIP
To avoid on-the-spot fines, be sure to stamp your ticket to validate your journey.

SPEED LIMIT

MOTORWAY

100 km/h
(62 mph)

MAIN ROADS

60 km/h
(37 mph)

SUBURBAN STREETS

50 km/h
(31 mph)

CITY CENTRES & SCHOOL ZONES

40 km/h
(25 mph)

Arriving by Air

Most international flights arrive into Australia's east coast. Sydney's Kingsford Smith, Melbourne's Tullamarine and Brisbane Airport are the three main gateways for long-haul flights, but flights from Asia also land at Cairns and those from Africa arrive into Perth.

For information on getting to and from Australia's main airports, see the table opposite.

Long-Distance Train Travel

Travelling between Australia's major cities by train is a convenient, comfortable and scenic way to get around the country. For a luxurious experience, choose **Journey Beyond Rail**'s *The Indian Pacific*, a three-day trip between Sydney and Perth, or *The Ghan*, another three-day service between Adelaide and Darwin, via Alice Springs. More affordable options include **Queensland Rail Travel**'s *Spirit of Queensland*, which links Brisbane and Cairns, and **NSW TrainLink**'s east coast services. Safety and hygiene measures, timetables, ticket information, transport maps and more can be obtained from individual operators' websites.

Journey Beyond Rail
w journeybeyondrail.com.au
NSW TrainLink
w transportnsw.info/regional
Queensland Rail Travel
w Queenslandrailtravel.com.au

Long-Distance Bus Travel

Coach travel is an inexpensive and efficient way to travel. The two main operators are **Greyhound Australia** and **Premier Motor Service**, which operates only on the east coast. Greyhound offers hop-on, hop-off passes for unlimited trips in one direction over 90 days, and a more expensive yearly pass for unlimited trips in any direction.

Greyhound Australia
w greyhound.com.au
Premier Motor Service
w premierms.com.au

GETTING TO AND FROM THE AIRPORT

Airport	Distance to city	Taxi fare	Public transport	Journey time	Price
Adelaide	6 km (4 miles)	$25	Bus	25 mins	$10
Brisbane	16 km (10 miles)	$55	Train	20 mins	$19.50
Cairns	6 km (4 miles)	$25	Shuttle bus	25 mins	$20
Canberra	8 km (5 miles)	$30	Bus	20 mins	$5
Darwin	13 km (8 miles)	$35	Shuttle bus	20 mins	$15
Hobart	22 km (14 miles)	$55	Skybus	25 mins	$19.50
Melbourne (Avalon)	49 km (30 miles)	$130	Skybus	50 mins	$27
Melbourne (Tullamarine)	22 km (14 miles)	$65	Skybus	25 mins	$24
Perth	15 km (9 miles)	$55	Bus	45 mins	$4.50
Sydney	9 km (6 miles)	$60	Train	20 mins	$19–25

CAR JOURNEY PLANNER

Plotting the main routes by journey time, this map is a rough guide to driving between Australia's main towns and cities. The times given reflect the fastest and most direct routes, where tolls may apply. Allow extra time for driving in bad weather, morning or evening rush hours, and high season, when roads will be busier.

••• Driving routes

Adelaide to Darwin	33 hrs		Hobart to Launceston	2.5 hrs
Adelaide to Perth	28 hrs		Melbourne to Adelaide	9 hrs
Brisbane to Sydney	10 hrs		Sydney to Canberra	3 hrs
Brisbane to Cairns	20 hrs		Sydney to Melbourne	10 hrs
Darwin to Alice Springs	15 hrs			

Long-Distance Boats and Ferries

Australia's vast island coastline makes it an international and domestic cruising destination. There are terminals in every state and territory except Canberra, but Sydney is Australia's largest and busiest port.

Car ferries link the mainland with Tasmania and Kangaroo Island. The **Spirit of Tasmania** travels between Melbourne and Devonport, and **SeaLink** reaches Kangaroo Island from Cape Jervis. Passenger ferries, including the **Rottnest Island Express**, transport visitors to Rottnest Island from Perth and Fremantle. Fast catamarans travel to the islands of the Great Barrier Reef from Cairns. Operators include **Great Adventures, Sunlover Reef Cruises** and **Fitzroy Island Adventures**. For slower journeys, float down the Murray River in a historic paddle steamer with **Murray River Paddlesteamers** or **PS Murray Princess**.

Fitzroy Island Adventures
🗑 fitzroyislandadventures.com
Great Adventures
🗑 greatadventures.com.au
Murray River Paddlesteamers
🗑 murrayriverpaddlesteamers.com.au
PS Murray Princess
🗑 murrayprincess.com.au
Rottnest Island Express
🗑 rottnestexpress.com.au
SeaLink
🗑 sealink.com.au
Spirit of Tasmania
🗑 spiritoftasmania.com.au
Sunlover Reef Cruises
🗑 sunlover.com.au

Public Transport

Public transport is run by individual state governments. Each state offers a range of efficient and cost-effective services. Most cities operate bus services, while city and suburban train, ferry and tram (also known as light rail) services are also common in capital cities. Each city and state transport website details safety and hygiene measures, route maps and timetables.

Adelaide
🗑 adelaidemetro.com.au
Canberra
🗑 transport.act.gov.au
New South Wales
🗑 transportnsw.info
Perth
🗑 transperth.wa.gov.au
Southeast Queensland
🗑 translink.com.au
Victoria
🗑 ptv.vic.gov.au

Tickets

Most of Australia's public transport services do not accept cash. Each state's public transport network accepts a different prepaid smartcard. Check individual websites for details. To use these cards, users tap on and off at the start and end of each journey. Fares are calculated based on distance travelled. Benefits can include daily and weekly caps on fares, and discounts for off-peak travel. Most cards can be topped up at transport hubs, newsagents, convenience stores and online.

Some states offer public transport passes that have been specifically designed for tourists. TransLink's "go seeQ" and "go explore" cards cover southeast Queensland, while the Adelaide Visitor metroCARD offers unlimited travel over three days in South Australia's capital.

Trains

Cities, including Sydney, Melbourne, Brisbane, Adelaide and Perth, offer metropolitan and suburban passenger train, or rapid transit metro, services. These services are particularly useful if you are staying outside the city centre. Note buses often replace trains on weekends when track maintenance work is being conducted.

Trams and Light Rail Services

Melbourne, Sydney, Canberra, the Gold Coast and Adelaide operate tram, or light rail, services. Melbourne and Adelaide even have free tram zones, where you don't need to pay for a ticket to ride the tram. The Sydney light rail network runs throughout the city and its inner west and eastern suburbs. Canberra's 13-stop light rail line runs from the northern town centre of Gungahlin to the city centre.

Buses

Australia's major cities all offer plentiful bus services, and some have dedicated lanes for buses. Buses plying in Brisbane's City Loop, the South Brisbane Loop, Canberra's Culture Loop and in Adelaide's City Connector Loop are all free of cost, covering city centres and stopping at major sights.

Ferries

Ferries ply the waterways in Sydney, Brisbane and Perth. Brisbane's CityHopper is a free inner-city ferry service. Be aware that Sydney's ferry service is more expensive than the city's other forms of public transport.

Taxis

Taxis are plentiful in every city. Raise an arm to flag down a vacant taxi (indicated by a light or illuminated "vacant" sign mounted on the roof), wait at a taxi rank or large hotel, or book ahead. The **13cabs** taxi network operates in all states. The two main taxi operators in Perth are **Black & White Cabs** and **Swan Taxis**.

Note that an airport access surcharge is added to fares for journeys to and from airports, and night tariffs mean higher fares after 10pm in some cities, including Sydney.

13cabs
🔽 13cabs.com.au
Black & White Cabs
🔽 blackandwhitecabs.com.au
Swan Taxis
🔽 swantaxis.com.au

Driving

The major cities' extensive public transport systems make it easy to be without a car but driving is the most convenient way to explore beyond urban centres. If you're planning on driving in the South Australian outback, get a **Multiple Entry Parks Pass**, allowing unlimited vehicular entry to several parks for one year.

Multiple Entry Parks Pass
🔽 parks.sa.gov.au

Car Rental
To rent a car or campervan you must be over the age of 21 and have held your licence for at least a year. Some rental companies charge an extra fee to drivers under the age of 25. Major car rental agencies have outlets at international airports and in all the major towns and cities.

Rules of the Road
Drive on the left and give way to the right at all times, unless otherwise indicated. Wearing seat belts is compulsory, as is using correctly fitted child seats. Drivers must give way to emergency vehicles by pulling to the left side of the road where possible.

Bus lanes, transit lanes (for vehicles with two or three occupants), no stopping and clearway zones are strictly enforced throughout the country. Melbourne also has additional laws that apply when driving near trams.

Drink driving laws are heavily policed, and roadside random breath testing and mobile drug testing is common. The legal blood alcohol limit is 0.05 per cent – zero for those without a full licence.

The use of mobile phones while driving is prohibited. Fixed and mobile speed cameras, red light cameras and mobile phone detection cameras are widely used.

Parking
Parking is limited and expensive in city centres, and at popular locations, including beaches. Local government rangers regularly patrol and fine drivers for parking illegally, or for longer than allowed or paid for.

Cycling

Cycling is an easy way to travel short distances within a city and a scenic option beyond urban centres. Bike paths and routes in and near the major cities are listed on the **Tourism Australia** website, and community cycling groups such as **Bicycle Network** post maps, rides, tips and resources online.

Companies, such as **AllTrails Bicycle Tours** and **Australian Cycling Holidays**, offer guided multi-day cycling holidays through the outback and along coastal trails, and facilitate self-guided tours with bike hire and cyclist support services.

AllTrails Bicycle Tours
🔽 alltrails.com.au
Australian Cycling Holidays
🔽 australiancyclingholidays.com.au
Bicycle Network
🔽 bicyclenetwork.com.au
Tourism Australia
🔽 australia.com

Bicycle Safety
Wearing a helmet is compulsory and donning high visibility clothing is also recommended. Cyclists must follow road rules at all times. Note adults in New South Wales, Victoria and Western Australia are also not allowed to ride on footpaths unless supervising a child rider.

Walking

With their large pavements and compact layouts, most city centres can easily be explored on foot. When walking around cities, wear sunscreen, carry water and stick to the shade where possible.

National parks are the best places to go bushwalking. Not only do they preserve the best of the country's natural heritage, but they also offer expert advice and well-marked trails for bushwalkers. Each state's national parks authority maintains a website with information on each park within its jurisdiction. Exceptional bushwalking regions include Cradle Mountain in Tasmania (*p296*), the MacDonnell Ranges in the Northern Territory (*p442*) and the Blue Mountains in New South Wales (*p160*).

When bushwalking, we recommend you download the **Emergency Plus** app and take some safety precautions. Plan your route carefully, check the weather forecast and tell someone where you are going. Wear comfortable shoes and clothing, a hat, sunscreen and insect repellent. It is also important to carry lots of water, plenty of provisions, and a fully charged mobile phone or satellite phone at all times.

Emergency Plus
🔽 emergencyplus.com.au

PRACTICAL
INFORMATION

A little know-how goes along way in Australia. Here, you can find all the essential advice and information you will need during your stay.

AT A GLANCE

EMERGENCY NUMBERS

GENERAL EMERGENCY

000

TIME ZONE
Australia spans three time zones: AEST/ACST/AWST. DST (Daylight Saving Time) is observed in South Australia, New South Wales, ACT, Victoria and Tasmania from the first Sunday in October to the first Sunday in April.

TAP WATER
Unless otherwise stated, tap water in Australia is safe to drink.

WEBSITES AND APPS

Tourism Australia
  Australia's national tourist board website (www.australia.com).
Bureau of Meteorology
  Check weather forecasts, warnings and rain radars throughout the country (www.bom.gov.au).
TripView
  Essential travel planning app for Sydney and Melbourne.
Beachsafe
  Surf Life Saving Australia's app offers safety information and advice.

Personal Security

Australia is generally safe, but petty crime does take place in the major cities. Pickpockets work known tourist areas and busy streets. Use your common sense, keep valuables in a safe place, and be alert to your surroundings. If you have anything stolen, report the crime as soon as possible at the nearest police station. Get a copy of the crime report in order to make a claim on your insurance. Contact your embassy or consulate immediately if your passport is stolen or in the event of a serious crime or accident.

As a rule, Australians are very accepting of all people, regardless of their race, gender or sexuality. The country does have one of the strictest immigration policies in the world, however, and small rural communities may be less tolerant of difference than people in the big cities. If you ever feel unsafe, head to the nearest police station or safe space.

Although same-sex marriage was only legalized in 2017, individual states and territories were granting partnership benefits and relationship recognition to same-sex couples from 2003. Today, New South Wales and Victoria have the largest LGBTQ+ populations and big cities' pride festivals, particularly the Sydney Gay and Lesbian Mardi Gras (p65), are world renowned. If you do feel unsafe, the **Safe Space Alliance** pinpoints your nearest place of refuge.

First Nations peoples have faced historic prejudice and discrimination. Aboriginal peoples and Torres Strait Islanders weren't included in the country's census until 1967, and inequality persists today.
Safe Space Alliance
🆆 safespacealliance.com

Health

Emergency medical care is free for visitors from countries with reciprocal health care agreements with Australia (p491). Find information on your nearest health care provider through the **Australian Department of Health**.

The sun is strong in Australia. Protect skin from harmful UV rays by wearing at least SPF 50

sunscreen, a hat, sunglasses and long-sleeved shirts. Check the day's UV rating on the **Bureau of Meteorology** website and find further safety information on **SunSmart**. Visitors to tropical areas should also use a DEET-based repellent to protect against mosquito-borne disease.

Bodies of water can be dangerous if simple precautions aren't followed. At beaches, always swim between the red-and-yellow flags and do not swim under the influence of alcohol or drugs, or at night. Wear a stinger suit between November and May in the country's north and always obey crocodile warning signs.

Australian Department of Health
W health.gov.au
Bureau of Meteorology
W bom.gov.au
SunSmart
W sunsmart.com.au

Smoking, Alcohol and Drugs

Smoking is banned in almost all public spaces. Signs indicate designated smoking areas. Alcohol and tobacco products cannot be sold or supplied to those under the age of 18. Illegal drug use, possession and supply is not tolerated. It is illegal to purchase a vape (e-cigarette) without a prescription. Travellers to Australia can only bring a maximum of two disposable vapes with them.

ID

Passports are required as ID at airports. Visits and tours to some government buildings require photo ID. Anyone who looks under 18 may be asked for ID as proof of age to enter licensed premises or to buy alcohol and cigarettes.

Visiting Places of Worship and Sacred Sites

Dress and act respectfully in places of worship and sacred sites. When visiting sites that are sacred for First Nations peoples, read signage carefully, keep to dedicated paths and camping areas, and show respect for the local community and their beliefs. It's best to explore a site in the company of an Aboriginal guide.

Mobile Phones and Wi-Fi

Telstra, Vodafone and **Optus** are Australia's major mobile network providers. Visitors can buy pay-as-you-go SIM cards at airports, phone stores, convenience stores and supermarkets, which can be used in compatible phones.

Free Wi-Fi is available in most public areas. Only connect to trusted networks.

Optus
W optus.com.au
Telstra
W telstra.com.au
Vodafone
W vodafone.com.au

Post

Australia Post is the national postal service. Standard post boxes are red, while Express Post boxes are yellow and require special prepaid envelopes. These envelopes and stamps are available at post offices.

Australia Post
W auspost.com.au

Taxes and Refunds

A 10 per cent goods and services tax (GST) is applied to most items and included in the price displayed. If you spend A$300 or more with a single store or business, you can claim back the GST paid through the **Tourist Refund Scheme**. To claim, you will need to submit your original tax invoices at an international airport's departure area, online or via a mobile app within 60 days of leaving Australia.

Tourist Refund Scheme
W abf.gov.au

Discount Cards

The **iVenture Card** is a prepaid card offering discounted entry to multiple attractions. Separate cards are available for Sydney, Melbourne and the Gold Coast, as well as a multi-city card covering all three destinations. It is worth considering carefully how many offers you are likely to take advantage of before purchasing one of these cards.

iVenture Card
W iventurecard.com

INDEX

501

Index

ACKNOWLEDGMENTS

DK would like to thank the following for their contribution to the previous edition:
Anita Isalska, Deborah Soden, Louise Bostock Lang, Jan Bowen, Paul Kloeden, Jacinta le Plaistrier, Ingrid Ohlsson, Sue Neales, Tamara Thiessen, Shelley Ware, Helen Peters.

The publisher would like to thank the following for their kind permission to reproduce their photographs:

(Key: a-above; b-below/bottom; c-centre; f-far; l-left; r-right; t-top)

123RF.com: Nils Versemann 60-61t.

Alamy Stock Photo: Marc Anderson 28bl, 112tc, Mark Andrews 105cra, Antiqua Print Gallery 44bl, Artokoloro 66t, Asia Photopress 25tr, Auscape International Pty Ltd / Michael Van Ewijk 333cla, Ian Beattie / Auscape International Pty Ltd 347, 396-97, John Fairhall / Auscape International Pty Ltd 275t, 299cra, Andrew Bain 55br, 56cra, 295b, 297cra, 377tr, 401, 402bc, 435tl, terry bamforth 32bl, Scott Barclay 167t, Susanna Bennett 436cla, martin berry 46bl, 123clb, 193t, 292bl, blickwinkel / Gemperle 428tl, blickwinkel / H. Baesemann 481tr, Paul Brown 22bl, camac 47bl, Have Camera Will Travel Australia 105tl, CandyAppleRed Images 260t, Jeffery Drewitz / Cephas Picture Library 466-67t, Trevor Collens 71crb, Cosmo Condina 53cl, CPA Media Pte Ltd 67tl, Mark Daffey 37cla, Ian Dagnall 252-53t, 315t, 385br, Ian G Dagnall 93br, 111b, 470bl, Kamila Delega 28crb, Peter Adams / DanitaDelimont.com 344c, 348-49, Walter Bibikow / DanitaDelimont.com 30cr, Design Pics / Radius Images 166tr, domonabike 223, 234b, Dorling Kindersley ltd 270b, downunder 270cl, Stephen Dwyer 123br, 222cr, Paul Dymond 62t, Sindre Ellingsen 155bl, 180-81, Frank Fichtmueller 176cla, Ana Flašker 87t, Lincoln Fowler 201b, 374bl, Nick Fox 88-89, jason freeman 129crb, Ganesha 34t, Ilya Genkin 144tl, 168-69t, GL Archive 229cra, 271bc, Ben Goode 324b, Manfred Gottschalk 64crb, 112bl, 145clb, Granger, NYC 69cra, Jeffrey Isaac Greenberg 10+ 356bl, Jeffrey Isaac Greenberg 6+ 353cra, Mike Greenslade / Australia 403br, Descamps Simon / Hemis.fr 69crb, Bibikow Walter / Hemis.fr 202bl, Chaput Franck / Hemis.fr 22crb, 318-19b, The Print Collector / Heritage Images 67tl, 70bl, Werner Forman Archive / Private collection / Heritage Images 427clb, Holli 138bc, Michael Holloway 321t, Cindy Hopkins 38cla, Dave G. Houser 421cla, Chris Howarth / Australia 200-01t, MD Rubai Huda 166bl, Horst Mahr / imageBROKER 8cl, imageBROKER / White Star / Monica Gumm 322tc, Norbert Probst / imageBROKER 385tl, Interfoto / Personalities 68-69t, Stephanie Jackson - Australian landscapes 19cb, 302-03, graham jepson 128t, Andrew Watson / John Warburton-Lee Photography 50crb, 59b, 411, 430-31, John White Photos 339br, Jon Arnold Images Ltd 20tl, 340-341,

Bjanka Kadic 22cr, 109br, Gina Kelley 48-49b, Keystone Pictures USA / ZUMAPRESS 70cla, Jason Knott 48tl, Alexander Kondakov 322bl, Krystyna Szulecka Photography 419cr, Takatoshi Kurikawa 64cla, Lakeview Images 69bc, lkpro 26-27ca, Suzanne Long 420-21b, Dennis Lound 457cl, Paul Lovelace 90-91b, De Luan 70tl, Marco Trovalusci Photography 42-43b, Photography By Marco 291br, Martin Norris Travel Photography 477cla, Regis Martin 421t, Iain Masterton 352cla, Marco Simoni / mauritius images GmbH 345, 364-65, Mauritius Images Gmbh / David & Micha Sheldon 237b, Walter Bibikow / mauritius images GmbH 30crb, MB_Photo 106-107t, 356-57t, 362clb, Andrew McInnes 161clb, #MilesTweedie Photography 63t, Richard Milnes 139t, 145cb, Martin Willis / Minden Pictures 38-39ca, model10 70-71t, David Tipling / Nature Picture Library 373cl, North Wind Picture Archives 66crb, 68tl, Terry Oakley 55cl, Ingo Oeland 47cr, Samantha Ohlsen 8cla, 60b, 249cr, 437t, Karl Phillipson / Optikal 276bl, Joseph Christopher Oropel 108-109t, Ozimages 375b, Jamie Paddock 189br, Paul Mayall Australia 54-55b, Shane Pedersen 392-93b, Phil Wills 57tr, Pictorial Press Ltd 68crb, Viktor Posnov 38-39t, Igor Prahin 225bl, John Quixley - Australia 64clb, 359t, Ray Warren Creative 317t, Sergi Reboredo 94t, redbrickstock.com / Paul Giggle 369clb, Edward Reeves 126tl, Ben Cooper / RGB Ventures / SuperStock 481tl, Jochen Schlenker / robertharding 299br, Michael Nolan / robertharding 476-77b, Michael Runkel / robertharding 426-27b, robertharding / Andrew Michael 115tr, robertharding / Marco Simoni 361br, Sally Robertson 461bl, William Robinson 37tr, Rolf_52 107tr, RooM the Agency / jamesphillips 274b, Russotwins 214c, 216-17, Erik Schlogl 107cl, ilse schrama 424t, Keith J Smith 468-69b, richard sowersby 378bl, Kumar Sriskandan 97tl, David Steele 21, James Talalay 277cl, WalkerPod Images / Tetra Images 13cr, Top Photo Corporation 317br, Piya Travel 243b, Travelscape Images 17bl, 26t, 56-57b, 194-195, 207bc, 466br, Ian Trower 178bl, Universal Art Archive 67cb, Genevieve Vallee 49t, 300b, 394t, 404t, 404-05b, Robin Weaver 111cl, Visions from Earth 370tr, 374tr, David Wall 292-93t, 451, 472-73, Robert Wallace / Wallace Media Network 164b, Ray Warren Australia 232tr, 299crb (Forest), Colin Waters 69tr, Andrew Watson 27tr, 421cra, Michael Willis 459b, ian woolcock 94cra, Chun Ju Wu 224t, Robert Wyatt 41tr, 288-89t, 297t, 400crb, 425br, 458bc, 468tl, Heesco / Khosnaran Khurelbaatar 61br, Zoonar / magann 80, 130-31, Bosiljka Zutich 137tl.

Art Gallery of New South Wales: 125br, AGNSW, Jenni Carter 12-13b, 124-25t, 125cra.

Australian Museum: AbramPowell 102-03t, 103br, Anna Kučera, Stuart Humphreys and Daniel Boud 103tr.

AWL Images: Marco Bottigelli 215tl, 244-45, 248, 460-61b, Tom Mackie 19tl, 278-79, Richard Stanley 2-3, 72-73, 155t, 170-71, 434-35b, Ian Trower 81, 142, 147tl, Andrew Watson 11t.

Bridgeman Images: NPL - DeA Picture Library / G. Sioen 45tr.

Courtesy Canberra Museum and Gallery: Brenton McGeachie 206-207t.

Courtesy of Tourism National Territory: 420-21b, 421tl, 421cla, Mark Sherwood 421cra.

Depositphotos Inc: christian__b 249cla, KonArt 58-59t, lkonya@optusnet.com.au 338b, lucidwaters 481cra, markrhiggins 360-61t, Mkenwoo 32cr, MLWilliams 105bc, ncousla 385cl, phuongphoto 319cra, phuongphoto 319cr, zstockphotos 368-69t, 372-73t.

Dreamstime.com: Adwo 114-15b, Andremichel 369crb, Leonid Andronov 90tr, Rafael Ben Ari 335b, 355t, Andrew Atkinson 10ca, Tamara Bauer 229bl, Benny-marty 43cl, Marcel Van Den Bos 227t, Marco Brivio 145bc, Richie Chan 110tl, 125cl, Daniela Constantinescu 422-23, Damian322 423cb, Stephane Debove 24t, Dinozzaver 52br, Dudlajzov 32crb, Ecophoto 43t, F11 photo 6-7, Filedimage 28cr, 186t, 255t, 276-277t, 290b, Markus Gann 65crb, Ben Goode 30t, Fritz Hiersche 441tc, 461cl, Richard Jacyno 480-81b, Jasmina 230-31t, Klodien 107br, 148-49t, 418bl, Laszlo Konya 259t, Serguei Levykin 327bc, Lizgiv 53b, Steve Lovegrove 34cla, 299tr, Marco Taliani De Marchio 59cl, Jakub Michankow 41cl, Bundit Minramun 149b, 169b, Andrey Moisseyev 30bl, Martin Pelanek 209t, Mariusz Prusaczyk 79bl, 118-19, Tanya Puntti 385cra, Rpianoshow 358-59b, Rudi1976 357b, Showface 42t, David Steele 12-13b, 446-47, Rostislav Stefanek 299crb, Stringerimages 36cra, Deborah Talan 299cr, THPStock 165t, 336-37t, Tsvibrav 185tr, 260-61b, Tunatura 384-85b, Martin Valigursky 378-79t, Julien Viry 123crb, 228t, 240clb, 442b, Taras Vyshnya 185cra, Bruce Whittingham 20cb, 128br, 406-07, Sharon Wills 320-21b, Ymgerman 234-235t, 327t, Zeytun Images 135bl, 259cr.

Getty Images: Vishal Bhandari / 500px 238-239t, AFP 199b, Saeed Khan / AFP 71tr, Mark Dadswell / Allsport 71bc, Carla Gottgens / Bloomberg 49cl, Cavan Images 40clb, Laurie Chamberlain 241cr, Nick Rains / Corbis Documentary 486-87b, PaulMorton / E+ 487br, Claudia Moser / EyeEm 49br, Yun Hung Huang / EyeEm 177b, Alan Lambert / The Age / Fairfax Media 443br, Fairfax Media 64cr, 135cra, Jouan / Rius / Gamma-Rapho 400br, Sylvain Grandadam / Gamma-Rapho 443t, Manfred Gottschalk 162-63b, Craig Heyton 485tr, Arthur Hoffmann 191b, Hulton Archive / Stringer 68bc, Mark Kolbe 44-45b, Leisa Tyler / LightRocket 284-85b, Glenn van der Knijff / Lonely Planet RF 215cb, 264-65, Peter Unger / Lonely Planet RF 376-77, Mint Images 144-45t, Moment / © Marco Bottigelli 324-25t, Moment / Bruno Carrillo Bertens 444-45t, Moment / Carolyn Hebbard 289b, Moment / Demosthenes Mateo Jr 354-55b, Moment / John Crux Photography 471t, Moment / Nigel Killeen 301t, Moment / Peter Pesta Photography 174-75b, Moment / Photo by Benjawan Sittidech 271tl,

Moment / Posnov 184-85b, 332-33b, Moment / Prasit photo 463t, Moment / Robert Lang Photography 312-13t, Moment / Southern Lightscapes-Australia 268-269, 294t, 333cra, Moment Open / John Crux Photography 390-91t, Moment Open / Migration Media - Underwater Imaging 485bc, Moment Open / Nigel Killeen 363t, Nigel Killeen / Moment 32t, Posnov / Moment 11cr, 41b, 346, 380-81, Martin Ollman 199t, Paparwin Tanupatarachai 282-83t, Jeremy Woodhouse / Photodisc 416t, Bill Heinsohn / Photographer's Choice RF 438-39t, Jeff Hunter / Photographer's Choice RF 10-11b, puyalroyo 440b, Mike Keating / Racing Photos 65clb, Richard I'Anson 61cla, RooM / janetteasche 287t, Science & Society Picture Library 67bl, Manfred Gottschalk / Stone 113t, Stone / Peter Unger 369br, Sergio Dionisio / stringer 103c, Jami Tarris 58-59b, Wendell Teodoro 65cr, Auscape / Universal Images Group 428-29b, 483cl, Jeff Greenberg / Universal Images Group 353cb, Martin Zwick / REDA&CO / Universal Images Group 258b, Paolo Picciotto / REDA&CO / Universal Images Group 402t, Jeremy Woodhouse 38tl, Krystle Wright 52-53t.

Getty Images / iStock: Andyworks 392tl, asiafoto 188-89t, atosan 319tc, BenGoode 50-51t, 306c, 308-09, benstevens 391cl, bjeayes 24-25t, Boyloso 236t, bschuitdesign 10clb, ChristianB 18, 210-11, ClaraNila 63br, coolendelkid 55t, CraigRJD 161crb, davidf 36-37t, DoraDalton 296b, 4FR / E+ 12t, funky-data 140-41t, Hanis 160-61t, jamenpercy 16c, 74-75, JensenChua 319cla, KarenHBlack 138tl, Stefan Keet 286cra, keiichihiki 46-47t, kokkai 136b, 204t, 226b, koshar 54tl, Kevin Lebre 307, 328-329, lovleah 17t, 150-51, lsarao 4, Nigel Marsh 190t, master2 13t, mastersky 337cra, miralex 263tr, Mlenny 79t, 98-99, NeoPhoto 456t, Kokkai Ng 220-21, offlines 298b, pniesen 387bl, RichardALock 464-65t, rudi_suardi 482b, scotto72 161br, sfe-co2 176t, StudioBarcelona 450c, 452-53, superjoseph 146-47b, takemax 230crb, timstarkey 192b, Totajla 127br, tracielouise 273b, travellinglight 78c, 82-83, trigga 169cr, Tsvibrav 326-27b, Uwe-Bergwitz 444tc, Julien Viry 92-93t, Yicai 203br.

Mary Evans Picture Library: John Frost Newspapers 70crb, Arthur Dorety / Stocktrek Images 66bc.

MONA - The Museum of Old and New Art: Jesse Hunniford 284tr.

National Gallery Of Australia, Canberra: 200-201t.

Shutterstock.com: 2021 Photography 423br, aiyoshi597 65tc, 221tr, alexroch 163tr, Alizada Studios 134t, Alvov 251t, Fimina Anna 65tl, Rudy Balasko 28t, Glen Berlin 291t, Bildagentur Zoonar GmbH 12clb, Blue Planet Studio 34-35ca, Stephane Bowker 209cra, John Carnemolla 429cr, Timothy Christianto 63cl, Alex Cimbal 202-03t, 336b, Mariangela Cruz 314bl, Luke Cummings 262bl, Debu55y 249br, Michael R Evans 334t, EQRoy 62-63b, 65cl, 352-53, 359bc, FiledIMAGE 256-57t, GotKom 272c, GTS Productions 423clb, Holli

64cra, Iacomino Frimages 410, 412-13, Yuki Ishii 36tl, Islandjems - Jemma Craig 26-27t, Tom Jastram 35tr, jax10289 236cl, josh.tagi 339t, juancsanchezherrera 13b, Julian Peters Photography 427tl, Olga Kashubin 8clb, Nicole Kwiatkowski 484t, Shuang Li 232t, lkonya 34-35t, Luke98 322-23t, Michael Major 51tr, marcobrivio.photo 87cra, Natalie Maro 395b, Claudine Van Massenhove 95bc, mastersky 333t, Maurizio De Mattei 388-89b, ms_pics_and_more 185cla, Nick Brundle Photography 419b, Oleksii G 299cra (Devil), pisaphotography 8-9, Thomas Rosenzweig 11br, Ryosue 26cla, Philip Schubert 39tr, 477tr, 478t, Darren Tierney 40-41t, Marco Tomasini 427cla, Tooykrub 116bl, Ksenija Toyechkina 22t, trabantos 233b, 483t, Steve Tritton 208b, VarnaK 154c, 156-57, Nils Versemann 222b, Taras Vyshnya 24-25ca, 64cl, 122-23t, 370-71b, Ashley Whitworth 427cl, Dr. Victor Wong 104-105b, Yunsun_Kim 488-89.

Cover images: Front and Spine: Getty Images: Photodisc / Matthew Micah Wrighta; *Back:* **Alamy Stock Photo:** blickwinkel / Gemperle cl; **Depositphotos Inc:** zstockphotos t; **Getty Images:** Photodisc / Matthew Micah Wrighta b; *Front Flap:* **AWL Images:** Andrew Watson t; **Dreamstime.com:** Tsvibrav br; **Getty Images:** Jami Tarris cla; **Getty Images / iStock:** keiichihiki cra, scotto72 bl; **Shutterstock.com:** Taras Vyshnya c; Back Flap: **Getty Images:** Jeff Hunter / Photographer's Choice RF c.

All other images © Dorling Kindersley Limited
For further information see: www.dkimages.com

Illustrators:

Richard Bonson, Jo Cameron, Stephen Conlin, Eugene Fleury, Chris Forsey, Steve Gyapay, Toni Hargreaves, Chris Orr, Robbie Polley, Kevin Robinson, Peter Ross, John Woodcock.

MIX
Paper | Supporting responsible forestry
FSC
www.fsc.org   FSC™ C018179

This book was made with Forest Stewardship Council™ certified paper – one small step in DK's commitment to a sustainable future.
Learn more at **www.dk.com/uk/ information/sustainability**

A NOTE FROM DK EYEWITNESS

The rate at which the world is changing is constantly keeping the DK travel team on our toes. While we've worked hard to ensure that this edition of Australia is accurate and up-to-date, we know that opening hours alter, standards shift, prices fluctuate, places close and new ones pop up in their stead. So, if you notice we've got something wrong or left something out, we want to hear about it. Please get in touch at travelguides@dk.com

First edition 1998
Published in Great Britain by Dorling Kindersley Limited, DK, One Embassy Gardens, 8 Viaduct Gardens, London SW11 7BW, UK

The authorised representative in the EEA is Dorling Kindersley Verlag GmbH. Arnulfstr. 124, 80636 Munich, Germany

Published in the United States by DK Publishing, 1745 Broadway, 20th Floor, New York, NY 10019, USA

Copyright © 1998, 2024 Dorling Kindersley Limited
A Penguin Random House Company

24 25 26 27 10 9 8 7 6 5 4 3 2 1

All rights reserved.

No part of this publication may be reproduced, stored in or introduced into a retrieval system, or transmitted, in any form, or by any means (electronic, mechanical, photocopying, recording, or otherwise), without the prior written permission of the copyright owner.

The publishers cannot accept responsibility for any consequences arising from the use of this book, nor for any material on third party websites, and cannot guarantee that any website address in this book will be a suitable source of travel information.

A CIP catalog record for this book is available from the British Library.

A catalog record for this book is available from the Library of Congress.

ISSN: 1542 1554
ISBN: 978 0 2416 7712 4
Printed and bound in China.
www.dk.com

DK Penguin Random House

Main Contributors Anita Isalska, Julia D'Orazio, Deborah Soden
Senior Editors Dipika Dasgupta, Keith Drew
Senior Art Editor Vinita Venugopal
Project Editors Abhijit Dutta, Anuroop Sanwalia
Editor Nandini Desiraju
Assistant Editors Ishita Chatterjee, Gauri Shukla
Assistant Art Editor Divyanshi Shreyaskar
Senior Picture Researcher Nishwan Rasool
Assistant Picture Research Administrator Manpreet Kaur
Picture Research Manager Taiyaba Khatoon
Publishing Assistant Simona Velikova
Jacket Designer Laura O'Brien
Project Cartographer Ashif
Cartography Manager Suresh Kumar
DTP Designer Rohit Rojal
Production Controller Kariss Ainsworth
Managing Editors Shikha Kulkarni, Beverly Smart, Hollie Teague
Managing Art Editor Gemma Doyle
Senior Managing Art Editor Priyanka Thakur
Art Director Maxine Pedliham
Publishing Director Georgina Dee